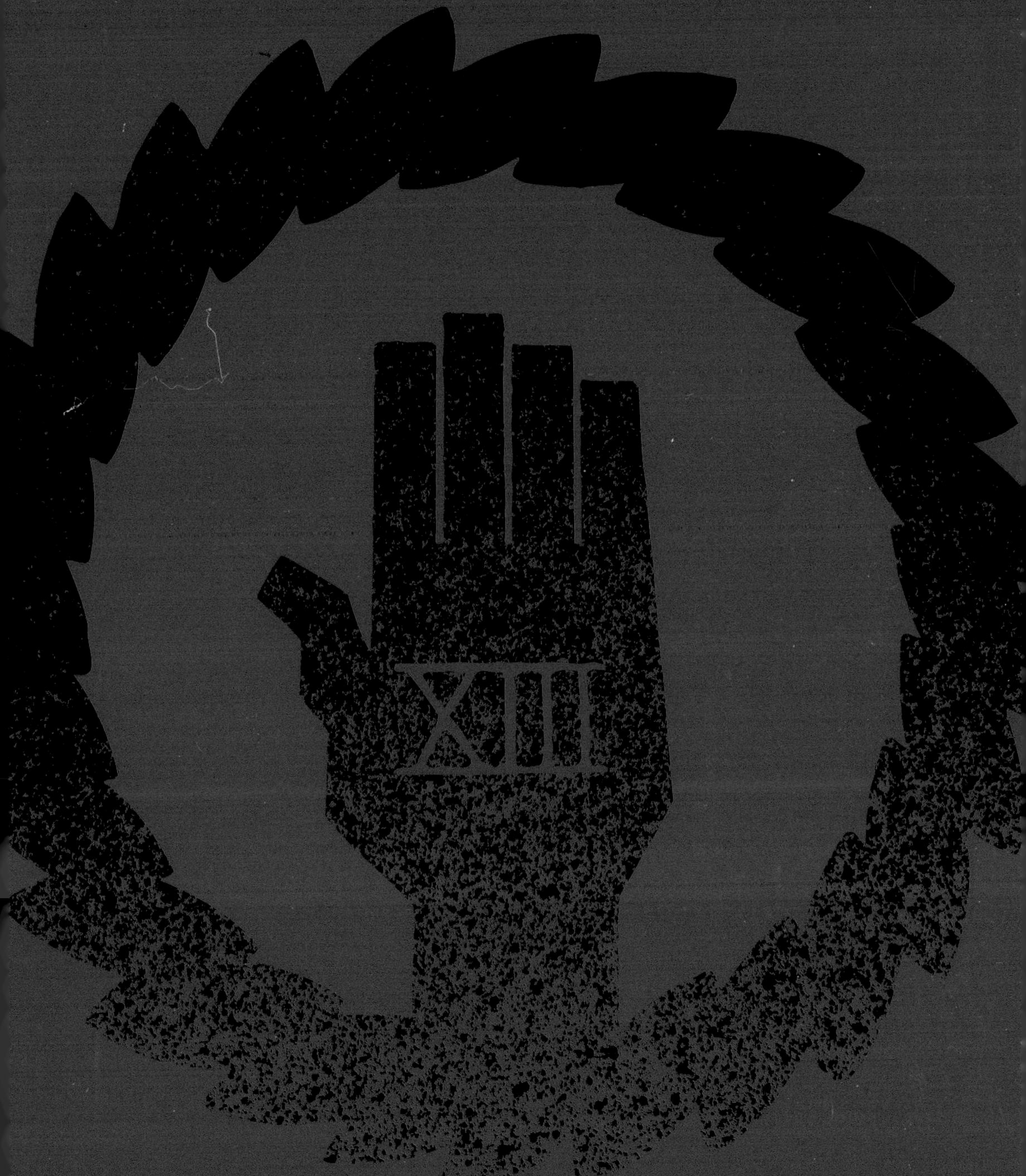
XIII

100 BULLETS

BOOK TWO

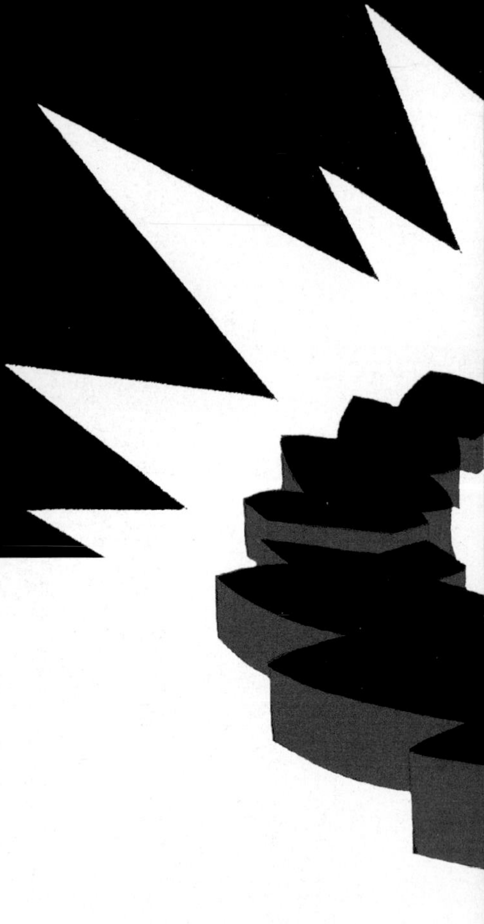

BRIAN AZZARELLO WRITER
EDUARDO RISSO ARTIST
LEE BERMEJO
JORDI BERNET
TIM BRADSTREET
MARK CHIARELLO
DAVE GIBBONS
J.G. JONES
JOE JUSKO
JIM LEE
FRANK MILLER
PAUL POPE GUEST ARTISTS

PATRICIA MULVIHILL COLORIST
CLEM ROBINS LETTERER
DAVE JOHNSON COVER ART AND ORIGINAL SERIES COVERS

100 BULLETS CREATED BY
BRIAN AZZARELLO AND **EDUARDO RISSO**

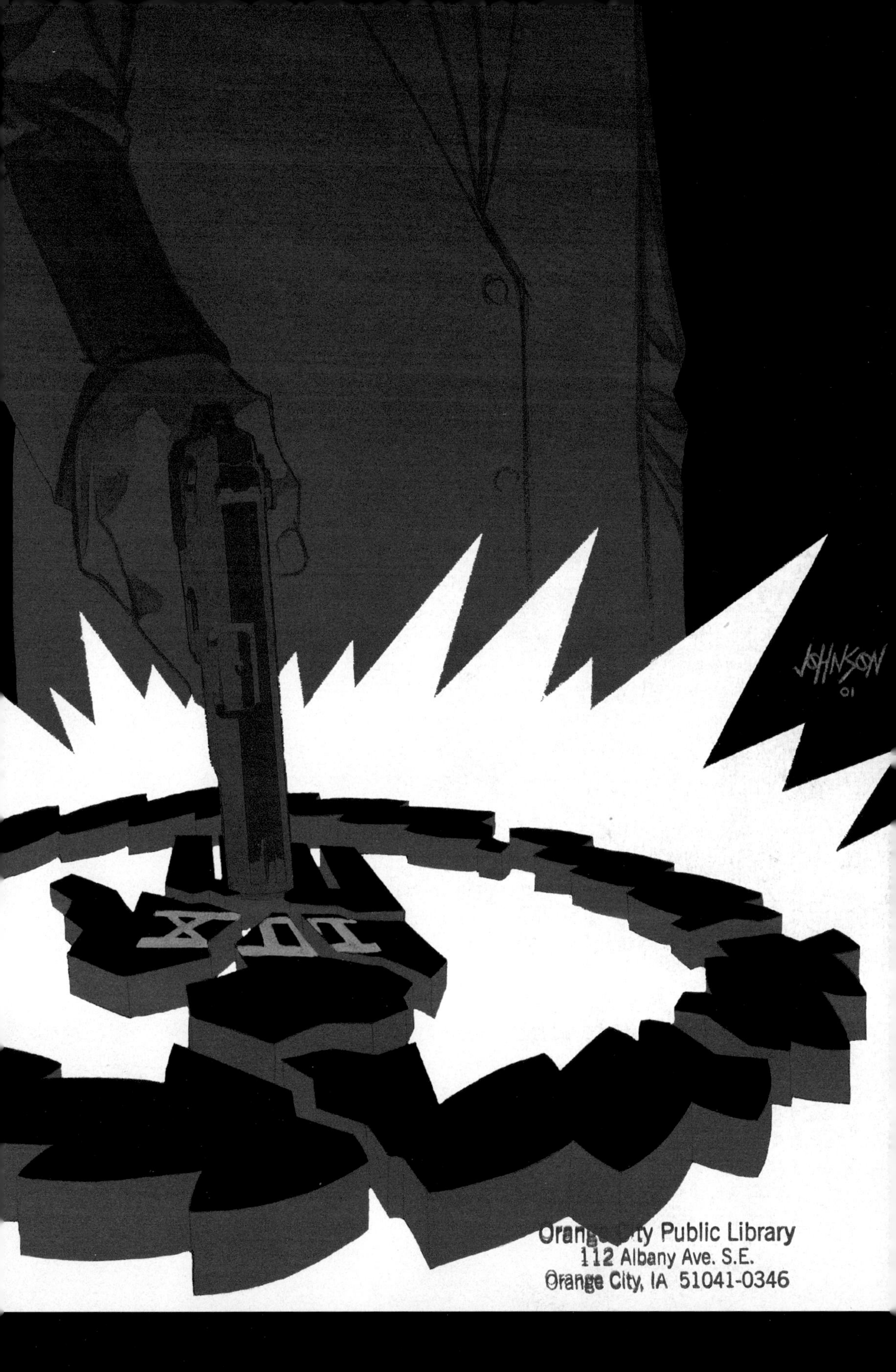
JOHNSON
01
XII

Will Dennis Editor - Original Series
Zachary Rau Assistant Editor - Original Series
Scott Nybakken Editor
Robbin Brosterman Design Director - Books
Louis Prandi Publication Design

Shelly Bond Executive Editor - Vertigo
Hank Kanalz Senior VP - Vertigo and Integrated Publishing

Special thanks to Nicolas Choisnel, Jean-Christophe Lips and Eduardo A. Santillan Marcus for their translating assistance.

DC Comics, 1700 Broadway, New York, NY 10019. A Warner Bros. Entertainment Company. Printed in the USA. First Printing. ISBN: 978-1-4012-5431-5
Library of Congress Cataloging-in-Publication Data is Available.

SUSTAINABLE FORESTRY INITIATIVE
Certified Chain of Custody
20% Certified Forest Content, 80% Certified Sourcing
www.sfiprogram.org
SFI-01042
APPLIES TO TEXT STOCK ONLY

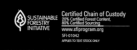

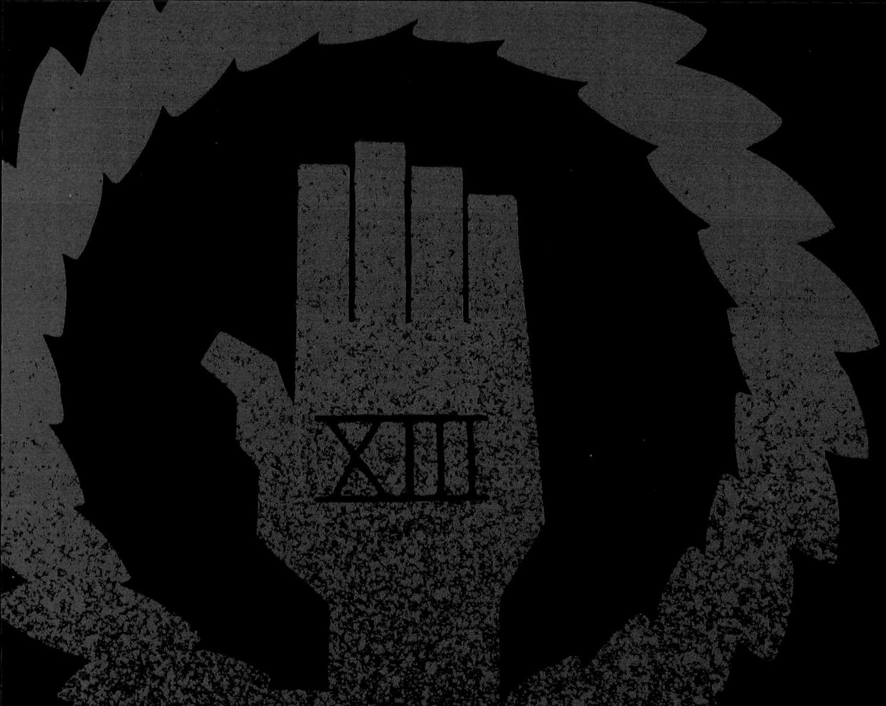
XIII

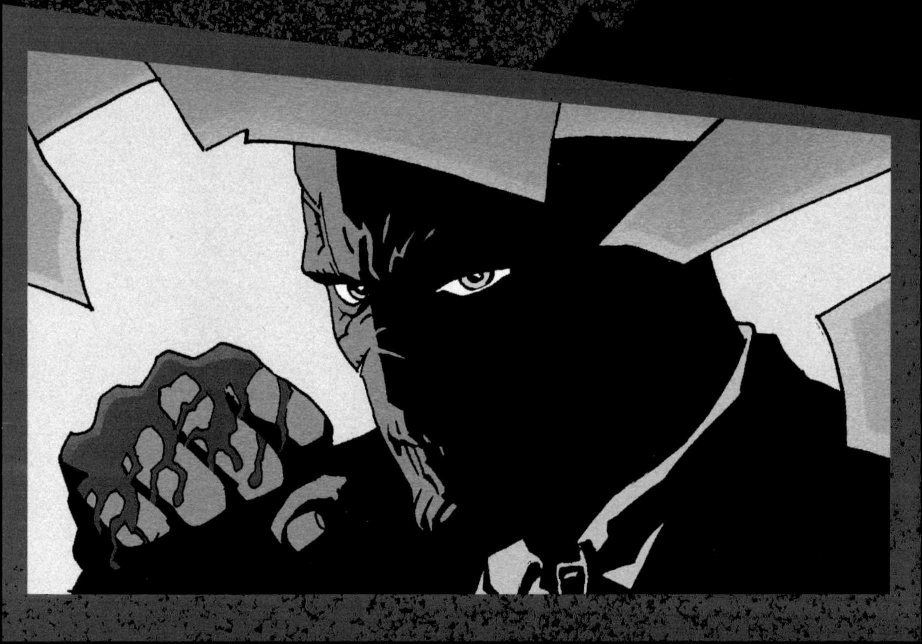

Table of Contents

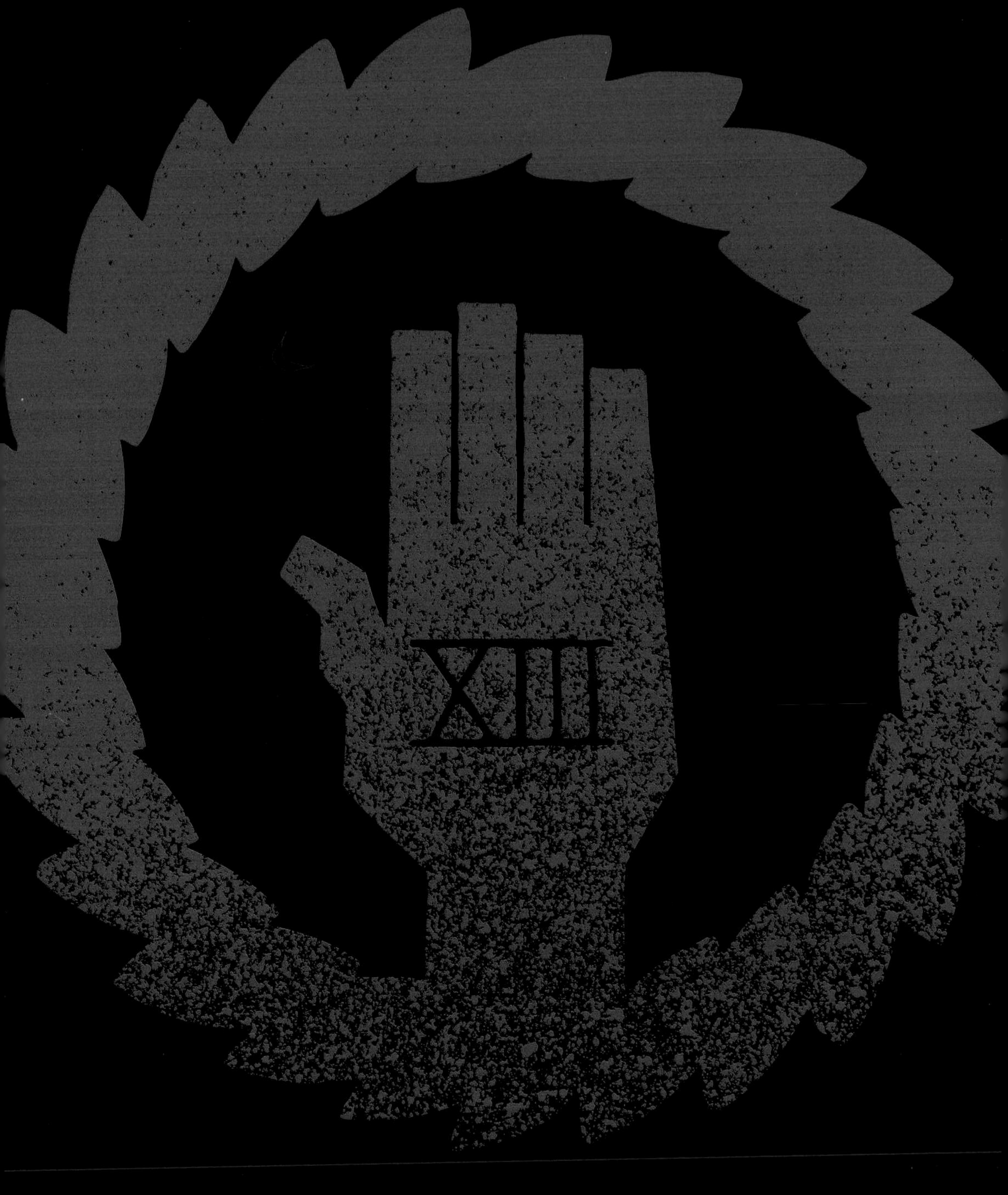
XIII

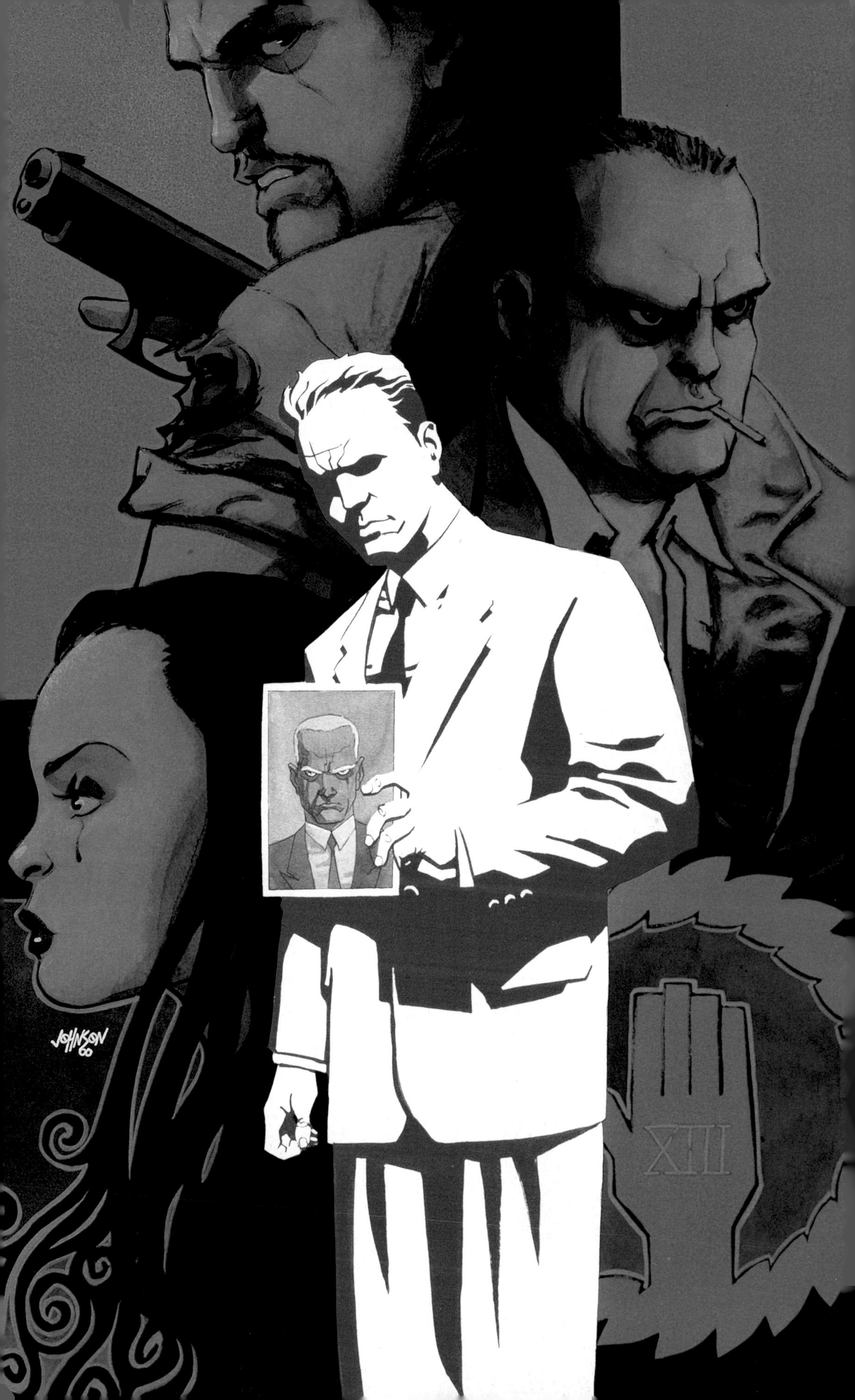
JOHNSON
XIII

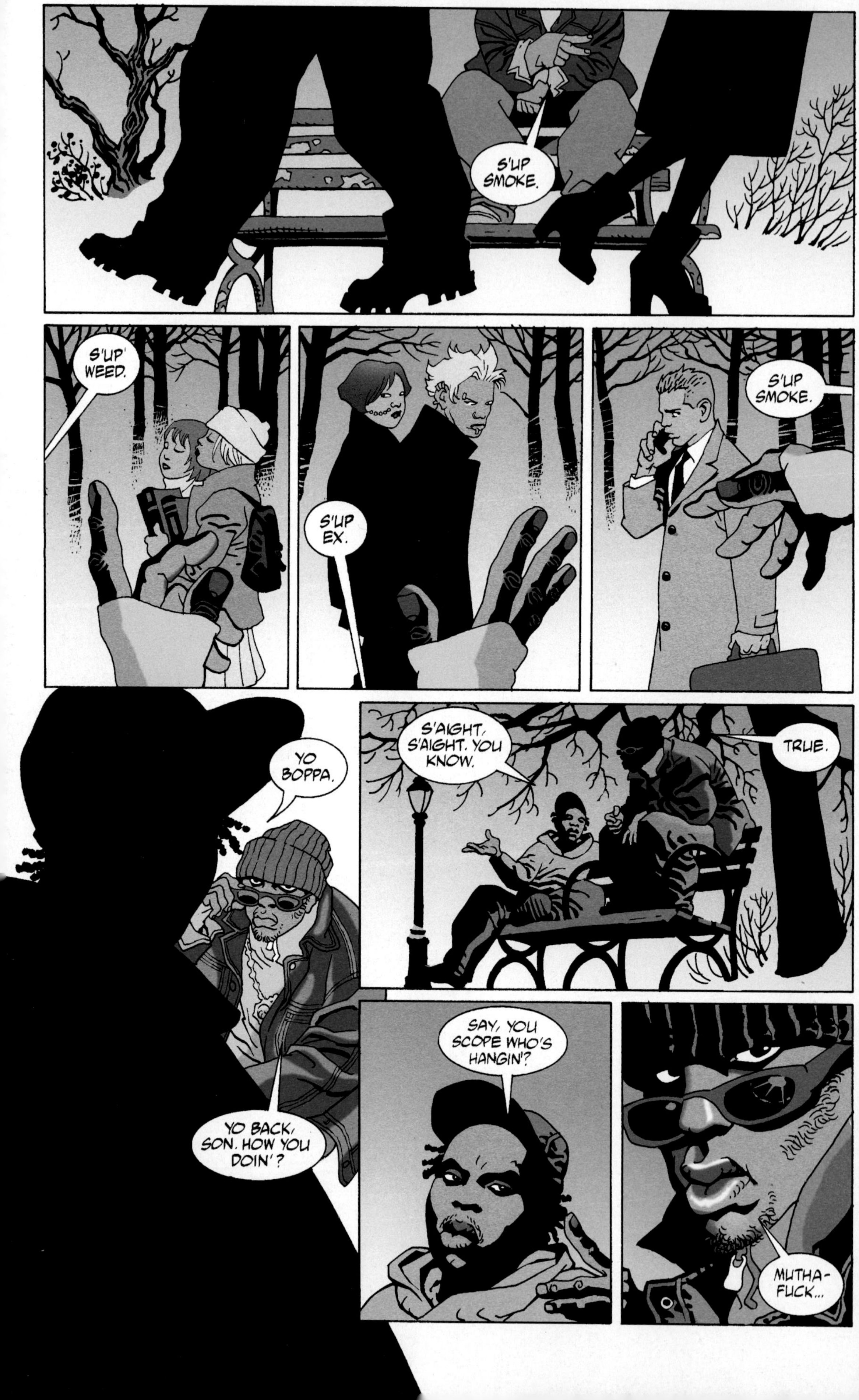
S'UP SMOKE.
S'UP' WEED.
S'UP EX.
S'UP SMOKE.
YO BOPPA.
YO BACK, SON. HOW YOU DOIN'?
S'AIGHT, S'AIGHT. YOU KNOW.
TRUE.
SAY, YOU SCOPE WHO'S HANGIN'?
MUTHA-FUCK...

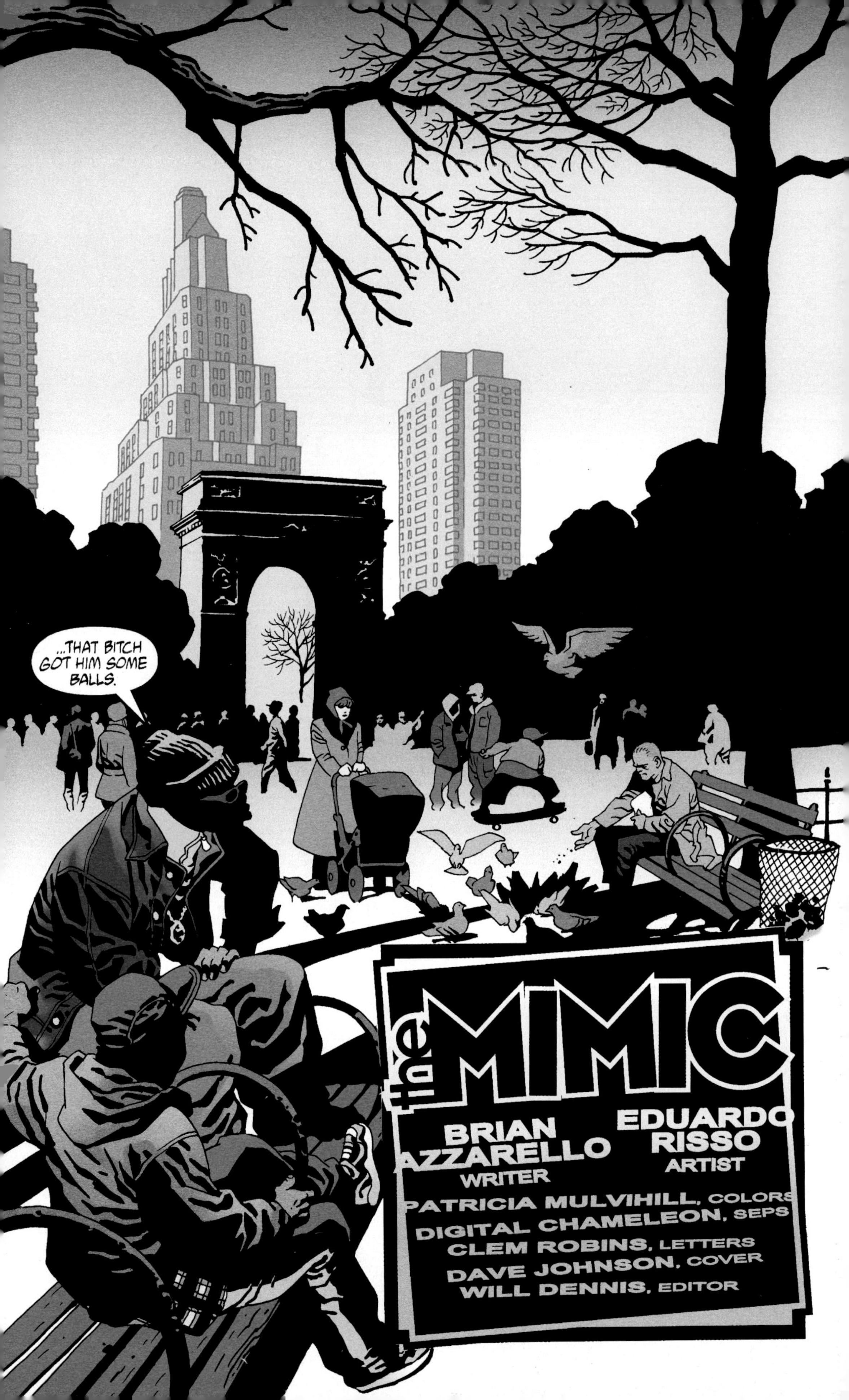

...THAT BITCH GOT HIM SOME BALLS.
the MIMIC
BRIAN AZZARELLO WRITER
EDUARDO RISSO ARTIST
PATRICIA MULVIHILL, COLORS
DIGITAL CHAMELEON, SEPS
CLEM ROBINS, LETTERS
DAVE JOHNSON, COVER
WILL DENNIS, EDITOR

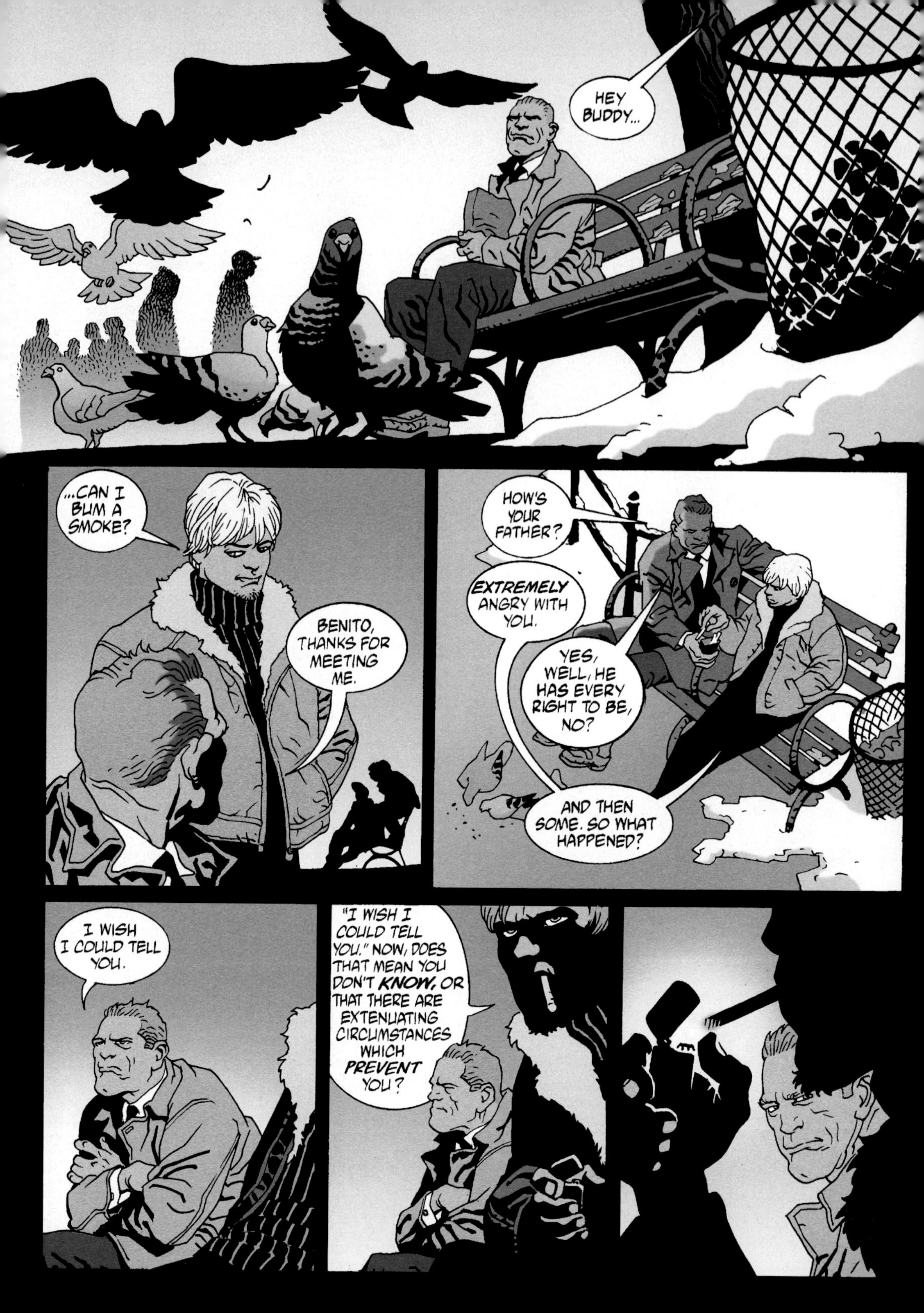
HEY BUDDY...
...CAN I BUM A SMOKE?
BENITO, THANKS FOR MEETING ME.
HOW'S YOUR FATHER?
EXTREMELY ANGRY WITH YOU.
YES, WELL, HE HAS EVERY RIGHT TO BE, NO?
AND THEN SOME. SO WHAT HAPPENED?
I WISH I COULD TELL YOU.
"I WISH I COULD TELL YOU." NOW, DOES THAT MEAN YOU DON'T KNOW, OR THAT THERE ARE EXTENUATING CIRCUMSTANCES WHICH PREVENT YOU?

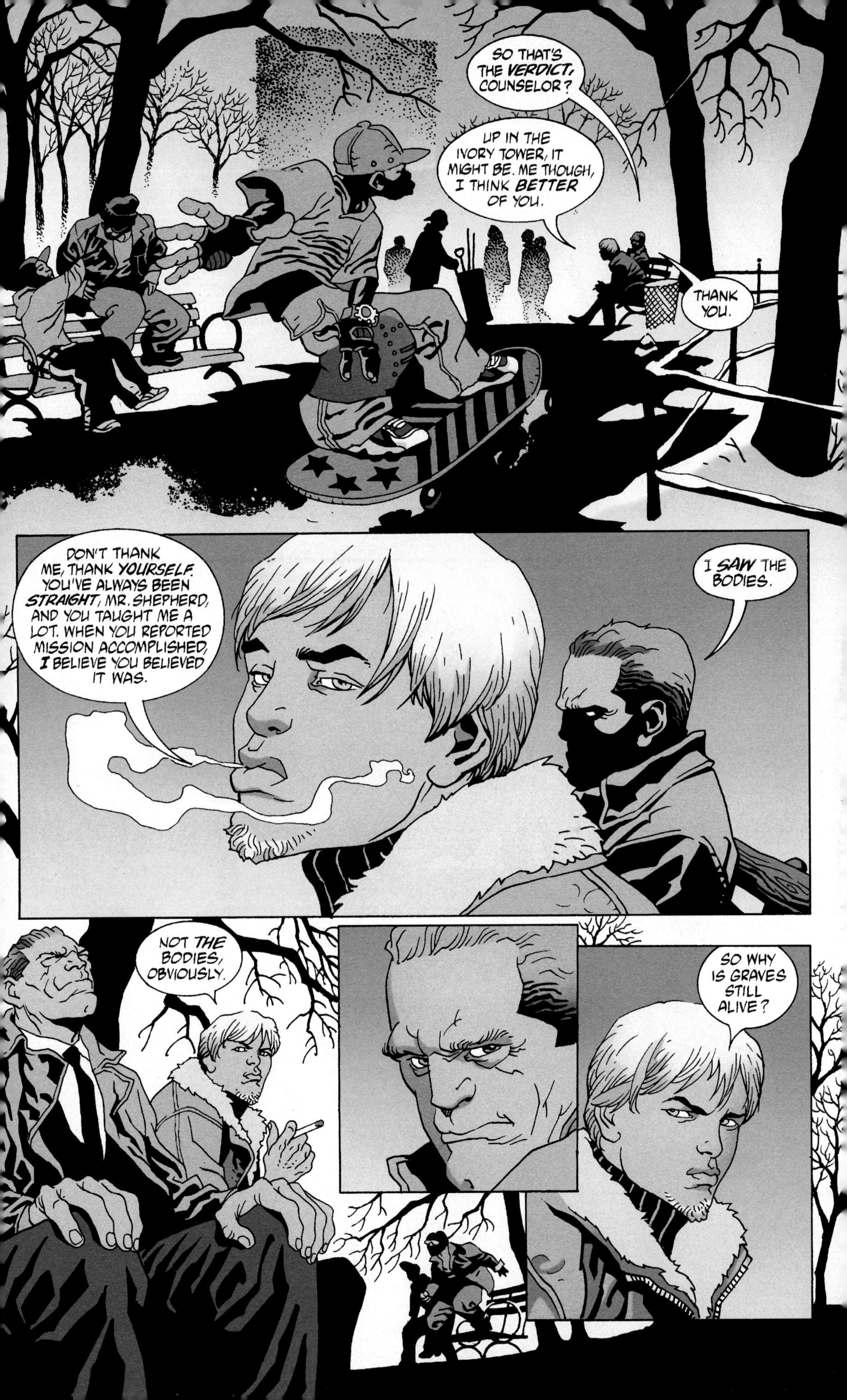
SO THAT'S THE VERDICT, COUNSELOR?
UP IN THE IVORY TOWER, IT MIGHT BE. ME THOUGH, I THINK BETTER OF YOU.
THANK YOU.
DON'T THANK ME, THANK YOURSELF. YOU'VE ALWAYS BEEN STRAIGHT, MR. SHEPHERD, AND YOU TAUGHT ME A LOT. WHEN YOU REPORTED MISSION ACCOMPLISHED, I BELIEVE YOU BELIEVED IT WAS.
I SAW THE BODIES.
NOT THE BODIES, OBVIOUSLY.
SO WHY IS GRAVES STILL ALIVE?

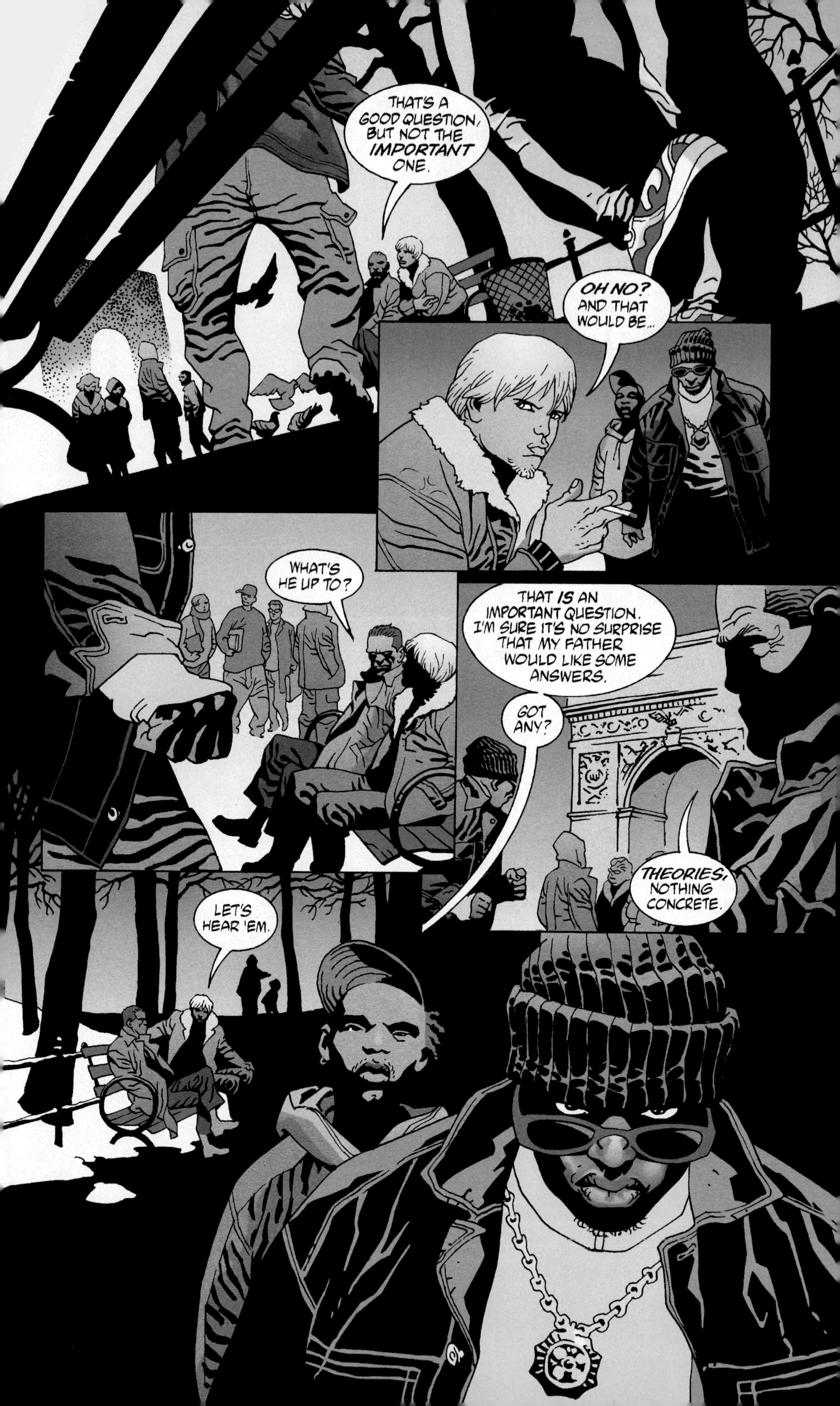
THAT'S A GOOD QUESTION, BUT NOT THE IMPORTANT ONE.
OH NO? AND THAT WOULD BE...
WHAT'S HE UP TO?
THAT IS AN IMPORTANT QUESTION. I'M SURE IT'S NO SURPRISE THAT MY FATHER WOULD LIKE SOME ANSWERS.
GOT ANY?
THEORIES, NOTHING CONCRETE.
LET'S HEAR 'EM.

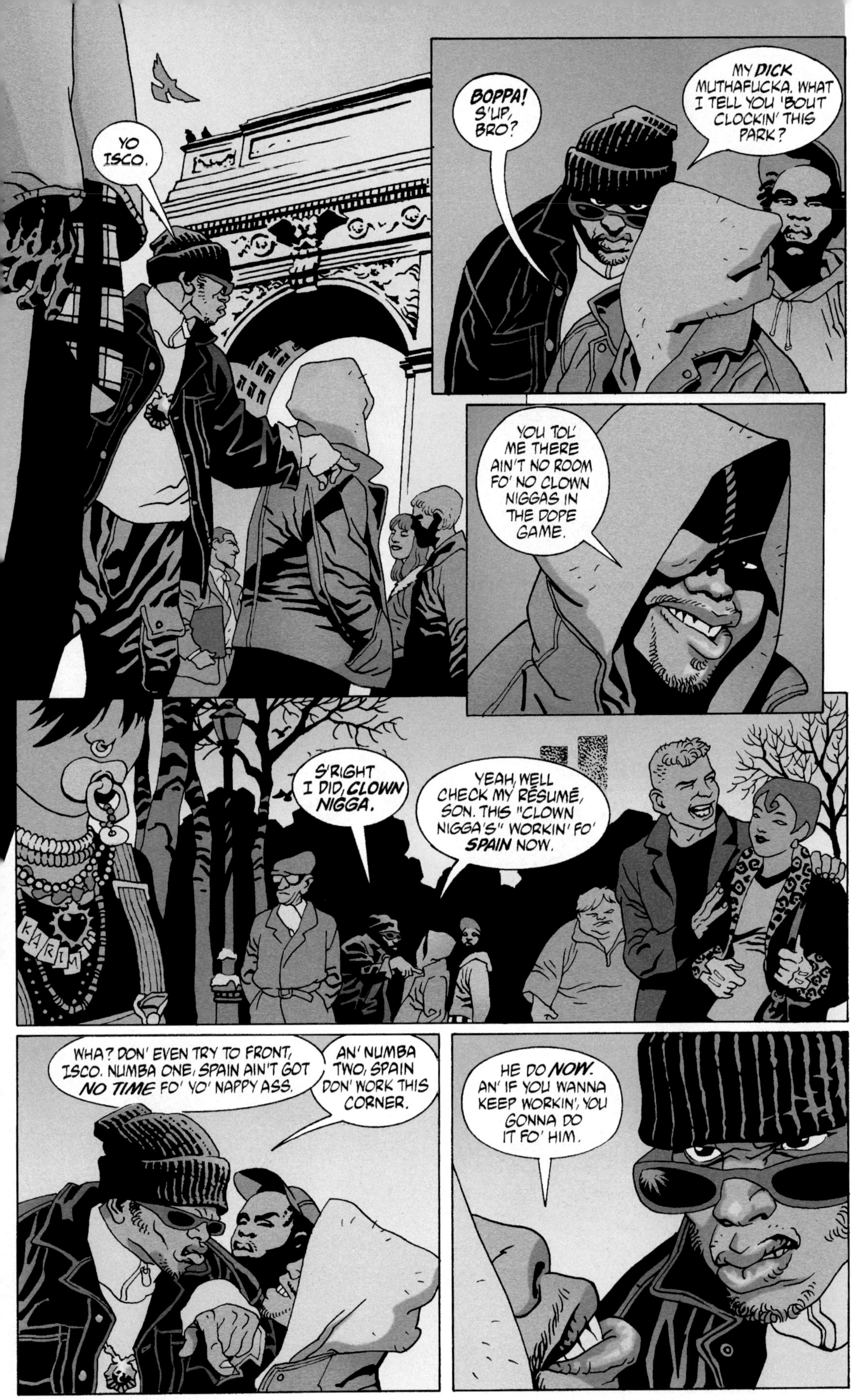
YO ISCO.
BOPPA! S'UP, BRO?
MY DICK MUTHAFUCKA. WHAT I TELL YOU 'BOUT CLOCKIN' THIS PARK?
YOU TOL' ME THERE AIN'T NO ROOM FO' NO CLOWN NIGGAS IN THE DOPE GAME.
S'RIGHT I DID, CLOWN NIGGA.
YEAH, WELL CHECK MY RÉSUMÉ, SON. THIS "CLOWN NIGGA'S" WORKIN' FO' SPAIN NOW.
KARIM
WHA? DON' EVEN TRY TO FRONT, ISCO. NUMBA ONE, SPAIN AIN'T GOT NO TIME FO' YO' NAPPY ASS.
AN' NUMBA TWO, SPAIN DON' WORK THIS CORNER.
HE DO NOW. AN' IF YOU WANNA KEEP WORKIN', YOU GONNA DO IT FO' HIM.

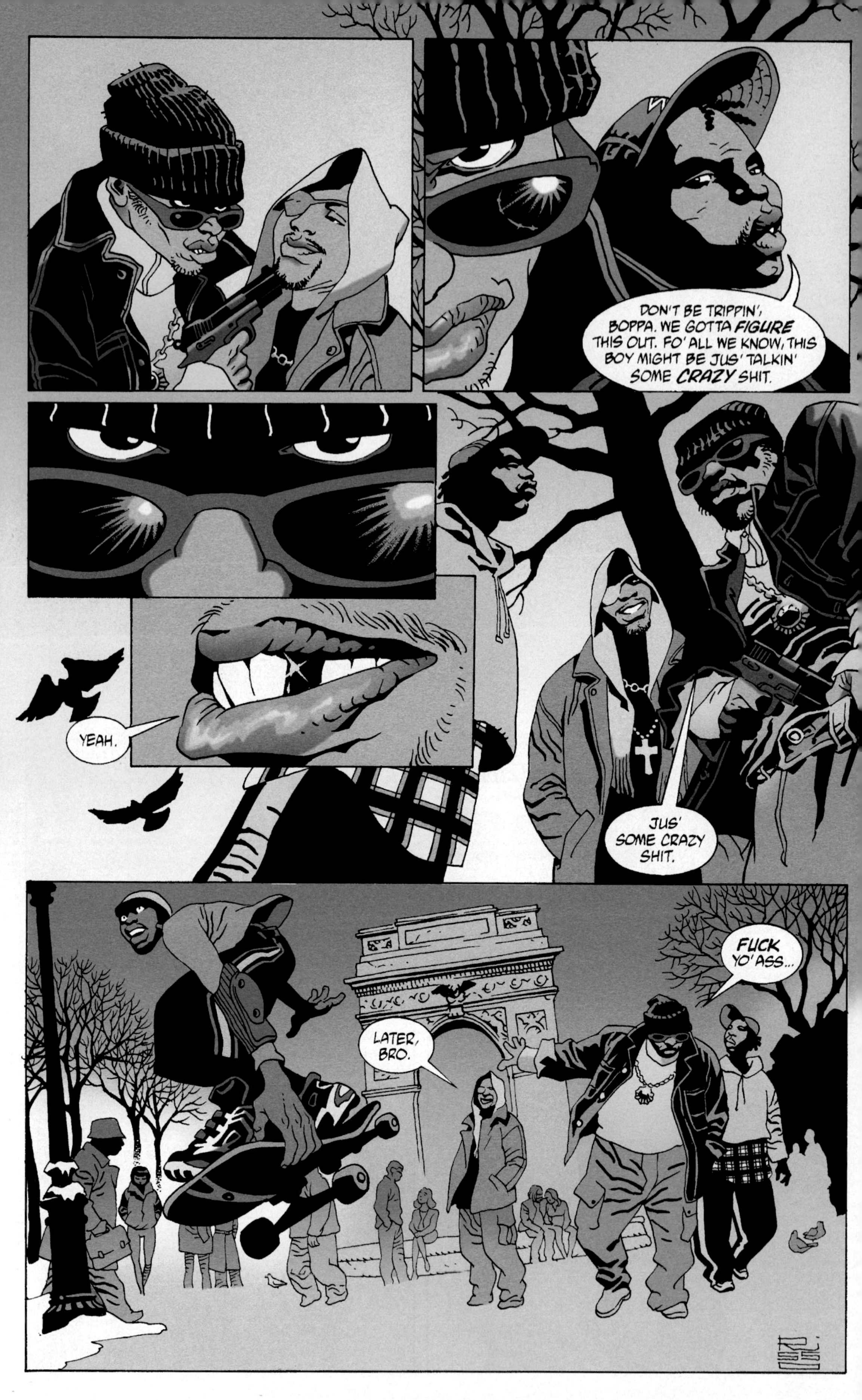
DON'T BE TRIPPIN', BOPPA. WE GOTTA FIGURE THIS OUT. FO' ALL WE KNOW, THIS BOY MIGHT BE JUS' TALKIN' SOME CRAZY SHIT.
YEAH.
JUS' SOME CRAZY SHIT.
FUCK YO' ASS...
LATER, BRO.

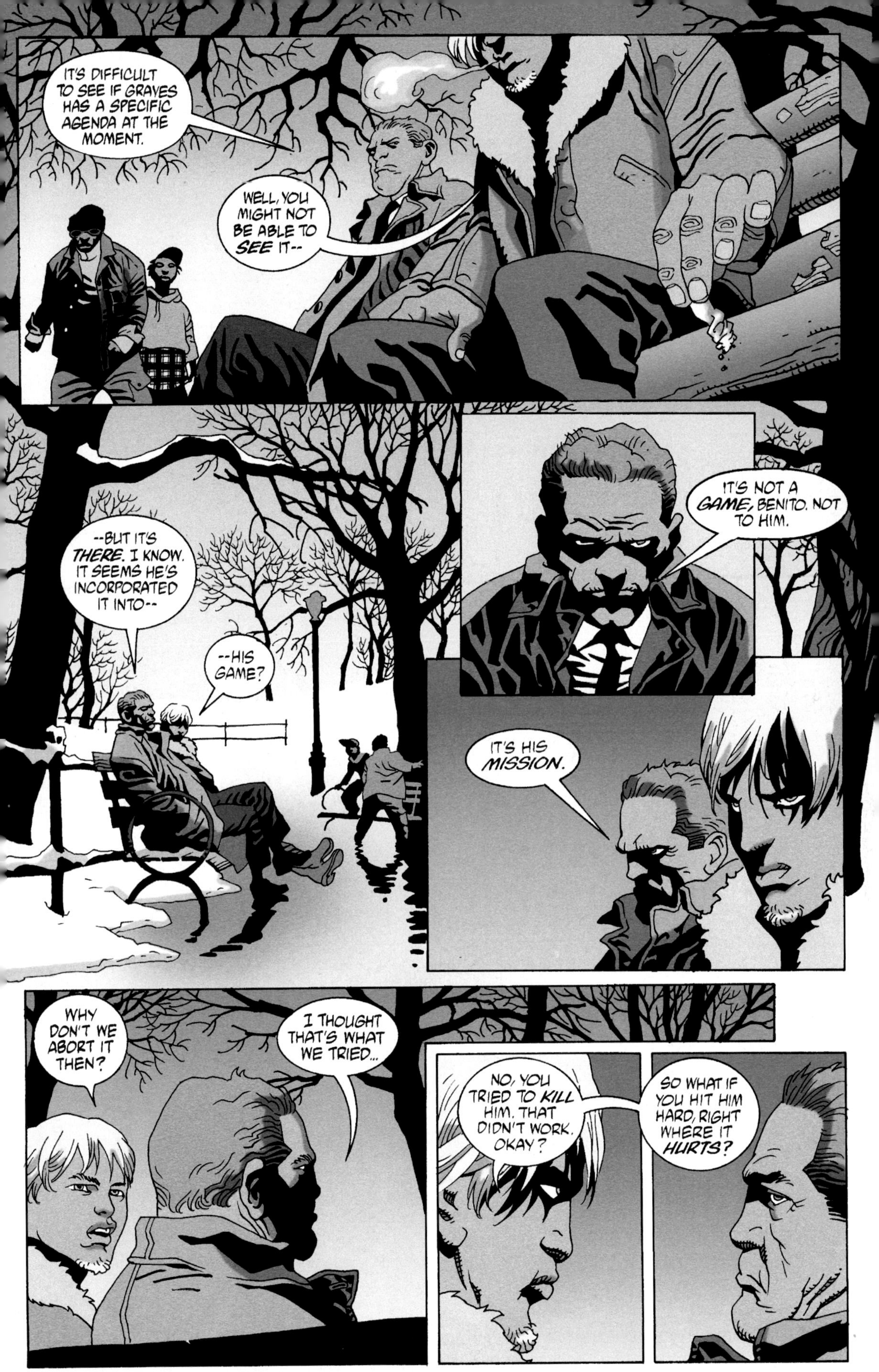
IT'S DIFFICULT TO SEE IF GRAVES HAS A SPECIFIC AGENDA AT THE MOMENT.
WELL, YOU MIGHT NOT BE ABLE TO SEE IT--
--BUT IT'S THERE. I KNOW. IT SEEMS HE'S INCORPORATED IT INTO--
--HIS GAME?
IT'S NOT A GAME, BENITO. NOT TO HIM.
IT'S HIS MISSION.
WHY DON'T WE ABORT IT THEN?
I THOUGHT THAT'S WHAT WE TRIED...
NO, YOU TRIED TO KILL HIM. THAT DIDN'T WORK. OKAY?
SO WHAT IF YOU HIT HIM HARD, RIGHT WHERE IT HURTS?

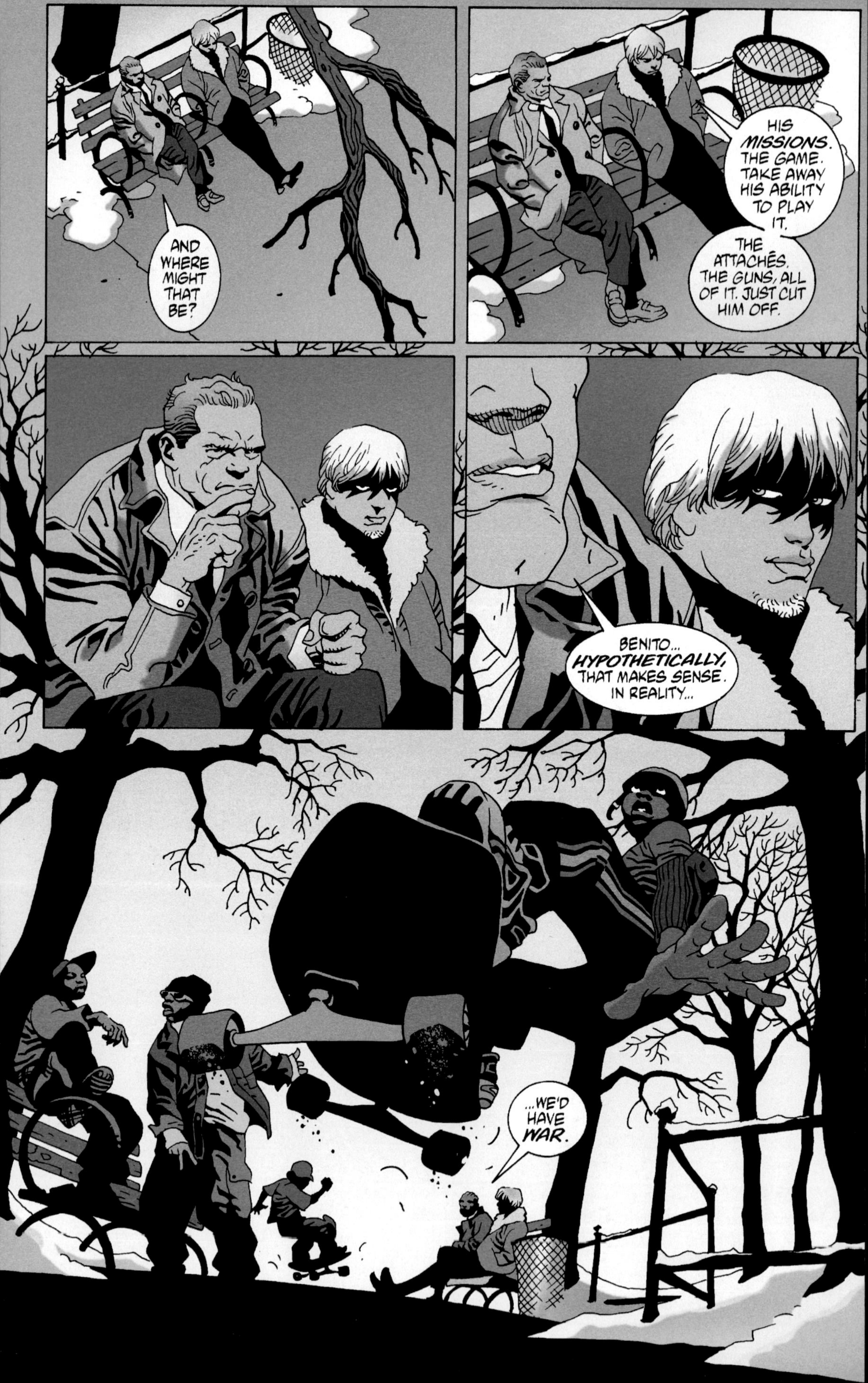
AND WHERE MIGHT THAT BE?
HIS MISSIONS. THE GAME. TAKE AWAY HIS ABILITY TO PLAY IT.
THE ATTACHÉS. THE GUNS, ALL OF IT. JUST CUT HIM OFF.
BENITO... HYPOTHETICALLY, THAT MAKES SENSE. IN REALITY...
...WE'D HAVE WAR.

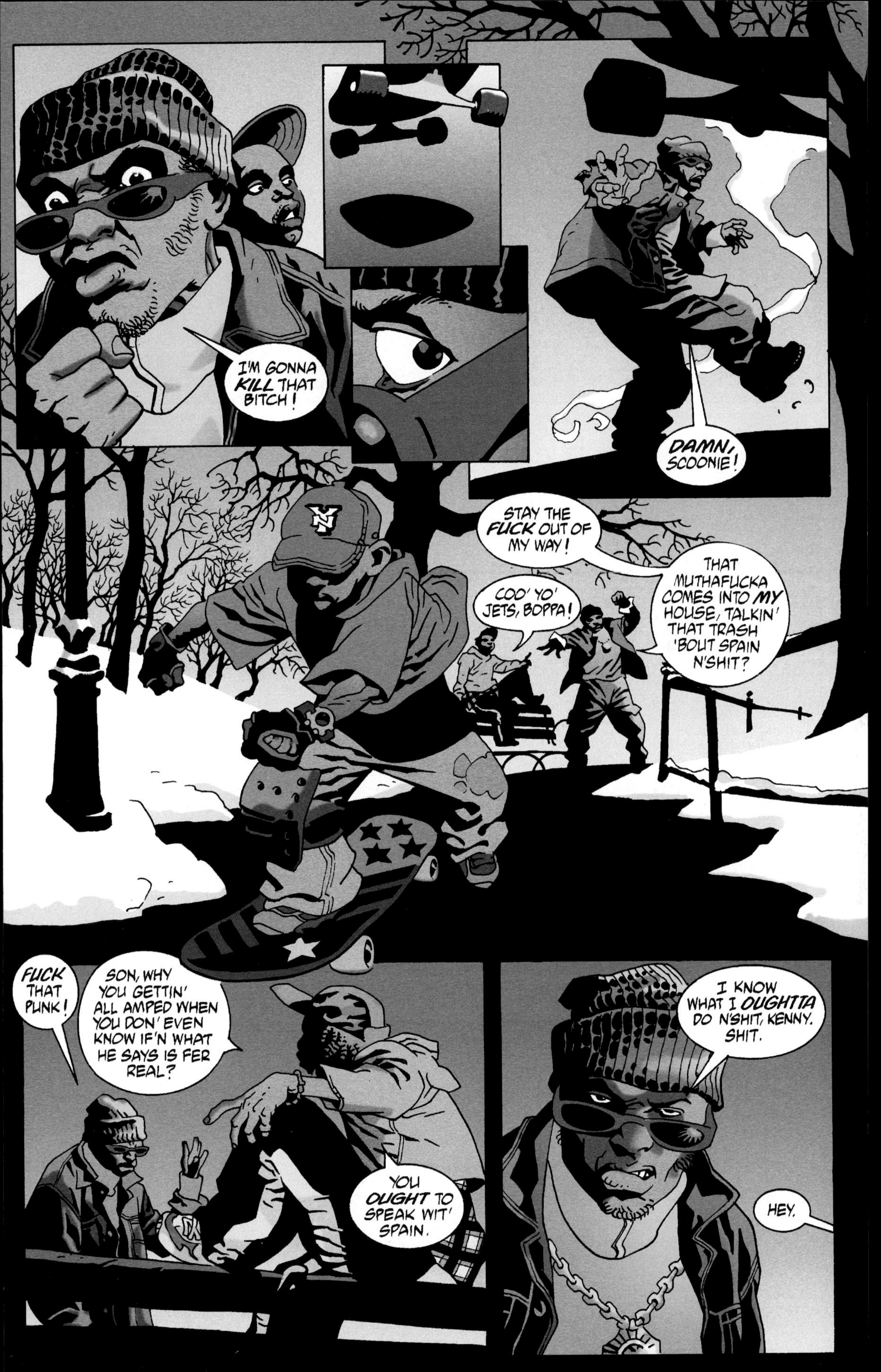
I'M GONNA KILL THAT BITCH!
DAMN, SCOONIE!
STAY THE FUCK OUT OF MY WAY!
THAT MUTHAFUCKA COMES INTO MY HOUSE, TALKIN' THAT TRASH 'BOUT SPAIN N'SHIT?
COO' YO' JETS, BOPPA!
FUCK THAT PUNK!
SON, WHY YOU GETTIN' ALL AMPED WHEN YOU DON' EVEN KNOW IF'N WHAT HE SAYS IS FER REAL?
YOU OUGHT TO SPEAK WIT' SPAIN.
I KNOW WHAT I OUGHTTA DO N'SHIT, KENNY. SHIT.
HEY.

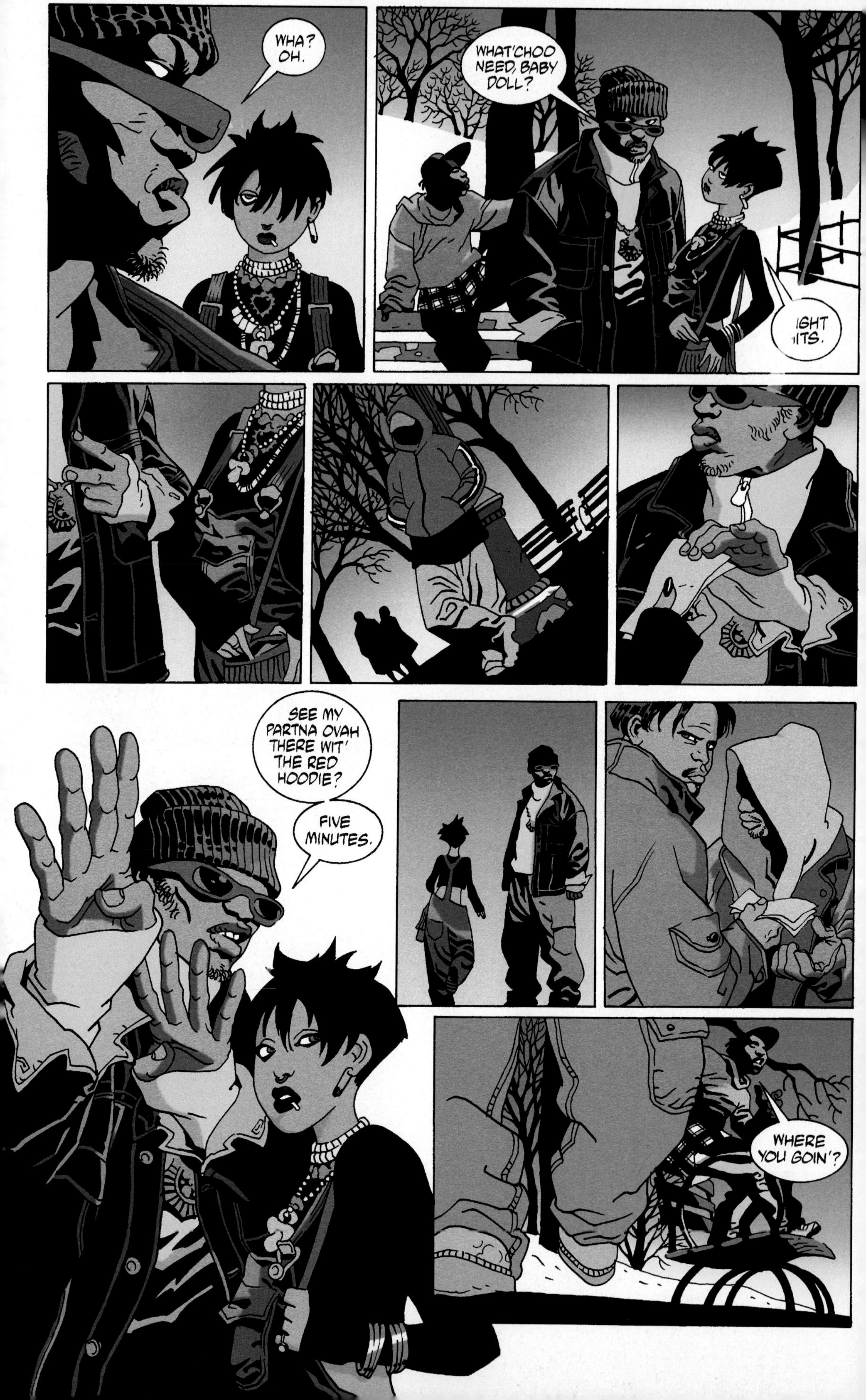
WHA? OH.
WHAT'CHOO NEED, BABY DOLL?
IGHT ITS.
SEE MY PARTNA OVAH THERE WIT' THE RED HOODIE?
FIVE MINUTES.
WHERE YOU GOIN'?

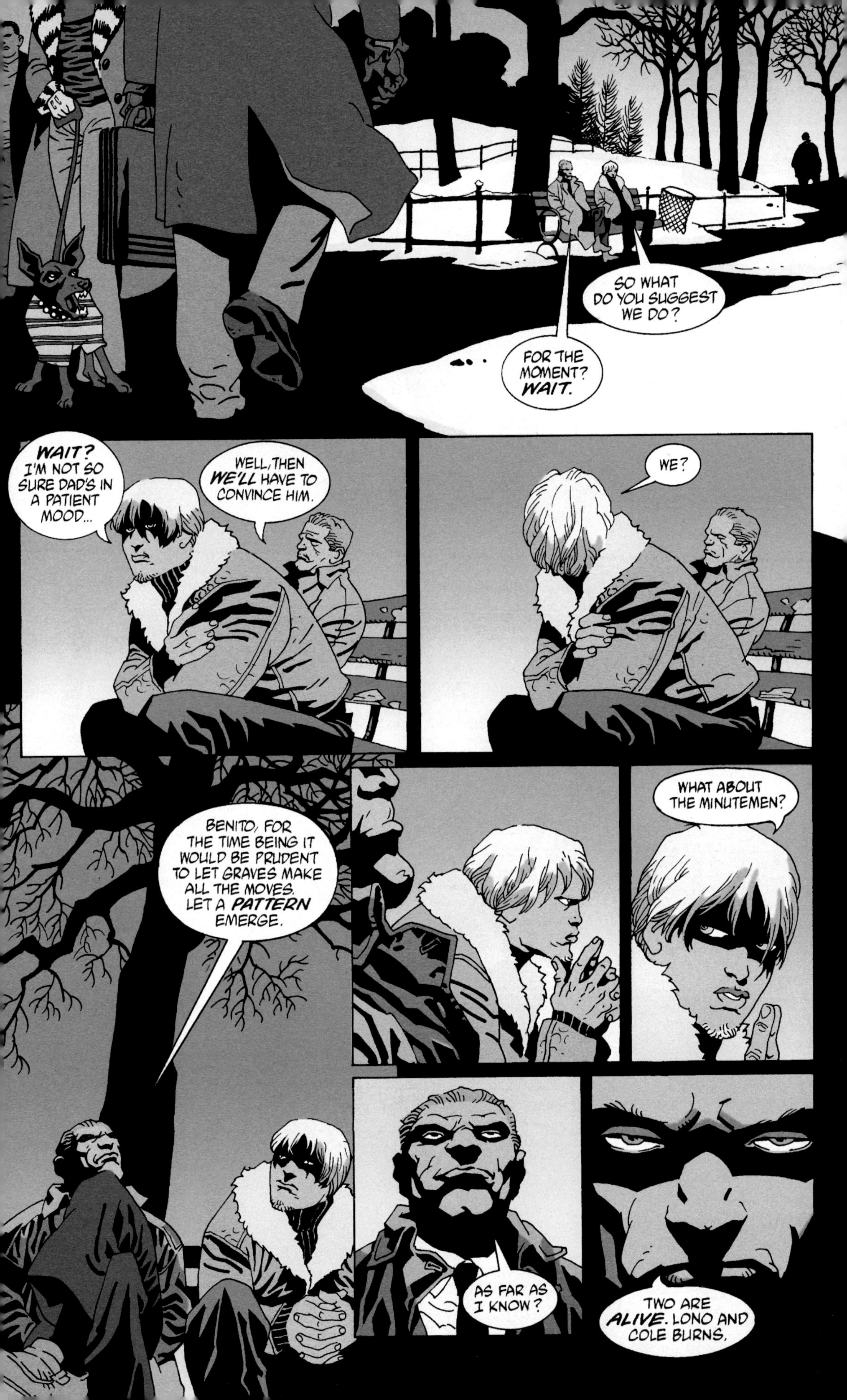

SO WHAT DO YOU SUGGEST WE DO?
FOR THE MOMENT? WAIT.
WAIT? I'M NOT SO SURE DAD'S IN A PATIENT MOOD...
WELL, THEN WE'LL HAVE TO CONVINCE HIM.
WE?
BENITO, FOR THE TIME BEING IT WOULD BE PRUDENT TO LET GRAVES MAKE ALL THE MOVES. LET A PATTERN EMERGE.
WHAT ABOUT THE MINUTEMEN?
AS FAR AS I KNOW?
TWO ARE ALIVE. LONO AND COLE BURNS.

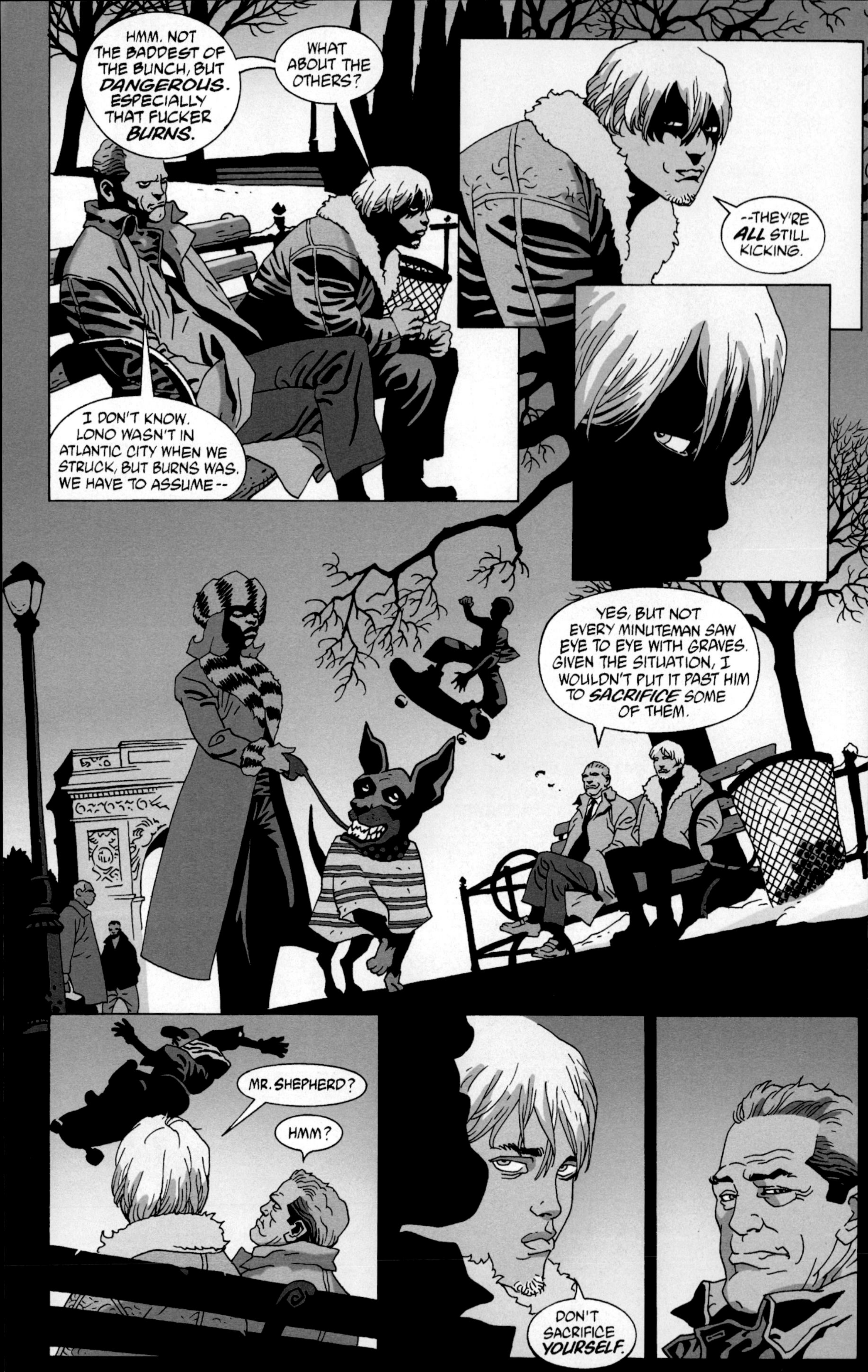
HMM. NOT THE BADDEST OF THE BUNCH, BUT **DANGEROUS.** ESPECIALLY THAT FUCKER **BURNS.**
WHAT ABOUT THE OTHERS?
I DON'T KNOW. LONO WASN'T IN ATLANTIC CITY WHEN WE STRUCK, BUT BURNS WAS. WE HAVE TO ASSUME--
--THEY'RE **ALL** STILL KICKING.
YES, BUT NOT EVERY MINUTEMAN SAW EYE TO EYE WITH GRAVES. GIVEN THE SITUATION, I WOULDN'T PUT IT PAST HIM TO **SACRIFICE** SOME OF THEM.
MR. SHEPHERD?
HMM?
DON'T SACRIFICE **YOURSELF.**

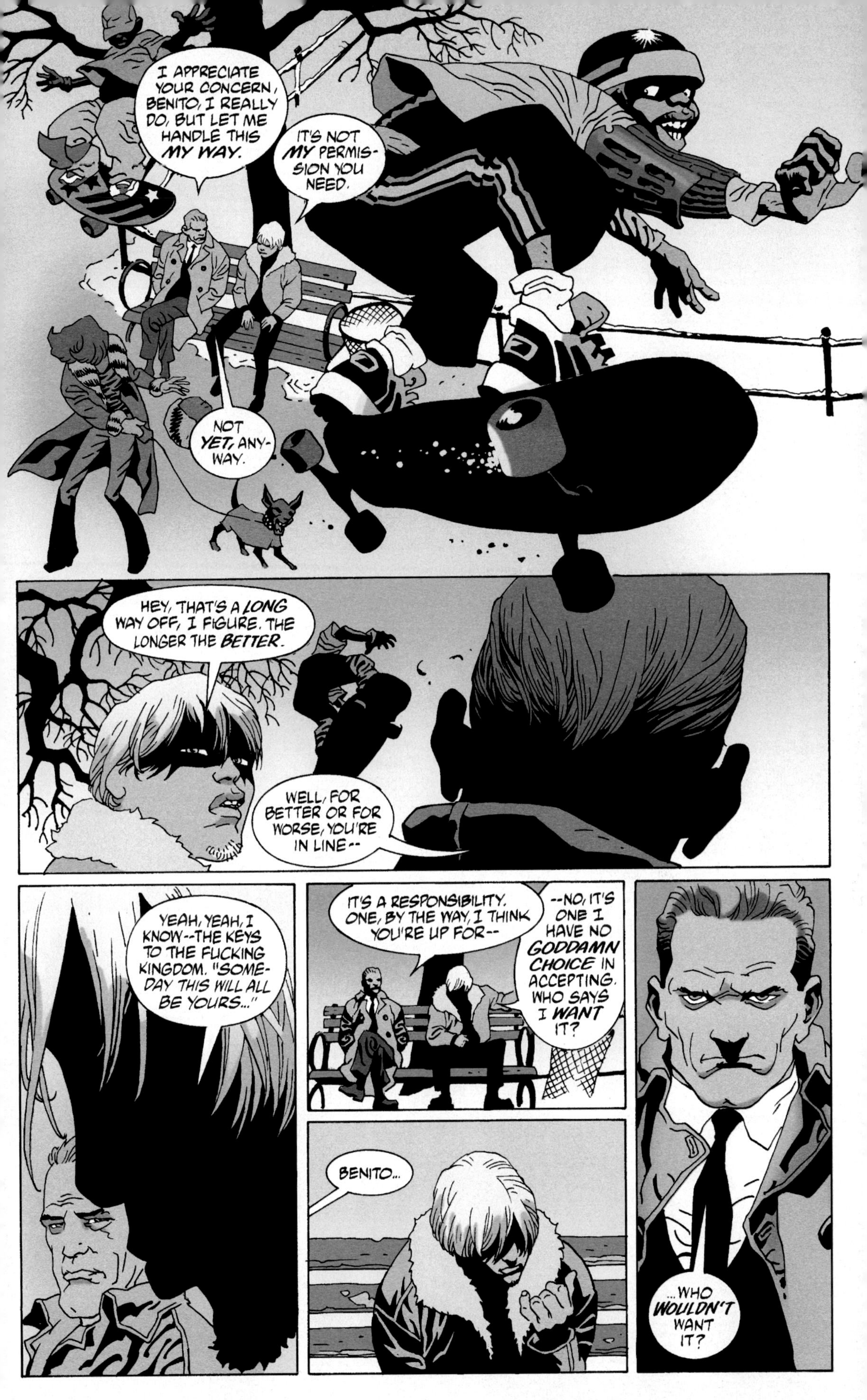
I APPRECIATE YOUR CONCERN, BENITO, I REALLY DO, BUT LET ME HANDLE THIS MY WAY.
IT'S NOT MY PERMISSION YOU NEED.
NOT YET, ANYWAY.
HEY, THAT'S A LONG WAY OFF, I FIGURE. THE LONGER THE BETTER.
WELL, FOR BETTER OR FOR WORSE, YOU'RE IN LINE--
YEAH, YEAH, I KNOW--THE KEYS TO THE FUCKING KINGDOM. "SOMEDAY THIS WILL ALL BE YOURS..."
IT'S A RESPONSIBILITY. ONE, BY THE WAY, I THINK YOU'RE UP FOR--
--NO, IT'S ONE I HAVE NO GODDAMN CHOICE IN ACCEPTING. WHO SAYS I WANT IT?
BENITO...
...WHO WOULDN'T WANT IT?

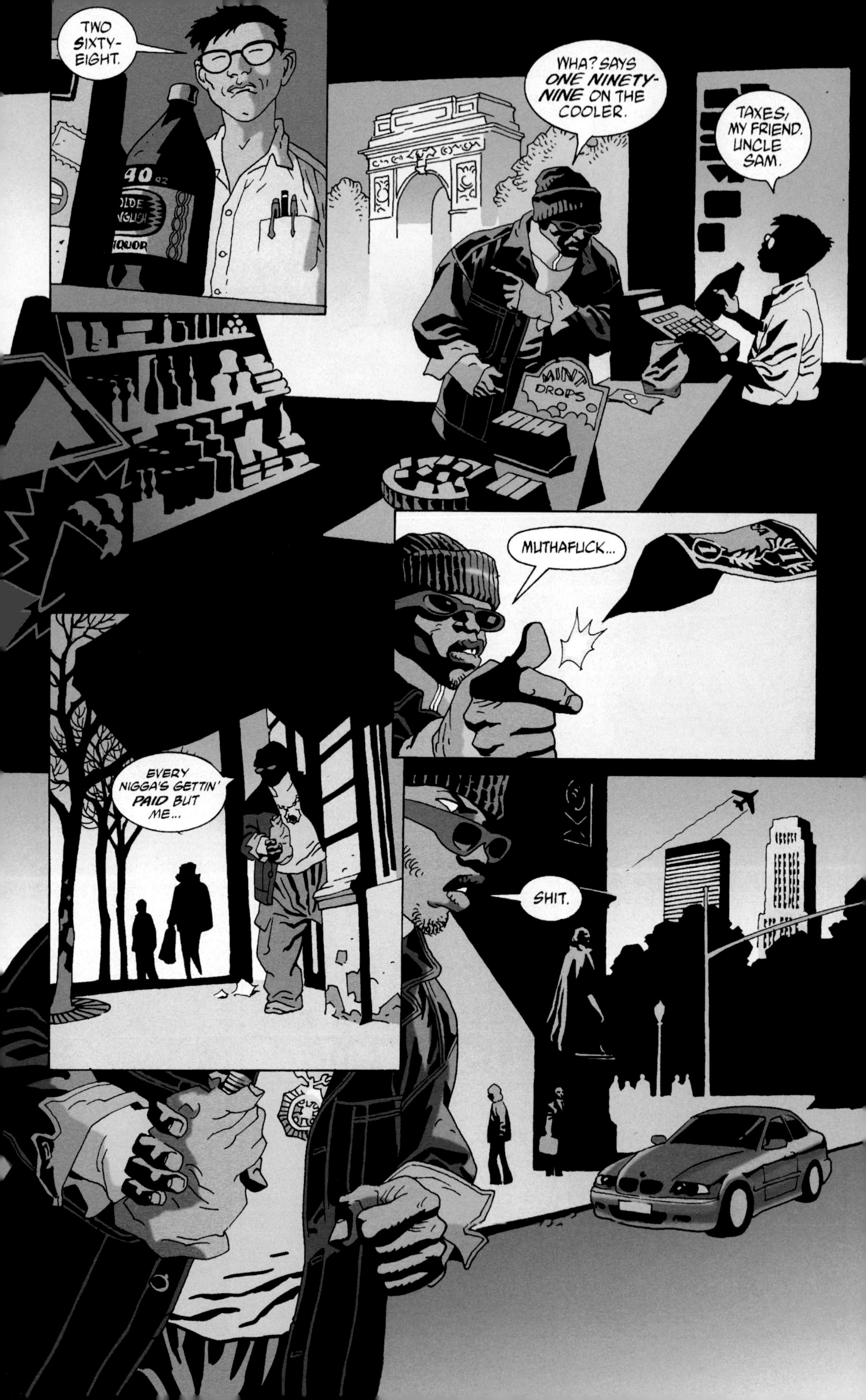

TWO SIXTY-EIGHT.
40 oz OLDE ENGLISH LIQUOR
WHA? SAYS ONE NINETY-NINE ON THE COOLER.
TAXES, MY FRIEND. UNCLE SAM.
MINT DROPS
MUTHAFUCK...
EVERY NIGGA'S GETTIN' PAID BUT ME...
SHIT.

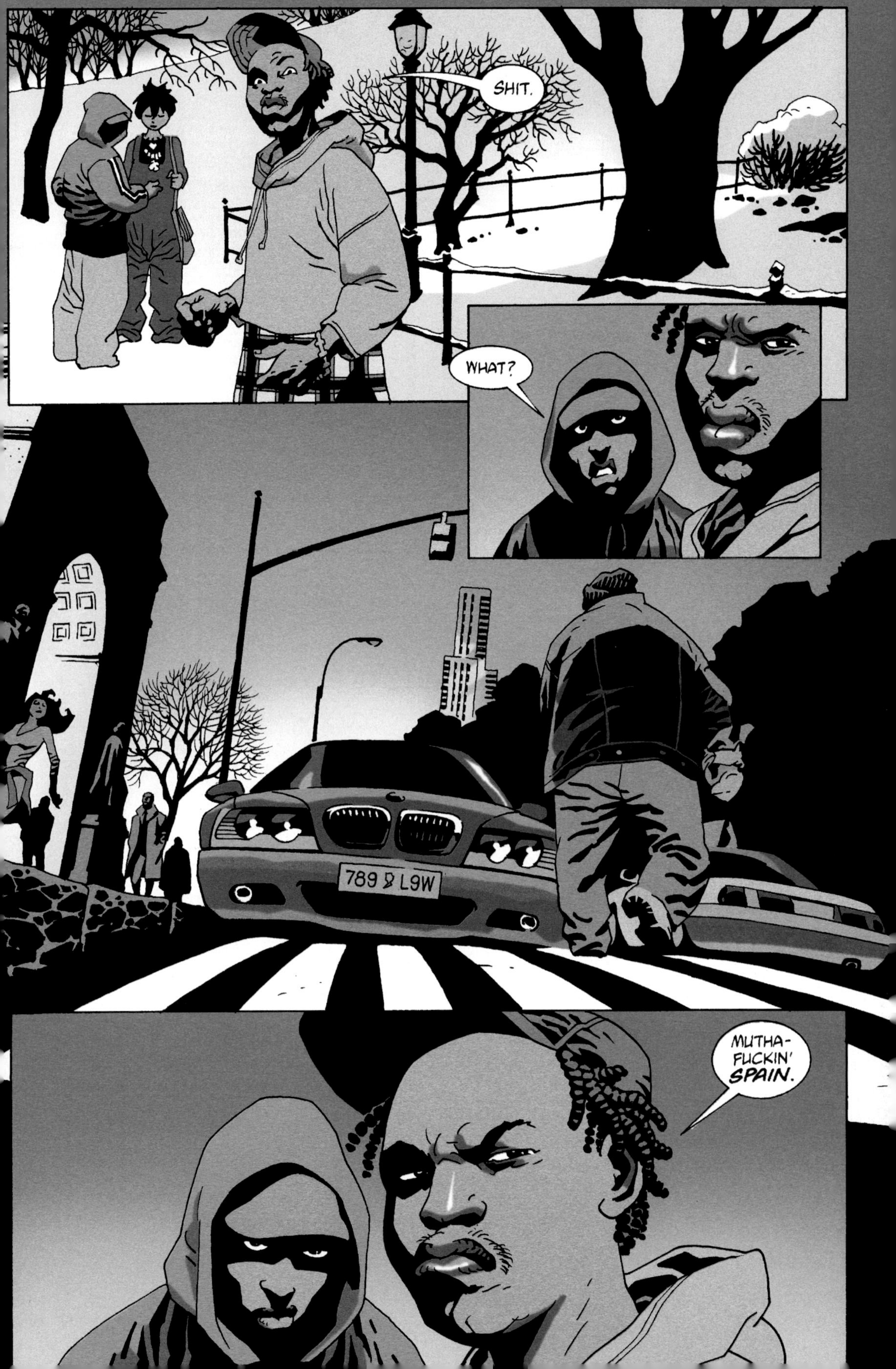
SHIT.
WHAT?
789 L9W
MUTHA-FUCKIN' *SPAIN*.

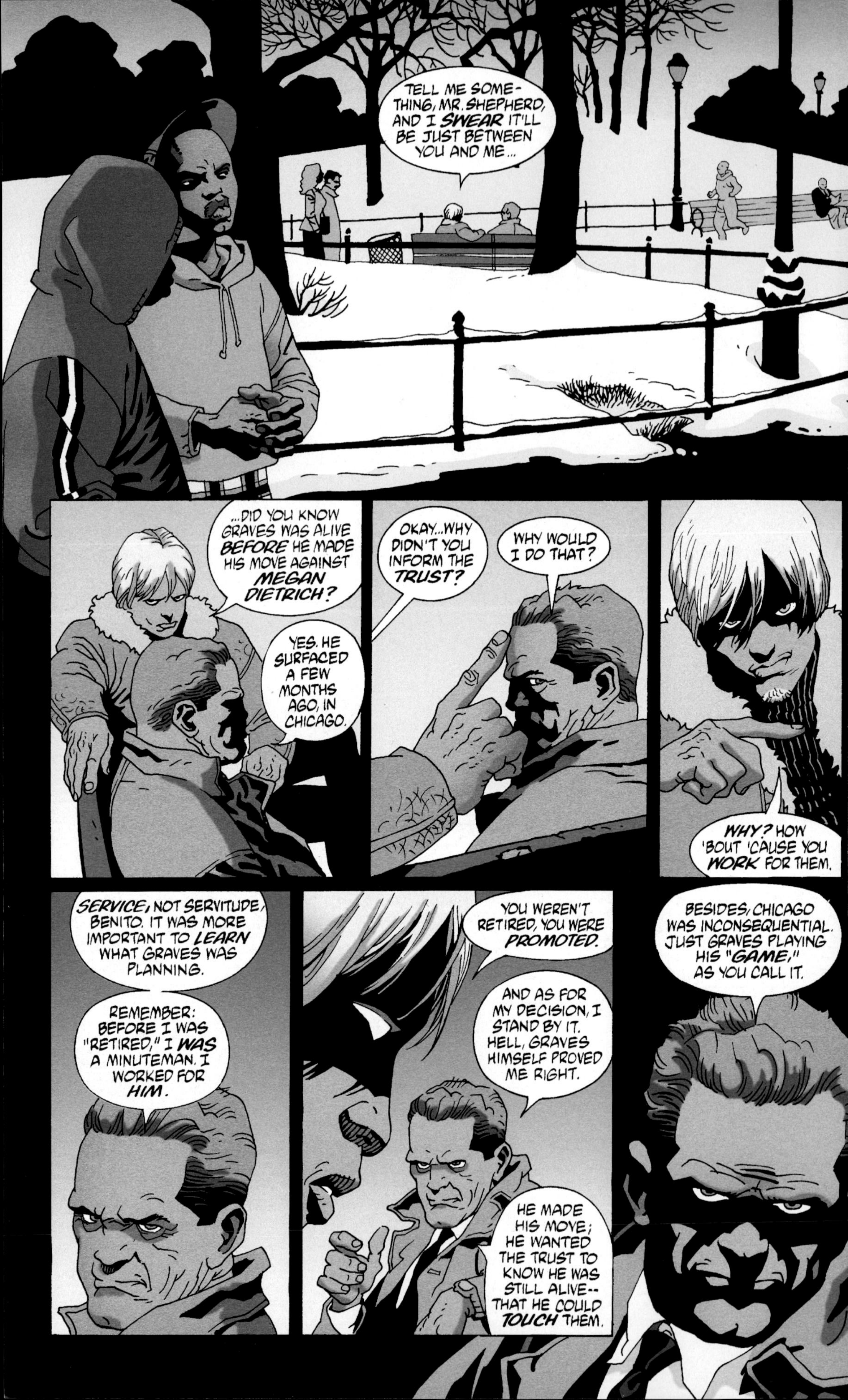

TELL ME SOME-THING, MR. SHEPHERD, AND I SWEAR IT'LL BE JUST BETWEEN YOU AND ME...
...DID YOU KNOW GRAVES WAS ALIVE BEFORE HE MADE HIS MOVE AGAINST MEGAN DIETRICH?
YES. HE SURFACED A FEW MONTHS AGO, IN CHICAGO.
OKAY...WHY DIDN'T YOU INFORM THE TRUST?
WHY WOULD I DO THAT?
WHY? HOW 'BOUT 'CAUSE YOU WORK FOR THEM.
SERVICE, NOT SERVITUDE, BENITO. IT WAS MORE IMPORTANT TO LEARN WHAT GRAVES WAS PLANNING.
REMEMBER: BEFORE I WAS "RETIRED," I WAS A MINUTEMAN. I WORKED FOR HIM.
YOU WEREN'T RETIRED, YOU WERE PROMOTED.
AND AS FOR MY DECISION, I STAND BY IT. HELL, GRAVES HIMSELF PROVED ME RIGHT.
HE MADE HIS MOVE; HE WANTED THE TRUST TO KNOW HE WAS STILL ALIVE-- THAT HE COULD TOUCH THEM.
BESIDES, CHICAGO WAS INCONSEQUENTIAL. JUST GRAVES PLAYING HIS "GAME," AS YOU CALL IT.

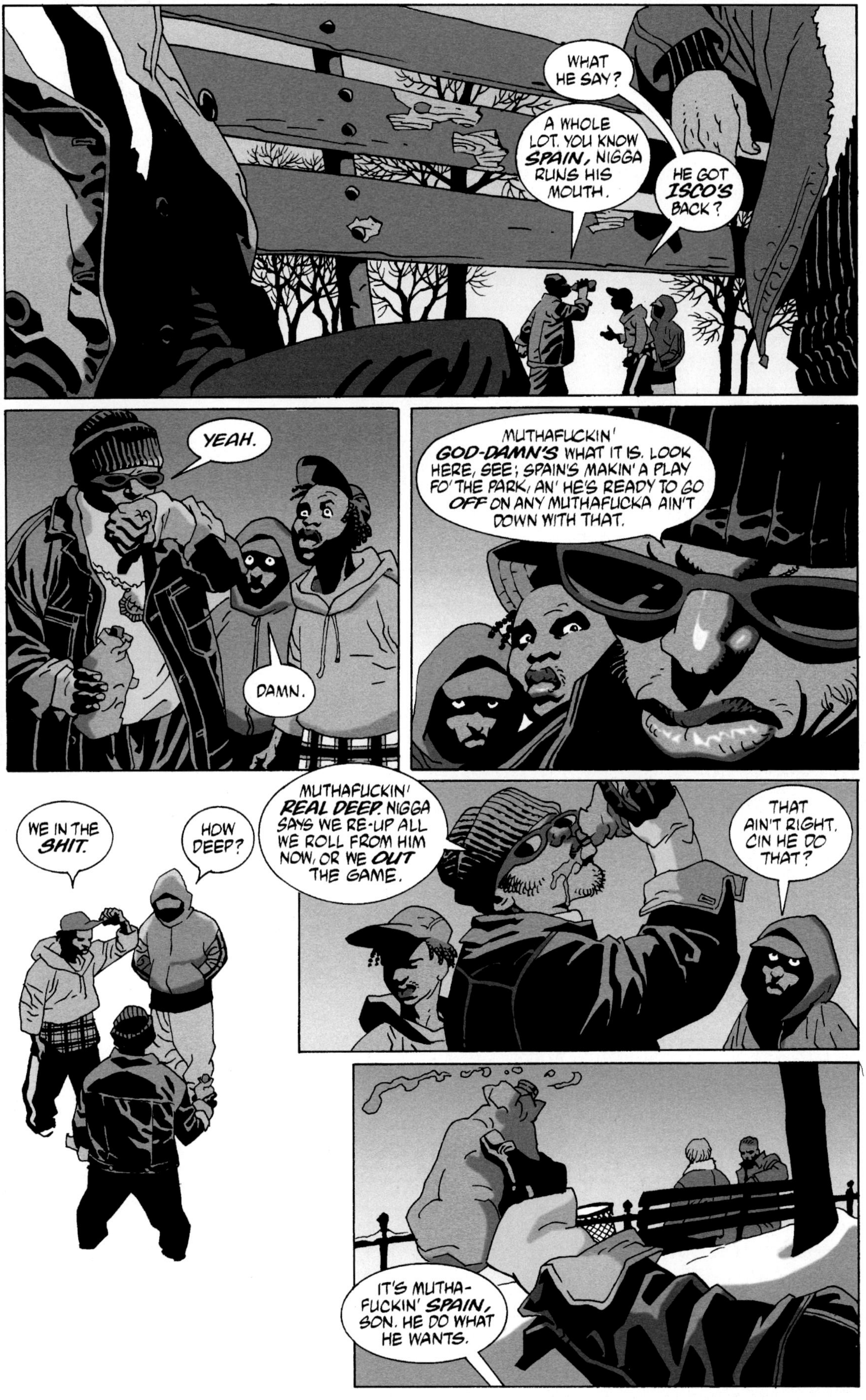
WHAT HE SAY?
A WHOLE LOT. YOU KNOW SPAIN, NIGGA RUNS HIS MOUTH.
HE GOT ISCO'S BACK?
YEAH.
DAMN.
MUTHAFUCKIN' GOD-DAMN'S WHAT IT IS. LOOK HERE, SEE; SPAIN'S MAKIN' A PLAY FO' THE PARK, AN' HE'S READY TO GO OFF ON ANY MUTHAFUCKA AIN'T DOWN WITH THAT.
WE IN THE SHIT.
HOW DEEP?
MUTHAFUCKIN' REAL DEEP. NIGGA SAYS WE RE-UP ALL WE ROLL FROM HIM NOW, OR WE OUT THE GAME.
THAT AIN'T RIGHT. CIN HE DO THAT?
IT'S MUTHA-FUCKIN' SPAIN, SON. HE DO WHAT HE WANTS.

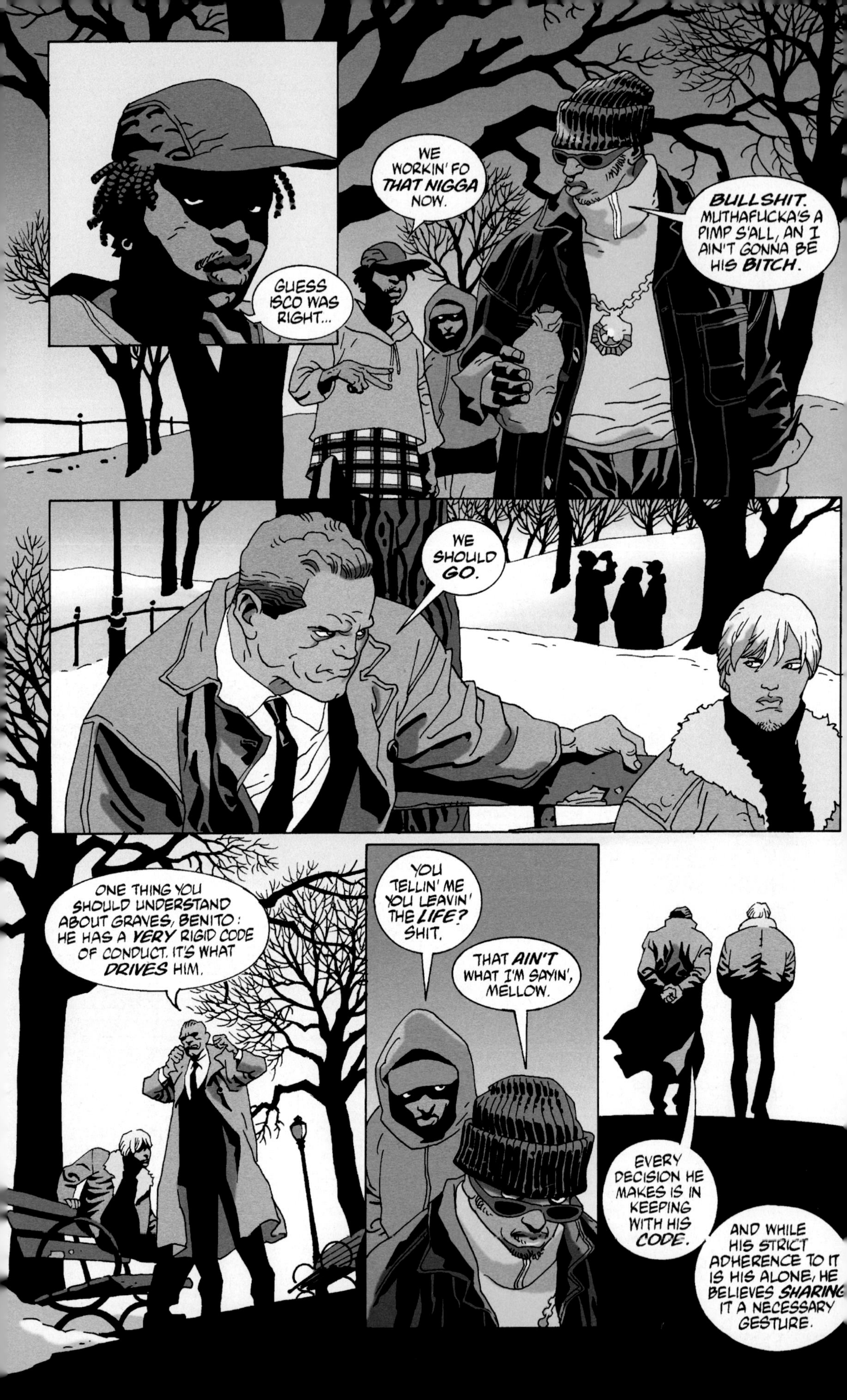

WE WORKIN' FO THAT NIGGA NOW.
GUESS ISCO WAS RIGHT...
BULLSHIT. MUTHAFUCKA'S A PIMP S'ALL, AN I AIN'T GONNA BE HIS BITCH.
WE SHOULD GO.
ONE THING YOU SHOULD UNDERSTAND ABOUT GRAVES, BENITO: HE HAS A VERY RIGID CODE OF CONDUCT. IT'S WHAT DRIVES HIM.
YOU TELLIN' ME YOU LEAVIN' THE LIFE? SHIT.
THAT AIN'T WHAT I'M SAYIN', MELLOW.
EVERY DECISION HE MAKES IS IN KEEPING WITH HIS CODE.
AND WHILE HIS STRICT ADHERENCE TO IT IS HIS ALONE, HE BELIEVES SHARING IT A NECESSARY GESTURE.

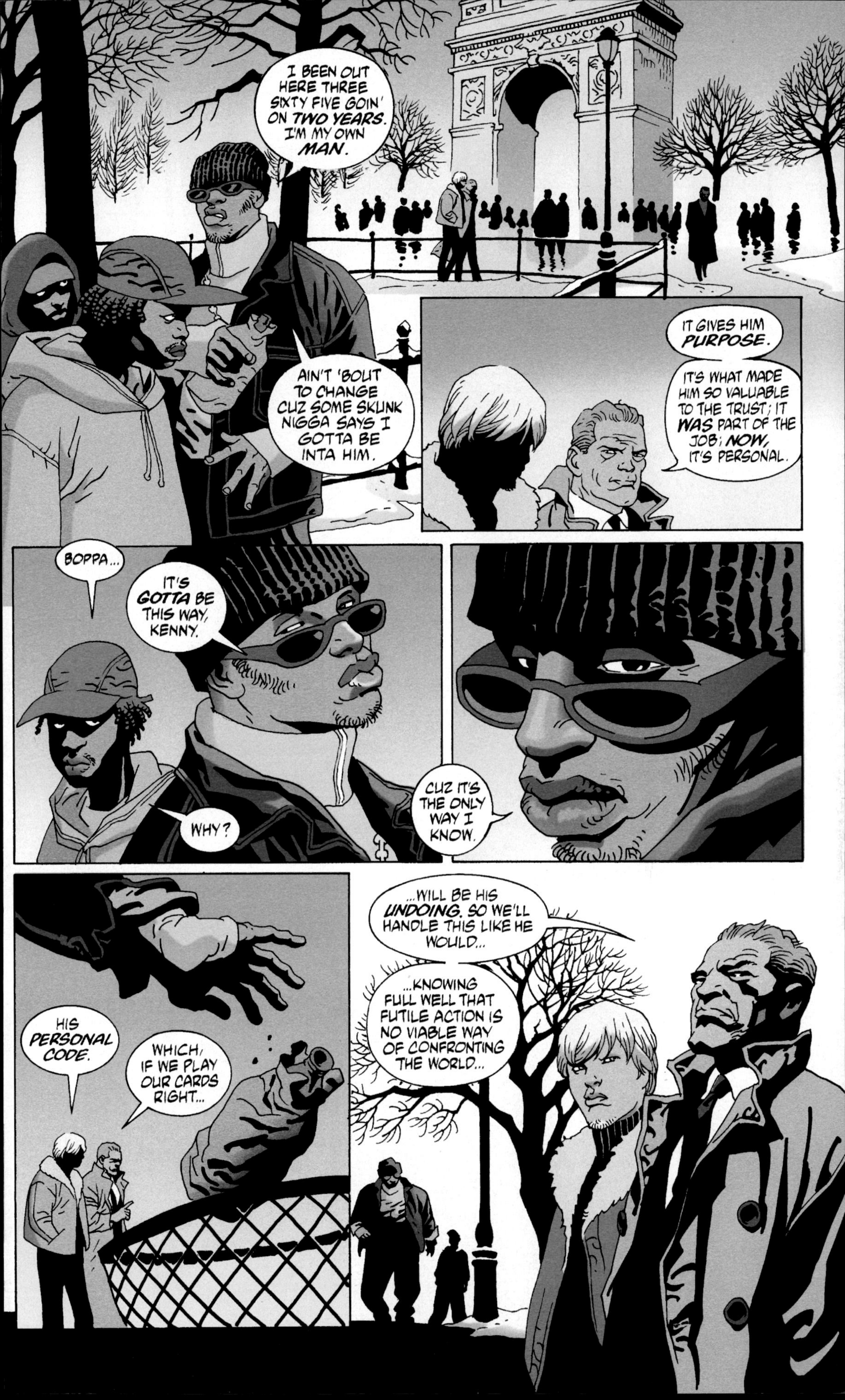
I BEEN OUT HERE THREE SIXTY FIVE GOIN' ON TWO YEARS. I'M MY OWN MAN.
AIN'T 'BOUT TO CHANGE CUZ SOME SKUNK NIGGA SAYS I GOTTA BE INTA HIM.
IT GIVES HIM PURPOSE.
IT'S WHAT MADE HIM SO VALUABLE TO THE TRUST; IT WAS PART OF THE JOB; NOW, IT'S PERSONAL.
BOPPA...
IT'S GOTTA BE THIS WAY, KENNY.
WHY?
CUZ IT'S THE ONLY WAY I KNOW.
HIS PERSONAL CODE.
WHICH, IF WE PLAY OUR CARDS RIGHT...
...WILL BE HIS UNDOING. SO WE'LL HANDLE THIS LIKE HE WOULD...
...KNOWING FULL WELL THAT FUTILE ACTION IS NO VIABLE WAY OF CONFRONTING THE WORLD...

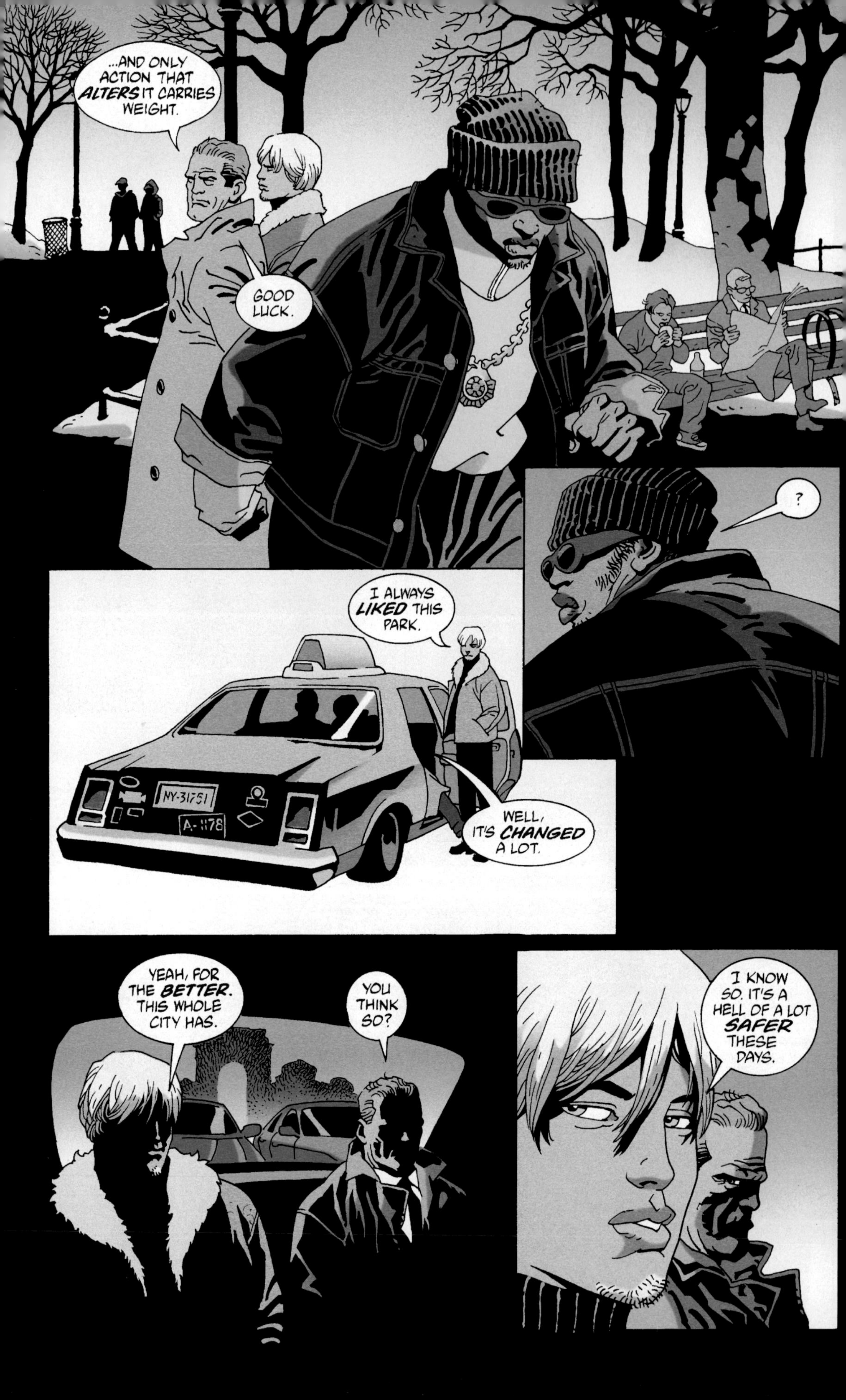
...AND ONLY ACTION THAT ALTERS IT CARRIES WEIGHT.
GOOD LUCK.
?
I ALWAYS LIKED THIS PARK.
NY-31751
A-1178
WELL, IT'S CHANGED A LOT.
YEAH, FOR THE BETTER. THIS WHOLE CITY HAS.
YOU THINK SO?
I KNOW SO. IT'S A HELL OF A LOT SAFER THESE DAYS.

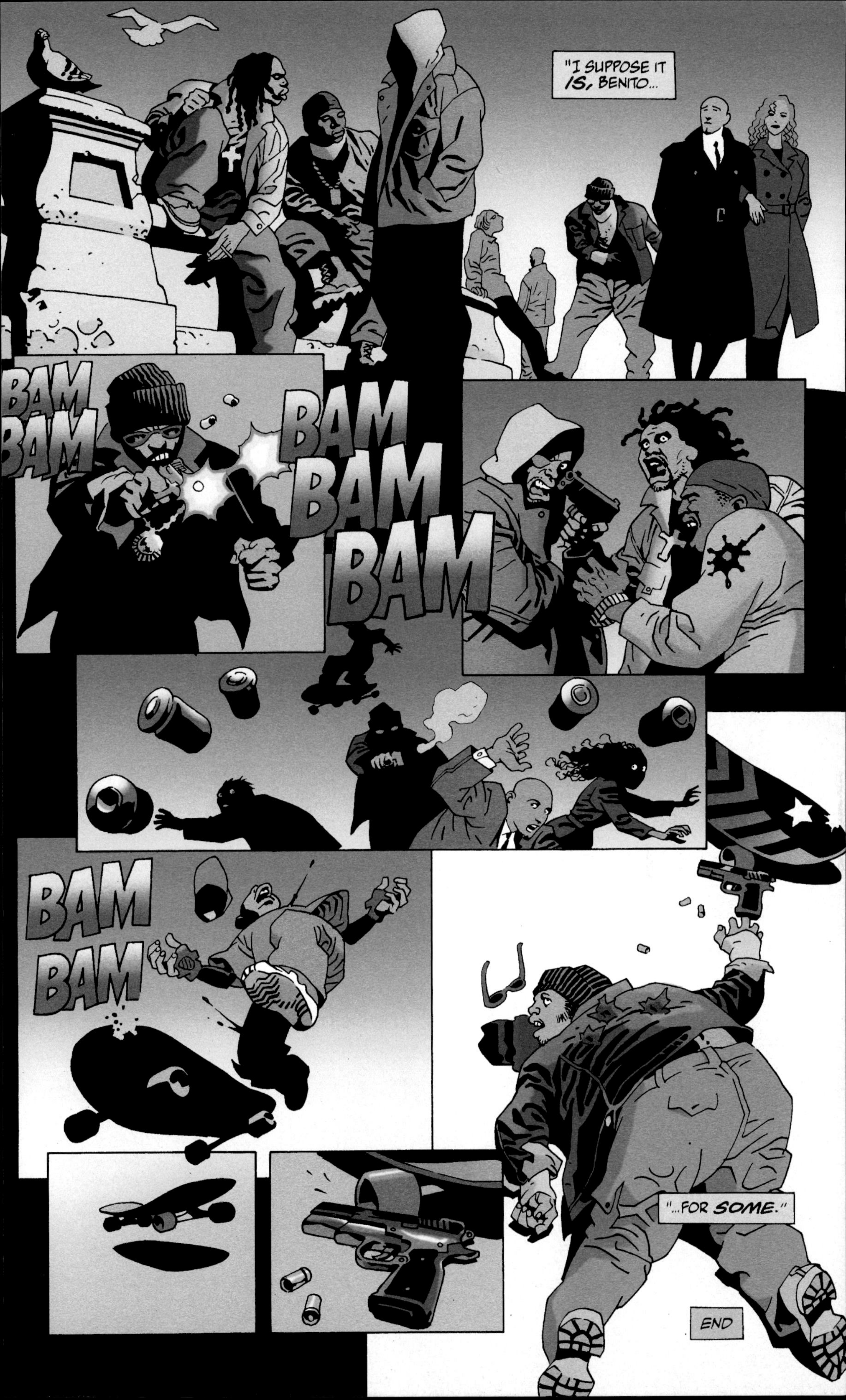

"I SUPPOSE IT IS, BENITO...
BAM
BAM
BAM
BAM
BAM
BAM
BAM
"...FOR SOME."
END

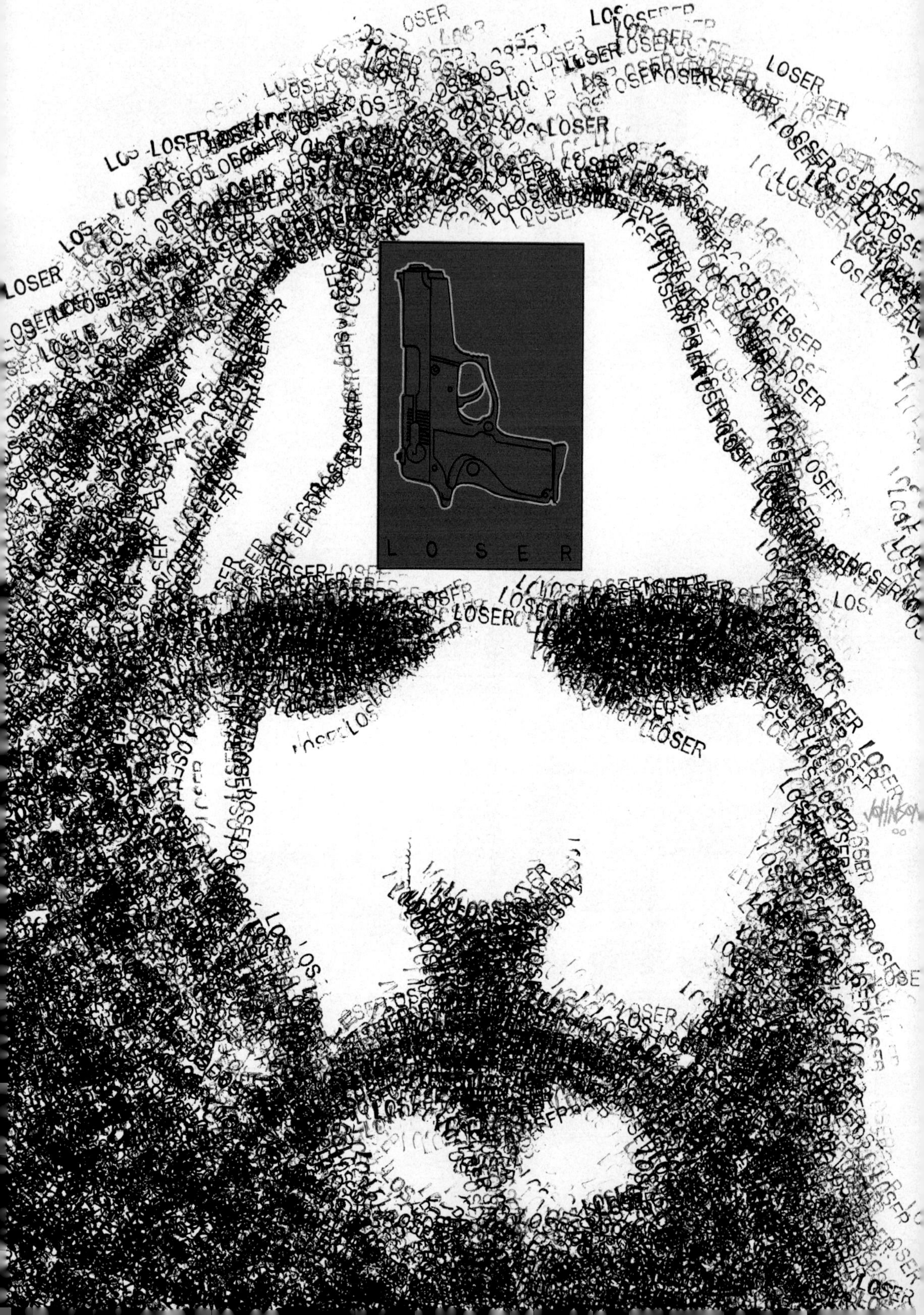
L O S E R

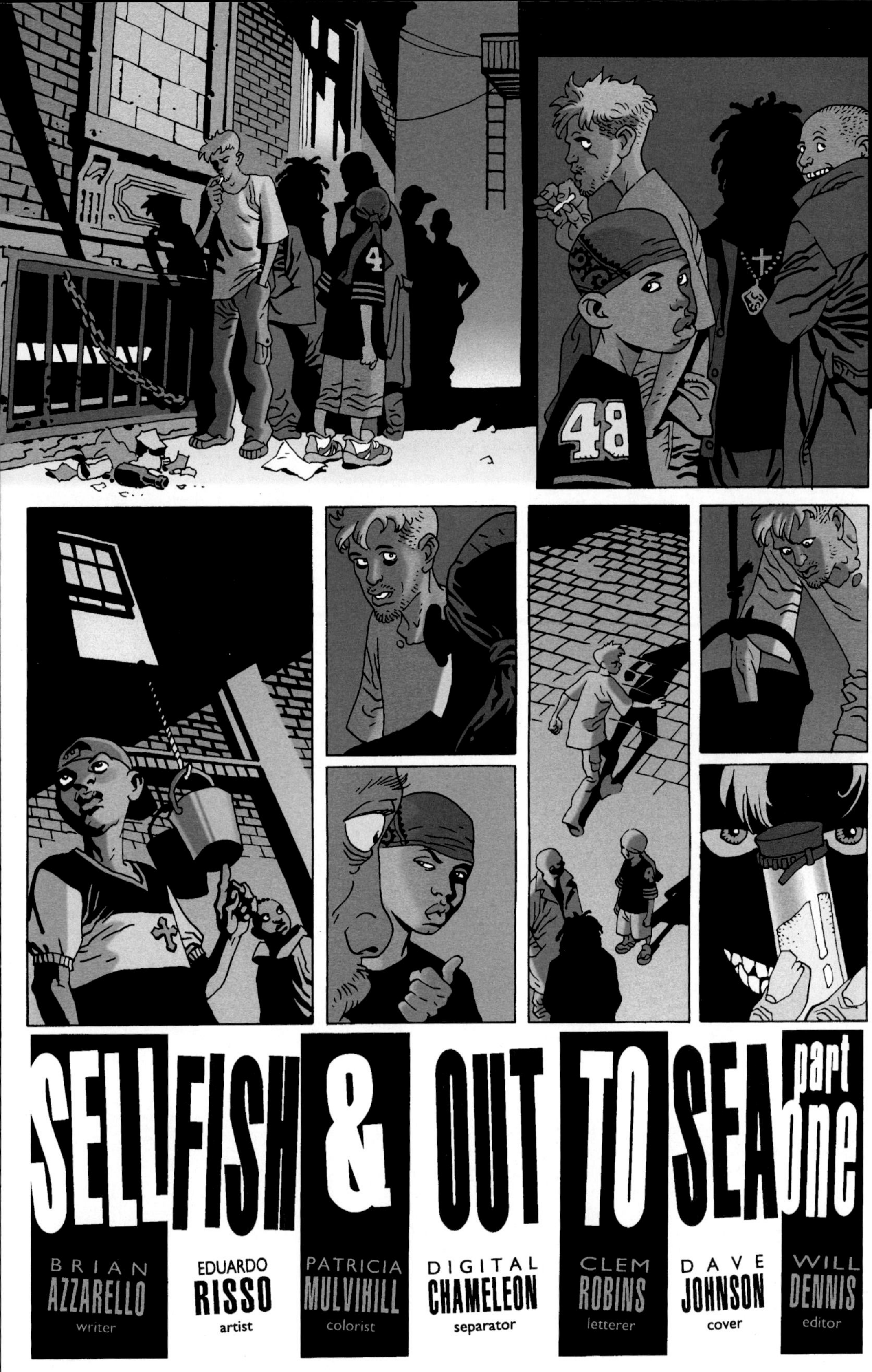
48

SELLFISH & OUT TO SEA part one

BRIAN AZZARELLO writer
EDUARDO RISSO artist
PATRICIA MULVIHILL colorist
DIGITAL CHAMELEON separator
CLEM ROBINS letterer
DAVE JOHNSON cover
WILL DENNIS editor

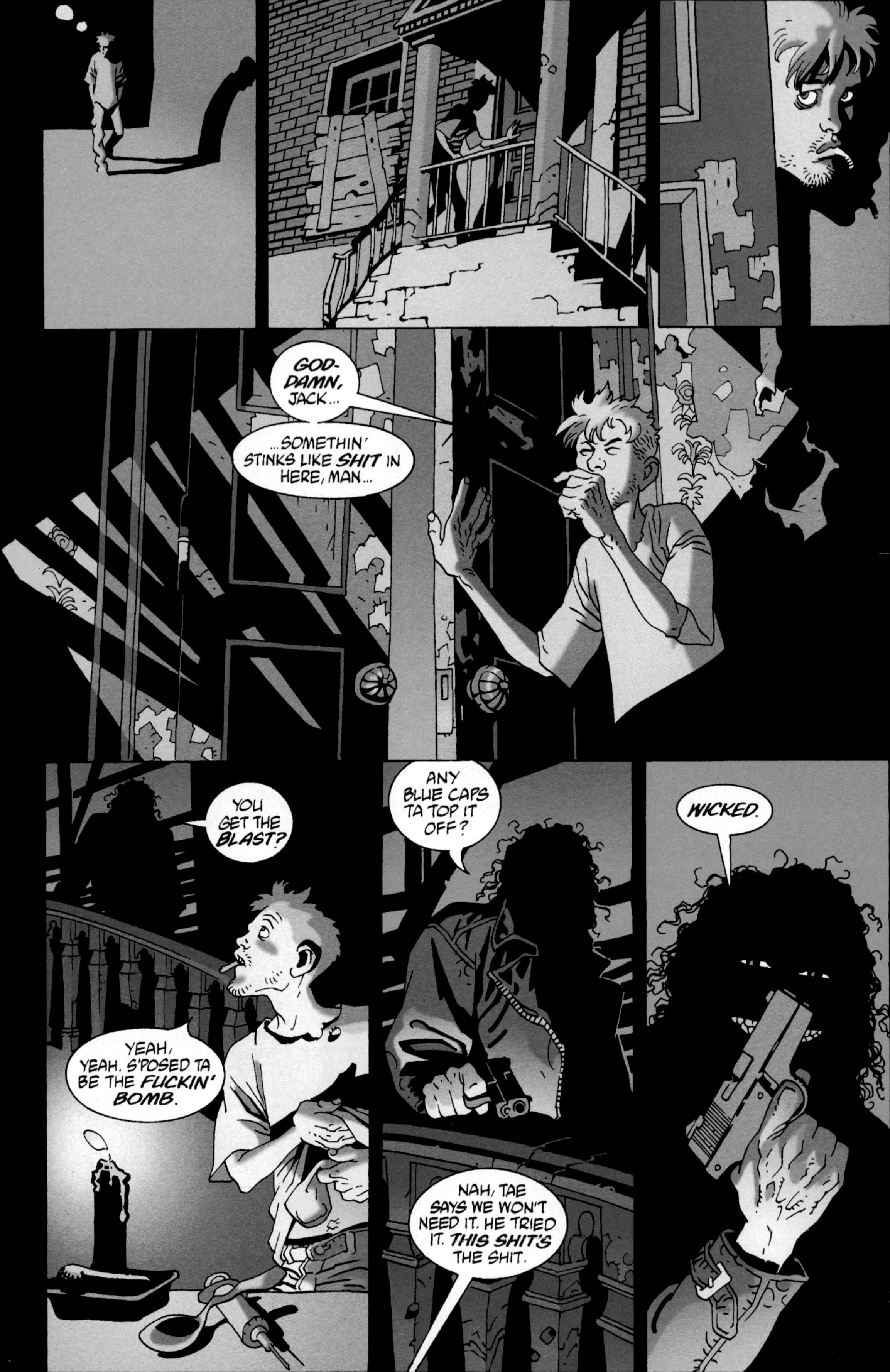
GOD-DAMN, JACK...
...SOMETHIN' STINKS LIKE SHIT IN HERE, MAN...
YOU GET THE BLAST?
YEAH, YEAH. S'POSED TA BE THE FUCKIN' BOMB.
ANY BLUE CAPS TA TOP IT OFF?
NAH, TAE SAYS WE WON'T NEED IT. HE TRIED IT. THIS SHIT'S THE SHIT.
WICKED.

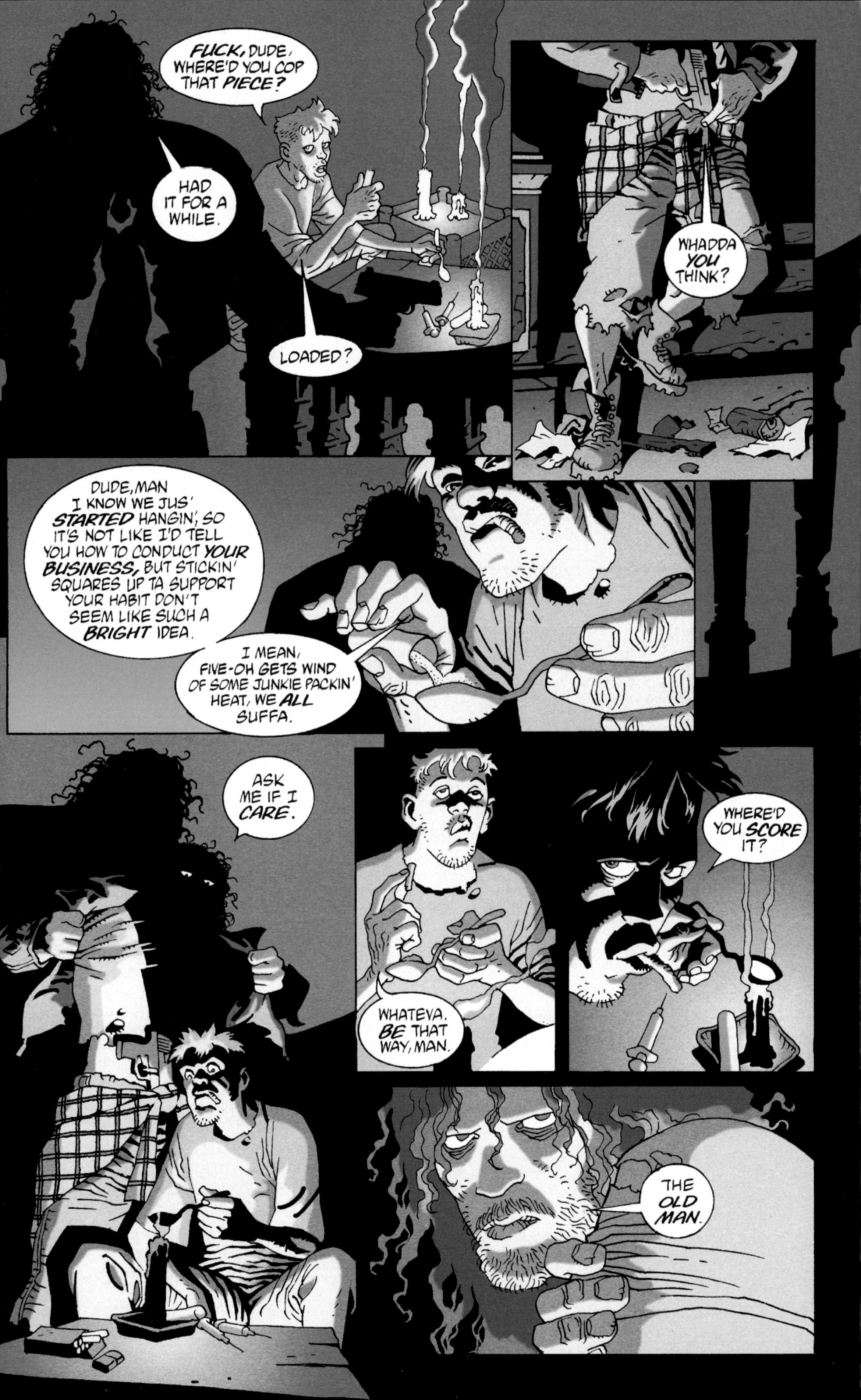
FUCK, DUDE, WHERE'D YOU COP THAT PIECE?
HAD IT FOR A WHILE.
LOADED?
WHADDA YOU THINK?
DUDE, MAN I KNOW WE JUS' STARTED HANGIN', SO IT'S NOT LIKE I'D TELL YOU HOW TO CONDUCT YOUR BUSINESS, BUT STICKIN' SQUARES UP TA SUPPORT YOUR HABIT DON'T SEEM LIKE SUCH A BRIGHT IDEA.
I MEAN, FIVE-OH GETS WIND OF SOME JUNKIE PACKIN' HEAT, WE ALL SUFFA.
ASK ME IF I CARE.
WHATEVA. BE THAT WAY, MAN.
WHERE'D YOU SCORE IT?
THE OLD MAN.

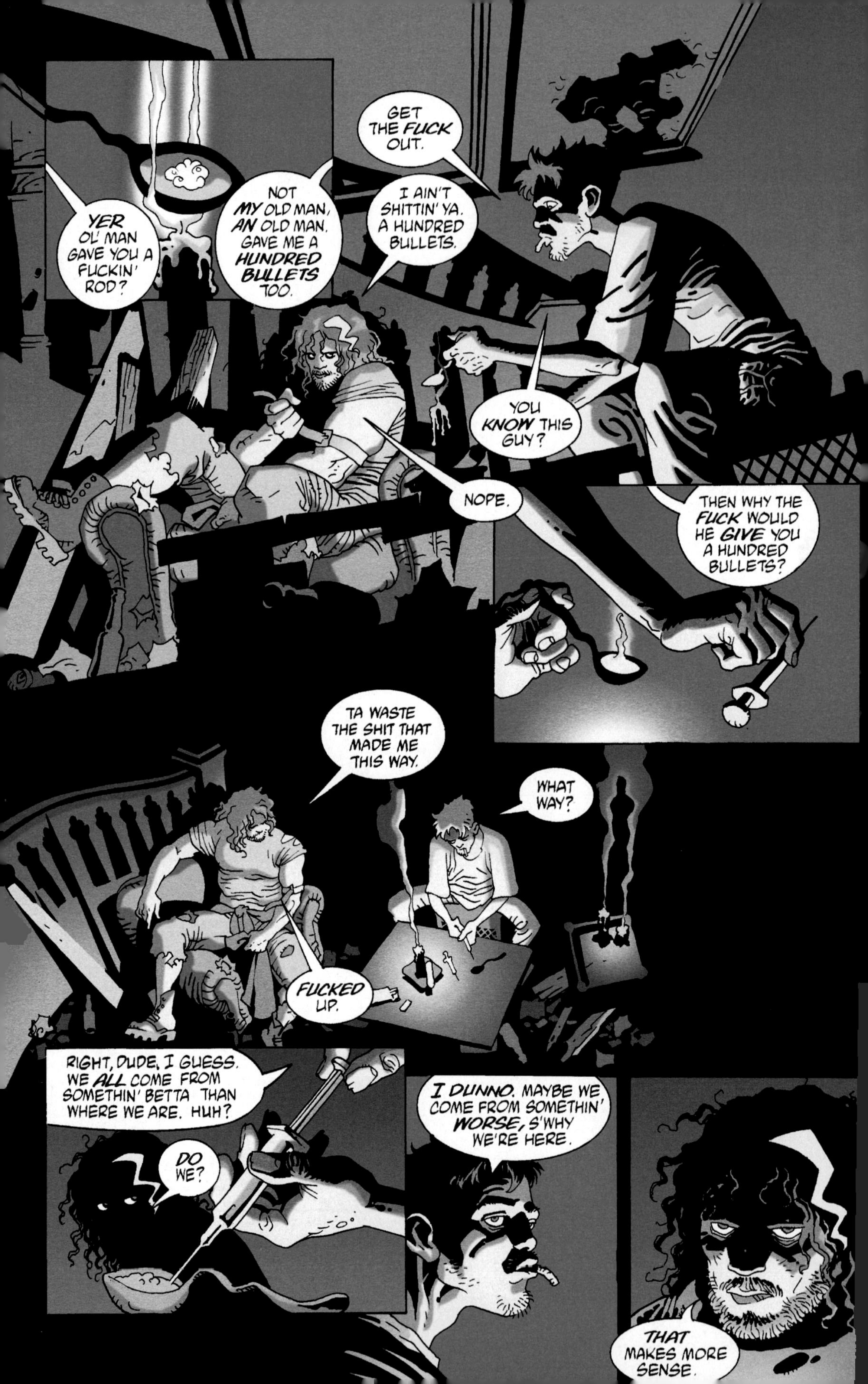

YER OL' MAN GAVE YOU A FUCKIN' ROD?
NOT MY OLD MAN, AN OLD MAN. GAVE ME A HUNDRED BULLETS TOO.
I AIN'T SHITTIN' YA. A HUNDRED BULLETS.
GET THE FUCK OUT.
YOU KNOW THIS GUY?
NOPE.
THEN WHY THE FUCK WOULD HE GIVE YOU A HUNDRED BULLETS?
TA WASTE THE SHIT THAT MADE ME THIS WAY.
WHAT WAY?
FUCKED UP.
RIGHT, DUDE, I GUESS. WE ALL COME FROM SOMETHIN' BETTA THAN WHERE WE ARE. HUH?
DO WE?
I DUNNO. MAYBE WE COME FROM SOMETHIN' WORSE, S'WHY WE'RE HERE.
THAT MAKES MORE SENSE.

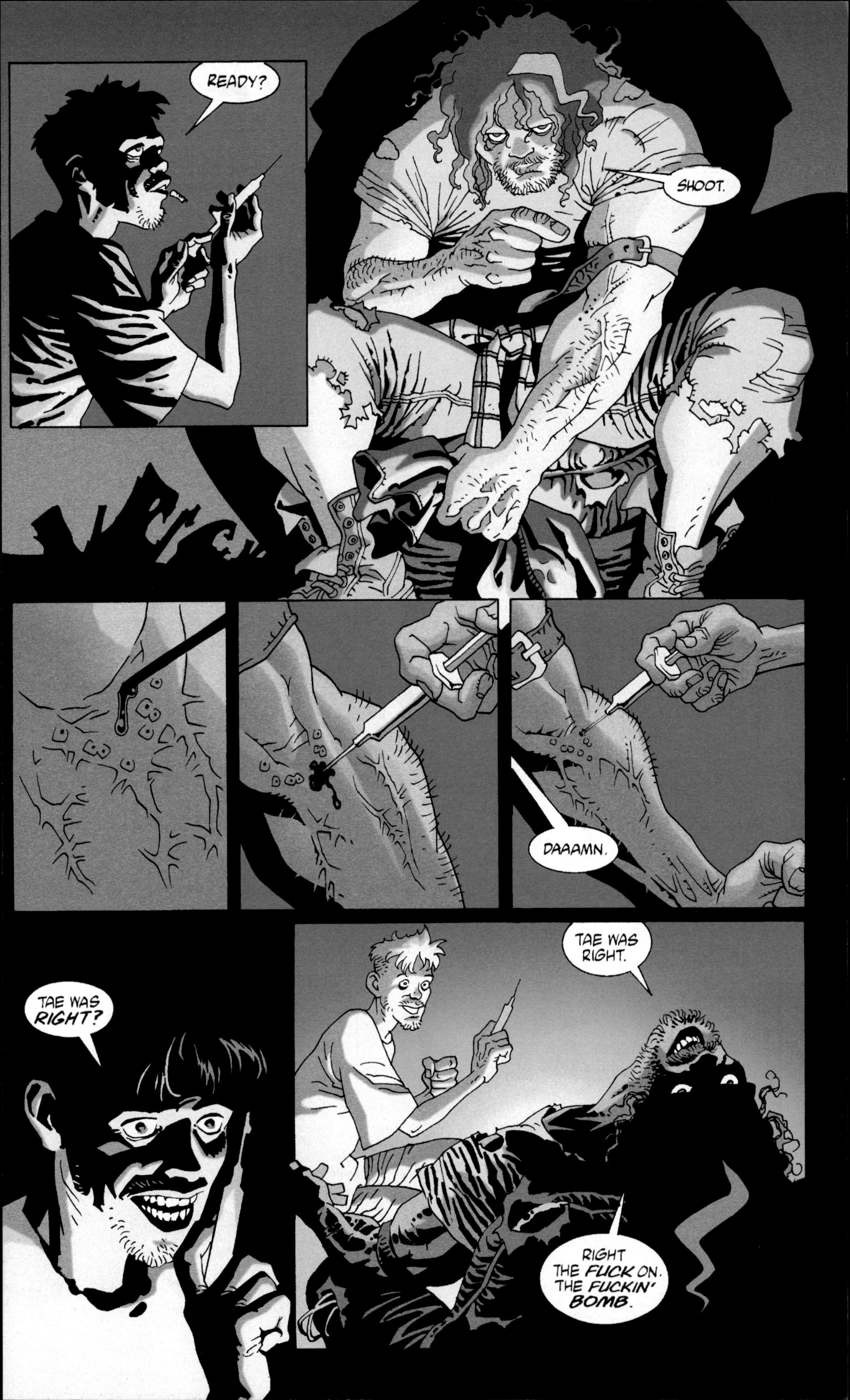
READY?
SHOOT.
DAAAMN.
TAE WAS RIGHT.
TAE WAS RIGHT?
RIGHT THE FUCK ON. THE FUCKIN' BOMB.

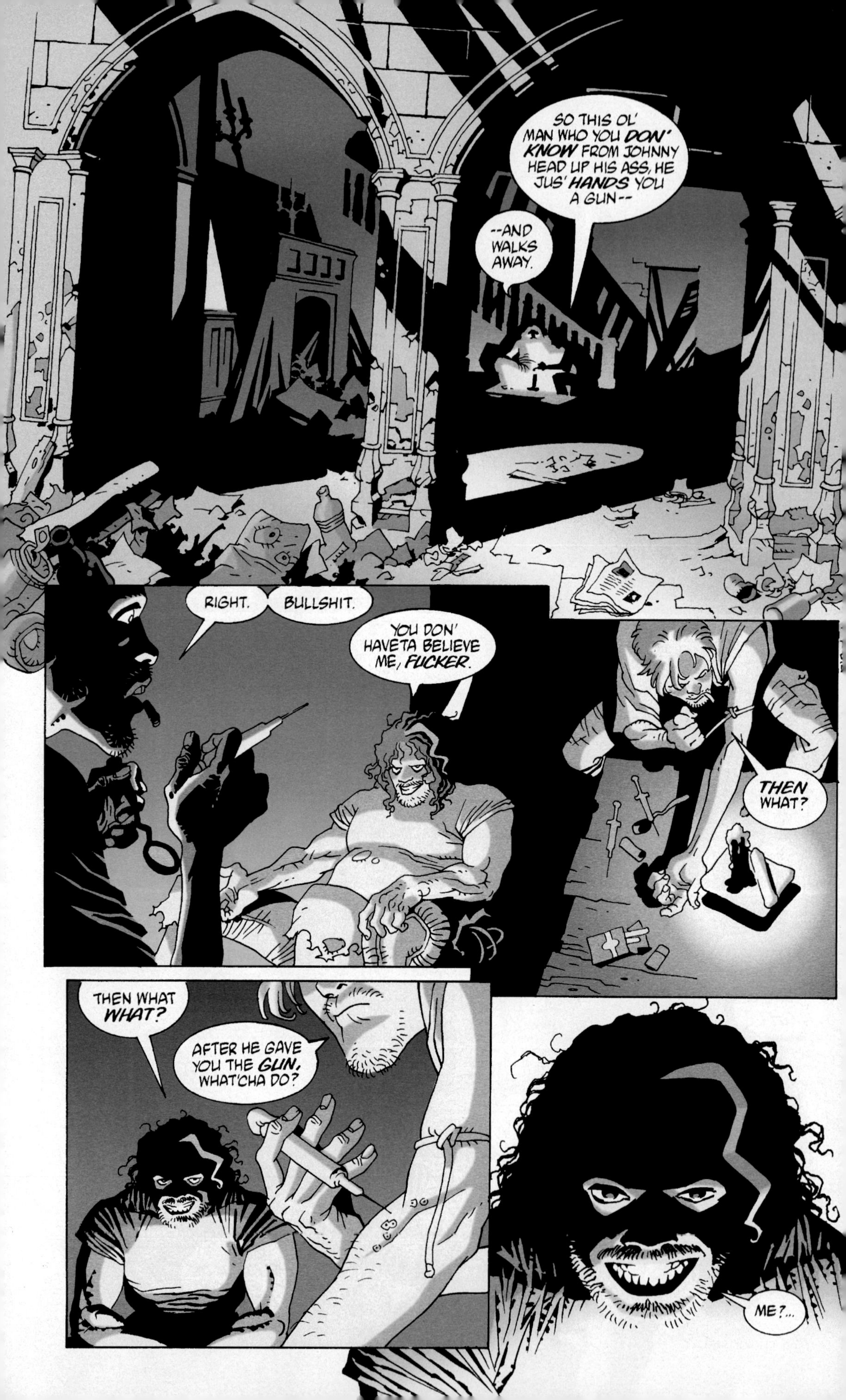

SO THIS OL' MAN WHO YOU DON' KNOW FROM JOHNNY HEAD UP HIS ASS, HE JUS' HANDS YOU A GUN--
--AND WALKS AWAY.
RIGHT.
BULLSHIT.
YOU DON' HAVETA BELIEVE ME, FUCKER.
THEN WHAT?
THEN WHAT WHAT?
AFTER HE GAVE YOU THE GUN, WHAT'CHA DO?
ME?...

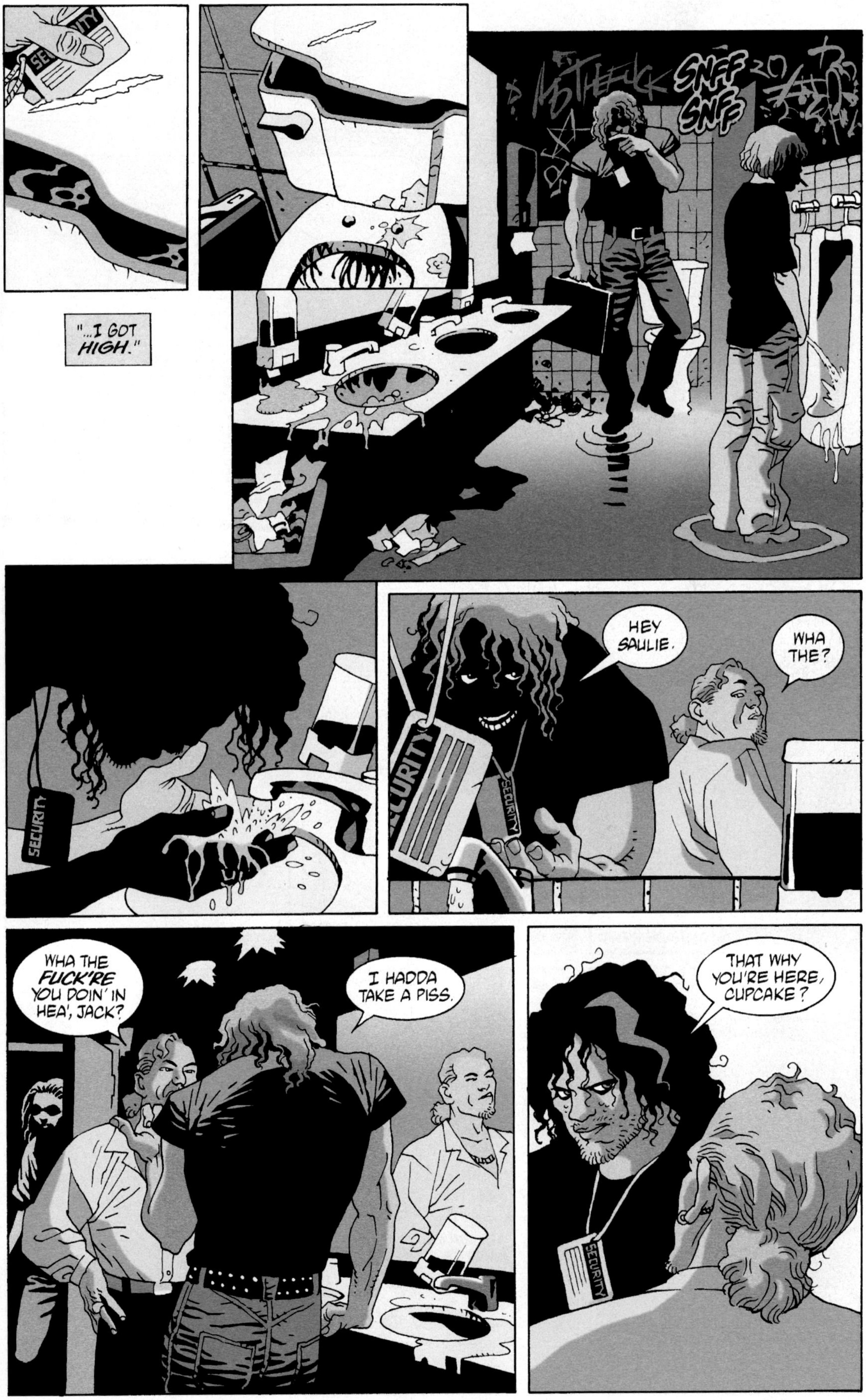
SECURITY
"...I GOT HIGH."
SNFF SNFF
SECURITY
HEY SAULIE.
WHA THE?
WHA THE FUCK'RE YOU DOIN' IN HEA', JACK?
I HADDA TAKE A PISS.
THAT WHY YOU'RE HERE, CUPCAKE?

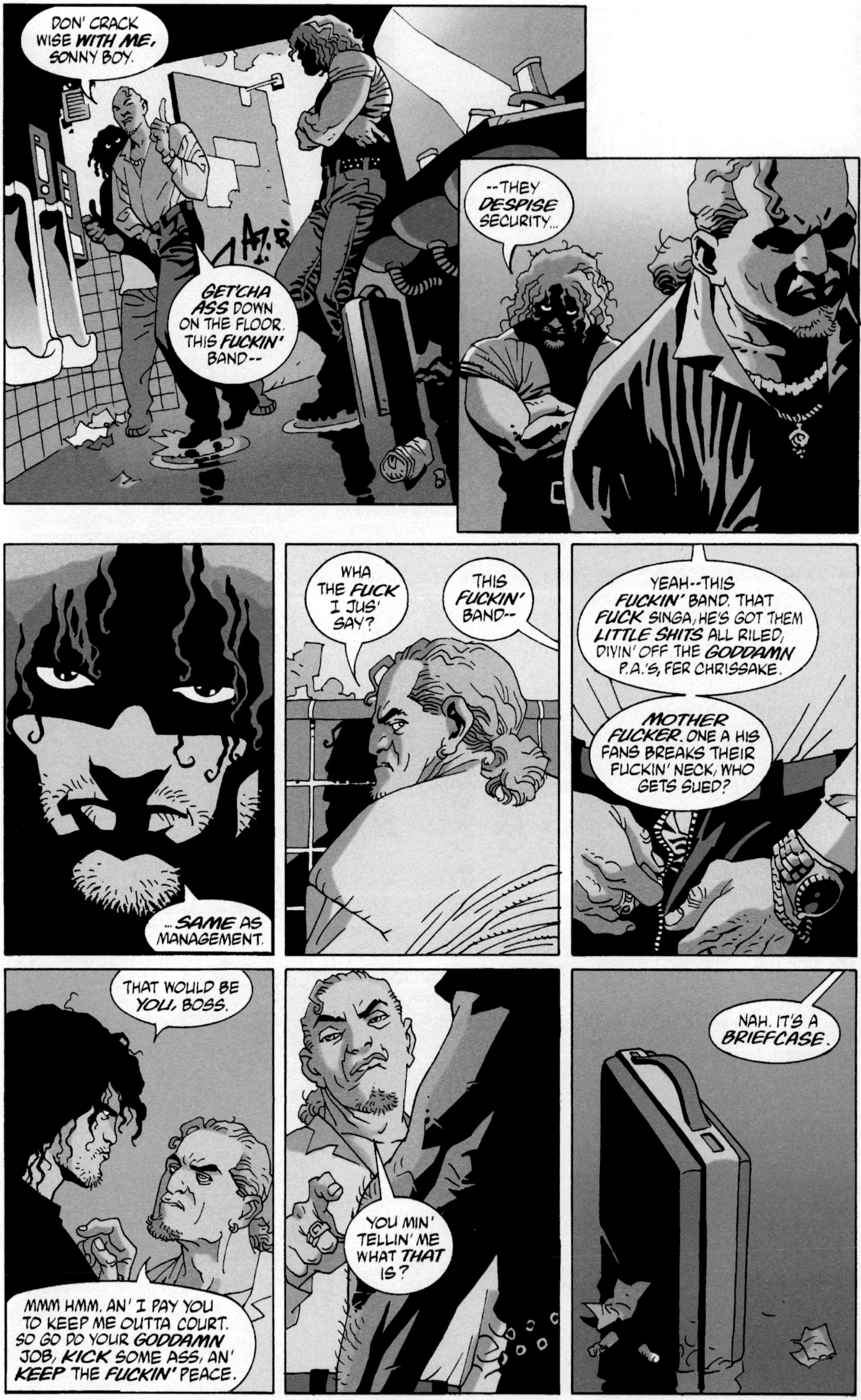

DON' CRACK WISE WITH ME, SONNY BOY.
GET'CHA ASS DOWN ON THE FLOOR. THIS FUCKIN' BAND--
--THEY DESPISE SECURITY...
...SAME AS MANAGEMENT.
WHA THE FUCK I JUS' SAY?
THIS FUCKIN' BAND--
YEAH--THIS FUCKIN' BAND. THAT FUCK SINGA, HE'S GOT THEM LITTLE SHITS ALL RILED, DIVIN' OFF THE GODDAMN P.A.'S, FER CHRISSAKE.
MOTHER FUCKER. ONE A HIS FANS BREAKS THEIR FUCKIN' NECK, WHO GETS SUED?
THAT WOULD BE YOU, BOSS.
MMM HMM. AN' I PAY YOU TO KEEP ME OUTTA COURT. SO GO DO YOUR GODDAMN JOB, KICK SOME ASS, AN' KEEP THE FUCKIN' PEACE.
YOU MIN' TELLIN' ME WHAT THAT IS?
NAH. IT'S A BRIEFCASE.

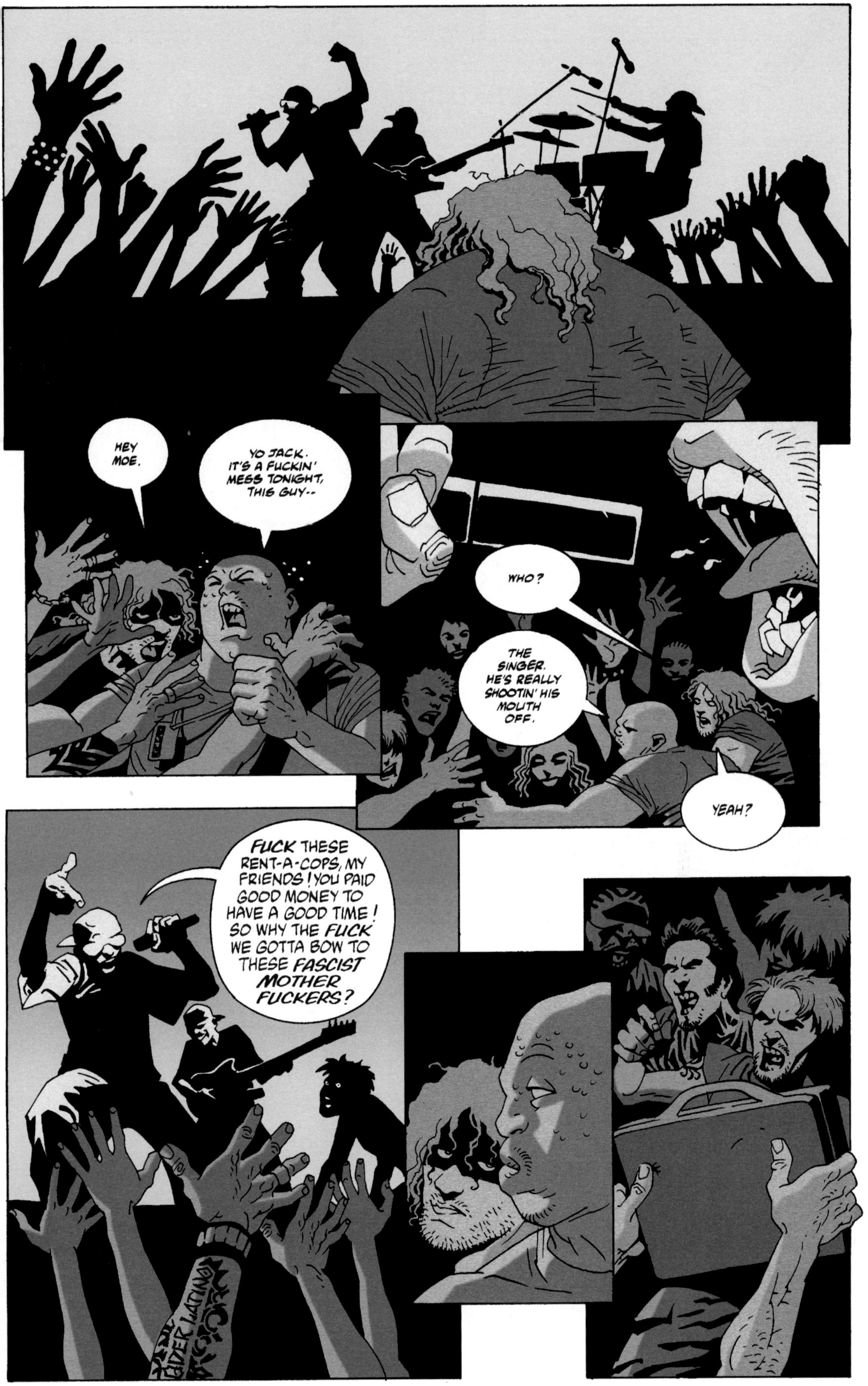
HEY MOE.
YO JACK. IT'S A FUCKIN' MESS TONIGHT, THIS GUY--
WHO?
THE SINGER. HE'S REALLY SHOOTIN' HIS MOUTH OFF.
YEAH?
FUCK THESE RENT-A-COPS, MY FRIENDS! YOU PAID GOOD MONEY TO HAVE A GOOD TIME! SO WHY THE FUCK WE GOTTA BOW TO THESE FASCIST MOTHER FUCKERS?

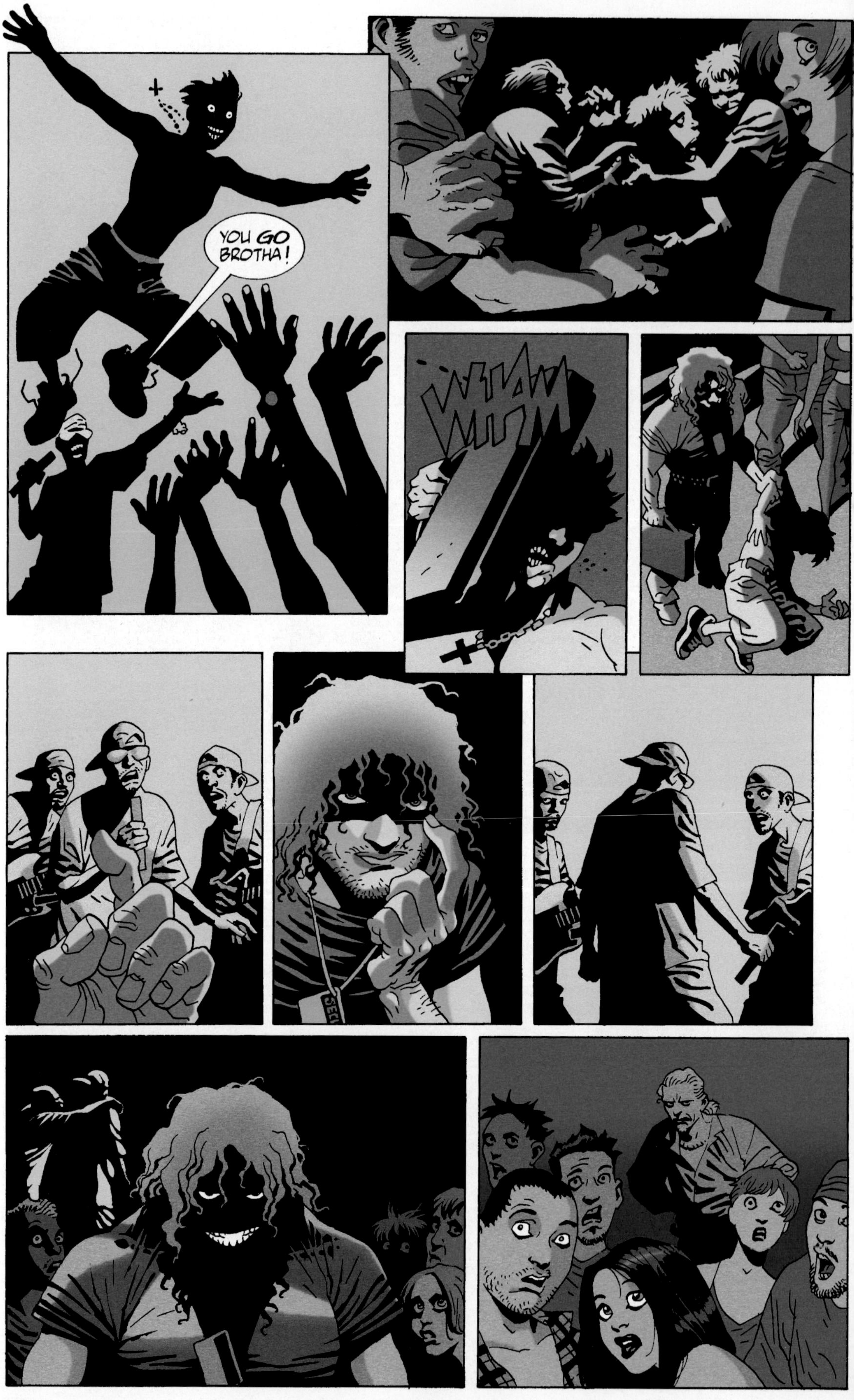
YOU GO BROTHA!
WHAM

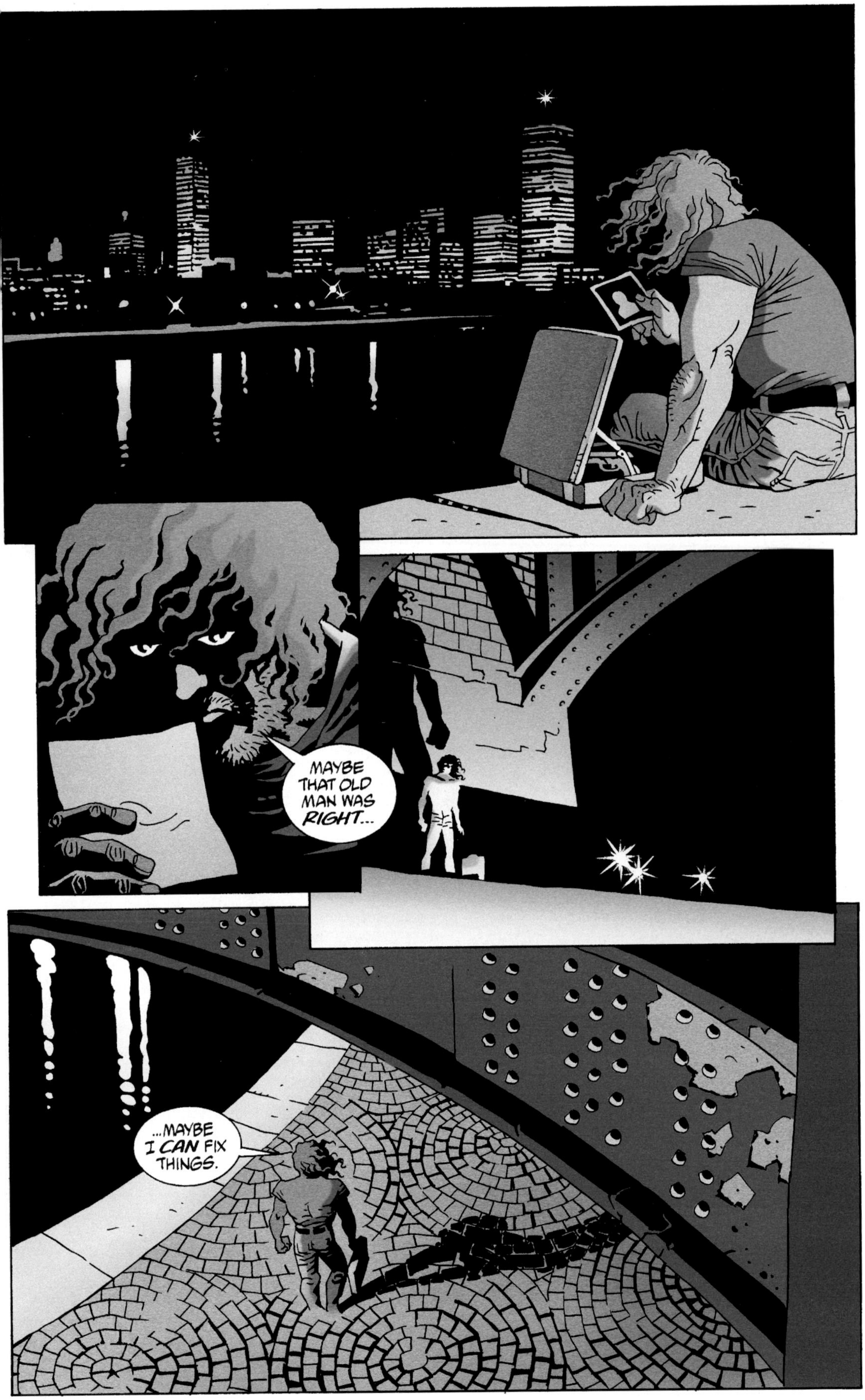
MAYBE THAT OLD MAN WAS RIGHT...
...MAYBE I CAN FIX THINGS.

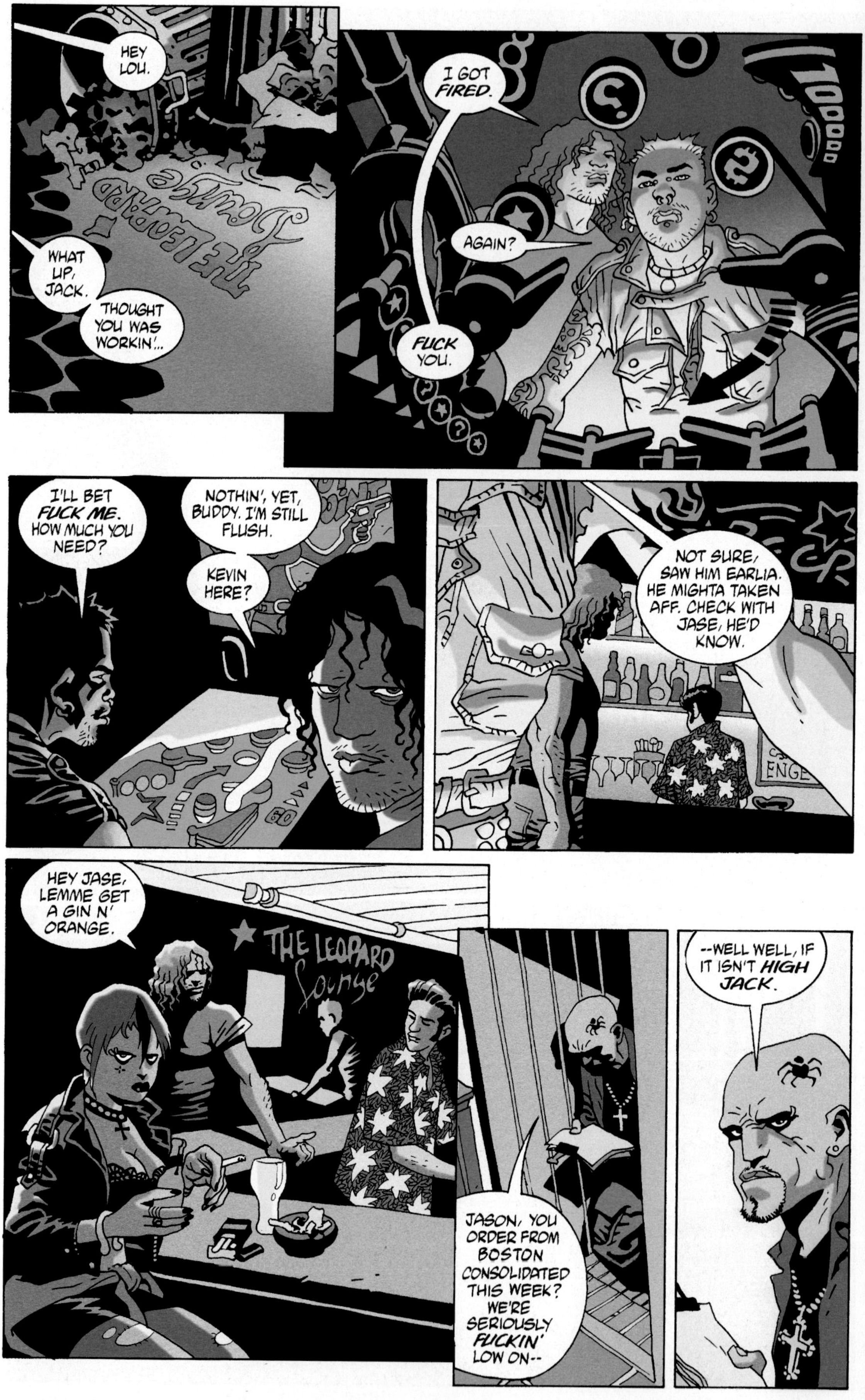
HEY LOU.
WHAT UP, JACK.
'THOUGHT YOU WAS WORKIN'...
I GOT FIRED.
AGAIN?
FUCK YOU.
I'LL BET FUCK ME. HOW MUCH YOU NEED?
NOTHIN', YET, BUDDY. I'M STILL FLUSH.
KEVIN HERE?
NOT SURE, SAW HIM EARLIA. HE MIGHTA TAKEN AFF. CHECK WITH JASE, HE'D KNOW.
HEY JASE, LEMME GET A GIN N' ORANGE.
THE LEOPARD Lounge
JASON, YOU ORDER FROM BOSTON CONSOLIDATED THIS WEEK? WE'RE SERIOUSLY FUCKIN' LOW ON--
--WELL WELL, IF IT ISN'T HIGH JACK.

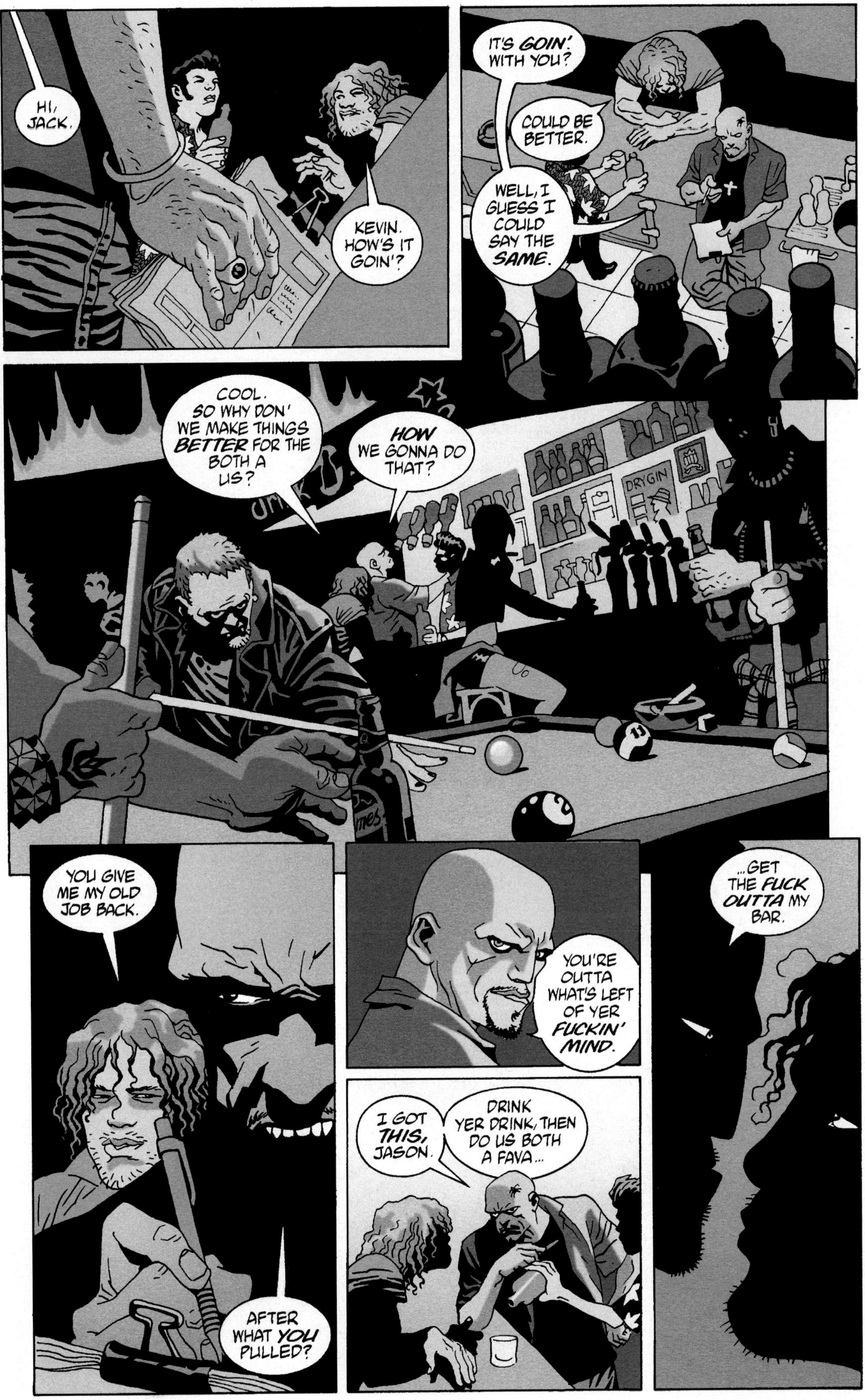
HI, JACK.
KEVIN. HOW'S IT GOIN'?
IT'S GOIN'. WITH YOU?
COULD BE BETTER.
WELL, I GUESS I COULD SAY THE SAME.
COOL. SO WHY DON' WE MAKE THINGS BETTER FOR THE BOTH A US?
HOW WE GONNA DO THAT?
DRY GIN
YOU GIVE ME MY OLD JOB BACK.
AFTER WHAT YOU PULLED?
YOU'RE OUTTA WHAT'S LEFT OF YER FUCKIN' MIND.
I GOT THIS, JASON.
DRINK YER DRINK, THEN DO US BOTH A FAVA...
...GET THE FUCK OUTTA MY BAR.

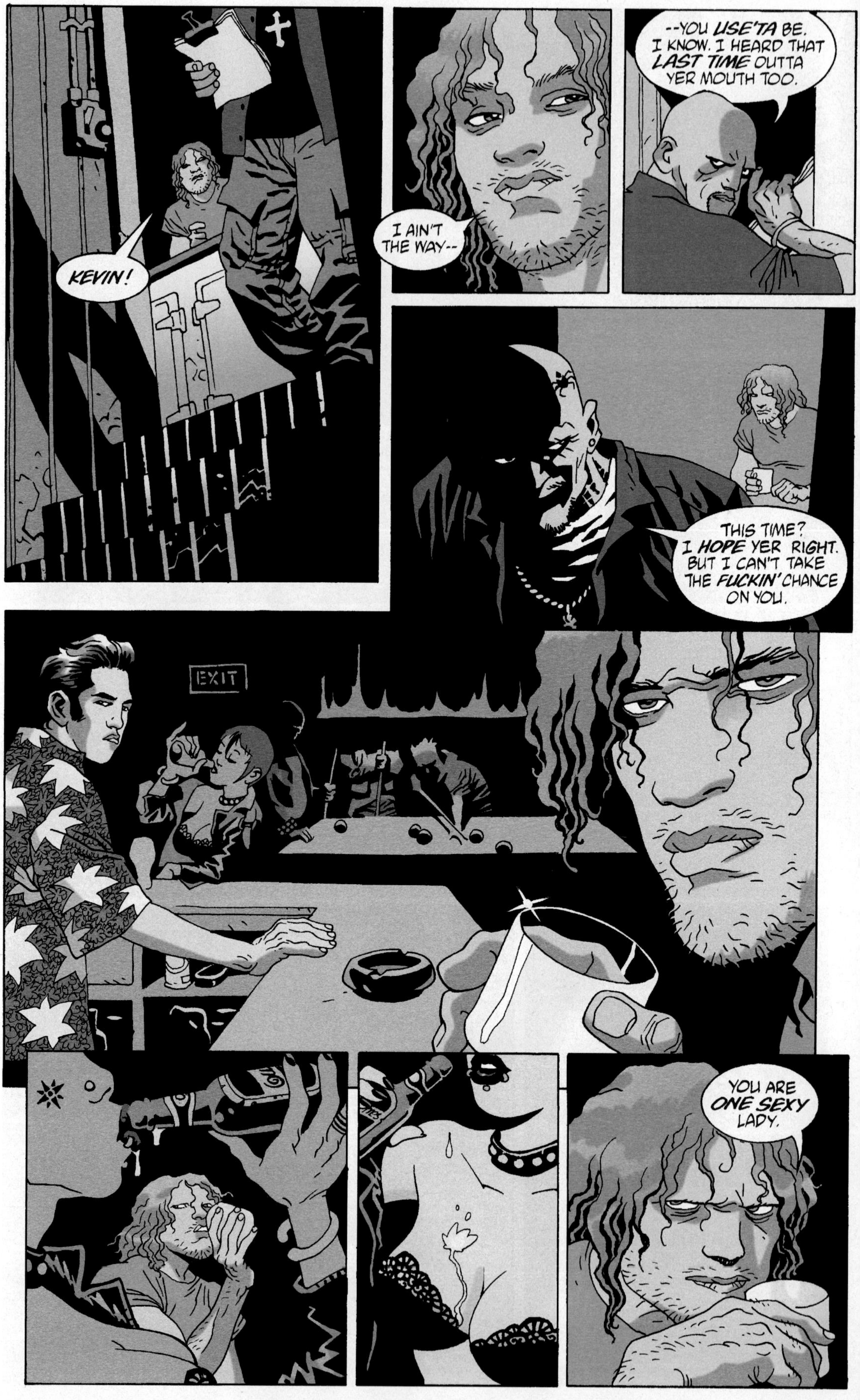
KEVIN!
I AIN'T THE WAY--
--YOU USE'TA BE. I KNOW. I HEARD THAT LAST TIME OUTTA YER MOUTH TOO.
THIS TIME? I HOPE YER RIGHT. BUT I CAN'T TAKE THE FUCKIN' CHANCE ON YOU.
EXIT
YOU ARE ONE SEXY LADY.

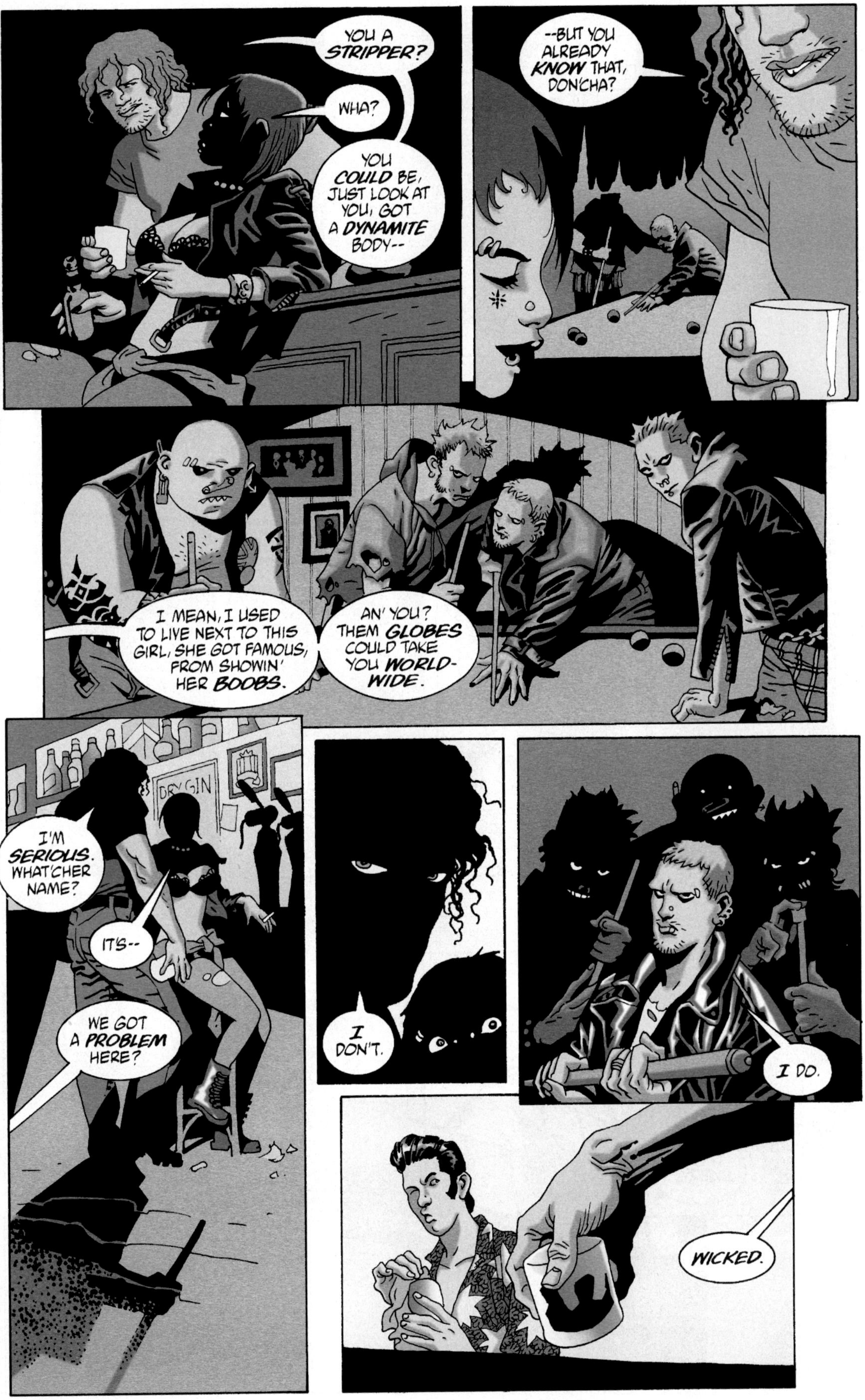

YOU A STRIPPER?
WHA?
YOU COULD BE, JUST LOOK AT YOU, GOT A DYNAMITE BODY--
--BUT YOU ALREADY KNOW THAT, DON'CHA?
I MEAN, I USED TO LIVE NEXT TO THIS GIRL, SHE GOT FAMOUS, FROM SHOWIN' HER BOOBS.
AN' YOU? THEM GLOBES COULD TAKE YOU WORLD-WIDE.
DRY GIN
I'M SERIOUS. WHAT'CHER NAME?
IT'S--
WE GOT A PROBLEM HERE?
I DON'T.
I DO.
WICKED.

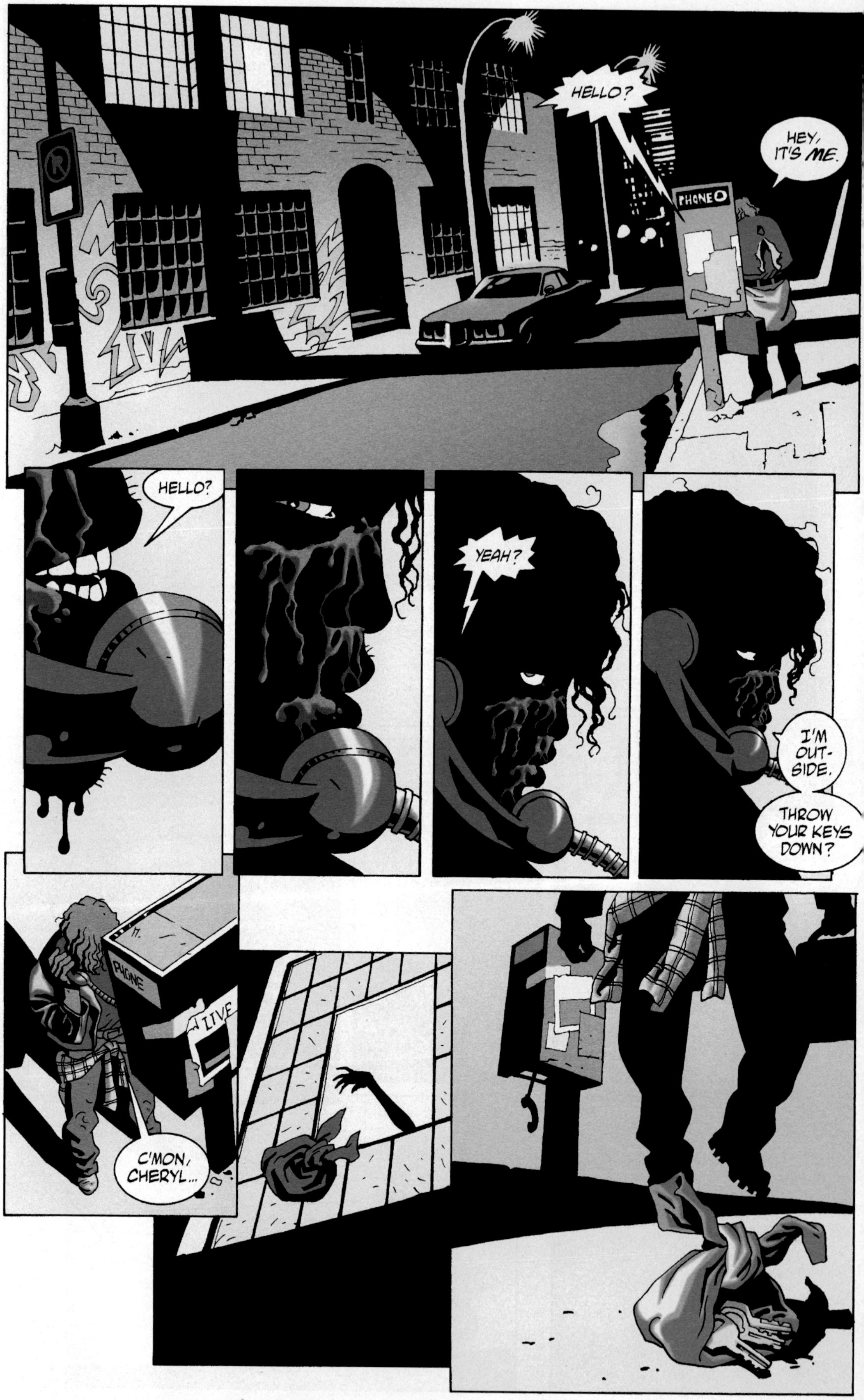
HELLO?
HEY, IT'S ME.
PHONE
HELLO?
YEAH?
I'M OUT-SIDE.
THROW YOUR KEYS DOWN?
PHONE
LIVE
C'MON, CHERYL...

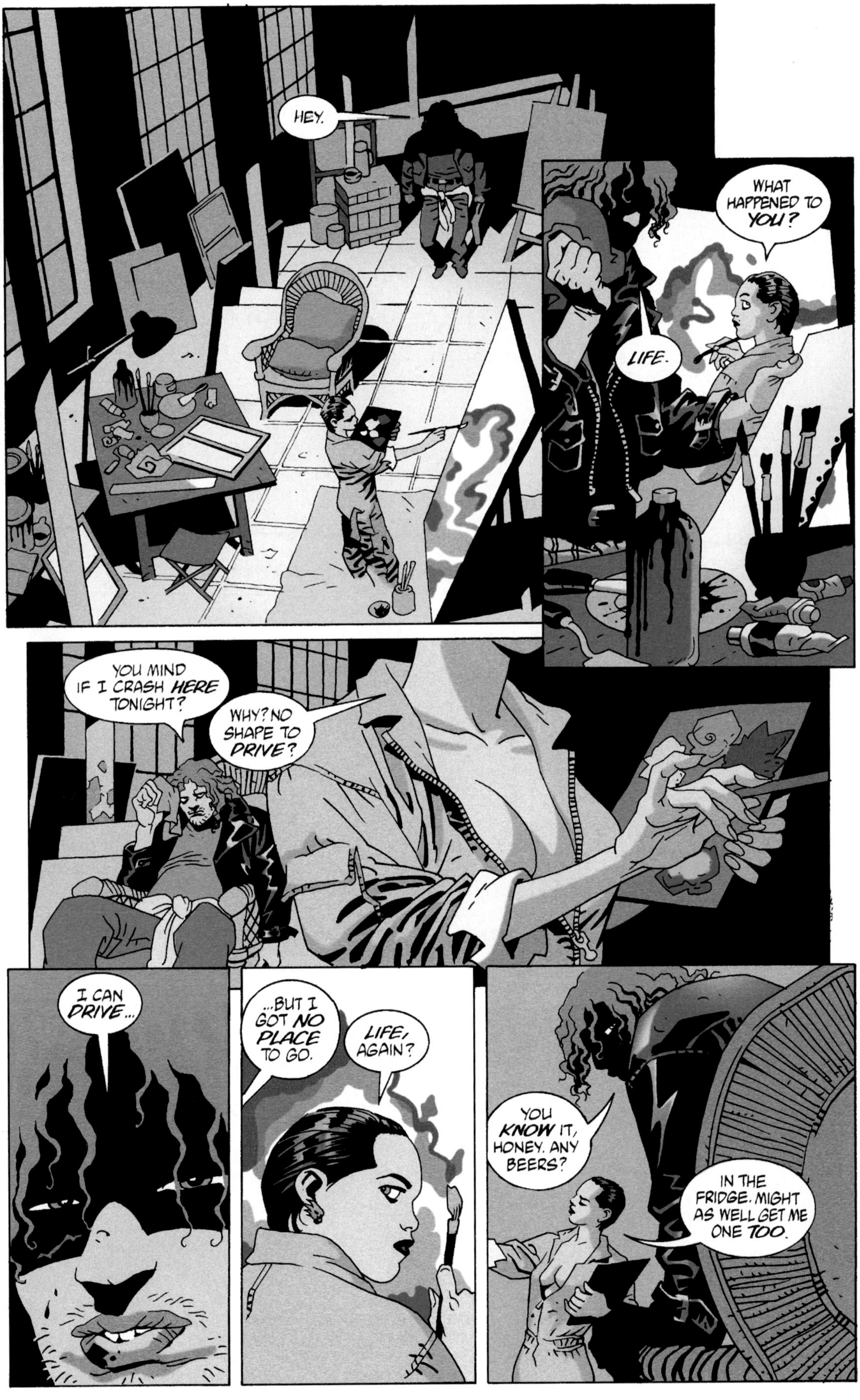

HEY.
WHAT HAPPENED TO YOU?
LIFE.
YOU MIND IF I CRASH HERE TONIGHT?
WHY? NO SHAPE TO DRIVE?
I CAN DRIVE...
...BUT I GOT NO PLACE TO GO.
LIFE, AGAIN?
YOU KNOW IT, HONEY. ANY BEERS?
IN THE FRIDGE. MIGHT AS WELL GET ME ONE TOO.

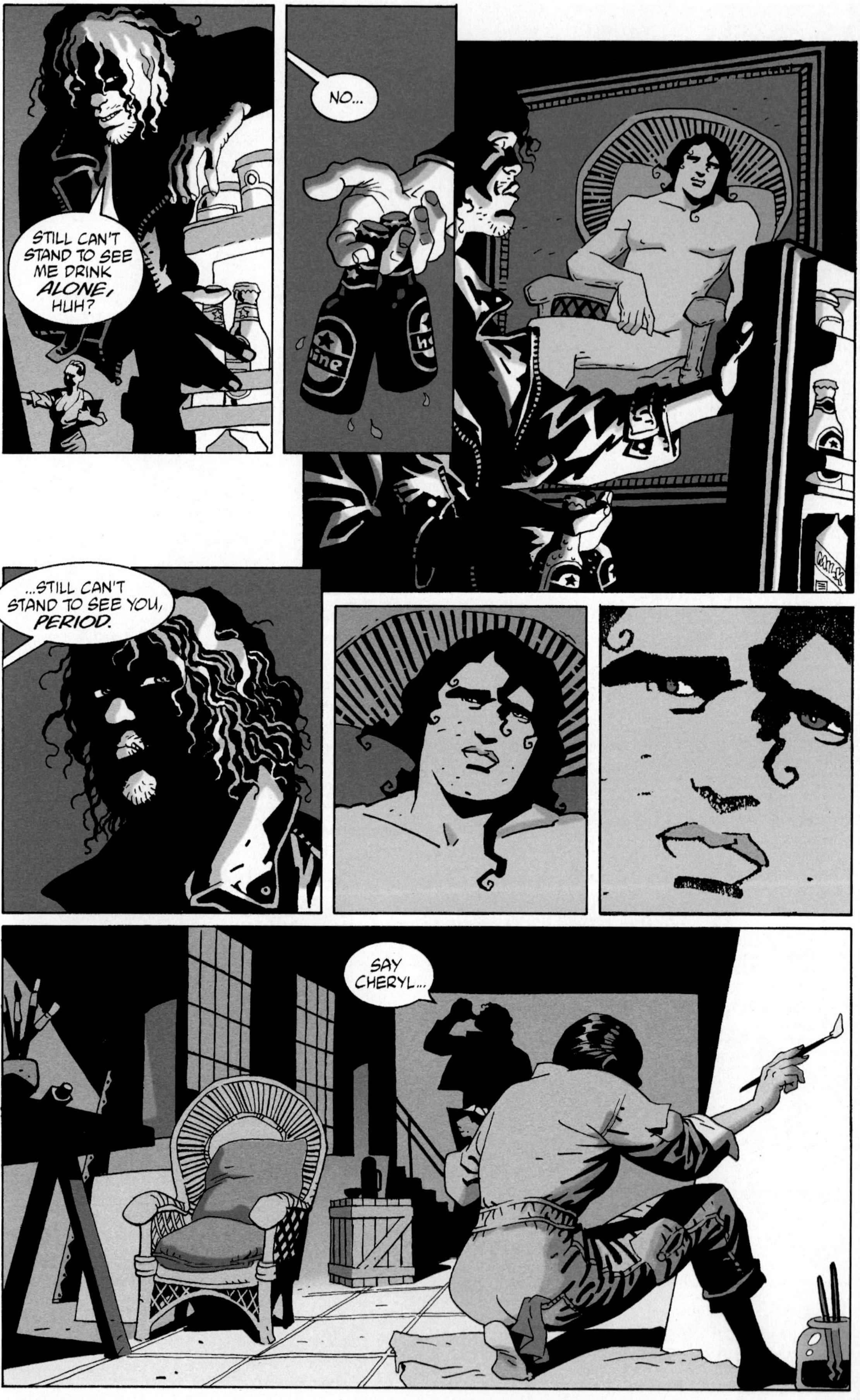
STILL CAN'T STAND TO SEE ME DRINK ALONE, HUH?
NO...
...STILL CAN'T STAND TO SEE YOU, PERIOD.
SAY CHERYL...

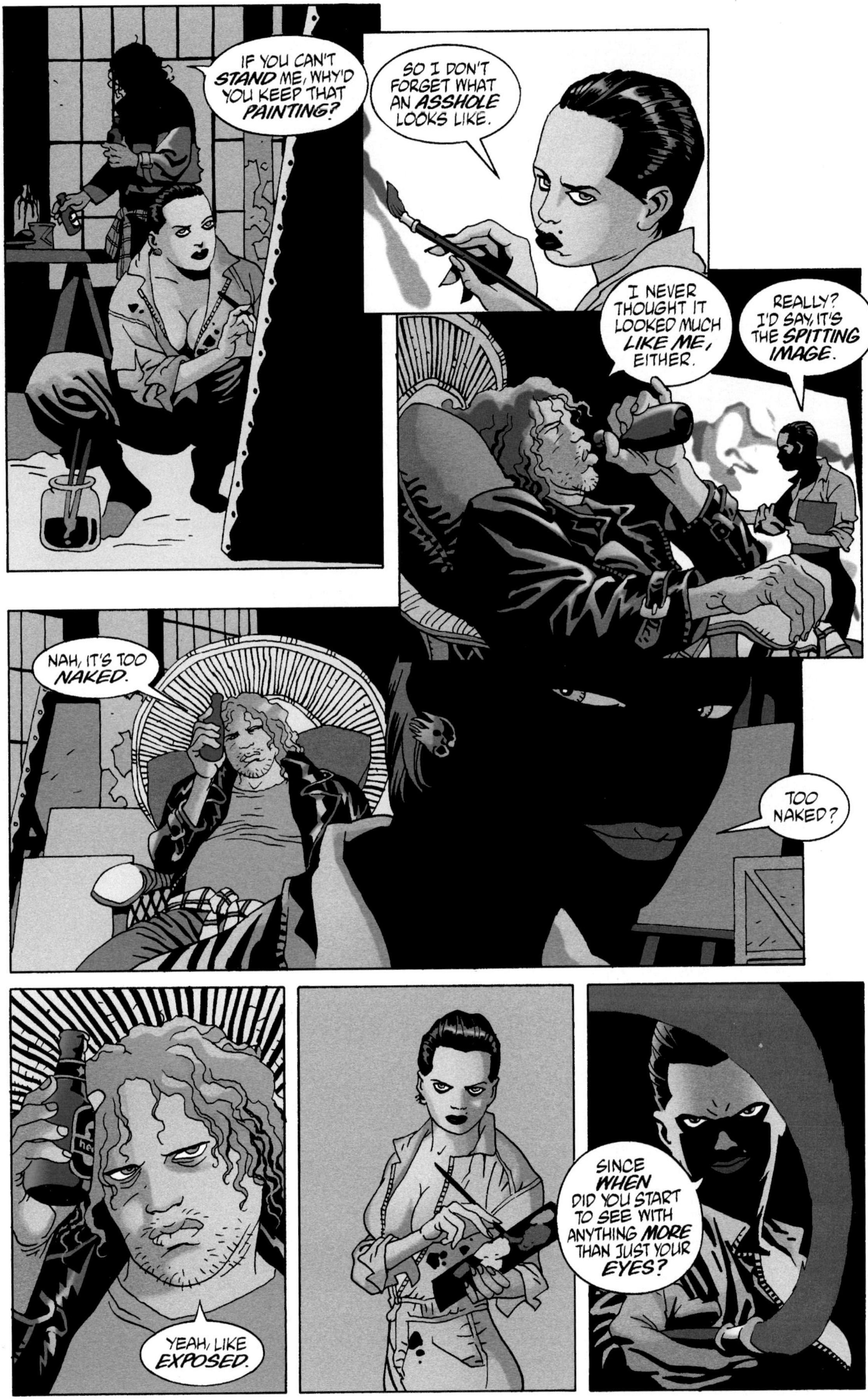
IF YOU CAN'T STAND ME, WHY'D YOU KEEP THAT PAINTING?
SO I DON'T FORGET WHAT AN ASSHOLE LOOKS LIKE.
I NEVER THOUGHT IT LOOKED MUCH LIKE ME, EITHER.
REALLY? I'D SAY, IT'S THE SPITTING IMAGE.
NAH, IT'S TOO NAKED.
TOO NAKED?
YEAH, LIKE EXPOSED.
SINCE WHEN DID YOU START TO SEE WITH ANYTHING MORE THAN JUST YOUR EYES?

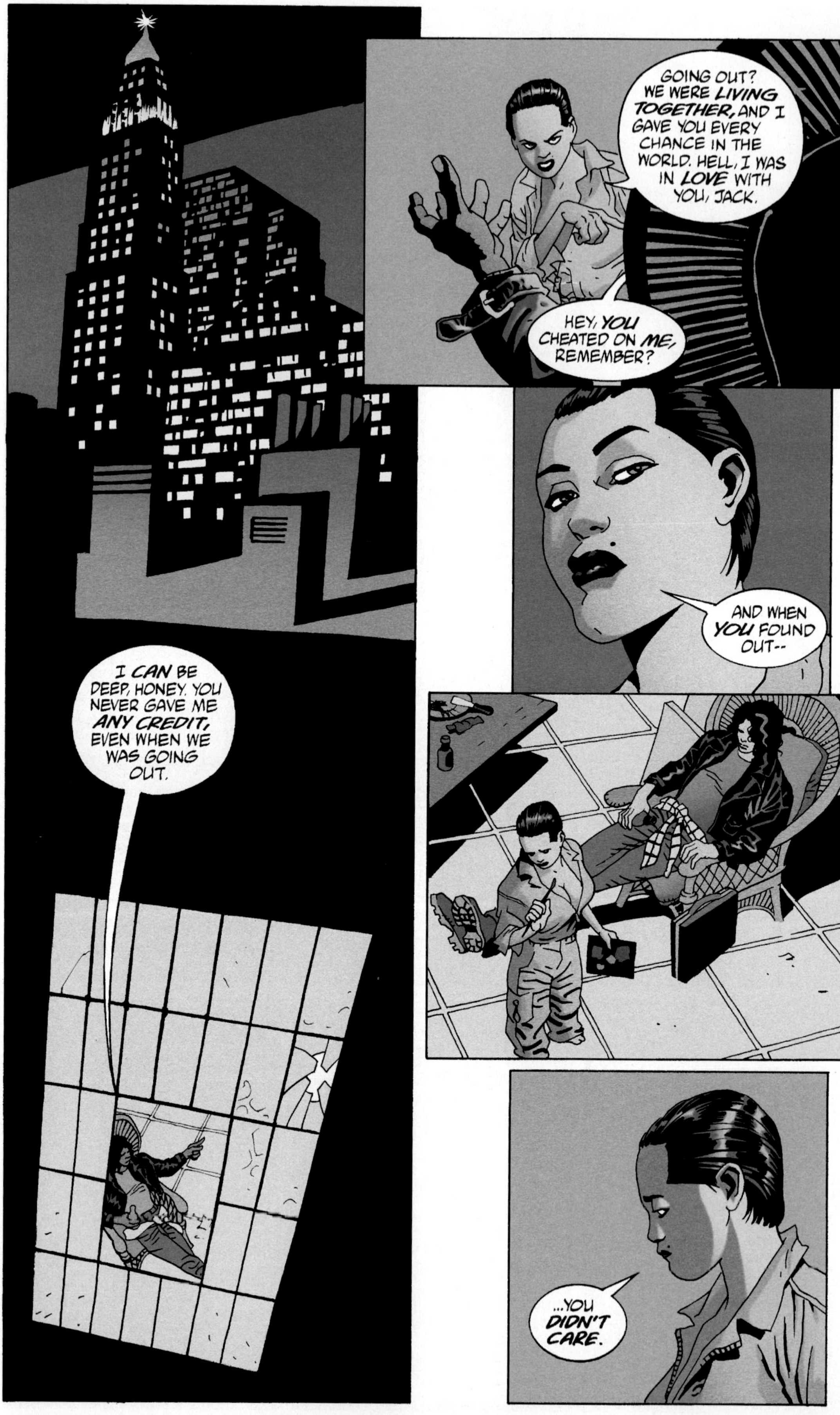
I CAN BE DEEP, HONEY. YOU NEVER GAVE ME ANY CREDIT, EVEN WHEN WE WAS GOING OUT.
GOING OUT? WE WERE LIVING TOGETHER, AND I GAVE YOU EVERY CHANCE IN THE WORLD. HELL, I WAS IN LOVE WITH YOU, JACK.
HEY, YOU CHEATED ON ME, REMEMBER?
AND WHEN YOU FOUND OUT--
...YOU DIDN'T CARE.

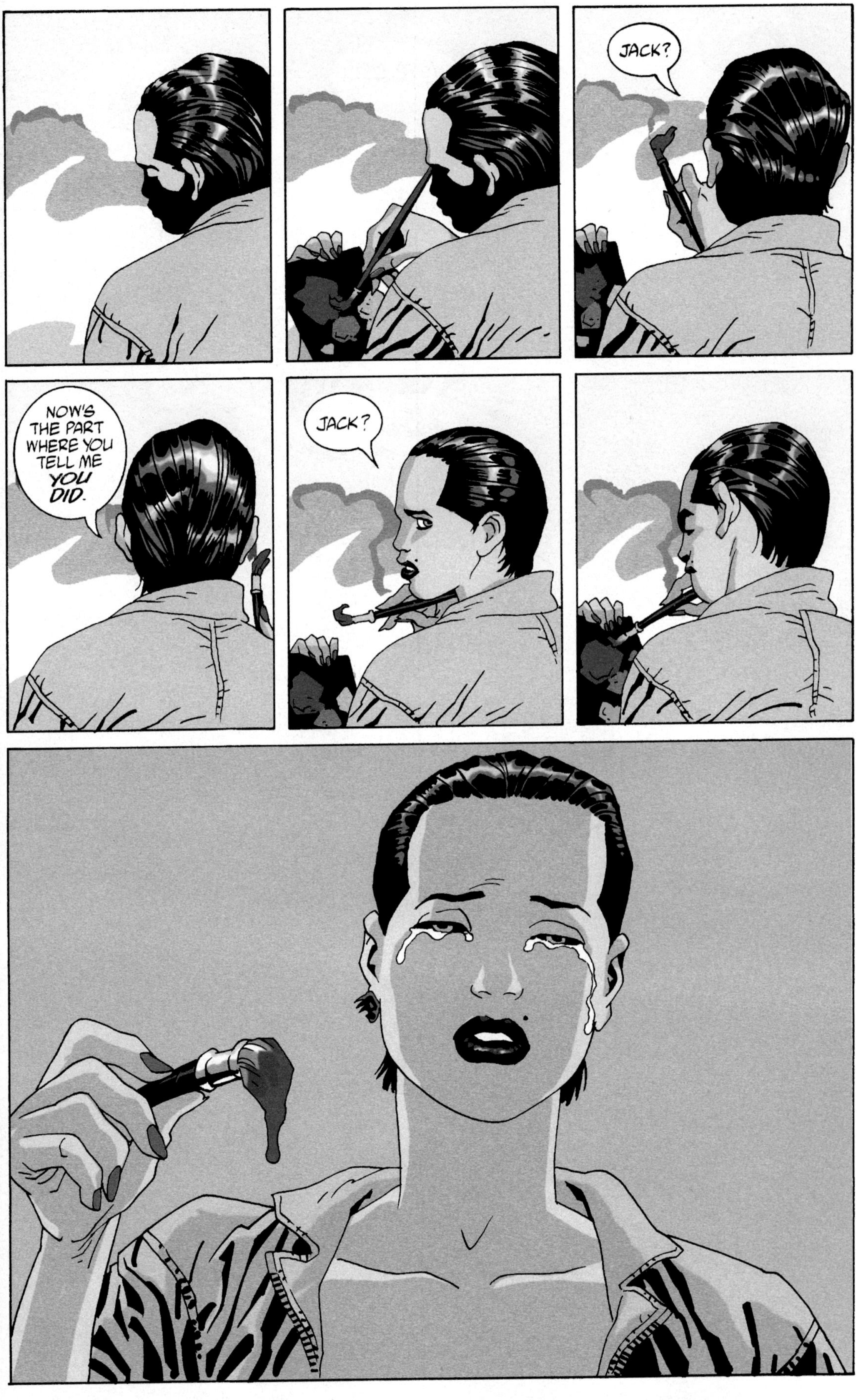
JACK?
NOW'S THE PART WHERE YOU TELL ME YOU DID.
JACK?

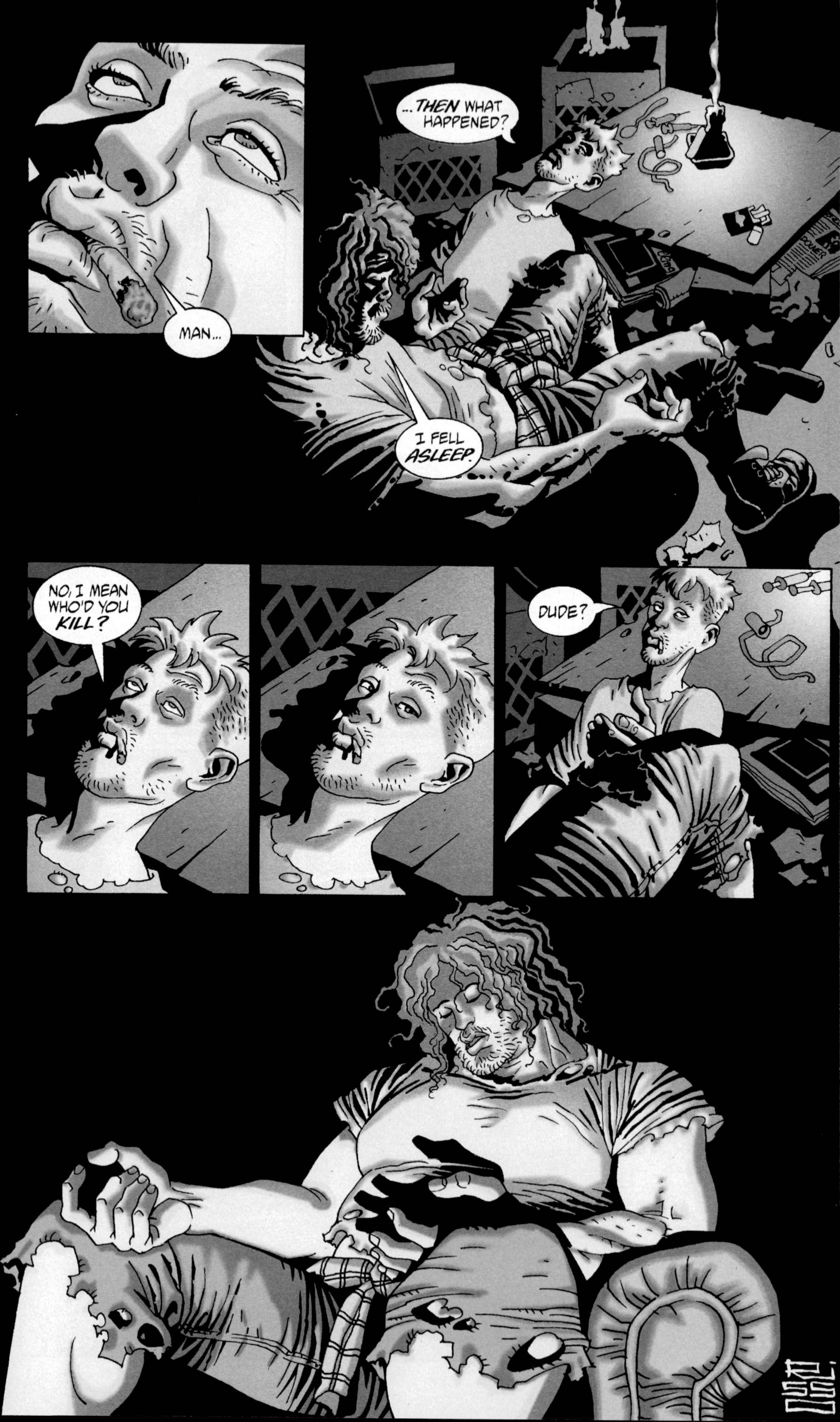
MAN...
...THEN WHAT HAPPENED?
I FELL ASLEEP.
NO, I MEAN WHO'D YOU KILL?
DUDE?

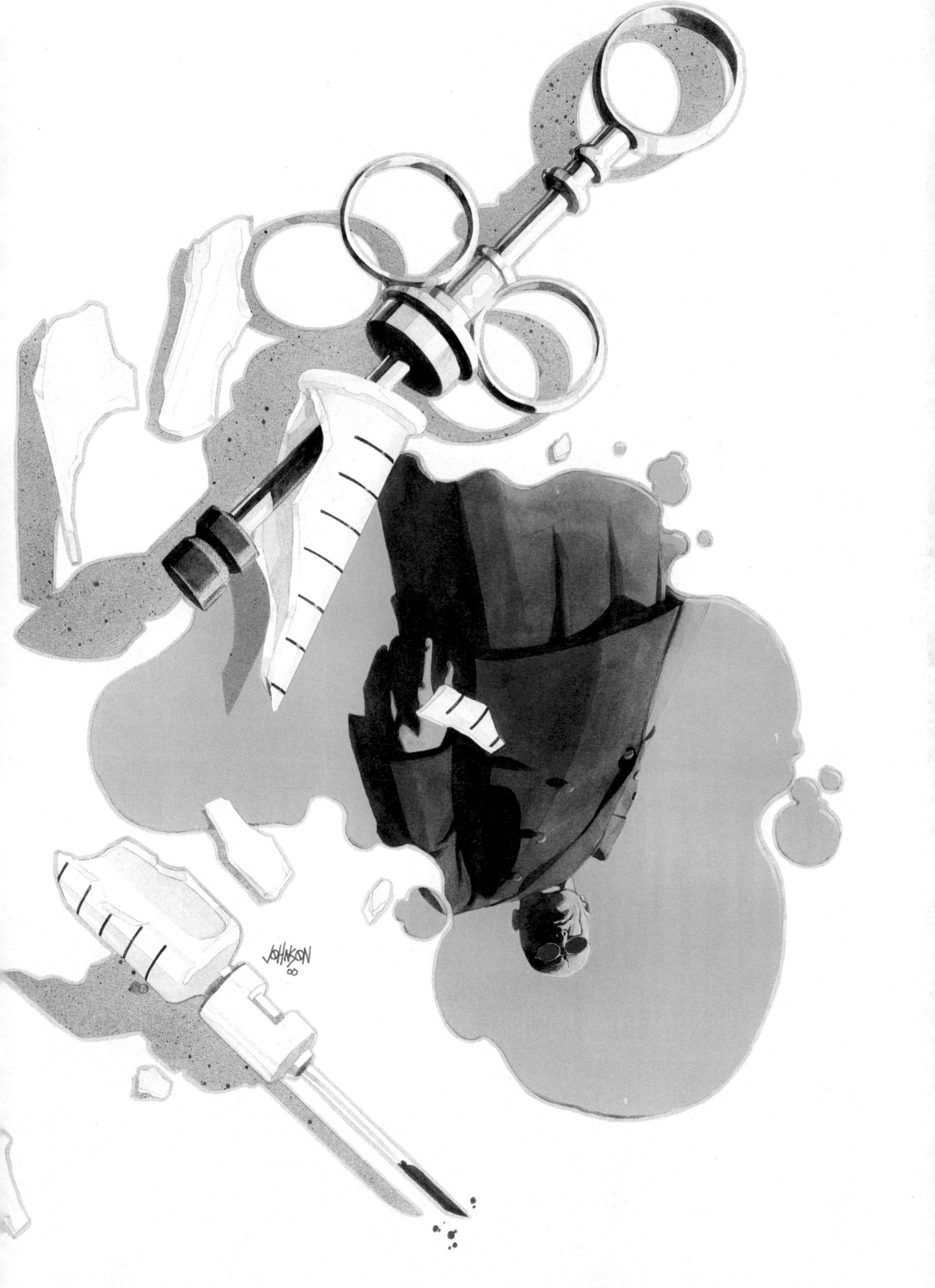
JOHNSON

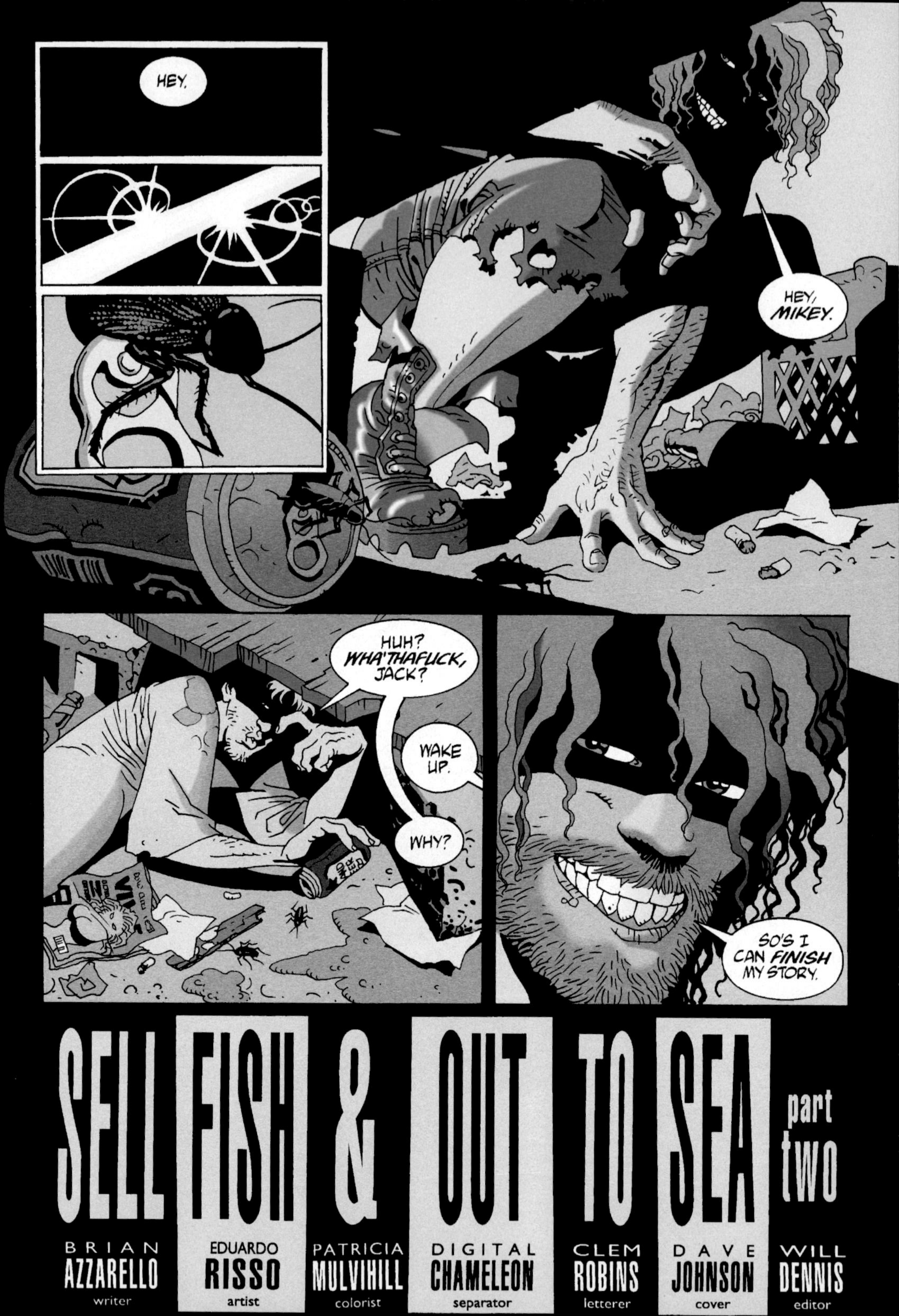
HEY.
HEY, MIKEY.
HUH? WHA'THAFUCK, JACK?
WAKE UP.
WHY?
SO'S I CAN FINISH MY STORY.

SELL FISH & OUT TO SEA part two

BRIAN **AZZARELLO** writer

EDUARDO **RISSO** artist

PATRICIA **MULVIHILL** colorist

DIGITAL **CHAMELEON** separator

CLEM **ROBINS** letterer

DAVE **JOHNSON** cover

WILL **DENNIS** editor

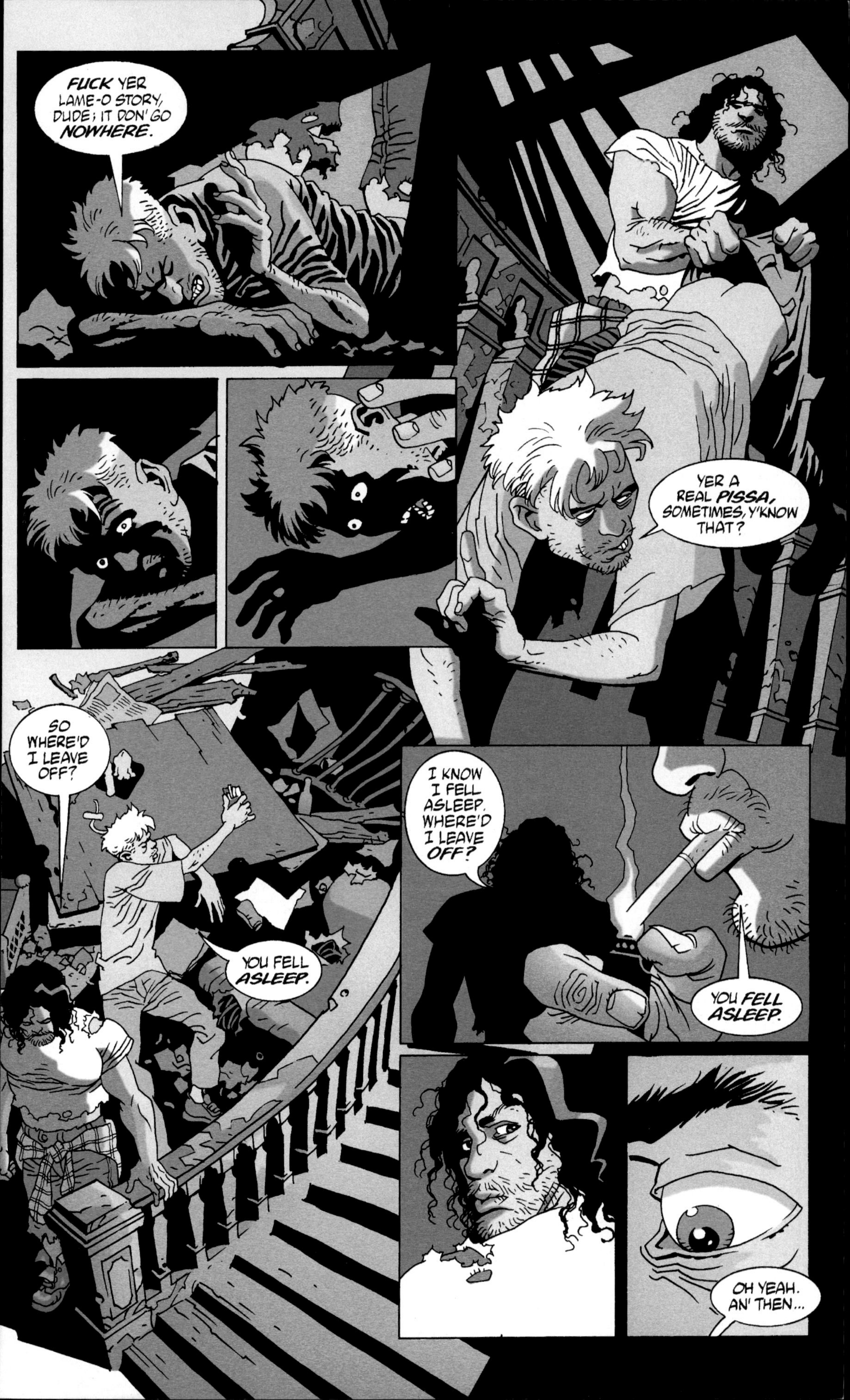
FUCK YER LAME-O STORY, DUDE; IT DON' GO NOWHERE.
YER A REAL PISSA, SOMETIMES, Y'KNOW THAT?
SO WHERE'D I LEAVE OFF?
YOU FELL ASLEEP.
I KNOW I FELL ASLEEP. WHERE'D I LEAVE OFF?
YOU FELL ASLEEP.
OH YEAH. AN' THEN...

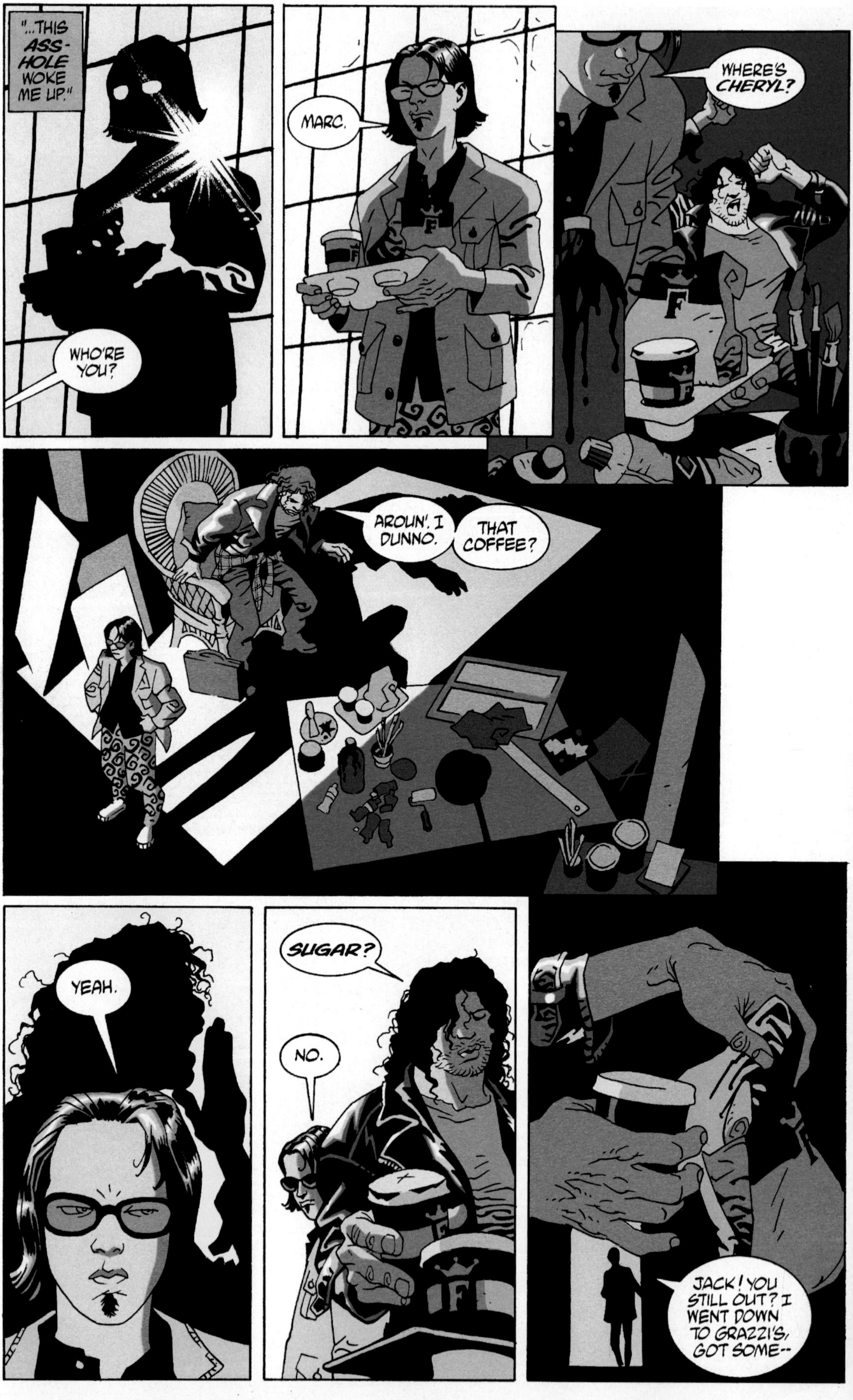
"...THIS ASS-HOLE WOKE ME UP."
WHO'RE YOU?
MARC.
WHERE'S CHERYL?
AROUN', I DUNNO.
THAT COFFEE?
YEAH.
SUGAR?
NO.
JACK! YOU STILL OUT? I WENT DOWN TO GRAZZI'S, GOT SOME--

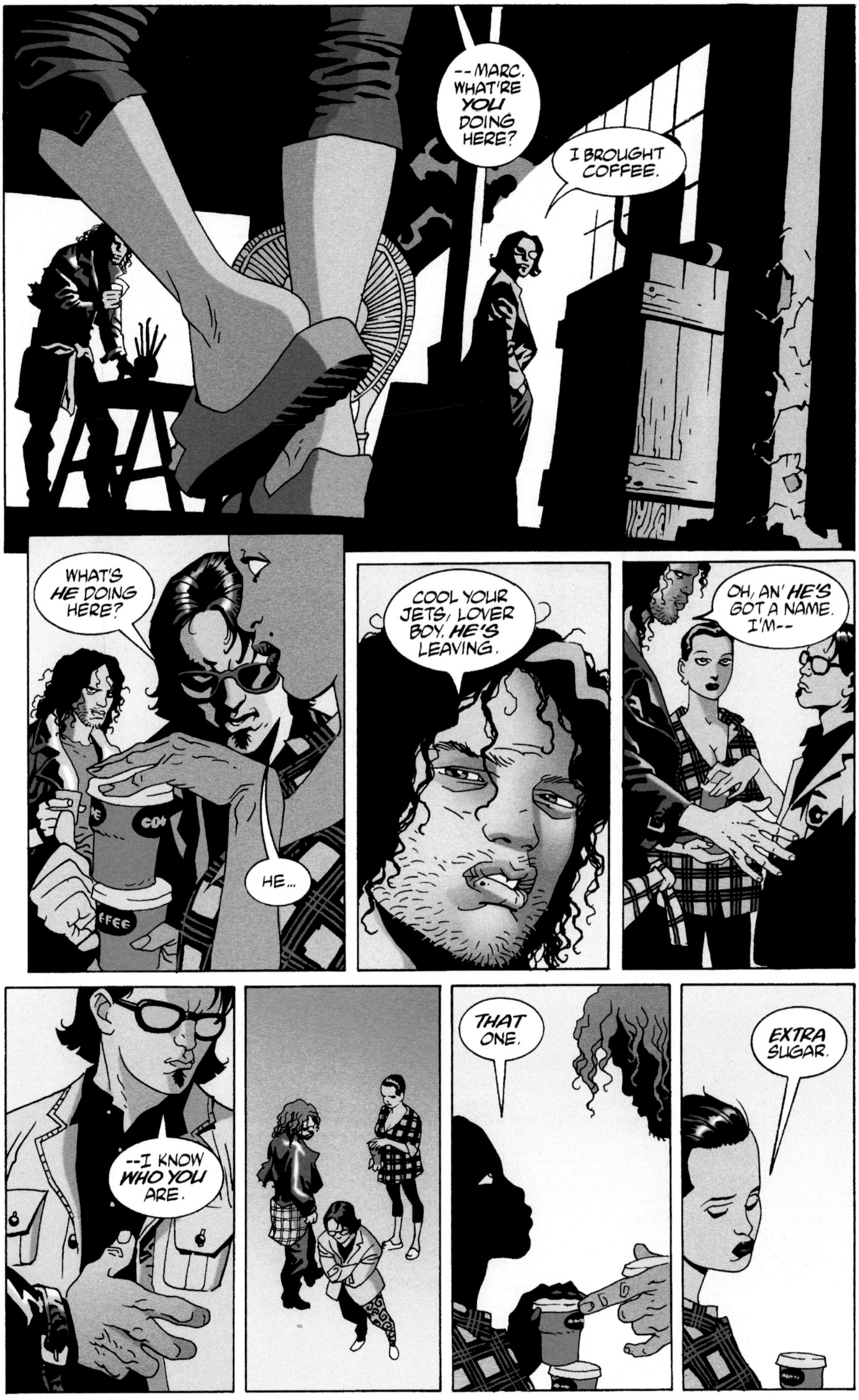
--MARC. WHAT'RE YOU DOING HERE?
I BROUGHT COFFEE.
WHAT'S HE DOING HERE?
HE...
COOL YOUR JETS, LOVER BOY. HE'S LEAVING.
OH, AN' HE'S GOT A NAME. I'M--
--I KNOW WHO YOU ARE.
THAT ONE.
EXTRA SUGAR.

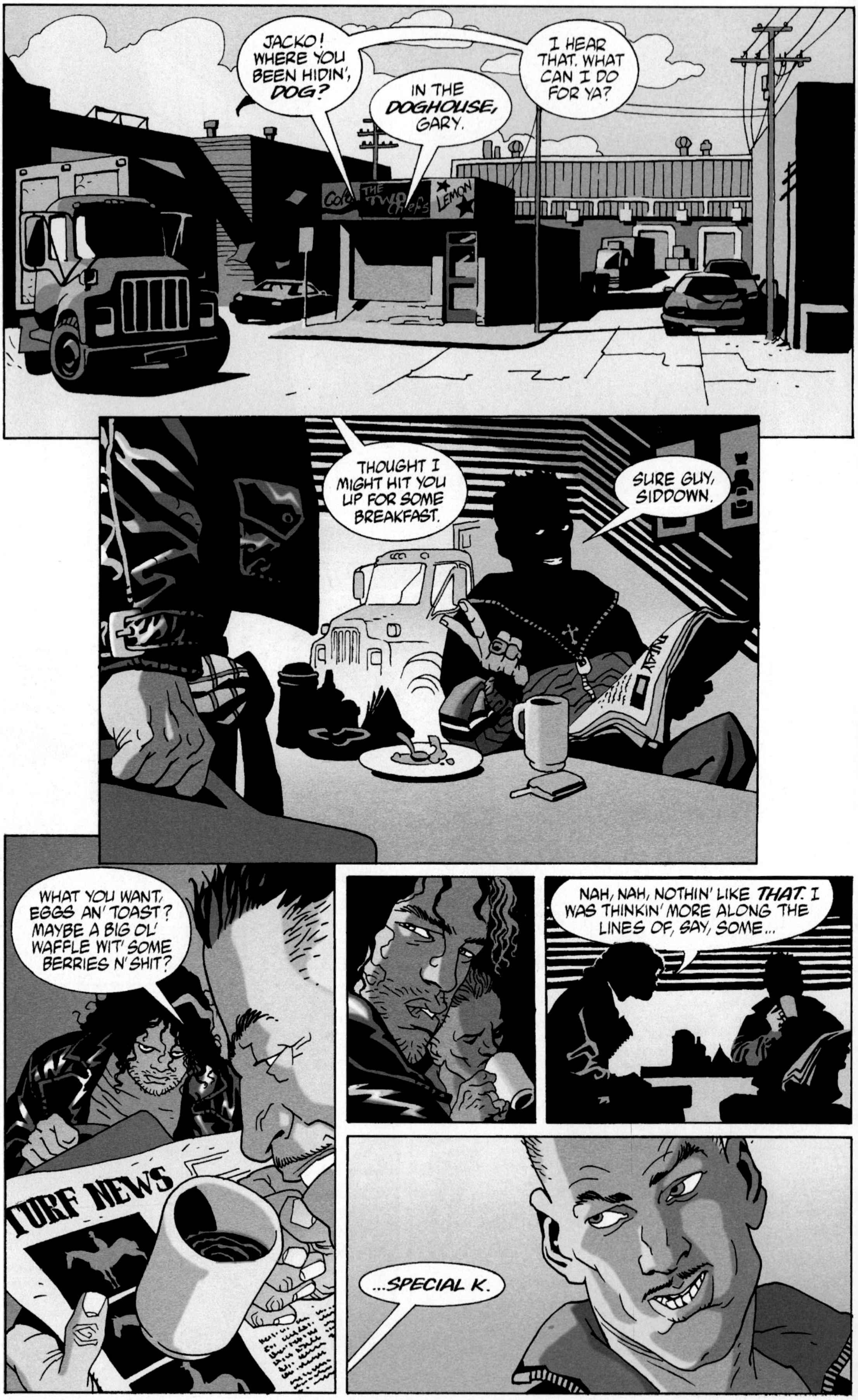
JACKO! WHERE YOU BEEN HIDIN', DOG?
IN THE DOGHOUSE, GARY.
I HEAR THAT. WHAT CAN I DO FOR YA?
THE TWO Chefs
LEMON
THOUGHT I MIGHT HIT YOU UP FOR SOME BREAKFAST.
SURE GUY, SIDDOWN.
WHAT YOU WANT, EGGS AN' TOAST? MAYBE A BIG OL' WAFFLE WIT' SOME BERRIES N' SHIT?
TURF NEWS
NAH, NAH, NOTHIN' LIKE THAT. I WAS THINKIN' MORE ALONG THE LINES OF, SAY, SOME...
...SPECIAL K.

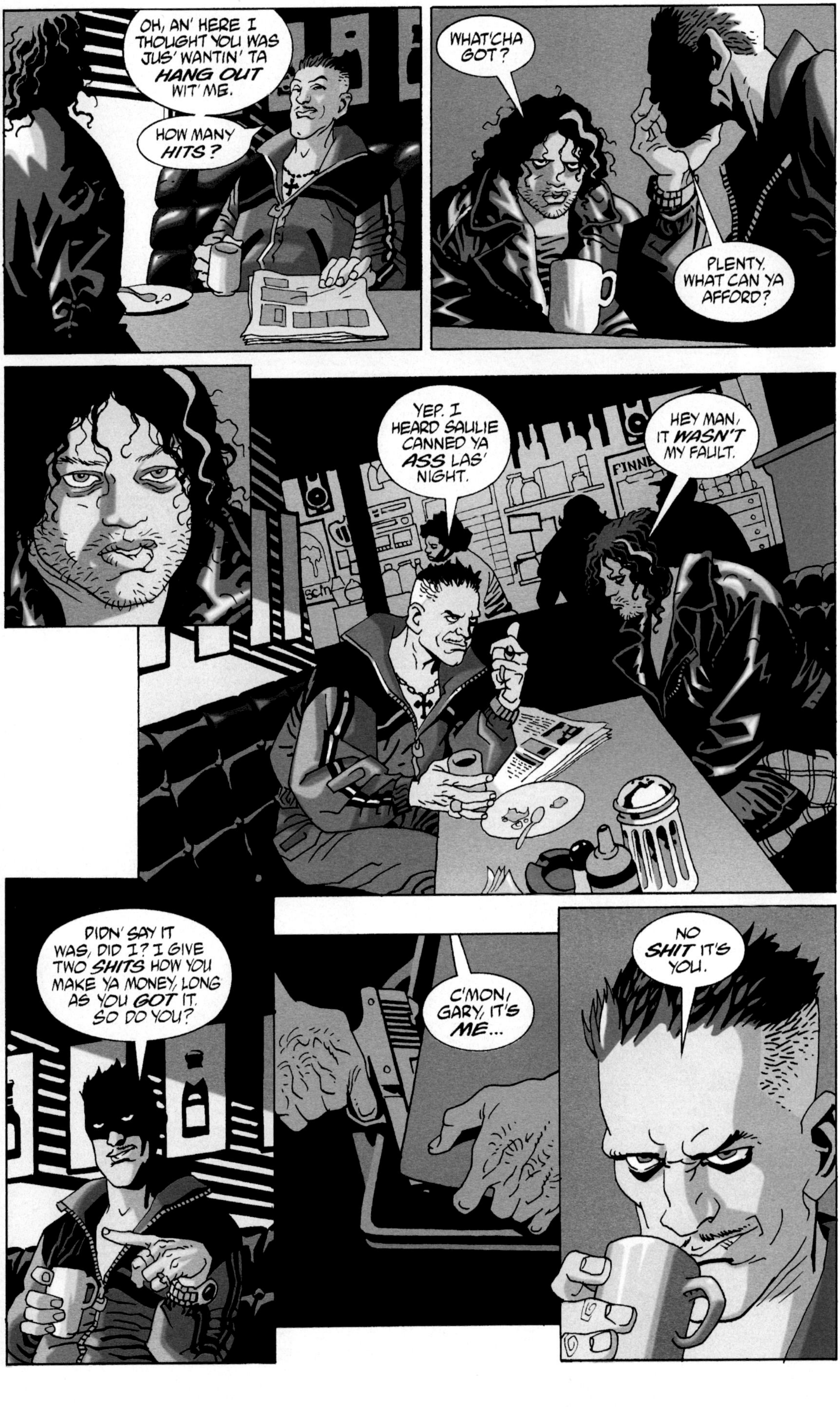
OH, AN' HERE I THOUGHT YOU WAS JUS' WANTIN' TA HANG OUT WIT' ME.
HOW MANY HITS?
WHAT'CHA GOT?
PLENTY. WHAT CAN YA AFFORD?
YEP. I HEARD SAULIE CANNED YA ASS LAS' NIGHT.
HEY MAN, IT WASN'T MY FAULT.
DIDN' SAY IT WAS, DID I? I GIVE TWO SHITS HOW YOU MAKE YA MONEY, LONG AS YOU GOT IT. SO DO YOU?
C'MON, GARY, IT'S ME...
NO SHIT IT'S YOU.

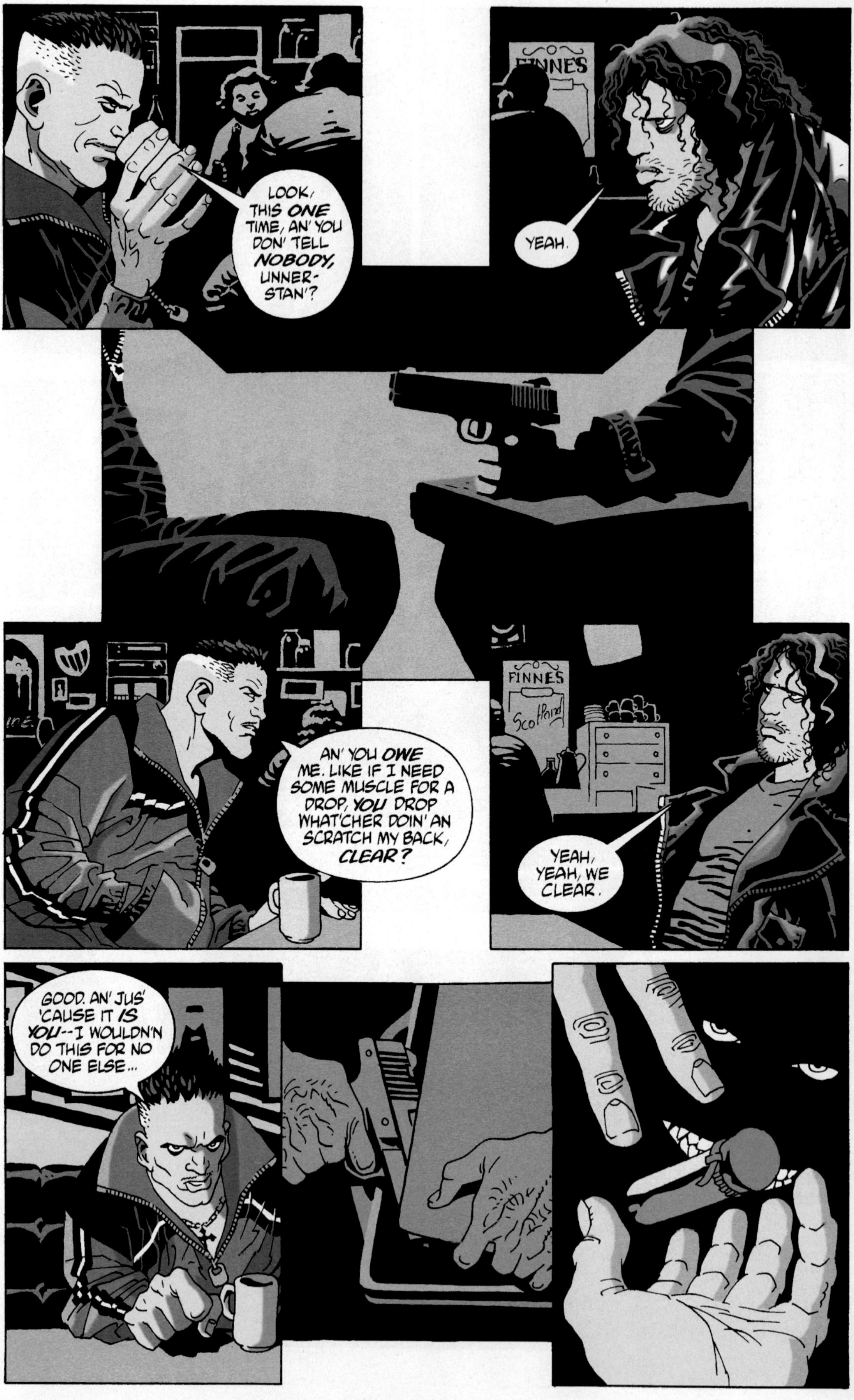
LOOK, THIS ONE TIME, AN' YOU DON' TELL NOBODY, UNNER-STAN'?
FINNES
YEAH.
AN' YOU OWE ME. LIKE IF I NEED SOME MUSCLE FOR A DROP, YOU DROP WHAT'CHER DOIN' AN SCRATCH MY BACK, CLEAR?
FINNES
Scotland
YEAH, YEAH, WE CLEAR.
GOOD. AN' JUS' 'CAUSE IT IS YOU--I WOULDN'N DO THIS FOR NO ONE ELSE...

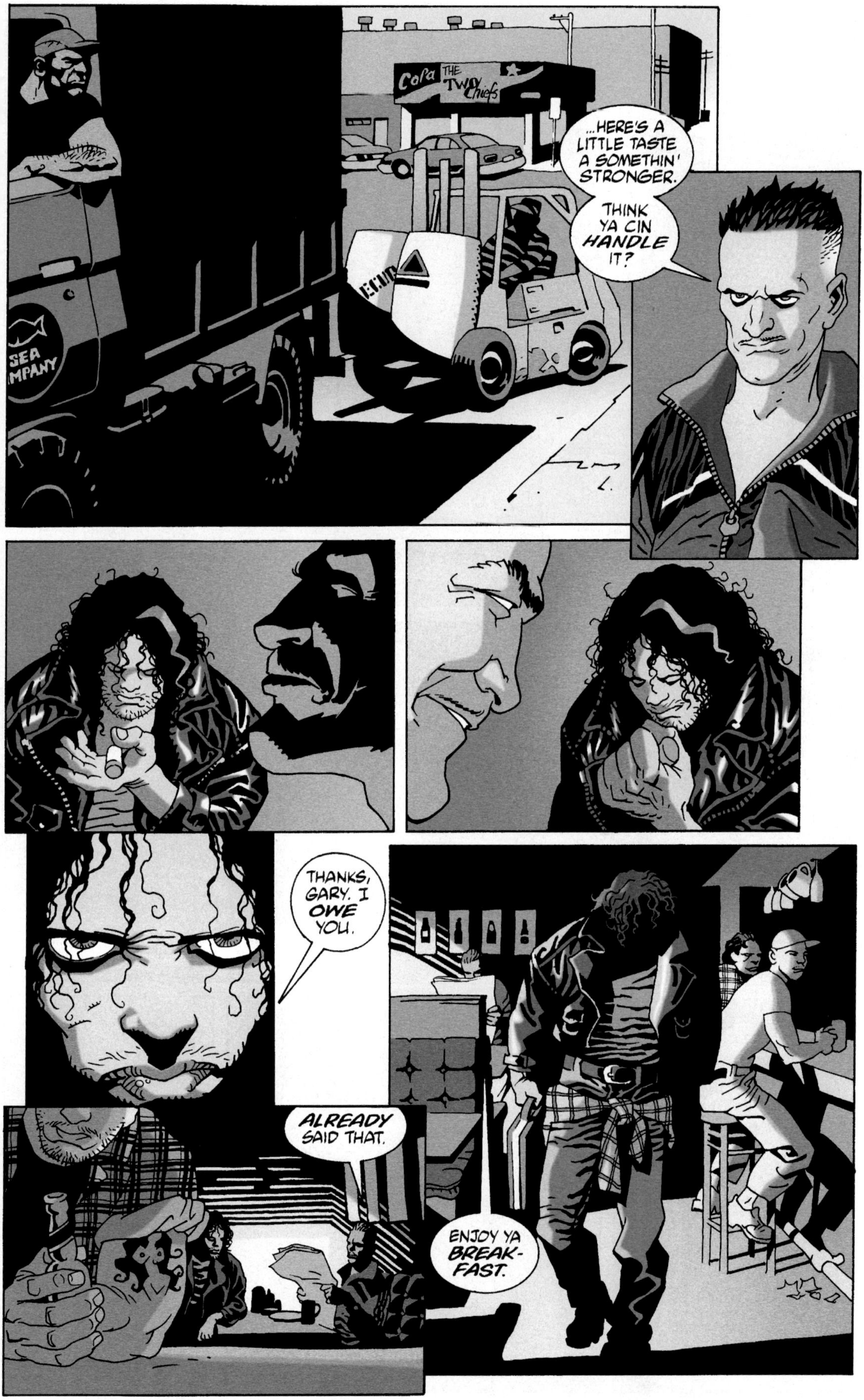
Cola THE TWO Chiefs
SEA
MPANY
...HERE'S A LITTLE TASTE A SOMETHIN' STRONGER.
THINK YA CIN HANDLE IT?
THANKS, GARY. I OWE YOU.
ALREADY SAID THAT.
ENJOY YA BREAK-FAST.

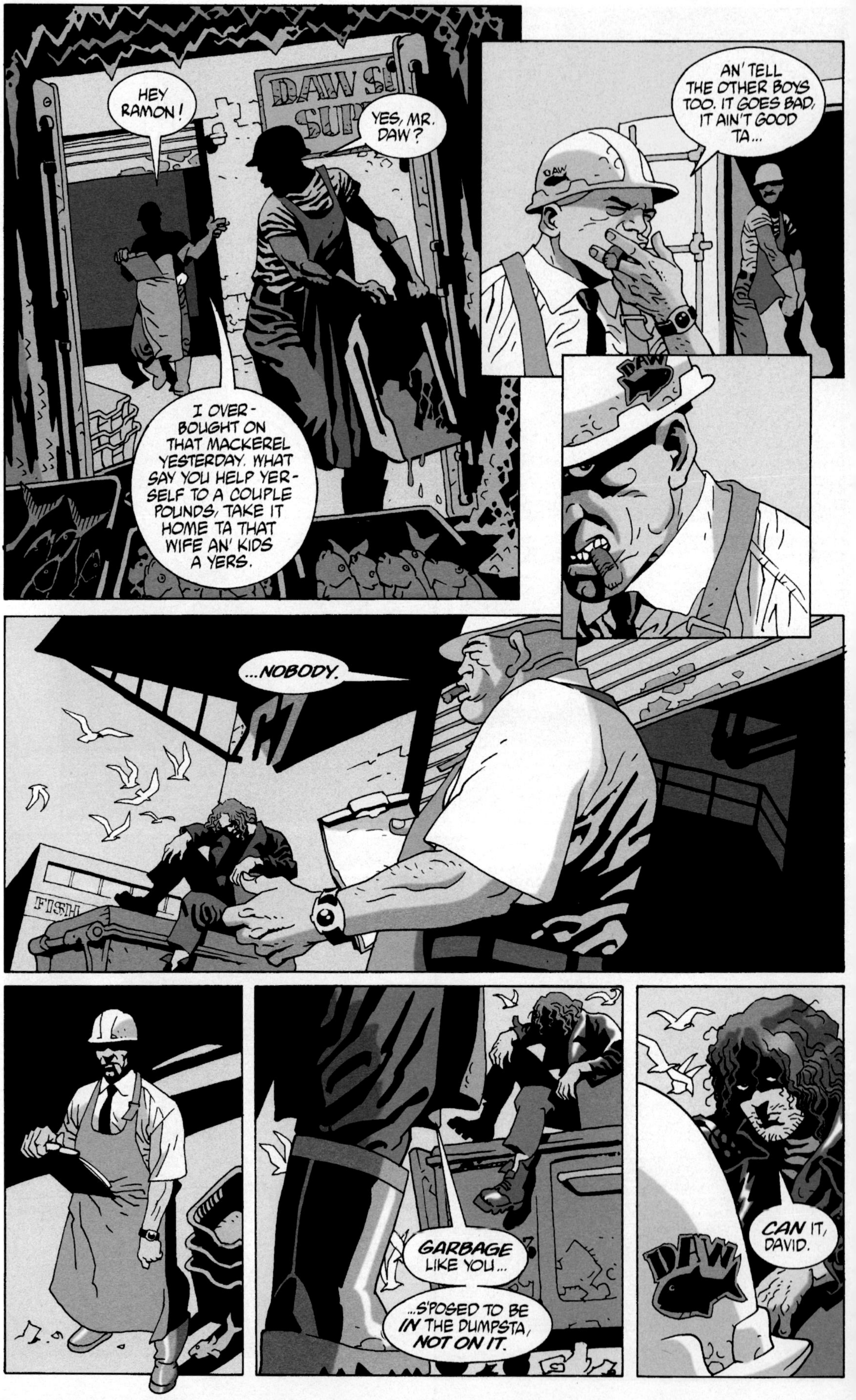
DAW S
SUP
HEY RAMON!
YES, MR. DAW?
I OVER-BOUGHT ON THAT MACKEREL YESTERDAY. WHAT SAY YOU HELP YER-SELF TO A COUPLE POUNDS, TAKE IT HOME TA THAT WIFE AN' KIDS A YERS.
AN' TELL THE OTHER BOYS TOO. IT GOES BAD, IT AIN'T GOOD TA...
DAW
DAW
...NOBODY.
FISH
GARBAGE LIKE YOU...
...S'POSED TO BE IN THE DUMPSTA, NOT ON IT.
DAW
CAN IT, DAVID.

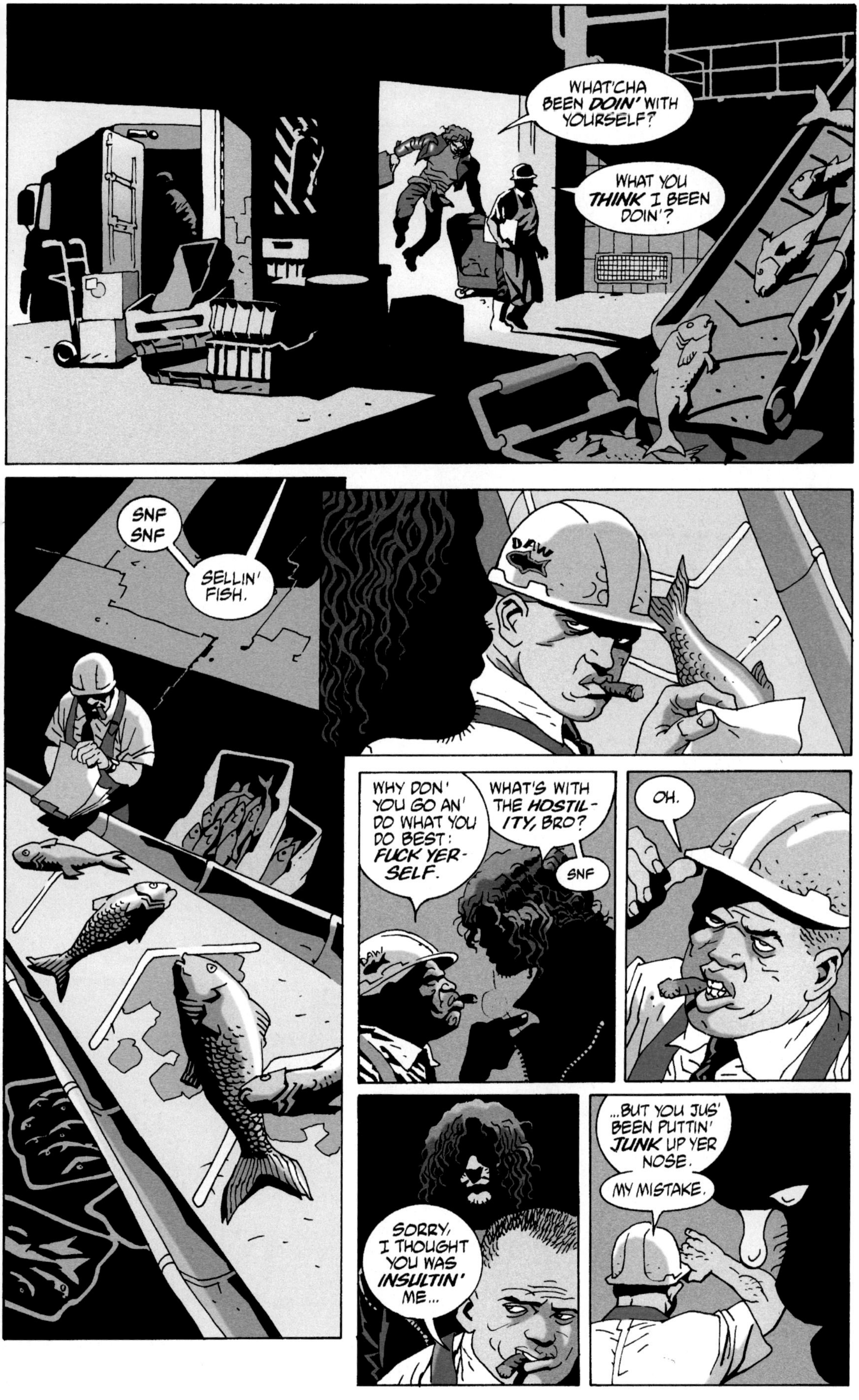
WHAT'CHA BEEN DOIN' WITH YOURSELF?
WHAT YOU THINK I BEEN DOIN'?
SNF SNF
SELLIN' FISH.
WHY DON' YOU GO AN' DO WHAT YOU DO BEST: FUCK YER-SELF.
WHAT'S WITH THE HOSTIL-ITY, BRO?
SNF
OH.
SORRY, I THOUGHT YOU WAS INSULTIN' ME...
...BUT YOU JUS' BEEN PUTTIN' JUNK UP YER NOSE.
MY MISTAKE.

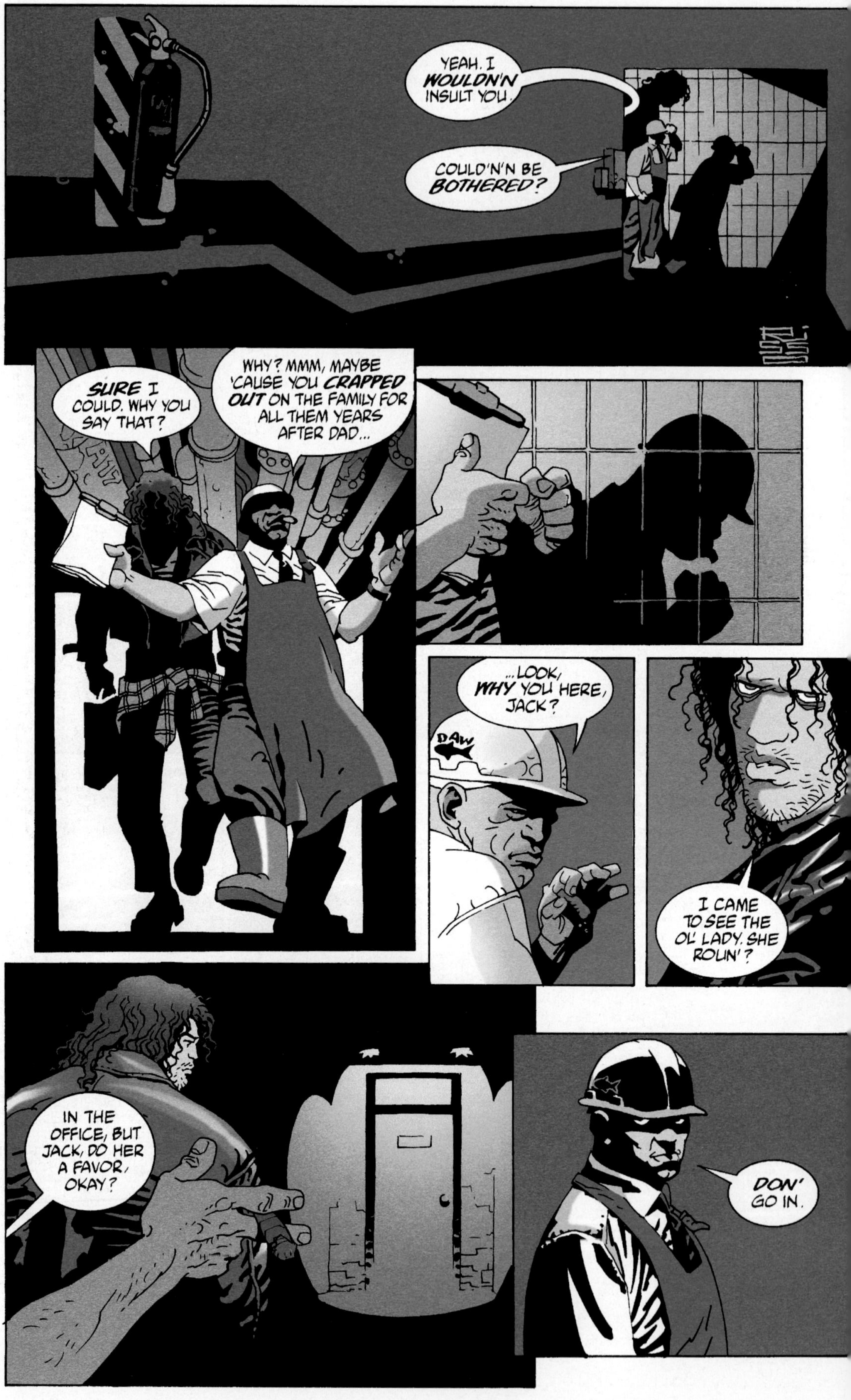
YEAH. I WOULDN'N INSULT YOU.
COULD'N'N BE BOTHERED?
SURE I COULD. WHY YOU SAY THAT?
WHY? MMM, MAYBE 'CAUSE YOU CRAPPED OUT ON THE FAMILY FOR ALL THEM YEARS AFTER DAD...
...LOOK, WHY YOU HERE, JACK?
DAW
I CAME TO SEE THE OL' LADY. SHE ROUN'?
IN THE OFFICE, BUT JACK, DO HER A FAVOR, OKAY?
DON' GO IN.

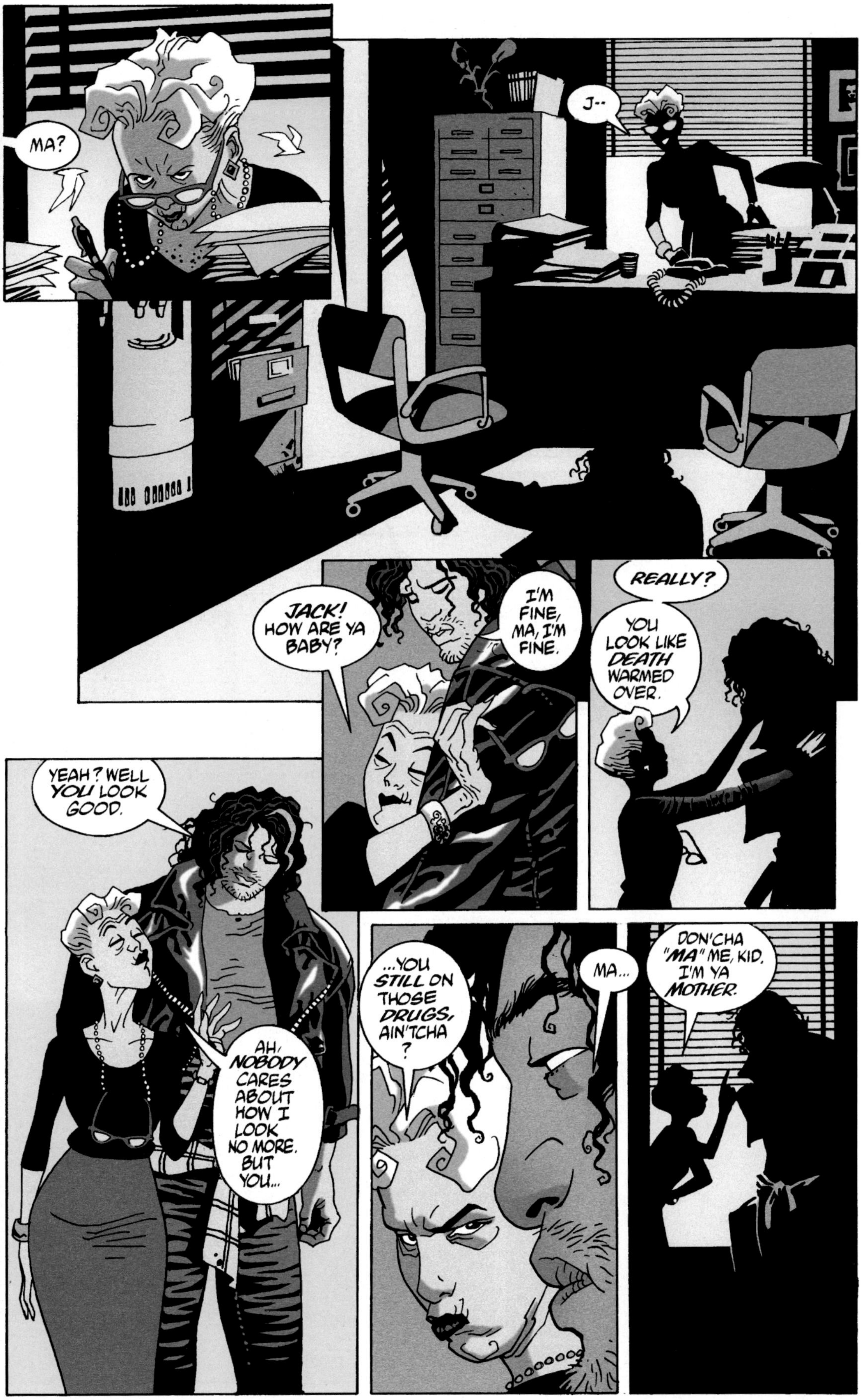
MA?
J--
JACK! HOW ARE YA BABY?
I'M FINE, MA, I'M FINE.
REALLY?
YOU LOOK LIKE DEATH WARMED OVER.
YEAH? WELL YOU LOOK GOOD.
AH, NOBODY CARES ABOUT HOW I LOOK NO MORE. BUT YOU...
...YOU STILL ON THOSE DRUGS, AIN'TCHA?
MA...
DON'CHA "MA" ME, KID, I'M YA MOTHER.

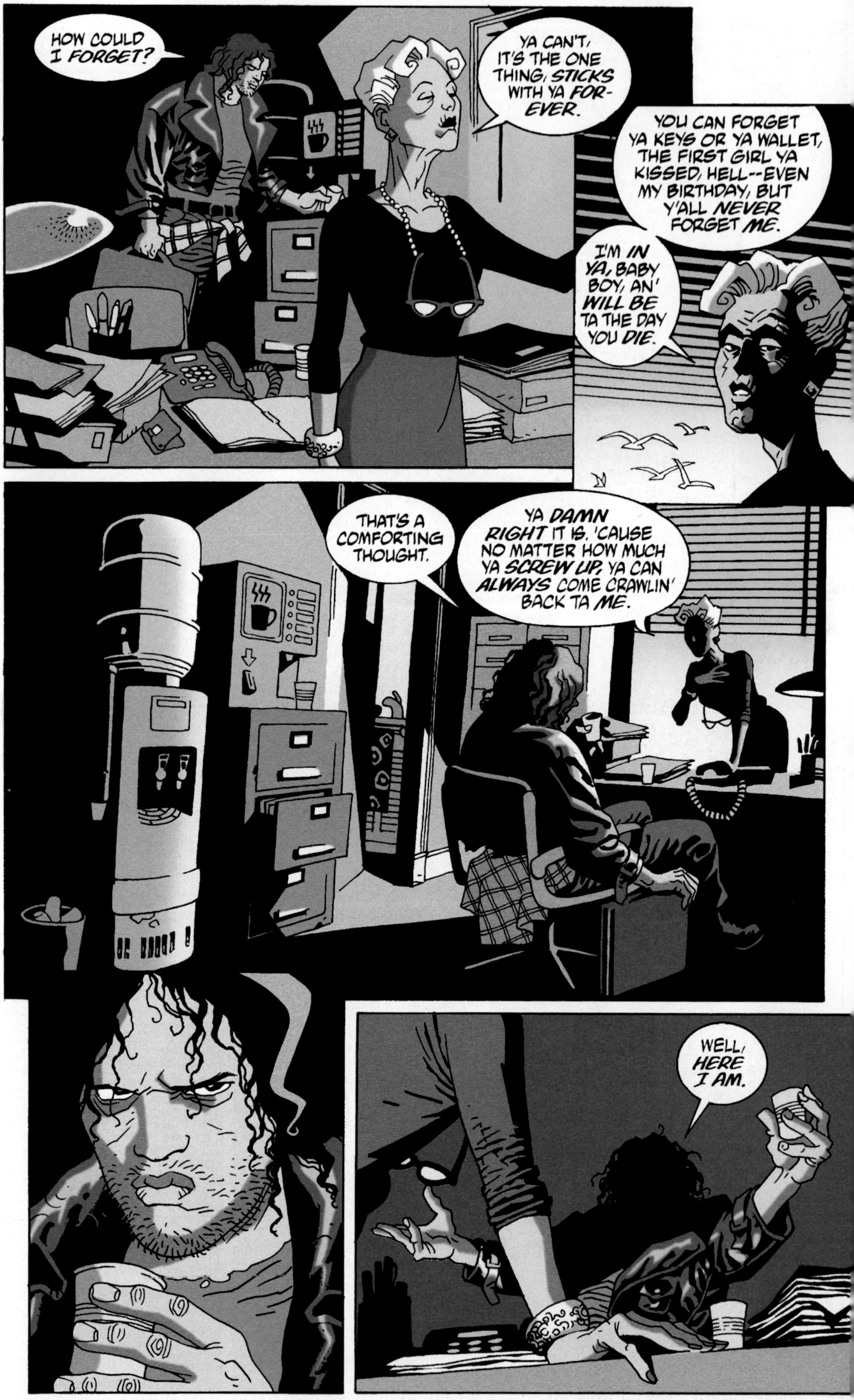
HOW COULD I *FORGET?*
YA CAN'T, IT'S THE ONE THING, *STICKS* WITH YA *FOREVER*.
YOU CAN FORGET YA KEYS OR YA WALLET, THE FIRST GIRL YA KISSED, HELL--EVEN MY BIRTHDAY, BUT Y'ALL *NEVER* FORGET *ME*.
I'M *IN YA*, BABY BOY, AN' *WILL BE* TA THE DAY YOU *DIE*.
THAT'S A COMFORTING THOUGHT.
YA *DAMN RIGHT* IT IS. 'CAUSE NO MATTER HOW MUCH YA *SCREW UP*, YA CAN *ALWAYS* COME CRAWLIN' BACK TA *ME*.
WELL, *HERE I AM*.

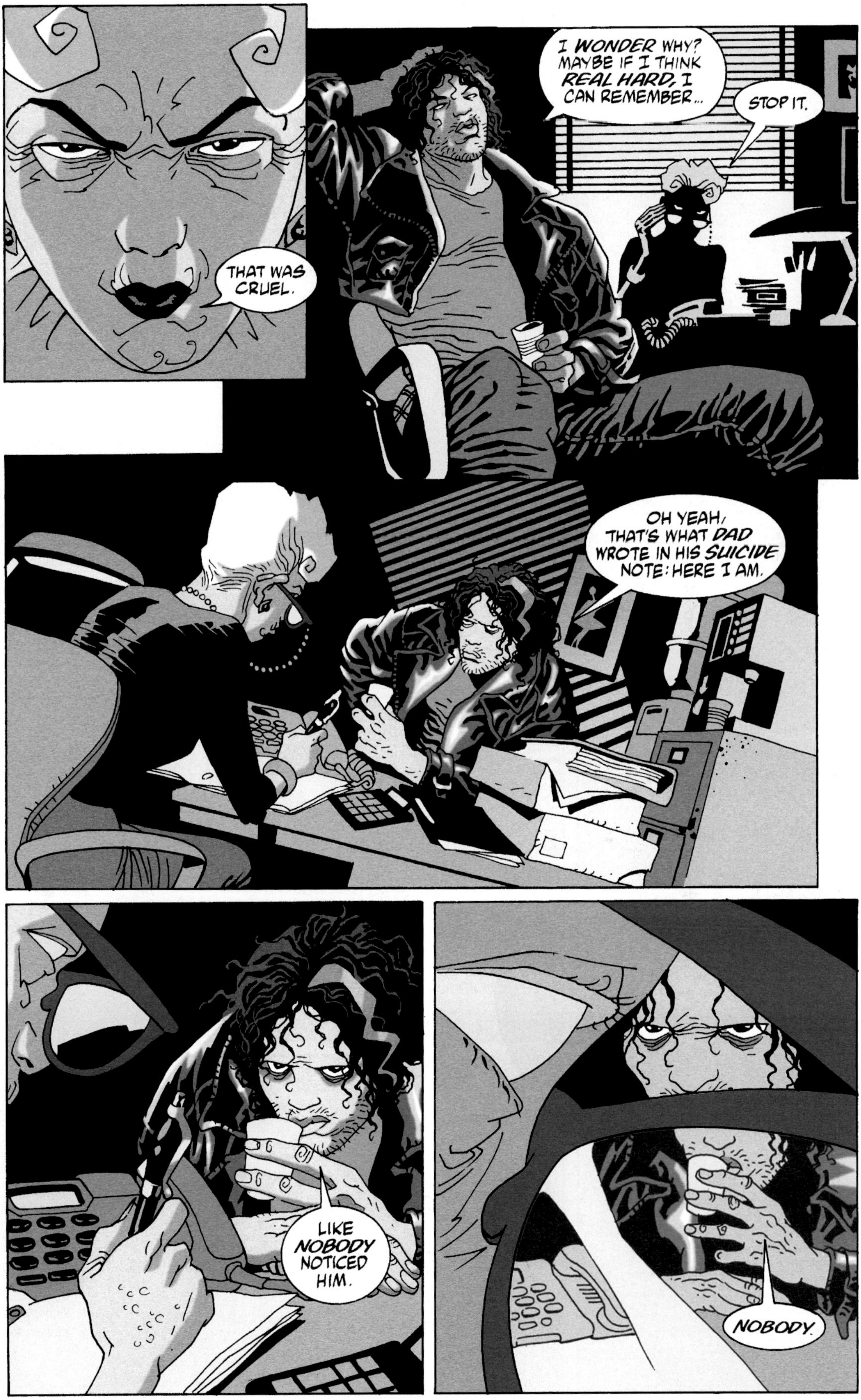
THAT WAS CRUEL.
I *WONDER* WHY? MAYBE IF I THINK *REAL HARD,* I CAN REMEMBER...
STOP IT.
OH YEAH, THAT'S WHAT *DAD* WROTE IN HIS *SUICIDE* NOTE: HERE I AM.
LIKE *NOBODY* NOTICED HIM.
NOBODY.

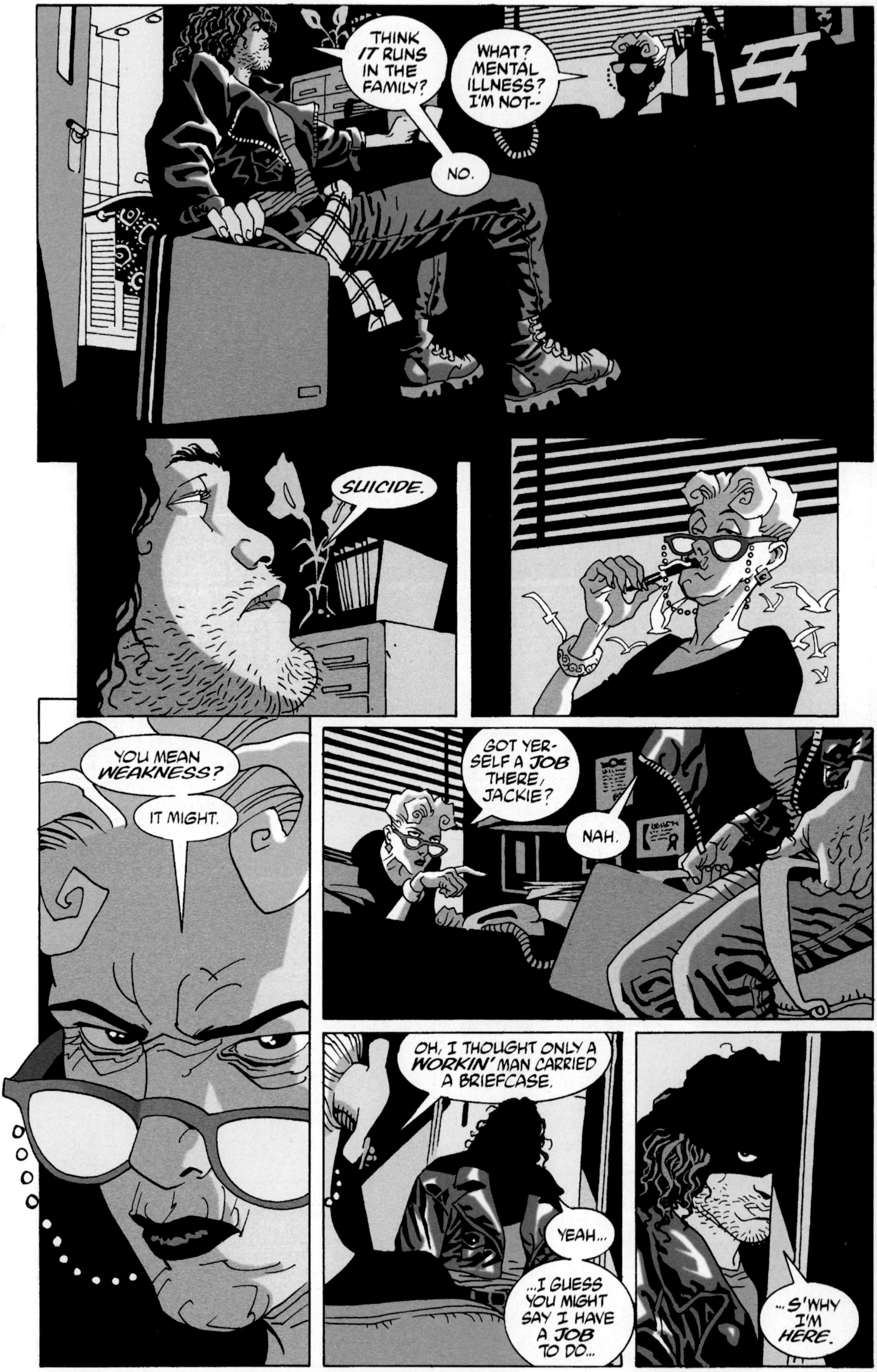
THINK *IT* RUNS IN THE FAMILY?
WHAT? MENTAL ILLNESS? I'M NOT--
NO.
SUICIDE.
YOU MEAN *WEAKNESS?*
IT MIGHT.
GOT YER-SELF A *JOB* THERE, JACKIE?
NAH.
OH, I THOUGHT ONLY A *WORKIN'* MAN CARRIED A BRIEFCASE.
YEAH...
...I GUESS YOU MIGHT SAY I HAVE A *JOB* TO DO...
...S'WHY I'M *HERE.*

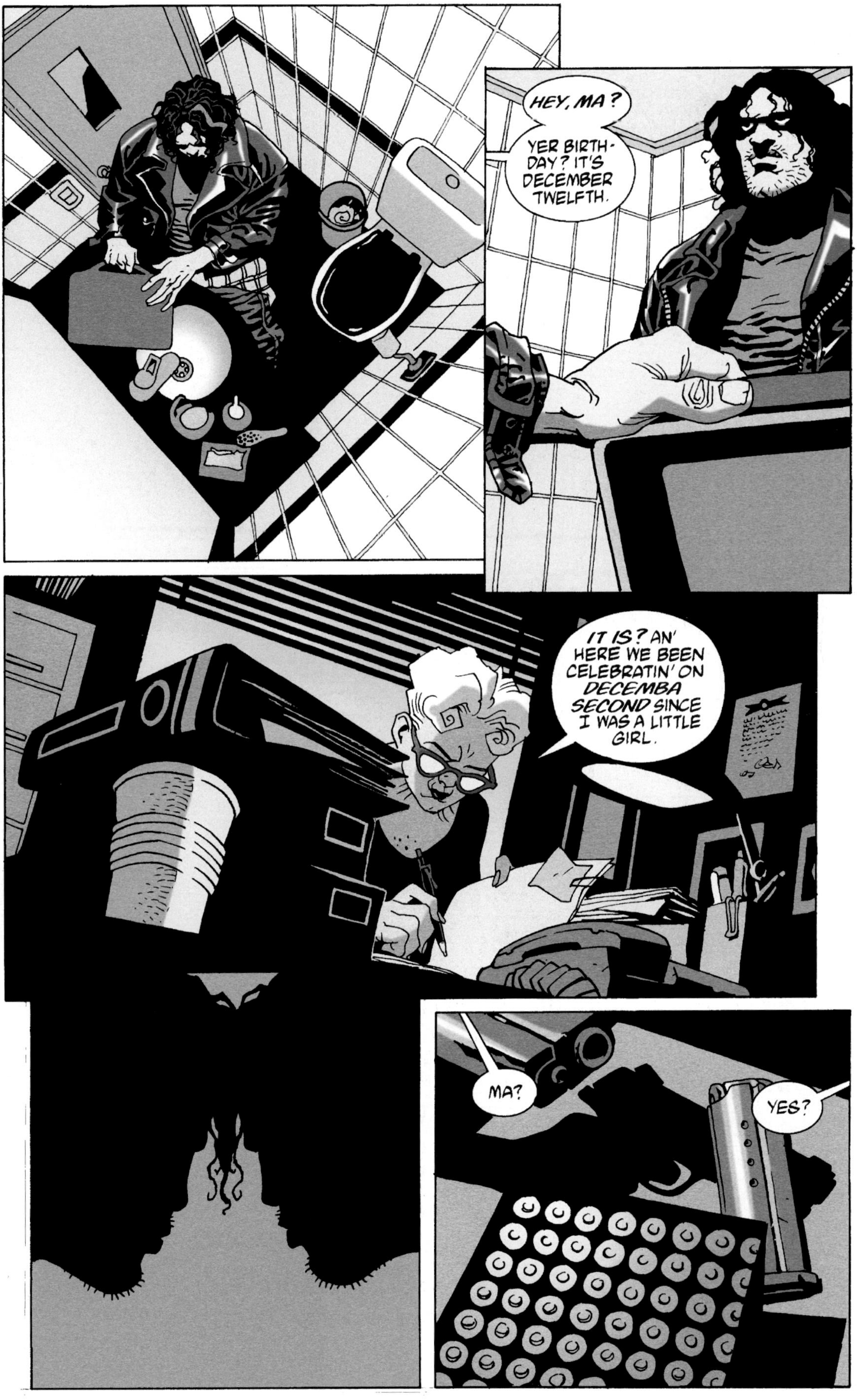
HEY, MA?
YER BIRTHDAY? IT'S DECEMBER TWELFTH.
IT IS? AN' HERE WE BEEN CELEBRATIN' ON DECEMBA SECOND SINCE I WAS A LITTLE GIRL.
MA?
YES?

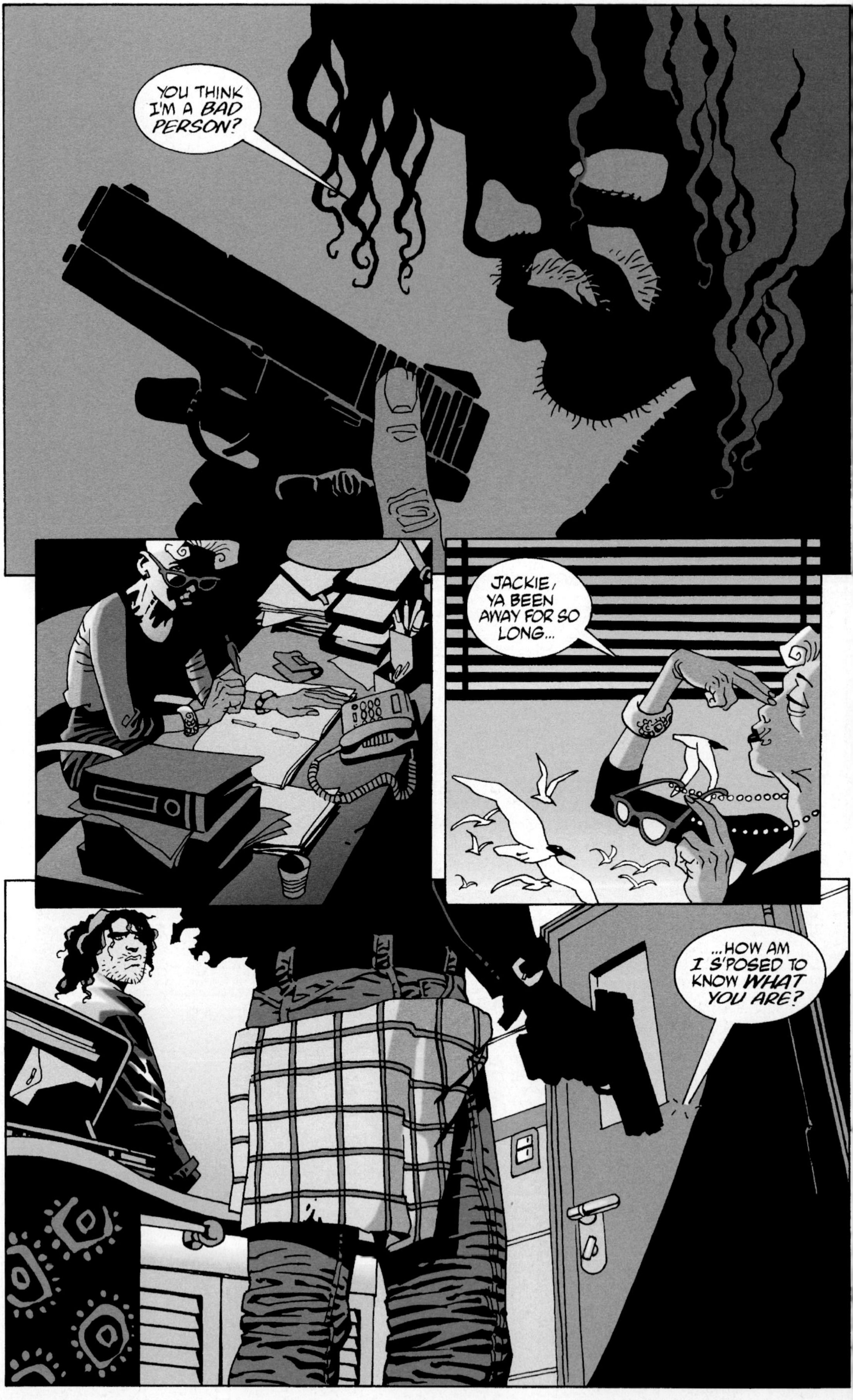
YOU THINK I'M A BAD PERSON?
JACKIE, YA BEEN AWAY FOR SO LONG...
...HOW AM I S'POSED TO KNOW WHAT YOU ARE?

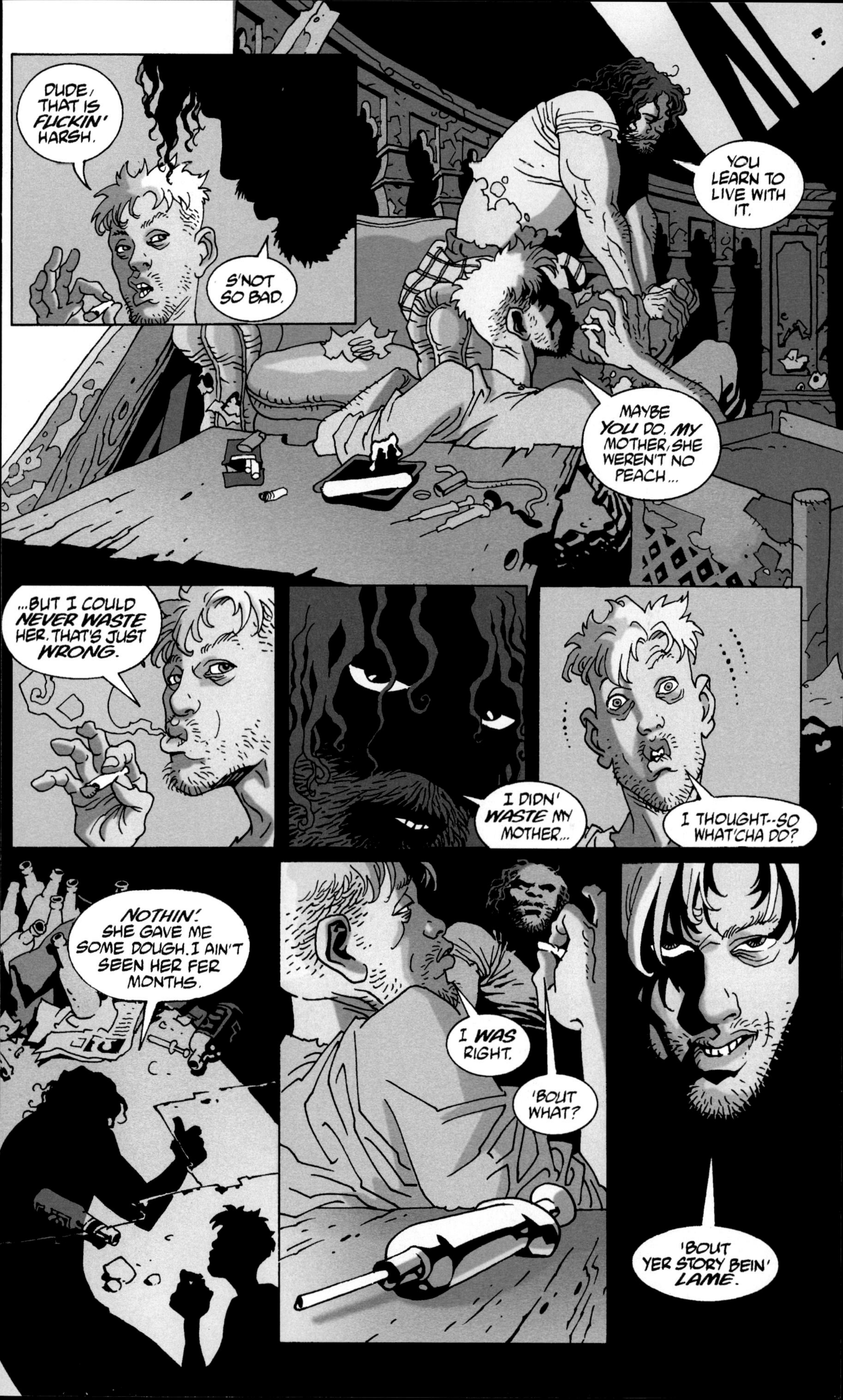
DUDE, THAT IS FUCKIN' HARSH.
S'NOT SO BAD.
YOU LEARN TO LIVE WITH IT.
MAYBE YOU DO. MY MOTHER, SHE WEREN'T NO PEACH...
...BUT I COULD NEVER WASTE HER. THAT'S JUST WRONG.
I DIDN' WASTE MY MOTHER...
I THOUGHT--SO WHAT'CHA DO?
NOTHIN'. SHE GAVE ME SOME DOUGH. I AIN'T SEEN HER FER MONTHS.
I WAS RIGHT.
'BOUT WHAT?
'BOUT YER STORY BEIN' LAME.

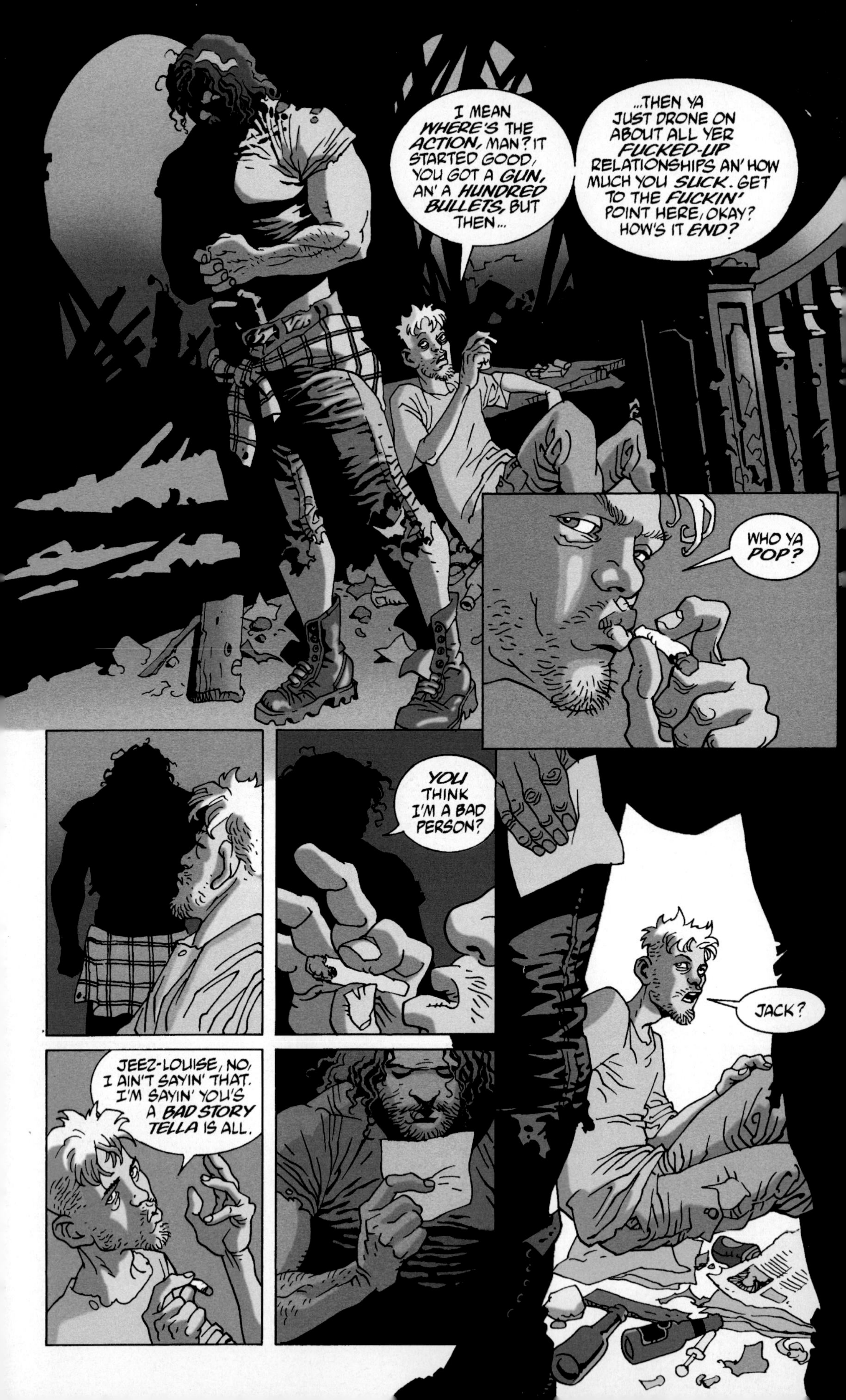
I MEAN WHERE'S THE ACTION, MAN? IT STARTED GOOD, YOU GOT A GUN, AN' A HUNDRED BULLETS, BUT THEN...
...THEN YA JUST DRONE ON ABOUT ALL YER FUCKED-UP RELATIONSHIPS AN' HOW MUCH YOU SUCK. GET TO THE FUCKIN' POINT HERE, OKAY? HOW'S IT END?
WHO YA POP?
YOU THINK I'M A BAD PERSON?
JEEZ-LOUISE, NO, I AIN'T SAYIN' THAT. I'M SAYIN' YOU'S A BAD STORY TELLA IS ALL.
JACK?

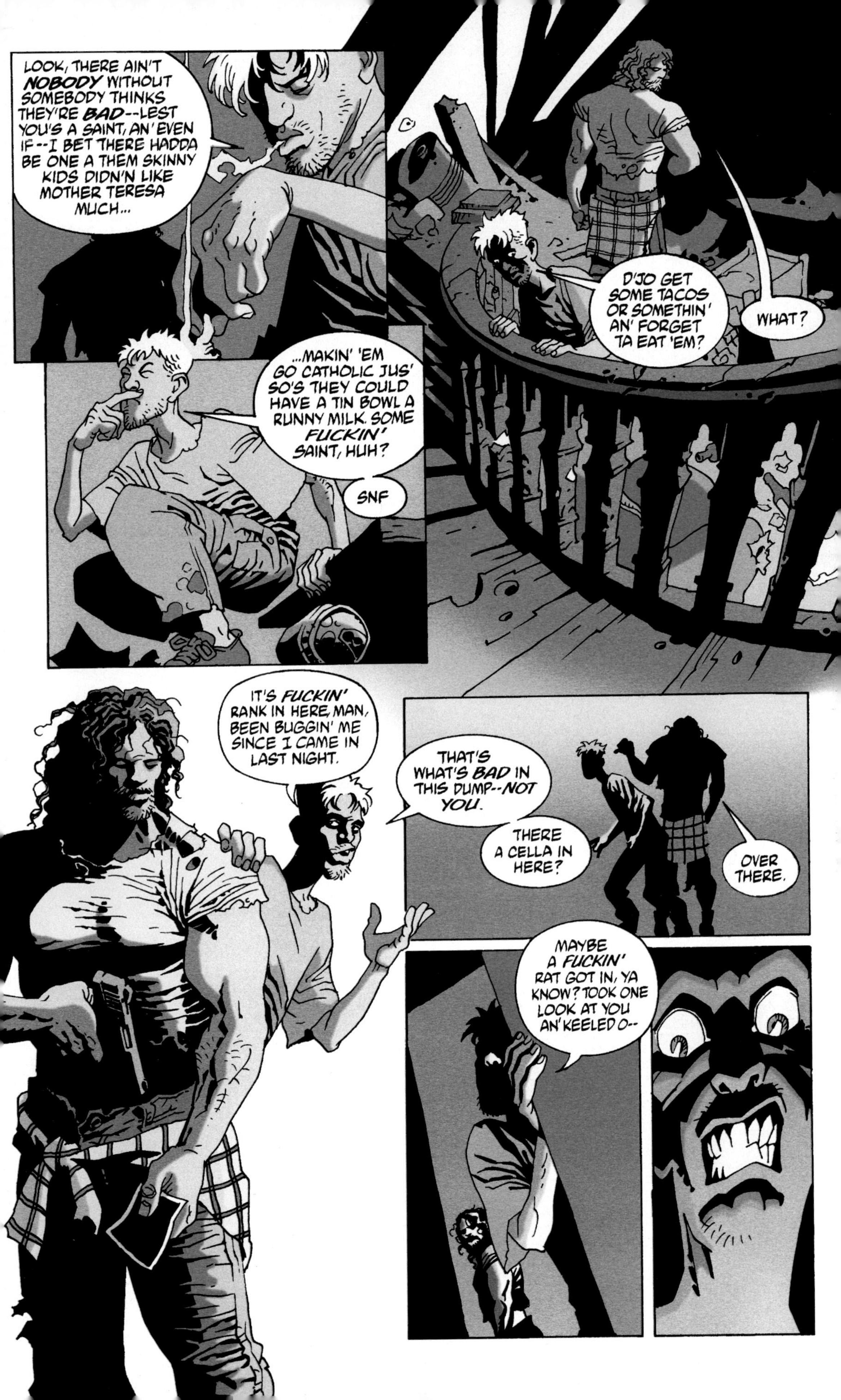
LOOK, THERE AIN'T NOBODY WITHOUT SOMEBODY THINKS THEY'RE BAD--LEST YOU'S A SAINT, AN' EVEN IF--I BET THERE HADDA BE ONE A THEM SKINNY KIDS DIDN'N LIKE MOTHER TERESA MUCH...
...MAKIN' 'EM GO CATHOLIC JUS' SO'S THEY COULD HAVE A TIN BOWL A RUNNY MILK. SOME FUCKIN' SAINT, HUH?
SNF
D'JO GET SOME TACOS OR SOMETHIN' AN' FORGET TA EAT 'EM?
WHAT?
IT'S FUCKIN' RANK IN HERE, MAN, BEEN BUGGIN' ME SINCE I CAME IN LAST NIGHT.
THAT'S WHAT'S BAD IN THIS DUMP--NOT YOU.
THERE A CELLA IN HERE?
OVER THERE.
MAYBE A FUCKIN' RAT GOT IN, YA KNOW? TOOK ONE LOOK AT YOU AN' KEELED O--

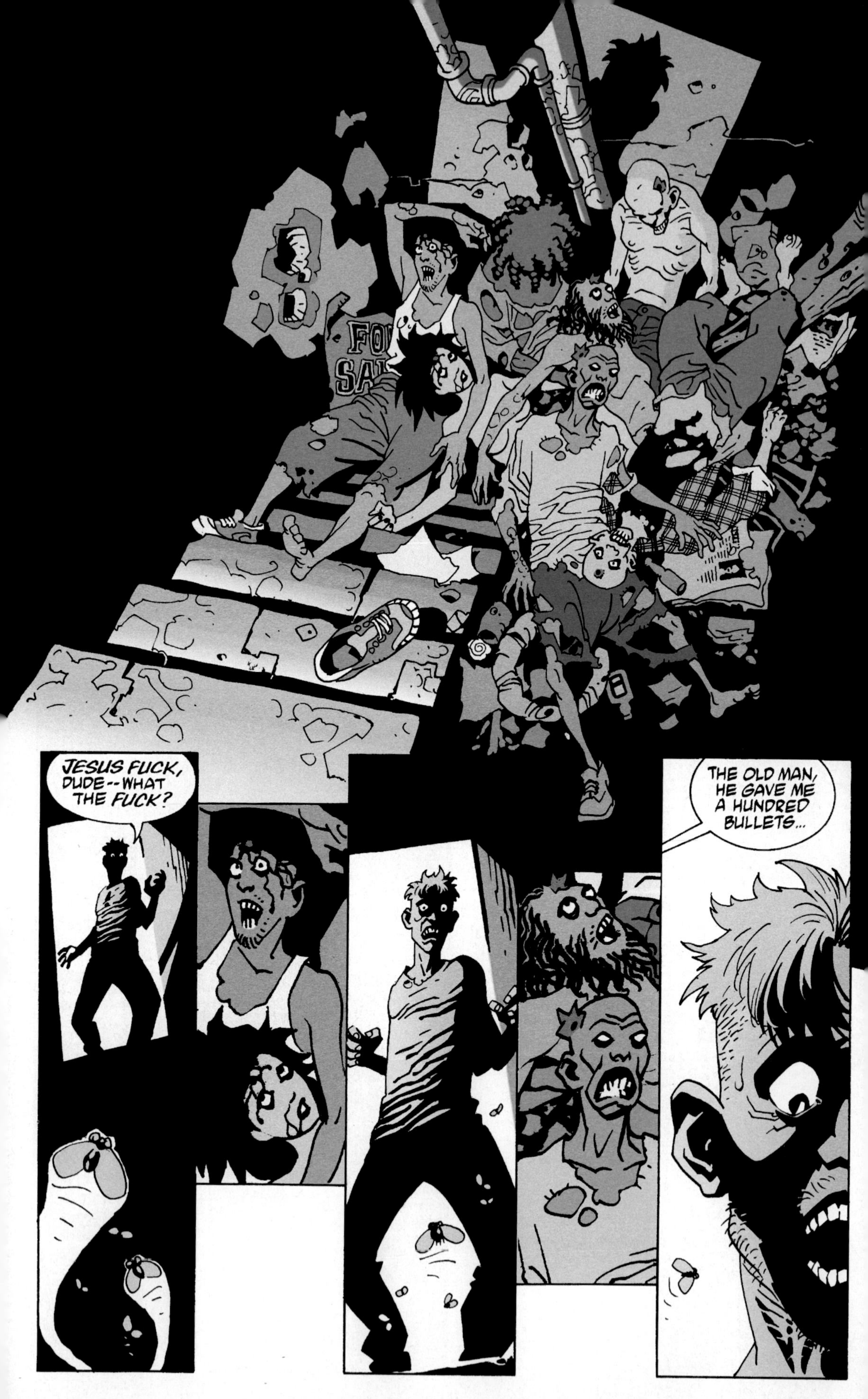
FOR SALE
JESUS FUCK, DUDE--WHAT THE FUCK?
THE OLD MAN, HE GAVE ME A HUNDRED BULLETS...

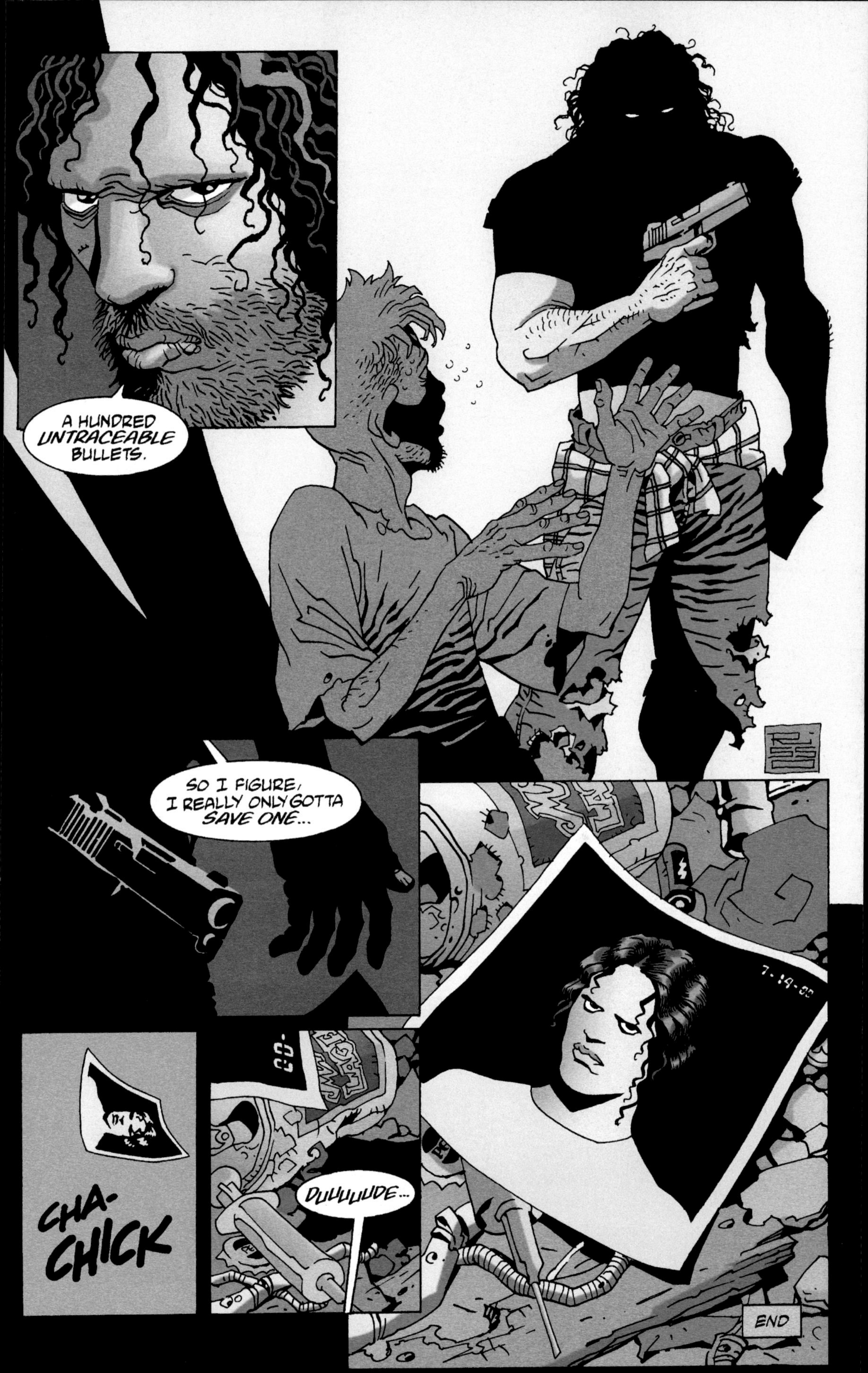
A HUNDRED UNTRACEABLE BULLETS.
SO I FIGURE, I REALLY ONLY GOTTA SAVE ONE...
7-19-00
CHA-CHICK
DUUUUUDE...
END

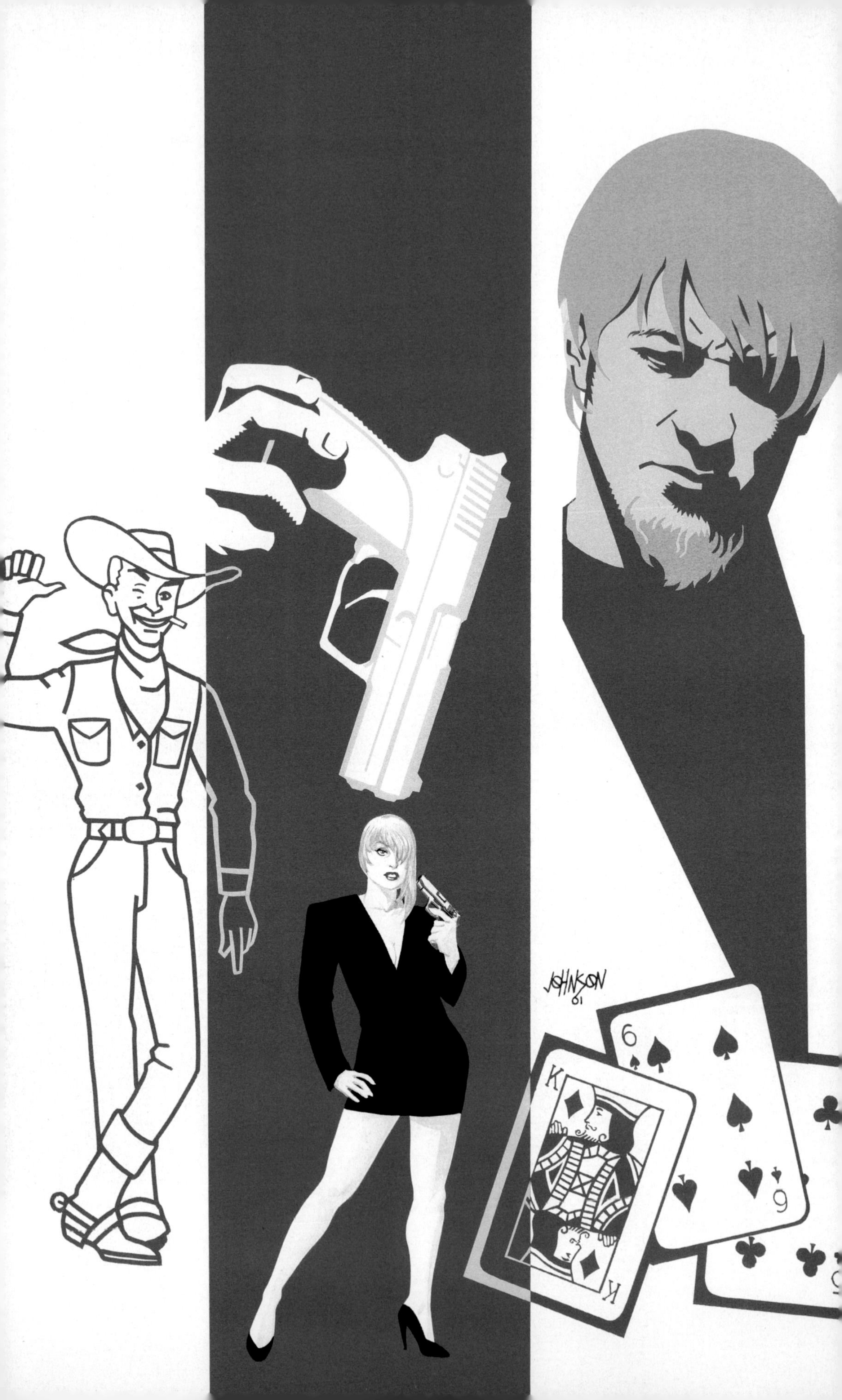
JOHNSON
01

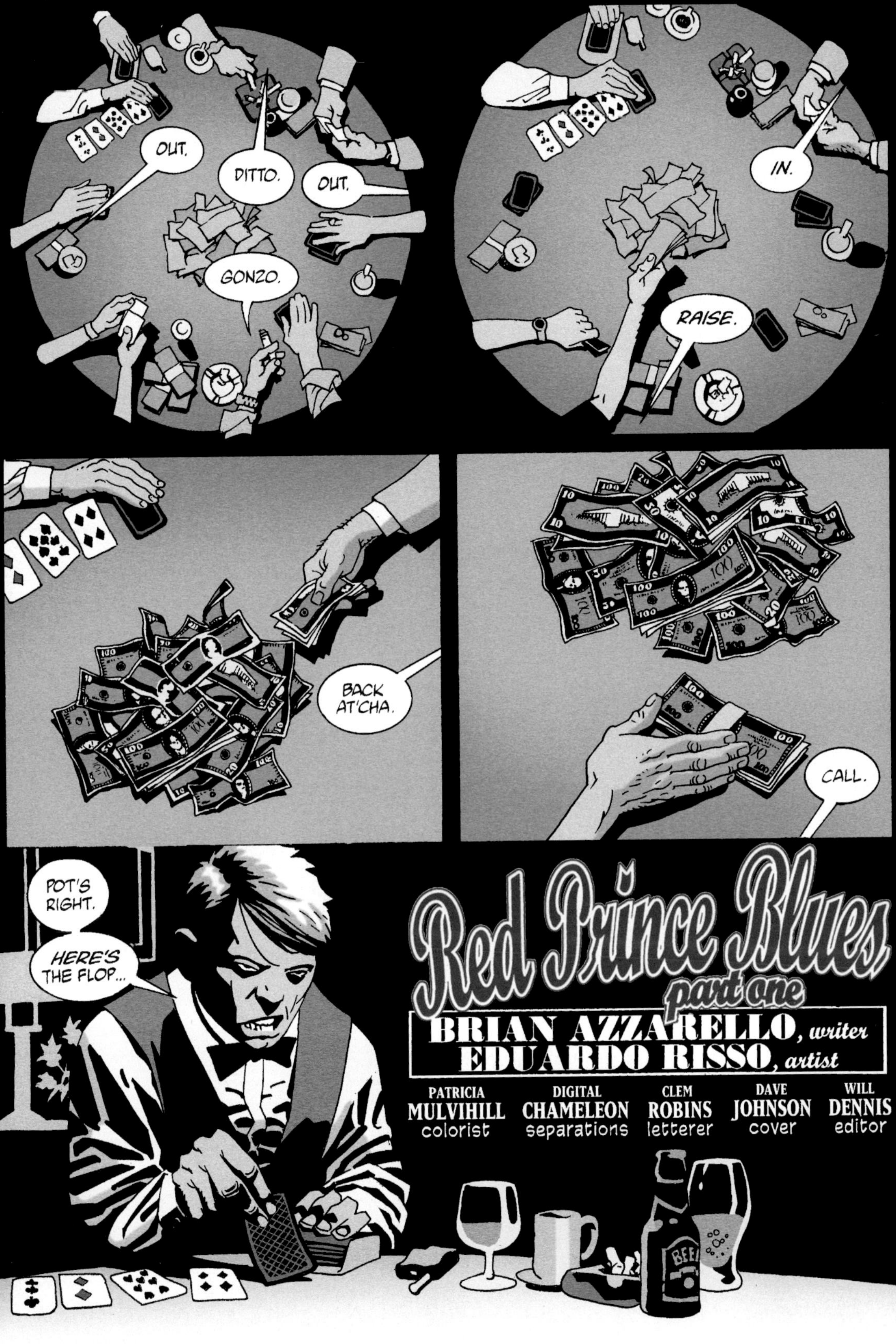
OUT.
DITTO.
OUT.
GONZO.
IN.
RAISE.
BACK AT'CHA.
CALL.
POT'S RIGHT.
HERE'S THE FLOP...
Red Prince Blues
part one
BRIAN AZZARELLO, writer
EDUARDO RISSO, artist
PATRICIA MULVIHILL colorist
DIGITAL CHAMELEON separations
CLEM ROBINS letterer
DAVE JOHNSON cover
WILL DENNIS editor

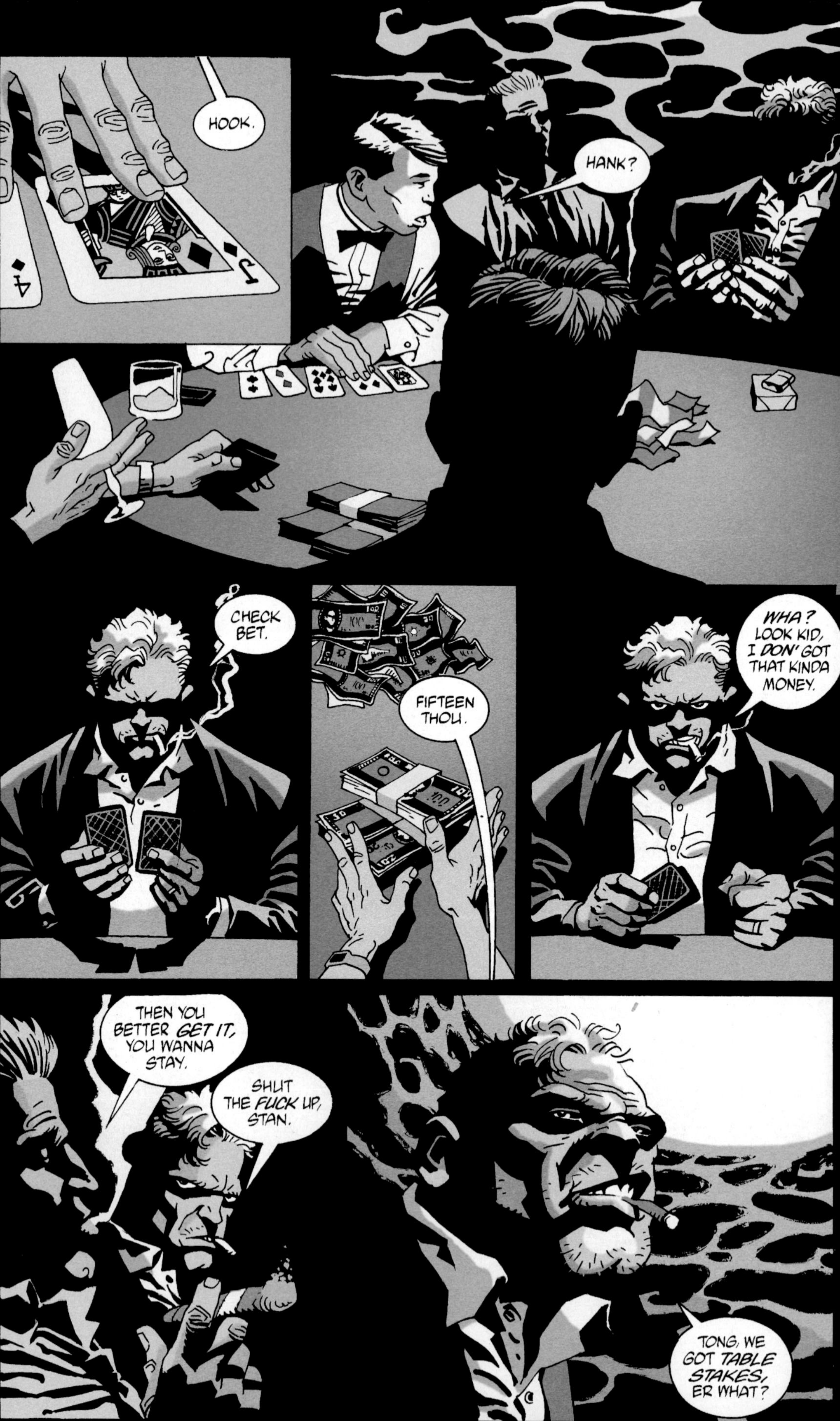
HOOK.
HANK?
CHECK BET.
FIFTEEN THOU.
WHA? LOOK KID, I DON' GOT THAT KINDA MONEY.
THEN YOU BETTER GET IT, YOU WANNA STAY.
SHUT THE FUCK UP, STAN.
TONG, WE GOT TABLE STAKES, ER WHAT?

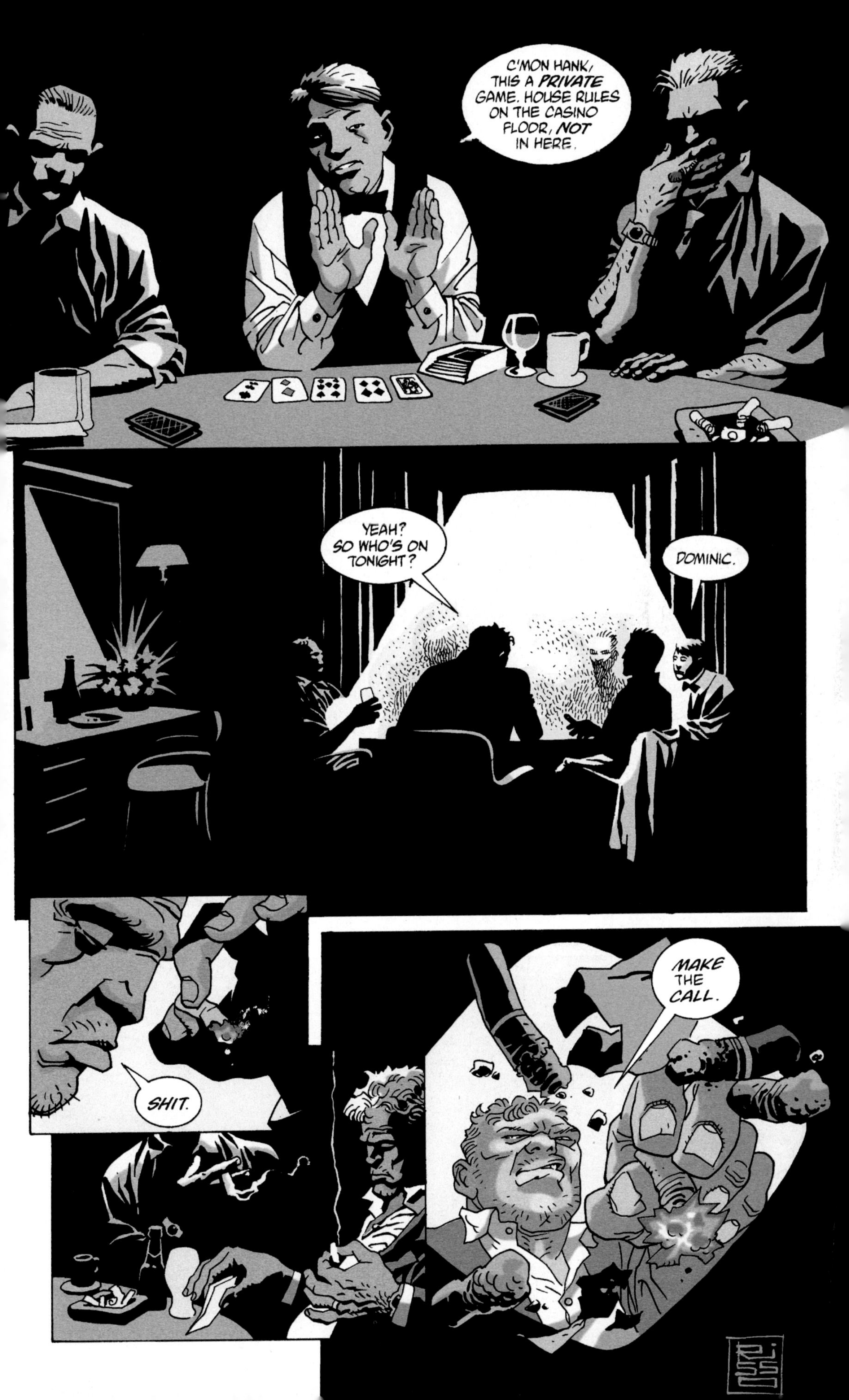
C'MON HANK, THIS A PRIVATE GAME. HOUSE RULES ON THE CASINO FLOOR, NOT IN HERE.
YEAH? SO WHO'S ON TONIGHT?
DOMINIC.
SHIT.
MAKE THE CALL.

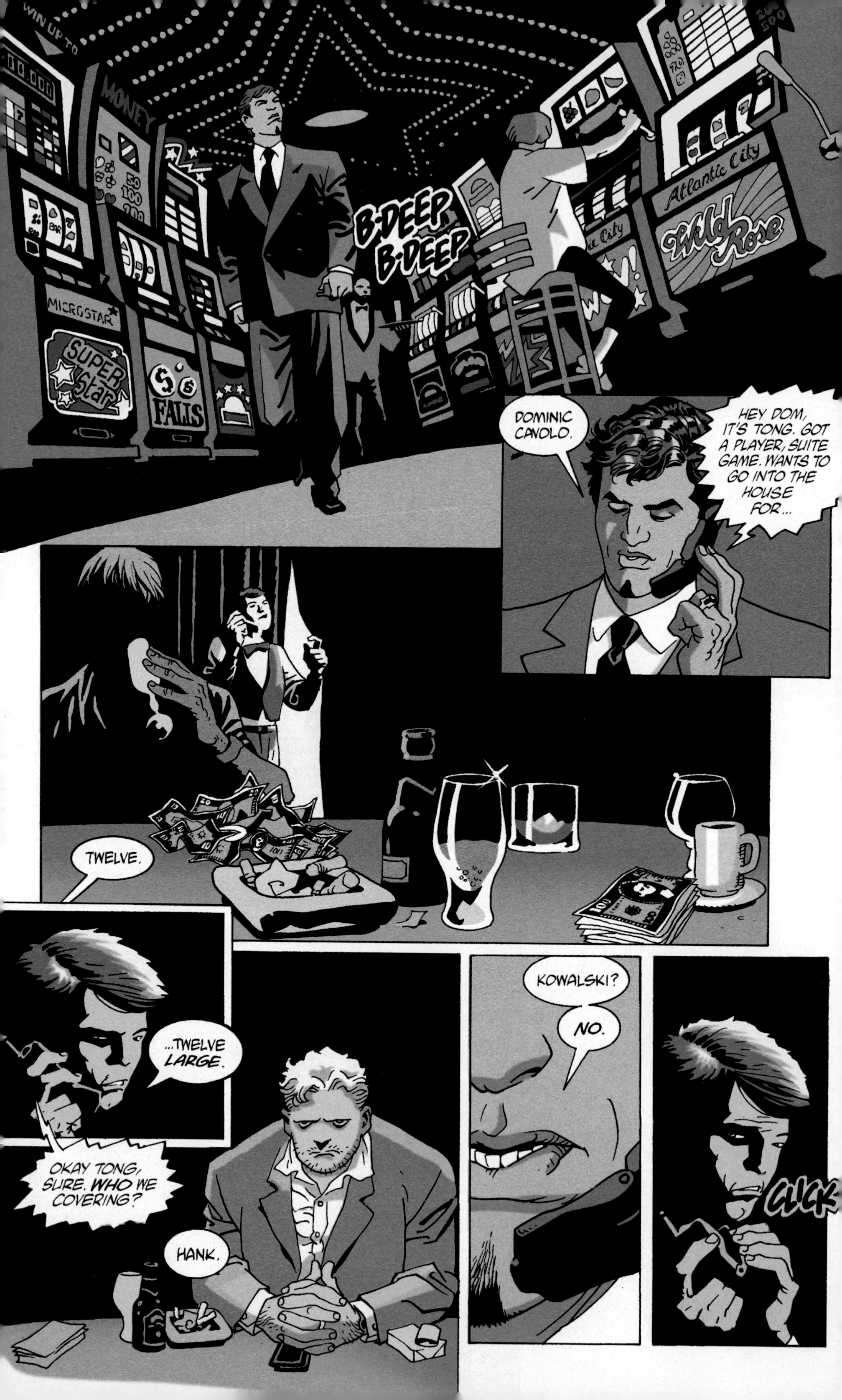
B-DEEP
B-DEEP
DOMINIC CAVOLO.
HEY DOM, IT'S TONG. GOT A PLAYER, SUITE GAME. WANTS TO GO INTO THE HOUSE FOR...
TWELVE.
...TWELVE LARGE.
OKAY TONG, SURE. WHO WE COVERING?
HANK.
KOWALSKI?
NO.
CLICK

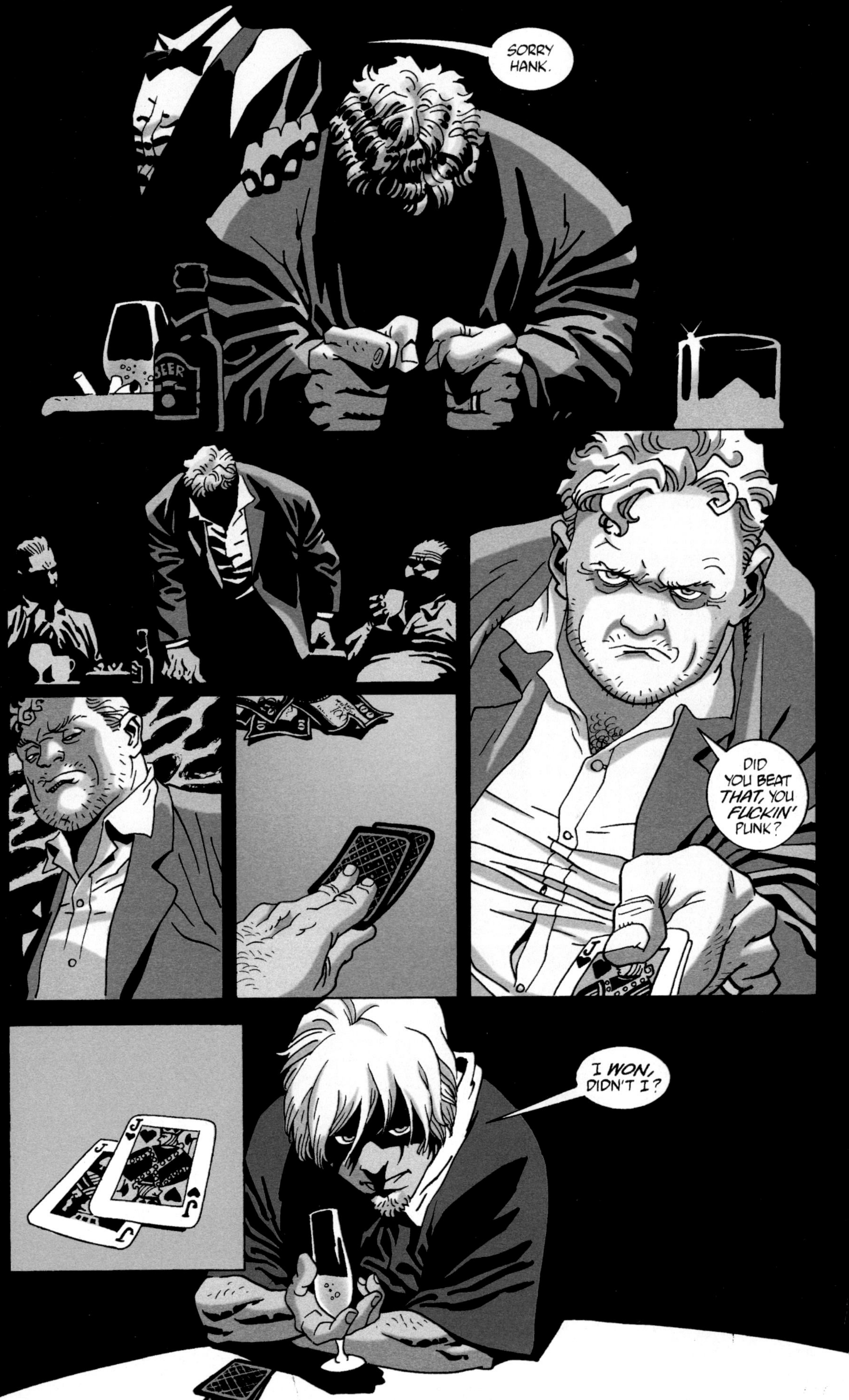
SORRY HANK.
DID YOU BEAT THAT, YOU FUCKIN' PUNK?
I WON, DIDN'T I?

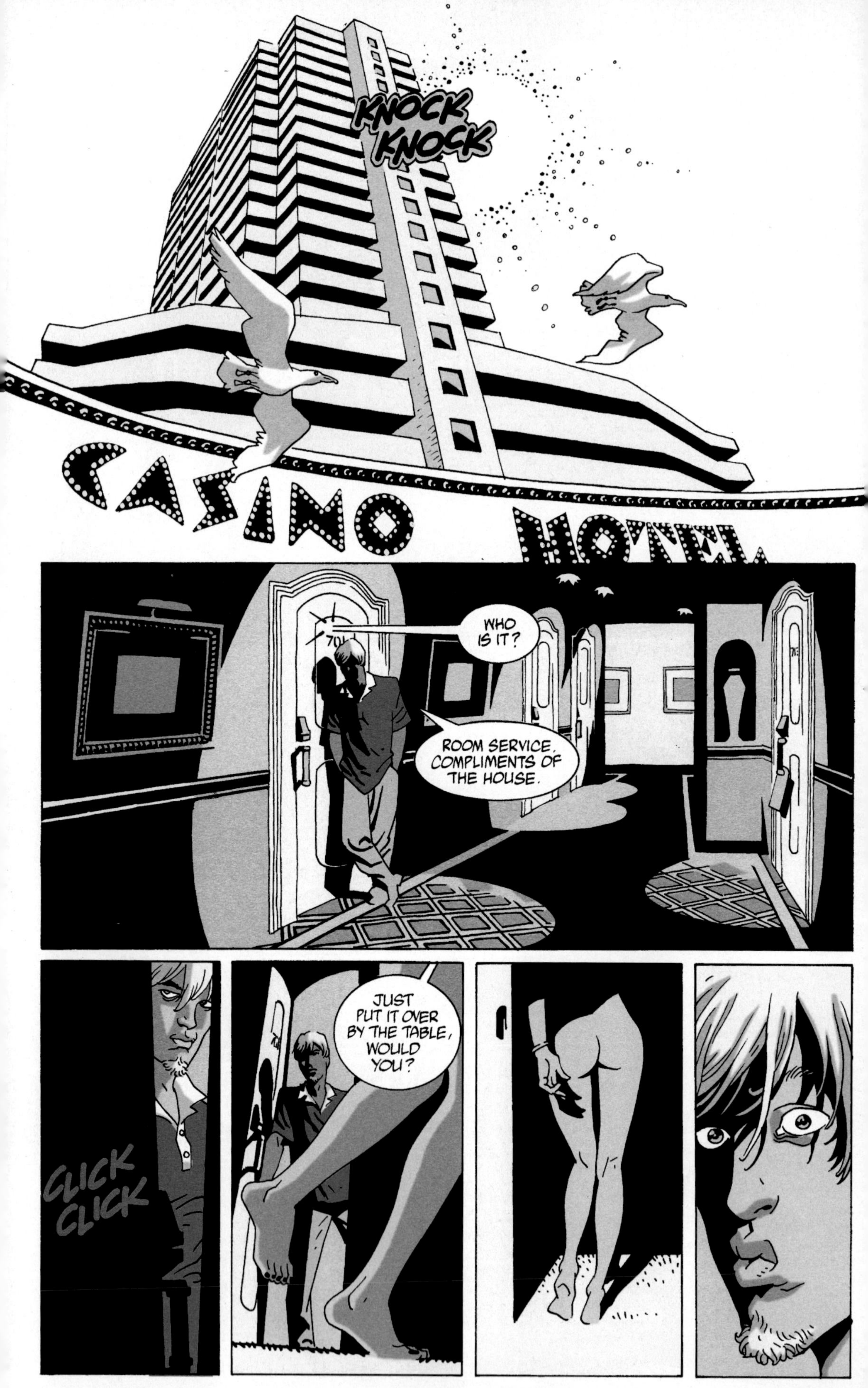
KNOCK KNOCK
CASINO HOTEL
WHO IS IT?
ROOM SERVICE, COMPLIMENTS OF THE HOUSE.
CLICK CLICK
JUST PUT IT OVER BY THE TABLE, WOULD YOU?

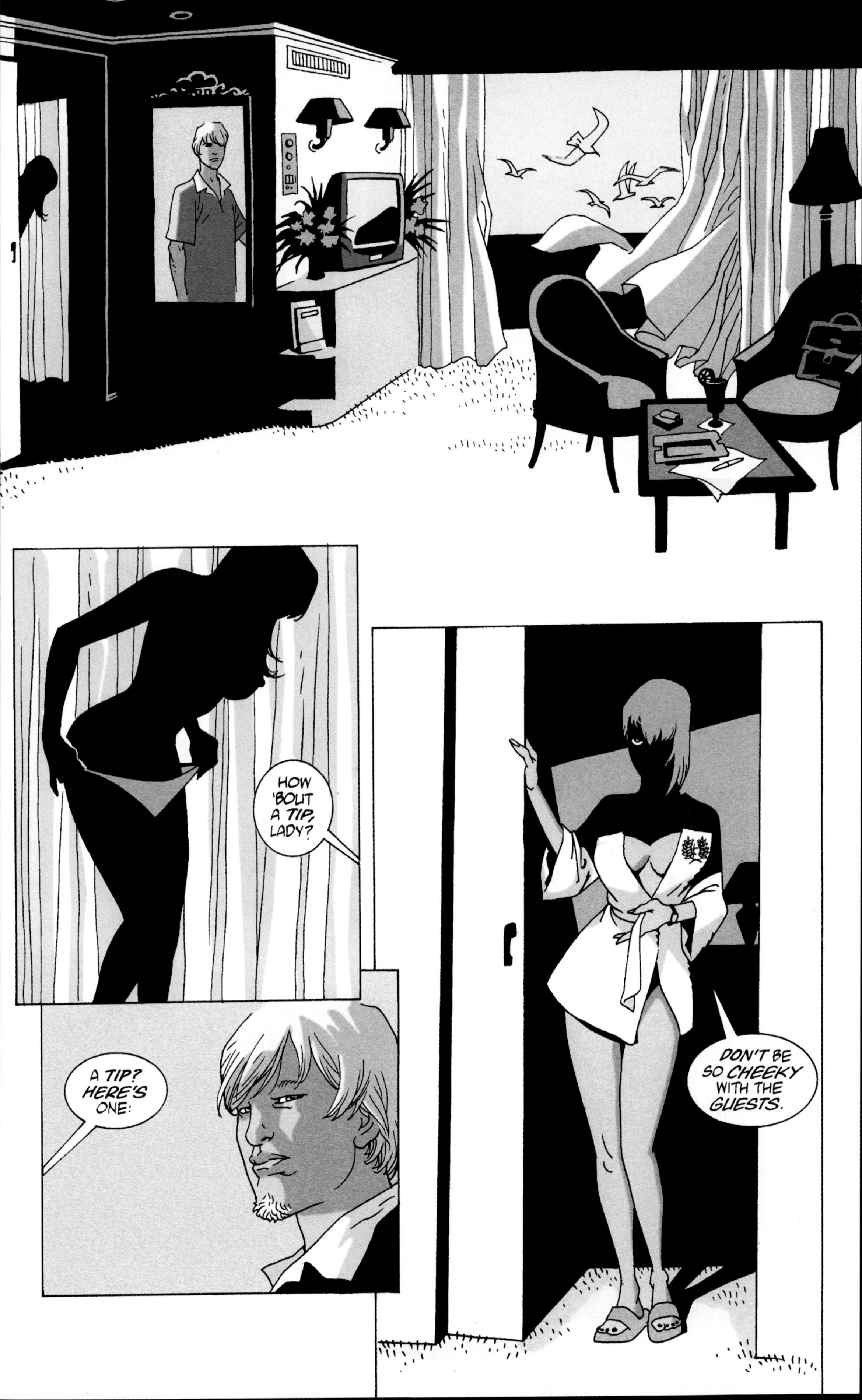
HOW 'BOUT A TIP, LADY?
DON'T BE SO CHEEKY WITH THE GUESTS.
A TIP? HERE'S ONE:

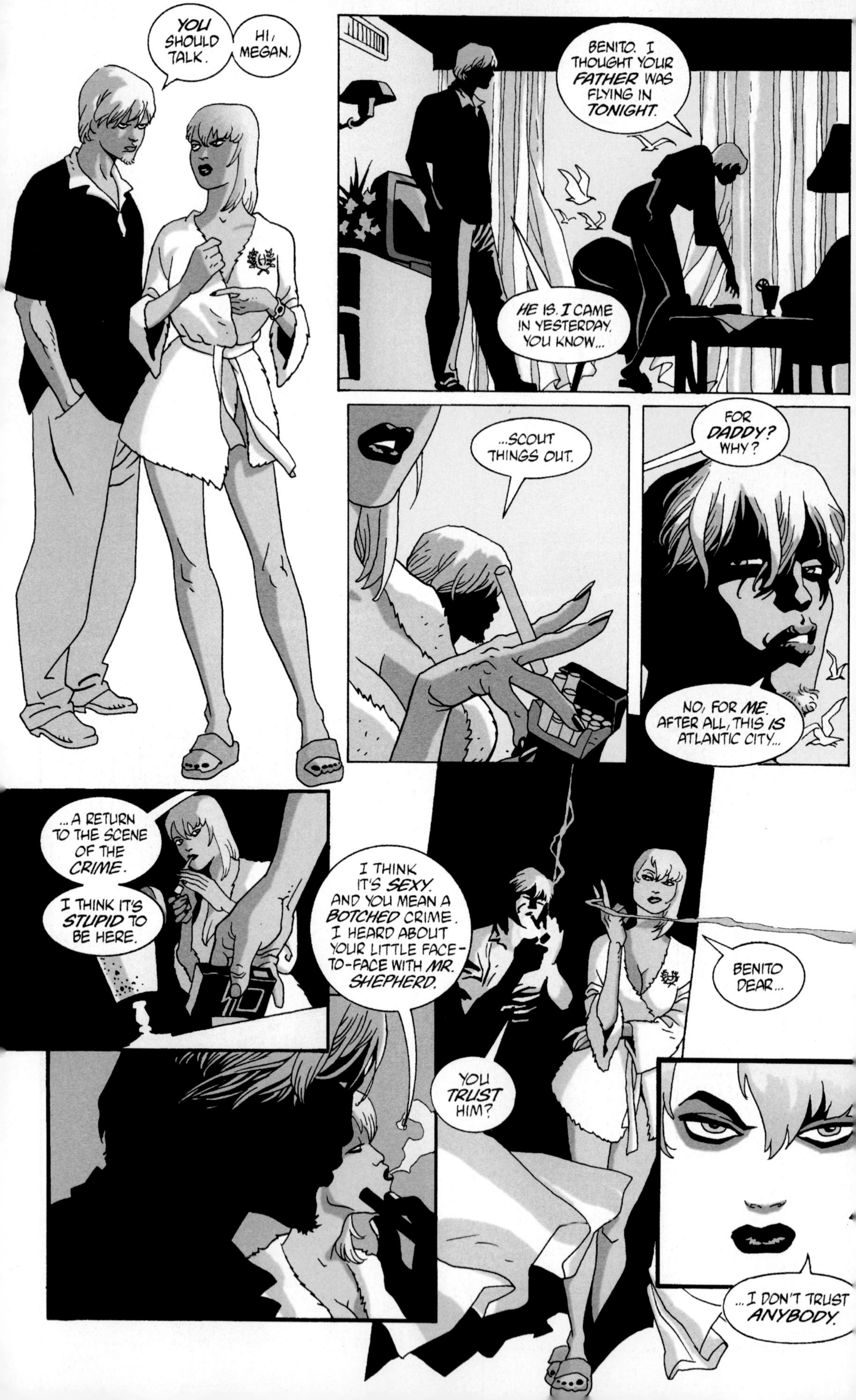
YOU SHOULD TALK.
HI, MEGAN.
BENITO. I THOUGHT YOUR FATHER WAS FLYING IN TONIGHT.
HE IS. I CAME IN YESTERDAY. YOU KNOW...
...SCOUT THINGS OUT.
FOR DADDY? WHY?
NO, FOR ME. AFTER ALL, THIS IS ATLANTIC CITY...
...A RETURN TO THE SCENE OF THE CRIME.
I THINK IT'S STUPID TO BE HERE.
I THINK IT'S SEXY. AND YOU MEAN A BOTCHED CRIME. I HEARD ABOUT YOUR LITTLE FACE-TO-FACE WITH MR. SHEPHERD.
BENITO DEAR...
YOU TRUST HIM?
...I DON'T TRUST ANYBODY.

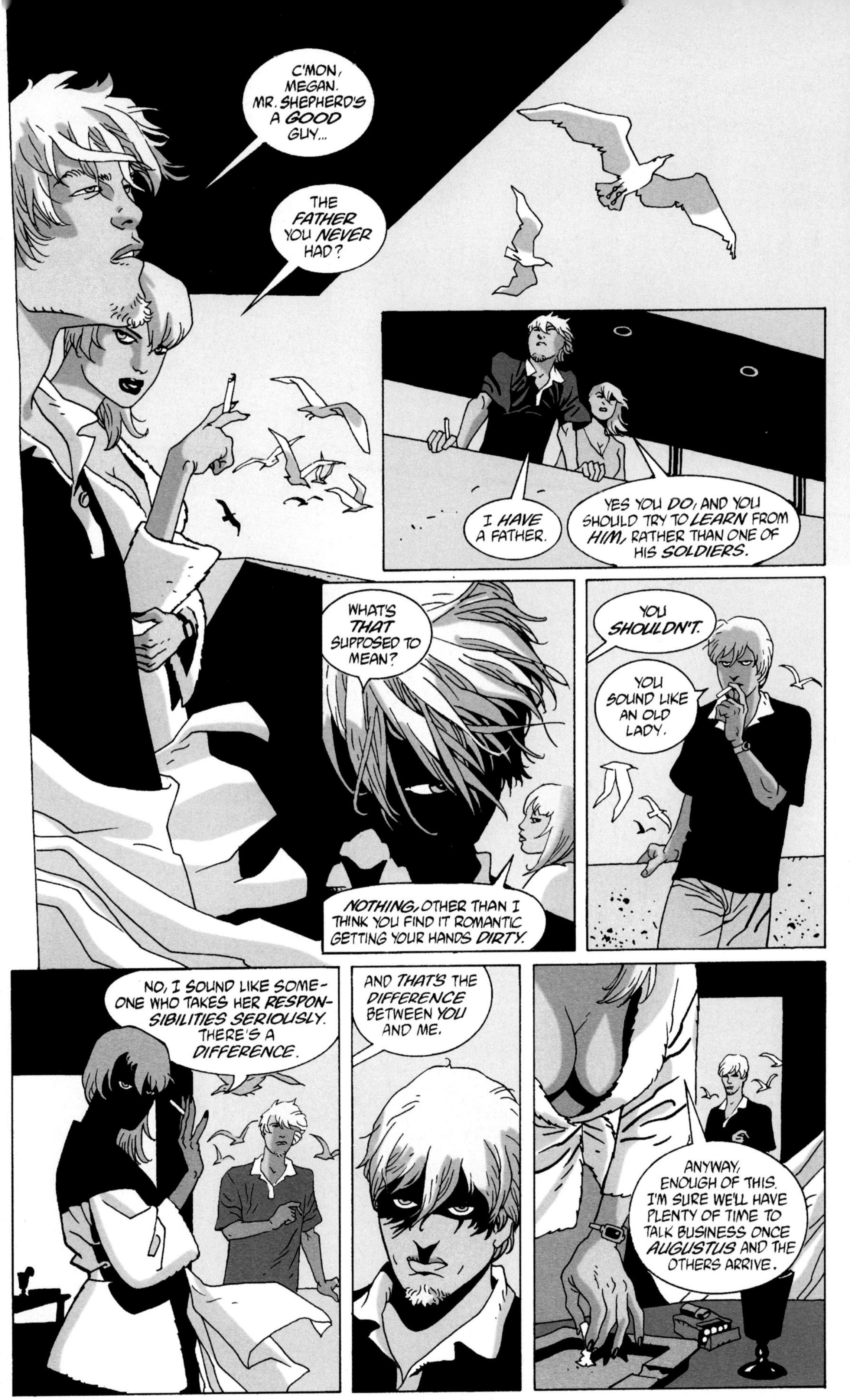
C'MON, MEGAN. MR. SHEPHERD'S A GOOD GUY...
THE FATHER YOU NEVER HAD?
I HAVE A FATHER.
YES YOU DO, AND YOU SHOULD TRY TO LEARN FROM HIM, RATHER THAN ONE OF HIS SOLDIERS.
WHAT'S THAT SUPPOSED TO MEAN?
NOTHING, OTHER THAN I THINK YOU FIND IT ROMANTIC GETTING YOUR HANDS DIRTY.
YOU SHOULDN'T.
YOU SOUND LIKE AN OLD LADY.
NO, I SOUND LIKE SOME-ONE WHO TAKES HER RESPON-SIBILITIES SERIOUSLY. THERE'S A DIFFERENCE.
AND THAT'S THE DIFFERENCE BETWEEN YOU AND ME.
ANYWAY, ENOUGH OF THIS. I'M SURE WE'LL HAVE PLENTY OF TIME TO TALK BUSINESS ONCE AUGUSTUS AND THE OTHERS ARRIVE.

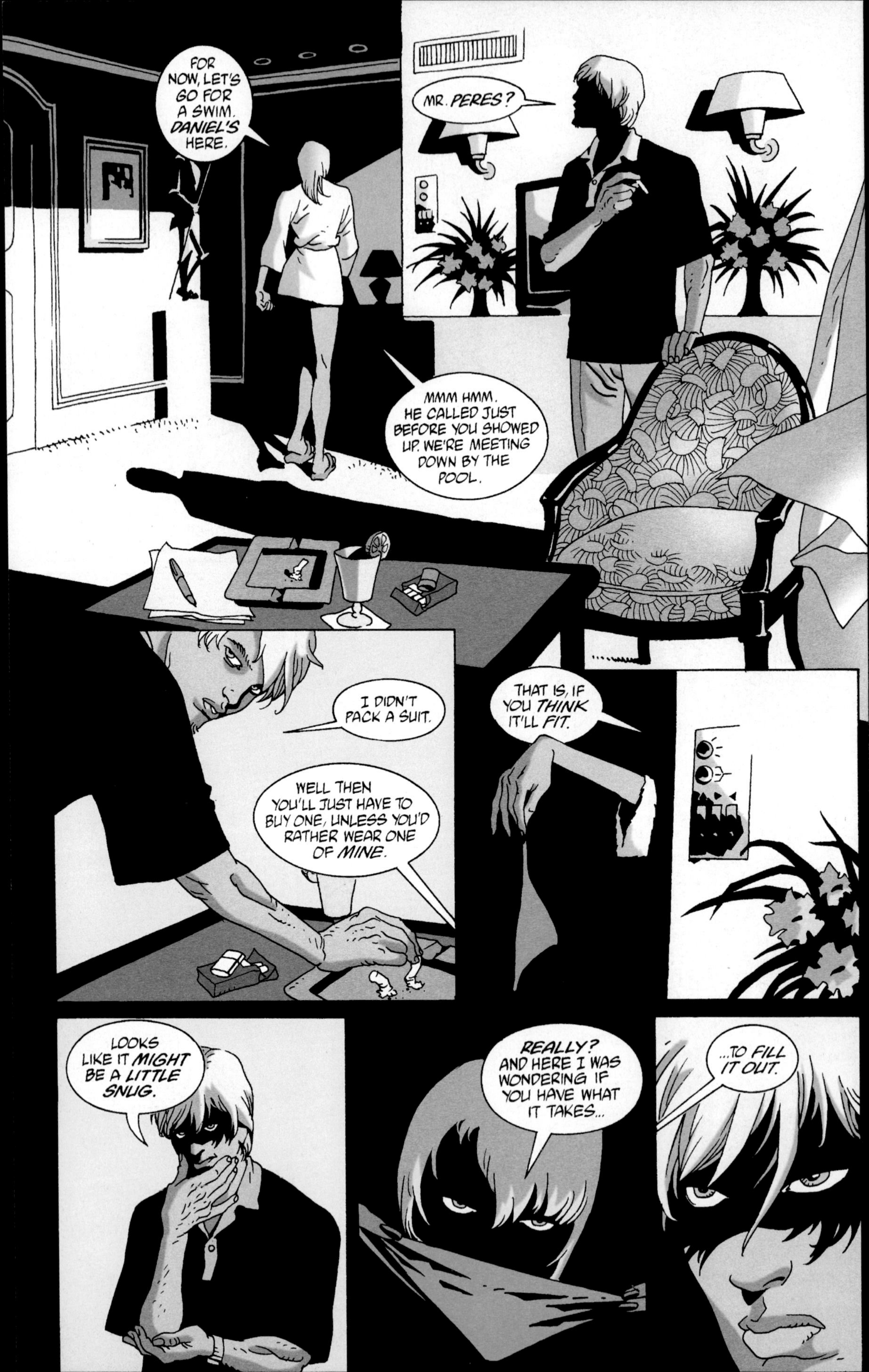
FOR NOW, LET'S GO FOR A SWIM. DANIEL'S HERE.
MR. PERES?
MMM HMM. HE CALLED JUST BEFORE YOU SHOWED UP. WE'RE MEETING DOWN BY THE POOL.
I DIDN'T PACK A SUIT.
WELL THEN YOU'LL JUST HAVE TO BUY ONE, UNLESS YOU'D RATHER WEAR ONE OF MINE.
THAT IS, IF YOU THINK IT'LL FIT.
LOOKS LIKE IT MIGHT BE A LITTLE SNUG.
REALLY? AND HERE I WAS WONDERING IF YOU HAVE WHAT IT TAKES...
...TO FILL IT OUT.

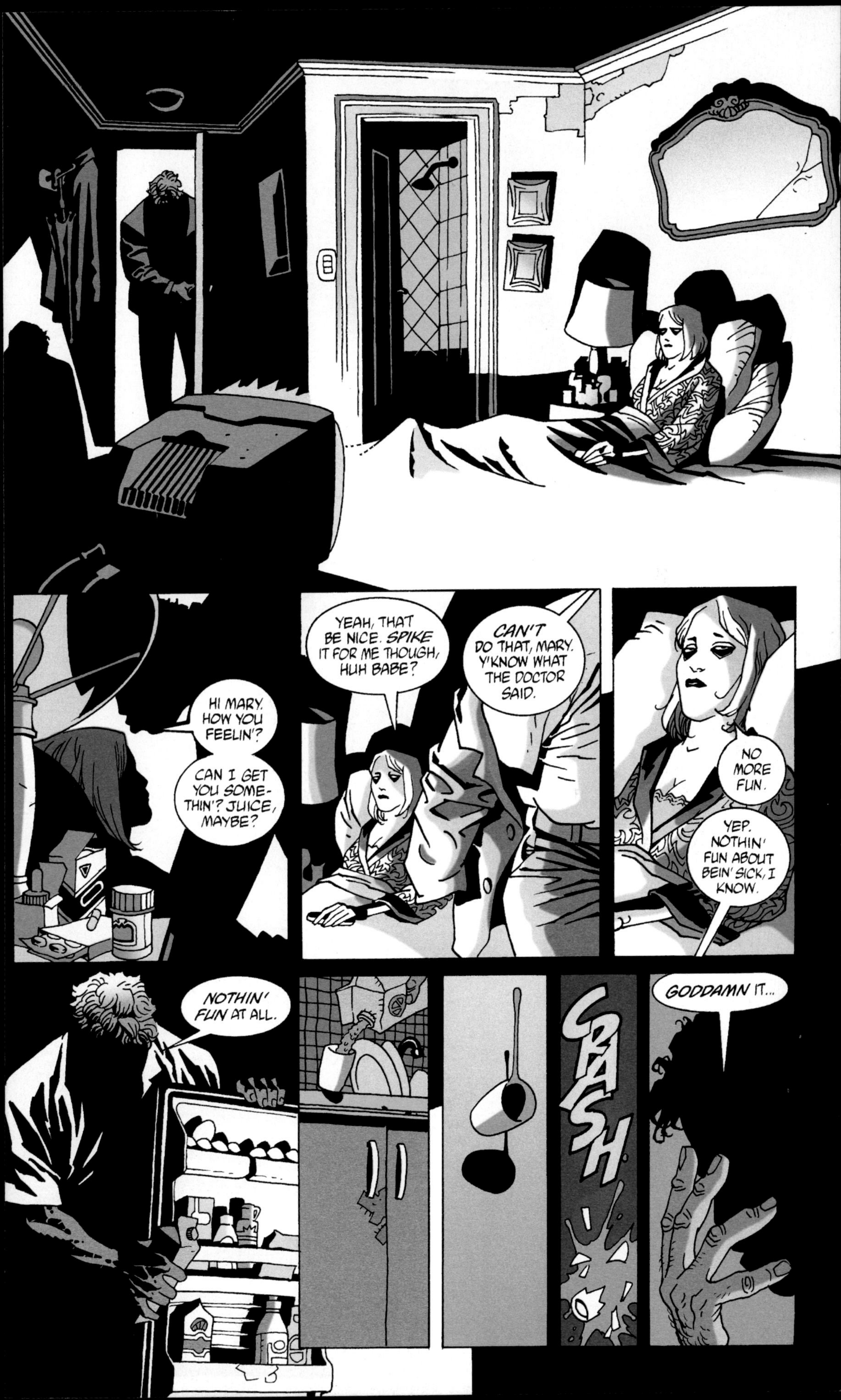
HI MARY. HOW YOU FEELIN'?
CAN I GET YOU SOME-THIN'? JUICE, MAYBE?
YEAH, THAT BE NICE. SPIKE IT FOR ME THOUGH, HUH BABE?
CAN'T DO THAT, MARY. Y'KNOW WHAT THE DOCTOR SAID.
NO MORE FUN.
YEP. NOTHIN' FUN ABOUT BEIN' SICK, I KNOW.
NOTHIN' FUN AT ALL.
CRASH
GODDAMN IT...

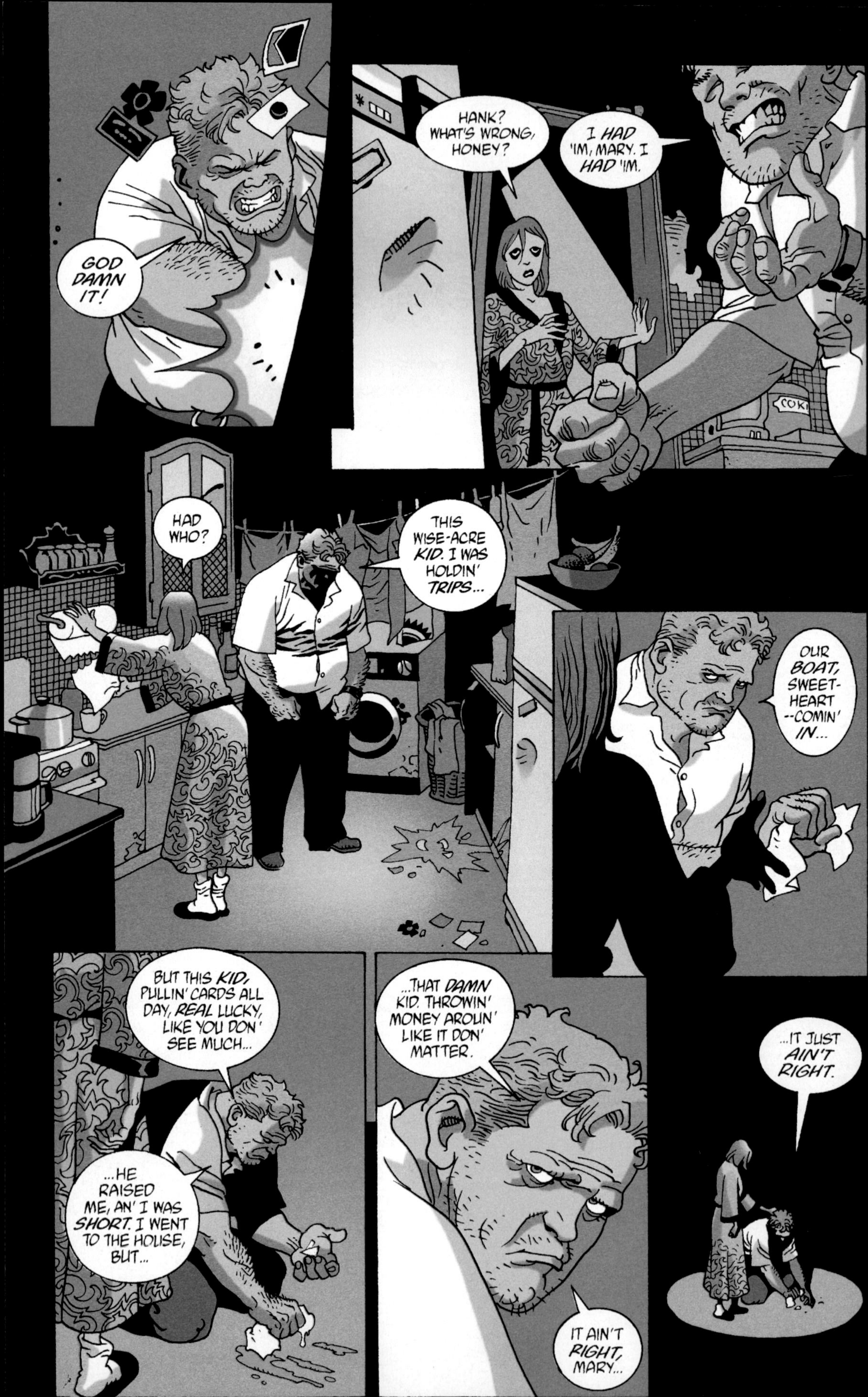
GOD DAMN IT!
HANK? WHAT'S WRONG, HONEY?
I HAD 'IM, MARY. I HAD 'IM.
HAD WHO?
THIS WISE-ACRE KID. I WAS HOLDIN' TRIPS...
OUR BOAT, SWEET-HEART --COMIN' IN...
BUT THIS KID, PULLIN' CARDS ALL DAY, REAL LUCKY, LIKE YOU DON' SEE MUCH...
...HE RAISED ME, AN' I WAS SHORT. I WENT TO THE HOUSE, BUT...
...THAT DAMN KID. THROWIN' MONEY AROUN' LIKE IT DON' MATTER.
IT AIN'T RIGHT, MARY...
...IT JUST AIN'T RIGHT.

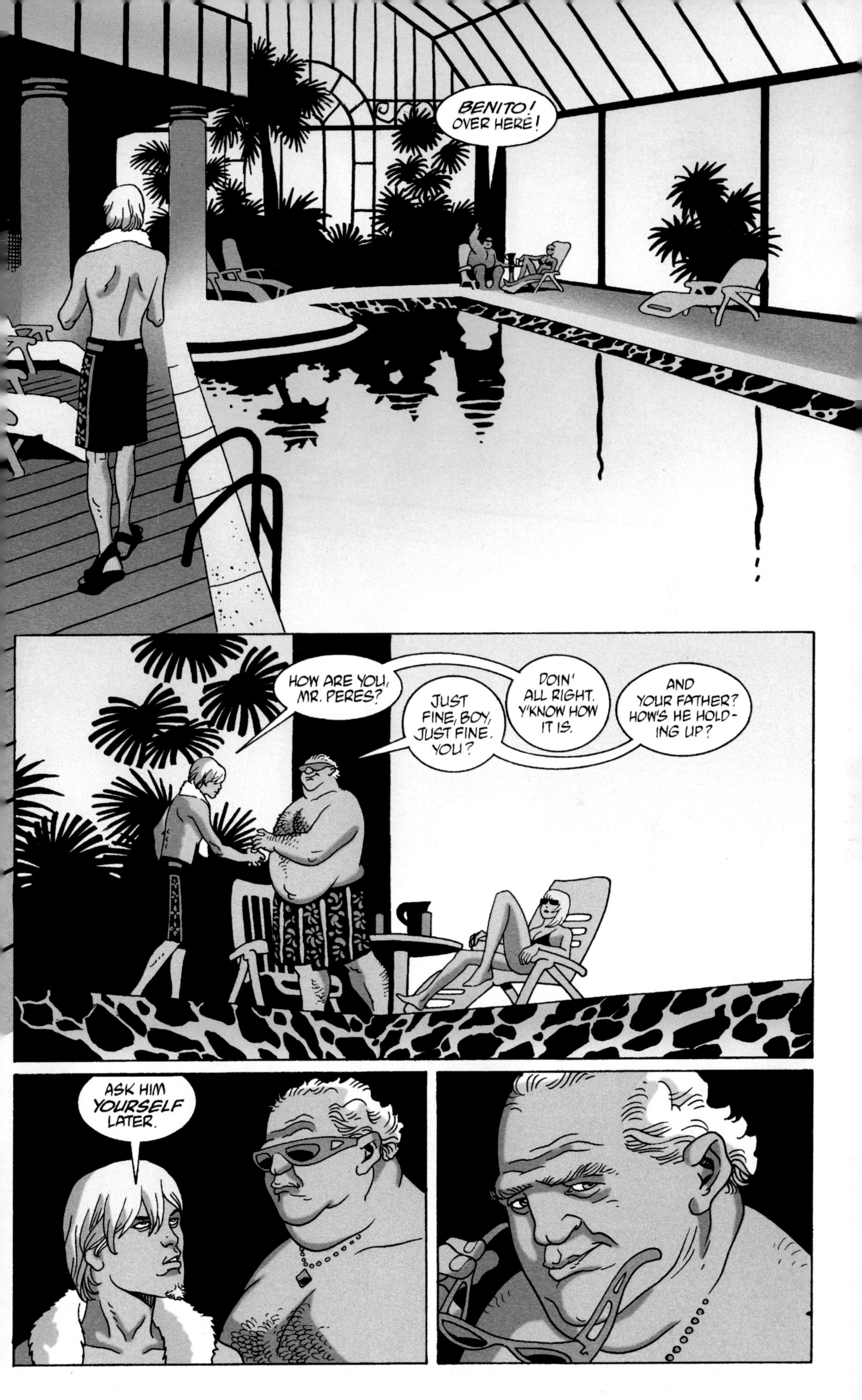
BENITO! OVER HERE!
HOW ARE YOU, MR. PERES?
JUST FINE, BOY, JUST FINE. YOU?
DOIN' ALL RIGHT. Y'KNOW HOW IT IS.
AND YOUR FATHER? HOW'S HE HOLDING UP?
ASK HIM YOURSELF LATER.

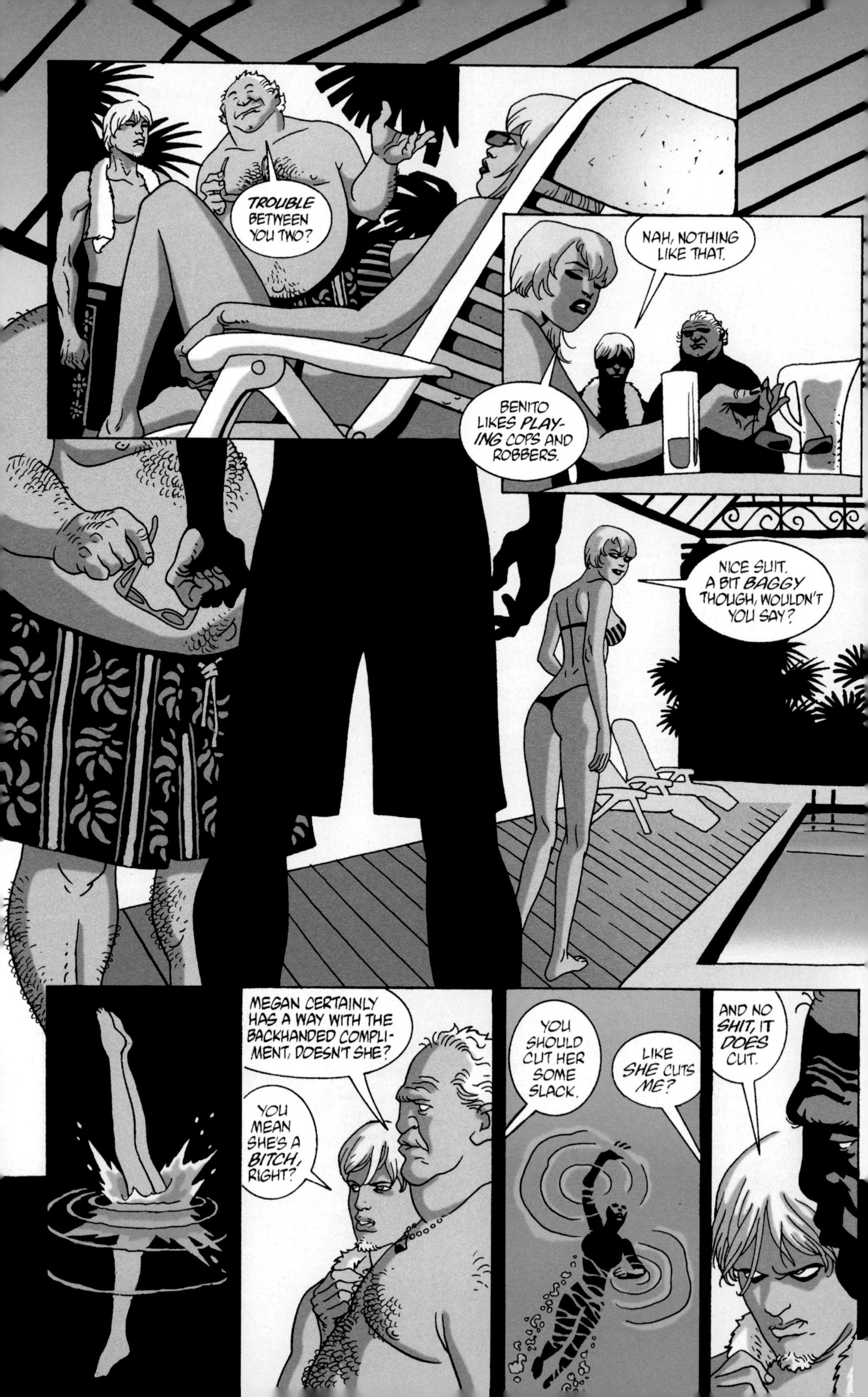
TROUBLE BETWEEN YOU TWO?
NAH, NOTHING LIKE THAT.
BENITO LIKES PLAY-ING COPS AND ROBBERS.
NICE SUIT. A BIT BAGGY THOUGH, WOULDN'T YOU SAY?
MEGAN CERTAINLY HAS A WAY WITH THE BACKHANDED COMPLI-MENT, DOESN'T SHE?
YOU MEAN SHE'S A BITCH, RIGHT?
YOU SHOULD CUT HER SOME SLACK.
LIKE SHE CUTS ME?
AND NO SHIT, IT DOES CUT.

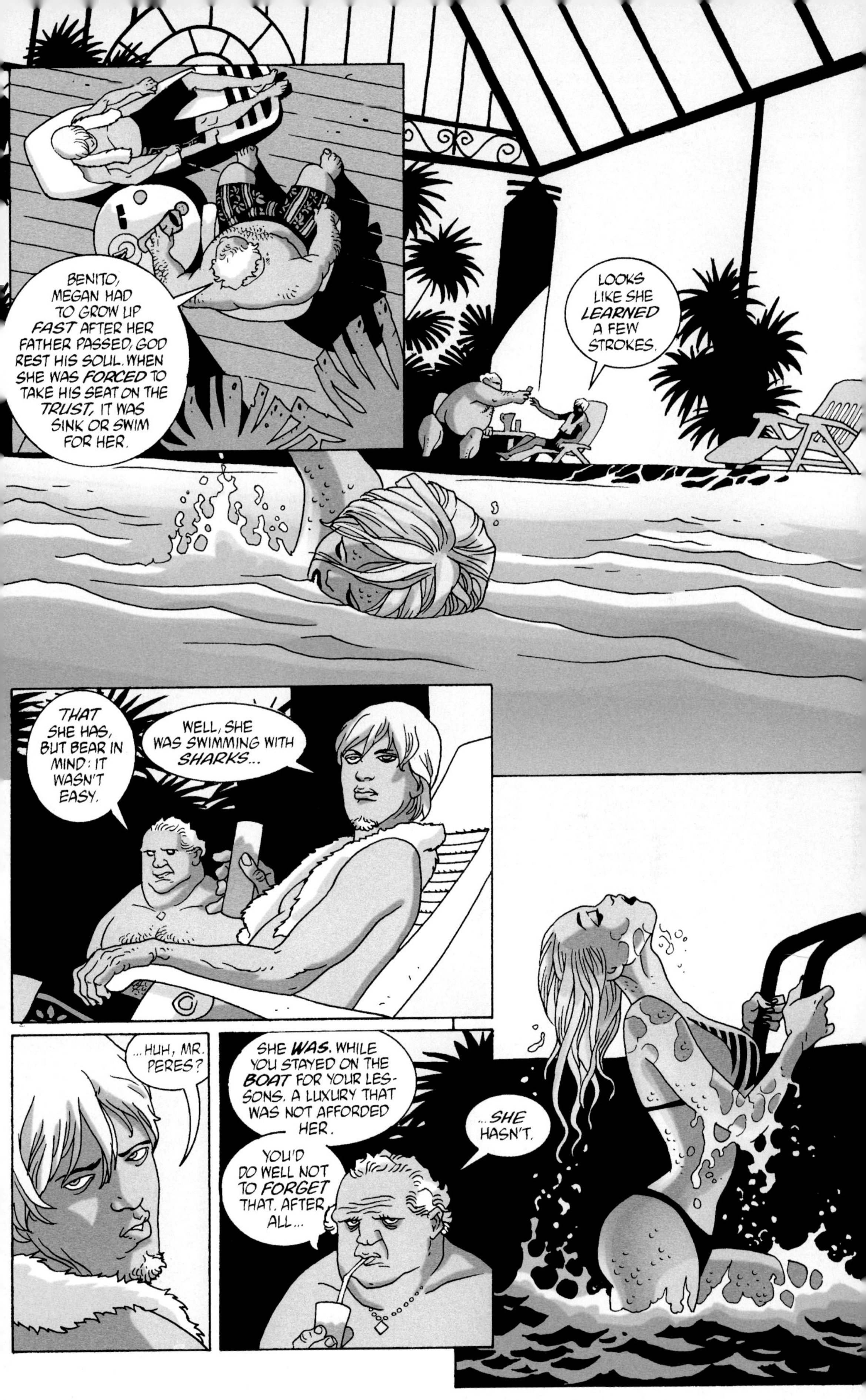
BENITO, MEGAN HAD TO GROW UP FAST AFTER HER FATHER PASSED, GOD REST HIS SOUL. WHEN SHE WAS FORCED TO TAKE HIS SEAT ON THE TRUST, IT WAS SINK OR SWIM FOR HER.
LOOKS LIKE SHE LEARNED A FEW STROKES.
THAT SHE HAS, BUT BEAR IN MIND: IT WASN'T EASY.
WELL, SHE WAS SWIMMING WITH SHARKS...
...HUH, MR. PERES?
SHE WAS. WHILE YOU STAYED ON THE BOAT FOR YOUR LESSONS. A LUXURY THAT WAS NOT AFFORDED HER.
YOU'D DO WELL NOT TO FORGET THAT. AFTER ALL...
...SHE HASN'T.

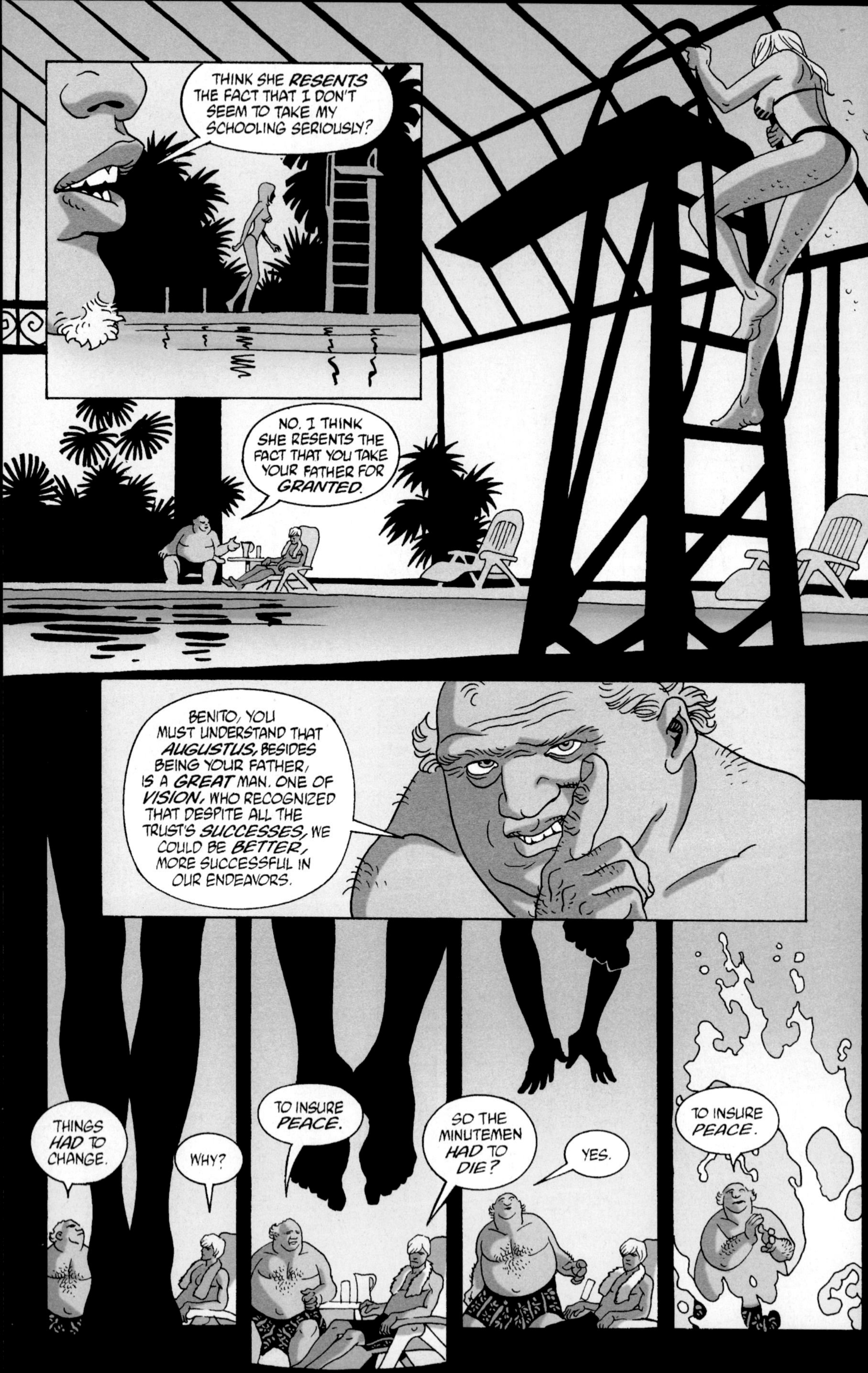
THINK SHE *RESENTS* THE FACT THAT I DON'T SEEM TO TAKE MY SCHOOLING SERIOUSLY?
NO. I THINK SHE RESENTS THE FACT THAT YOU TAKE YOUR FATHER FOR *GRANTED*.
BENITO, YOU MUST UNDERSTAND THAT *AUGUSTUS,* BESIDES BEING YOUR FATHER, IS A *GREAT* MAN. ONE OF *VISION,* WHO RECOGNIZED THAT DESPITE ALL THE TRUST'S *SUCCESSES,* WE COULD BE *BETTER,* MORE SUCCESSFUL IN OUR ENDEAVORS.
THINGS *HAD* TO CHANGE.
WHY?
TO INSURE *PEACE*.
SO THE MINUTEMEN *HAD* TO *DIE?*
YES.
TO INSURE *PEACE*.

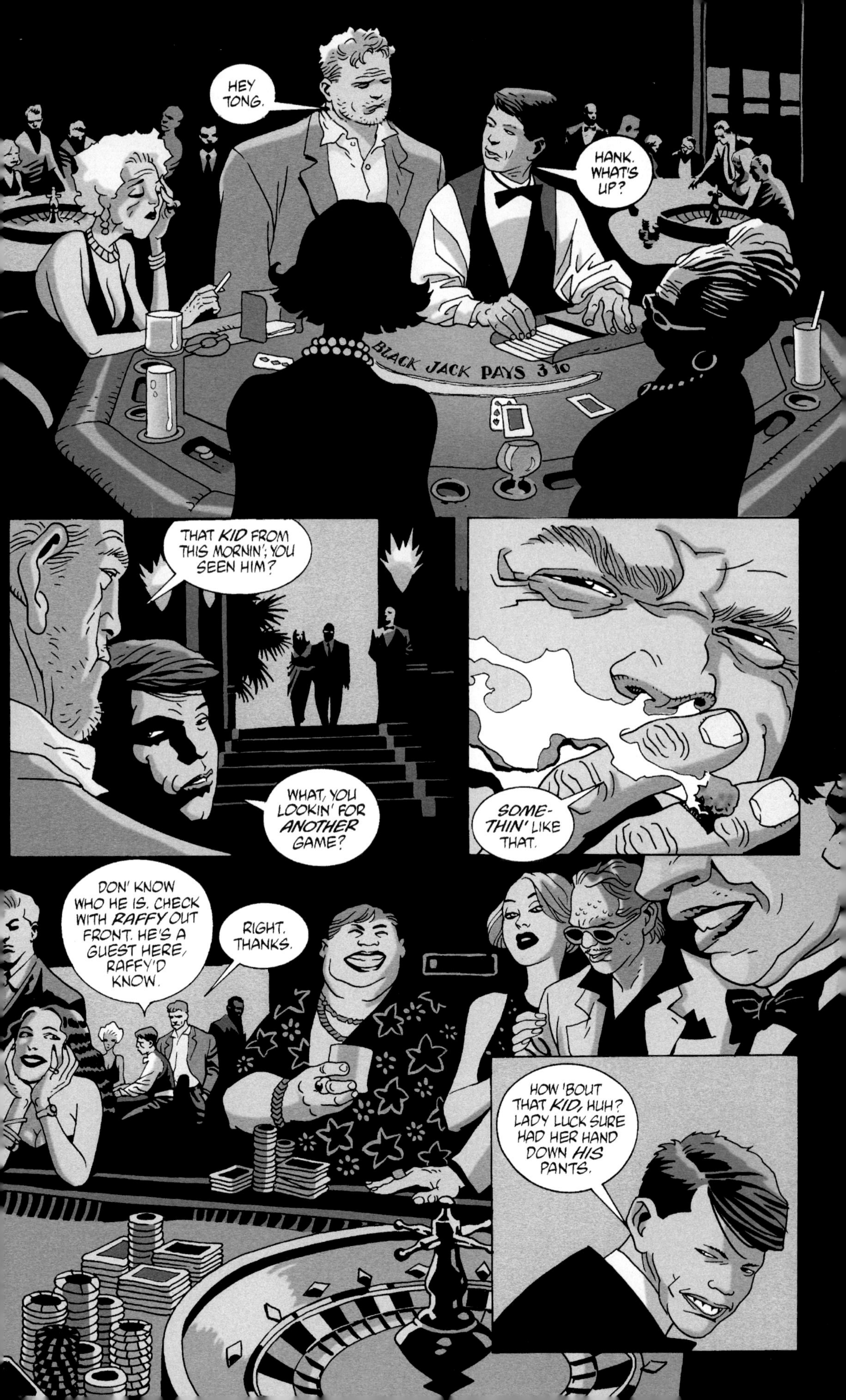
HEY TONG.
HANK. WHAT'S UP?
BLACK JACK PAYS 3 to
THAT KID FROM THIS MORNIN'; YOU SEEN HIM?
WHAT, YOU LOOKIN' FOR ANOTHER GAME?
SOME-THIN' LIKE THAT.
DON' KNOW WHO HE IS. CHECK WITH RAFFY OUT FRONT. HE'S A GUEST HERE, RAFFY'D KNOW.
RIGHT. THANKS.
HOW 'BOUT THAT KID, HUH? LADY LUCK SURE HAD HER HAND DOWN HIS PANTS.

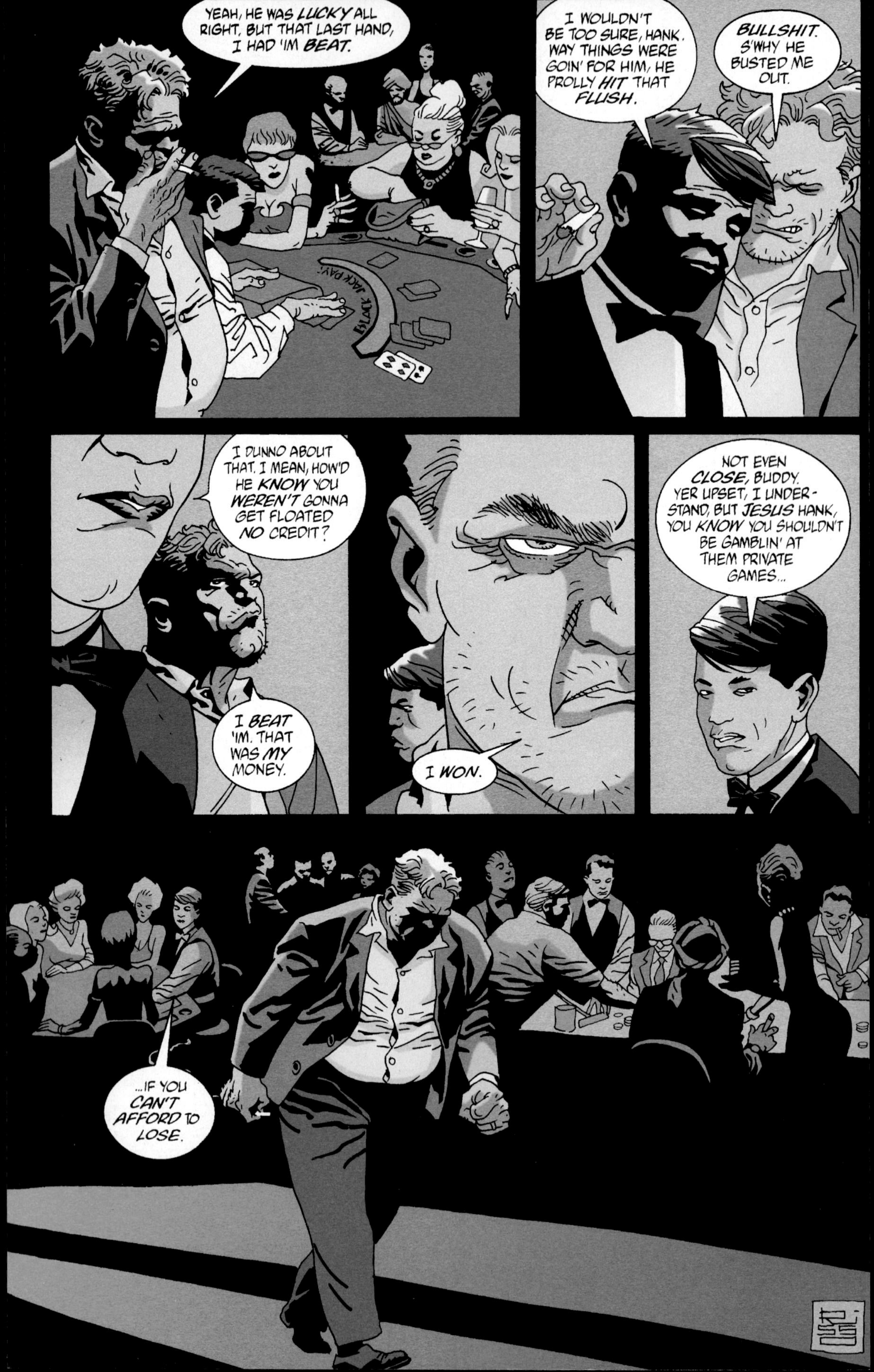
YEAH, HE WAS LUCKY ALL RIGHT, BUT THAT LAST HAND, I HAD 'IM BEAT.
BLACK JACK PAYS
I WOULDN'T BE TOO SURE, HANK. WAY THINGS WERE GOIN' FOR HIM, HE PROLLY HIT THAT FLUSH.
BULLSHIT. S'WHY HE BUSTED ME OUT.
I DUNNO ABOUT THAT. I MEAN, HOW'D HE KNOW YOU WEREN'T GONNA GET FLOATED NO CREDIT?
I BEAT 'IM. THAT WAS MY MONEY.
I WON.
NOT EVEN CLOSE, BUDDY. YER UPSET, I UNDER-STAND, BUT JESUS HANK, YOU KNOW YOU SHOULDN'T BE GAMBLIN' AT THEM PRIVATE GAMES...
...IF YOU CAN'T AFFORD TO LOSE.

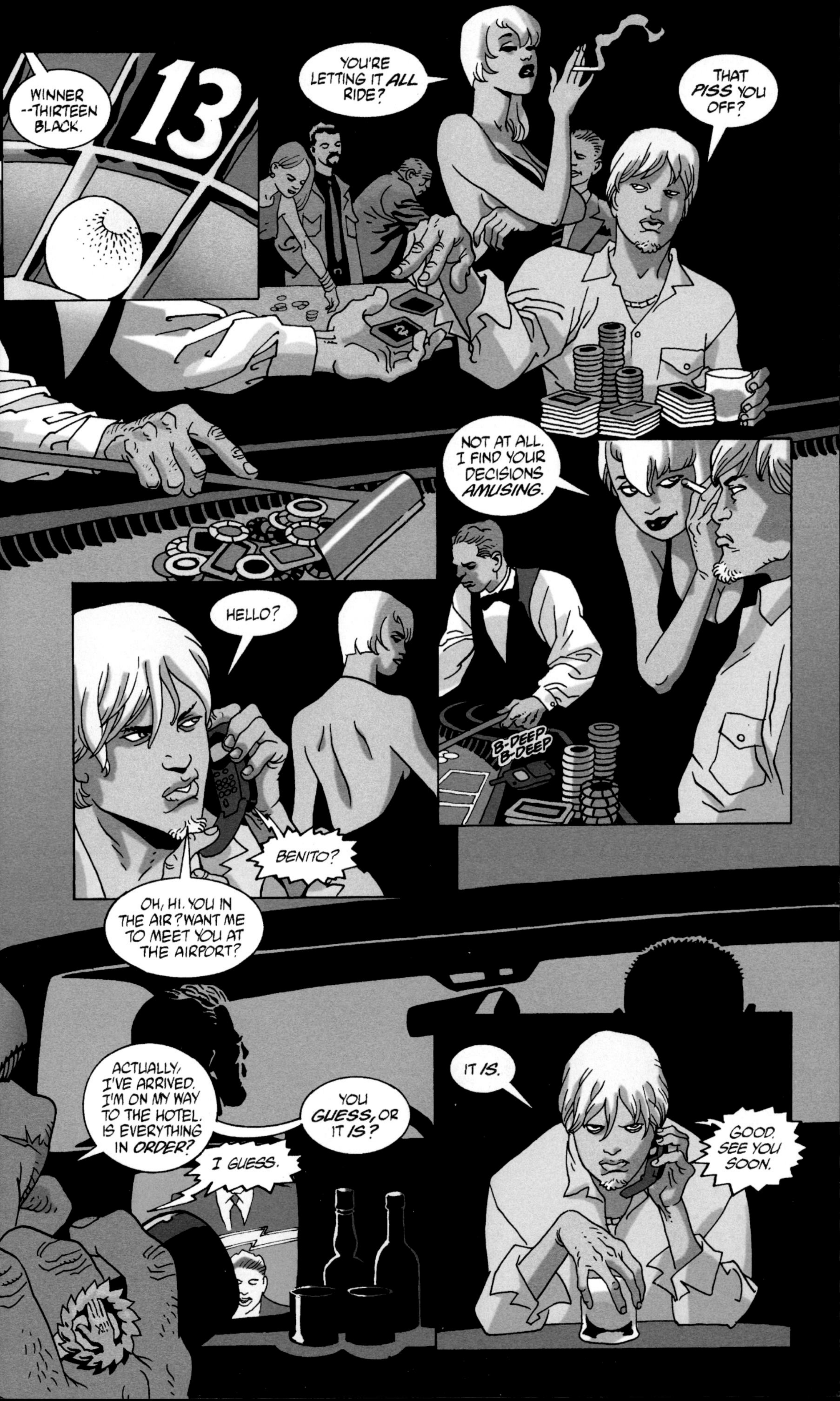
WINNER --THIRTEEN BLACK.
13
YOU'RE LETTING IT ALL RIDE?
THAT PISS YOU OFF?
NOT AT ALL. I FIND YOUR DECISIONS AMUSING.
B-DEEP B-DEEP
HELLO?
BENITO?
OH, HI. YOU IN THE AIR? WANT ME TO MEET YOU AT THE AIRPORT?
ACTUALLY, I'VE ARRIVED. I'M ON MY WAY TO THE HOTEL. IS EVERYTHING IN ORDER?
I GUESS.
YOU GUESS, OR IT IS?
IT IS.
GOOD. SEE YOU SOON.

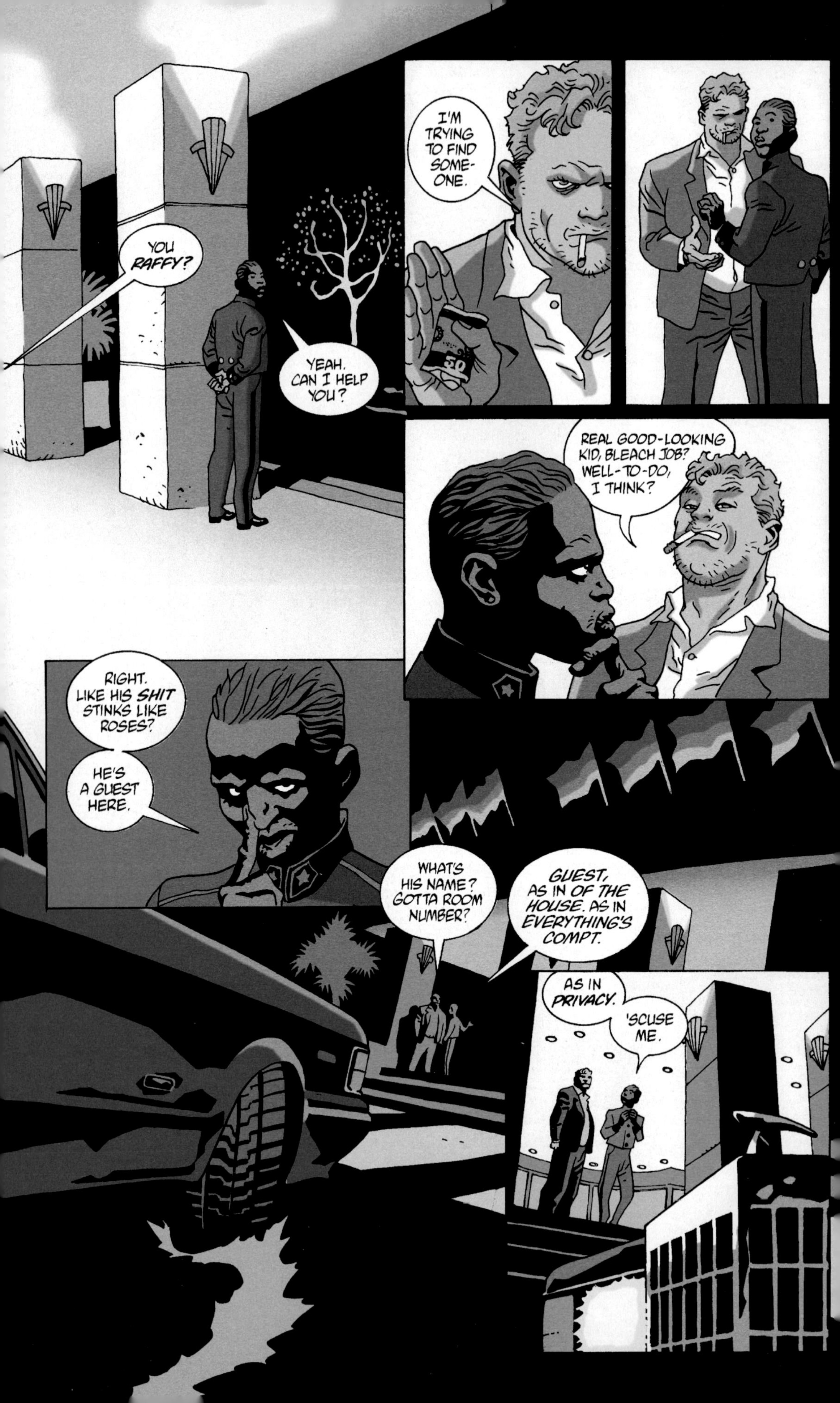
YOU RAFFY?
YEAH. CAN I HELP YOU?
I'M TRYING TO FIND SOME-ONE.
REAL GOOD-LOOKING KID, BLEACH JOB? WELL-TO-DO, I THINK?
RIGHT. LIKE HIS SHIT STINKS LIKE ROSES?
HE'S A GUEST HERE.
WHAT'S HIS NAME? GOTTA ROOM NUMBER?
GUEST, AS IN OF THE HOUSE. AS IN EVERYTHING'S COMPT.
AS IN PRIVACY.
'SCUSE ME.

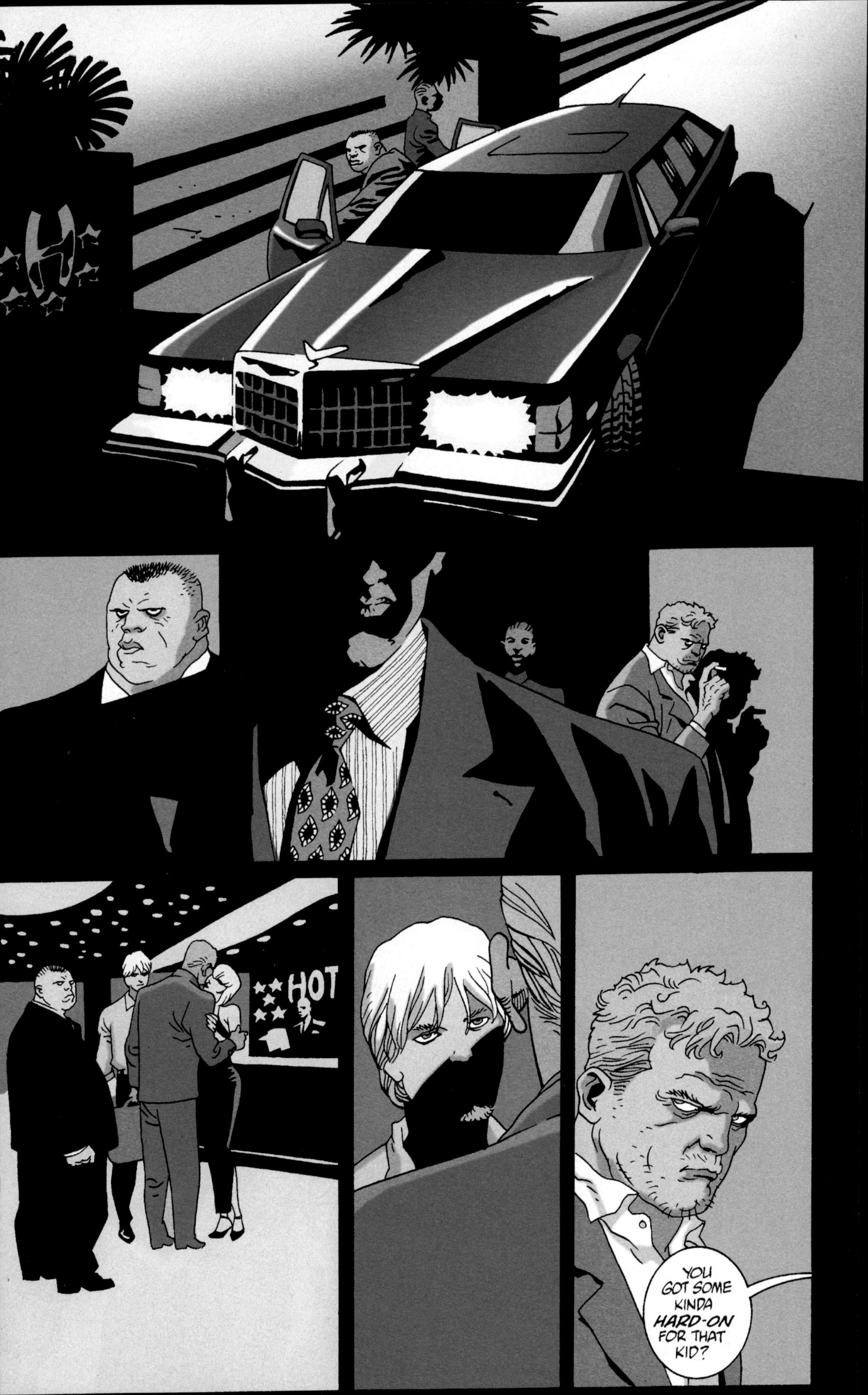

HOT
HOT
YOU GOT SOME KINDA HARD-ON FOR THAT KID?

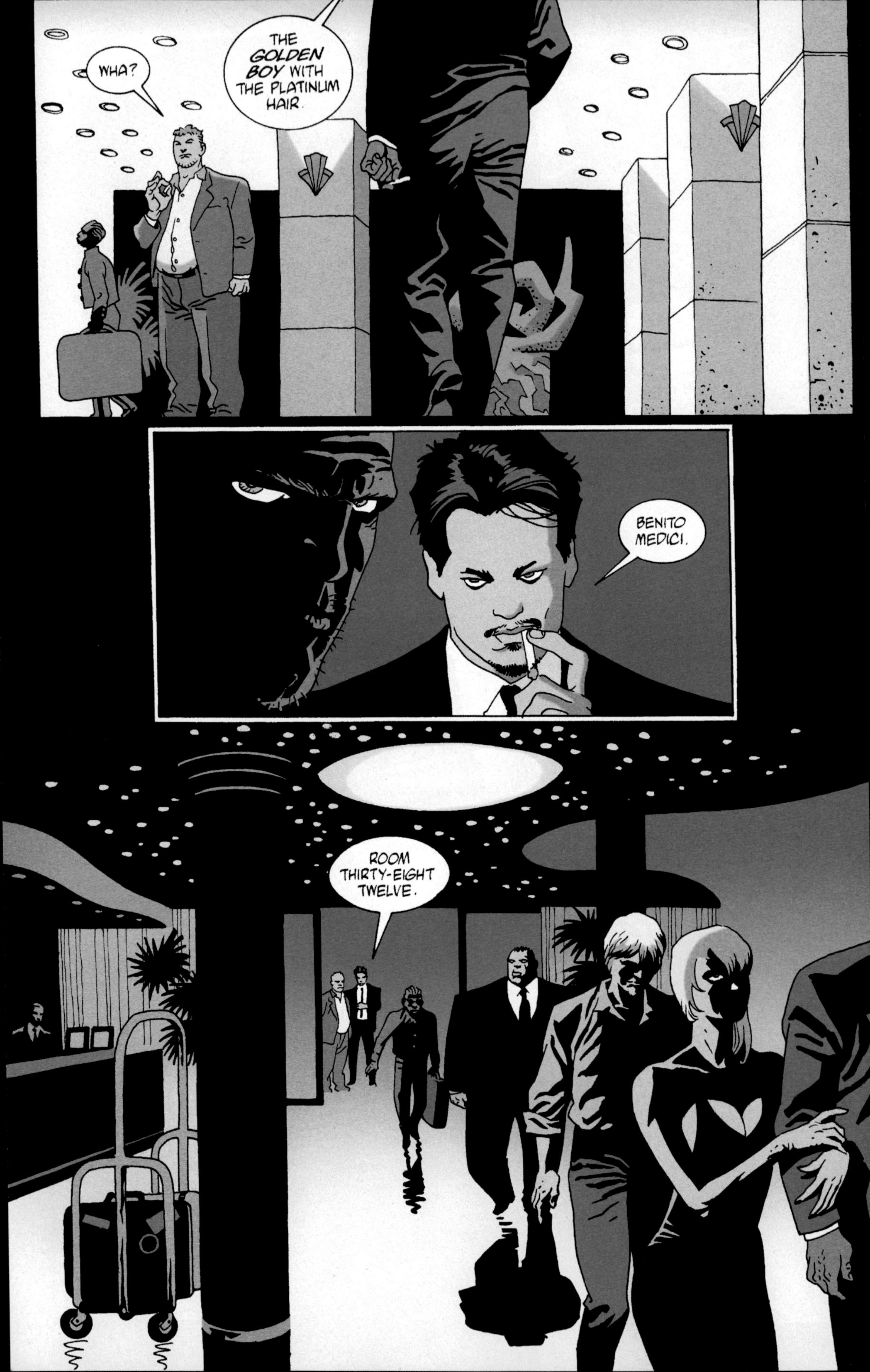
WHA?
THE GOLDEN BOY WITH THE PLATINUM HAIR.
BENITO MEDICI.
ROOM THIRTY-EIGHT TWELVE.

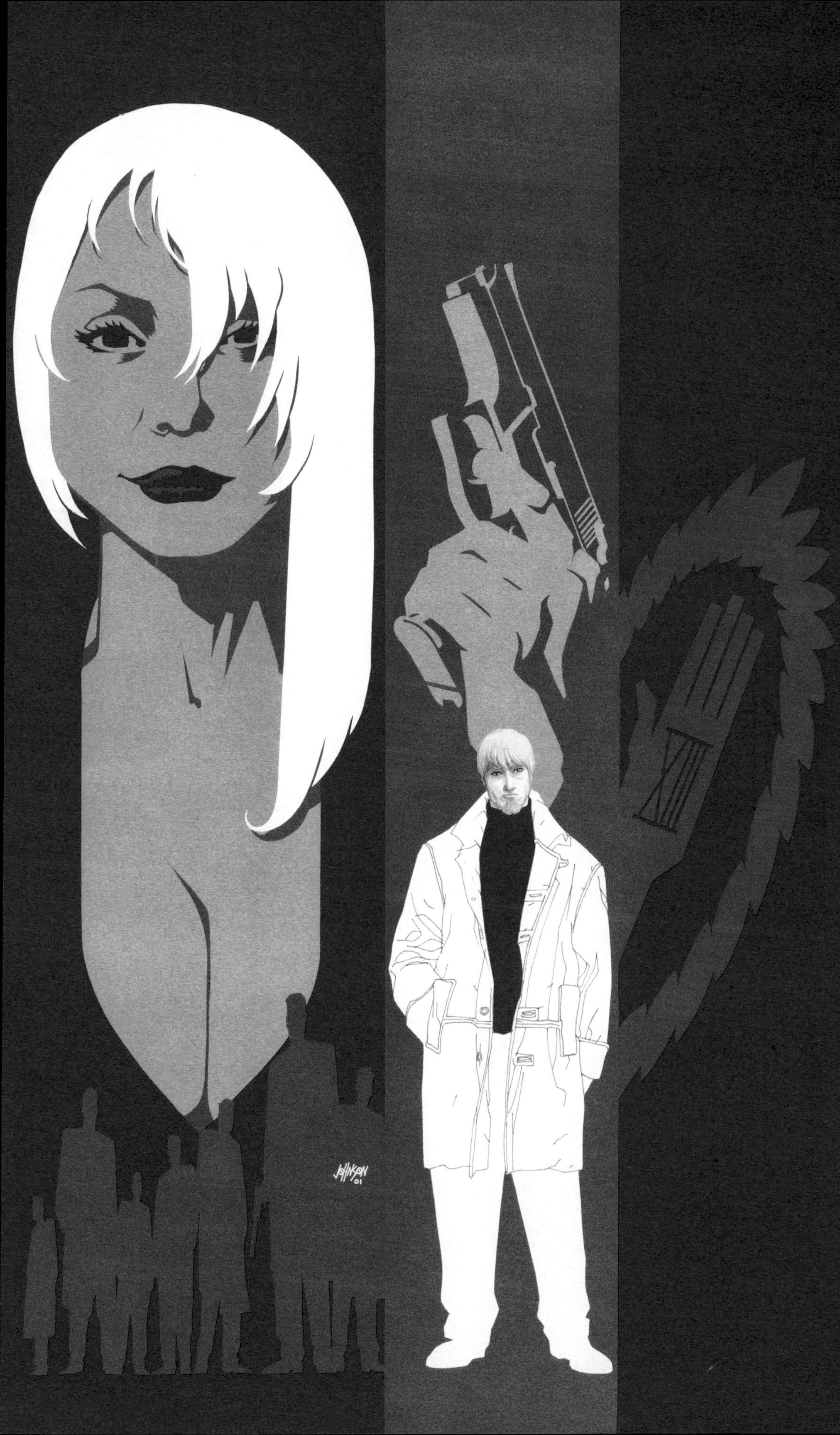
JOHNSON '01

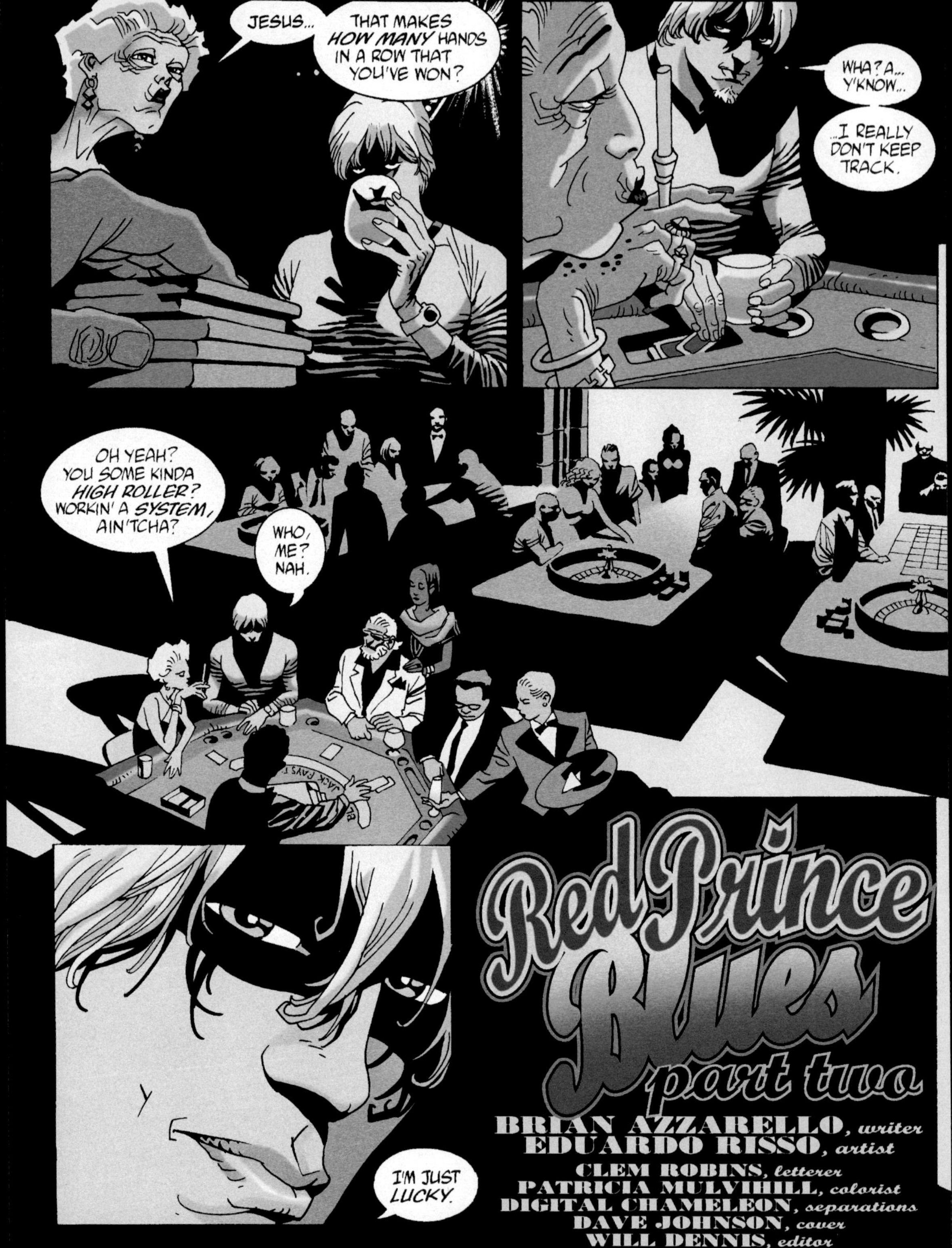

JESUS...
THAT MAKES *HOW MANY* HANDS IN A ROW THAT YOU'VE WON?
WHA? A... Y'KNOW...
...I REALLY DON'T KEEP TRACK.
OH YEAH? YOU SOME KINDA *HIGH ROLLER?* WORKIN' A *SYSTEM,* AIN'TCHA?
WHO, ME? NAH.
I'M JUST *LUCKY.*
Red Prince Blues
part two
BRIAN AZZARELLO, writer
EDUARDO RISSO, artist
CLEM ROBINS, letterer
PATRICIA MULVIHILL, colorist
DIGITAL CHAMELEON, separations
DAVE JOHNSON, cover
WILL DENNIS, editor

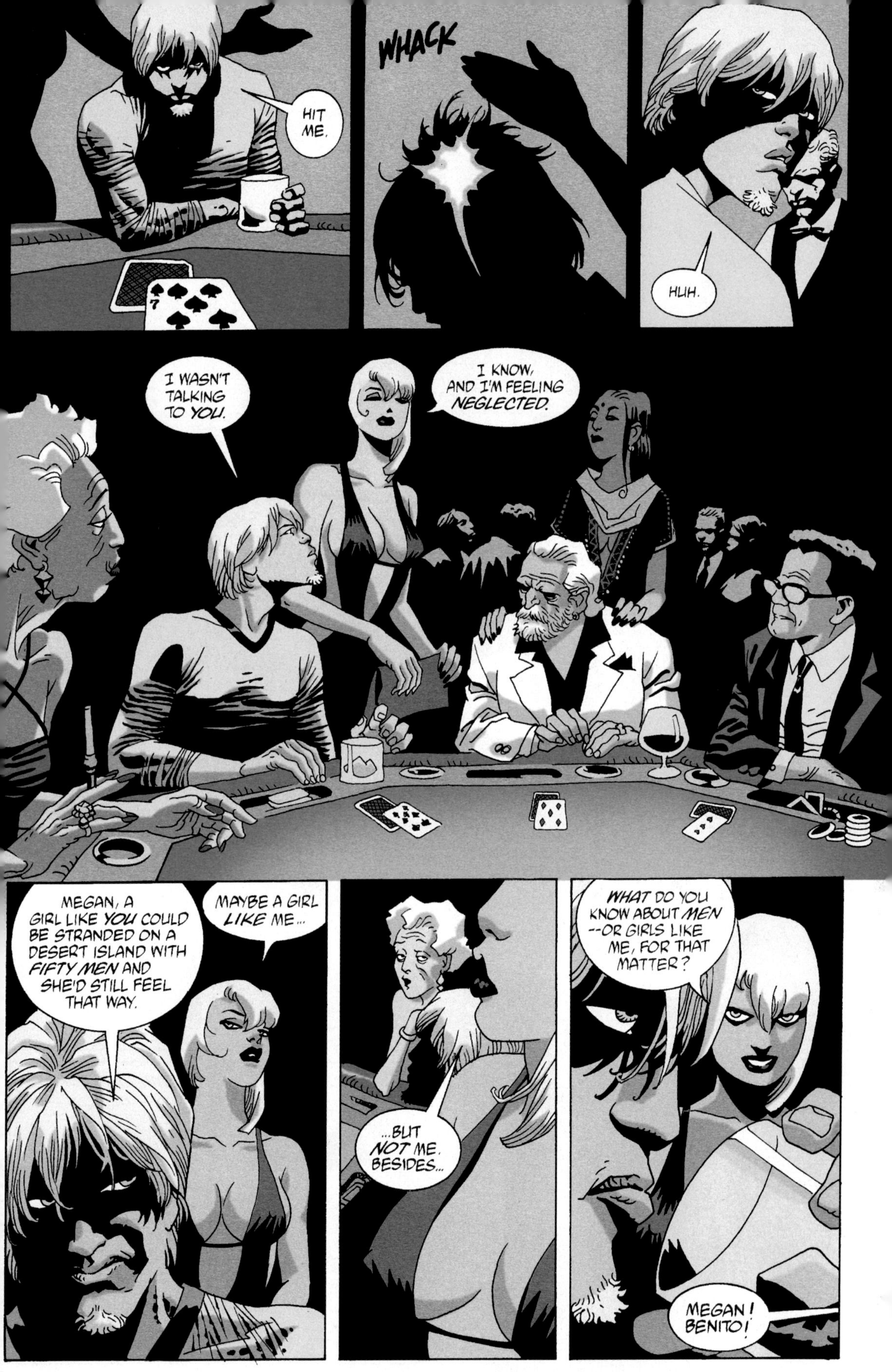
HIT ME.
WHACK
HUH.
I WASN'T TALKING TO YOU.
I KNOW, AND I'M FEELING NEGLECTED.
MEGAN, A GIRL LIKE YOU COULD BE STRANDED ON A DESERT ISLAND WITH FIFTY MEN AND SHE'D STILL FEEL THAT WAY.
MAYBE A GIRL LIKE ME...
...BUT NOT ME. BESIDES...
WHAT DO YOU KNOW ABOUT MEN --OR GIRLS LIKE ME, FOR THAT MATTER?
MEGAN! BENITO!

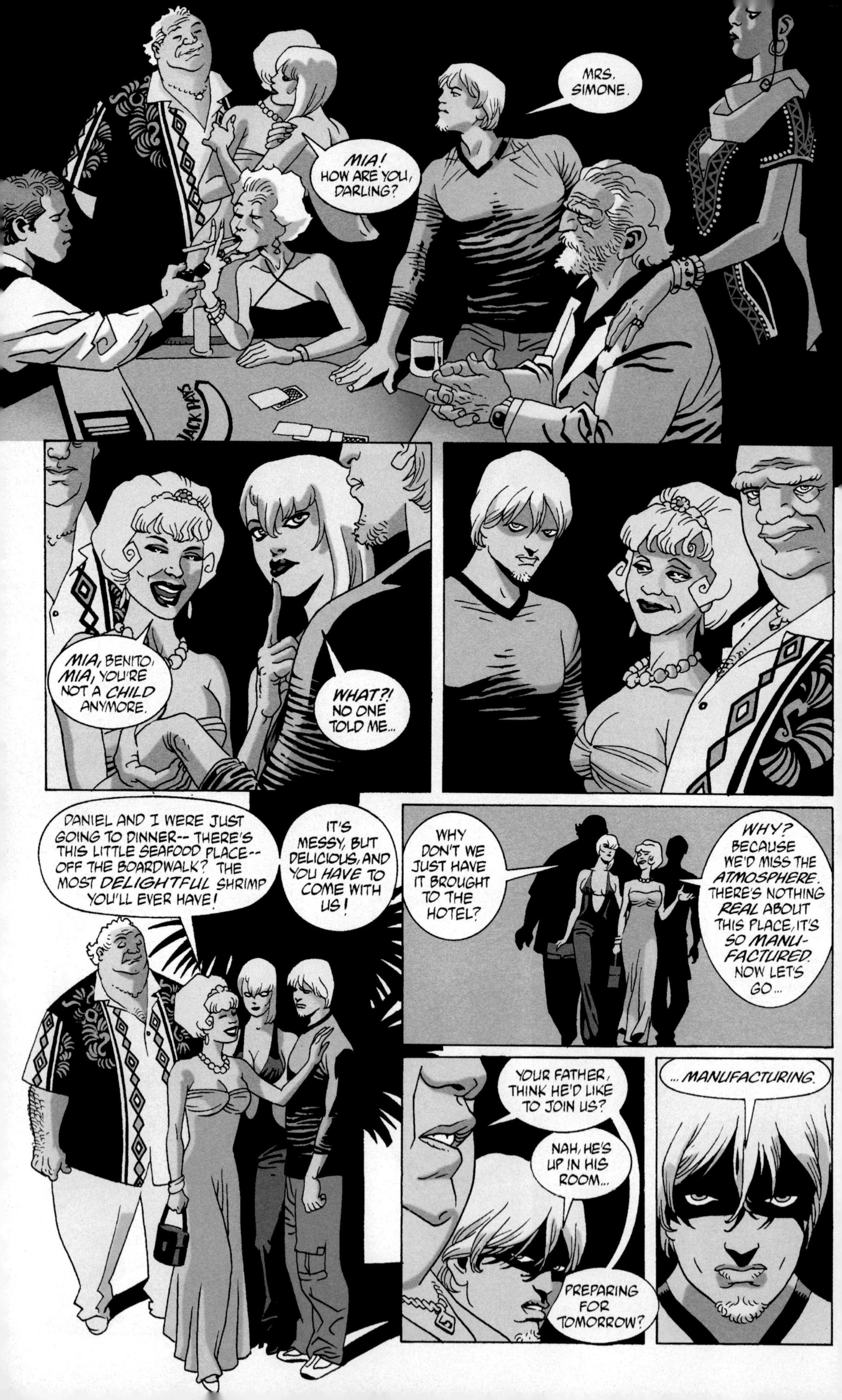
MRS. SIMONE.
MIA! HOW ARE YOU, DARLING?
MIA, BENITO. MIA, YOU'RE NOT A CHILD ANYMORE.
WHAT?! NO ONE TOLD ME...
DANIEL AND I WERE JUST GOING TO DINNER-- THERE'S THIS LITTLE SEAFOOD PLACE-- OFF THE BOARDWALK? THE MOST DELIGHTFUL SHRIMP YOU'LL EVER HAVE!
IT'S MESSY, BUT DELICIOUS, AND YOU HAVE TO COME WITH US!
WHY DON'T WE JUST HAVE IT BROUGHT TO THE HOTEL?
WHY? BECAUSE WE'D MISS THE ATMOSPHERE. THERE'S NOTHING REAL ABOUT THIS PLACE, IT'S SO MANUFACTURED. NOW LET'S GO...
YOUR FATHER, THINK HE'D LIKE TO JOIN US?
NAH, HE'S UP IN HIS ROOM...
PREPARING FOR TOMORROW?
...MANUFACTURING.

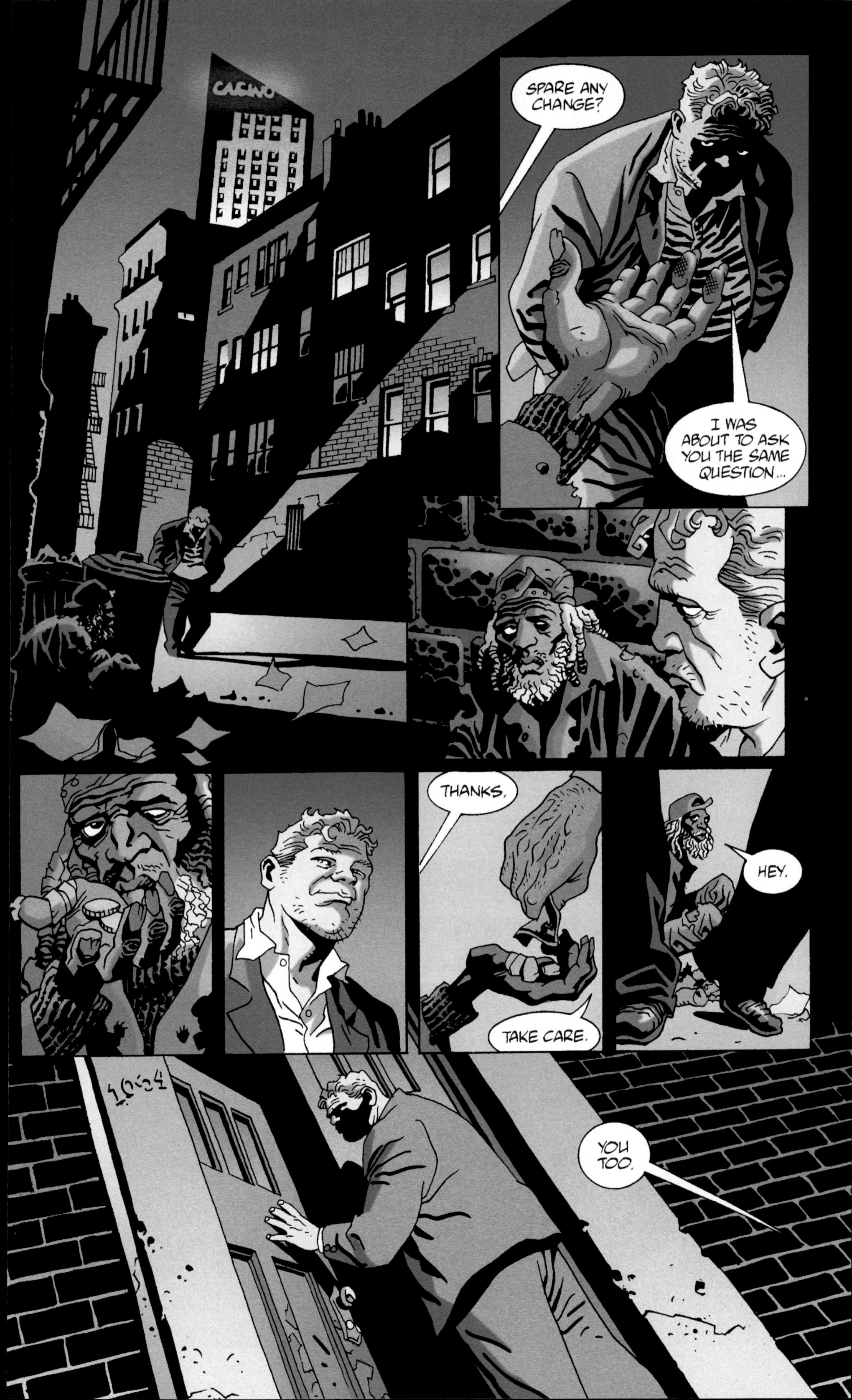
CASINO
SPARE ANY CHANGE?
I WAS ABOUT TO ASK YOU THE SAME QUESTION...
THANKS.
TAKE CARE.
HEY.
YOU TOO.

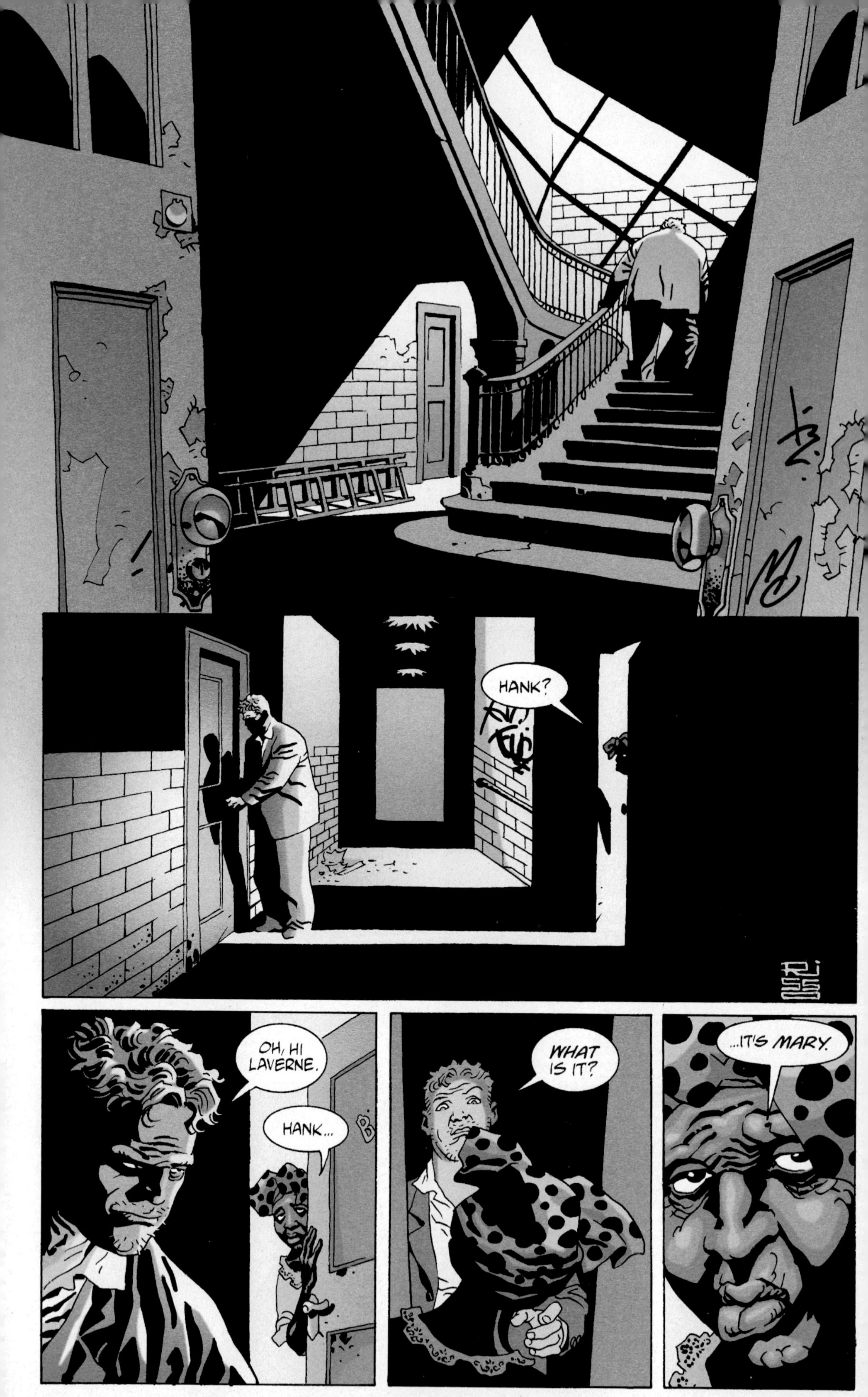

HANK?
OH, HI LAVERNE.
HANK...
WHAT IS IT?
...IT'S MARY.

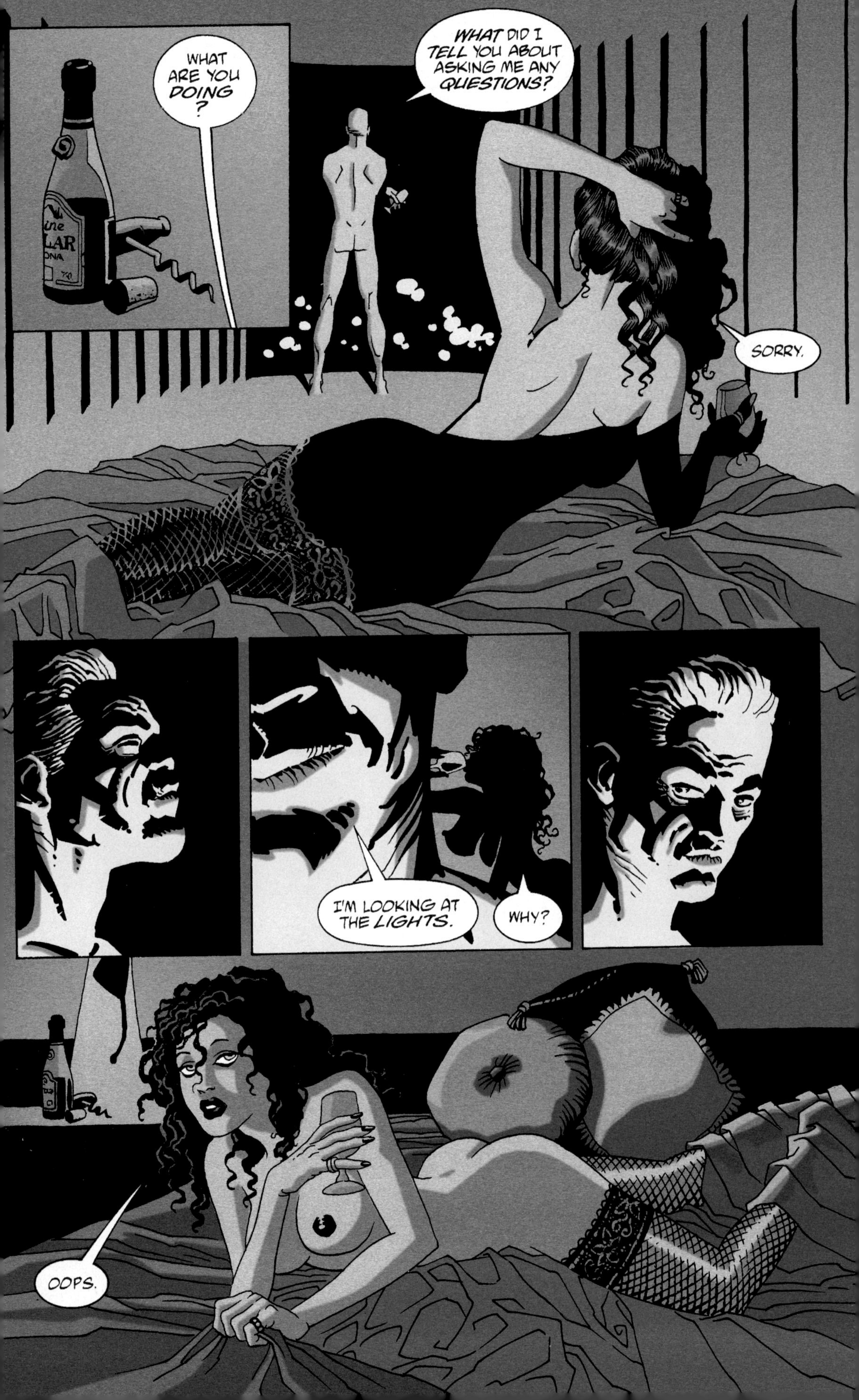

WHAT ARE YOU DOING ?
WHAT DID I TELL YOU ABOUT ASKING ME ANY QUESTIONS?
SORRY.
I'M LOOKING AT THE LIGHTS.
WHY?
OOPS.

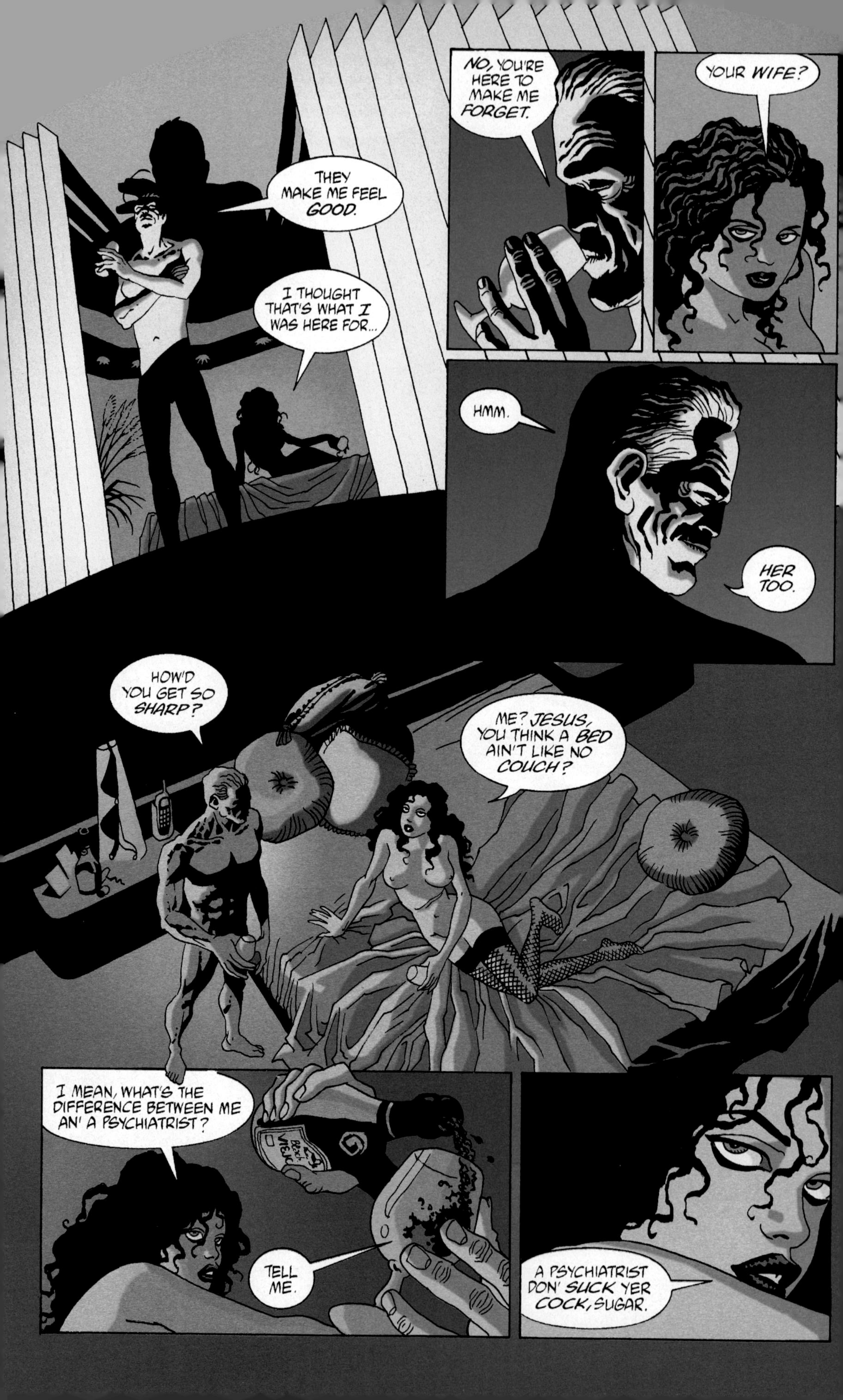
THEY MAKE ME FEEL GOOD.
I THOUGHT THAT'S WHAT I WAS HERE FOR...
NO, YOU'RE HERE TO MAKE ME FORGET.
YOUR WIFE?
HMM.
HER TOO.
HOW'D YOU GET SO SHARP?
ME? JESUS, YOU THINK A BED AIN'T LIKE NO COUCH?
I MEAN, WHAT'S THE DIFFERENCE BETWEEN ME AN' A PSYCHIATRIST?
TELL ME.
A PSYCHIATRIST DON' SUCK YER COCK, SUGAR.

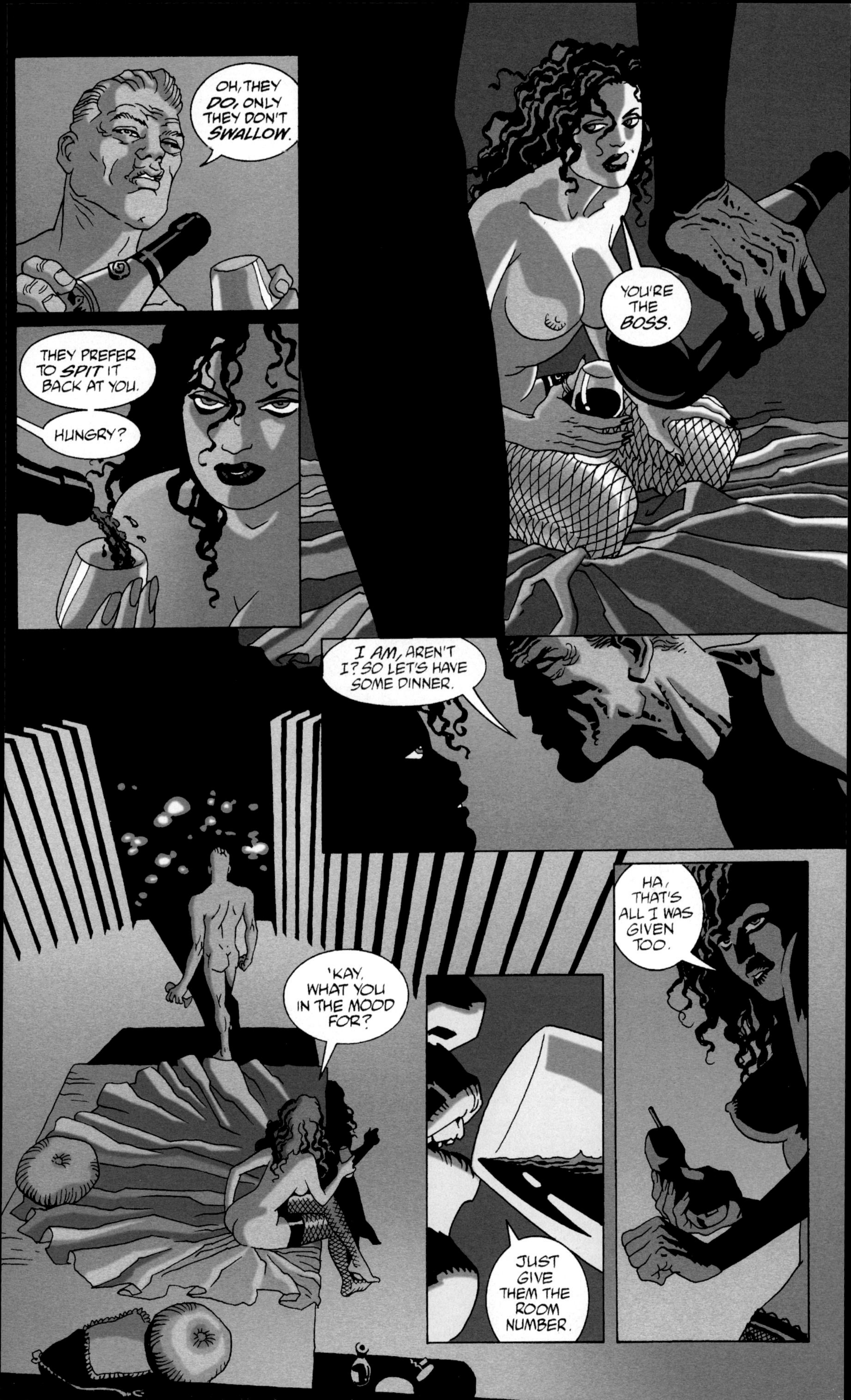
OH, THEY DO, ONLY THEY DON'T SWALLOW.
THEY PREFER TO SPIT IT BACK AT YOU.
HUNGRY?
YOU'RE THE BOSS.
I AM, AREN'T I? SO LET'S HAVE SOME DINNER.
'KAY, WHAT YOU IN THE MOOD FOR?
JUST GIVE THEM THE ROOM NUMBER.
HA, THAT'S ALL I WAS GIVEN TOO.

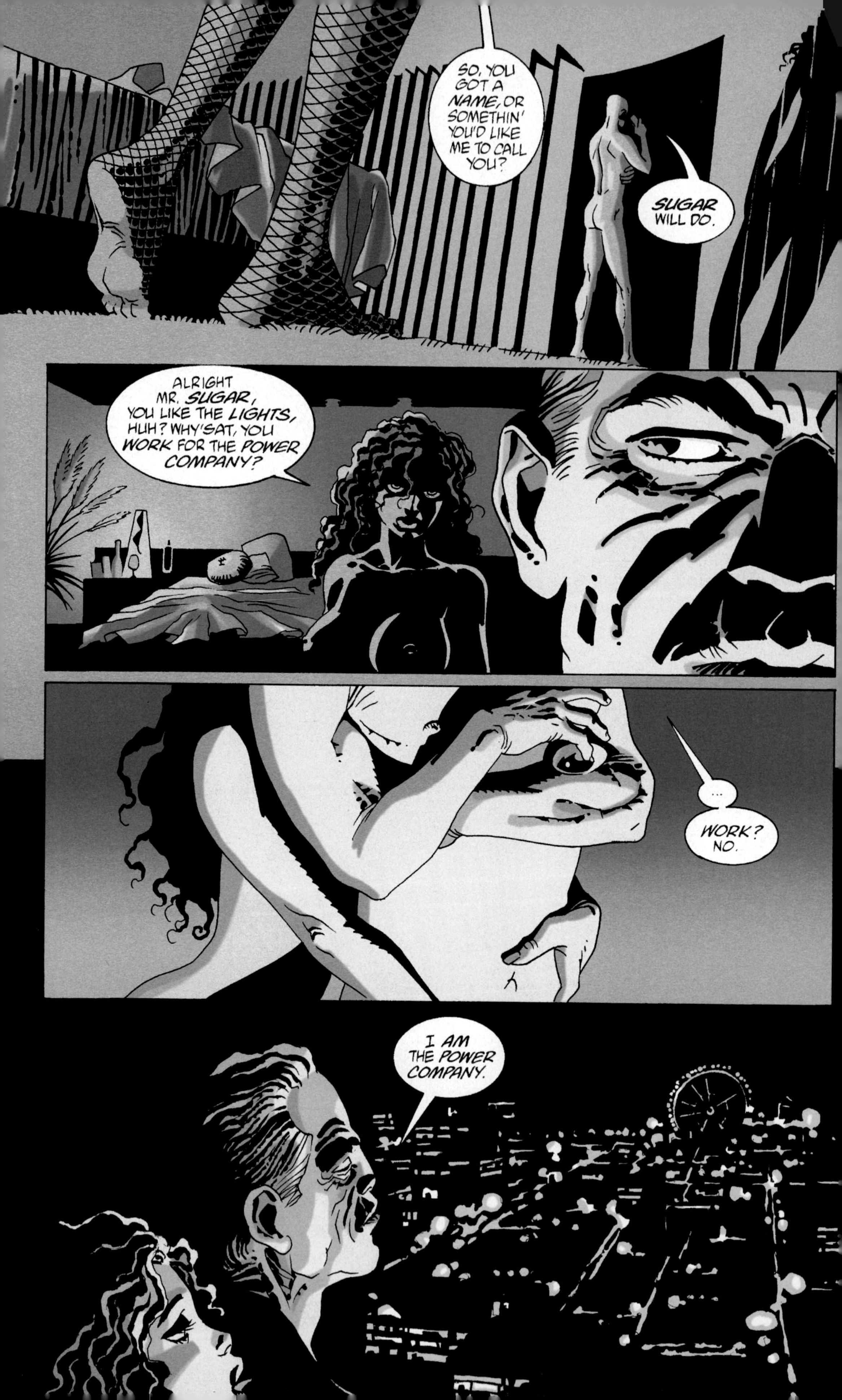
SO, YOU GOT A NAME, OR SOMETHIN' YOU'D LIKE ME TO CALL YOU?
SUGAR WILL DO.
ALRIGHT MR. SUGAR, YOU LIKE THE LIGHTS, HUH? WHY'SAT, YOU WORK FOR THE POWER COMPANY?
...
WORK? NO.
I AM THE POWER COMPANY.

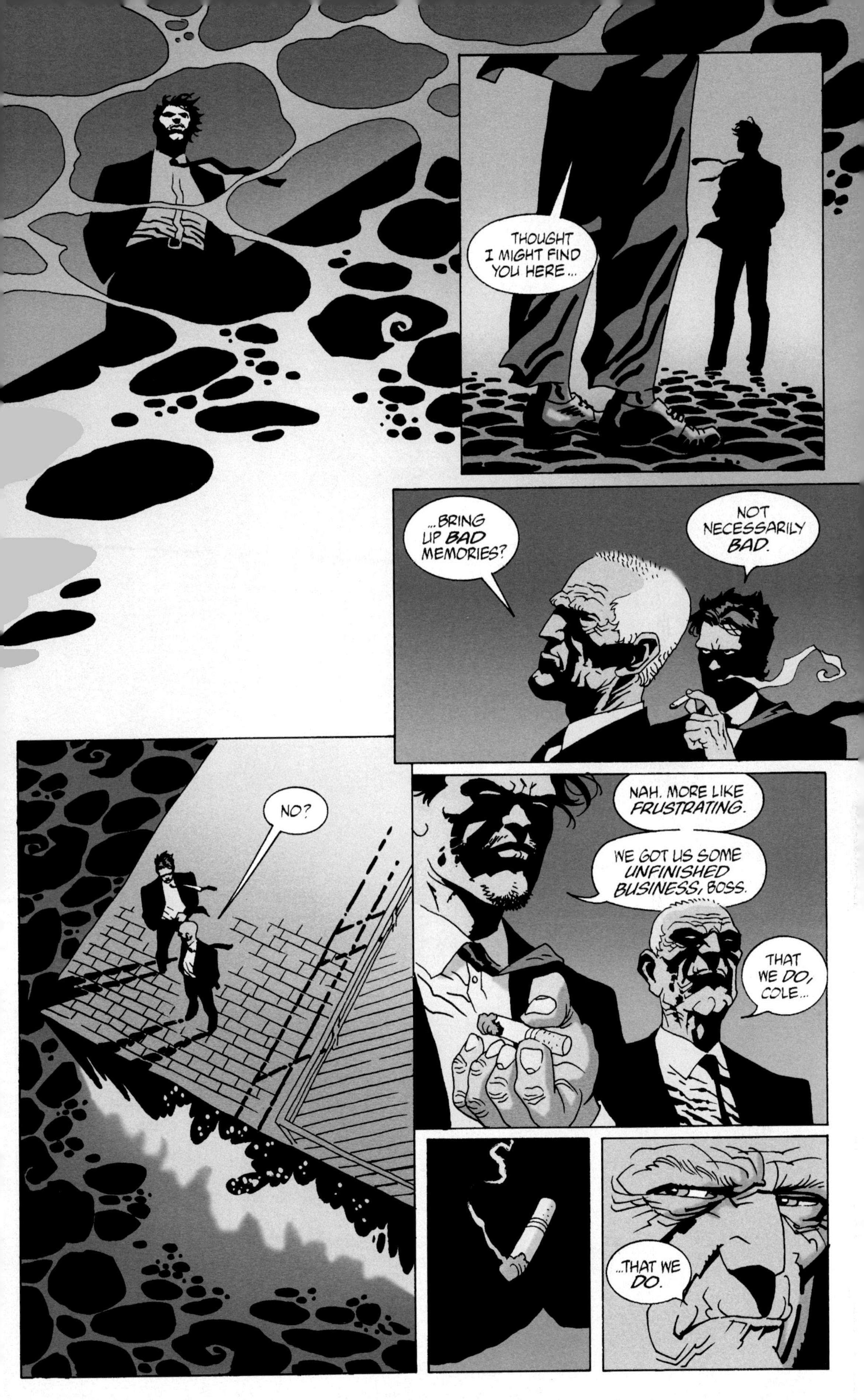
THOUGHT I MIGHT FIND YOU HERE...
...BRING UP BAD MEMORIES?
NOT NECESSARILY BAD.
NO?
NAH. MORE LIKE FRUSTRATING.
WE GOT US SOME UNFINISHED BUSINESS, BOSS.
THAT WE DO, COLE...
...THAT WE DO.

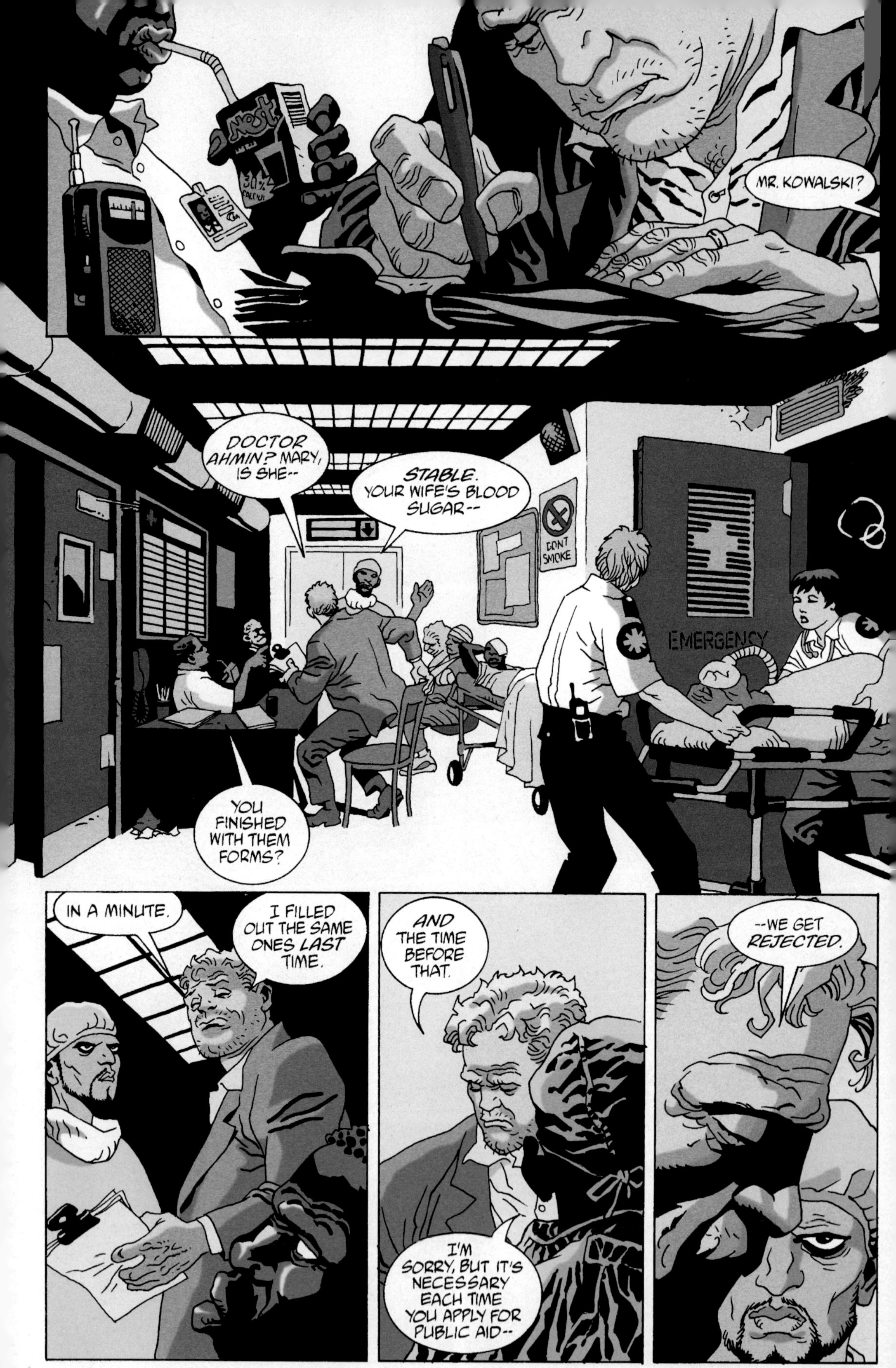

MR. KOWALSKI?
DOCTOR AHMIN? MARY, IS SHE--
STABLE. YOUR WIFE'S BLOOD SUGAR--
DON'T SMOKE
EMERGENCY
YOU FINISHED WITH THEM FORMS?
IN A MINUTE.
I FILLED OUT THE SAME ONES LAST TIME.
AND THE TIME BEFORE THAT.
I'M SORRY, BUT IT'S NECESSARY EACH TIME YOU APPLY FOR PUBLIC AID--
--WE GET REJECTED.

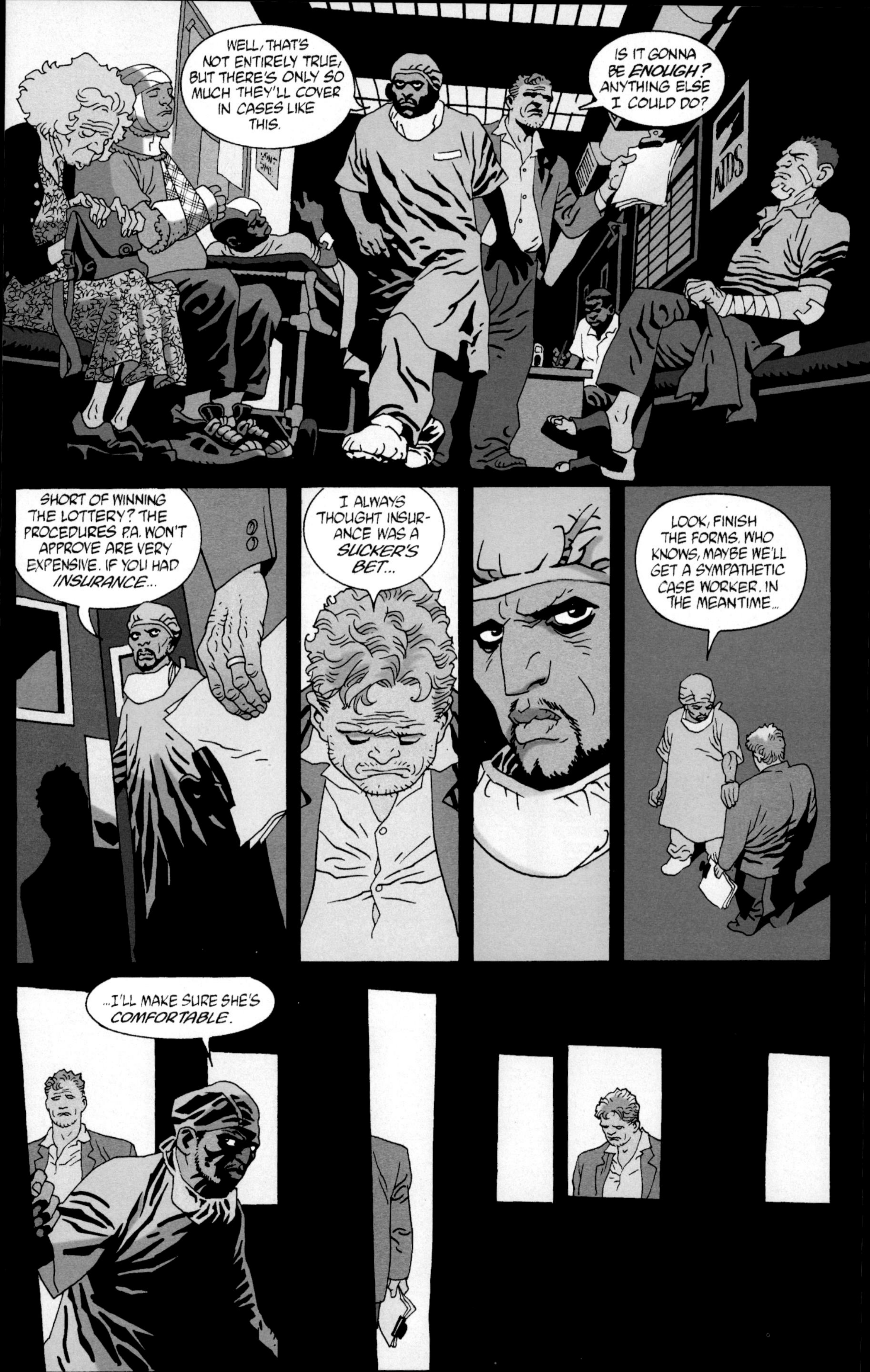
WELL, THAT'S NOT ENTIRELY TRUE, BUT THERE'S ONLY SO MUCH THEY'LL COVER IN CASES LIKE THIS.
IS IT GONNA BE *ENOUGH?* ANYTHING ELSE I COULD DO?
AIDS
SHORT OF WINNING THE LOTTERY? THE PROCEDURES P.A. WON'T APPROVE ARE VERY EXPENSIVE. IF YOU HAD *INSURANCE*...
I ALWAYS THOUGHT INSURANCE WAS A *SUCKER'S* BET...
LOOK, FINISH THE FORMS. WHO KNOWS, MAYBE WE'LL GET A SYMPATHETIC CASE WORKER. IN THE MEANTIME...
...I'LL MAKE SURE SHE'S *COMFORTABLE*.

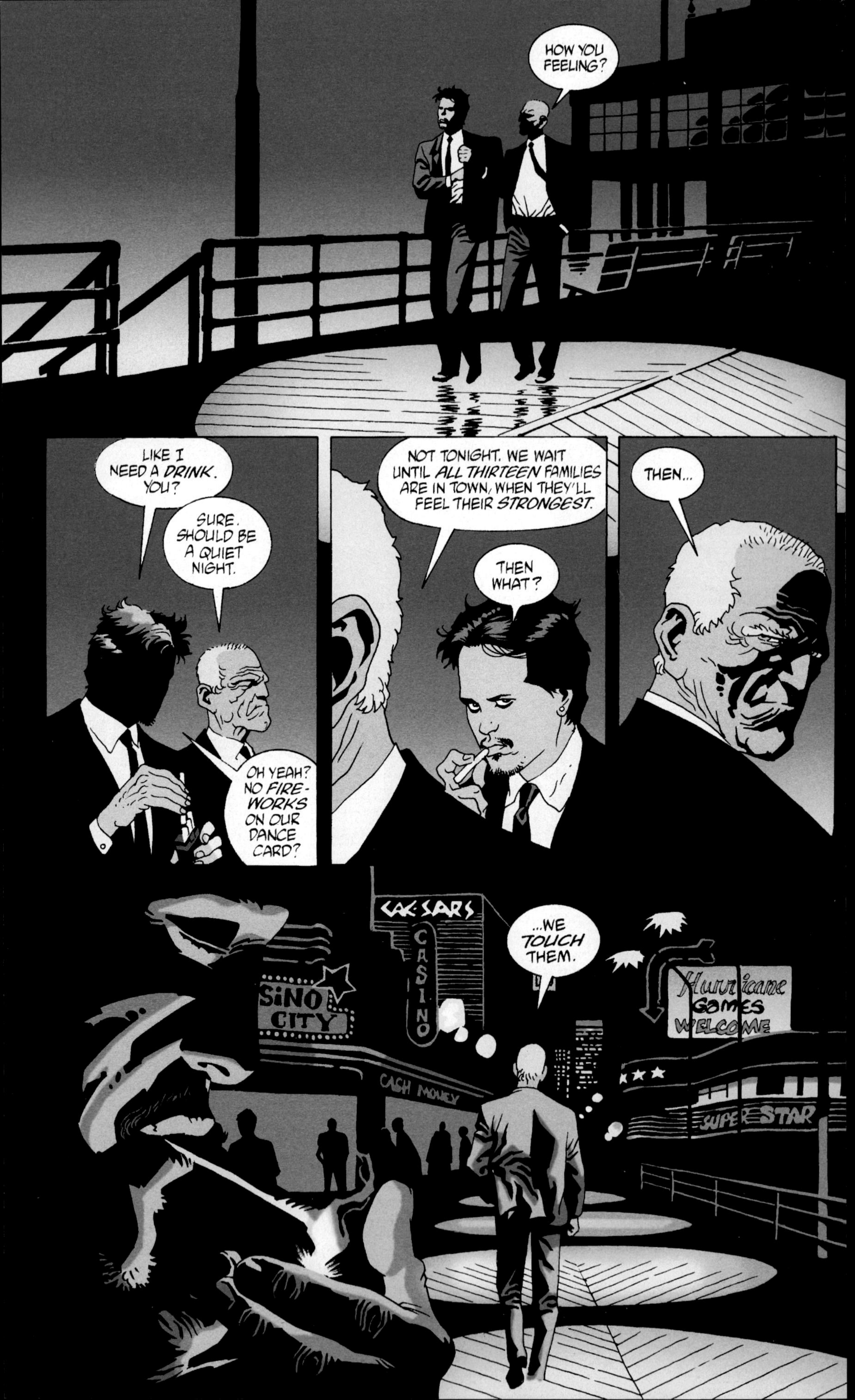
HOW YOU FEELING?
LIKE I NEED A DRINK. YOU?
SURE. SHOULD BE A QUIET NIGHT.
OH YEAH? NO FIRE-WORKS ON OUR DANCE CARD?
NOT TONIGHT. WE WAIT UNTIL ALL THIRTEEN FAMILIES ARE IN TOWN, WHEN THEY'LL FEEL THEIR STRONGEST.
THEN WHAT?
THEN...
...WE TOUCH THEM.
CAESARS
CASINO
SINO CITY
CASH MONEY
Hurricane Games WELCOME
SUPER STAR

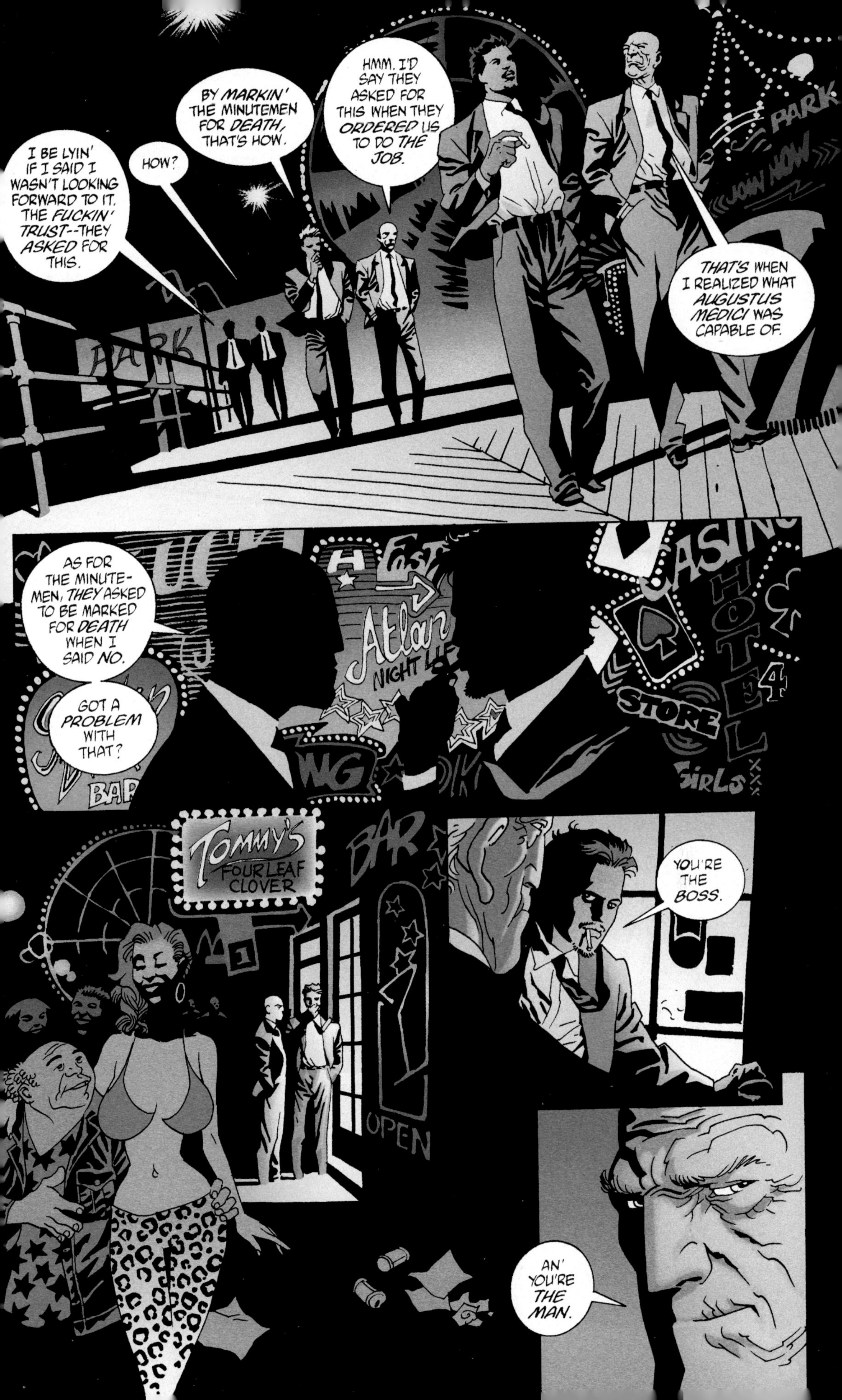
I BE LYIN' IF I SAID I WASN'T LOOKING FORWARD TO IT. THE FUCKIN' TRUST--THEY ASKED FOR THIS.
HOW?
BY MARKIN' THE MINUTEMEN FOR DEATH, THAT'S HOW.
HMM. I'D SAY THEY ASKED FOR THIS WHEN THEY ORDERED US TO DO THE JOB.
THAT'S WHEN I REALIZED WHAT AUGUSTUS MEDICI WAS CAPABLE OF.
PARK
JOIN NOW
AS FOR THE MINUTE-MEN, THEY ASKED TO BE MARKED FOR DEATH WHEN I SAID NO.
GOT A PROBLEM WITH THAT?
NIGHT LI
HOTEL
STORE
GIRLS
BAR
TOMMY'S FOUR LEAF CLOVER
BAR
OPEN
YOU'RE THE BOSS.
AN' YOU'RE THE MAN.

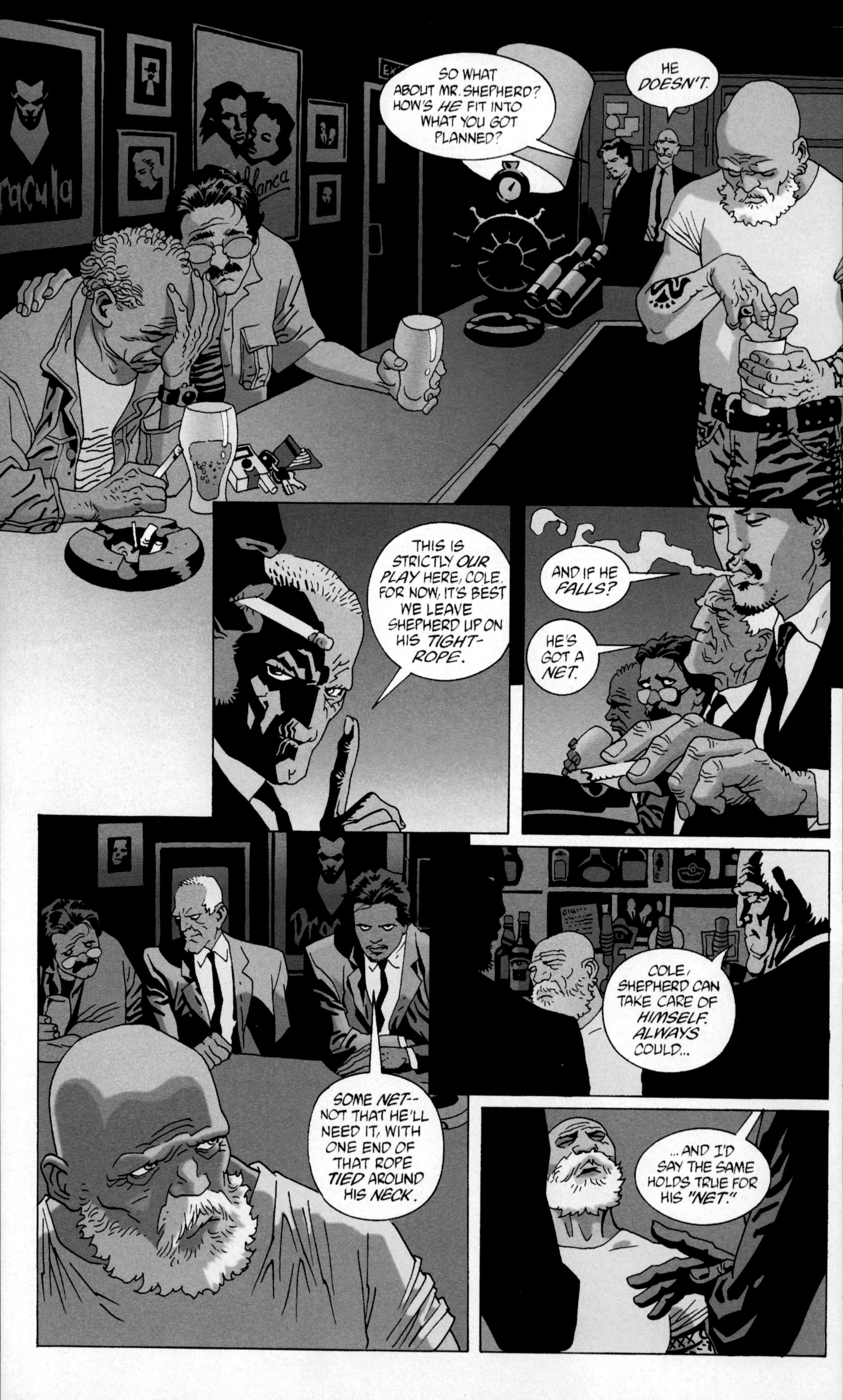

SO WHAT ABOUT MR. SHEPHERD? HOW'S HE FIT INTO WHAT YOU GOT PLANNED?
HE DOESN'T.
THIS IS STRICTLY OUR PLAY HERE, COLE. FOR NOW, IT'S BEST WE LEAVE SHEPHERD UP ON HIS TIGHT-ROPE.
AND IF HE FALLS?
HE'S GOT A NET.
SOME NET-- NOT THAT HE'LL NEED IT, WITH ONE END OF THAT ROPE TIED AROUND HIS NECK.
COLE, SHEPHERD CAN TAKE CARE OF HIMSELF. ALWAYS COULD...
...AND I'D SAY THE SAME HOLDS TRUE FOR HIS "NET."

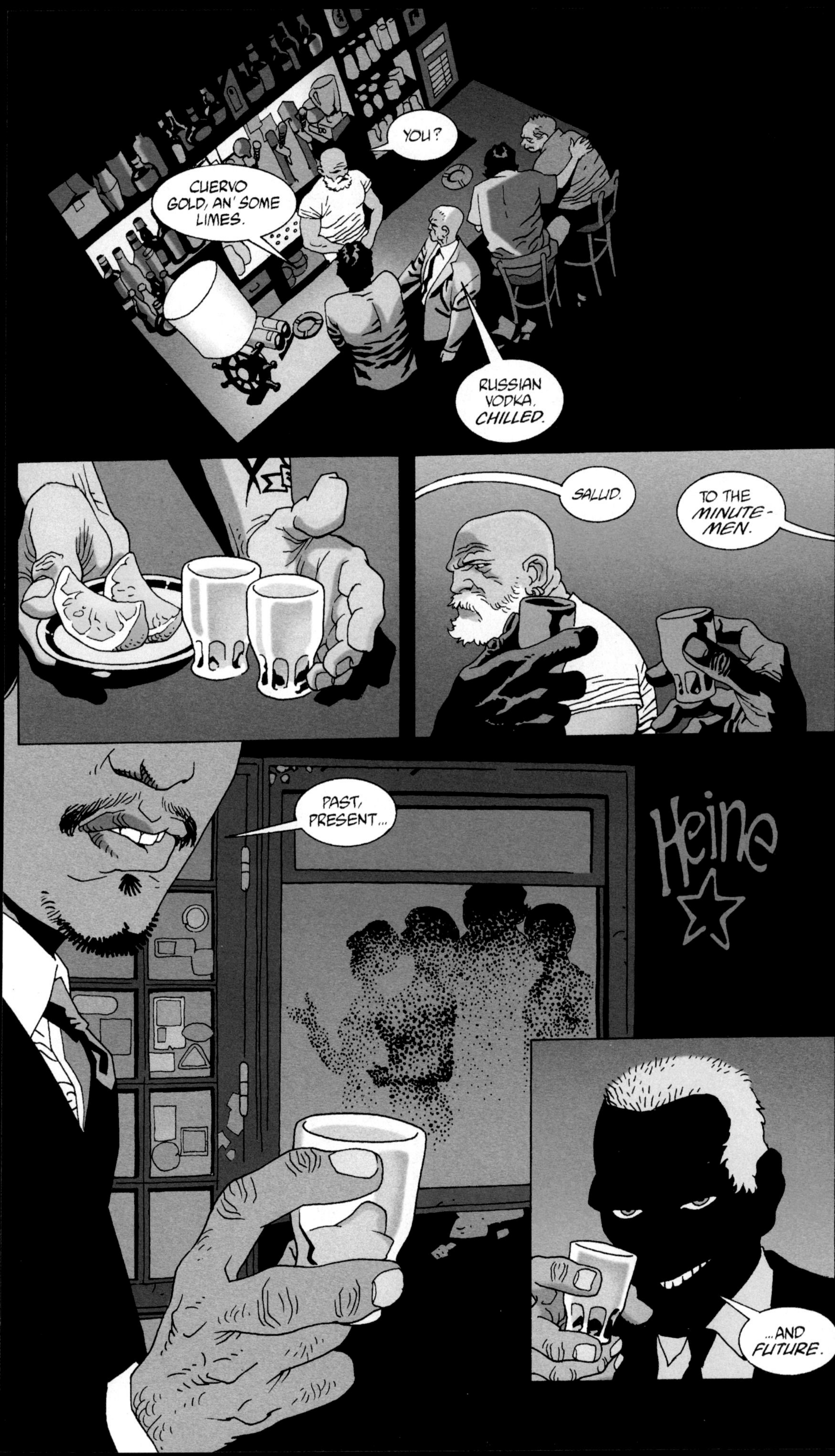
YOU?
CUERVO GOLD, AN' SOME LIMES.
RUSSIAN VODKA, CHILLED.
SALUD.
TO THE MINUTE-MEN.
PAST, PRESENT...
Heine
...AND FUTURE.

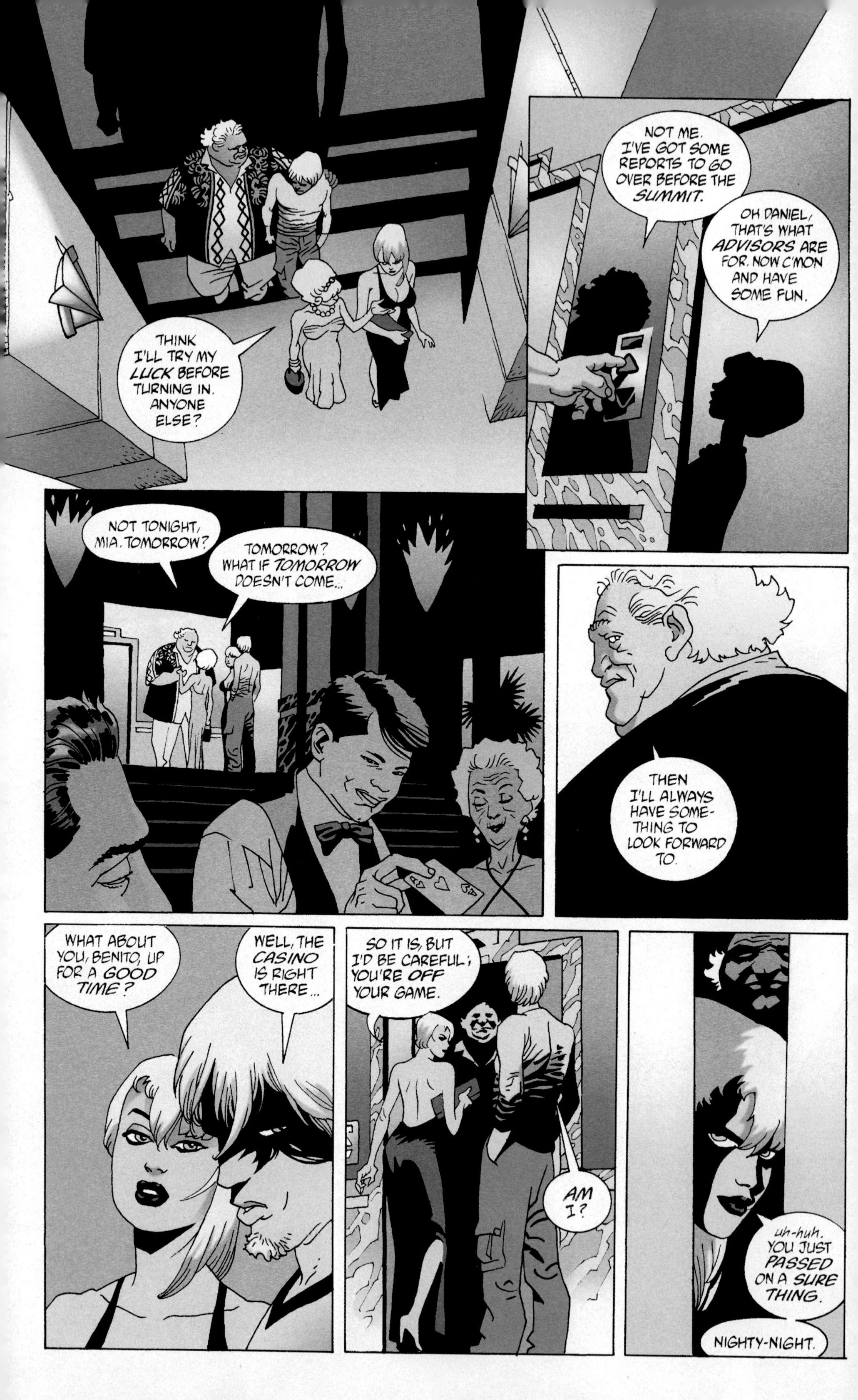
THINK I'LL TRY MY LUCK BEFORE TURNING IN. ANYONE ELSE?
NOT ME. I'VE GOT SOME REPORTS TO GO OVER BEFORE THE SUMMIT.
OH DANIEL, THAT'S WHAT ADVISORS ARE FOR. NOW C'MON AND HAVE SOME FUN.
NOT TONIGHT, MIA. TOMORROW?
TOMORROW? WHAT IF TOMORROW DOESN'T COME...
THEN I'LL ALWAYS HAVE SOME-THING TO LOOK FORWARD TO.
WHAT ABOUT YOU, BENITO, UP FOR A GOOD TIME?
WELL, THE CASINO IS RIGHT THERE...
SO IT IS, BUT I'D BE CAREFUL; YOU'RE OFF YOUR GAME.
AM I?
uh-huh. YOU JUST PASSED ON A SURE THING.
NIGHTY-NIGHT.

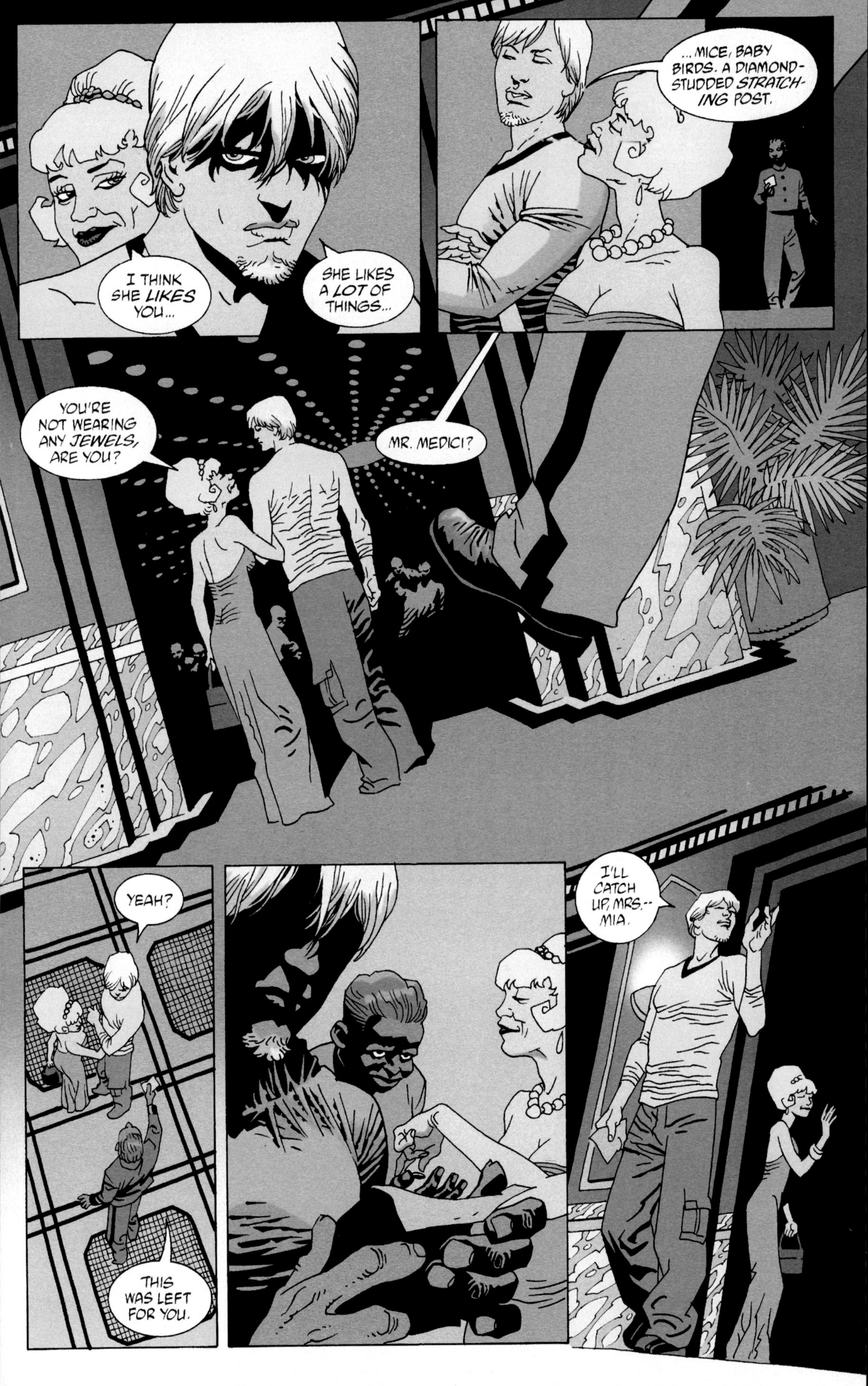
I THINK SHE *LIKES* YOU...
SHE LIKES A *LOT* OF THINGS...
...MICE, BABY BIRDS. A DIAMOND-STUDDED *STRATCHING* POST.
YOU'RE NOT WEARING ANY *JEWELS*, ARE YOU?
MR. MEDICI?
YEAH?
THIS WAS LEFT FOR YOU.
I'LL CATCH UP, MRS.-- MIA.

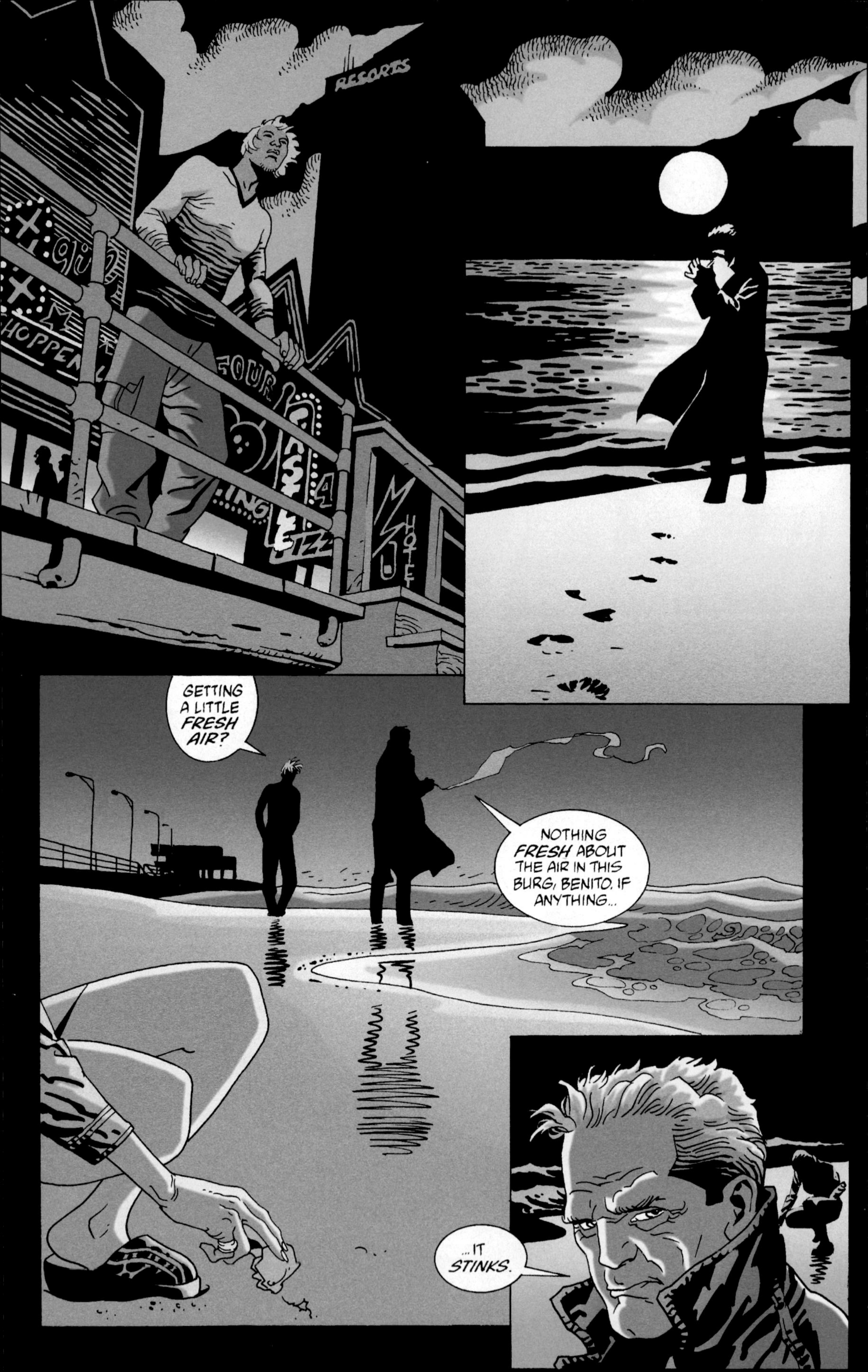
RESORTS
FOUR
GETTING A LITTLE FRESH AIR?
NOTHING FRESH ABOUT THE AIR IN THIS BURG, BENITO. IF ANYTHING...
...IT STINKS.

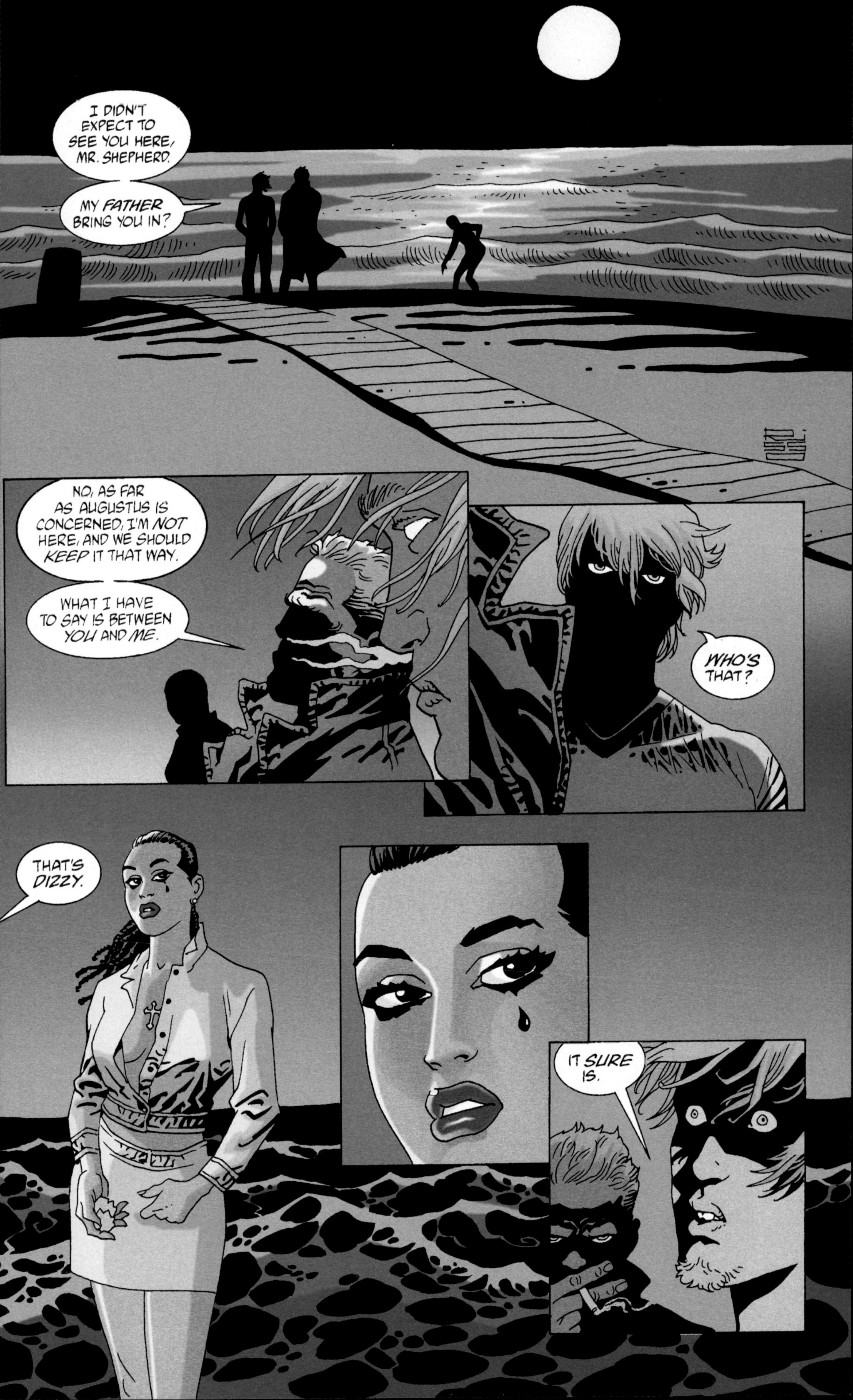
I DIDN'T EXPECT TO SEE YOU HERE, MR. SHEPHERD.
MY *FATHER* BRING YOU IN?
NO, AS FAR AS AUGUSTUS IS CONCERNED, I'M *NOT* HERE, AND WE SHOULD *KEEP* IT THAT WAY.
WHAT I HAVE TO SAY IS BETWEEN *YOU* AND *ME*.
WHO'S THAT?
THAT'S *DIZZY*.
IT *SURE* IS.

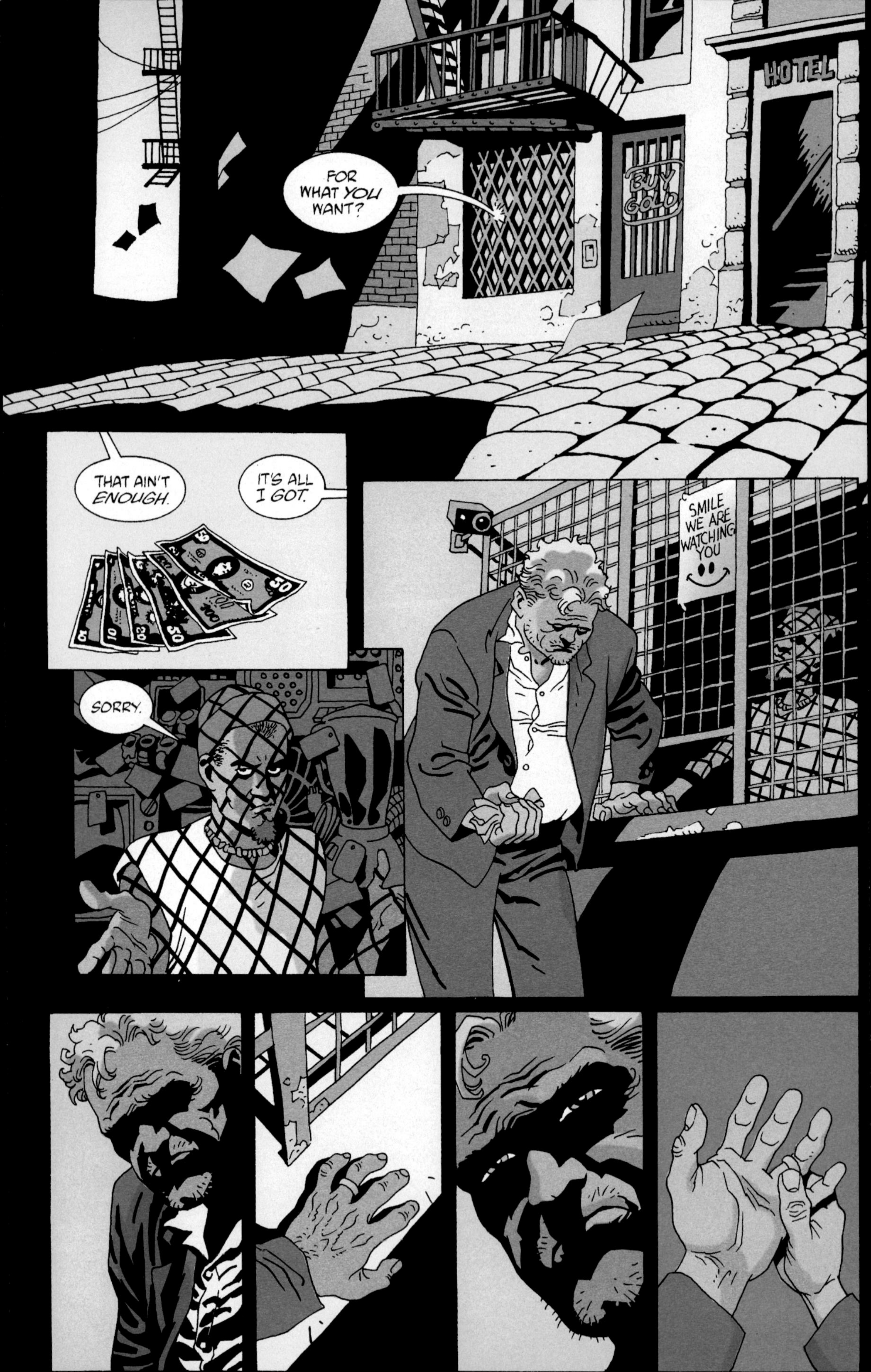
HOTEL
FOR WHAT YOU WANT?
BUY GOLD
THAT AIN'T ENOUGH.
IT'S ALL I GOT.
SMILE WE ARE WATCHING YOU
SORRY.

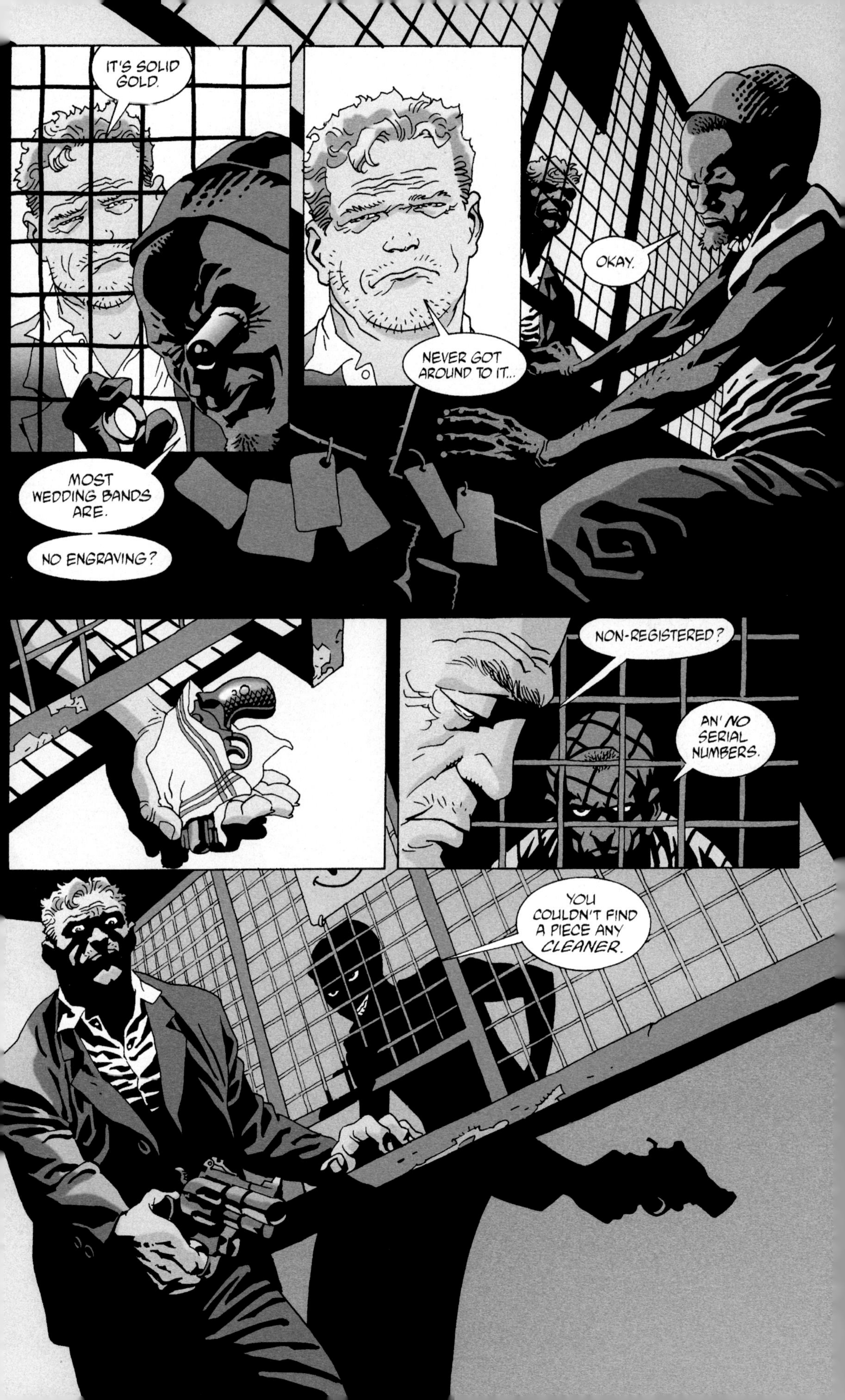
IT'S SOLID GOLD.
NEVER GOT AROUND TO IT...
OKAY.
MOST WEDDING BANDS ARE.
NO ENGRAVING?
NON-REGISTERED?
AN' NO SERIAL NUMBERS.
YOU COULDN'T FIND A PIECE ANY CLEANER.

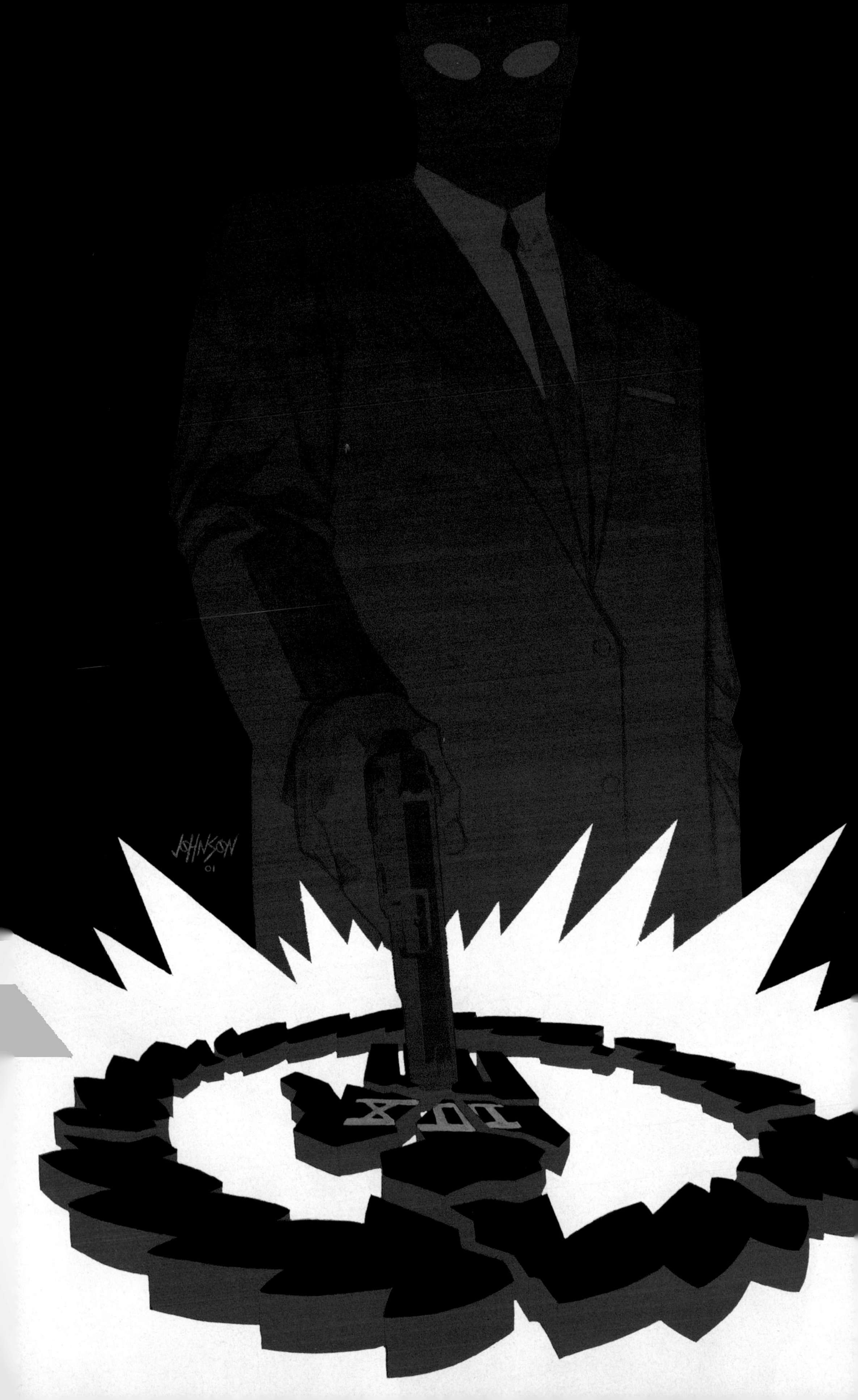
JOHNSON
01

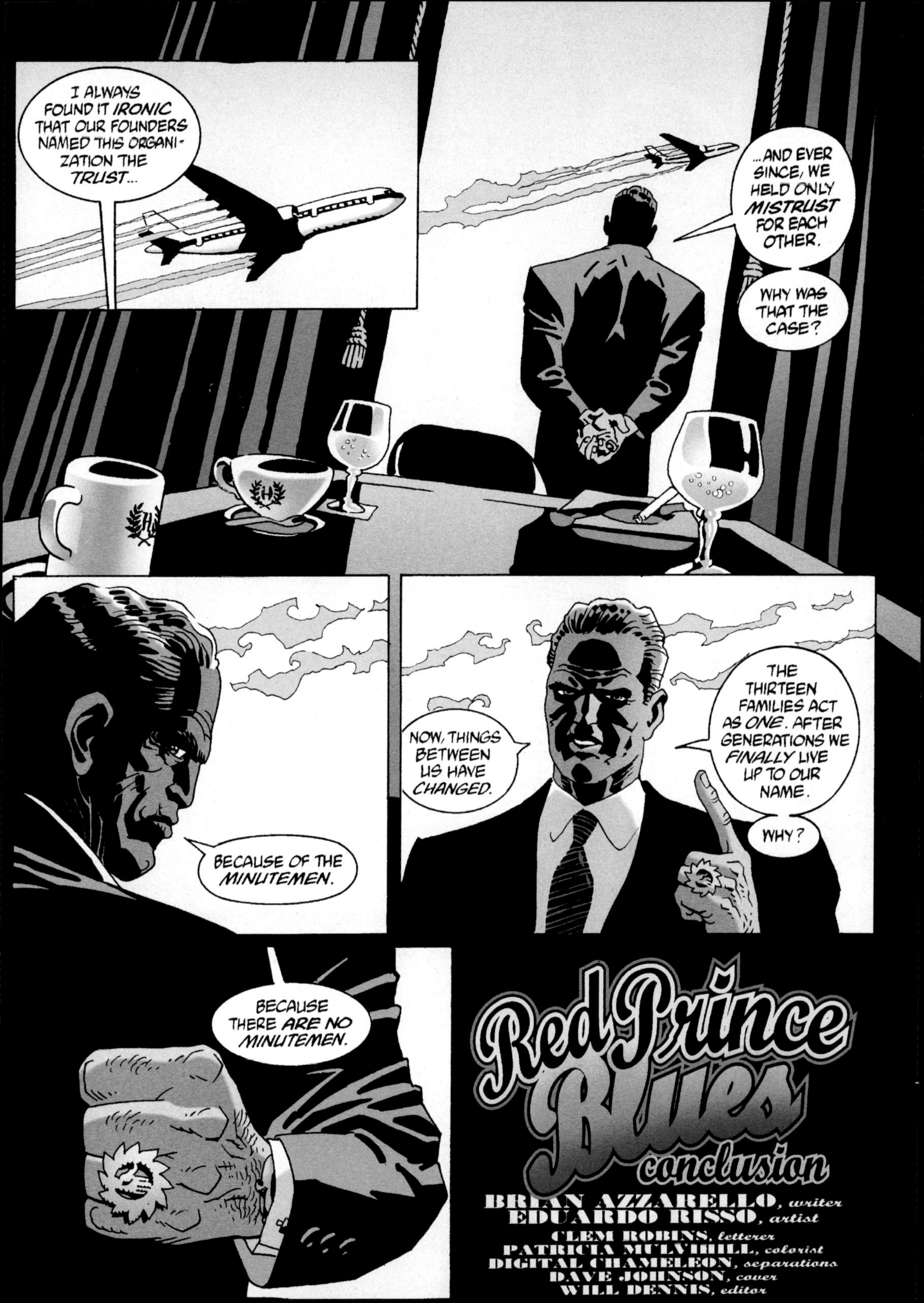

I ALWAYS FOUND IT IRONIC THAT OUR FOUNDERS NAMED THIS ORGANI-ZATION THE TRUST...
...AND EVER SINCE, WE HELD ONLY MISTRUST FOR EACH OTHER.
WHY WAS THAT THE CASE?
BECAUSE OF THE MINUTEMEN.
NOW, THINGS BETWEEN US HAVE CHANGED.
THE THIRTEEN FAMILIES ACT AS ONE. AFTER GENERATIONS WE FINALLY LIVE UP TO OUR NAME.
WHY?
BECAUSE THERE ARE NO MINUTEMEN.
Red Prince Blues
conclusion
BRIAN AZZARELLO, writer
EDUARDO RISSO, artist
CLEM ROBINS, letterer
PATRICIA MULVIHILL, colorist
DIGITAL CHAMELEON, separations
DAVE JOHNSON, cover
WILL DENNIS, editor

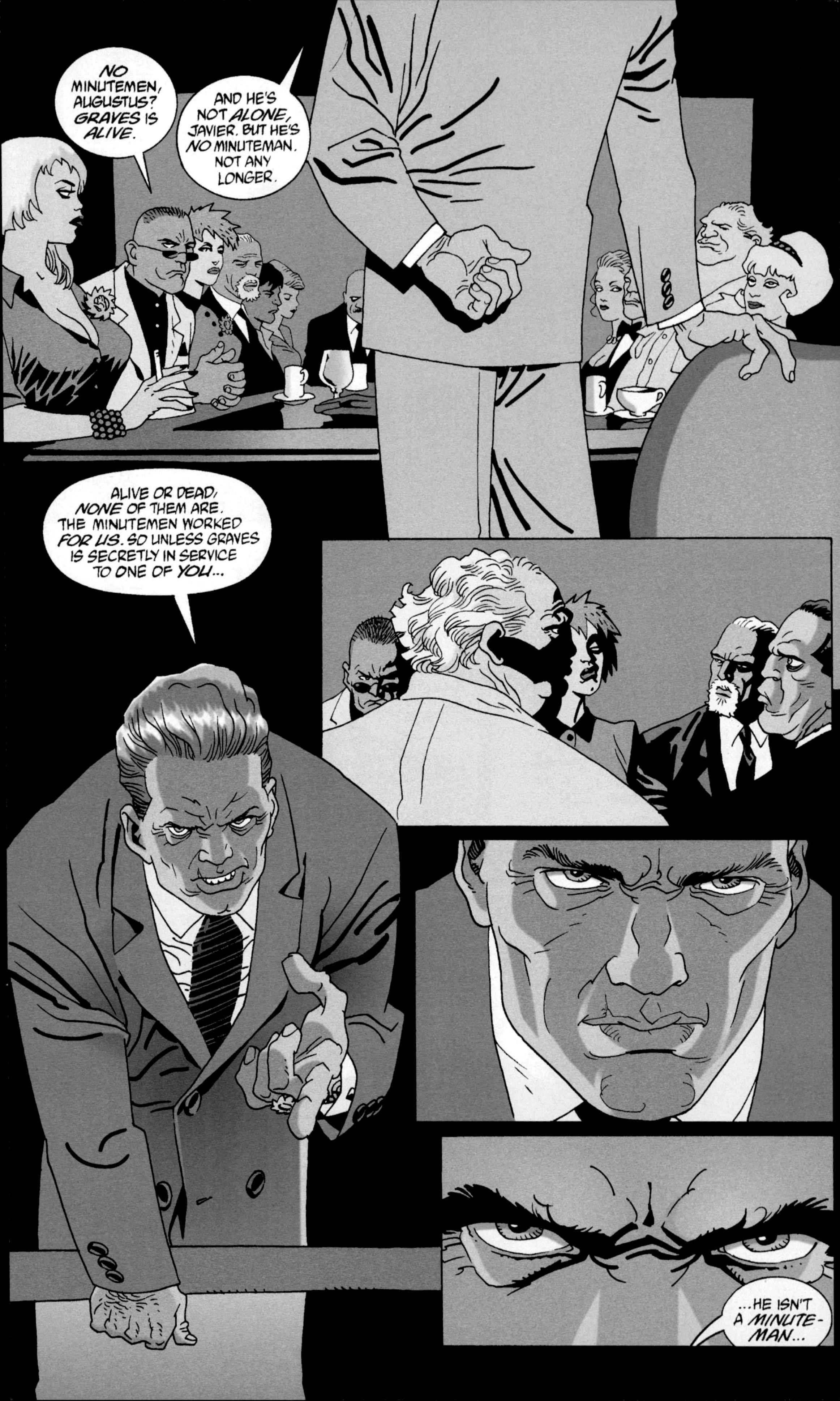
NO MINUTEMEN, AUGUSTUS? GRAVES IS ALIVE.
AND HE'S NOT ALONE, JAVIER. BUT HE'S NO MINUTEMAN. NOT ANY LONGER.
ALIVE OR DEAD, NONE OF THEM ARE. THE MINUTEMEN WORKED FOR US. SO UNLESS GRAVES IS SECRETLY IN SERVICE TO ONE OF YOU...
...HE ISN'T A MINUTE-MAN...

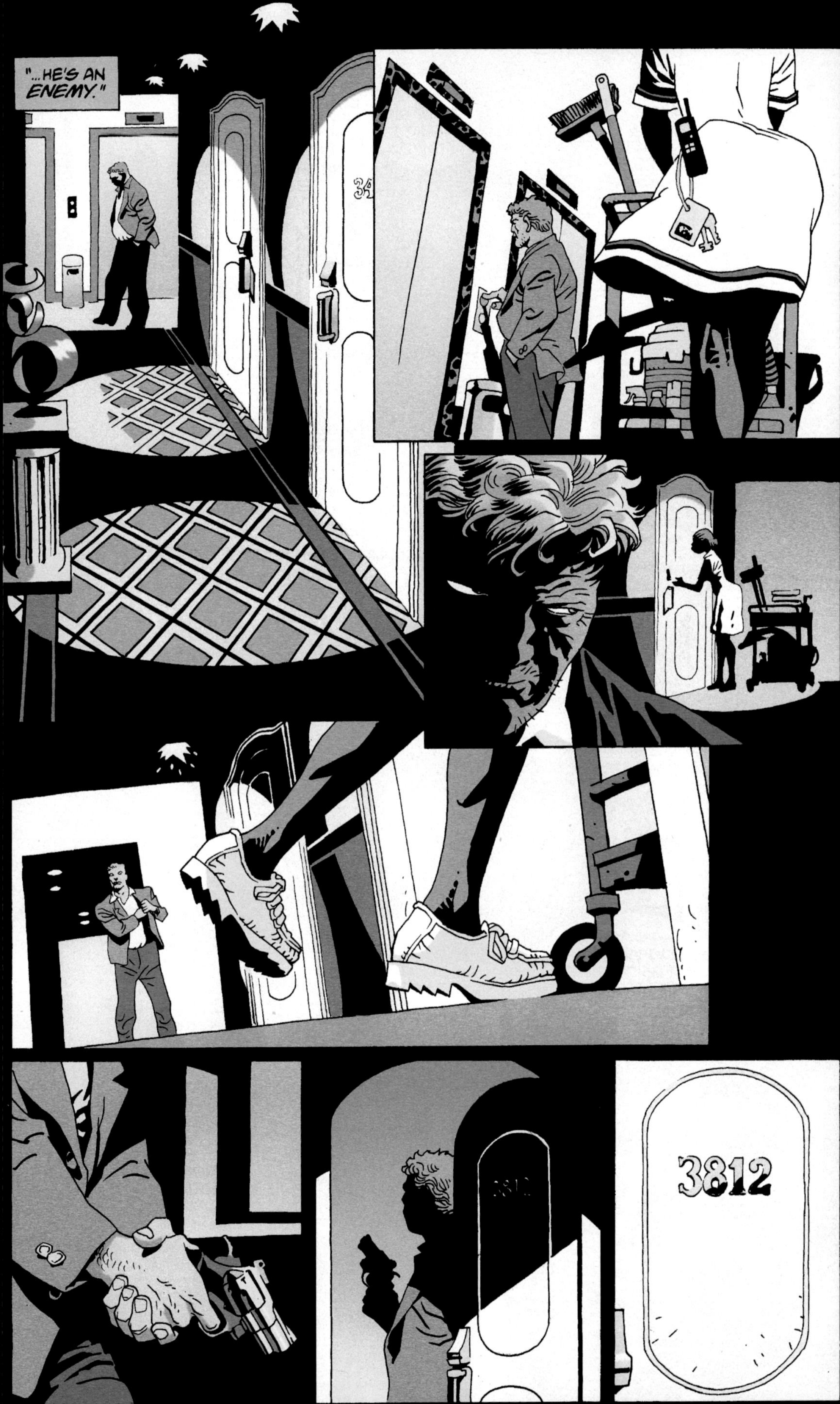
"...HE'S AN ENEMY."
3A
3812

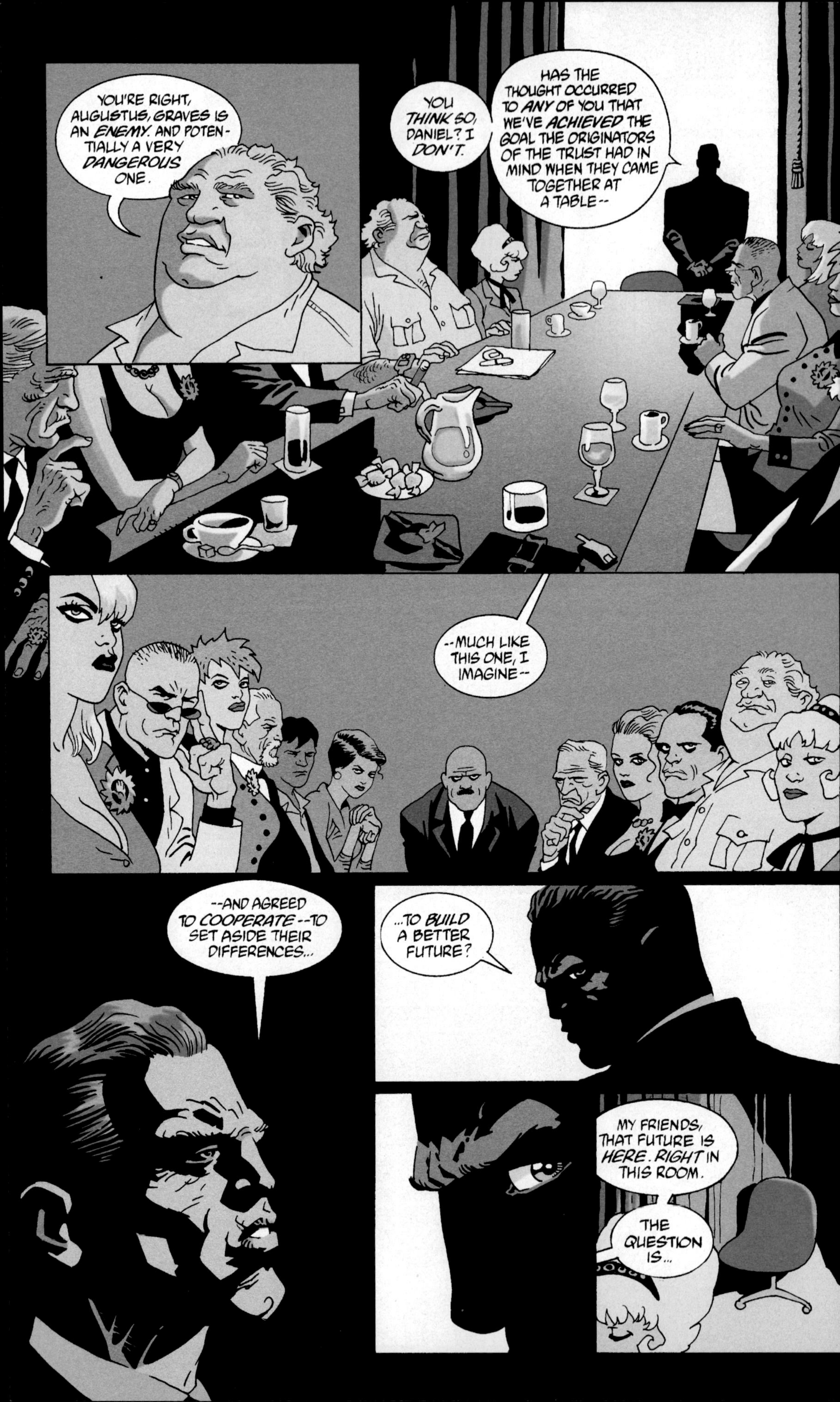
YOU'RE RIGHT, AUGUSTUS, GRAVES IS AN ENEMY. AND POTENTIALLY A VERY DANGEROUS ONE.
YOU THINK SO, DANIEL? I DON'T.
HAS THE THOUGHT OCCURRED TO ANY OF YOU THAT WE'VE ACHIEVED THE GOAL THE ORIGINATORS OF THE TRUST HAD IN MIND WHEN THEY CAME TOGETHER AT A TABLE--
--MUCH LIKE THIS ONE, I IMAGINE--
--AND AGREED TO COOPERATE--TO SET ASIDE THEIR DIFFERENCES...
...TO BUILD A BETTER FUTURE?
MY FRIENDS, THAT FUTURE IS HERE. RIGHT IN THIS ROOM.
THE QUESTION IS...

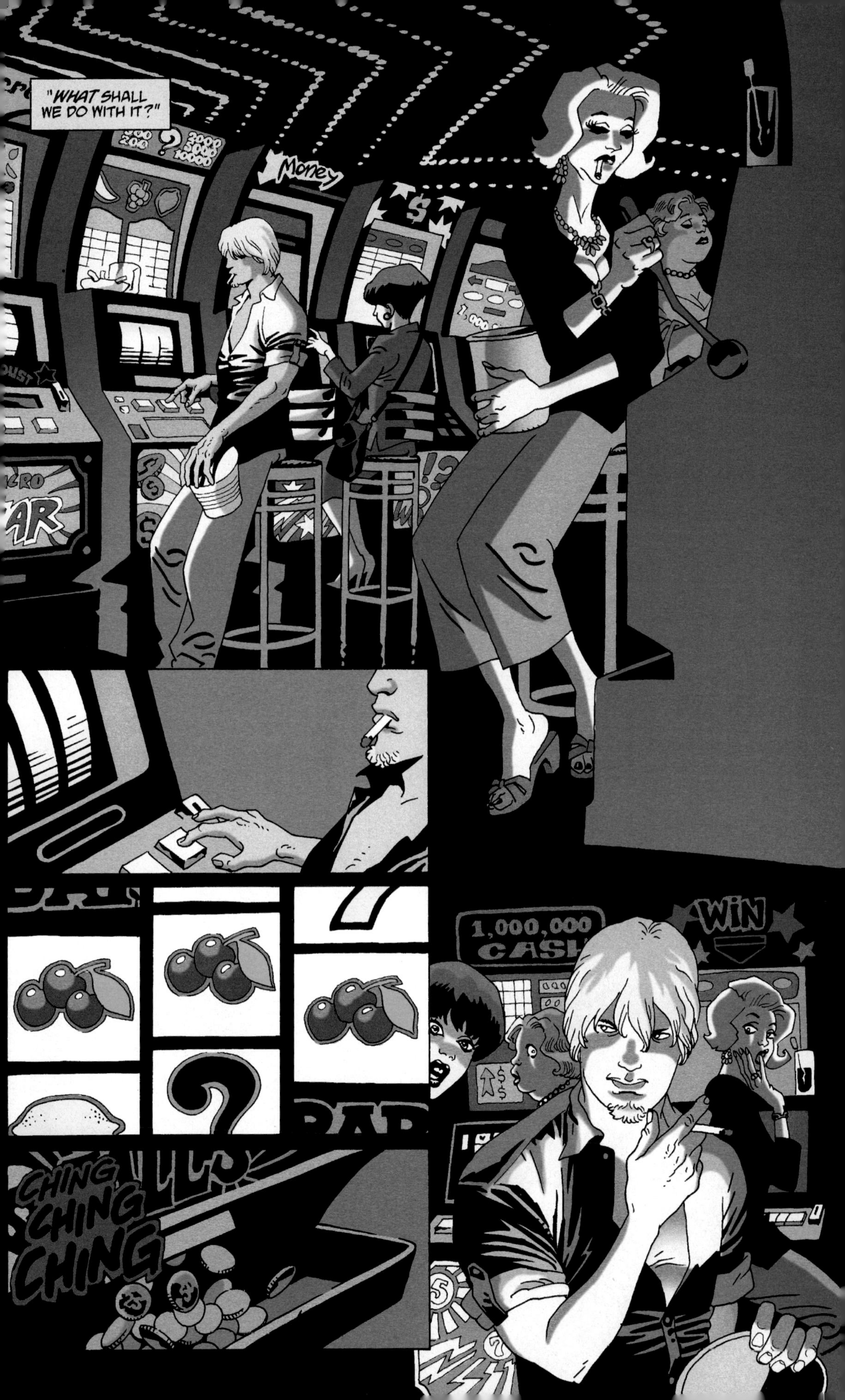
"WHAT SHALL WE DO WITH IT?"
Money
$
1,000,000 CASH
WIN
CHING CHING CHING

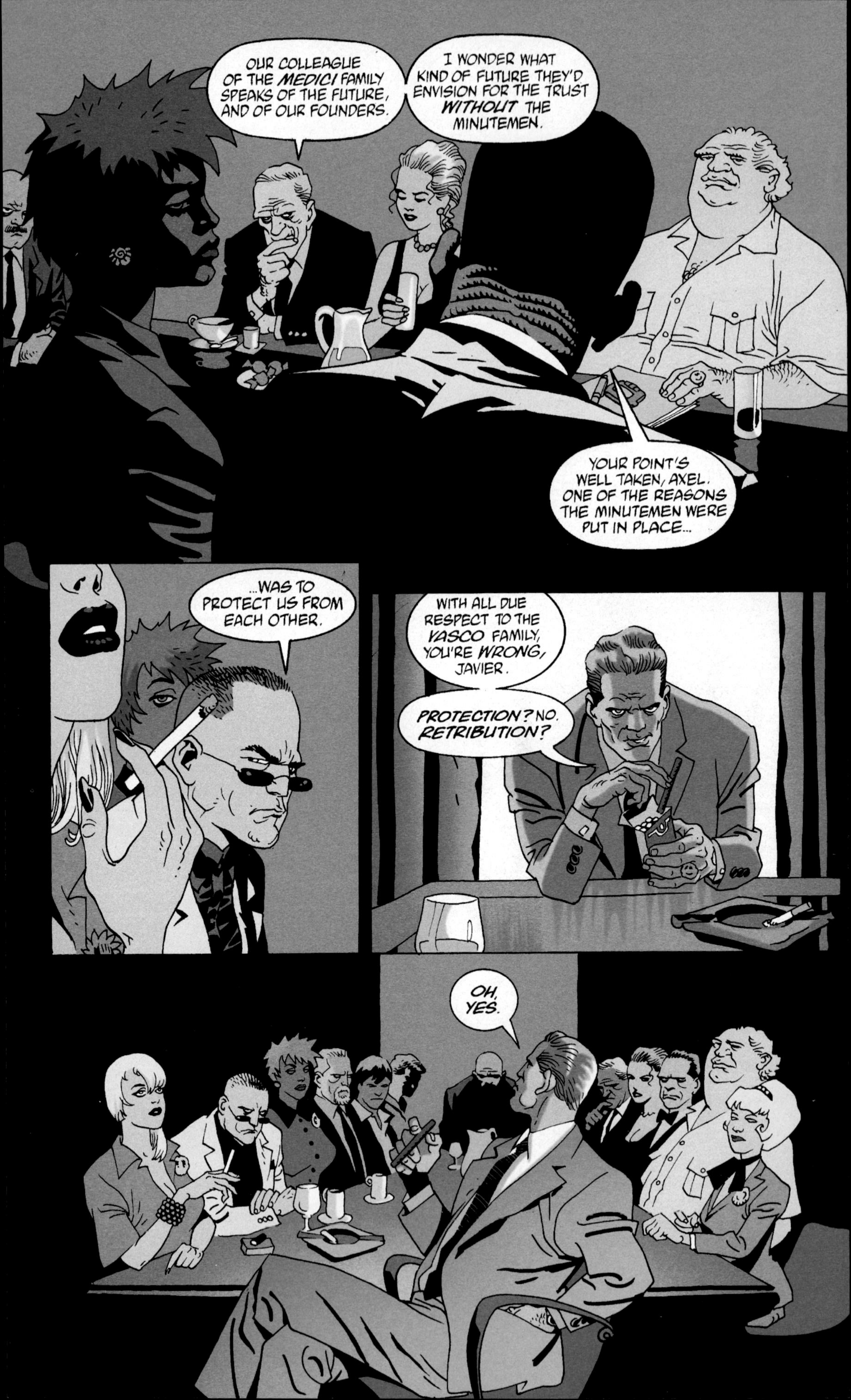
OUR COLLEAGUE OF THE MEDICI FAMILY SPEAKS OF THE FUTURE, AND OF OUR FOUNDERS.
I WONDER WHAT KIND OF FUTURE THEY'D ENVISION FOR THE TRUST WITHOUT THE MINUTEMEN.
YOUR POINT'S WELL TAKEN, AXEL. ONE OF THE REASONS THE MINUTEMEN WERE PUT IN PLACE...
...WAS TO PROTECT US FROM EACH OTHER.
WITH ALL DUE RESPECT TO THE VASCO FAMILY, YOU'RE WRONG, JAVIER.
PROTECTION? NO. RETRIBUTION?
OH, YES.

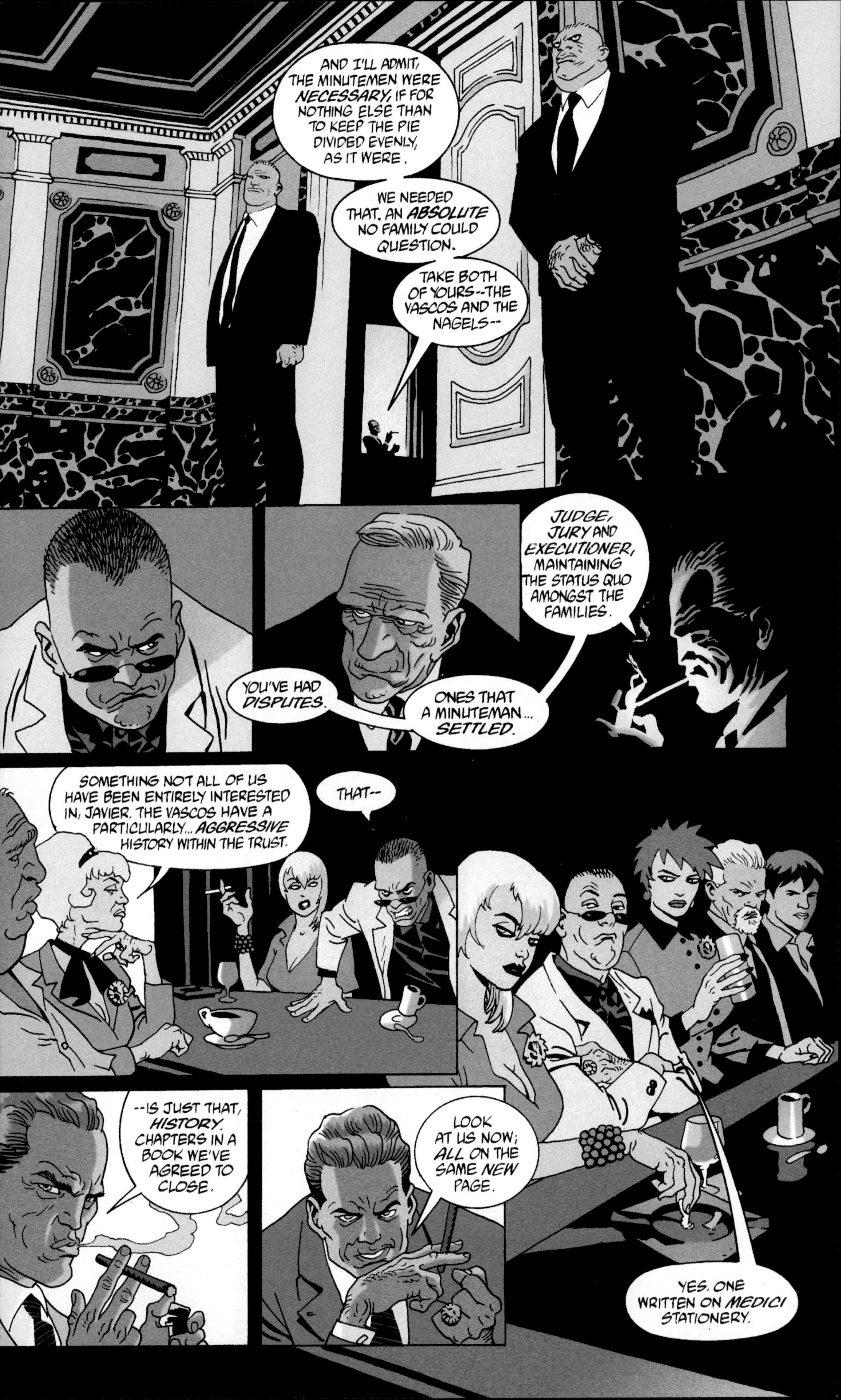
AND I'LL ADMIT, THE MINUTEMEN WERE NECESSARY, IF FOR NOTHING ELSE THAN TO KEEP THE PIE DIVIDED EVENLY, AS IT WERE.
WE NEEDED THAT. AN ABSOLUTE NO FAMILY COULD QUESTION.
TAKE BOTH OF YOURS--THE VASCOS AND THE NAGELS--
YOU'VE HAD DISPUTES.
ONES THAT A MINUTEMAN... SETTLED.
JUDGE, JURY AND EXECUTIONER, MAINTAINING THE STATUS QUO AMONGST THE FAMILIES.
SOMETHING NOT ALL OF US HAVE BEEN ENTIRELY INTERESTED IN, JAVIER. THE VASCOS HAVE A PARTICULARLY... AGGRESSIVE HISTORY WITHIN THE TRUST.
THAT--
--IS JUST THAT, HISTORY. CHAPTERS IN A BOOK WE'VE AGREED TO CLOSE.
LOOK AT US NOW; ALL ON THE SAME NEW PAGE.
YES. ONE WRITTEN ON MEDICI STATIONERY.

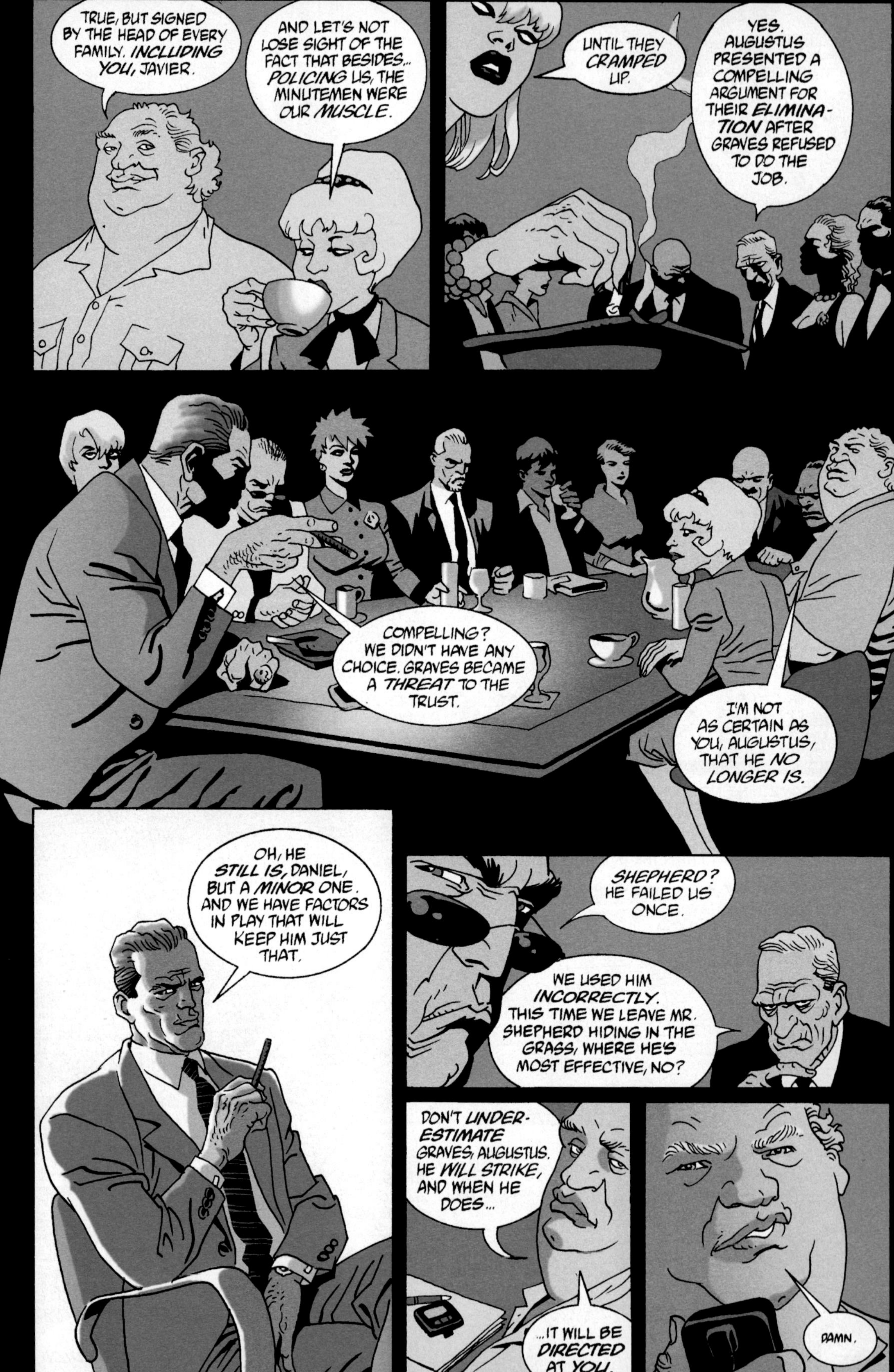
TRUE, BUT SIGNED BY THE HEAD OF EVERY FAMILY. INCLUDING YOU, JAVIER.
AND LET'S NOT LOSE SIGHT OF THE FACT THAT BESIDES... POLICING US, THE MINUTEMEN WERE OUR MUSCLE.
UNTIL THEY CRAMPED UP.
YES. AUGUSTUS PRESENTED A COMPELLING ARGUMENT FOR THEIR ELIMINATION AFTER GRAVES REFUSED TO DO THE JOB.
COMPELLING? WE DIDN'T HAVE ANY CHOICE. GRAVES BECAME A THREAT TO THE TRUST.
I'M NOT AS CERTAIN AS YOU, AUGUSTUS, THAT HE NO LONGER IS.
OH, HE STILL IS, DANIEL, BUT A MINOR ONE. AND WE HAVE FACTORS IN PLAY THAT WILL KEEP HIM JUST THAT.
SHEPHERD? HE FAILED US ONCE.
WE USED HIM INCORRECTLY. THIS TIME WE LEAVE MR. SHEPHERD HIDING IN THE GRASS, WHERE HE'S MOST EFFECTIVE, NO?
DON'T UNDER-ESTIMATE GRAVES, AUGUSTUS. HE WILL STRIKE, AND WHEN HE DOES...
...IT WILL BE DIRECTED AT YOU.
DAMN.

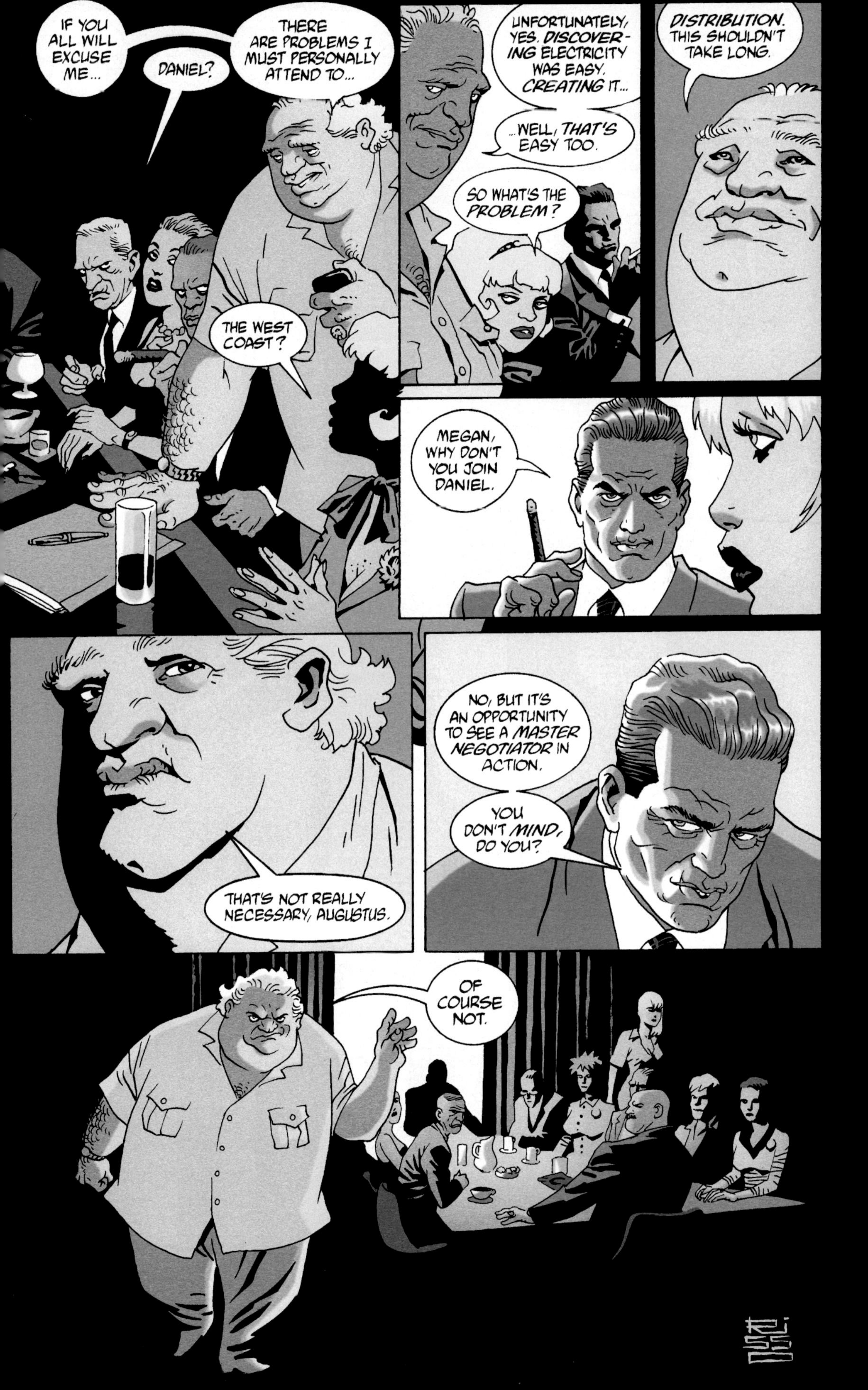
IF YOU ALL WILL EXCUSE ME...
THERE ARE PROBLEMS I MUST PERSONALLY ATTEND TO...
DANIEL?
THE WEST COAST?
UNFORTUNATELY, YES. DISCOVERING ELECTRICITY WAS EASY. CREATING IT...
...WELL, THAT'S EASY TOO.
SO WHAT'S THE PROBLEM?
DISTRIBUTION. THIS SHOULDN'T TAKE LONG.
MEGAN, WHY DON'T YOU JOIN DANIEL.
THAT'S NOT REALLY NECESSARY, AUGUSTUS.
NO, BUT IT'S AN OPPORTUNITY TO SEE A MASTER NEGOTIATOR IN ACTION.
YOU DON'T MIND, DO YOU?
OF COURSE NOT.

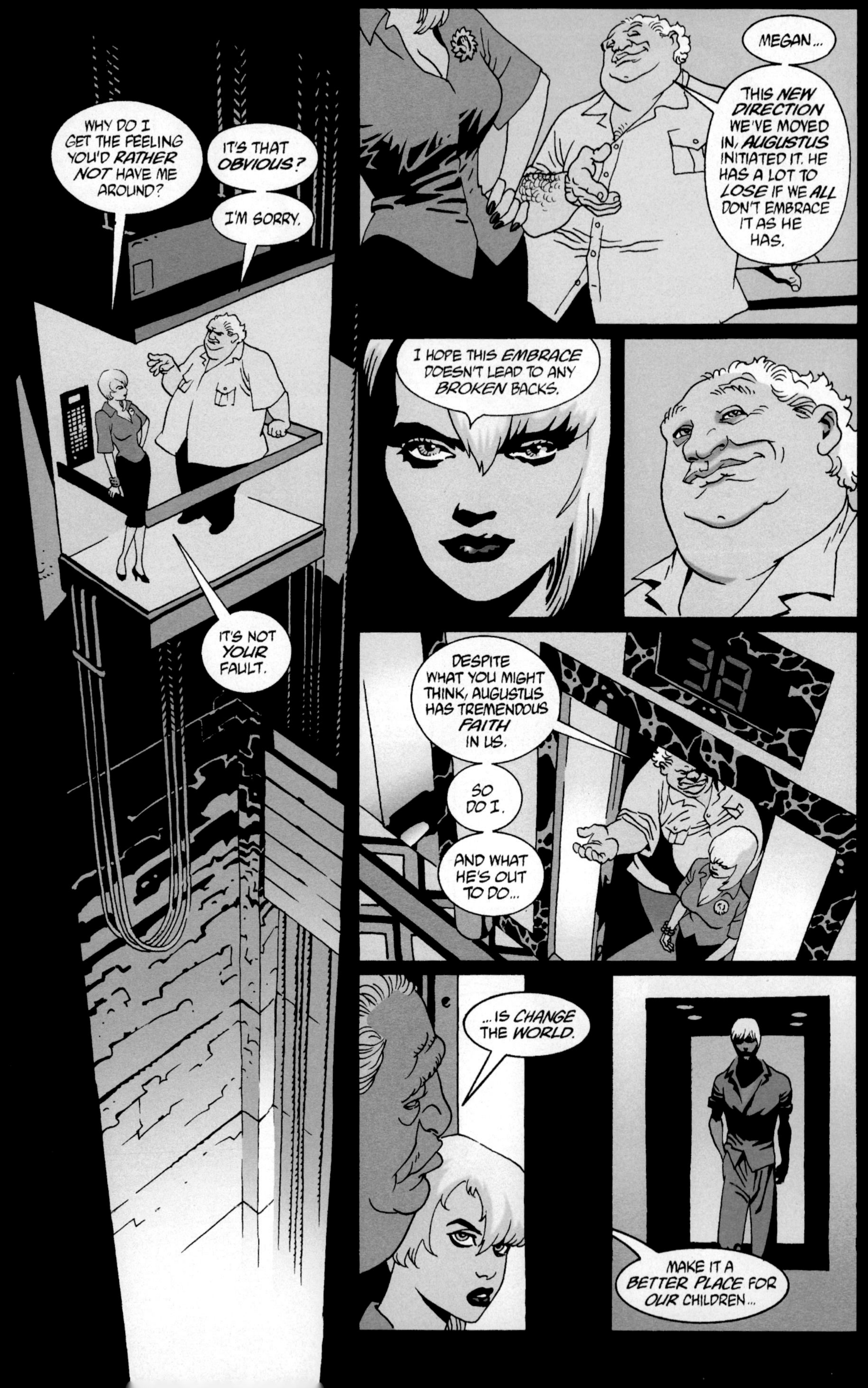
WHY DO I GET THE FEELING YOU'D RATHER NOT HAVE ME AROUND?
IT'S THAT OBVIOUS?
I'M SORRY.
IT'S NOT YOUR FAULT.
MEGAN...
THIS NEW DIRECTION WE'VE MOVED IN, AUGUSTUS INITIATED IT. HE HAS A LOT TO LOSE IF WE ALL DON'T EMBRACE IT AS HE HAS.
I HOPE THIS EMBRACE DOESN'T LEAD TO ANY BROKEN BACKS.
DESPITE WHAT YOU MIGHT THINK, AUGUSTUS HAS TREMENDOUS FAITH IN US.
SO DO I.
AND WHAT HE'S OUT TO DO...
...IS CHANGE THE WORLD.
MAKE IT A BETTER PLACE FOR OUR CHILDREN...

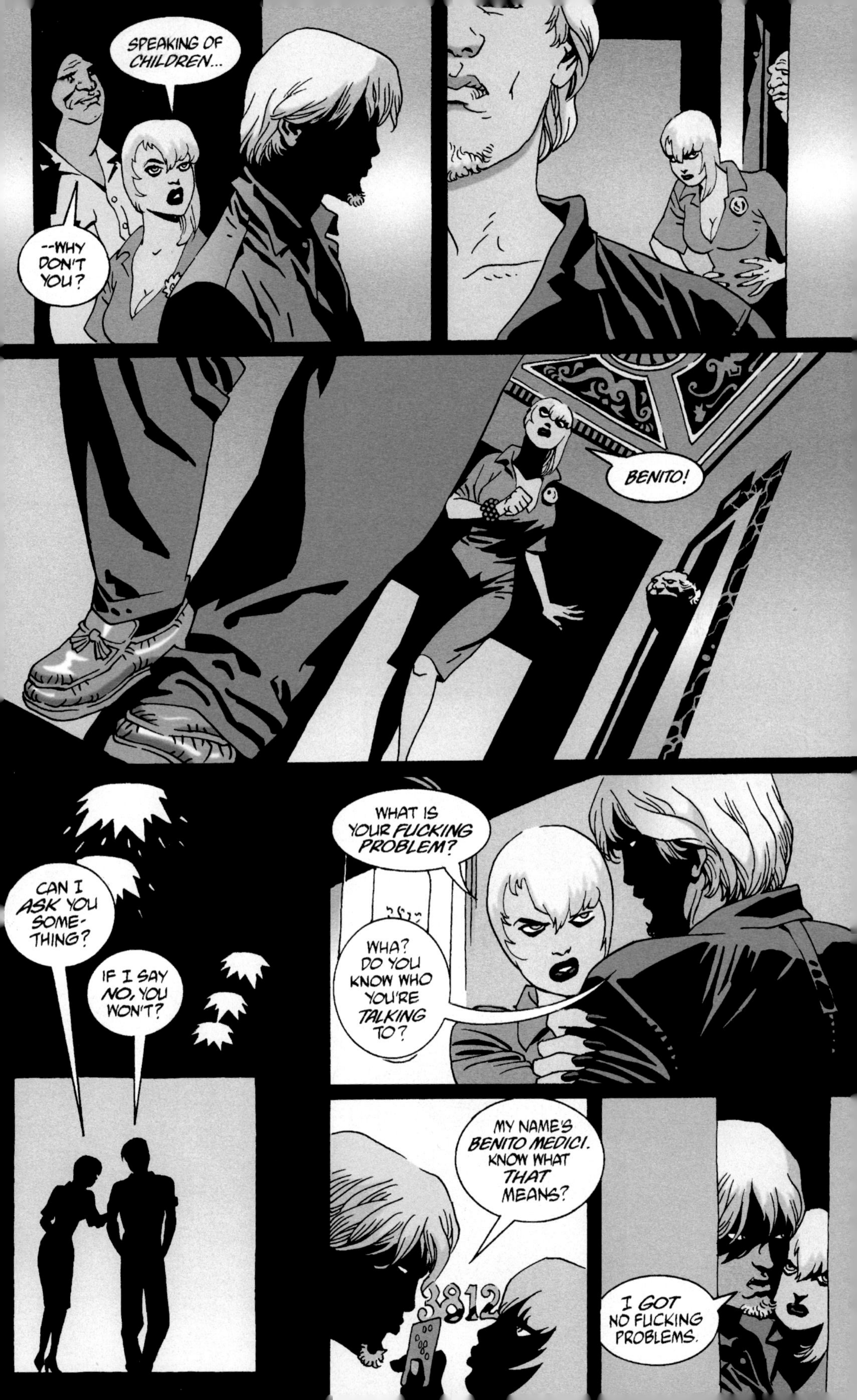
SPEAKING OF CHILDREN...
--WHY DON'T YOU?
BENITO!
CAN I ASK YOU SOME-THING?
IF I SAY NO, YOU WON'T?
WHAT IS YOUR FUCKING PROBLEM?
WHA? DO YOU KNOW WHO YOU'RE TALKING TO?
MY NAME'S BENITO MEDICI. KNOW WHAT THAT MEANS?
3812
I GOT NO FUCKING PROBLEMS.

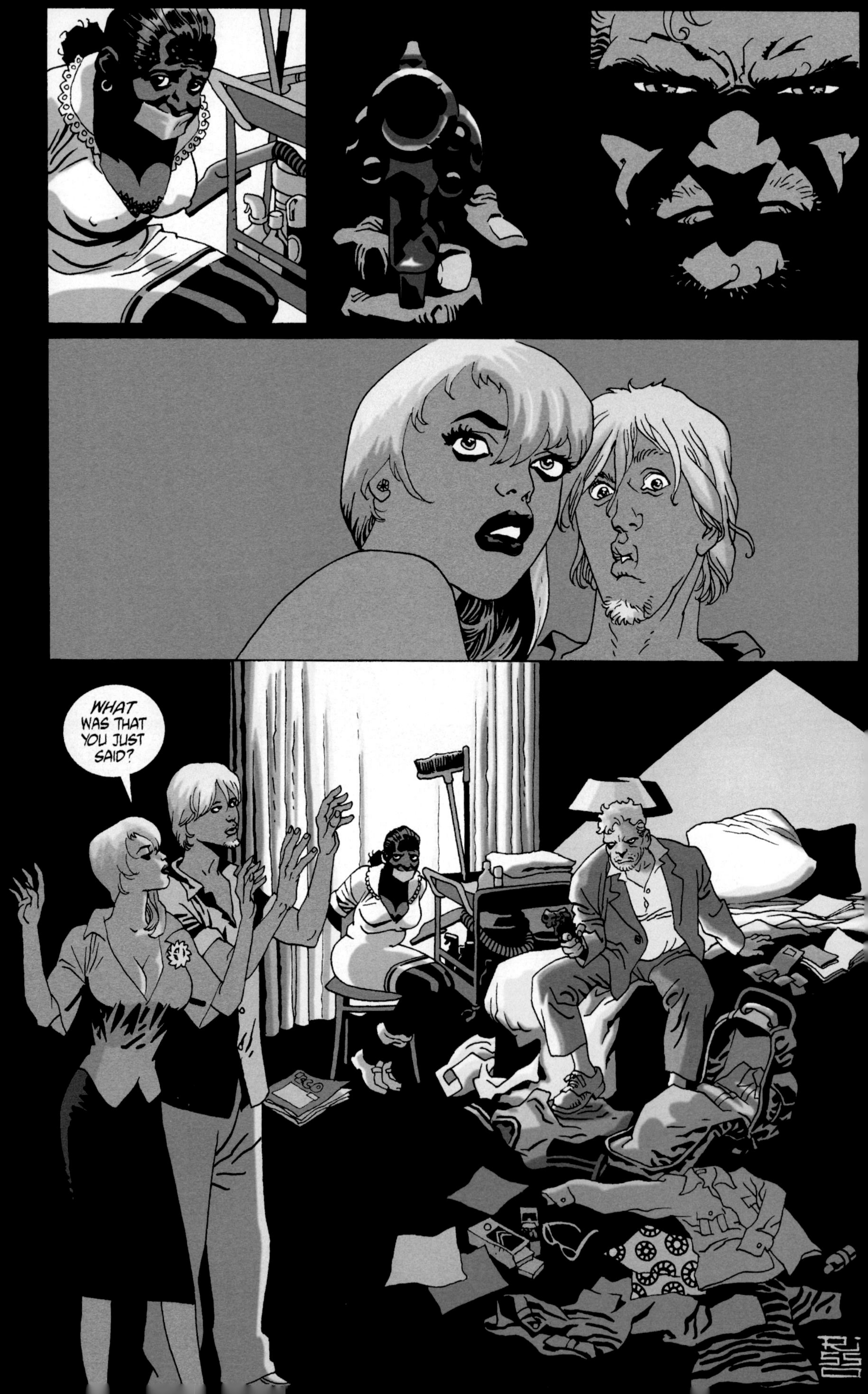
WHAT WAS THAT YOU JUST SAID?

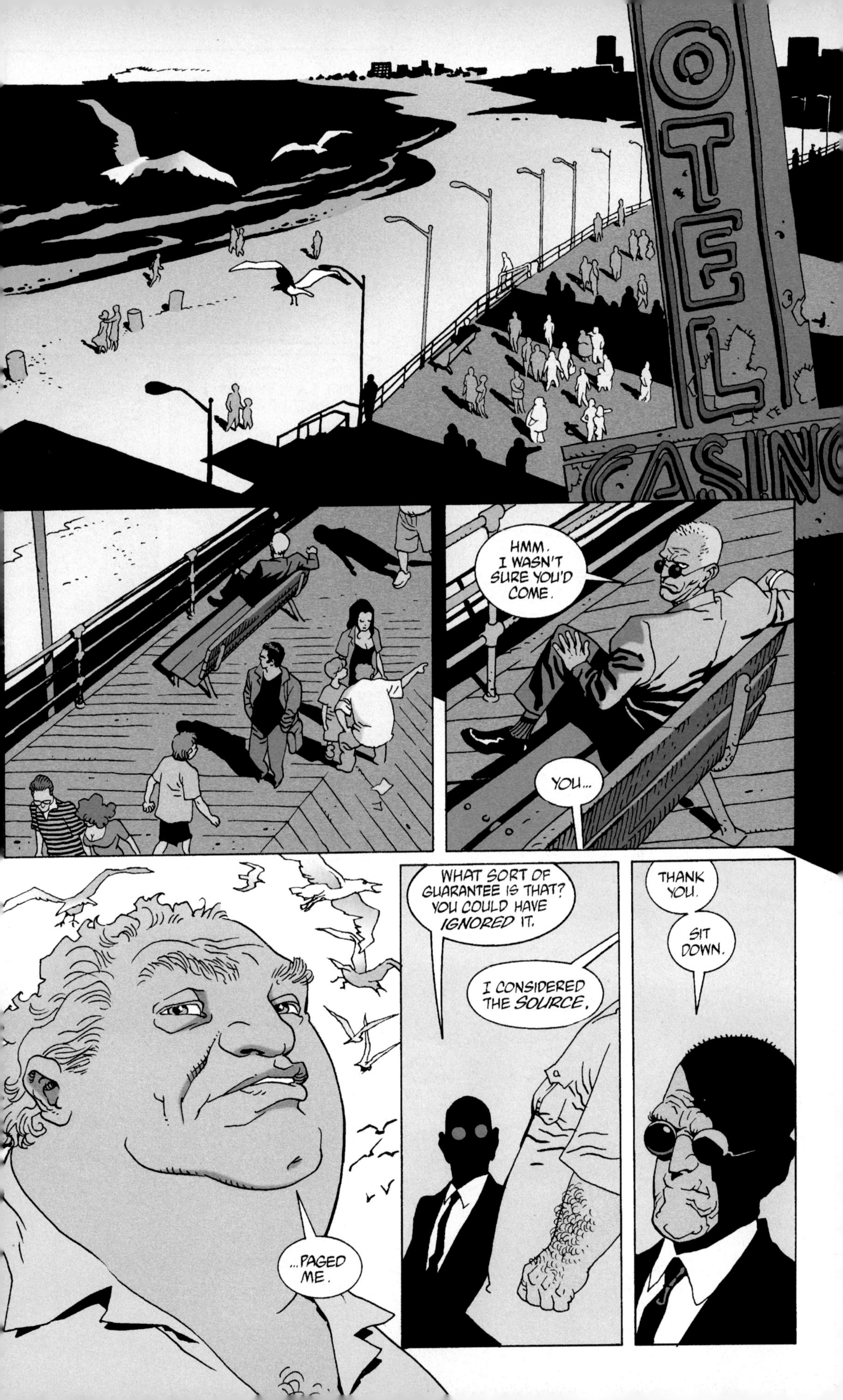
OTEL
CASINO
HMM. I WASN'T SURE YOU'D COME.
YOU...
...PAGED ME.
WHAT SORT OF GUARANTEE IS THAT? YOU COULD HAVE *IGNORED* IT.
I CONSIDERED THE *SOURCE*.
THANK YOU.
SIT DOWN.

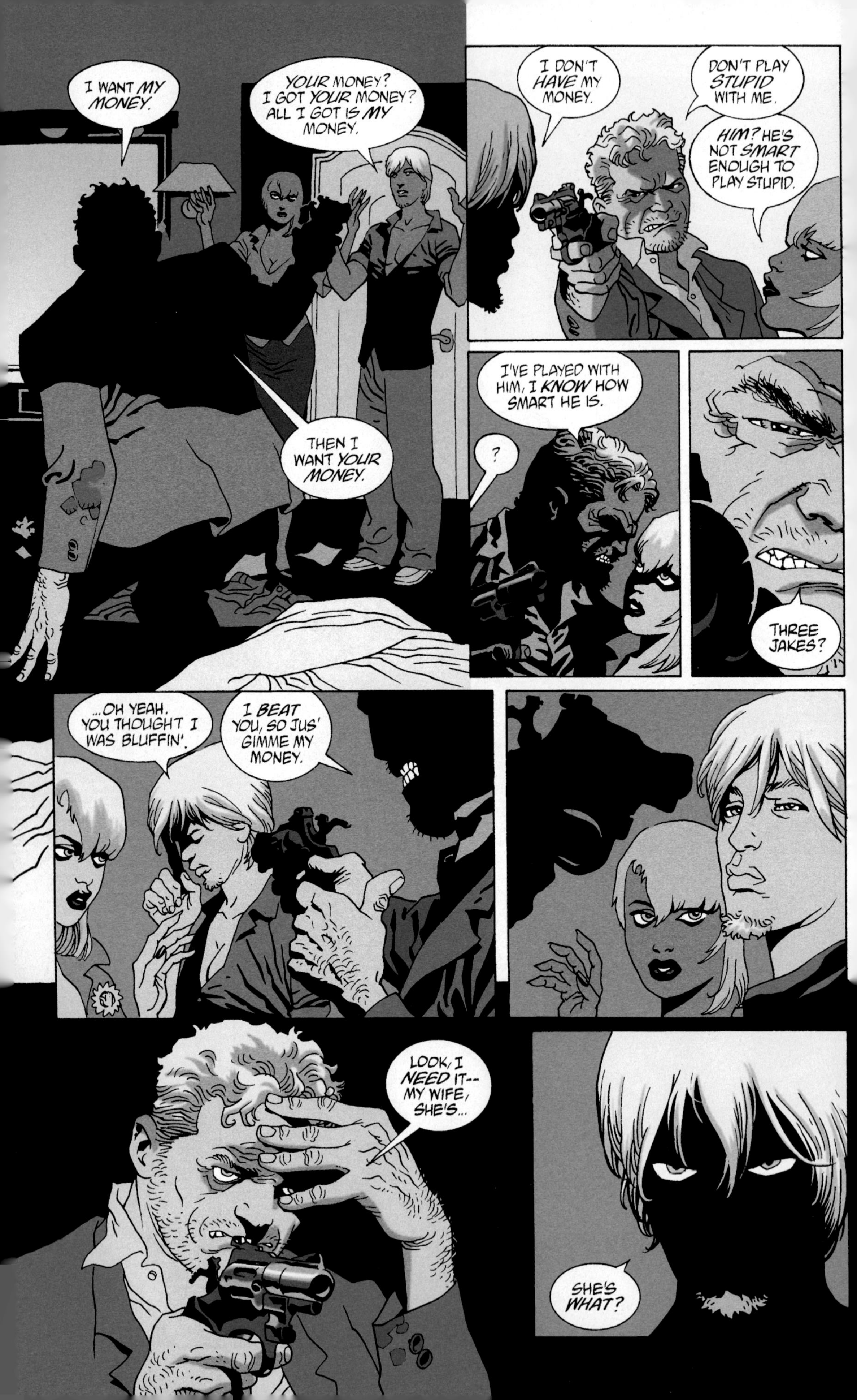

I WANT MY MONEY.
YOUR MONEY? I GOT YOUR MONEY? ALL I GOT IS MY MONEY.
THEN I WANT YOUR MONEY.
I DON'T HAVE MY MONEY.
DON'T PLAY STUPID WITH ME.
HIM? HE'S NOT SMART ENOUGH TO PLAY STUPID.
I'VE PLAYED WITH HIM, I KNOW HOW SMART HE IS.
?
THREE JAKES?
...OH YEAH. YOU THOUGHT I WAS BLUFFIN'.
I BEAT YOU, SO JUS' GIMME MY MONEY.
LOOK, I NEED IT-- MY WIFE, SHE'S...
SHE'S WHAT?

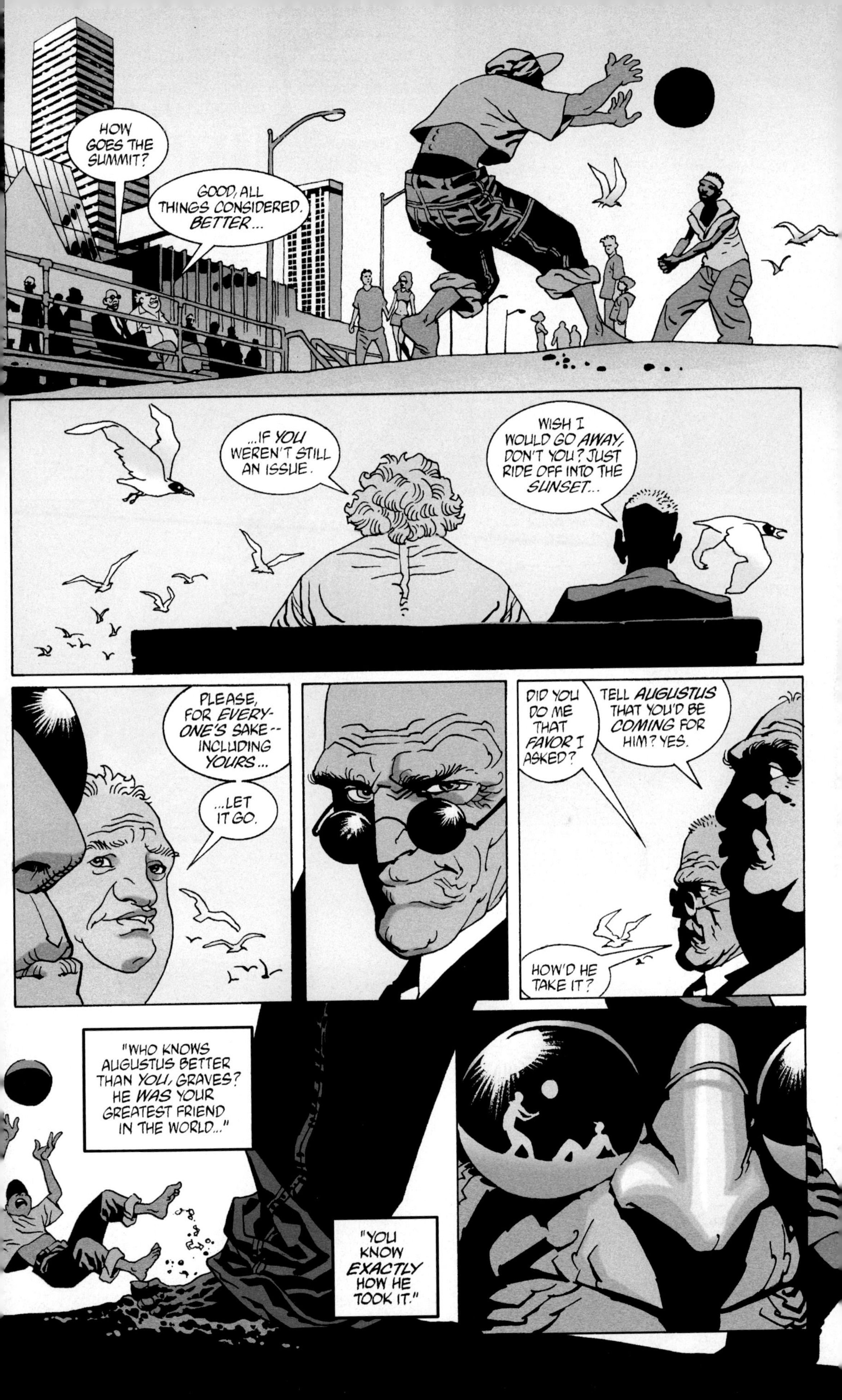
HOW GOES THE SUMMIT?
GOOD, ALL THINGS CONSIDERED. BETTER...
...IF YOU WEREN'T STILL AN ISSUE.
WISH I WOULD GO AWAY, DON'T YOU? JUST RIDE OFF INTO THE SUNSET...
PLEASE, FOR EVERYONE'S SAKE-- INCLUDING YOURS...
...LET IT GO.
DID YOU DO ME THAT FAVOR I ASKED?
TELL AUGUSTUS THAT YOU'D BE COMING FOR HIM? YES.
HOW'D HE TAKE IT?
"WHO KNOWS AUGUSTUS BETTER THAN YOU, GRAVES? HE WAS YOUR GREATEST FRIEND IN THE WORLD..."
"YOU KNOW EXACTLY HOW HE TOOK IT."

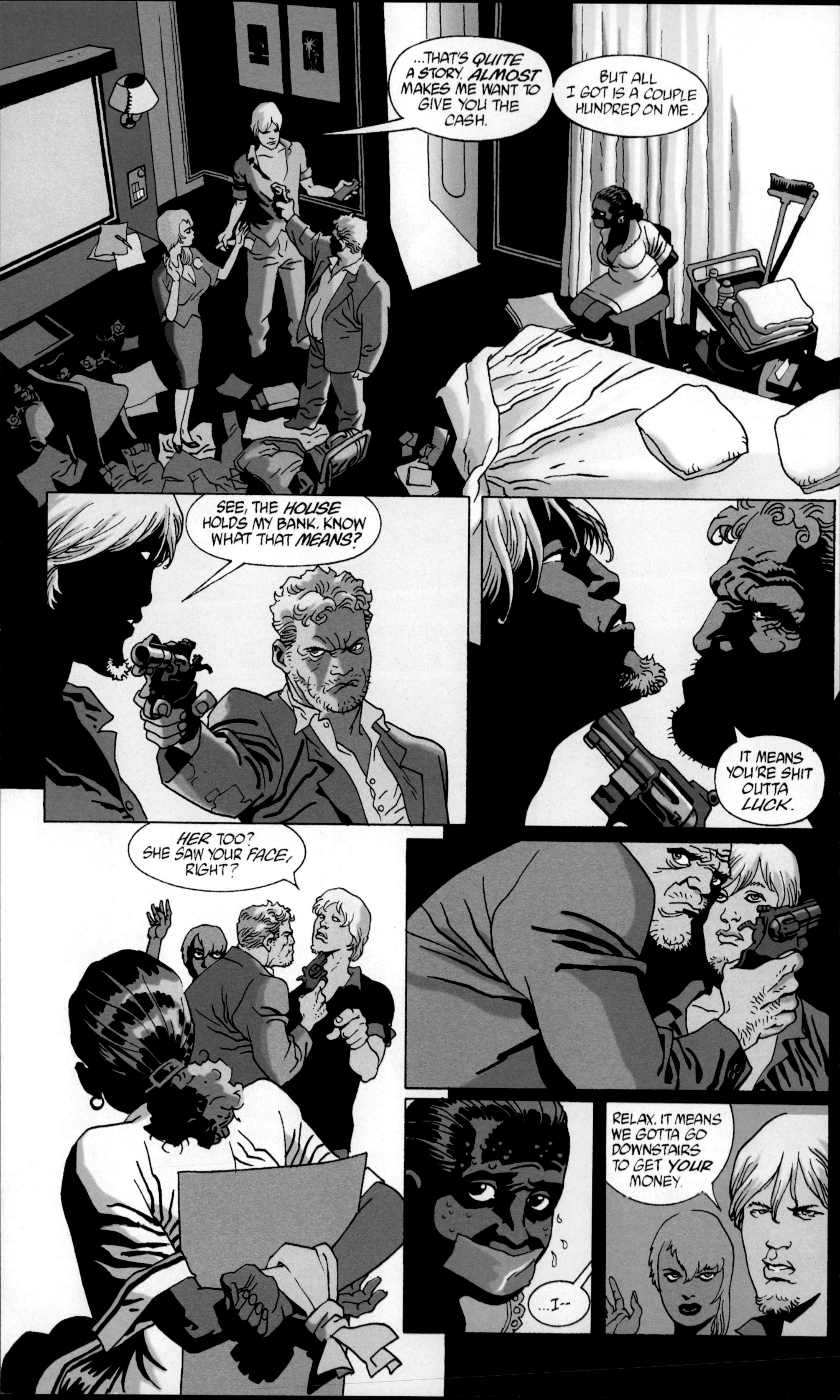
...THAT'S QUITE A STORY. ALMOST MAKES ME WANT TO GIVE YOU THE CASH.
BUT ALL I GOT IS A COUPLE HUNDRED ON ME.
SEE, THE HOUSE HOLDS MY BANK. KNOW WHAT THAT MEANS?
IT MEANS YOU'RE SHIT OUTTA LUCK.
HER TOO? SHE SAW YOUR FACE, RIGHT?
...I--
RELAX. IT MEANS WE GOTTA GO DOWNSTAIRS TO GET YOUR MONEY.

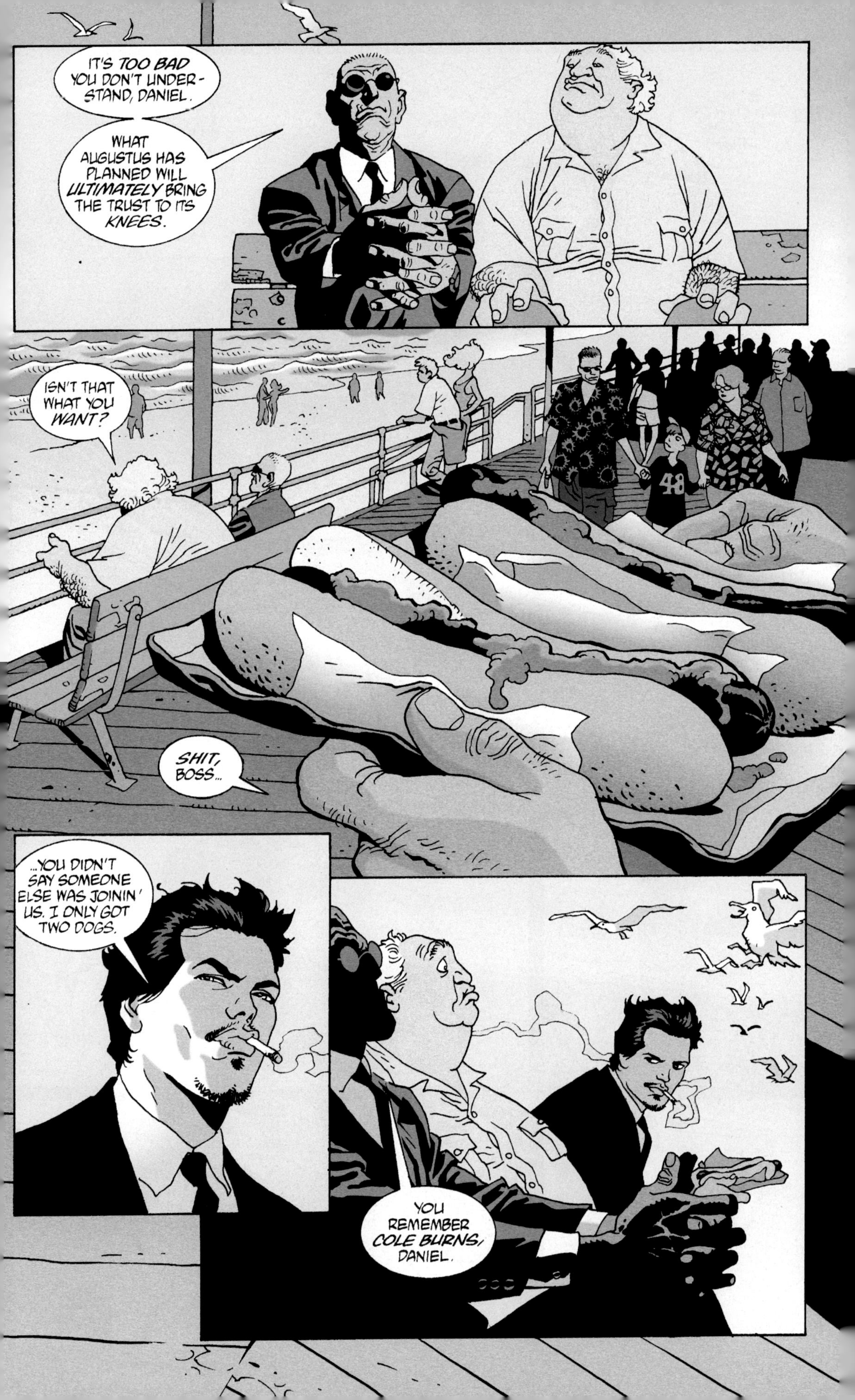
IT'S TOO BAD YOU DON'T UNDERSTAND, DANIEL.
WHAT AUGUSTUS HAS PLANNED WILL ULTIMATELY BRING THE TRUST TO ITS KNEES.
ISN'T THAT WHAT YOU WANT?
SHIT, BOSS...
...YOU DIDN'T SAY SOMEONE ELSE WAS JOININ' US. I ONLY GOT TWO DOGS.
YOU REMEMBER COLE BURNS, DANIEL.

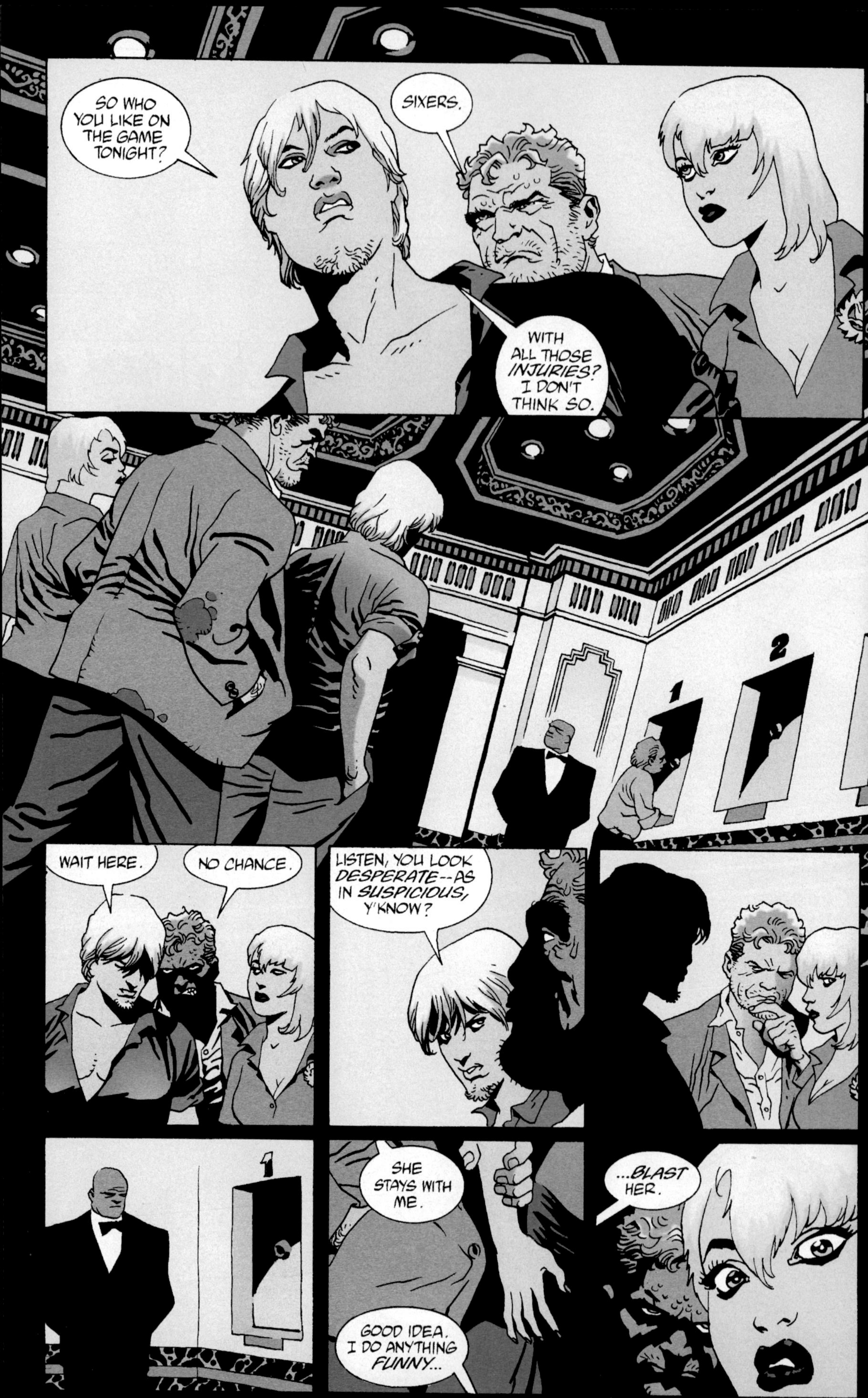
SO WHO YOU LIKE ON THE GAME TONIGHT?
SIXERS.
WITH ALL THOSE INJURIES? I DON'T THINK SO.
1
2
WAIT HERE.
NO CHANCE.
LISTEN, YOU LOOK DESPERATE--AS IN SUSPICIOUS, Y'KNOW?
1
SHE STAYS WITH ME.
GOOD IDEA. I DO ANYTHING FUNNY...
...BLAST HER.

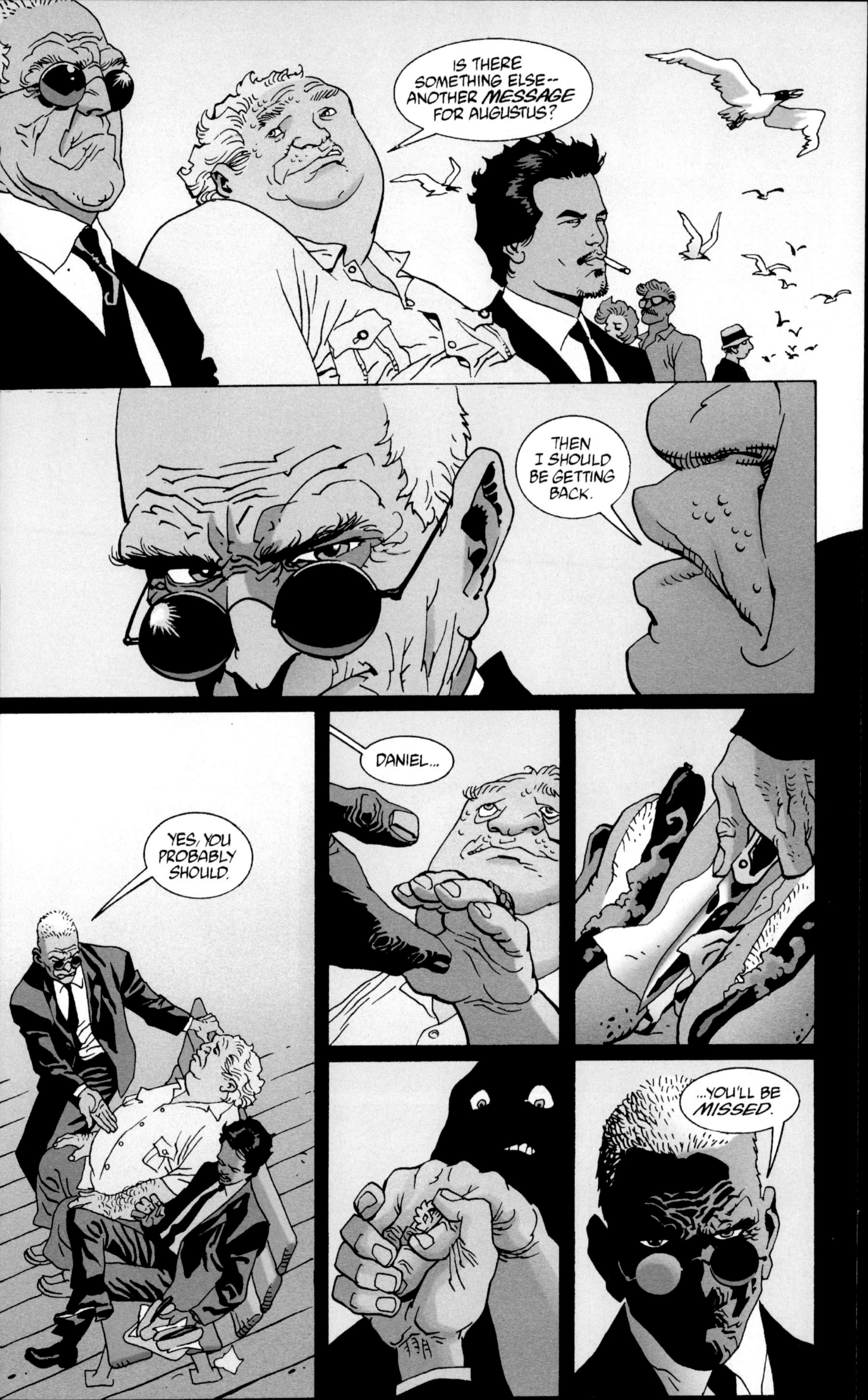
IS THERE SOMETHING ELSE-- ANOTHER MESSAGE FOR AUGUSTUS?
THEN I SHOULD BE GETTING BACK.
YES, YOU PROBABLY SHOULD.
DANIEL...
...YOU'LL BE MISSED.

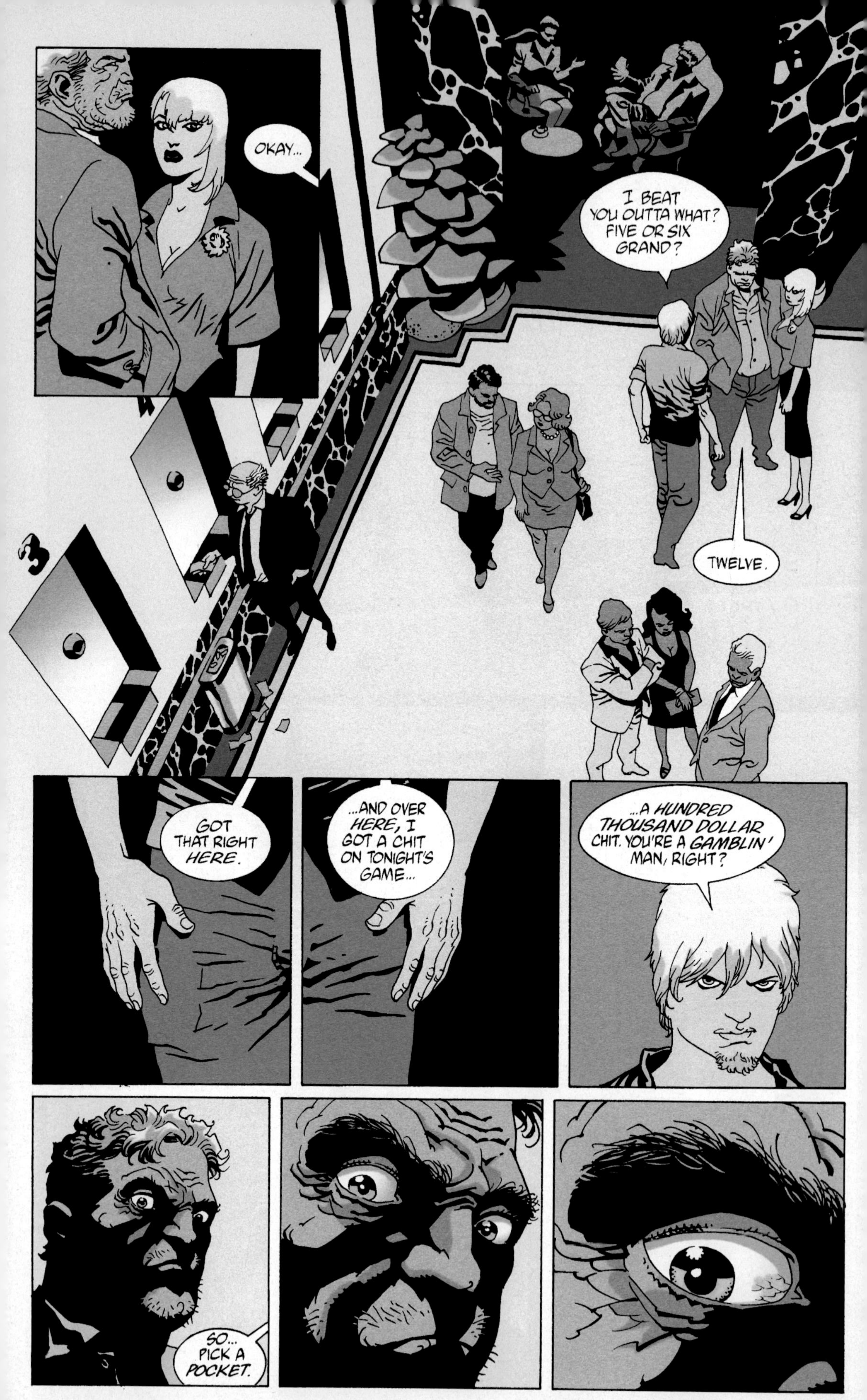
OKAY...
I BEAT YOU OUTTA WHAT? FIVE OR SIX GRAND?
TWELVE.
3
GOT THAT RIGHT HERE.
...AND OVER HERE, I GOT A CHIT ON TONIGHT'S GAME...
...A HUNDRED THOUSAND DOLLAR CHIT. YOU'RE A GAMBLIN' MAN, RIGHT?
SO... PICK A POCKET.

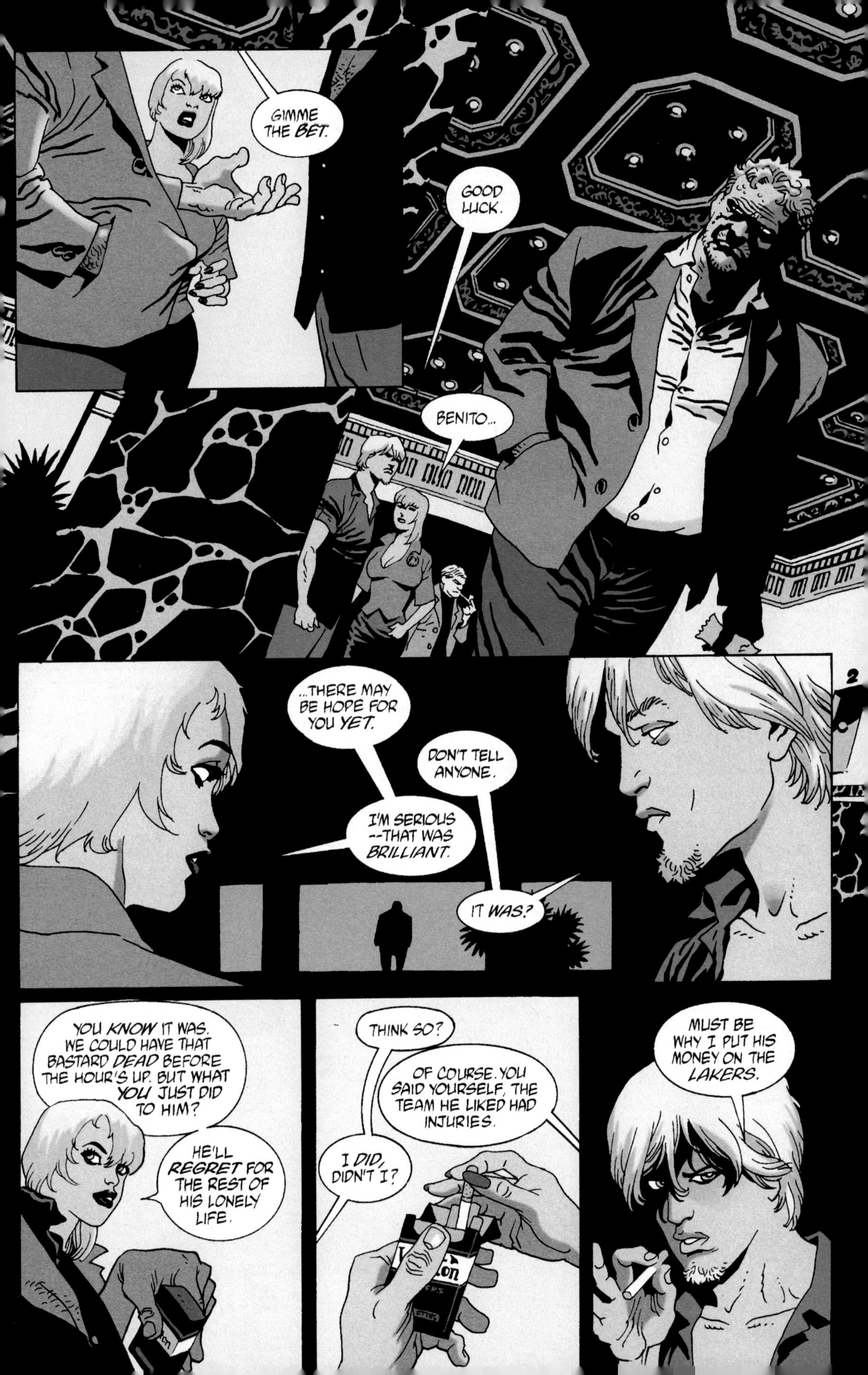
GIMME THE BET.
GOOD LUCK.
BENITO...
...THERE MAY BE HOPE FOR YOU YET.
DON'T TELL ANYONE.
I'M SERIOUS --THAT WAS BRILLIANT.
IT WAS?
YOU KNOW IT WAS. WE COULD HAVE THAT BASTARD DEAD BEFORE THE HOUR'S UP. BUT WHAT YOU JUST DID TO HIM?
HE'LL REGRET FOR THE REST OF HIS LONELY LIFE.
THINK SO?
OF COURSE. YOU SAID YOURSELF, THE TEAM HE LIKED HAD INJURIES.
I DID, DIDN'T I?
MUST BE WHY I PUT HIS MONEY ON THE LAKERS.

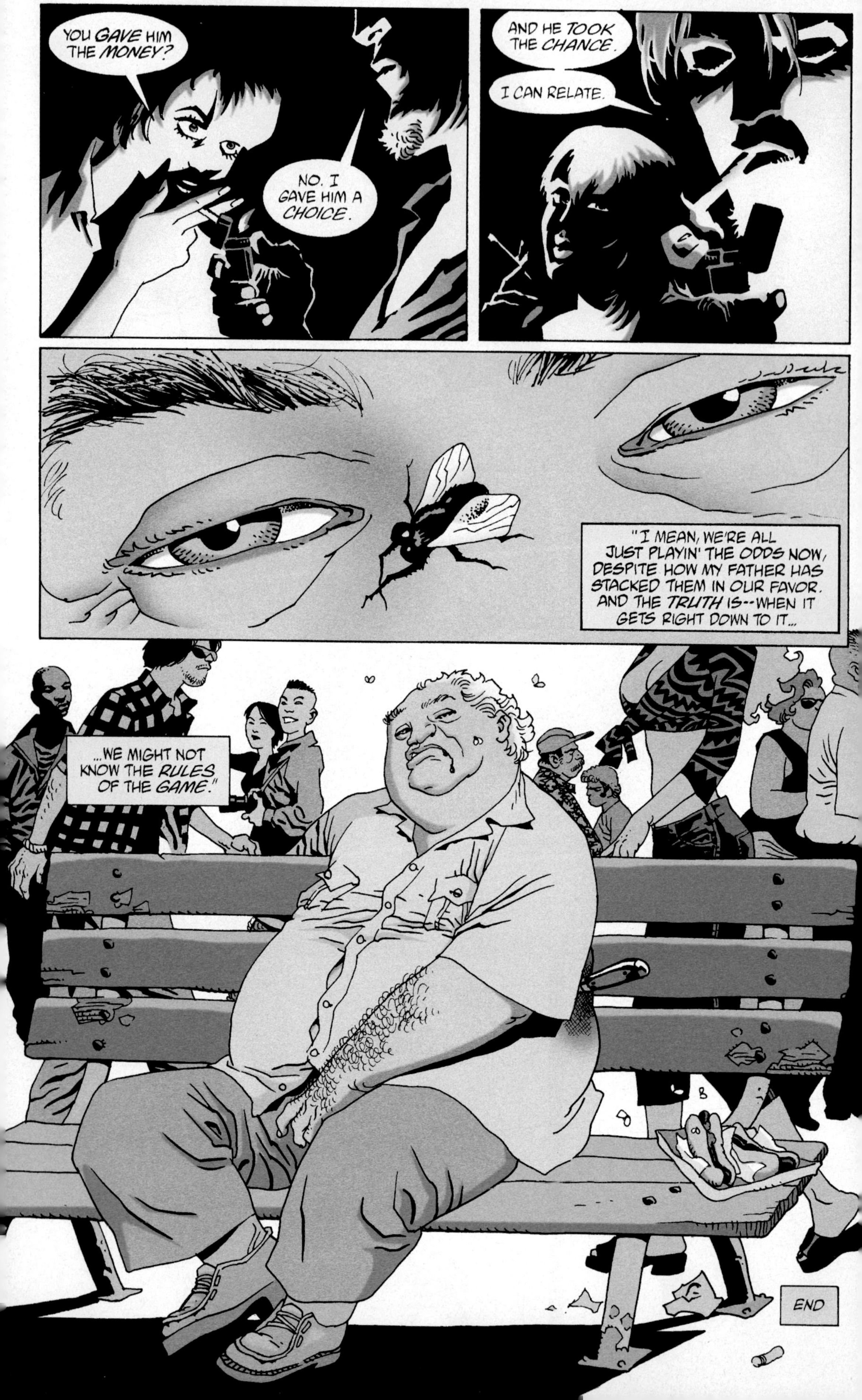
YOU GAVE HIM THE MONEY?
NO. I GAVE HIM A CHOICE.
AND HE TOOK THE CHANCE.
I CAN RELATE.
"I MEAN, WE'RE ALL JUST PLAYIN' THE ODDS NOW, DESPITE HOW MY FATHER HAS STACKED THEM IN OUR FAVOR. AND THE TRUTH IS--WHEN IT GETS RIGHT DOWN TO IT...
...WE MIGHT NOT KNOW THE RULES OF THE GAME."
END

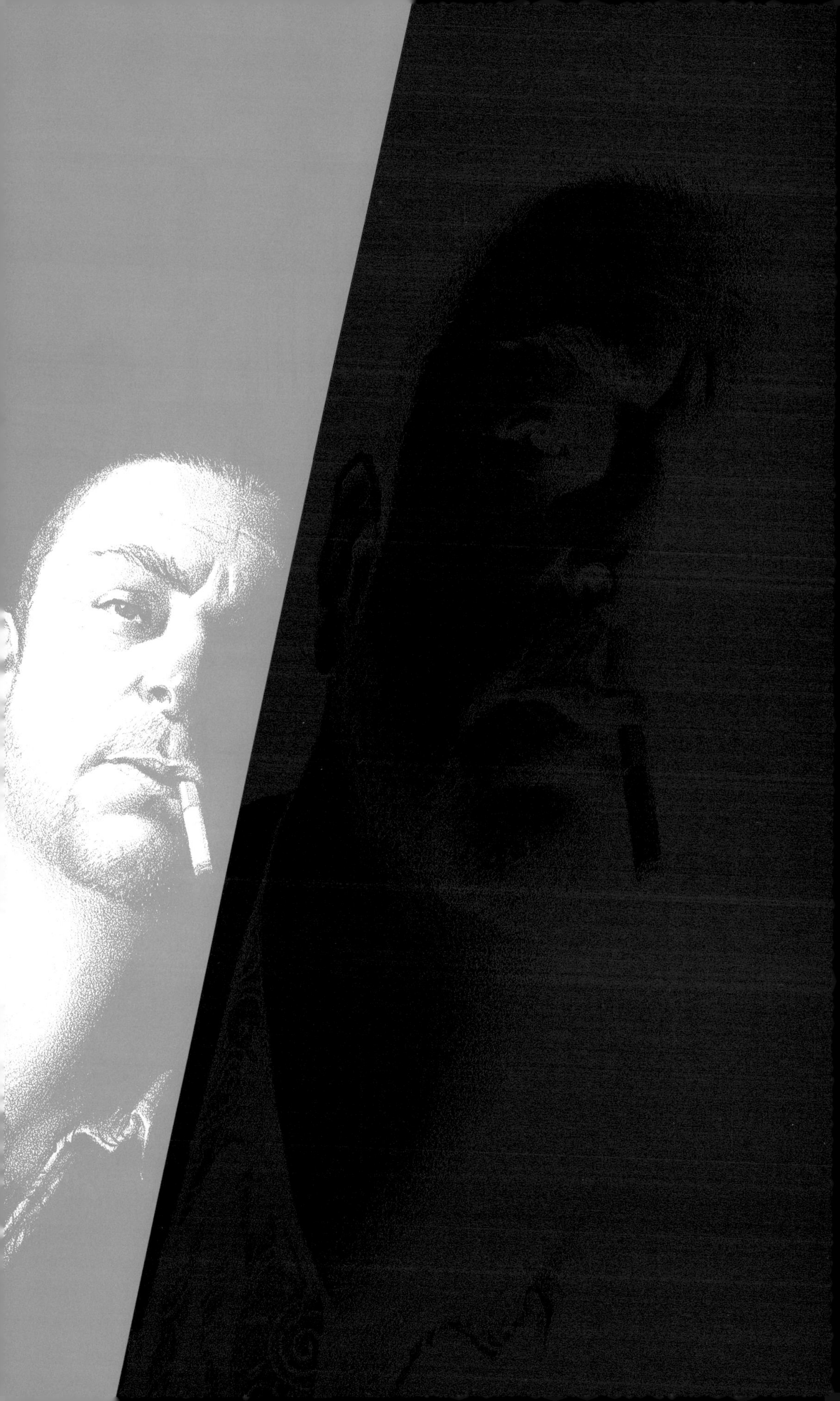

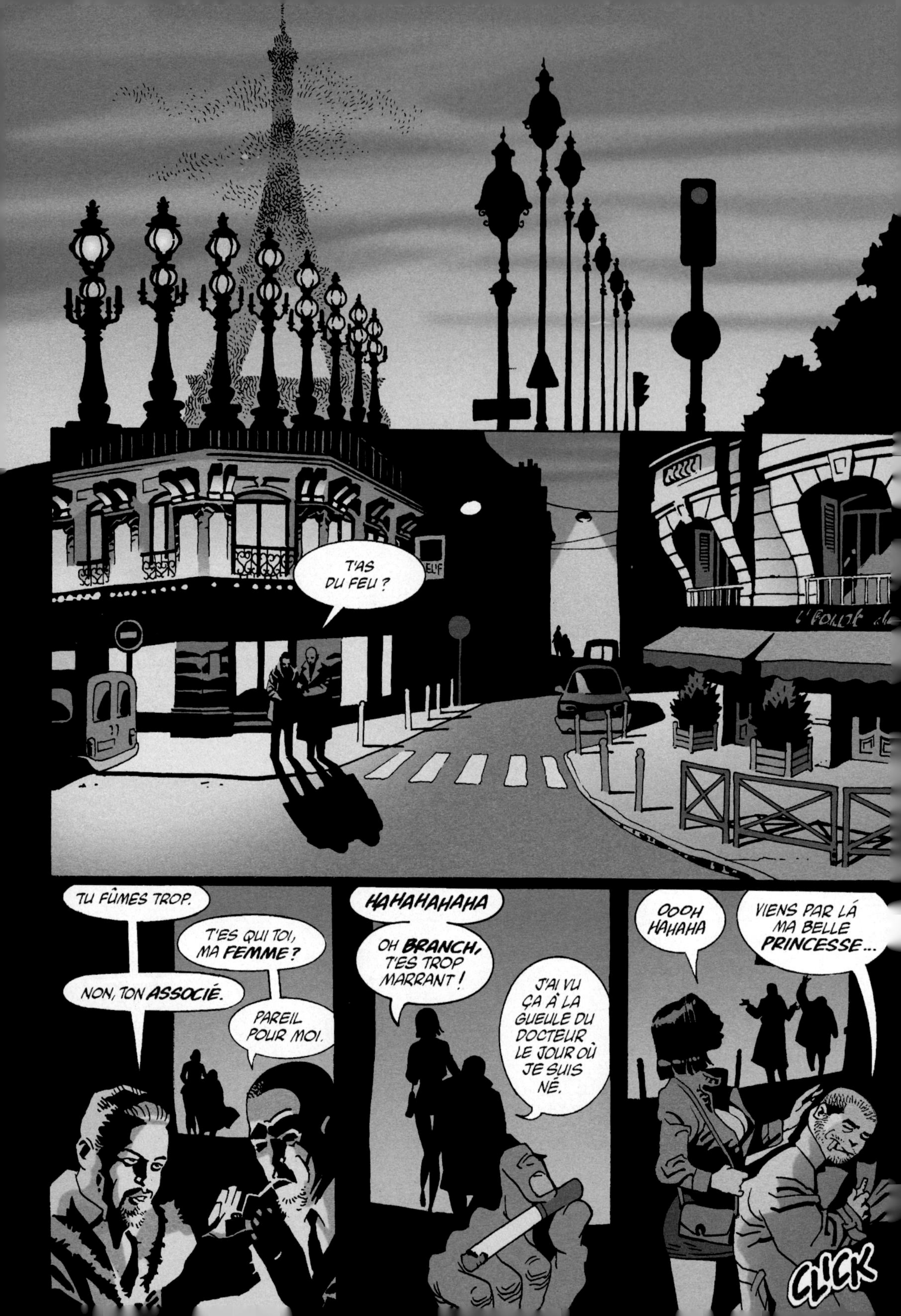

EL'F
T'AS DU FEU ?
TU FÛMES TROP.
T'ES QUI TOI, MA FEMME ?
NON, TON ASSOCIÉ.
PAREIL POUR MOI.
HAHAHAHAHA
OH BRANCH, T'ES TROP MARRANT !
J'AI VU ÇA À LA GUEULE DU DOCTEUR LE JOUR OÙ JE SUIS NÉ.
OOOH HAHAHA
VIENS PAR LÁ MA BELLE PRINCESSE...
CLICK

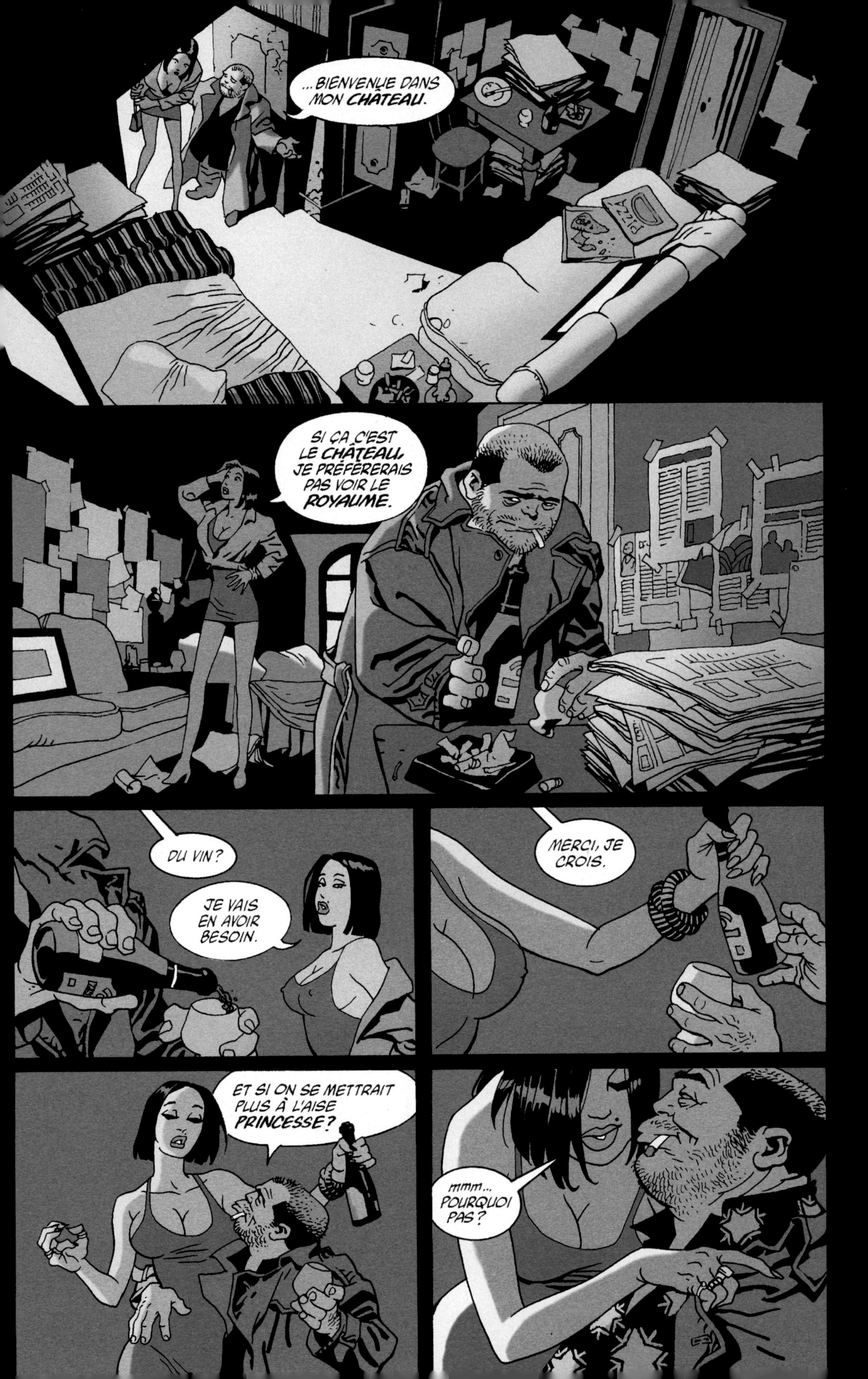
...BIENVENUE DANS MON CHÂTEAU.
SI ÇA C'EST LE CHÂTEAU, JE PRÉFÉRERAIS PAS VOIR LE ROYAUME.
DU VIN?
JE VAIS EN AVOIR BESOIN.
MERCI, JE CROIS.
ET SI ON SE METTRAIT PLUS À L'AISE PRINCESSE?
mmm... POURQUOI PAS?

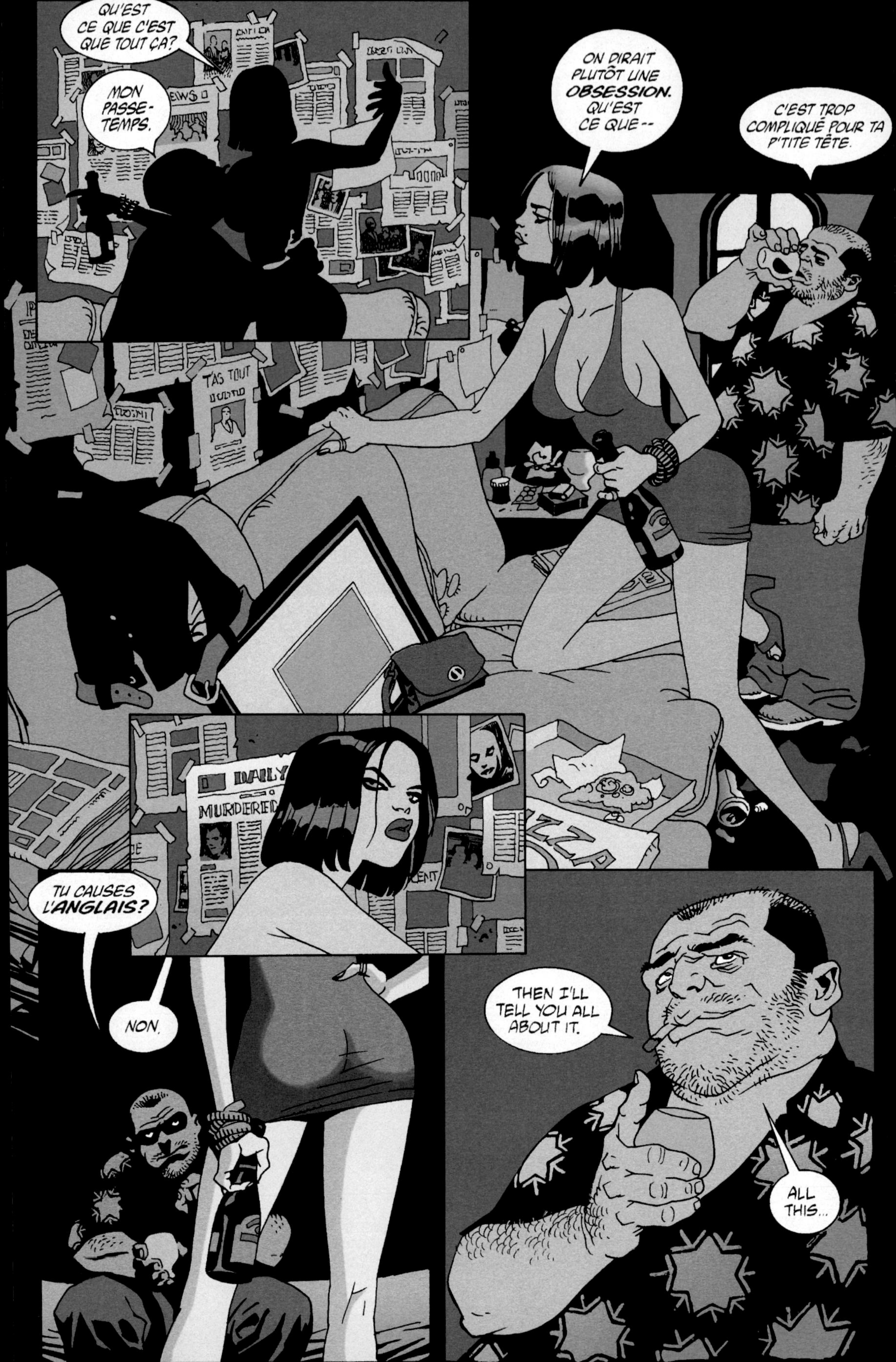
QU'EST CE QUE C'EST QUE TOUT ÇA?
MON PASSE-TEMPS.
ON DIRAIT PLUTÔT UNE OBSESSION. QU'EST CE QUE --
C'EST TROP COMPLIQUÉ POUR TA P'TITE TÊTE.
TU CAUSES L'ANGLAIS?
NON.
THEN I'LL TELL YOU ALL ABOUT IT.
ALL THIS...

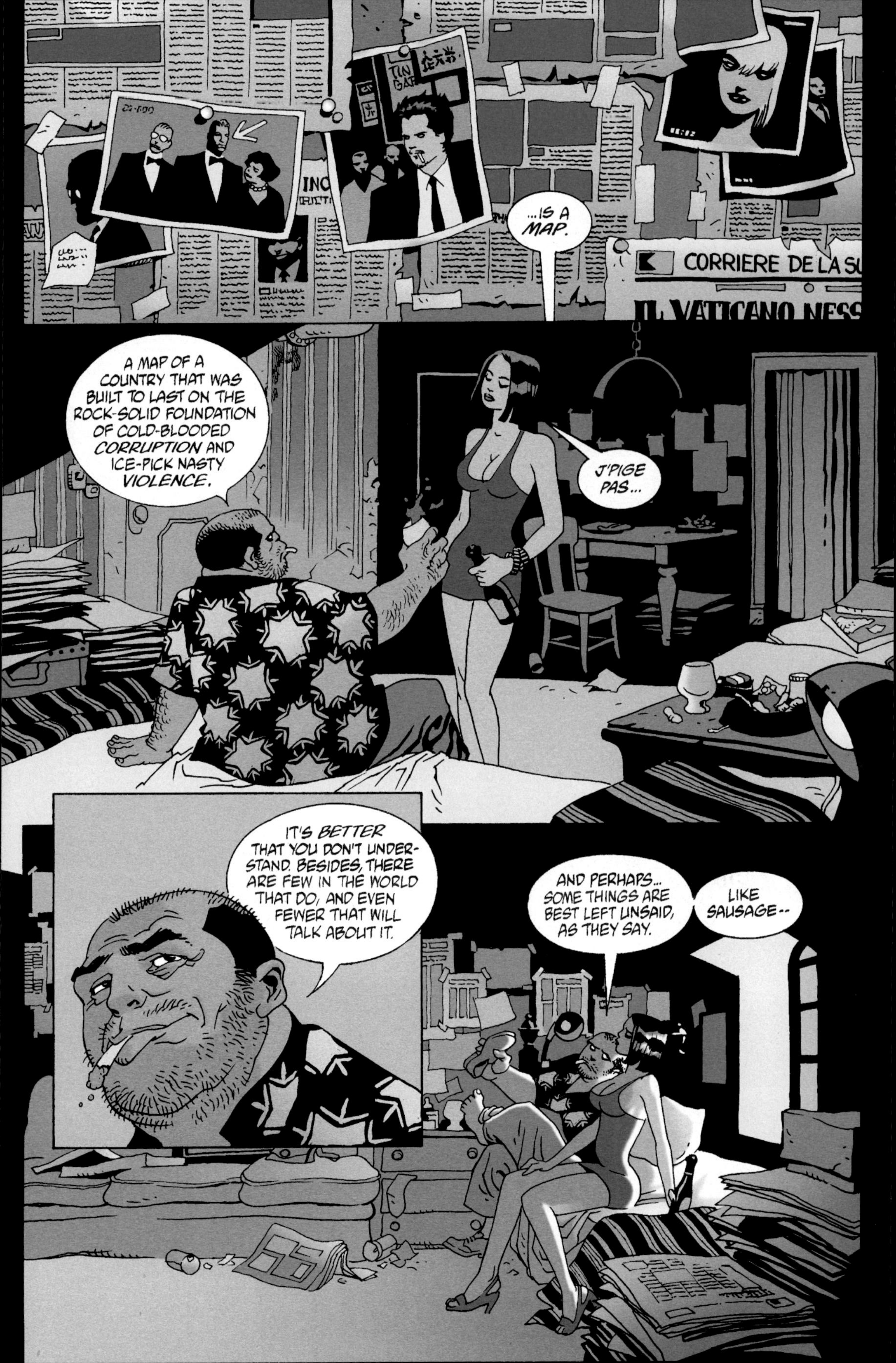

CORRIERE DE LA SU
IL VATICANO NESS
...IS A MAP.
A MAP OF A COUNTRY THAT WAS BUILT TO LAST ON THE ROCK-SOLID FOUNDATION OF COLD-BLOODED CORRUPTION AND ICE-PICK NASTY VIOLENCE.
J'PIGE PAS...
IT'S BETTER THAT YOU DON'T UNDERSTAND. BESIDES, THERE ARE FEW IN THE WORLD THAT DO, AND EVEN FEWER THAT WILL TALK ABOUT IT.
AND PERHAPS... SOME THINGS ARE BEST LEFT UNSAID, AS THEY SAY.
LIKE SAUSAGE--

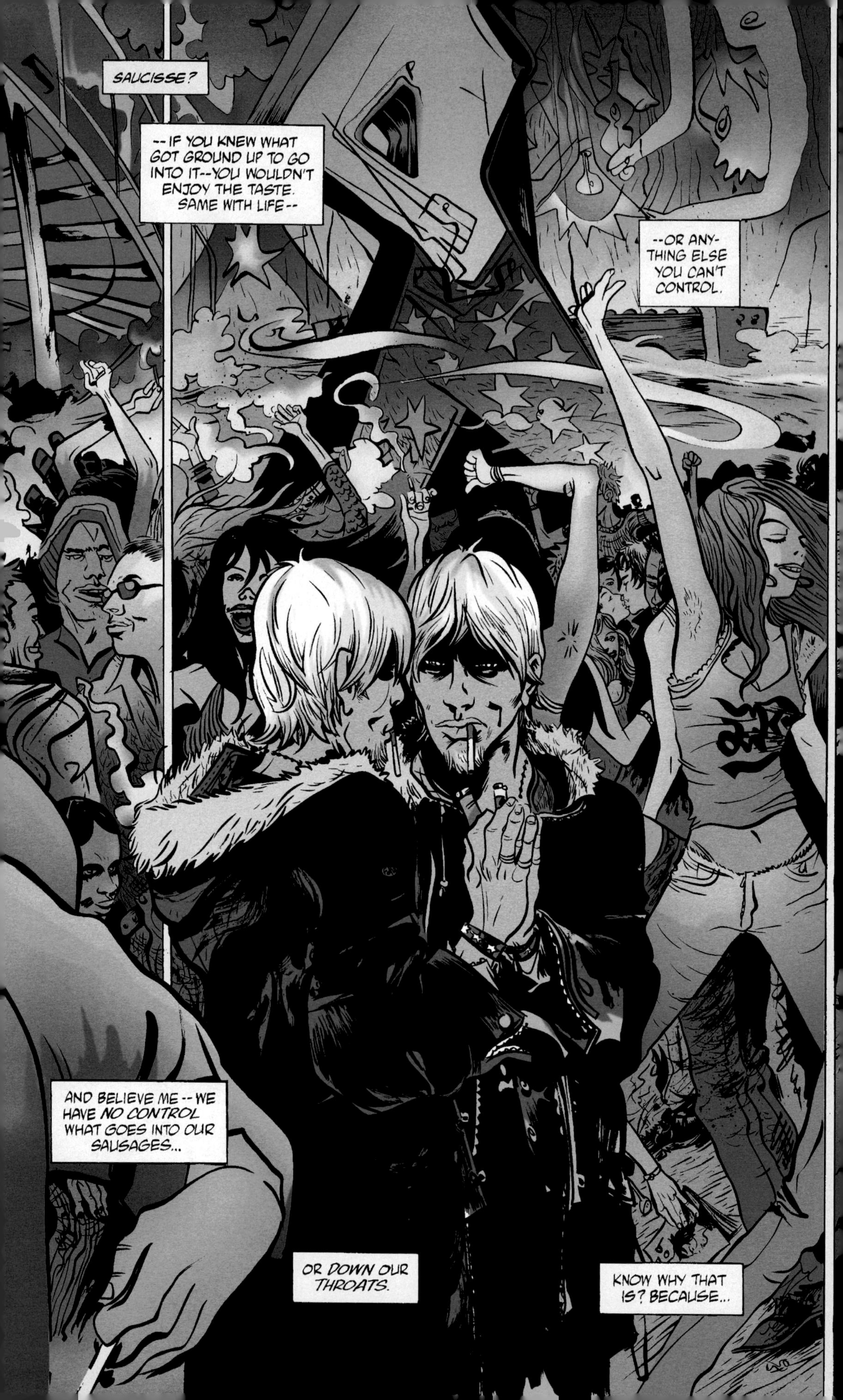
SAUCISSE?
--IF YOU KNEW WHAT GOT GROUND UP TO GO INTO IT--YOU WOULDN'T ENJOY THE TASTE. SAME WITH LIFE--
--OR ANYTHING ELSE YOU CAN'T CONTROL.
AND BELIEVE ME--WE HAVE NO CONTROL WHAT GOES INTO OUR SAUSAGES...
OR DOWN OUR THROATS.
KNOW WHY THAT IS? BECAUSE...

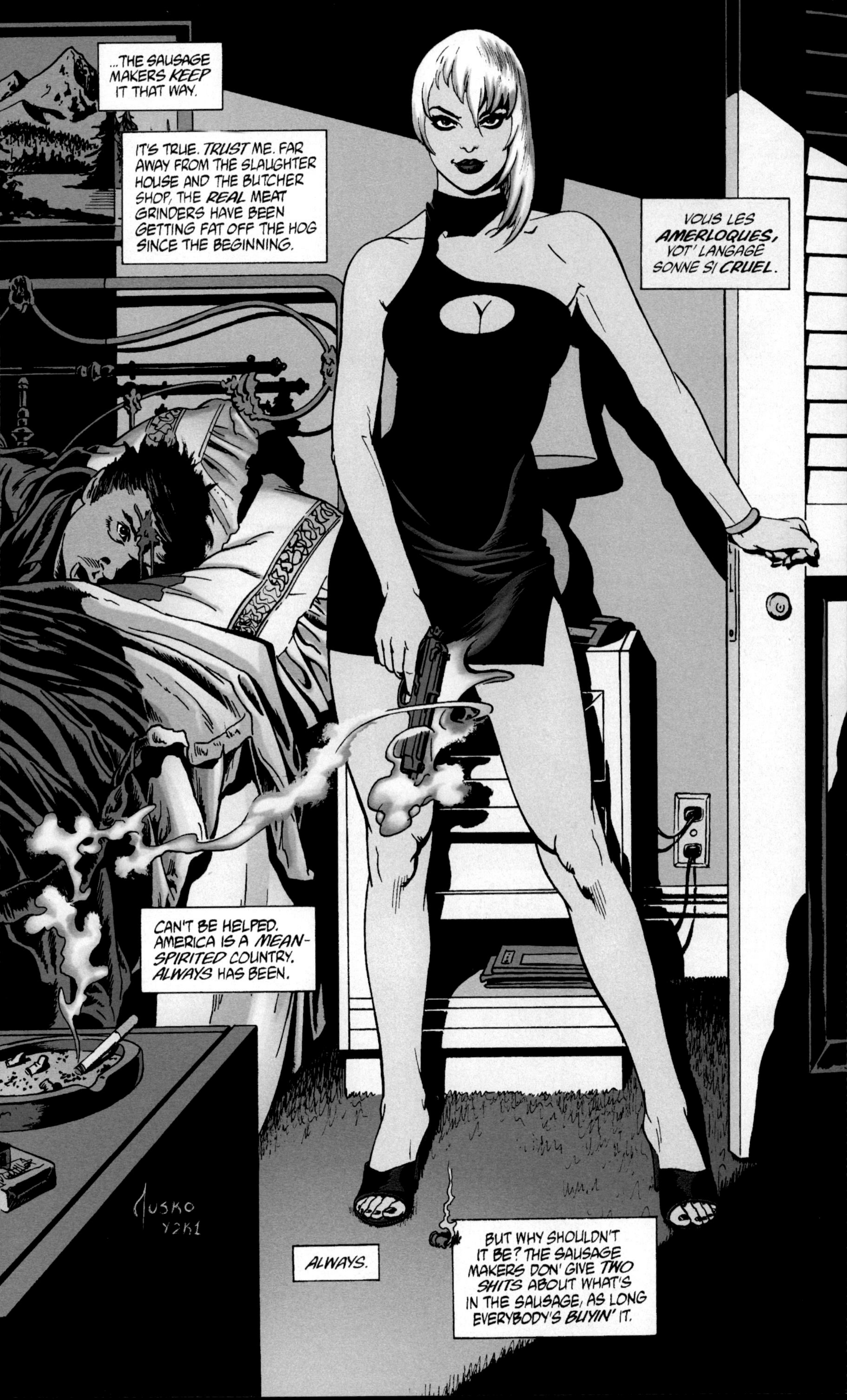
...THE SAUSAGE MAKERS KEEP IT THAT WAY.
IT'S TRUE. TRUST ME. FAR AWAY FROM THE SLAUGHTER HOUSE AND THE BUTCHER SHOP, THE REAL MEAT GRINDERS HAVE BEEN GETTING FAT OFF THE HOG SINCE THE BEGINNING.
VOUS LES AMERLOQUES, VOT' LANGAGE SONNE SI CRUEL.
CAN'T BE HELPED. AMERICA IS A MEAN-SPIRITED COUNTRY. ALWAYS HAS BEEN.
ALWAYS.
BUT WHY SHOULDN'T IT BE? THE SAUSAGE MAKERS DON' GIVE TWO SHITS ABOUT WHAT'S IN THE SAUSAGE, AS LONG EVERYBODY'S BUYIN' IT.
JUSKO Y2K1

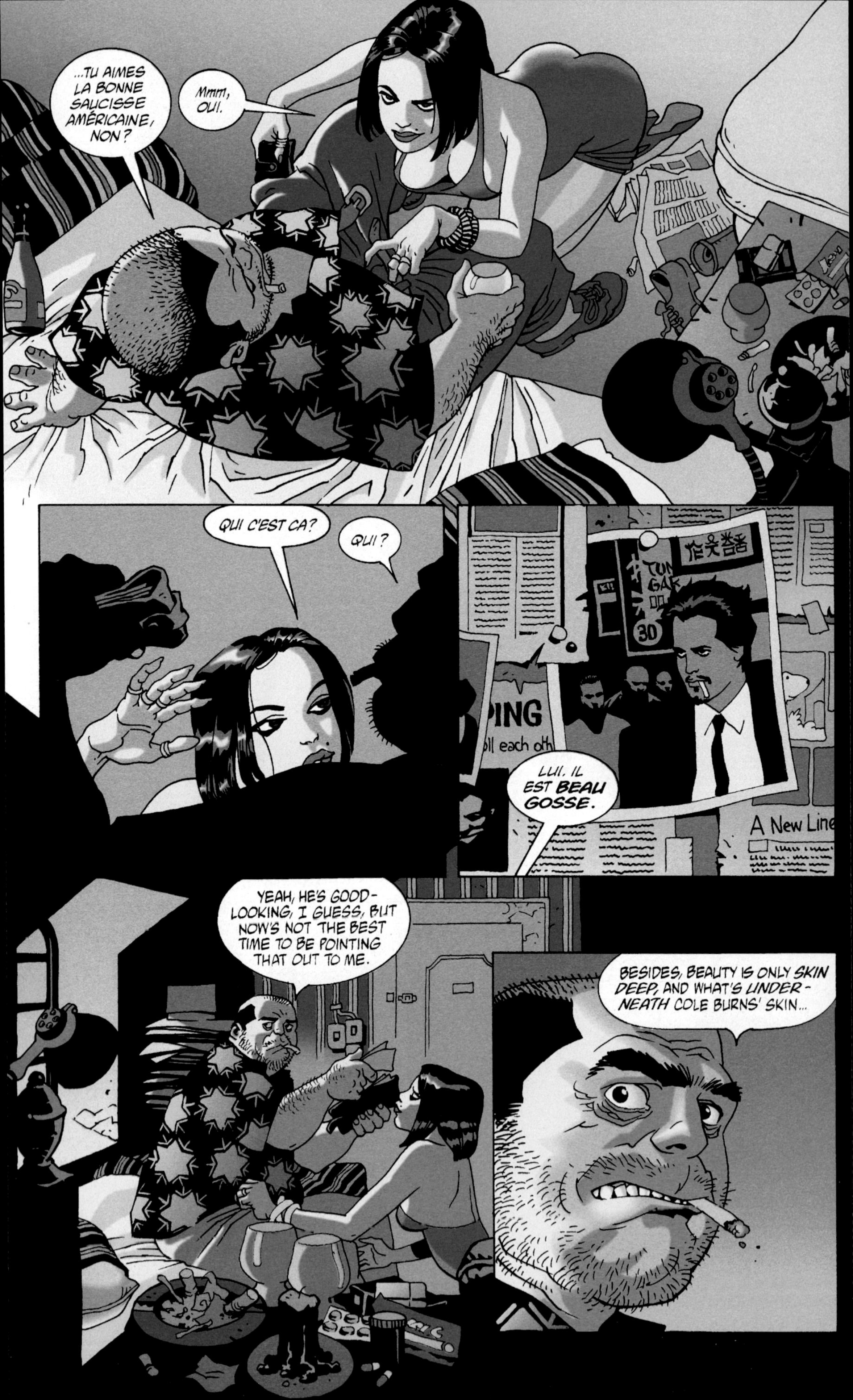
...TU AIMES LA BONNE SAUCISSE AMÉRICAINE, NON?
MMM, OUI.
QUI C'EST CA?
QUI?
LUI. IL EST BEAU GOSSE.
PING
A New Line
YEAH, HE'S GOOD-LOOKING, I GUESS, BUT NOW'S NOT THE BEST TIME TO BE POINTING THAT OUT TO ME.
BESIDES, BEAUTY IS ONLY SKIN DEEP, AND WHAT'S UNDERNEATH COLE BURNS' SKIN...

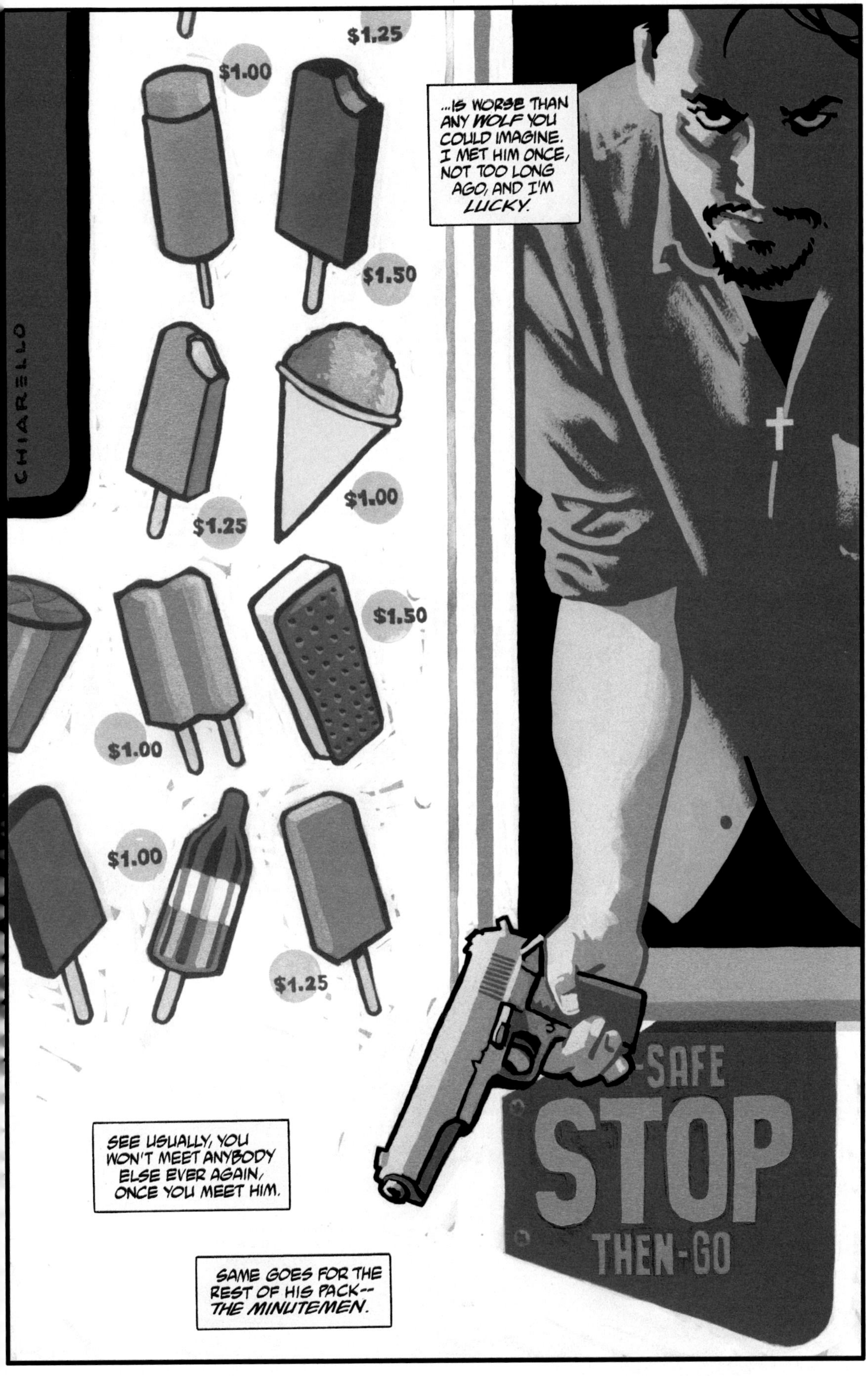

...IS WORSE THAN ANY WOLF YOU COULD IMAGINE. I MET HIM ONCE, NOT TOO LONG AGO, AND I'M LUCKY.
SEE USUALLY, YOU WON'T MEET ANYBODY ELSE EVER AGAIN, ONCE YOU MEET HIM.
SAME GOES FOR THE REST OF HIS PACK-- THE MINUTEMEN.
$1.25
$1.00
$1.50
$1.00
$1.25
$1.50
$1.00
$1.00
$1.25
-SAFE
STOP
THEN-GO
CHIARELLO

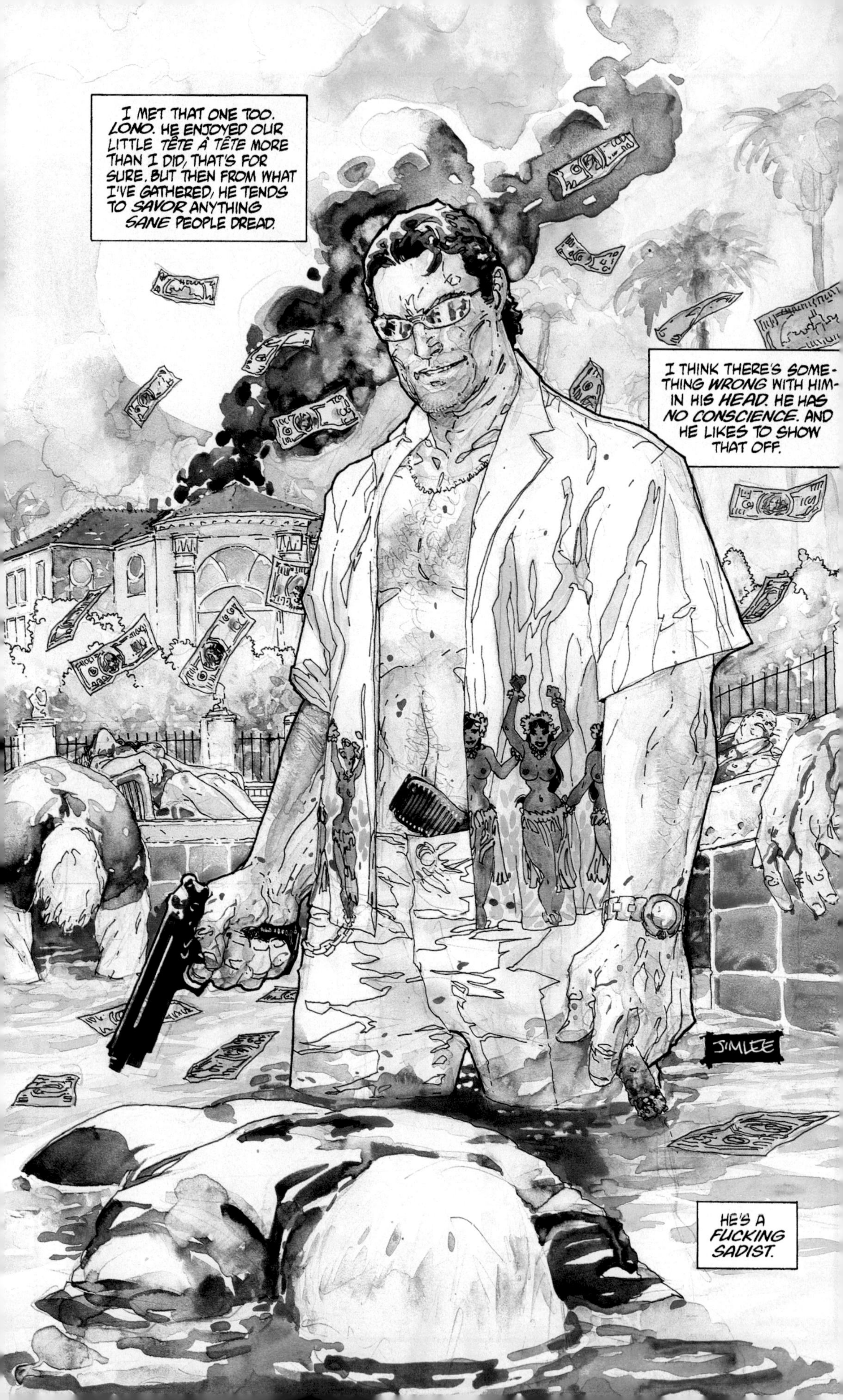
I MET THAT ONE TOO. LONO. HE ENJOYED OUR LITTLE TÊTE À TÊTE MORE THAN I DID, THAT'S FOR SURE. BUT THEN FROM WHAT I'VE GATHERED, HE TENDS TO SAVOR ANYTHING SANE PEOPLE DREAD.
I THINK THERE'S SOMETHING WRONG WITH HIM-IN HIS HEAD. HE HAS NO CONSCIENCE. AND HE LIKES TO SHOW THAT OFF.
HE'S A FUCKING SADIST.
JIMLEE

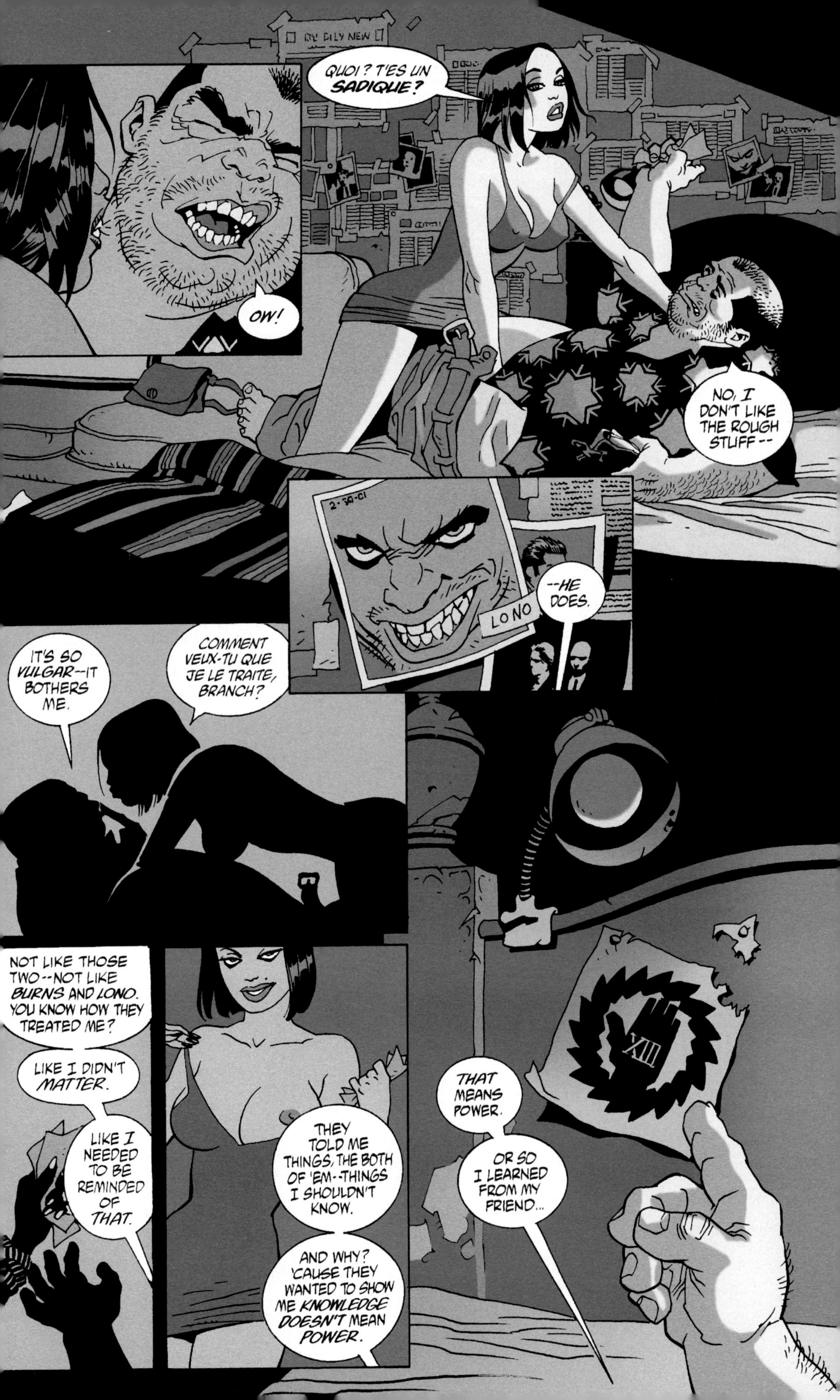
QUOI? T'ES UN SADIQUE?
OW!
NO, I DON'T LIKE THE ROUGH STUFF--
--HE DOES.
LONO
IT'S SO VULGAR--IT BOTHERS ME.
COMMENT VEUX-TU QUE JE LE TRAITE, BRANCH?
NOT LIKE THOSE TWO--NOT LIKE BURNS AND LONO. YOU KNOW HOW THEY TREATED ME?
LIKE I DIDN'T MATTER.
LIKE I NEEDED TO BE REMINDED OF THAT.
THEY TOLD ME THINGS, THE BOTH OF 'EM--THINGS I SHOULDN'T KNOW.
AND WHY? 'CAUSE THEY WANTED TO SHOW ME KNOWLEDGE DOESN'T MEAN POWER.
THAT MEANS POWER.
OR SO I LEARNED FROM MY FRIEND...
XIII

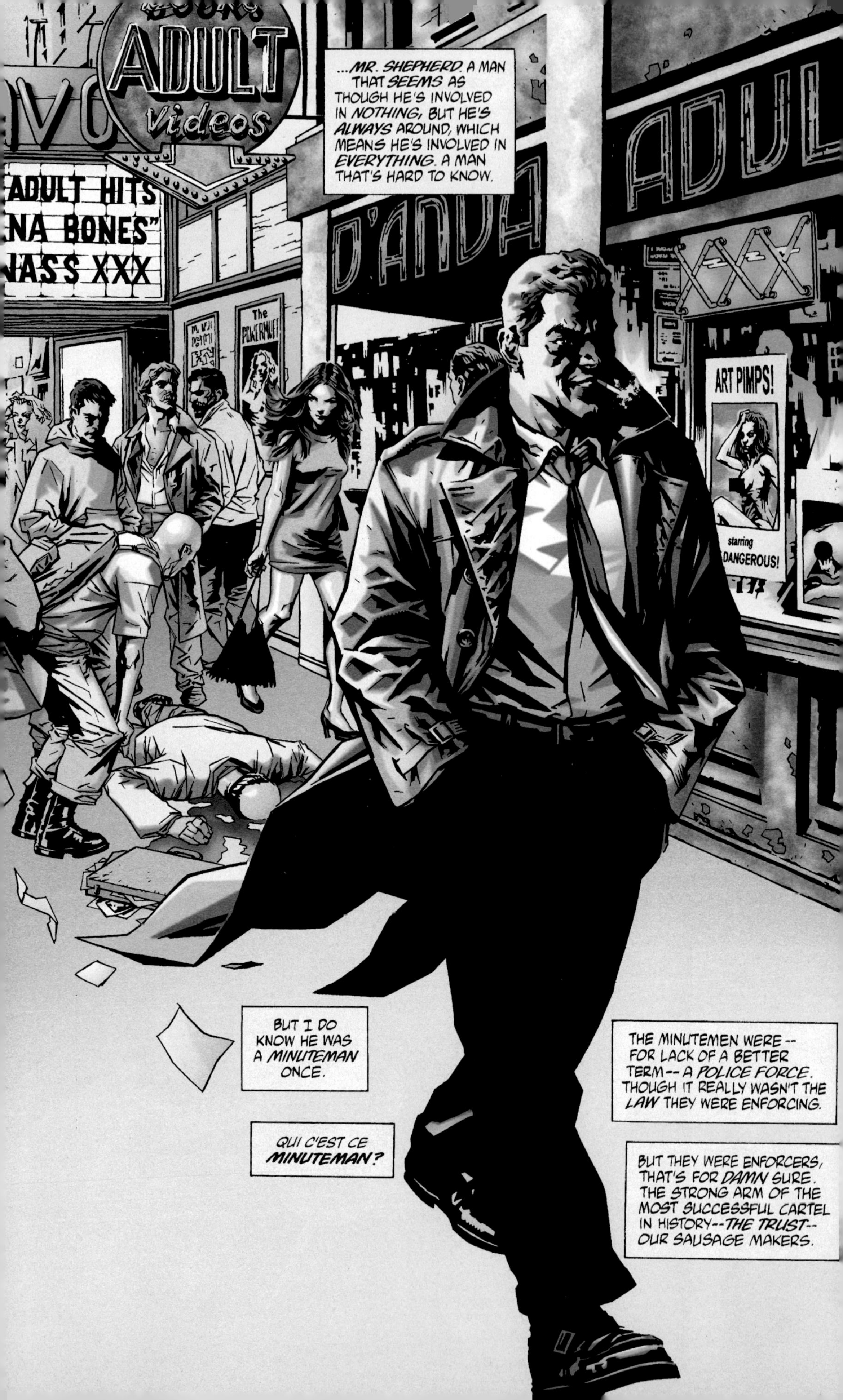
...MR. SHEPHERD. A MAN THAT SEEMS AS THOUGH HE'S INVOLVED IN NOTHING; BUT HE'S ALWAYS AROUND, WHICH MEANS HE'S INVOLVED IN EVERYTHING. A MAN THAT'S HARD TO KNOW.
BUT I DO KNOW HE WAS A MINUTEMAN ONCE.
QUI C'EST CE MINUTEMAN?
THE MINUTEMEN WERE -- FOR LACK OF A BETTER TERM -- A POLICE FORCE. THOUGH IT REALLY WASN'T THE LAW THEY WERE ENFORCING.
BUT THEY WERE ENFORCERS, THAT'S FOR DAMN SURE. THE STRONG ARM OF THE MOST SUCCESSFUL CARTEL IN HISTORY--THE TRUST-- OUR SAUSAGE MAKERS.
ADULT Videos
ADULT HITS
NA BONES"
NASS XXX
D'ANDA
ADUL
XXX
ART PIMPS!
starring
DANGEROUS!
The POWERMUFF

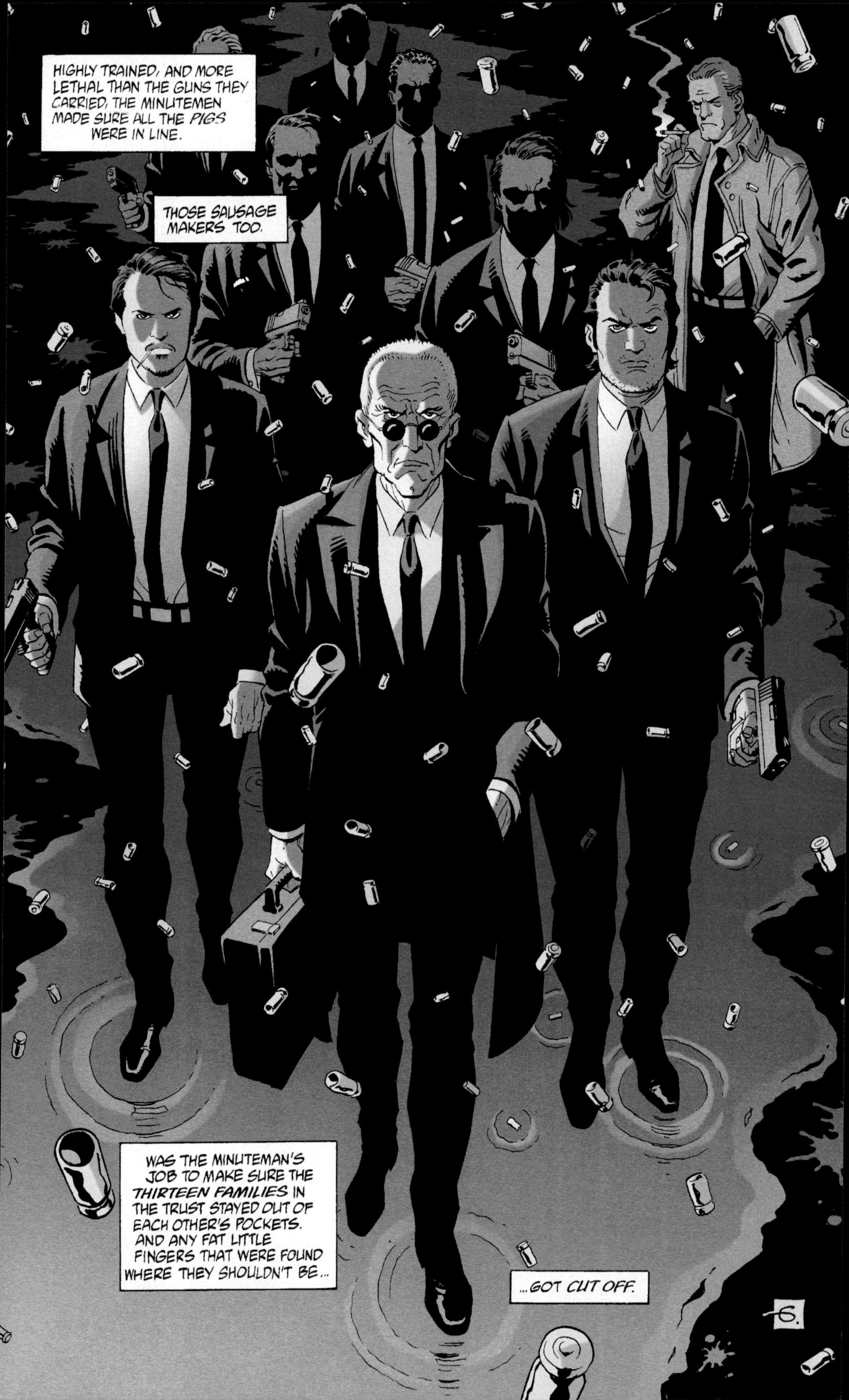
HIGHLY TRAINED, AND MORE LETHAL THAN THE GUNS THEY CARRIED, THE MINUTEMEN MADE SURE ALL THE *PIGS* WERE IN LINE.
THOSE SAUSAGE MAKERS TOO.
WAS THE MINUTEMAN'S JOB TO MAKE SURE THE *THIRTEEN FAMILIES* IN THE TRUST STAYED OUT OF EACH OTHER'S POCKETS. AND ANY FAT LITTLE FINGERS THAT WERE FOUND WHERE THEY SHOULDN'T BE...
...GOT CUT OFF.

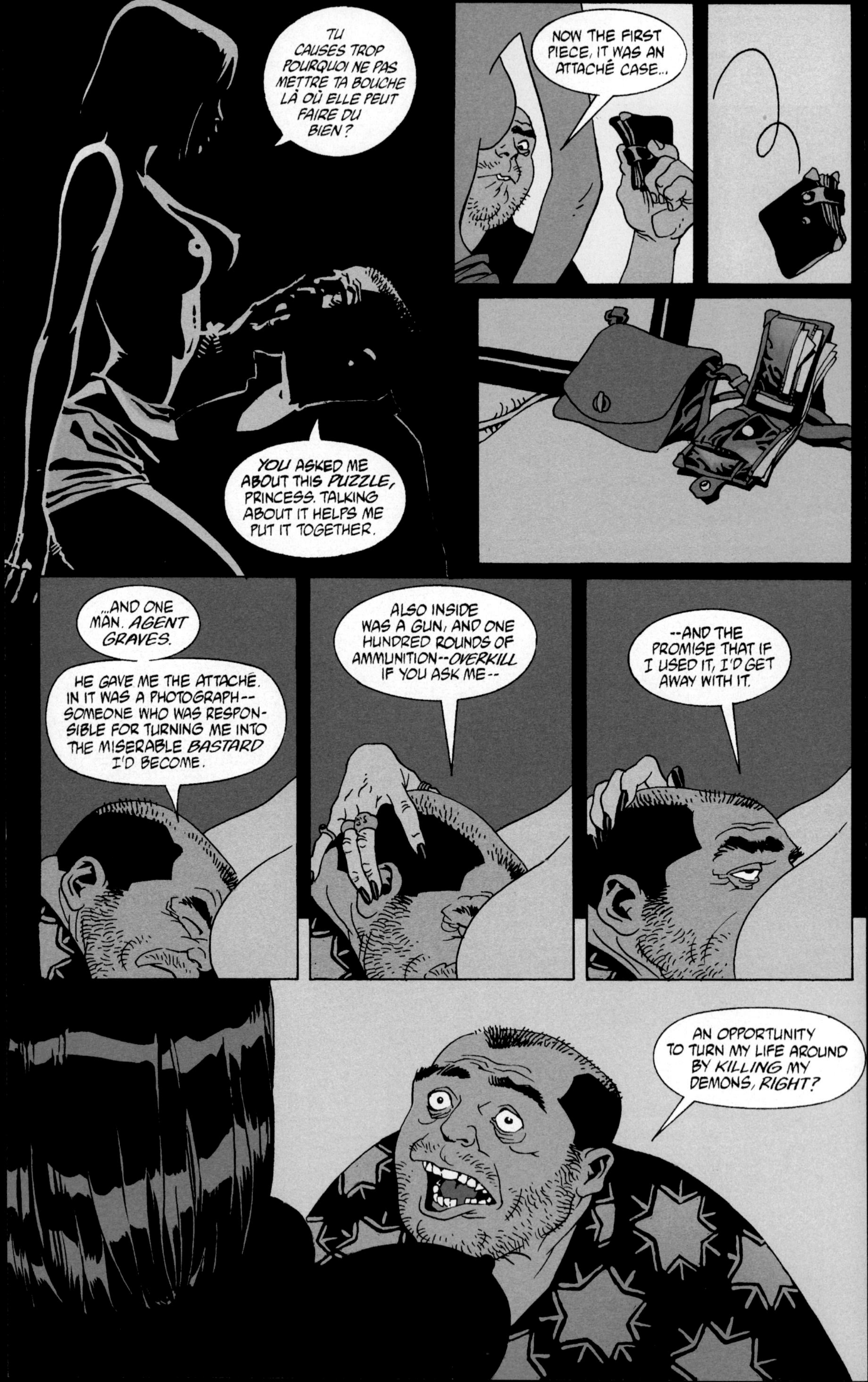
TU CAUSES TROP POURQUOI NE PAS METTRE TA BOUCHE LÀ OÙ ELLE PEUT FAIRE DU BIEN?
YOU ASKED ME ABOUT THIS PUZZLE, PRINCESS. TALKING ABOUT IT HELPS ME PUT IT TOGETHER.
NOW THE FIRST PIECE, IT WAS AN ATTACHÉ CASE...
...AND ONE MAN. AGENT GRAVES.
HE GAVE ME THE ATTACHÉ. IN IT WAS A PHOTOGRAPH-- SOMEONE WHO WAS RESPONSIBLE FOR TURNING ME INTO THE MISERABLE BASTARD I'D BECOME.
ALSO INSIDE WAS A GUN, AND ONE HUNDRED ROUNDS OF AMMUNITION--OVERKILL IF YOU ASK ME--
--AND THE PROMISE THAT IF I USED IT, I'D GET AWAY WITH IT.
AN OPPORTUNITY TO TURN MY LIFE AROUND BY KILLING MY DEMONS, RIGHT?

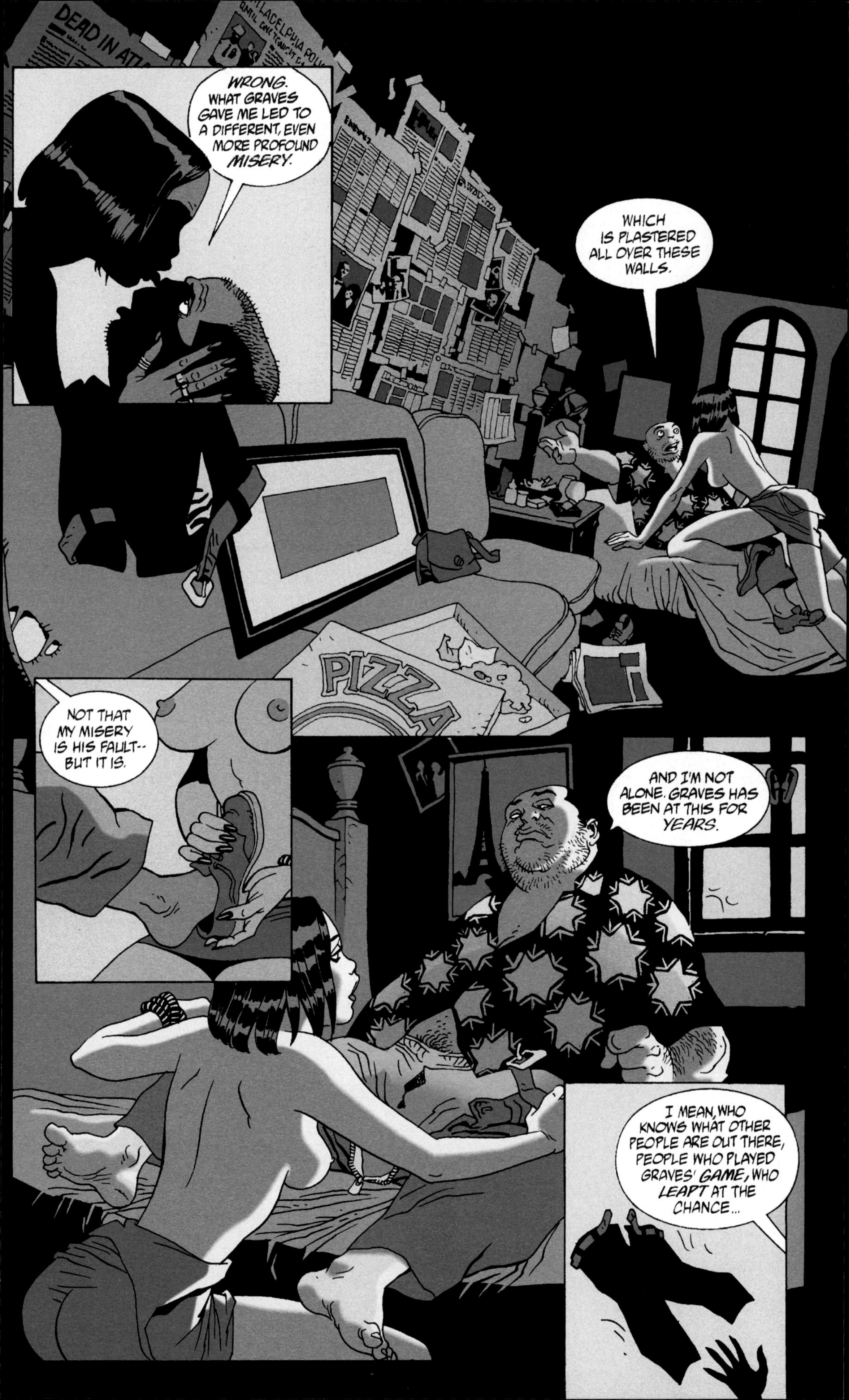
WRONG. WHAT GRAVES GAVE ME LED TO A DIFFERENT, EVEN MORE PROFOUND MISERY.
WHICH IS PLASTERED ALL OVER THESE WALLS.
PIZZA
NOT THAT MY MISERY IS HIS FAULT-- BUT IT IS.
AND I'M NOT ALONE. GRAVES HAS BEEN AT THIS FOR YEARS.
I MEAN, WHO KNOWS WHAT OTHER PEOPLE ARE OUT THERE, PEOPLE WHO PLAYED GRAVES' GAME, WHO LEAPT AT THE CHANCE...

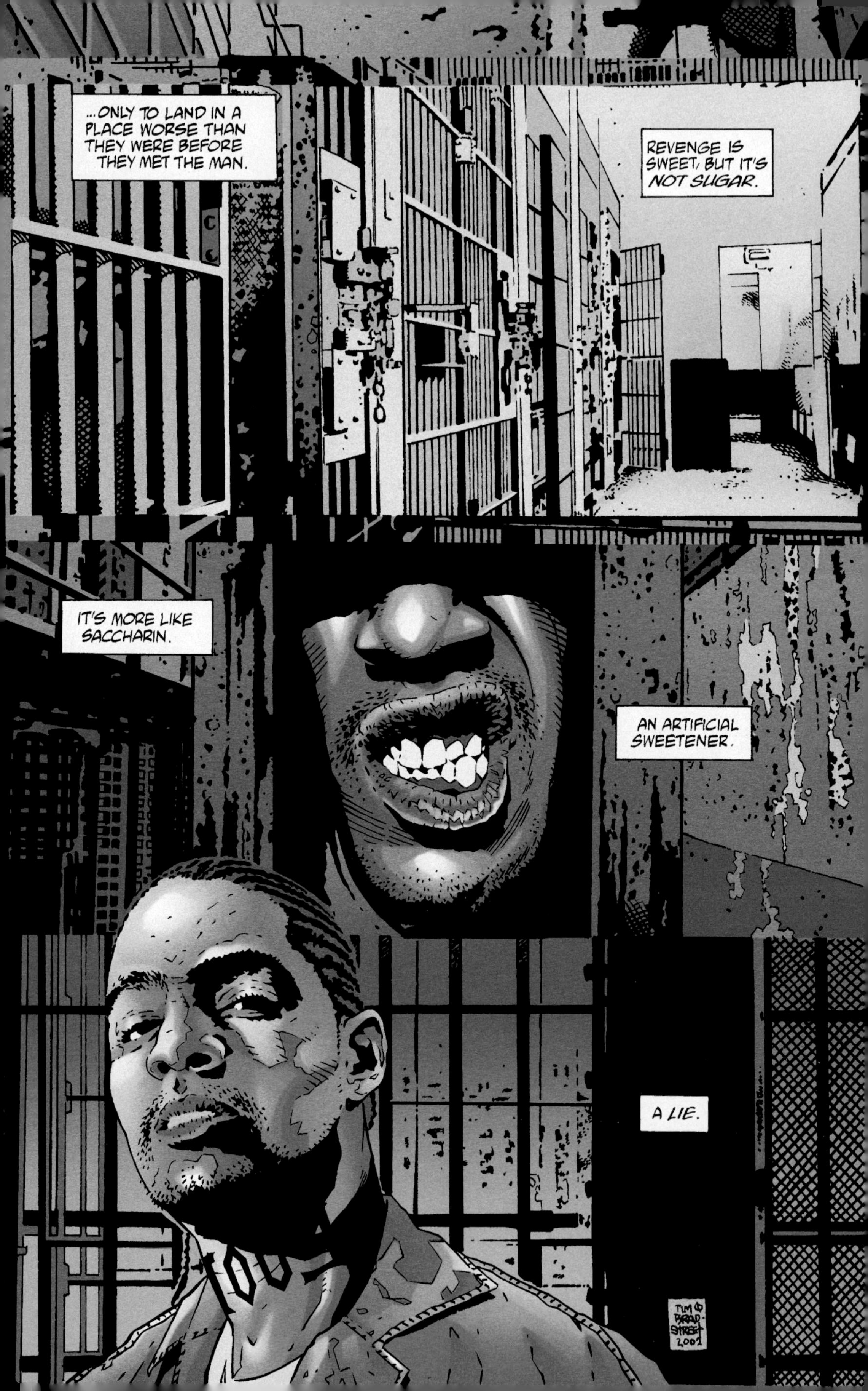
...ONLY TO LAND IN A PLACE WORSE THAN THEY WERE BEFORE THEY MET THE MAN.
REVENGE IS SWEET, BUT IT'S NOT SUGAR.
IT'S MORE LIKE SACCHARIN.
AN ARTIFICIAL SWEETENER.
A LIE.
TIM BRADSTREET 2001

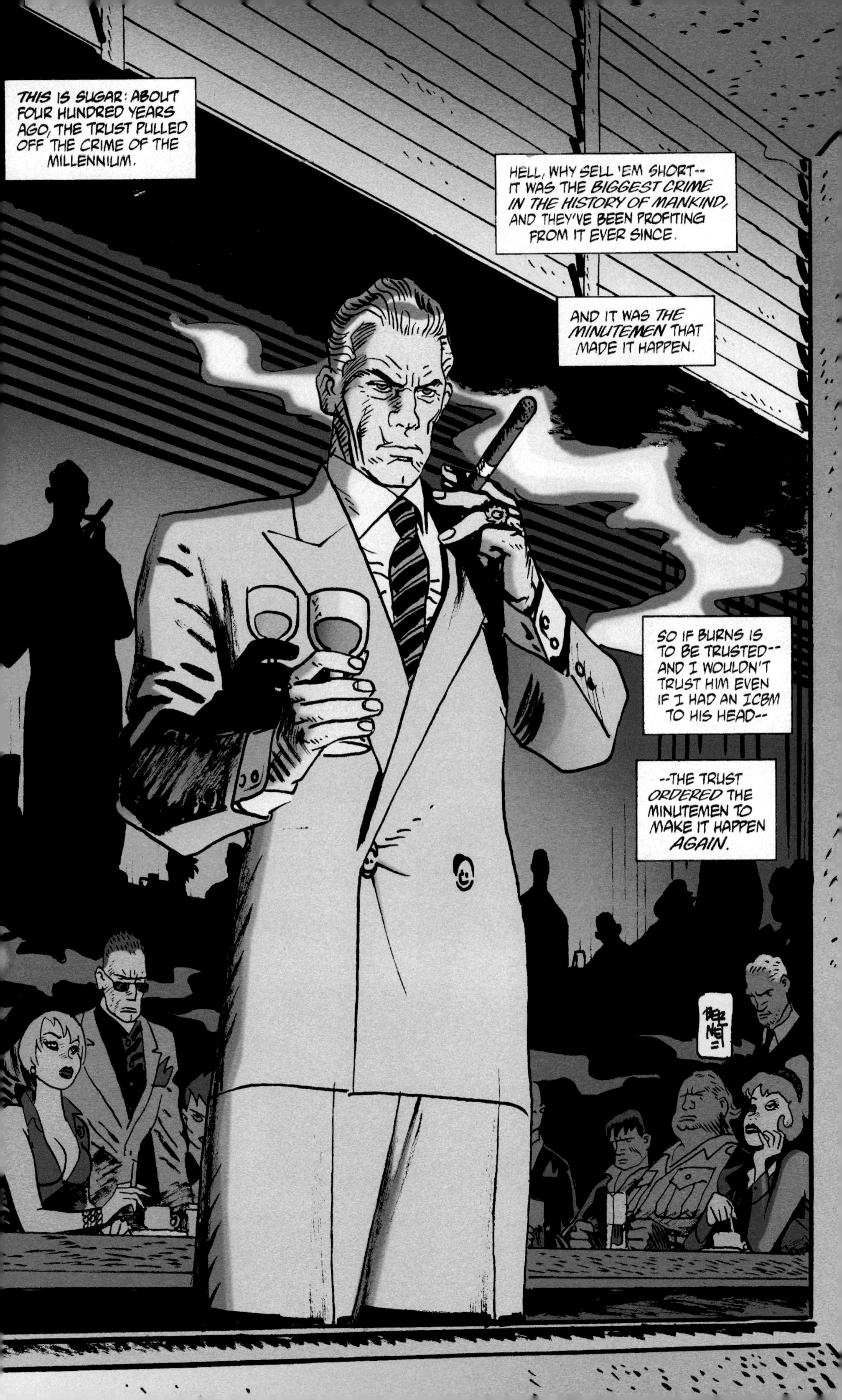
THIS IS SUGAR: ABOUT FOUR HUNDRED YEARS AGO, THE TRUST PULLED OFF THE CRIME OF THE MILLENNIUM.
HELL, WHY SELL 'EM SHORT-- IT WAS THE BIGGEST CRIME IN THE HISTORY OF MANKIND, AND THEY'VE BEEN PROFITING FROM IT EVER SINCE.
AND IT WAS THE MINUTEMEN THAT MADE IT HAPPEN.
SO IF BURNS IS TO BE TRUSTED-- AND I WOULDN'T TRUST HIM EVEN IF I HAD AN ICBM TO HIS HEAD--
--THE TRUST ORDERED THE MINUTEMEN TO MAKE IT HAPPEN AGAIN.

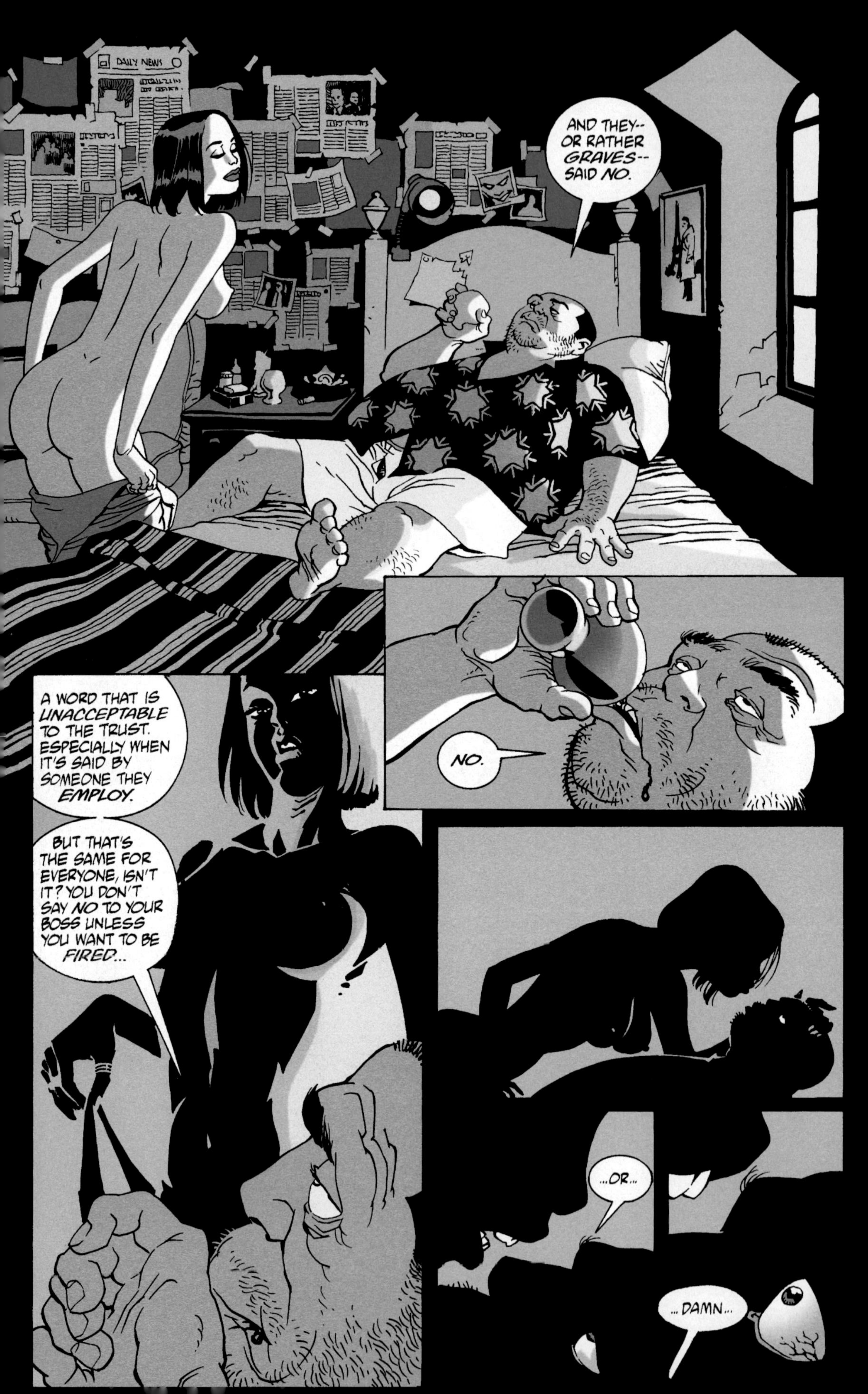
DAILY NEWS
AND THEY-- OR RATHER *GRAVES*-- SAID *NO*.
NO.
A WORD THAT IS *UNACCEPTABLE* TO THE TRUST. ESPECIALLY WHEN IT'S SAID BY SOMEONE THEY *EMPLOY*.
BUT THAT'S THE SAME FOR EVERYONE, ISN'T IT? YOU DON'T SAY *NO* TO YOUR BOSS UNLESS YOU WANT TO BE *FIRED*...
...OR...
...DAMN...

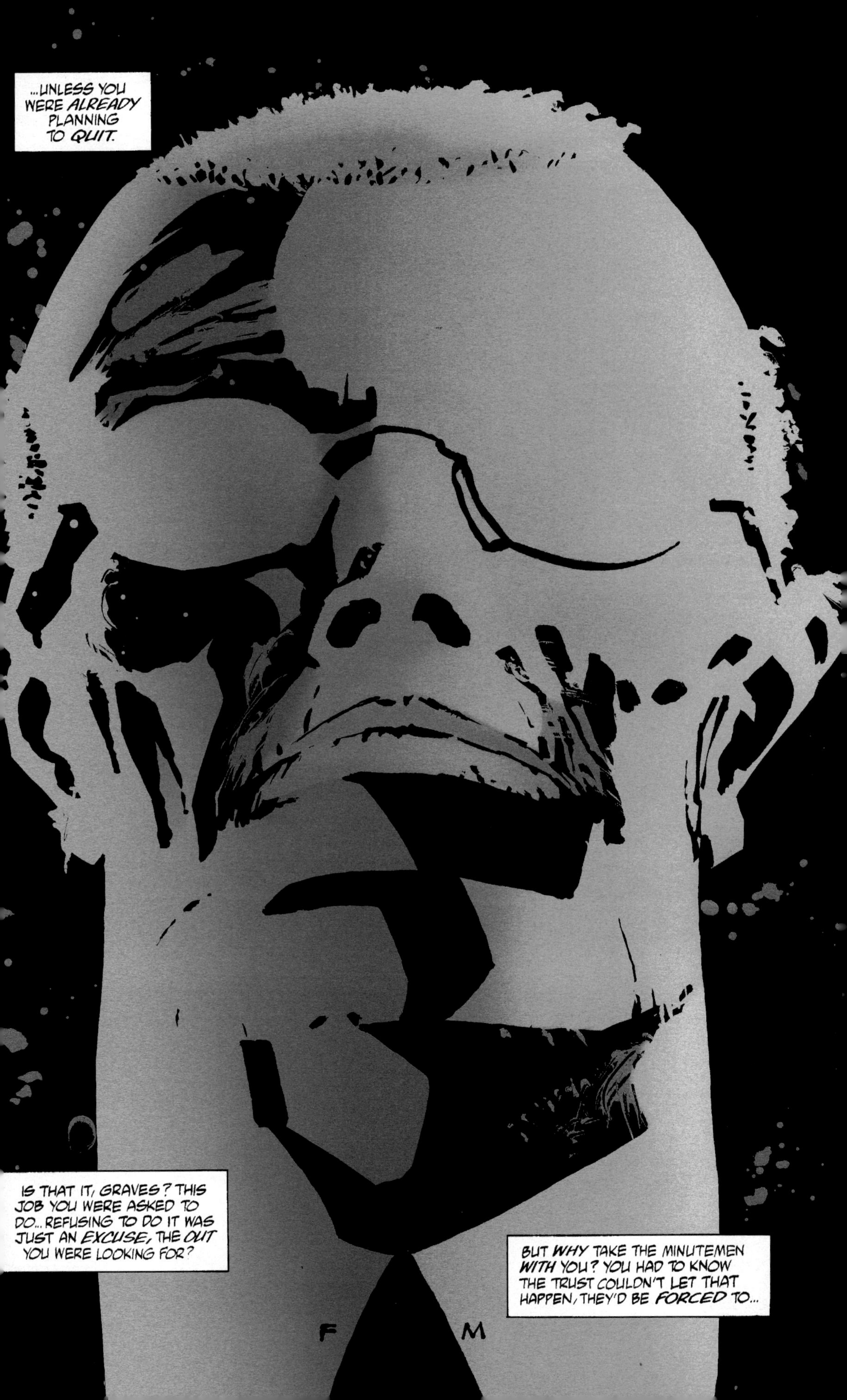
...UNLESS YOU WERE ALREADY PLANNING TO QUIT.
IS THAT IT, GRAVES? THIS JOB YOU WERE ASKED TO DO... REFUSING TO DO IT WAS JUST AN EXCUSE, THE OUT YOU WERE LOOKING FOR?
BUT WHY TAKE THE MINUTEMEN WITH YOU? YOU HAD TO KNOW THE TRUST COULDN'T LET THAT HAPPEN, THEY'D BE FORCED TO...
F M

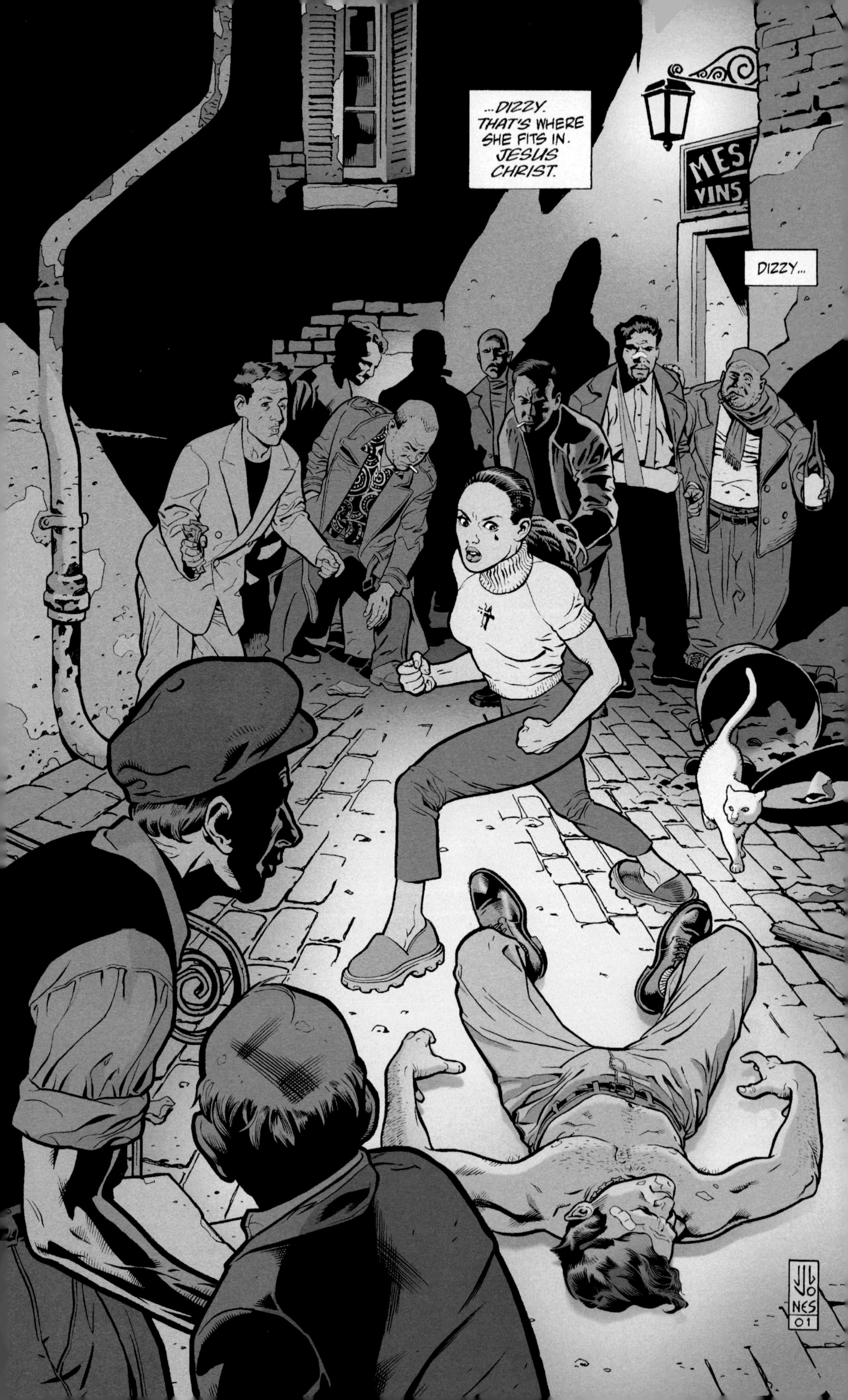
...DIZZY. THAT'S WHERE SHE FITS IN. JESUS CHRIST.
MES
VINS
DIZZY...
JG JONES 01

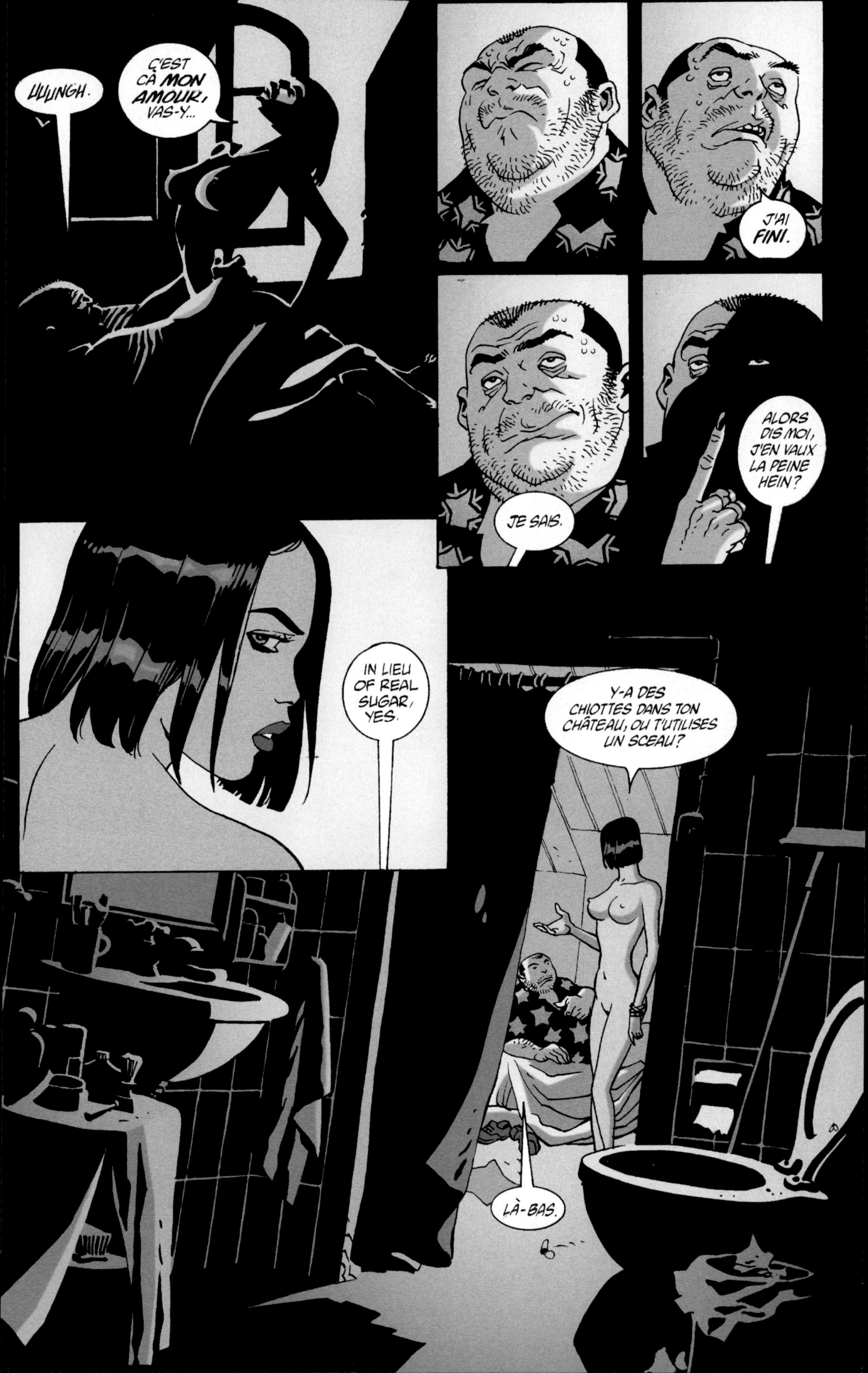
UUUNGH.
C'EST ÇA MON AMOUR, VAS-Y...
J'AI FINI.
JE SAIS.
ALORS DIS MOI, J'EN VAUX LA PEINE HEIN?
IN LIEU OF REAL SUGAR, YES.
Y-A DES CHIOTTES DANS TON CHÂTEAU, OU T'UTILISES UN SCEAU?
LÀ-BAS.

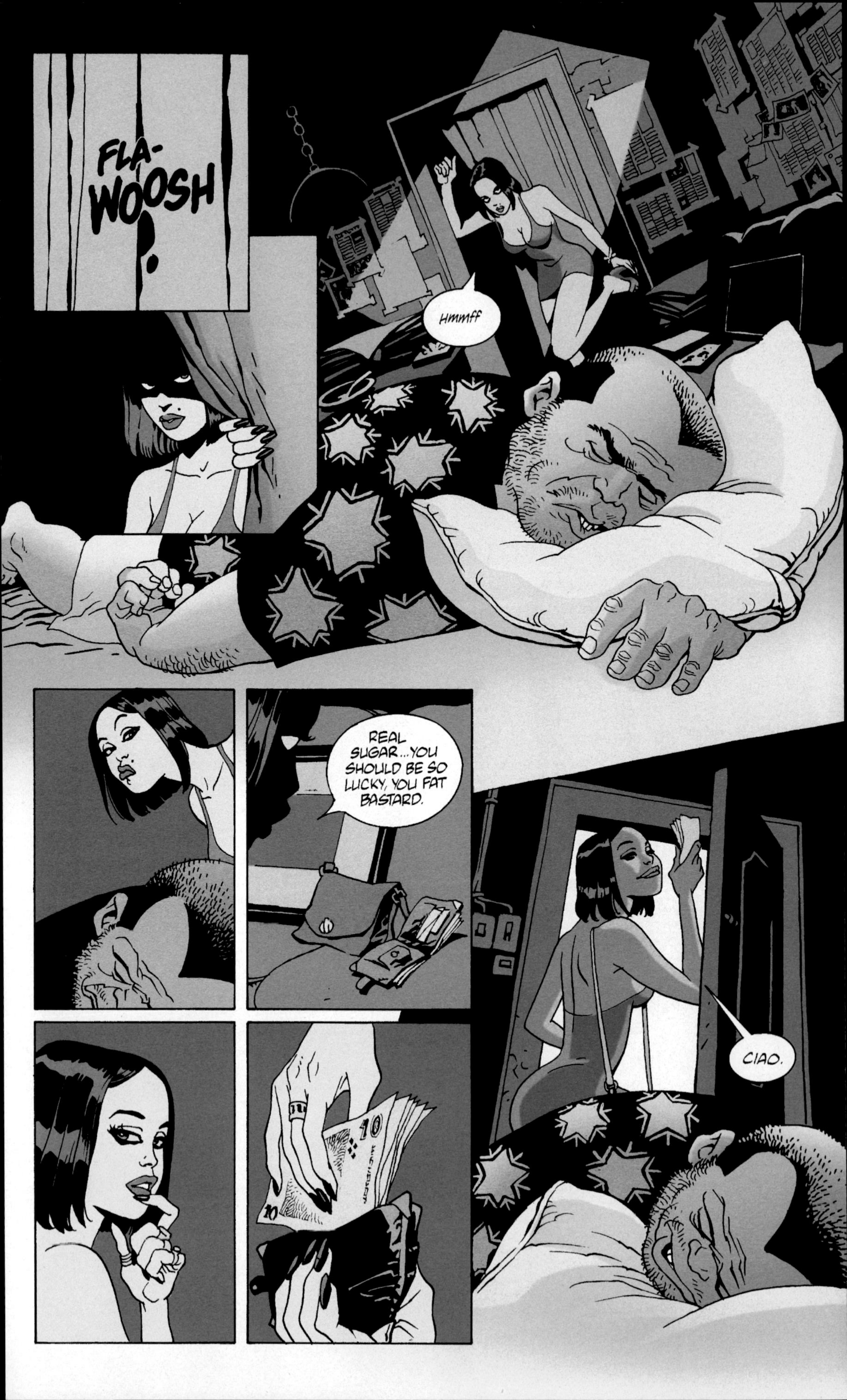
FLA-WOOSH
Hmmff
REAL SUGAR...YOU SHOULD BE SO LUCKY, YOU FAT BASTARD.
CIAO.

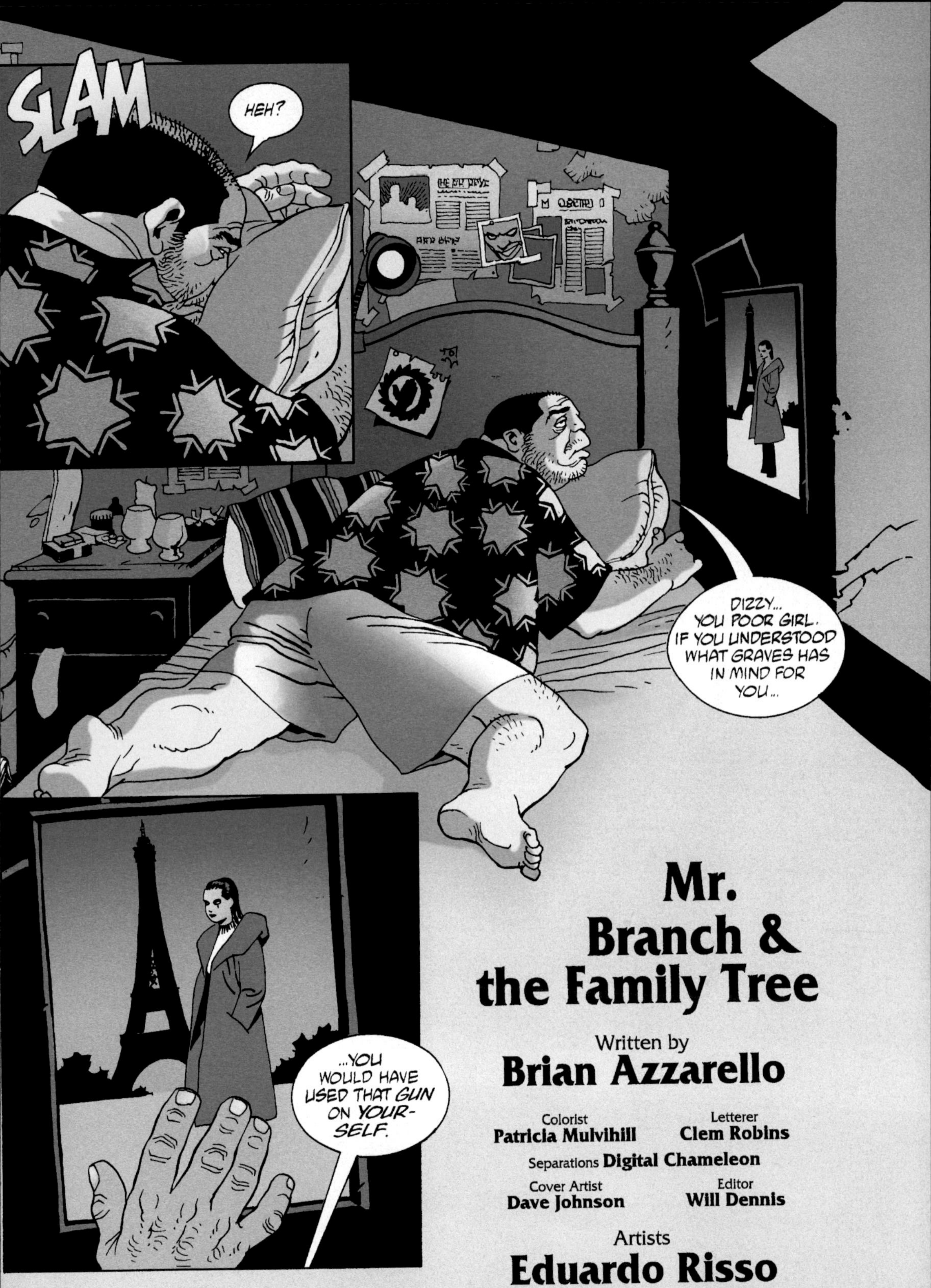
SLAM
HEH?
DIZZY... YOU POOR GIRL. IF YOU UNDERSTOOD WHAT GRAVES HAS IN MIND FOR YOU...
...YOU WOULD HAVE USED THAT GUN ON YOURSELF.

Mr. Branch & the Family Tree

Written by
Brian Azzarello

Colorist **Patricia Mulvihill**
Letterer **Clem Robins**
Separations **Digital Chameleon**
Cover Artist **Dave Johnson**
Editor **Will Dennis**

Artists
Eduardo Risso
Pgs. 146-149, 152, 155, 158-159, 162, 165-167

Paul Pope Pg. 150: Benito Medici
Joe Jusko Pg. 151: Megan Dietrich
Mark Chiarello Pg. 153: Cole Burns
Jim Lee Pg. 154: Lono
Lee Bermejo Pg. 156: Mr. Shepherd
Dave Gibbons Pg. 157: The Minutemen
Tim Bradstreet Pg. 160: Loop Hughes
Jordi Bernet Pg. 161: Augustus Medici
Frank Miller Pg. 163: Agent Graves
J.G. Jones Pg. 164: Dizzy Cordova

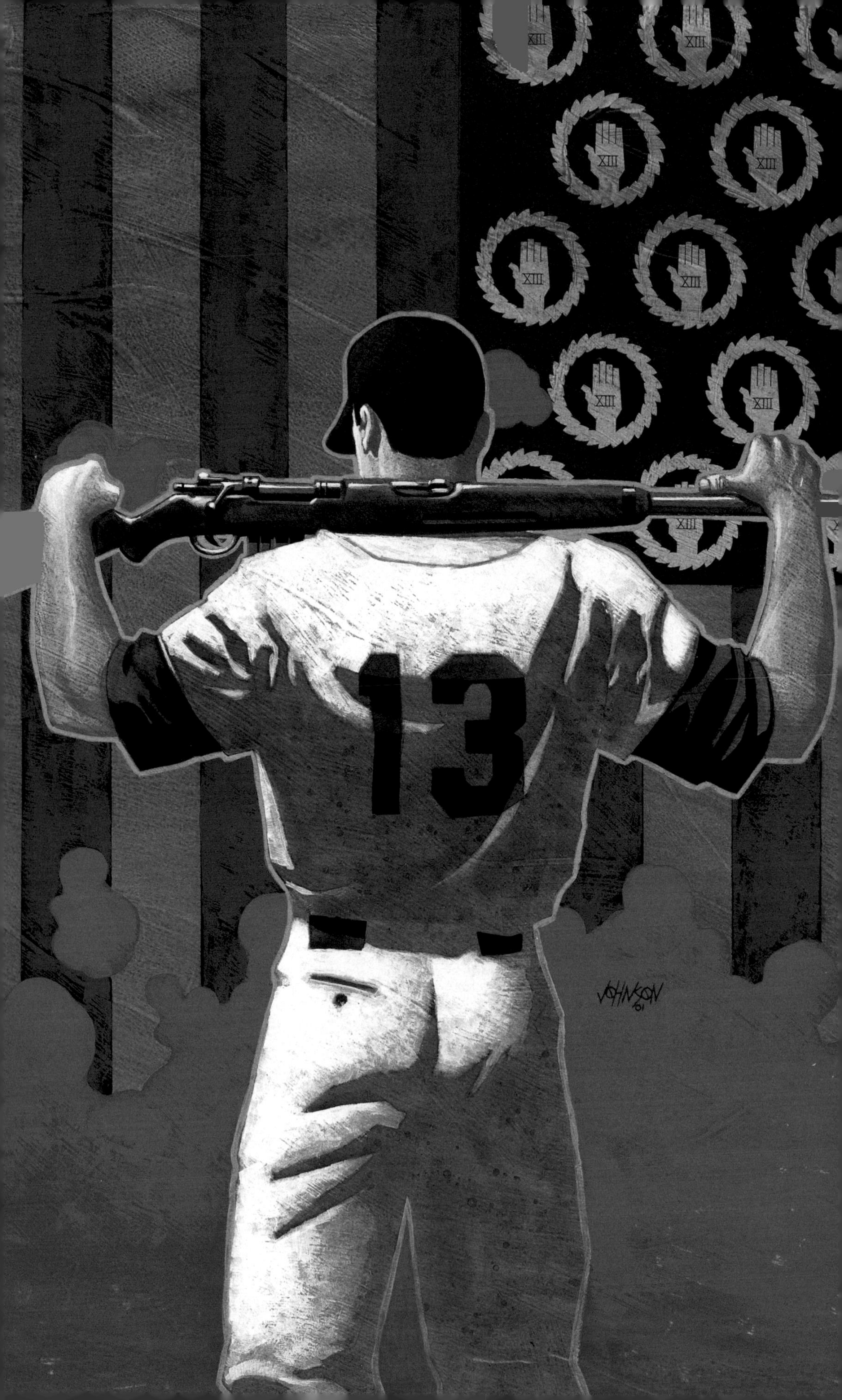
13
JOHNSON '01

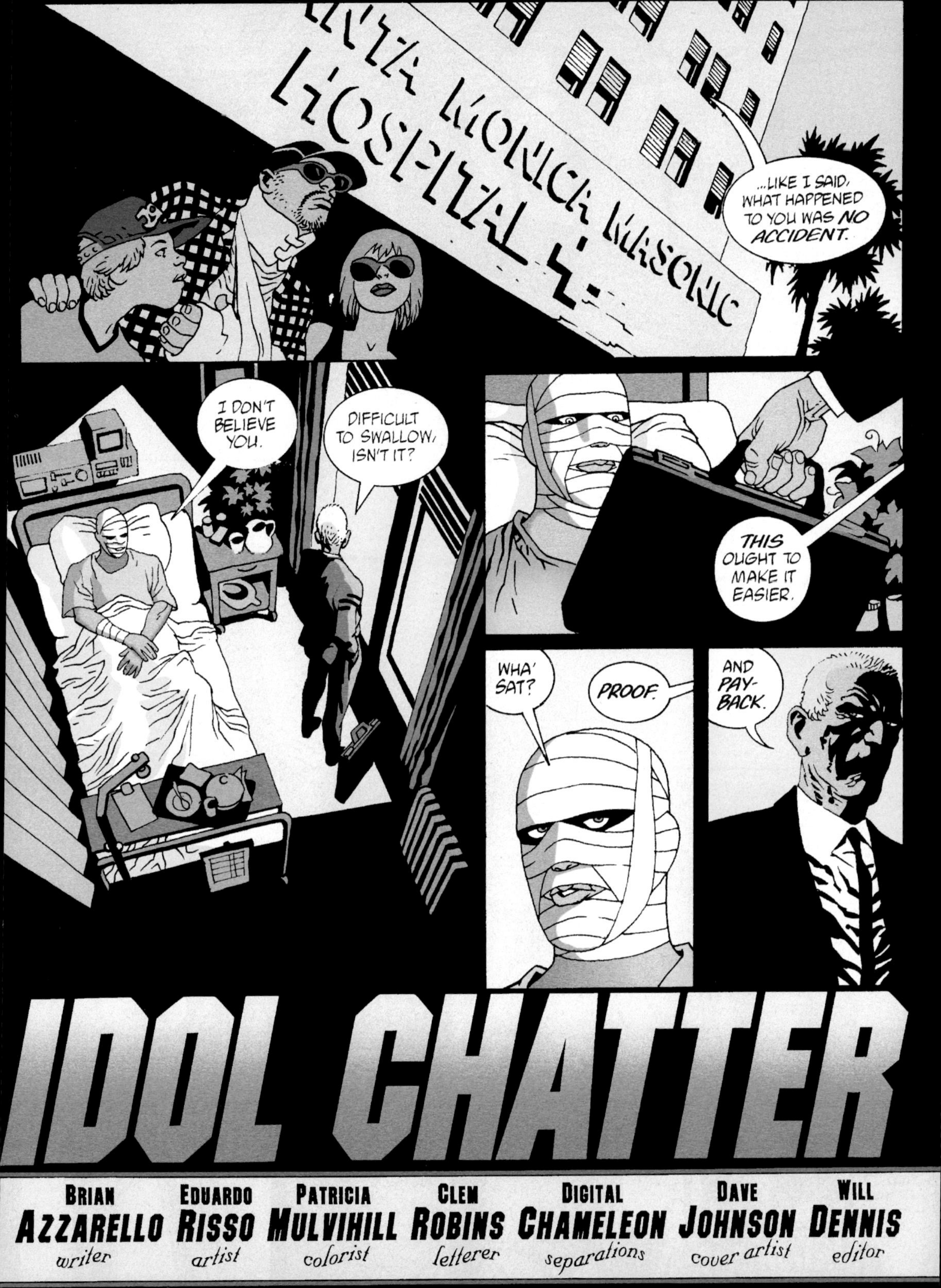
MONICA MASONIC
HOSPITAL
...LIKE I SAID, WHAT HAPPENED TO YOU WAS NO ACCIDENT.
I DON'T BELIEVE YOU.
DIFFICULT TO SWALLOW, ISN'T IT?
THIS OUGHT TO MAKE IT EASIER.
WHA' SAT?
PROOF.
AND PAY-BACK.

IDOL CHATTER

BRIAN AZZARELLO *writer*
EDUARDO RISSO *artist*
PATRICIA MULVIHILL *colorist*
CLEM ROBINS *letterer*
DIGITAL CHAMELEON *separations*
DAVE JOHNSON *cover artist*
WILL DENNIS *editor*

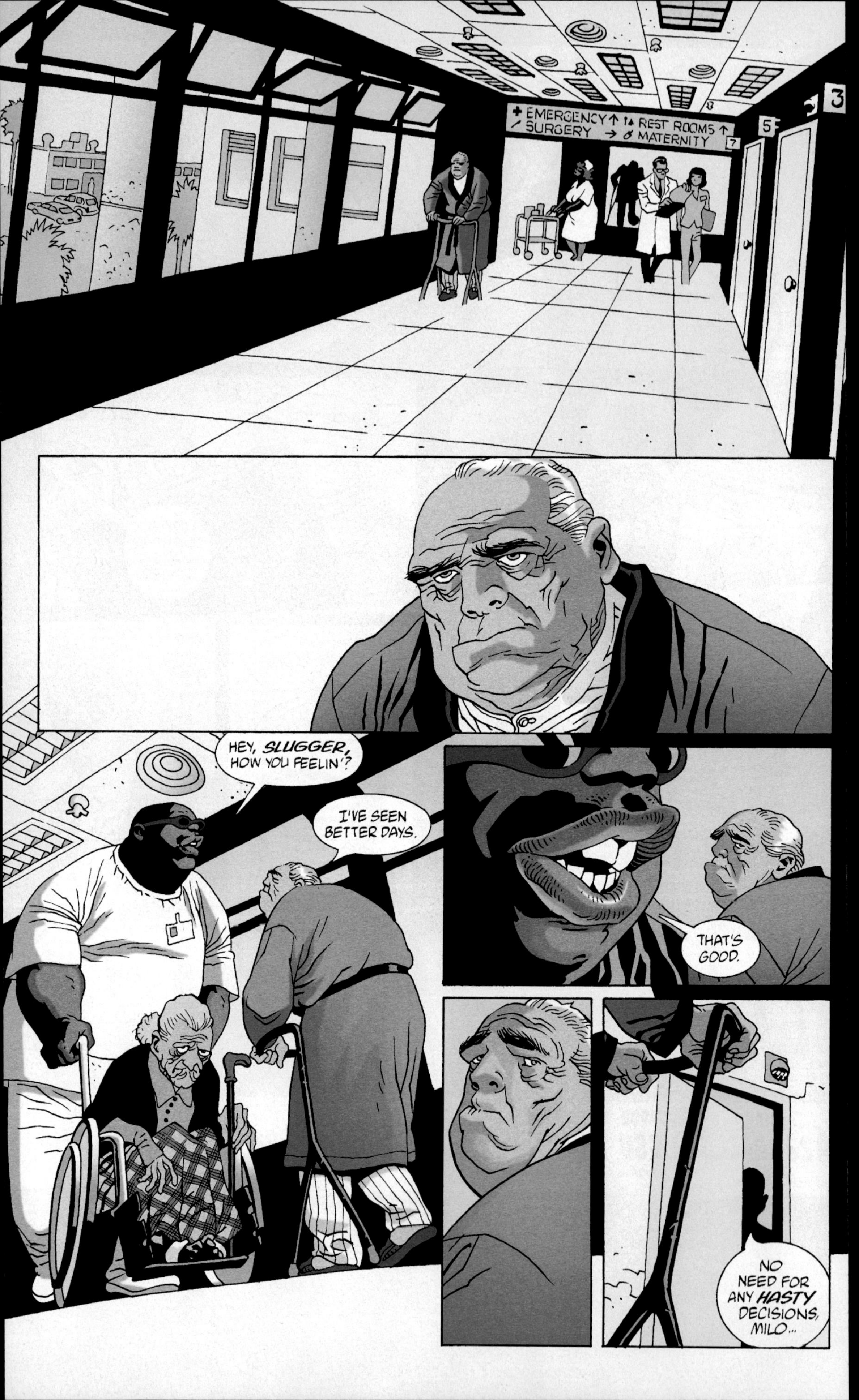
EMERGENCY ↑ REST ROOMS ↑
SURGERY → MATERNITY
HEY, SLUGGER, HOW YOU FEELIN'?
I'VE SEEN BETTER DAYS.
THAT'S GOOD.
NO NEED FOR ANY HASTY DECISIONS, MILO...

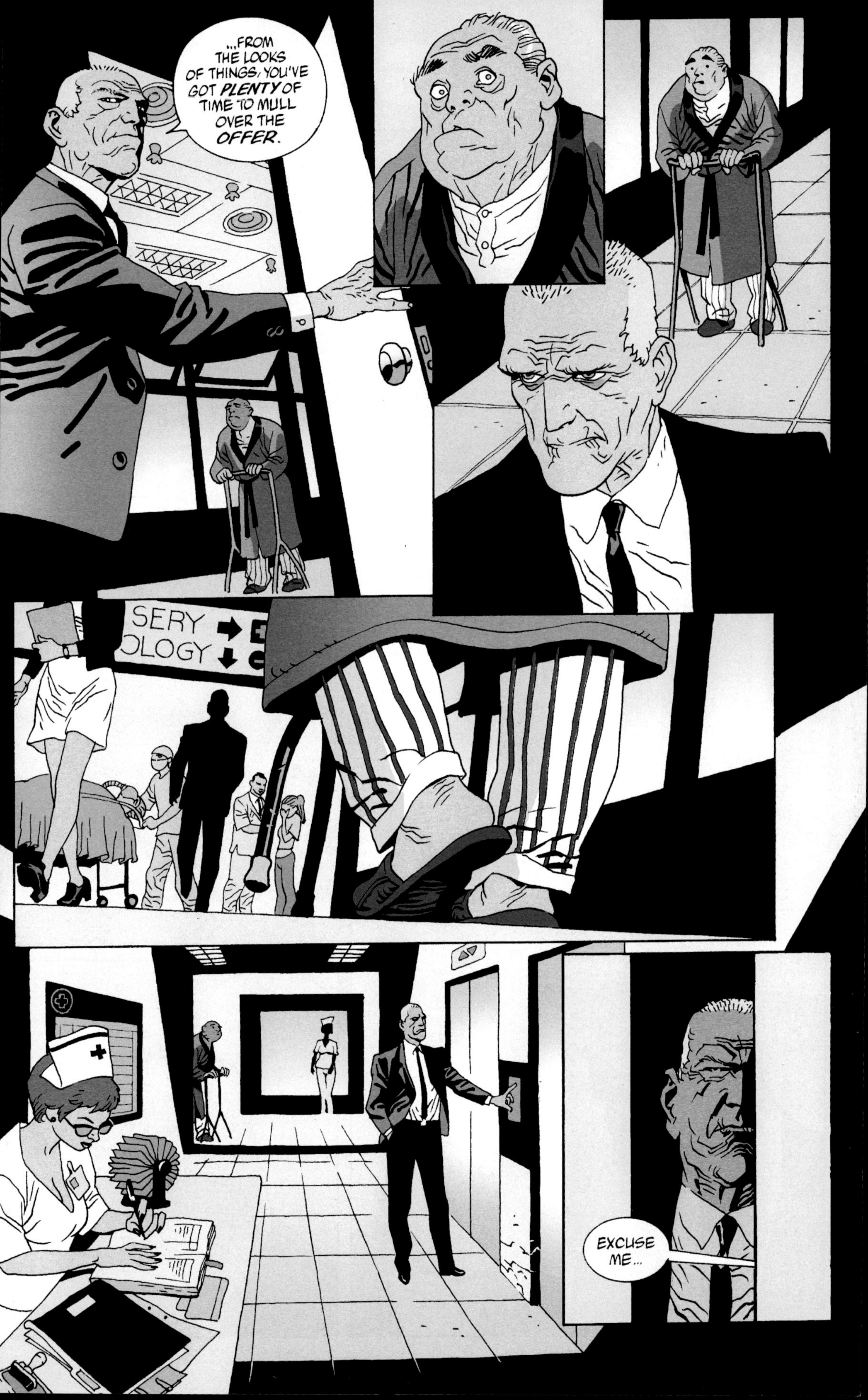
...FROM THE LOOKS OF THINGS, YOU'VE GOT PLENTY OF TIME TO MULL OVER THE OFFER.
SERY
OLOGY
EXCUSE ME...

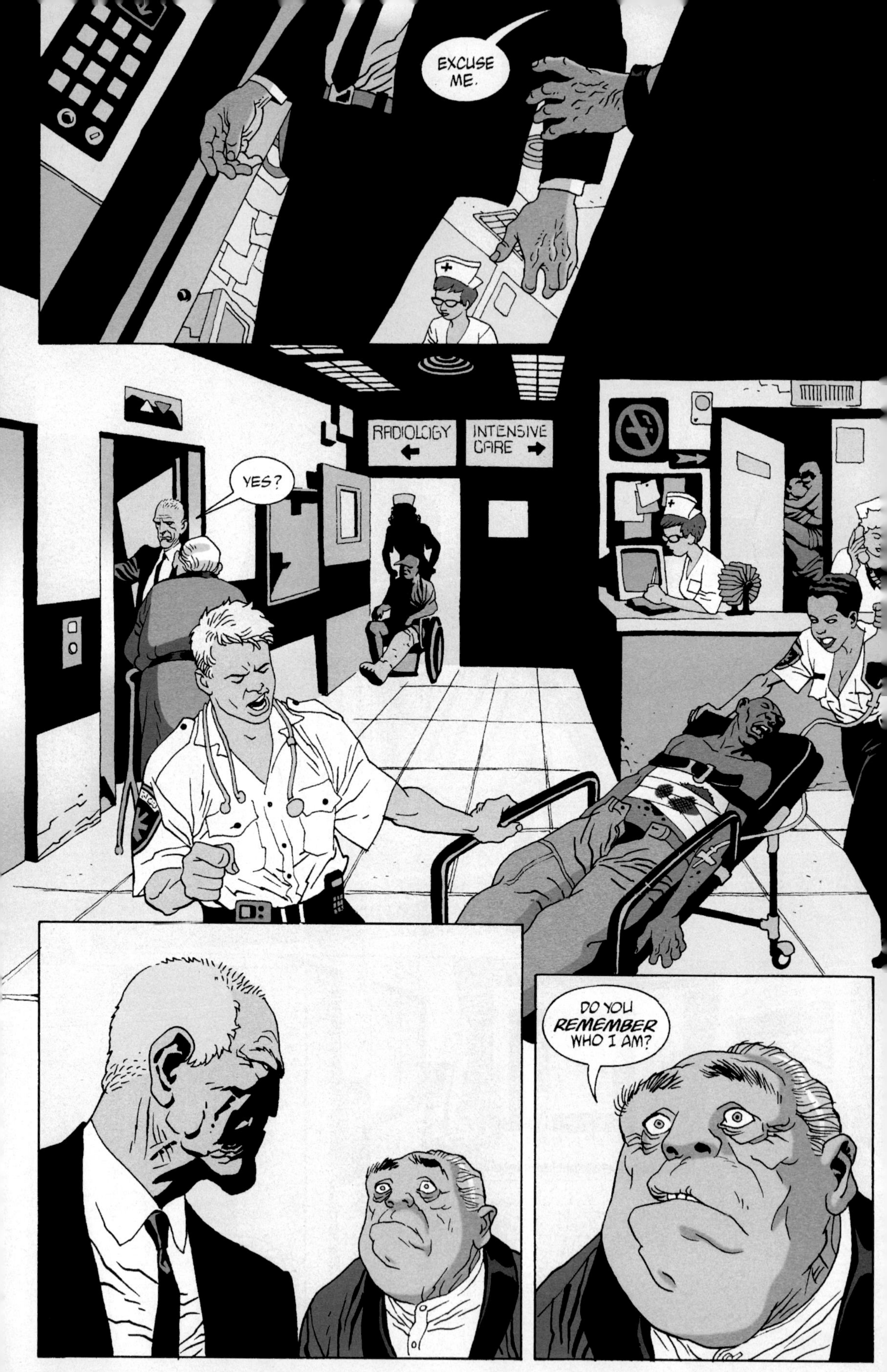
EXCUSE ME.
RADIOLOGY
INTENSIVE CARE
YES?
DO YOU *REMEMBER* WHO I AM?

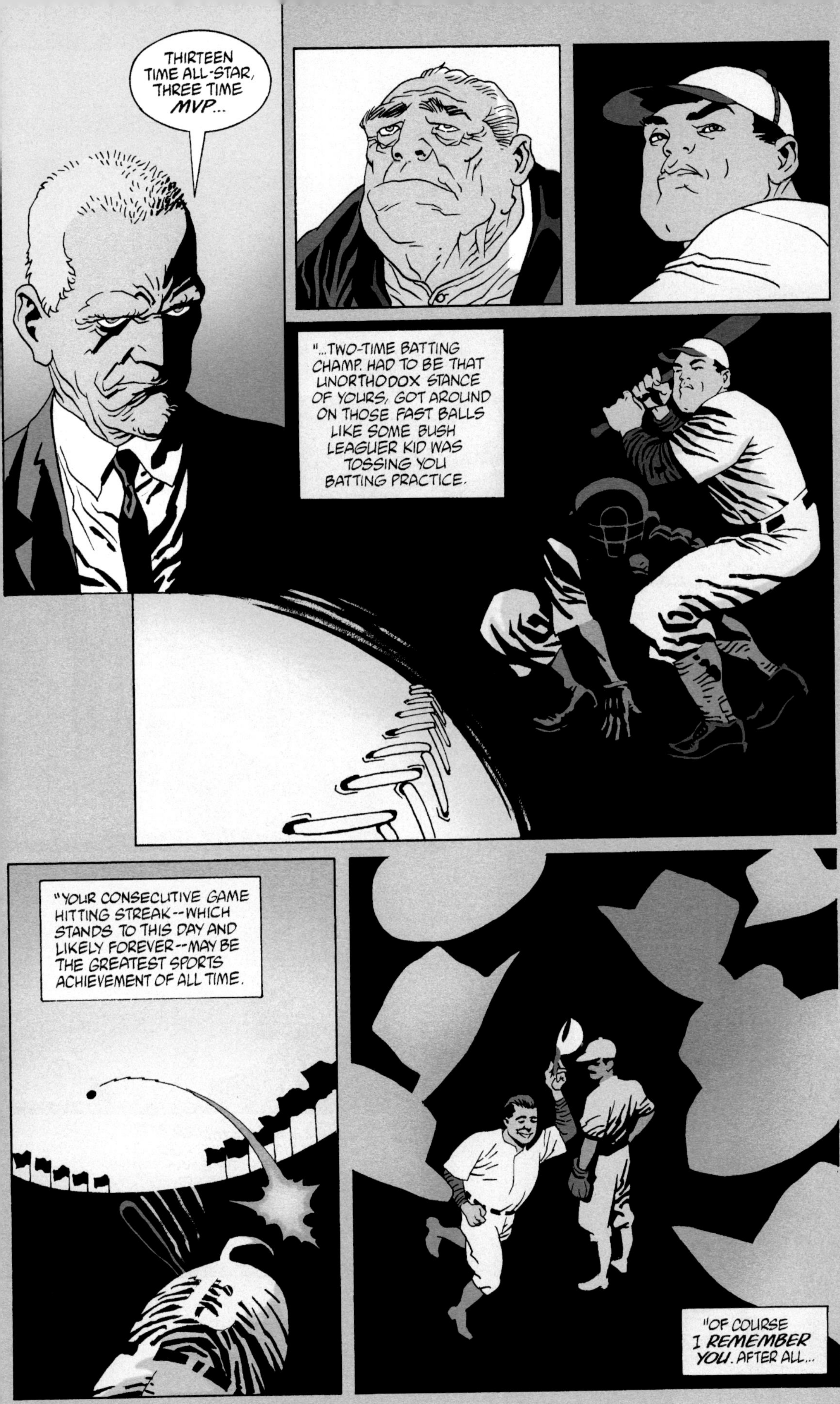
THIRTEEN TIME ALL-STAR, THREE TIME MVP...
"...TWO-TIME BATTING CHAMP. HAD TO BE THAT UNORTHODOX STANCE OF YOURS, GOT AROUND ON THOSE FAST BALLS LIKE SOME BUSH LEAGUER KID WAS TOSSING YOU BATTING PRACTICE.
"YOUR CONSECUTIVE GAME HITTING STREAK--WHICH STANDS TO THIS DAY AND LIKELY FOREVER--MAY BE THE GREATEST SPORTS ACHIEVEMENT OF ALL TIME.
"OF COURSE I REMEMBER YOU. AFTER ALL...

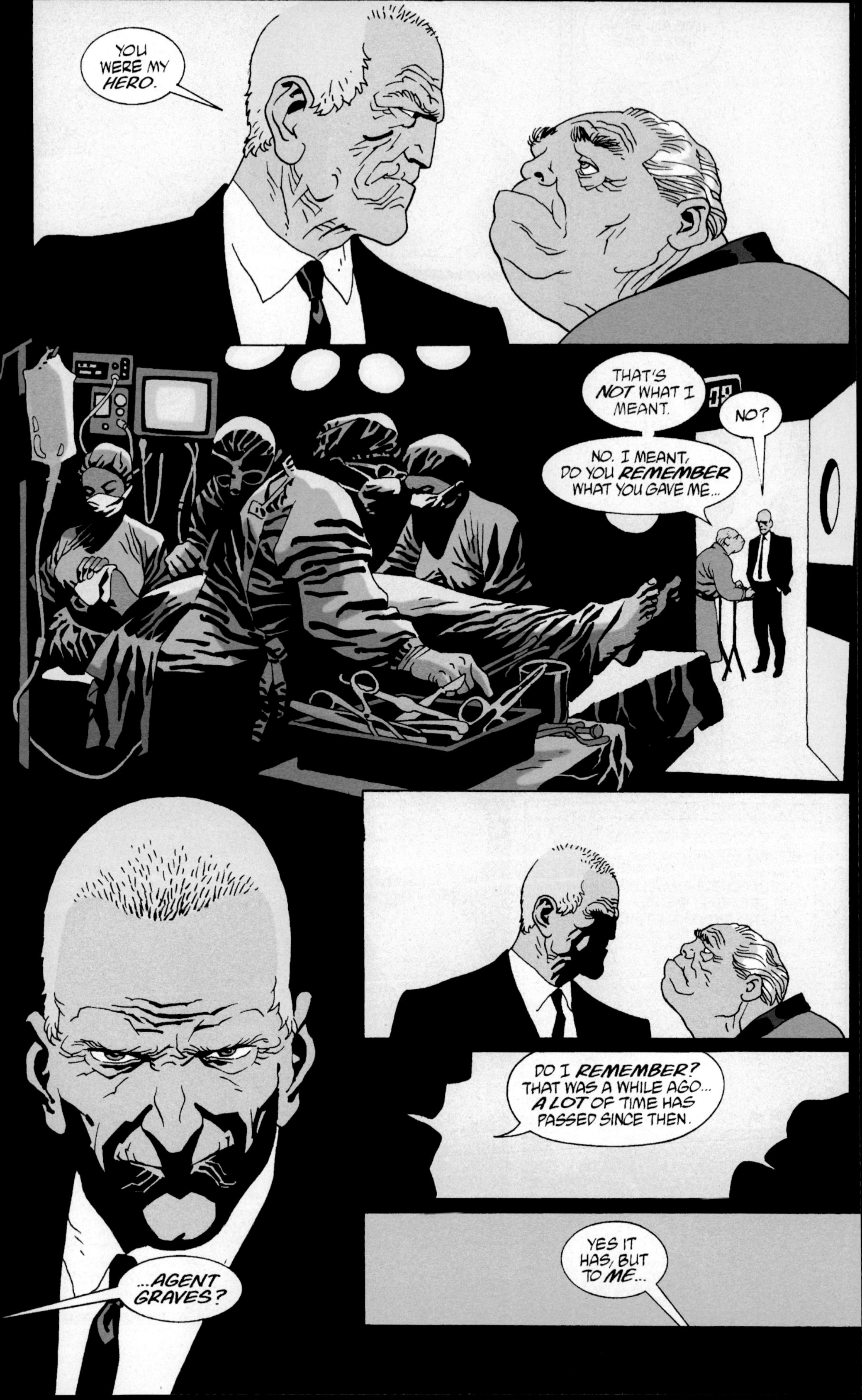
YOU WERE MY HERO.
THAT'S NOT WHAT I MEANT.
NO?
NO. I MEANT, DO YOU REMEMBER WHAT YOU GAVE ME...
...AGENT GRAVES?
DO I REMEMBER? THAT WAS A WHILE AGO... A LOT OF TIME HAS PASSED SINCE THEN.
YES IT HAS, BUT TO ME...

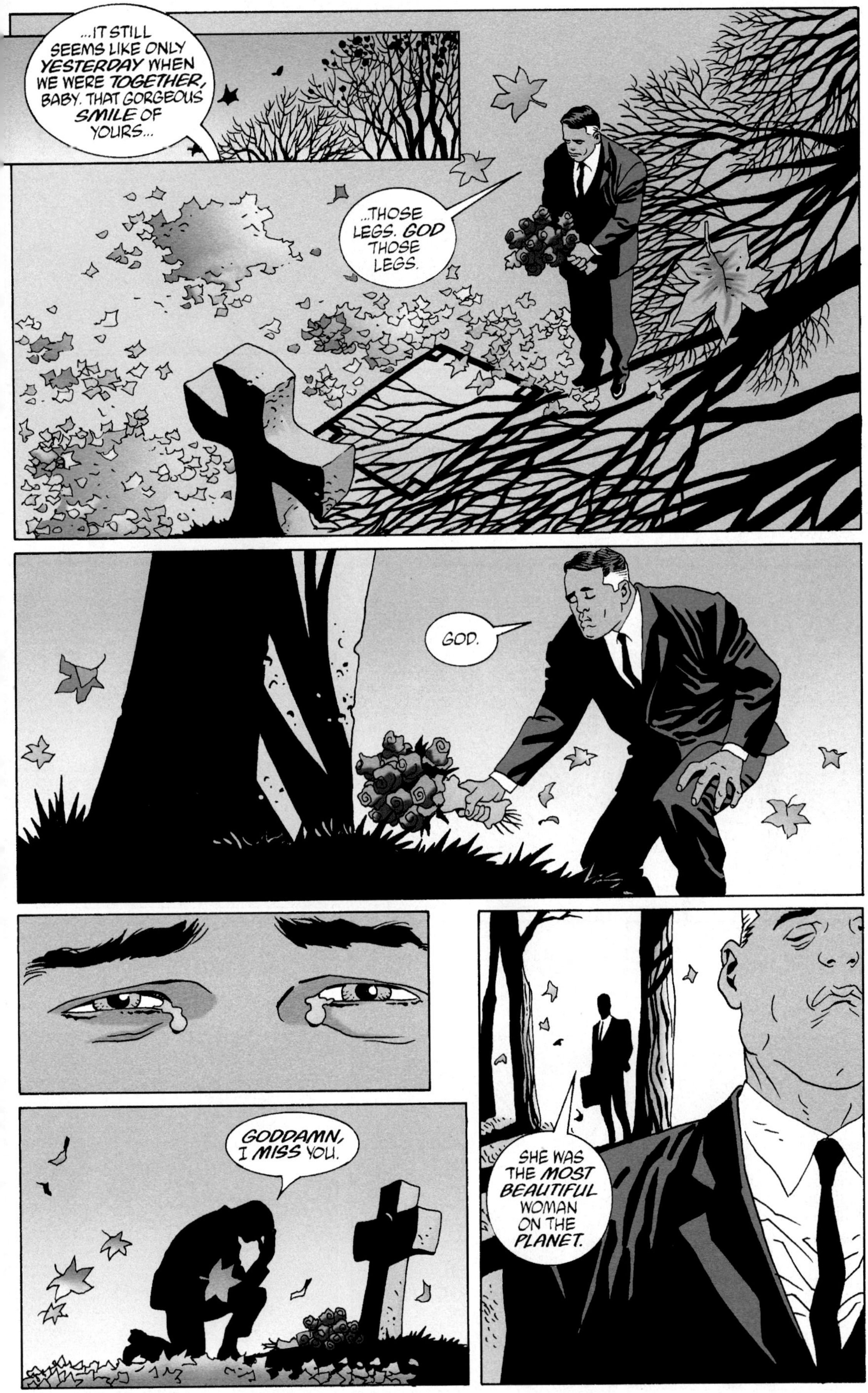
...IT STILL SEEMS LIKE ONLY YESTERDAY WHEN WE WERE TOGETHER, BABY. THAT GORGEOUS SMILE OF YOURS...
...THOSE LEGS. GOD THOSE LEGS.
GOD.
GODDAMN, I MISS YOU.
SHE WAS THE MOST BEAUTIFUL WOMAN ON THE PLANET.

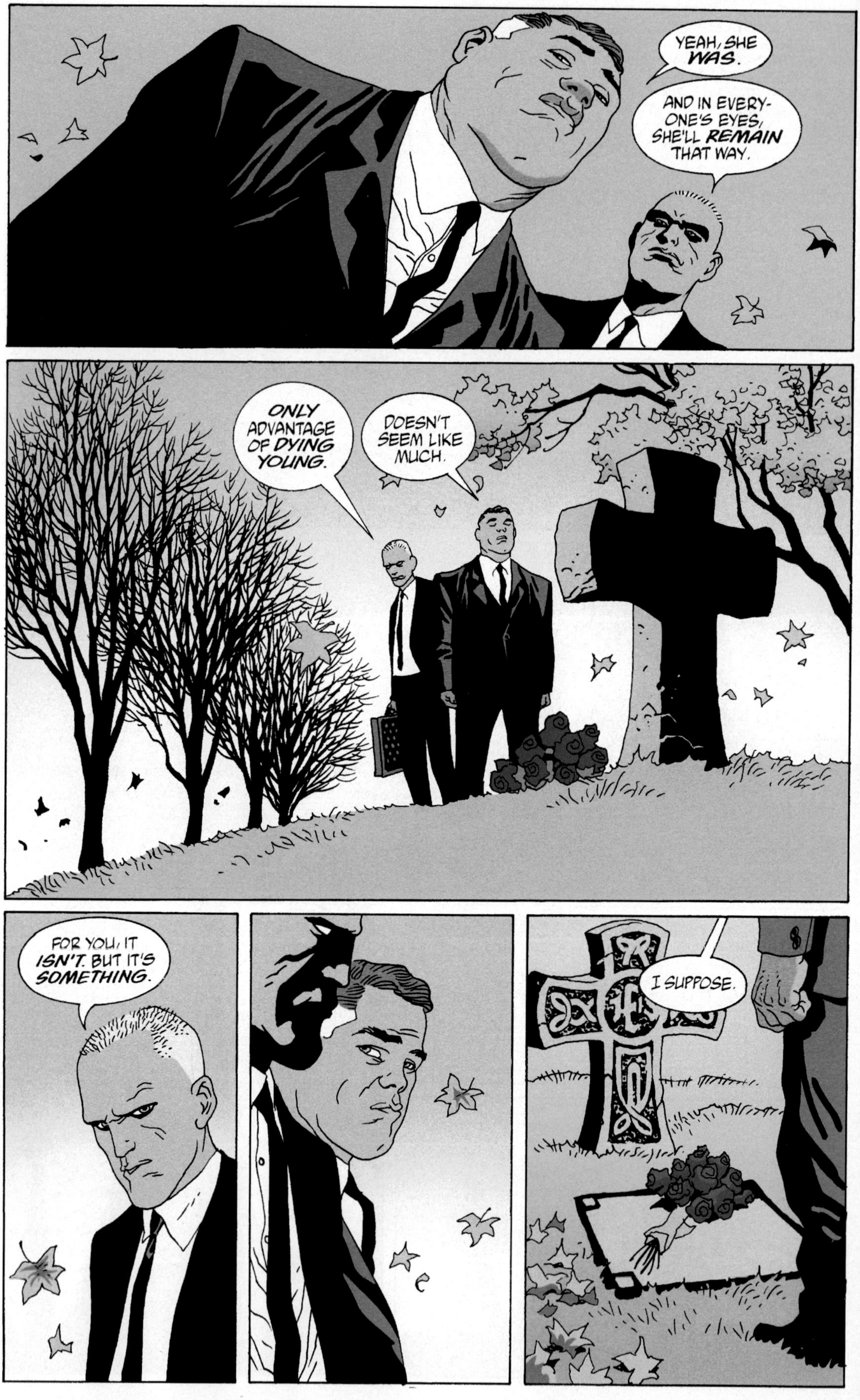
YEAH, SHE WAS.
AND IN EVERY-ONE'S EYES, SHE'LL REMAIN THAT WAY.
ONLY ADVANTAGE OF DYING YOUNG.
DOESN'T SEEM LIKE MUCH.
FOR YOU, IT ISN'T. BUT IT'S SOMETHING.
I SUPPOSE.

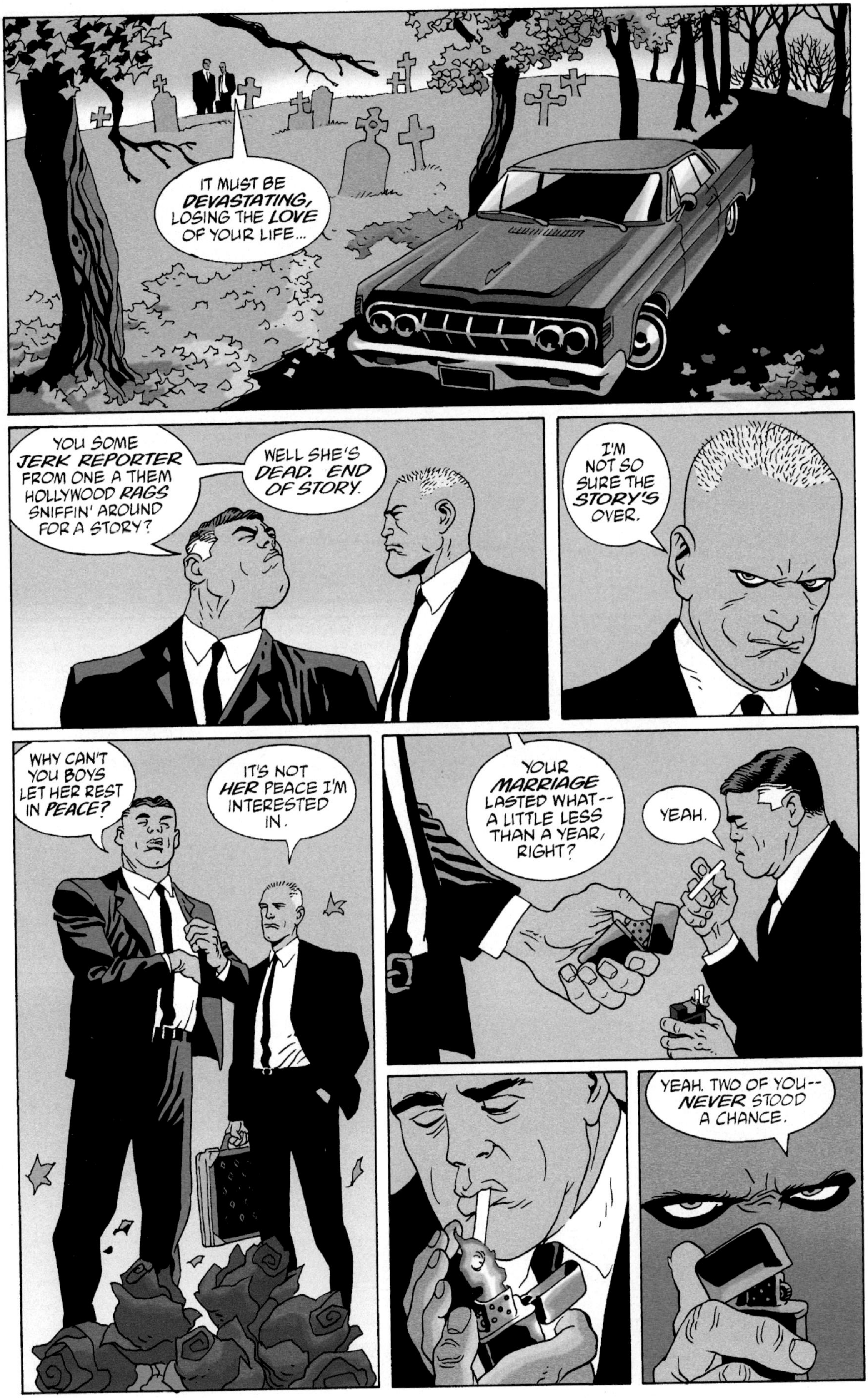
IT MUST BE DEVASTATING, LOSING THE LOVE OF YOUR LIFE...
YOU SOME JERK REPORTER FROM ONE A THEM HOLLYWOOD RAGS SNIFFIN' AROUND FOR A STORY?
WELL SHE'S DEAD. END OF STORY.
I'M NOT SO SURE THE STORY'S OVER.
WHY CAN'T YOU BOYS LET HER REST IN PEACE?
IT'S NOT HER PEACE I'M INTERESTED IN.
YOUR MARRIAGE LASTED WHAT-- A LITTLE LESS THAN A YEAR, RIGHT?
YEAH.
YEAH. TWO OF YOU-- NEVER STOOD A CHANCE.

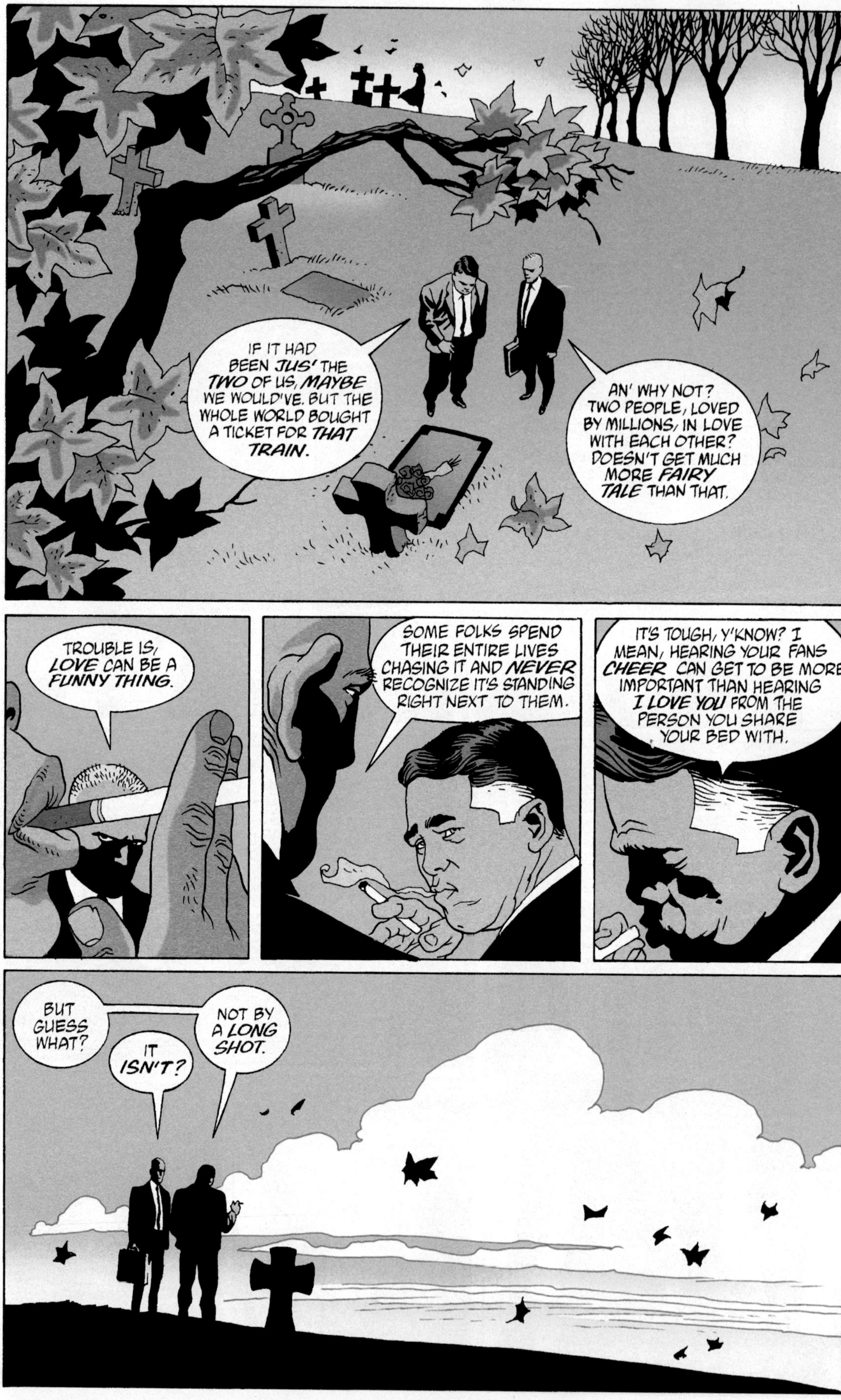
IF IT HAD BEEN JUS' THE TWO OF US, MAYBE WE WOULD'VE. BUT THE WHOLE WORLD BOUGHT A TICKET FOR THAT TRAIN.
AN' WHY NOT? TWO PEOPLE, LOVED BY MILLIONS, IN LOVE WITH EACH OTHER? DOESN'T GET MUCH MORE FAIRY TALE THAN THAT.
TROUBLE IS, LOVE CAN BE A FUNNY THING.
SOME FOLKS SPEND THEIR ENTIRE LIVES CHASING IT AND NEVER RECOGNIZE IT'S STANDING RIGHT NEXT TO THEM.
IT'S TOUGH, Y'KNOW? I MEAN, HEARING YOUR FANS CHEER CAN GET TO BE MORE IMPORTANT THAN HEARING I LOVE YOU FROM THE PERSON YOU SHARE YOUR BED WITH.
BUT GUESS WHAT?
IT ISN'T?
NOT BY A LONG SHOT.

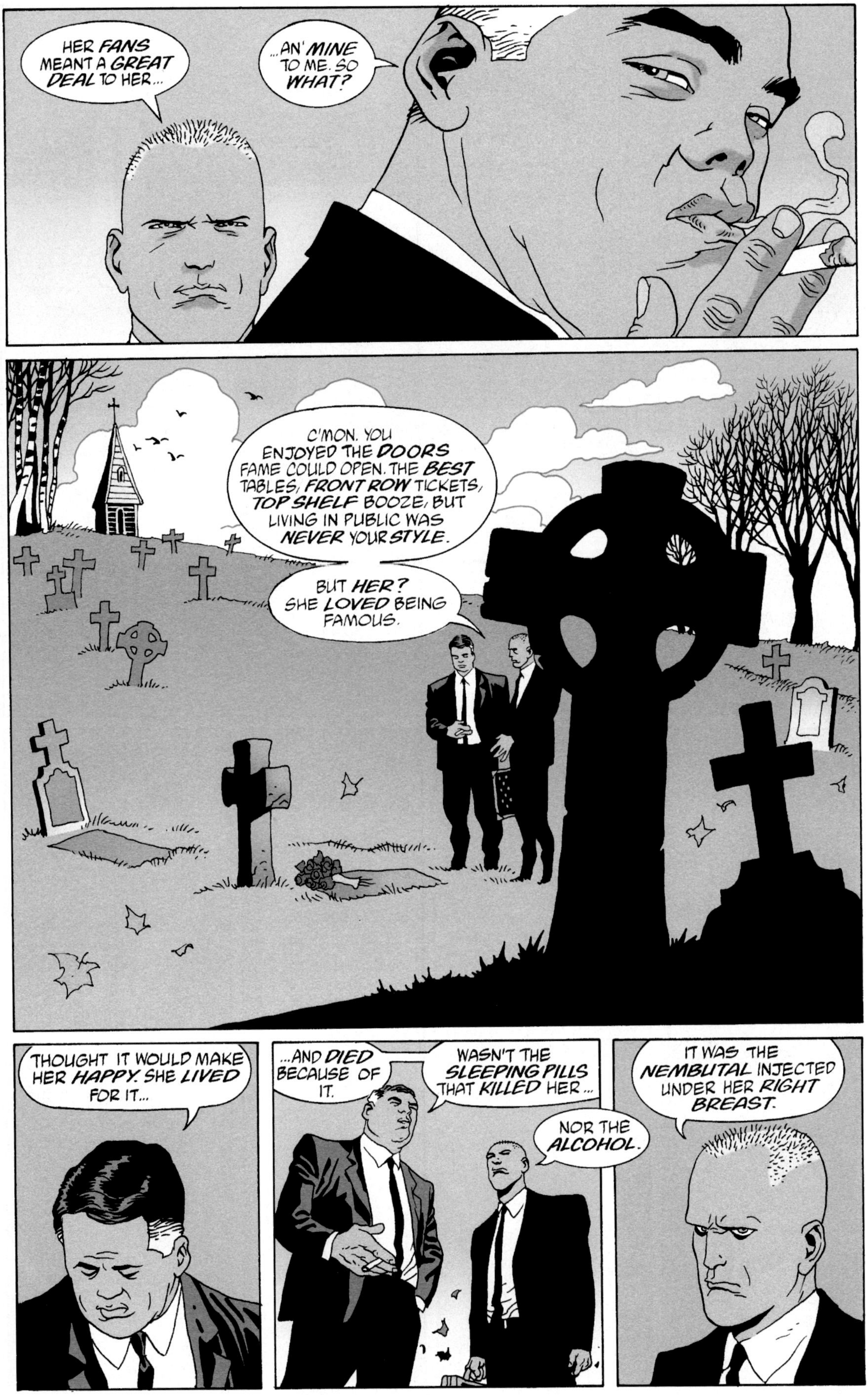
HER FANS MEANT A GREAT DEAL TO HER...
...AN' MINE TO ME. SO WHAT?
C'MON. YOU ENJOYED THE DOORS FAME COULD OPEN. THE BEST TABLES, FRONT ROW TICKETS, TOP SHELF BOOZE, BUT LIVING IN PUBLIC WAS NEVER YOUR STYLE.
BUT HER? SHE LOVED BEING FAMOUS.
THOUGHT IT WOULD MAKE HER HAPPY. SHE LIVED FOR IT...
...AND DIED BECAUSE OF IT.
WASN'T THE SLEEPING PILLS THAT KILLED HER...
NOR THE ALCOHOL.
IT WAS THE NEMBUTAL INJECTED UNDER HER RIGHT BREAST.

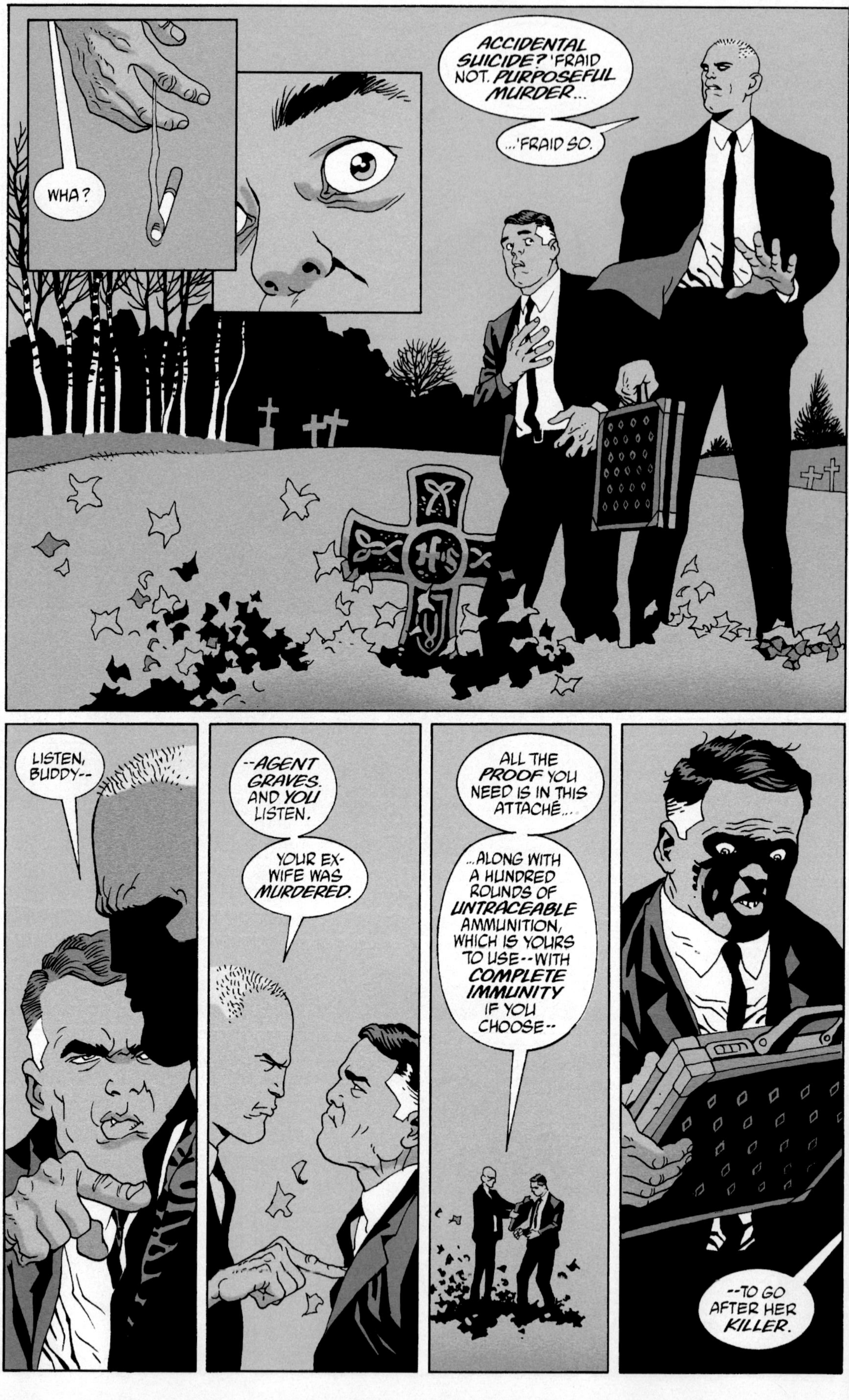
WHA?
ACCIDENTAL SUICIDE? 'FRAID NOT. PURPOSEFUL MURDER...
...'FRAID SO.
LISTEN, BUDDY--
--AGENT GRAVES. AND YOU LISTEN.
YOUR EX-WIFE WAS MURDERED.
ALL THE PROOF YOU NEED IS IN THIS ATTACHÉ...
...ALONG WITH A HUNDRED ROUNDS OF UNTRACEABLE AMMUNITION, WHICH IS YOURS TO USE--WITH COMPLETE IMMUNITY IF YOU CHOOSE--
--TO GO AFTER HER KILLER.

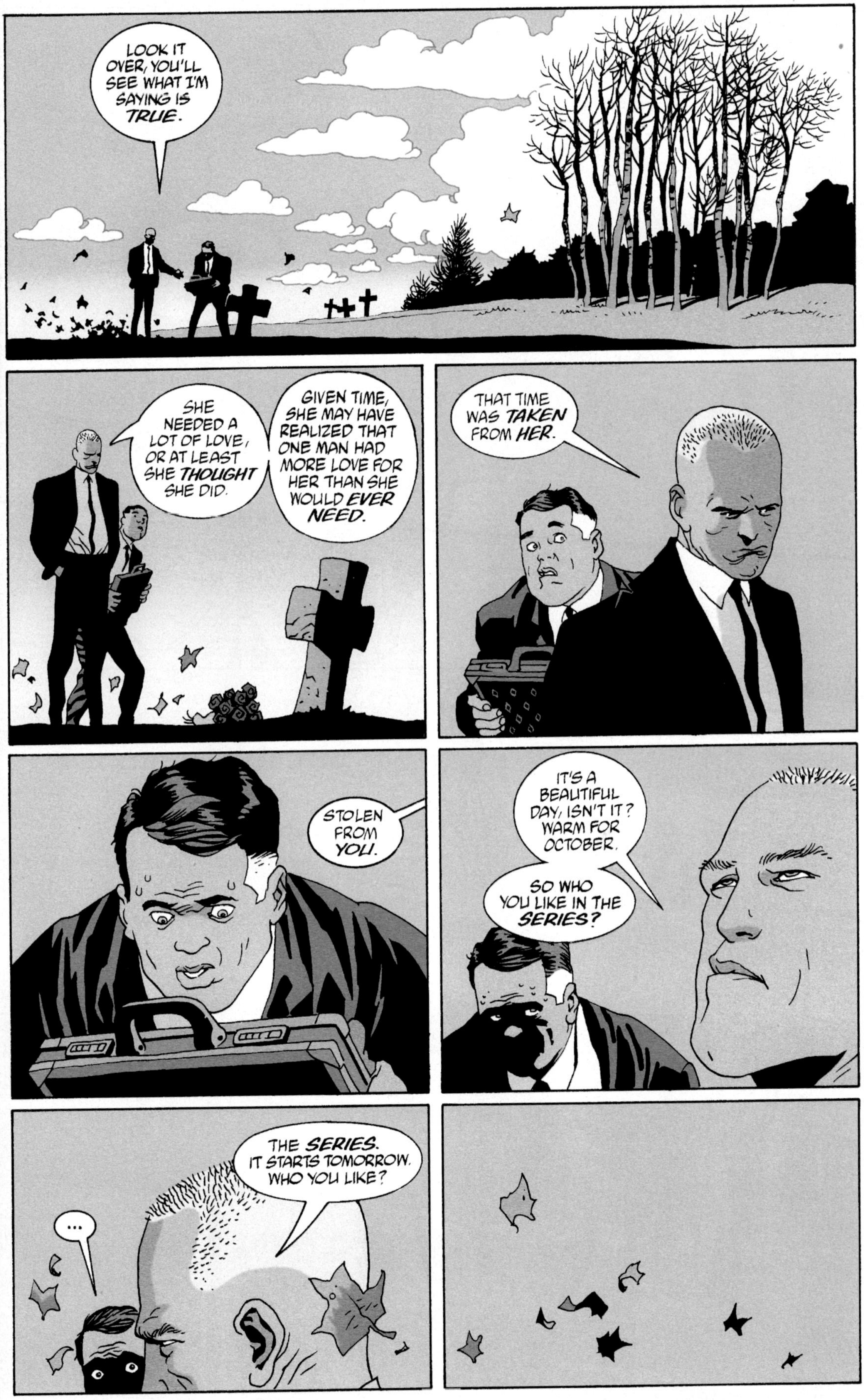
LOOK IT OVER, YOU'LL SEE WHAT I'M SAYING IS TRUE.
SHE NEEDED A LOT OF LOVE, OR AT LEAST SHE THOUGHT SHE DID.
GIVEN TIME, SHE MAY HAVE REALIZED THAT ONE MAN HAD MORE LOVE FOR HER THAN SHE WOULD EVER NEED.
THAT TIME WAS TAKEN FROM HER.
STOLEN FROM YOU.
IT'S A BEAUTIFUL DAY, ISN'T IT? WARM FOR OCTOBER.
SO WHO YOU LIKE IN THE SERIES?
...
THE SERIES. IT STARTS TOMORROW. WHO YOU LIKE?

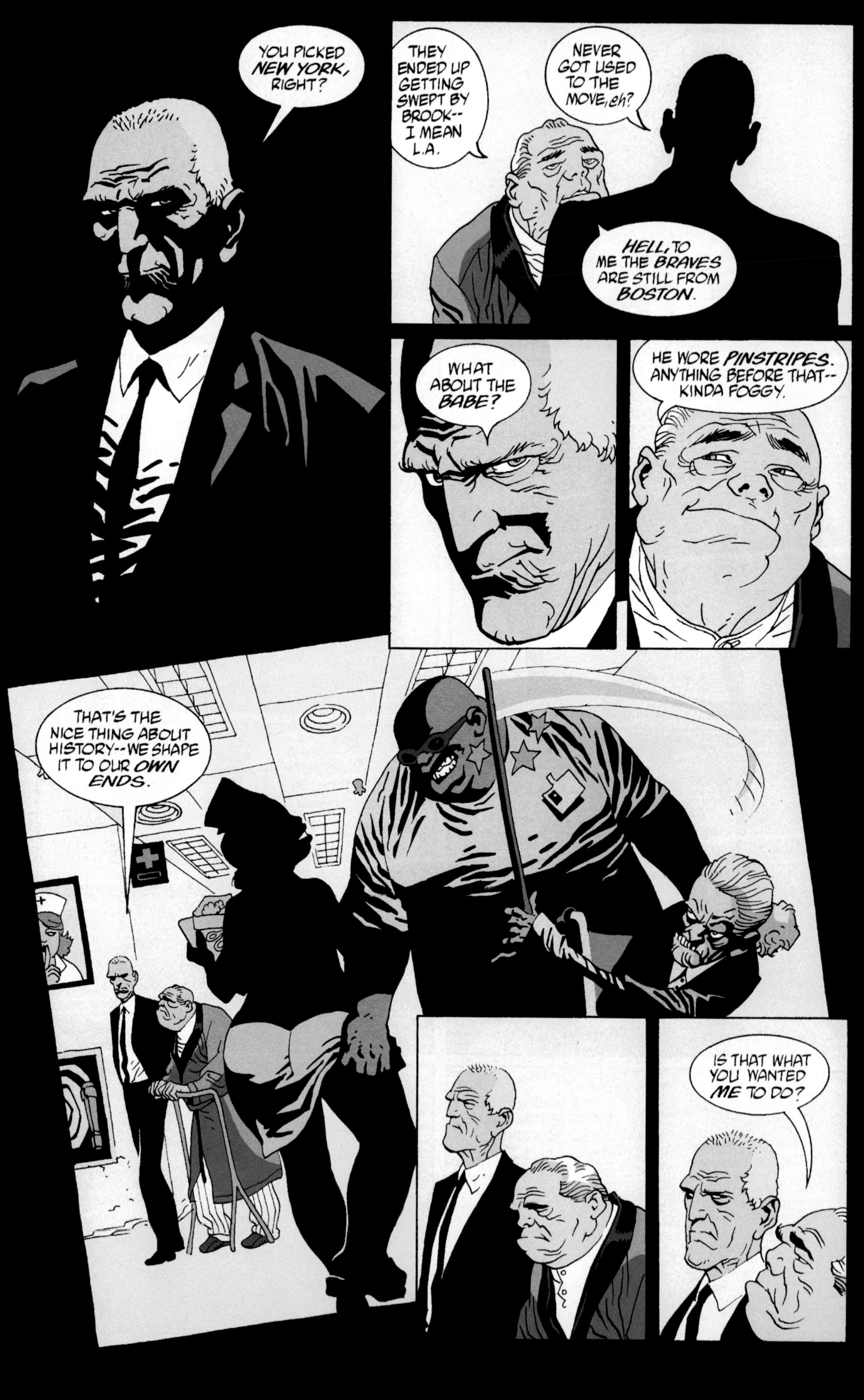
YOU PICKED NEW YORK, RIGHT?
THEY ENDED UP GETTING SWEPT BY BROOK-- I MEAN L.A.
NEVER GOT USED TO THE MOVE, eh?
HELL, TO ME THE BRAVES ARE STILL FROM BOSTON.
WHAT ABOUT THE BABE?
HE WORE PINSTRIPES. ANYTHING BEFORE THAT-- KINDA FOGGY.
THAT'S THE NICE THING ABOUT HISTORY--WE SHAPE IT TO OUR OWN ENDS.
IS THAT WHAT YOU WANTED ME TO DO?

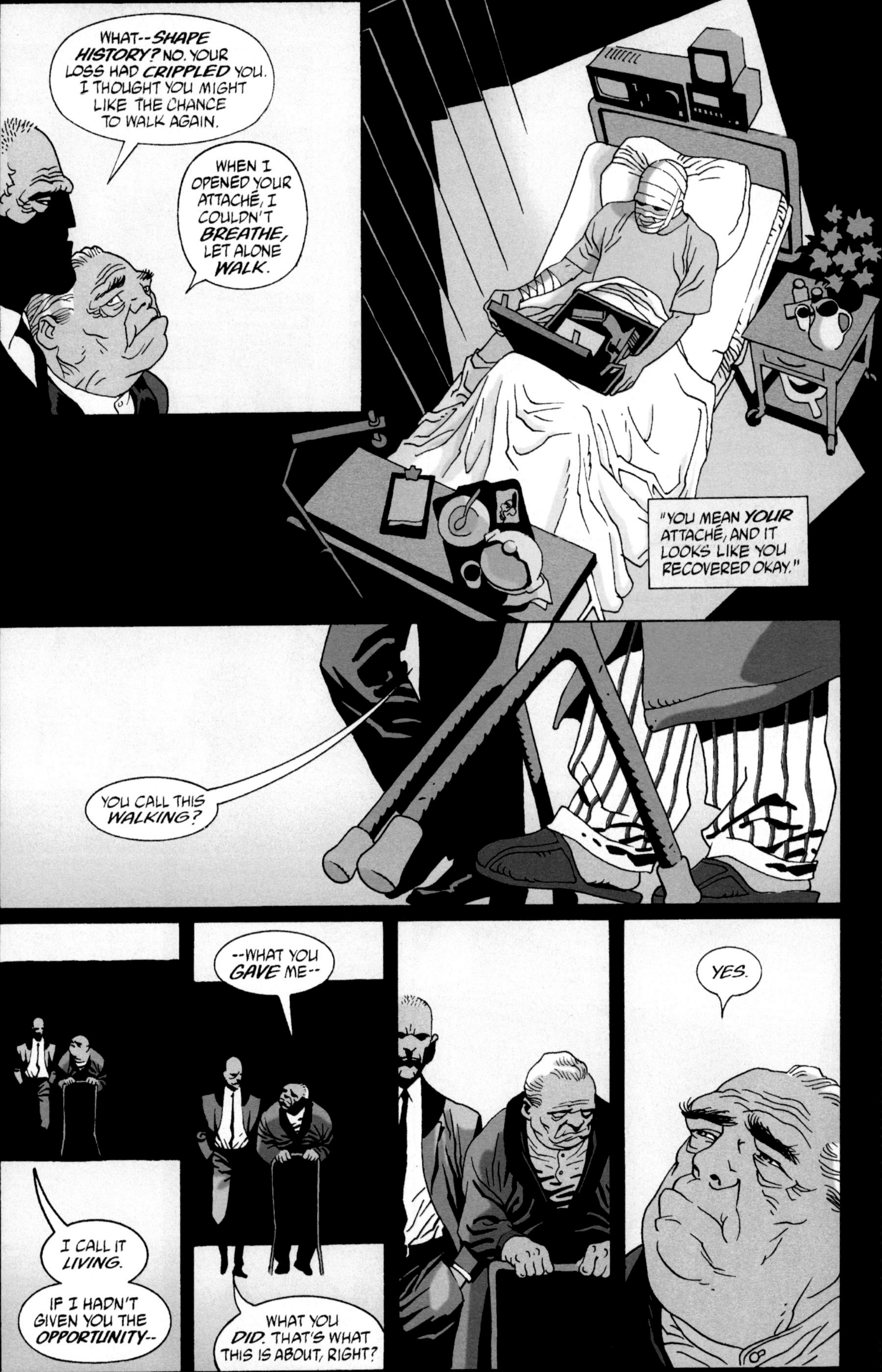
WHAT--SHAPE HISTORY? NO. YOUR LOSS HAD CRIPPLED YOU. I THOUGHT YOU MIGHT LIKE THE CHANCE TO WALK AGAIN.
WHEN I OPENED YOUR ATTACHÉ, I COULDN'T BREATHE, LET ALONE WALK.
"YOU MEAN YOUR ATTACHÉ, AND IT LOOKS LIKE YOU RECOVERED OKAY."
YOU CALL THIS WALKING?
I CALL IT LIVING.
IF I HADN'T GIVEN YOU THE OPPORTUNITY--
--WHAT YOU GAVE ME--
WHAT YOU DID. THAT'S WHAT THIS IS ABOUT, RIGHT?
YES.

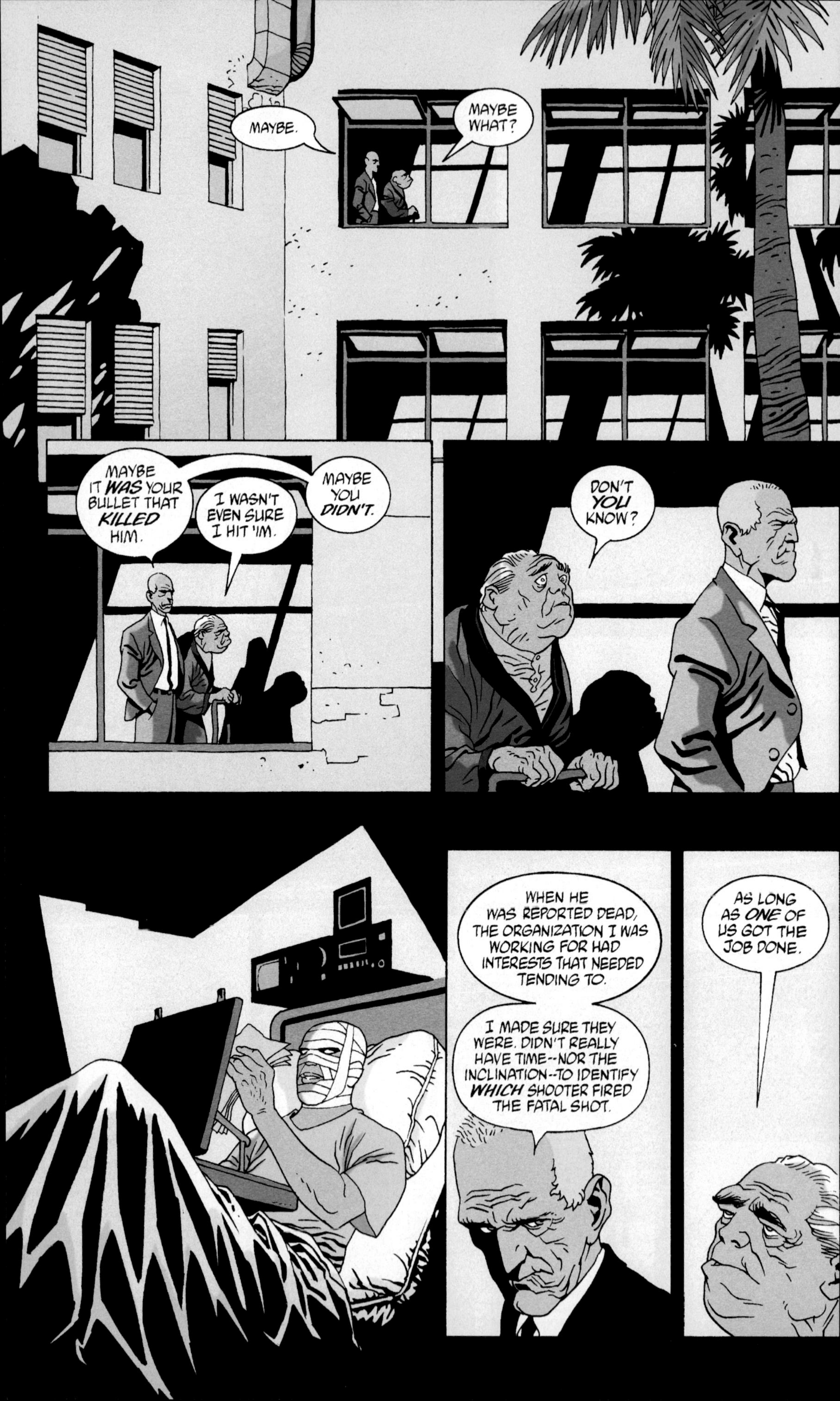
MAYBE.
MAYBE WHAT?
MAYBE IT WAS YOUR BULLET THAT KILLED HIM.
I WASN'T EVEN SURE I HIT 'IM.
MAYBE YOU DIDN'T.
DON'T YOU KNOW?
WHEN HE WAS REPORTED DEAD, THE ORGANIZATION I WAS WORKING FOR HAD INTERESTS THAT NEEDED TENDING TO.
I MADE SURE THEY WERE. DIDN'T REALLY HAVE TIME--NOR THE INCLINATION--TO IDENTIFY WHICH SHOOTER FIRED THE FATAL SHOT.
AS LONG AS ONE OF US GOT THE JOB DONE.

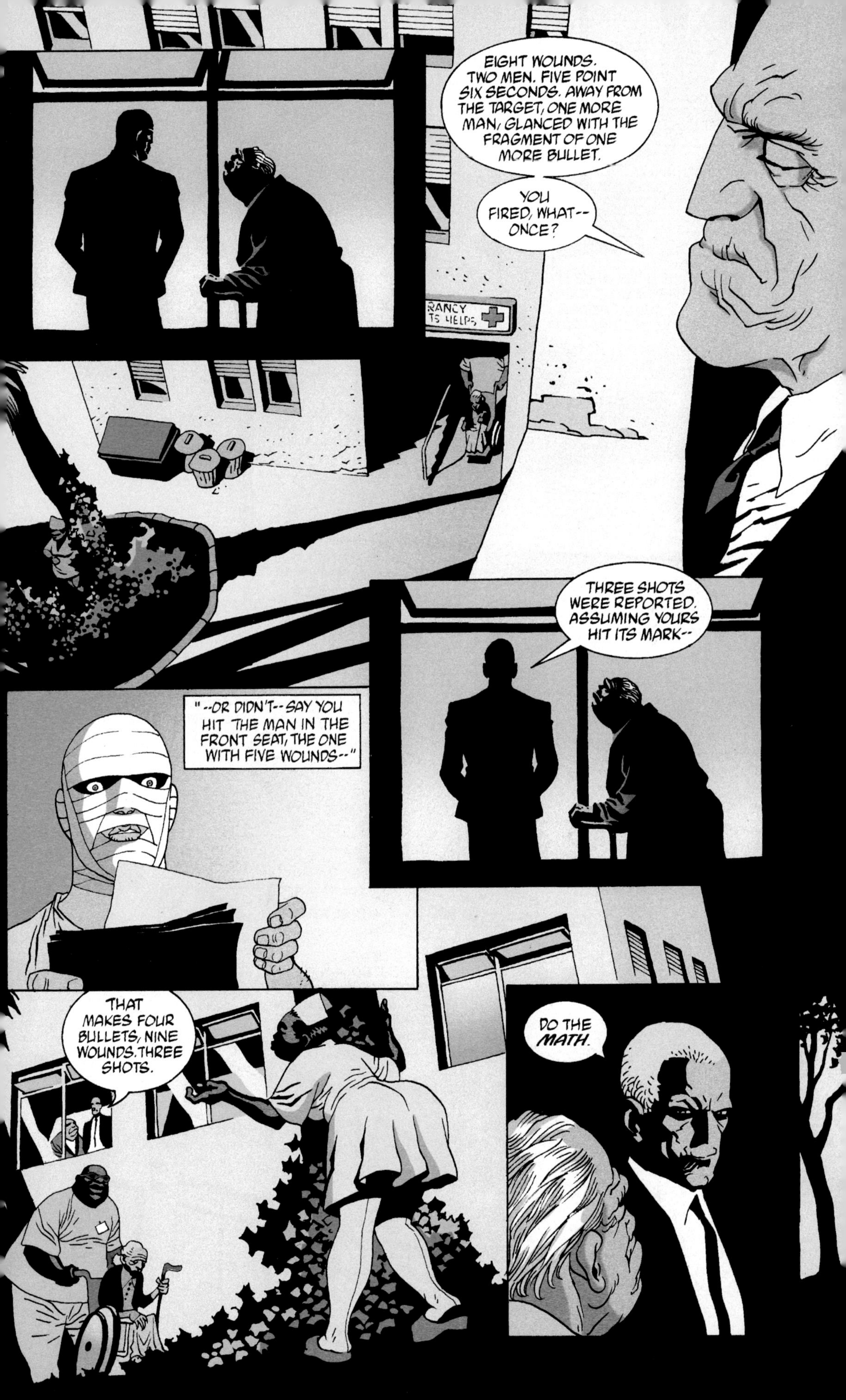
EIGHT WOUNDS. TWO MEN. FIVE POINT SIX SECONDS. AWAY FROM THE TARGET, ONE MORE MAN, GLANCED WITH THE FRAGMENT OF ONE MORE BULLET.
YOU FIRED, WHAT-- ONCE?
RANCY
TS HELPS
THREE SHOTS WERE REPORTED. ASSUMING YOURS HIT ITS MARK--
"--OR DIDN'T--SAY YOU HIT THE MAN IN THE FRONT SEAT, THE ONE WITH FIVE WOUNDS--"
THAT MAKES FOUR BULLETS, NINE WOUNDS. THREE SHOTS.
DO THE *MATH*.

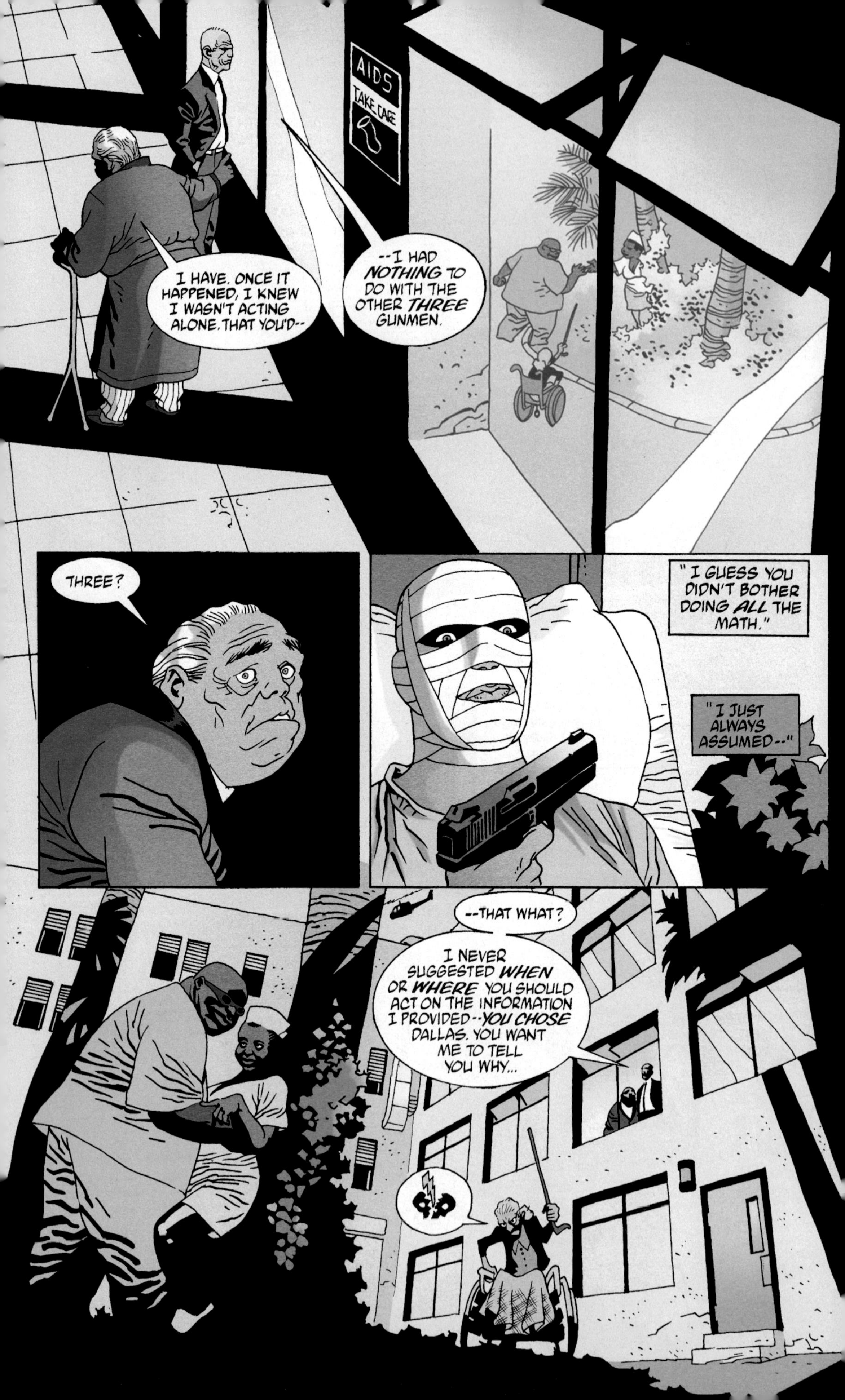
AIDS
TAKE CARE
I HAVE. ONCE IT HAPPENED, I KNEW I WASN'T ACTING ALONE. THAT YOU'D--
--I HAD NOTHING TO DO WITH THE OTHER THREE GUNMEN.
THREE?
"I GUESS YOU DIDN'T BOTHER DOING ALL THE MATH."
"I JUST ALWAYS ASSUMED--"
--THAT WHAT?
I NEVER SUGGESTED WHEN OR WHERE YOU SHOULD ACT ON THE INFORMATION I PROVIDED--YOU CHOSE DALLAS. YOU WANT ME TO TELL YOU WHY...

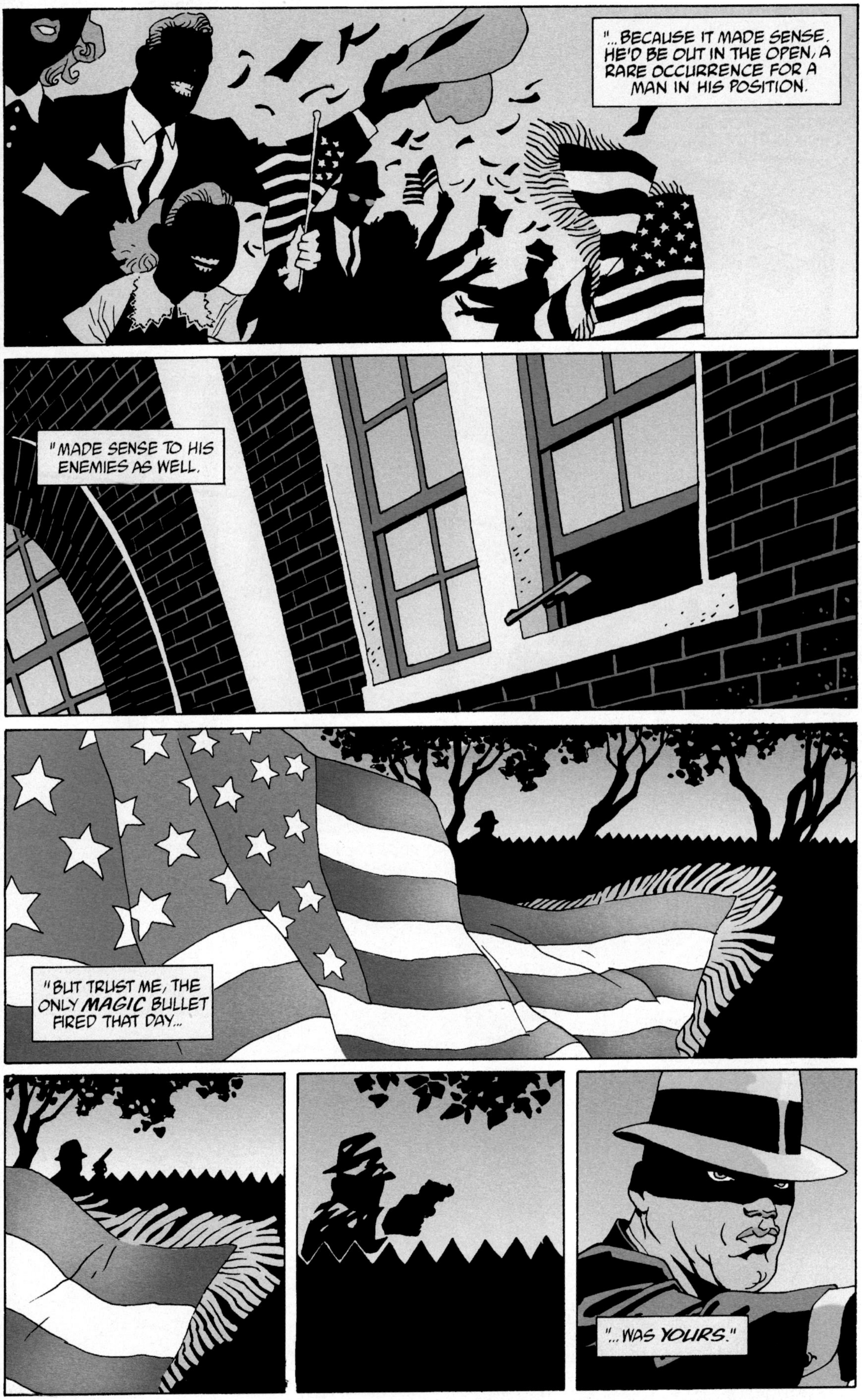
"...BECAUSE IT MADE SENSE. HE'D BE OUT IN THE OPEN, A RARE OCCURRENCE FOR A MAN IN HIS POSITION.
"MADE SENSE TO HIS ENEMIES AS WELL.
"BUT TRUST ME, THE ONLY MAGIC BULLET FIRED THAT DAY...
"...WAS YOURS."

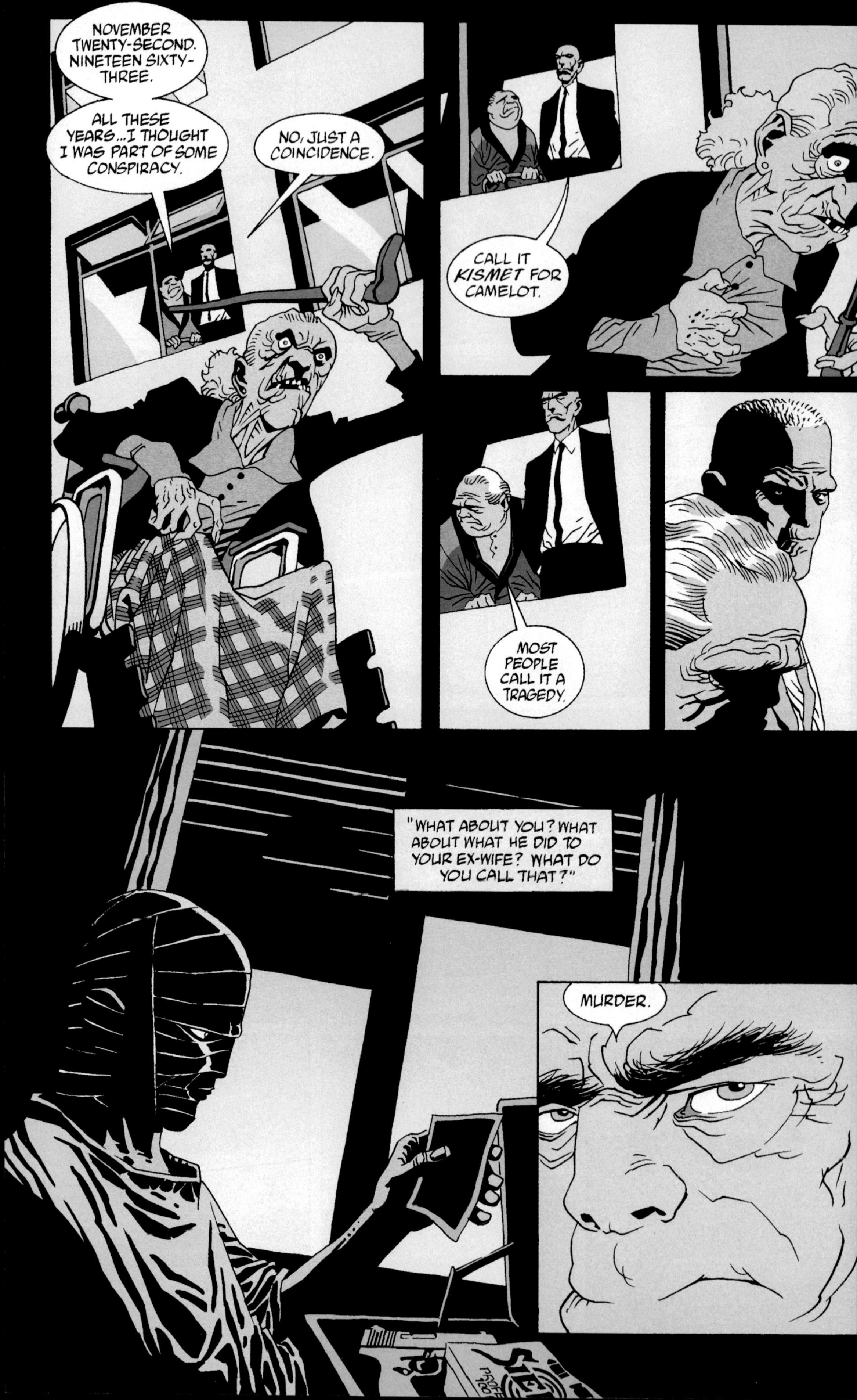
NOVEMBER TWENTY-SECOND. NINETEEN SIXTY-THREE.
ALL THESE YEARS...I THOUGHT I WAS PART OF SOME CONSPIRACY.
NO, JUST A COINCIDENCE.
CALL IT KISMET FOR CAMELOT.
MOST PEOPLE CALL IT A TRAGEDY.
"WHAT ABOUT YOU? WHAT ABOUT WHAT HE DID TO YOUR EX-WIFE? WHAT DO YOU CALL THAT?"
MURDER.

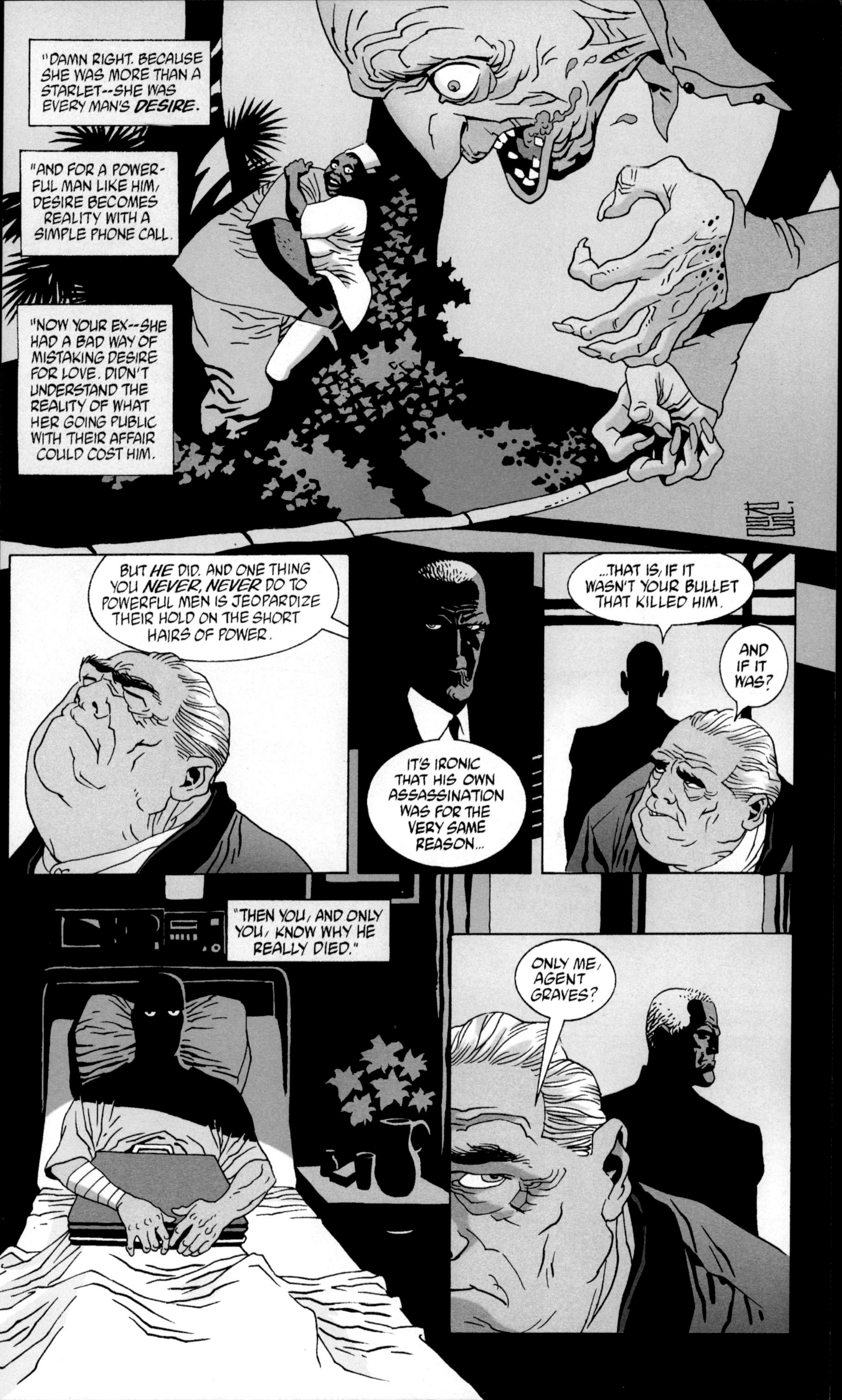
"DAMN RIGHT. BECAUSE SHE WAS MORE THAN A STARLET--SHE WAS EVERY MAN'S DESIRE.
"AND FOR A POWERFUL MAN LIKE HIM, DESIRE BECOMES REALITY WITH A SIMPLE PHONE CALL.
"NOW YOUR EX--SHE HAD A BAD WAY OF MISTAKING DESIRE FOR LOVE. DIDN'T UNDERSTAND THE REALITY OF WHAT HER GOING PUBLIC WITH THEIR AFFAIR COULD COST HIM.
BUT HE DID. AND ONE THING YOU NEVER, NEVER DO TO POWERFUL MEN IS JEOPARDIZE THEIR HOLD ON THE SHORT HAIRS OF POWER.
IT'S IRONIC THAT HIS OWN ASSASSINATION WAS FOR THE VERY SAME REASON...
...THAT IS, IF IT WASN'T YOUR BULLET THAT KILLED HIM.
AND IF IT WAS?
"THEN YOU, AND ONLY YOU, KNOW WHY HE REALLY DIED."
ONLY ME, AGENT GRAVES?

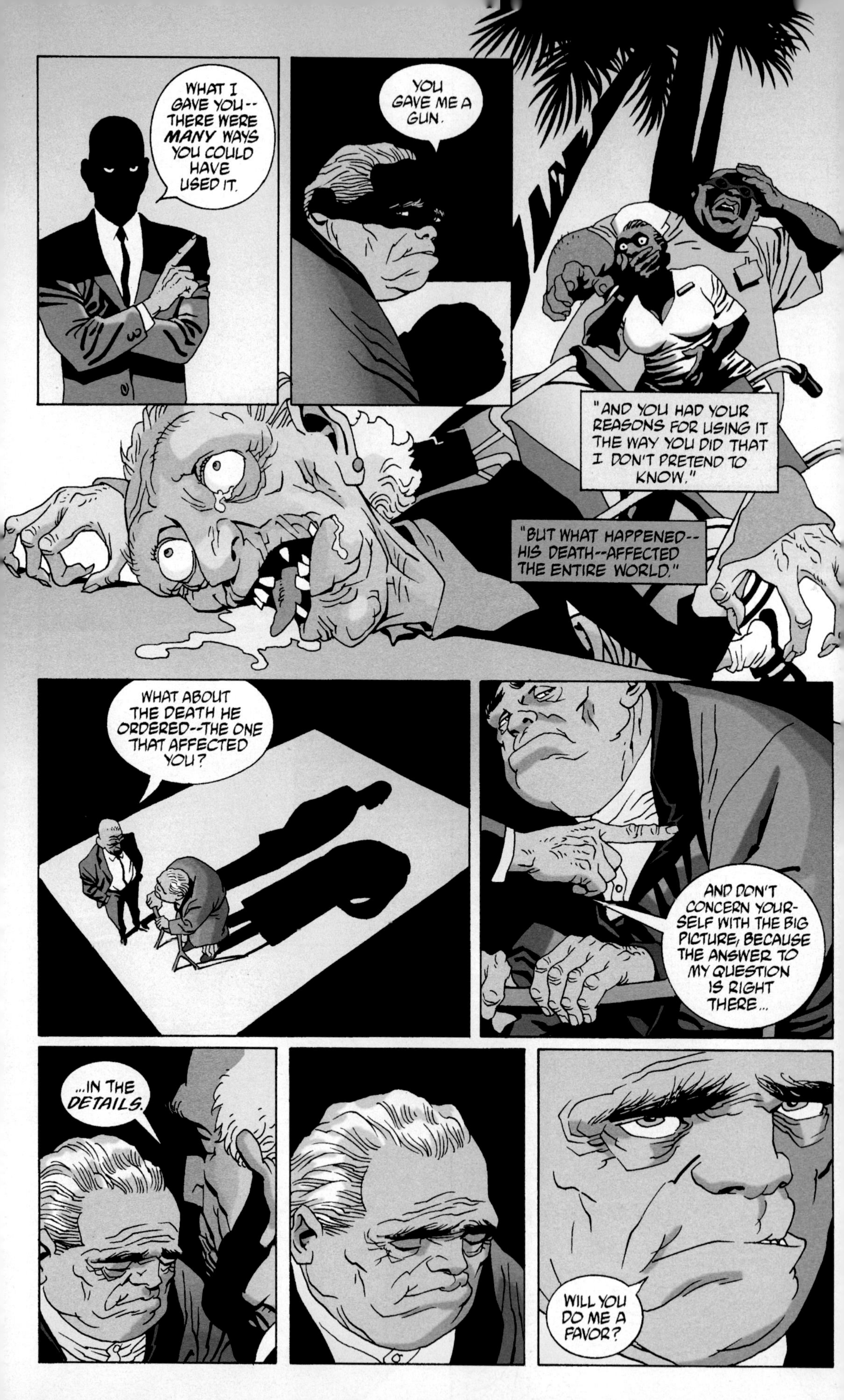
WHAT I GAVE YOU-- THERE WERE *MANY* WAYS YOU COULD HAVE USED IT.
YOU GAVE ME A GUN.
"AND YOU HAD YOUR REASONS FOR USING IT THE WAY YOU DID THAT I DON'T PRETEND TO KNOW."
"BUT WHAT HAPPENED-- HIS DEATH--AFFECTED THE ENTIRE WORLD."
WHAT ABOUT THE DEATH HE ORDERED--THE ONE THAT AFFECTED YOU?
AND DON'T CONCERN YOUR-SELF WITH THE BIG PICTURE, BECAUSE THE ANSWER TO MY QUESTION IS RIGHT THERE...
...IN THE *DETAILS.*
WILL YOU DO ME A FAVOR?

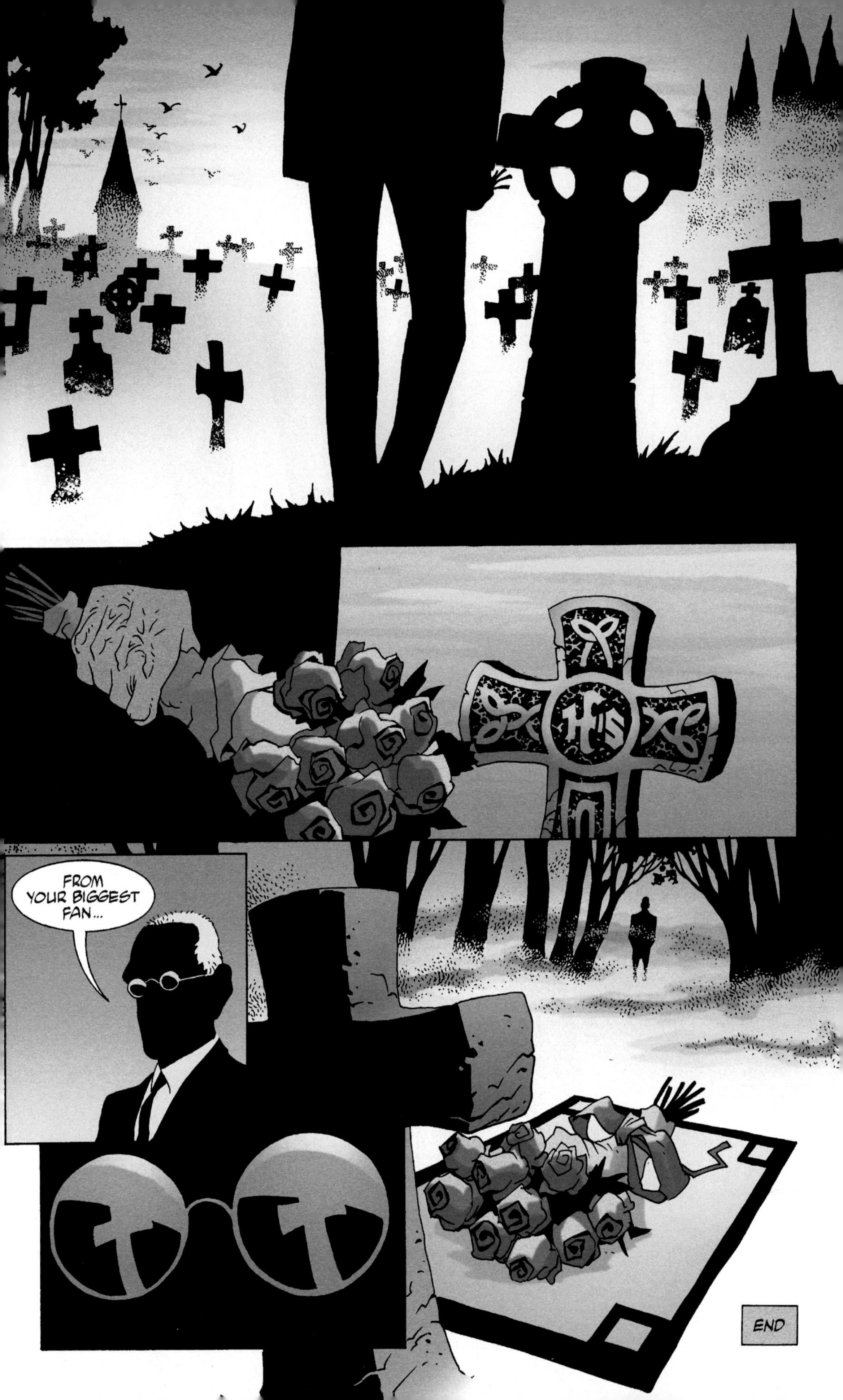
FROM YOUR BIGGEST FAN...
END

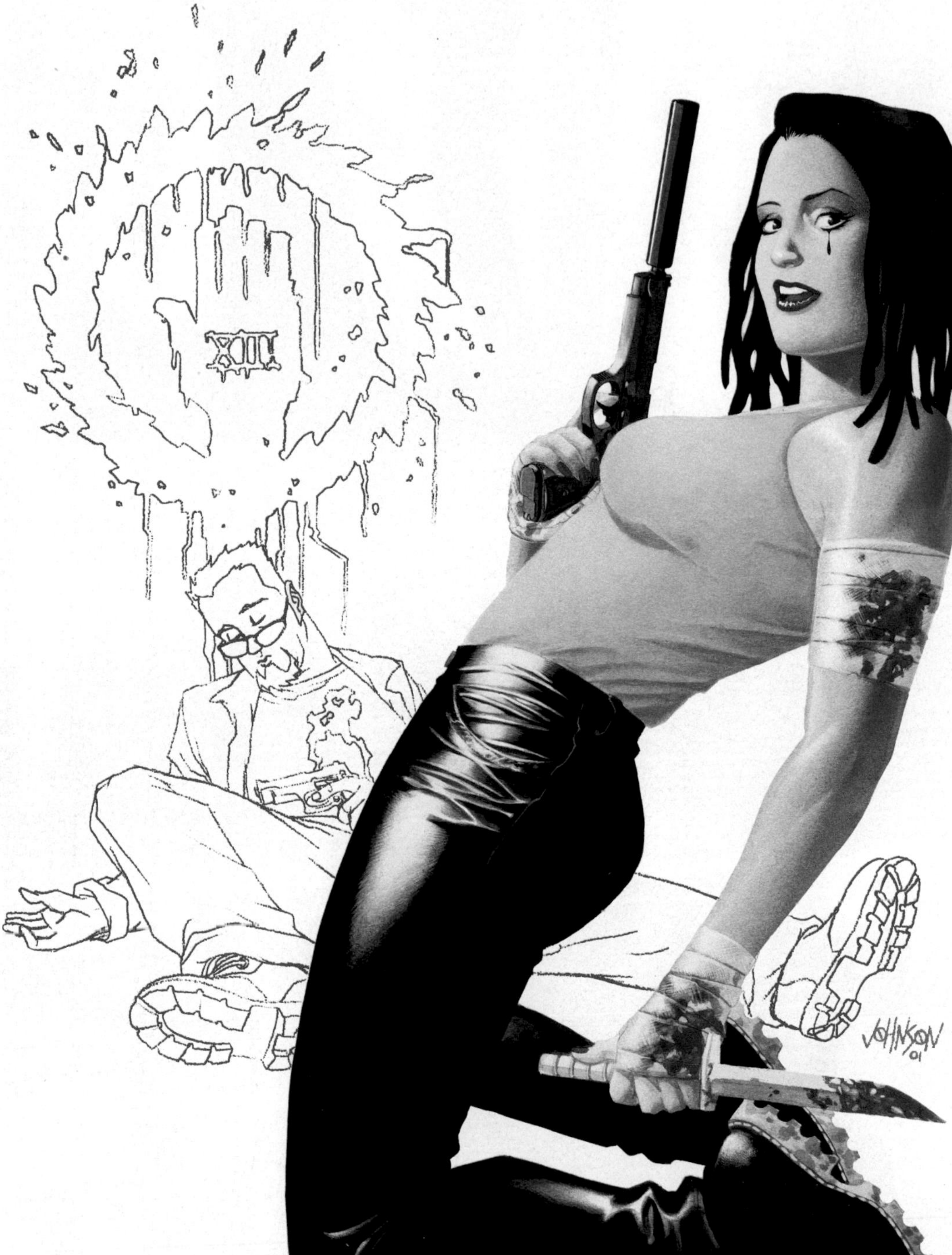
XIII
JOHNSON '01

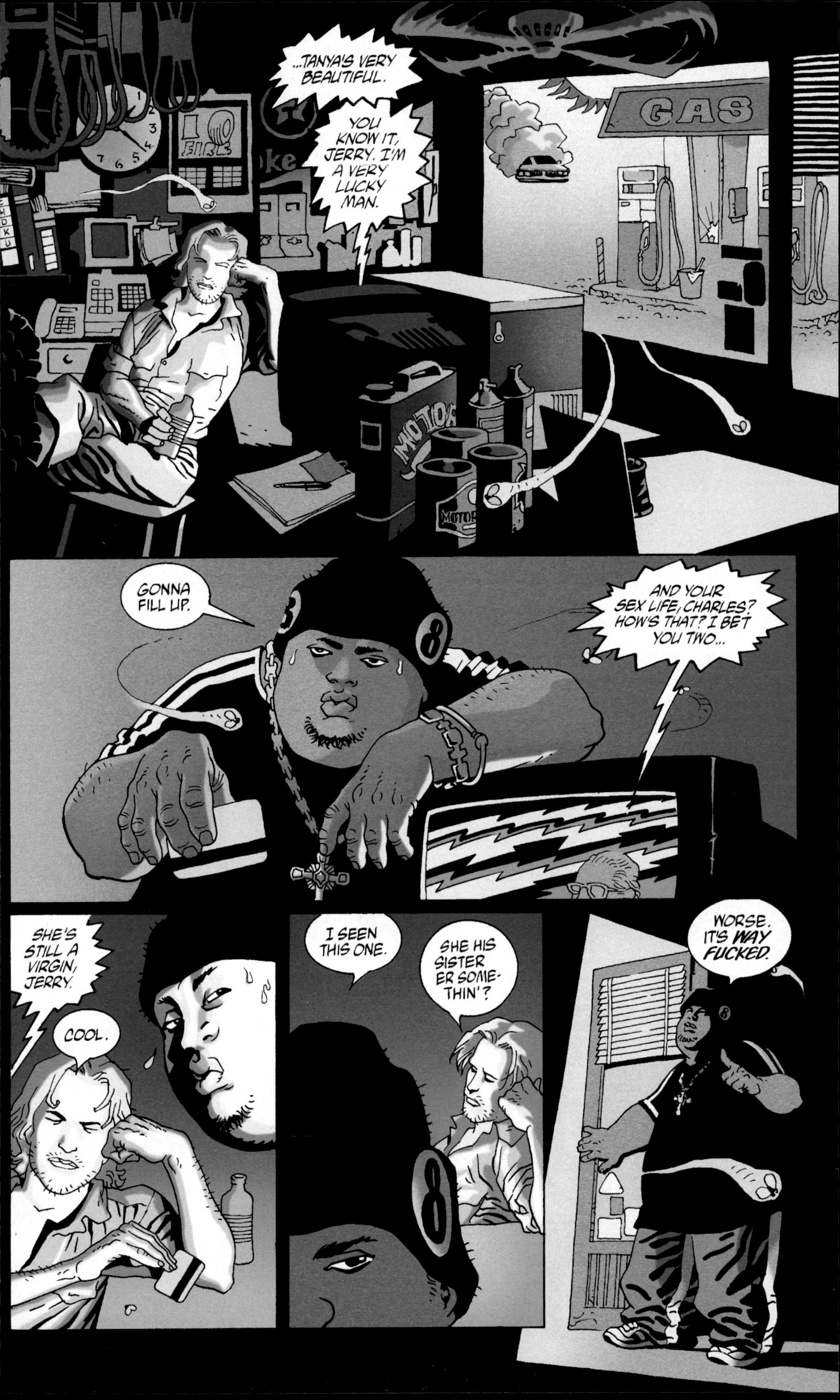
...TANYA'S VERY BEAUTIFUL.
YOU KNOW IT, JERRY. I'M A VERY LUCKY MAN.
GAS
GONNA FILL UP.
AND YOUR SEX LIFE, CHARLES? HOW'S THAT? I BET YOU TWO...
SHE'S STILL A VIRGIN, JERRY.
COOL.
I SEEN THIS ONE.
SHE HIS SISTER ER SOME-THIN'?
WORSE. IT'S WAY FUCKED.

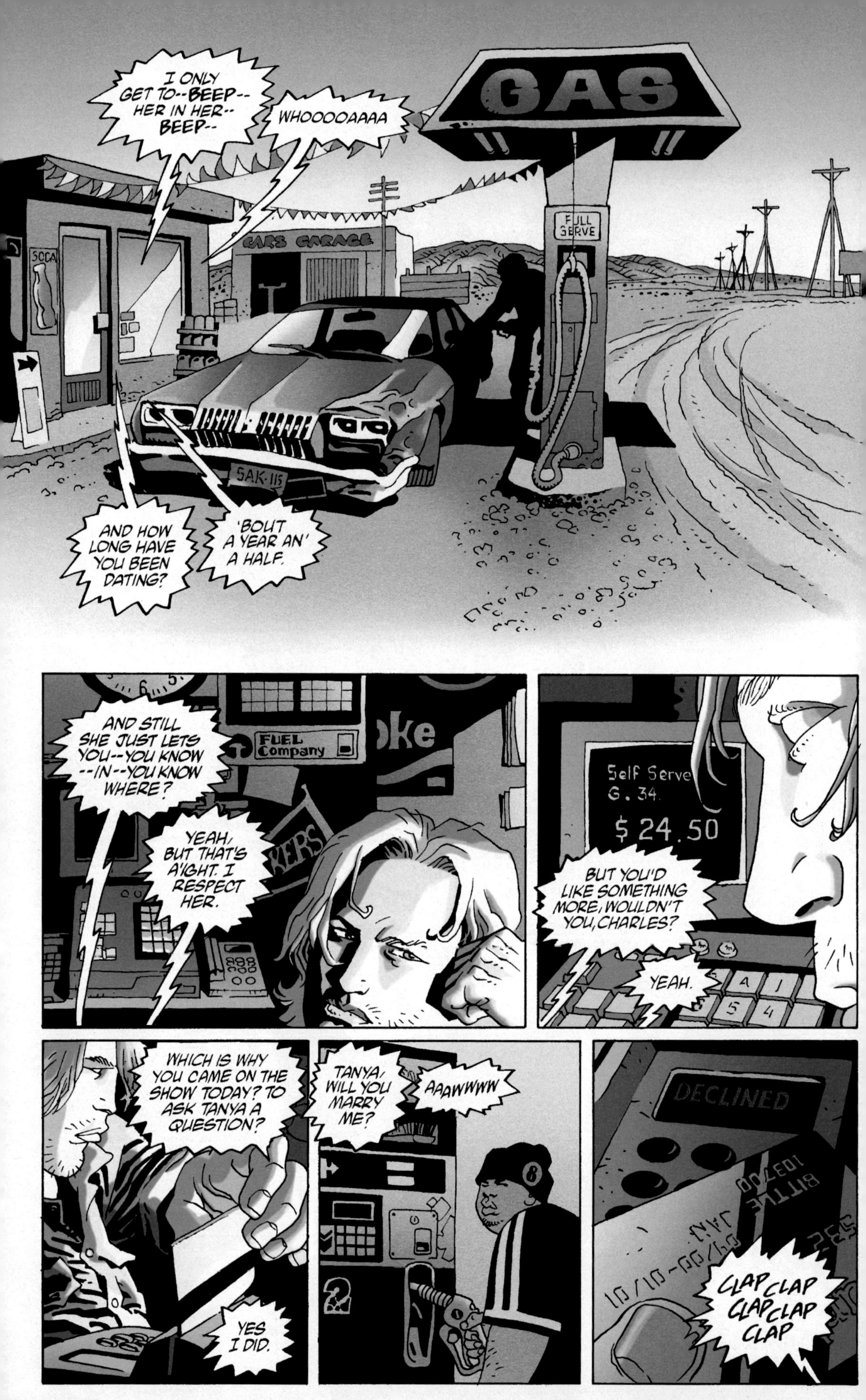

I ONLY GET TO--BEEP-- HER IN HER-- BEEP--
WHOOOOAAAA
GAS
FULL SERVE
GARS GARAGE
SODA
SAK-115
AND HOW LONG HAVE YOU BEEN DATING?
'BOUT A YEAR AN' A HALF.
AND STILL SHE JUST LETS YOU--YOU KNOW --IN--YOU KNOW WHERE?
FUEL Company
YEAH, BUT THAT'S A'IGHT. I RESPECT HER.
Self Serve
G. 34.
$ 24.50
BUT YOU'D LIKE SOMETHING MORE, WOULDN'T YOU, CHARLES?
YEAH.
WHICH IS WHY YOU CAME ON THE SHOW TODAY? TO ASK TANYA A QUESTION?
YES I DID.
TANYA, WILL YOU MARRY ME?
AAAWWWW
DECLINED
CLAP CLAP CLAP CLAP CLAP

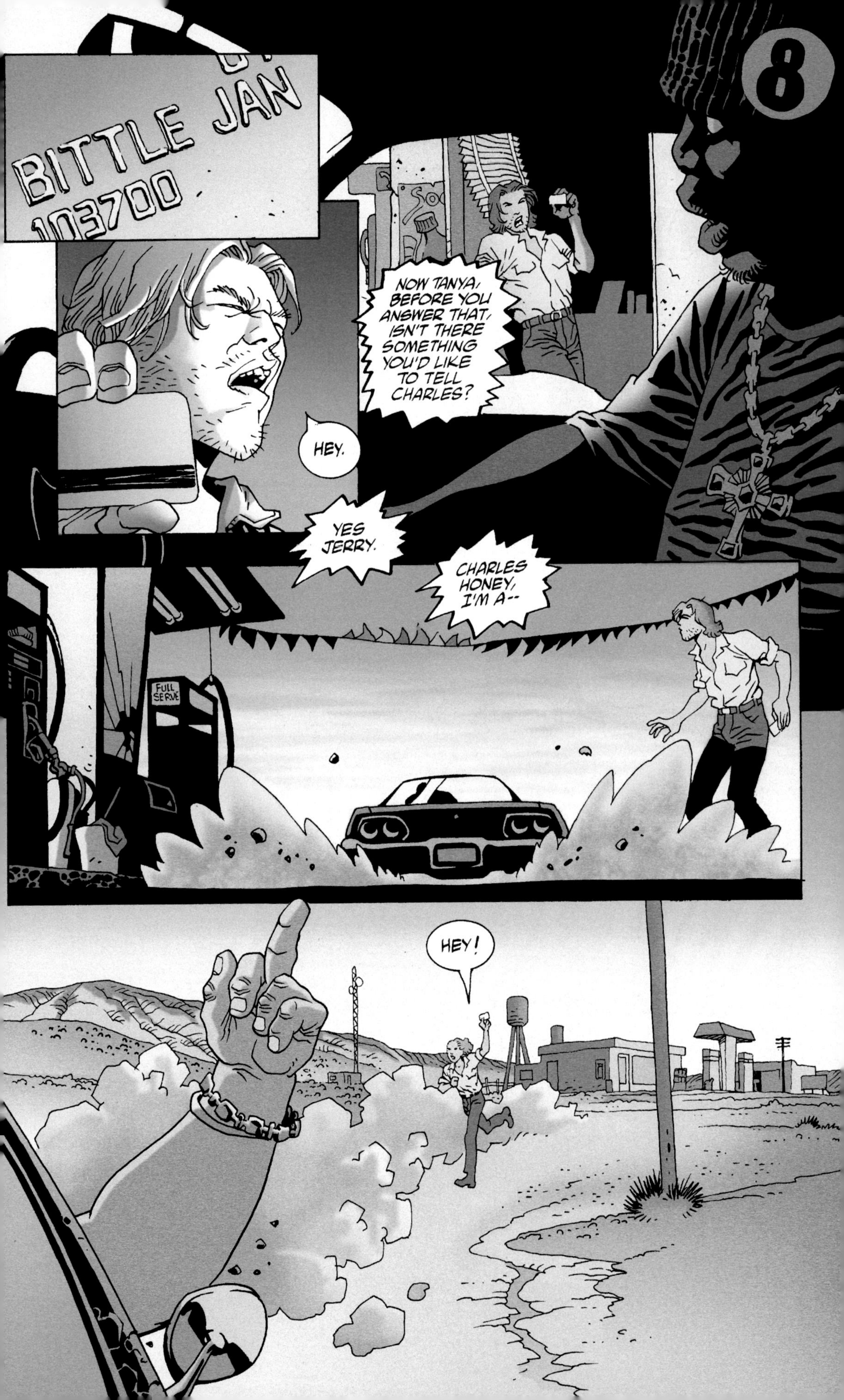
8
BITTLE JAN
103700
NOW TANYA, BEFORE YOU ANSWER THAT, ISN'T THERE SOMETHING YOU'D LIKE TO TELL CHARLES?
HEY.
YES JERRY.
CHARLES HONEY, I'M A--
FULL SERVE
HEY!

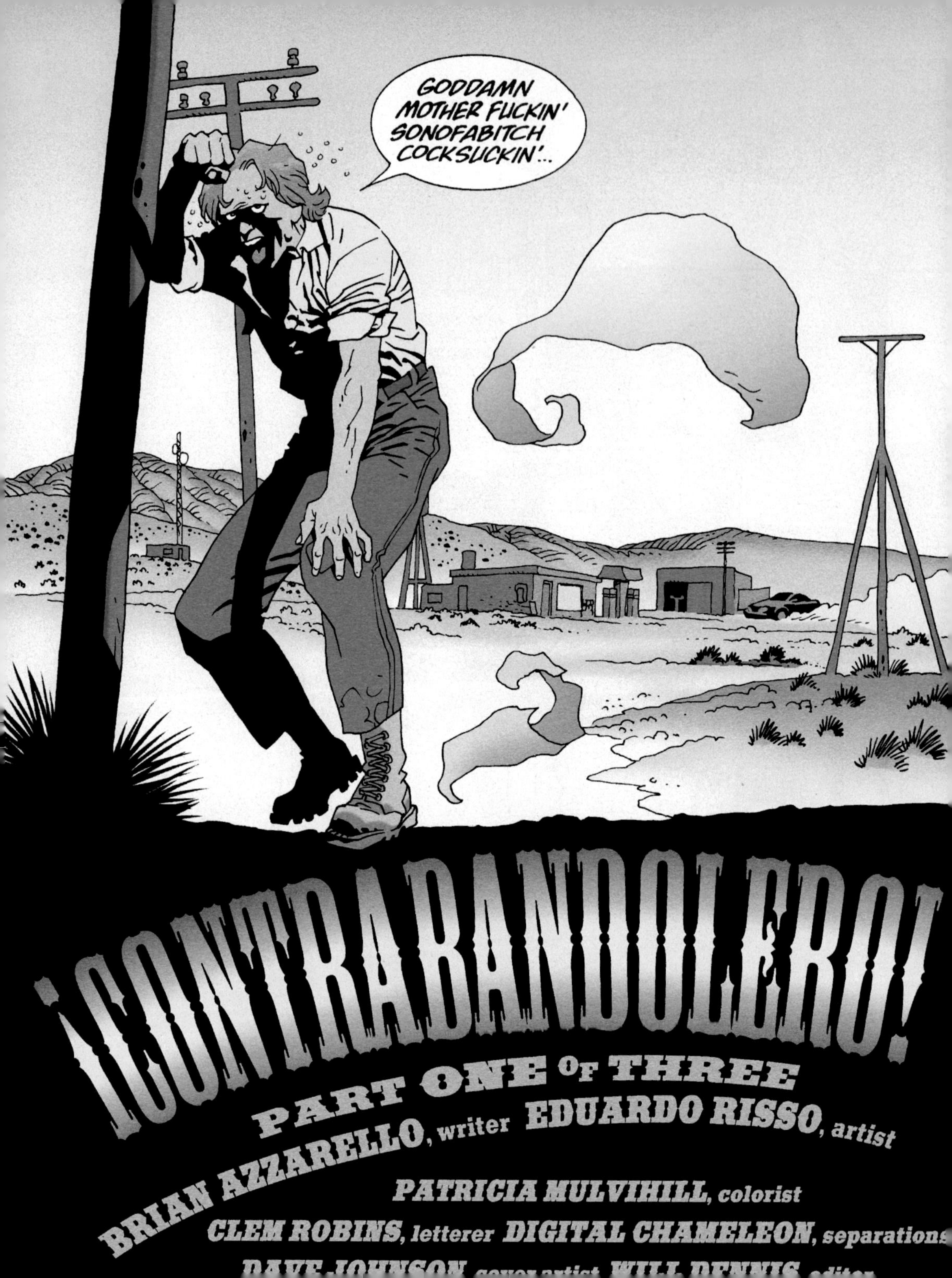
GODDAMN MOTHER FUCKIN' SONOFABITCH COCKSUCKIN'...
¡CONTRABANDOLERO!
PART ONE OF THREE
BRIAN AZZARELLO, writer EDUARDO RISSO, artist
PATRICIA MULVIHILL, colorist
CLEM ROBINS, letterer DIGITAL CHAMELEON, separations

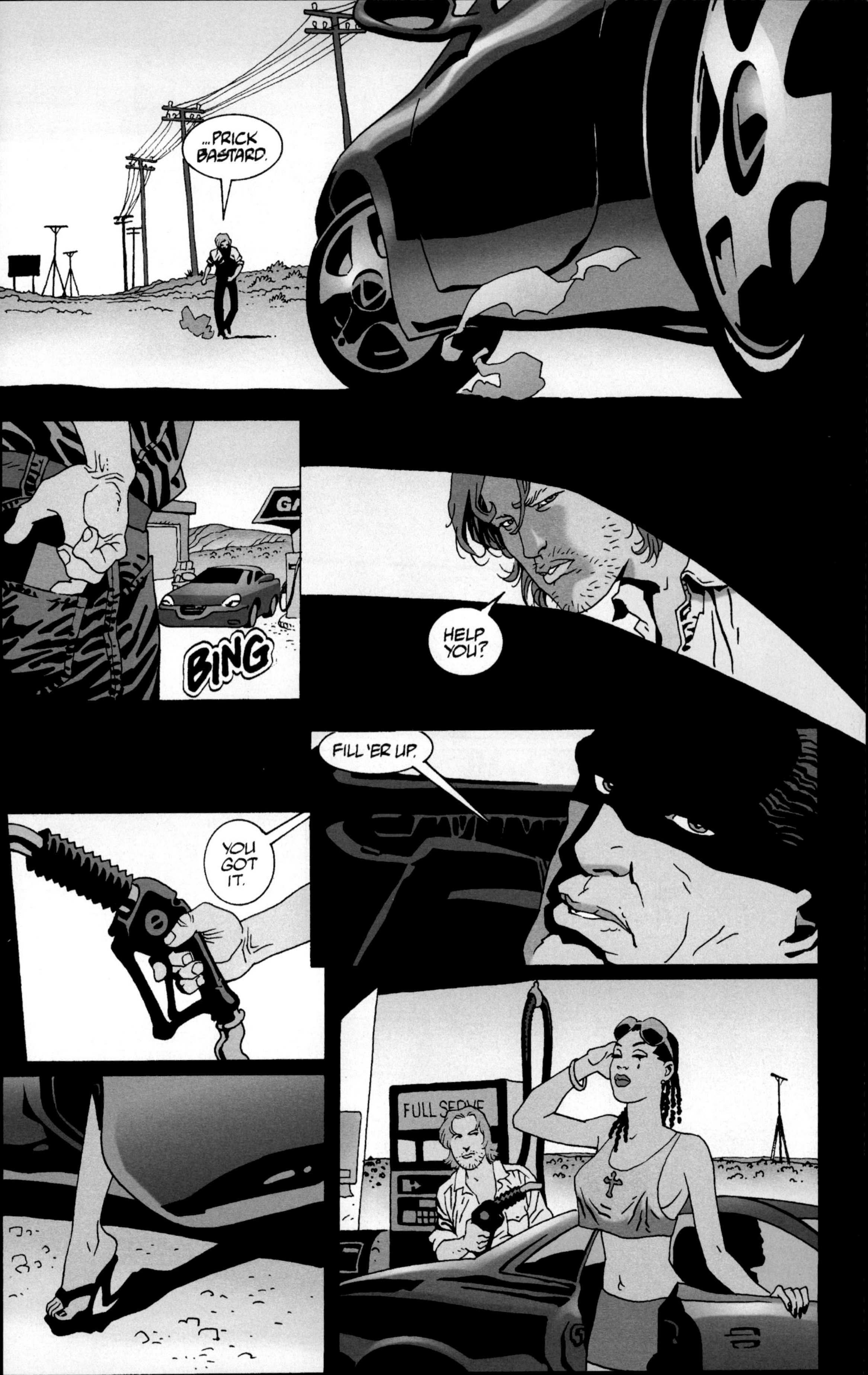
...PRICK BASTARD.
BING
HELP YOU?
FILL 'ER UP.
YOU GOT IT.
FULL SERVE

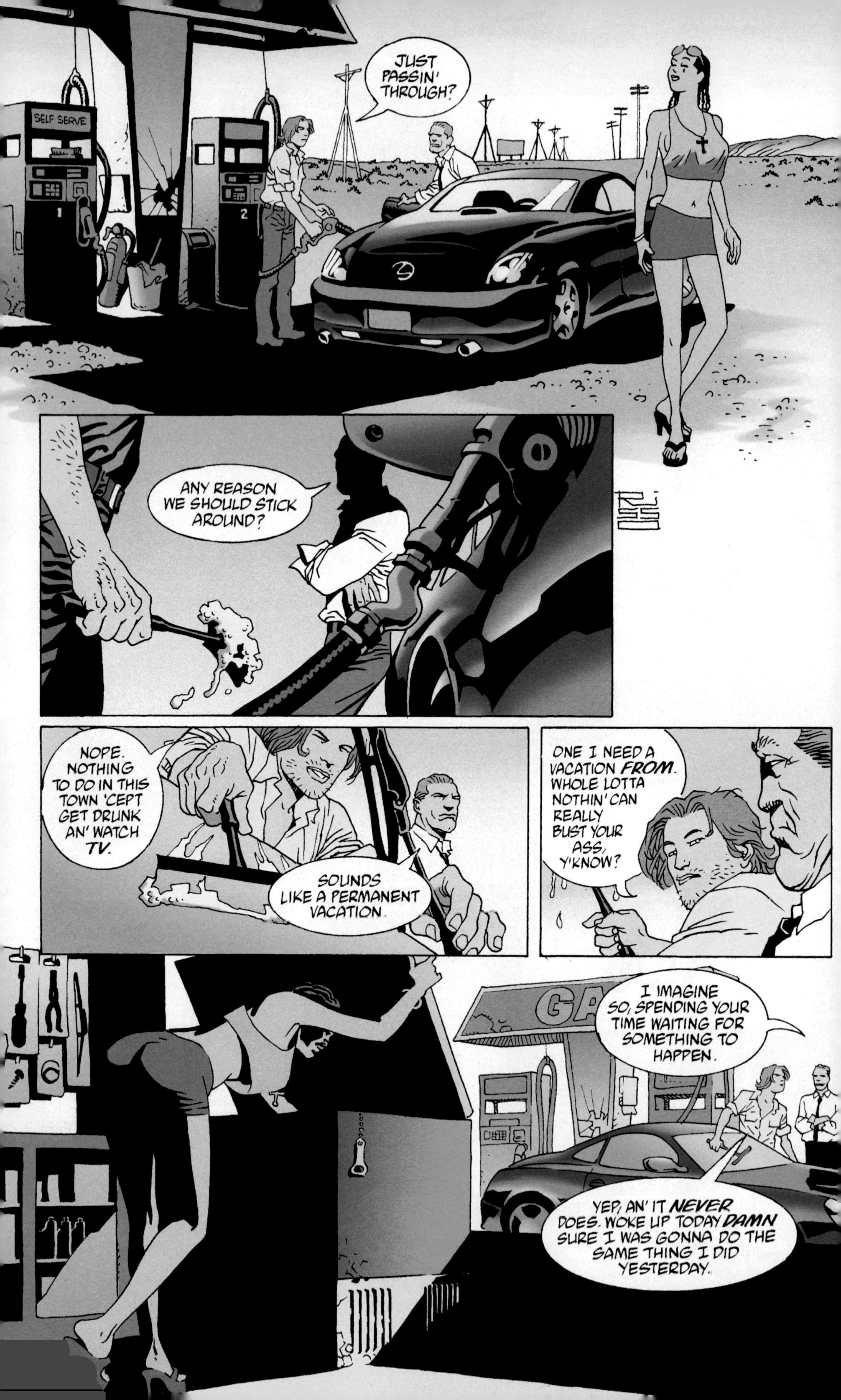
SELF SERVE
JUST PASSIN' THROUGH?
ANY REASON WE SHOULD STICK AROUND?
NOPE. NOTHING TO DO IN THIS TOWN 'CEPT GET DRUNK AN' WATCH TV.
SOUNDS LIKE A PERMANENT VACATION.
ONE I NEED A VACATION FROM. WHOLE LOTTA NOTHIN' CAN REALLY BUST YOUR ASS, Y'KNOW?
I IMAGINE SO, SPENDING YOUR TIME WAITING FOR SOMETHING TO HAPPEN.
YEP, AN' IT NEVER DOES. WOKE UP TODAY DAMN SURE I WAS GONNA DO THE SAME THING I DID YESTERDAY.

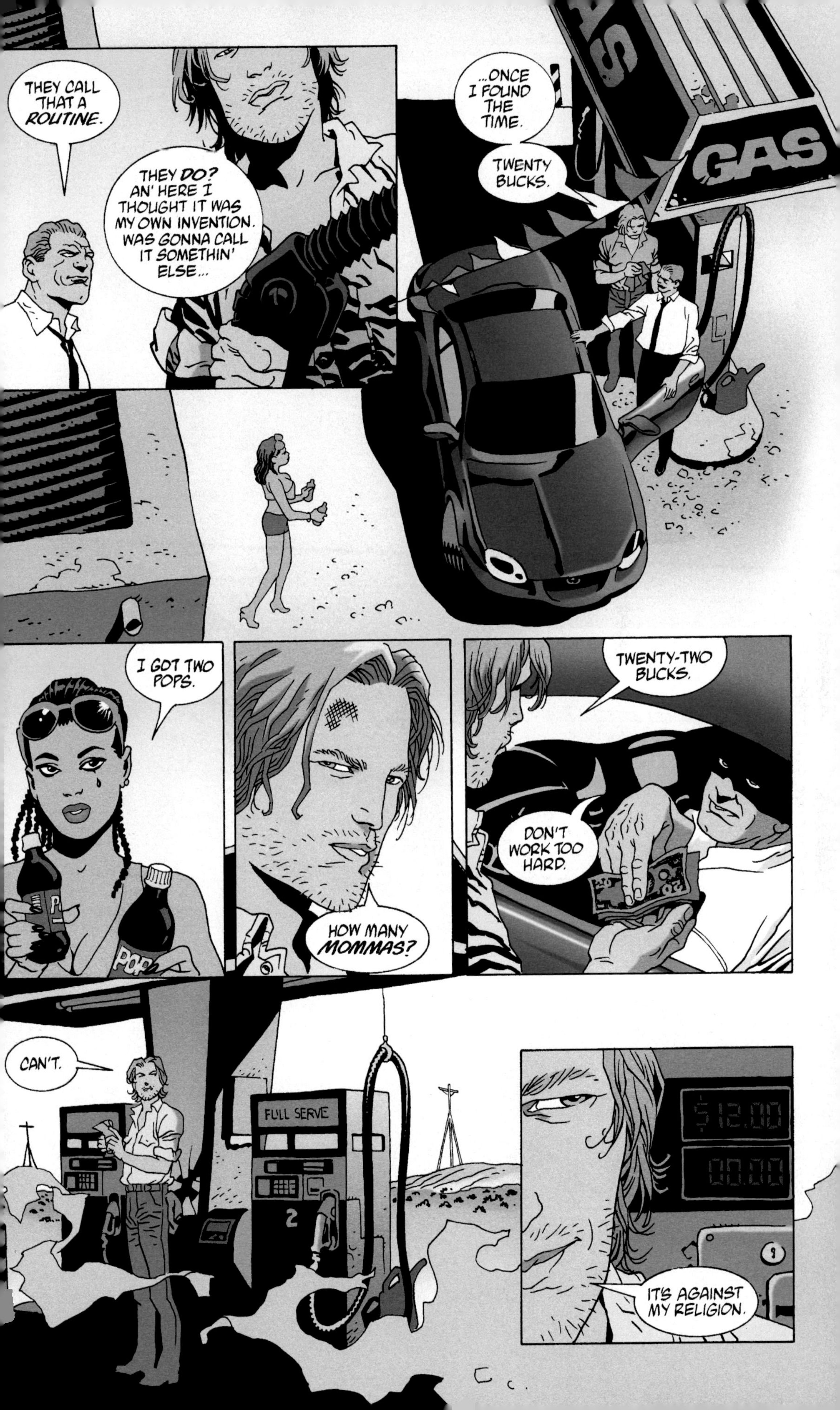
THEY CALL THAT A ROUTINE.
THEY DO? AN' HERE I THOUGHT IT WAS MY OWN INVENTION. WAS GONNA CALL IT SOMETHIN' ELSE...
...ONCE I FOUND THE TIME.
TWENTY BUCKS.
GAS
GAS
I GOT TWO POPS.
HOW MANY MOMMAS?
TWENTY-TWO BUCKS.
DON'T WORK TOO HARD.
CAN'T.
FULL SERVE
$12.00
00.00
IT'S AGAINST MY RELIGION.

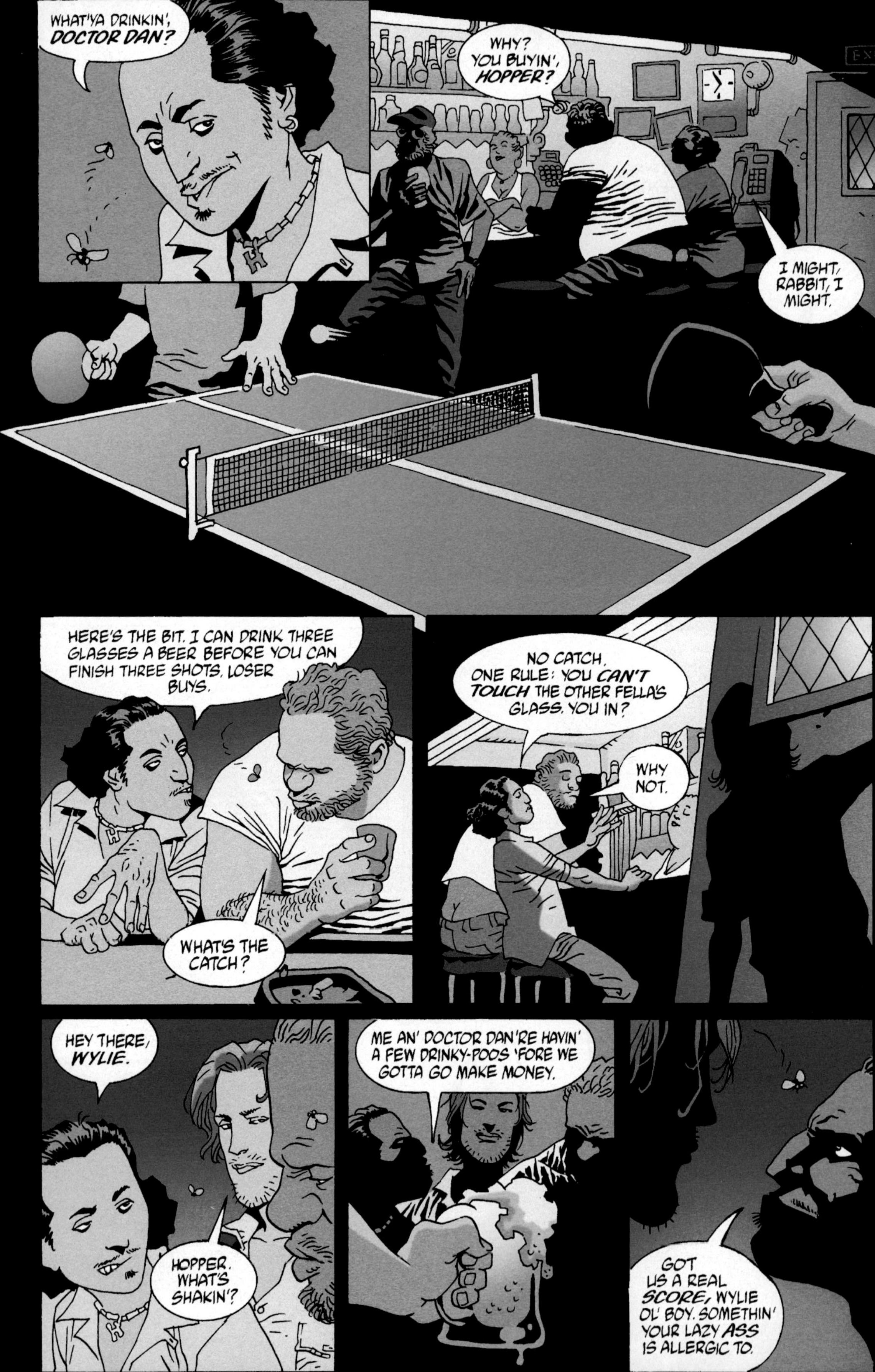
WHAT'YA DRINKIN', DOCTOR DAN?
WHY? YOU BUYIN', HOPPER?
I MIGHT, RABBIT, I MIGHT.
HERE'S THE BIT. I CAN DRINK THREE GLASSES A BEER BEFORE YOU CAN FINISH THREE SHOTS. LOSER BUYS.
WHAT'S THE CATCH?
NO CATCH. ONE RULE: YOU CAN'T TOUCH THE OTHER FELLA'S GLASS. YOU IN?
WHY NOT.
HEY THERE, WYLIE.
HOPPER. WHAT'S SHAKIN'?
ME AN' DOCTOR DAN'RE HAVIN' A FEW DRINKY-POOS 'FORE WE GOTTA GO MAKE MONEY.
GOT US A REAL SCORE, WYLIE OL' BOY. SOMETHIN' YOUR LAZY ASS IS ALLERGIC TO.

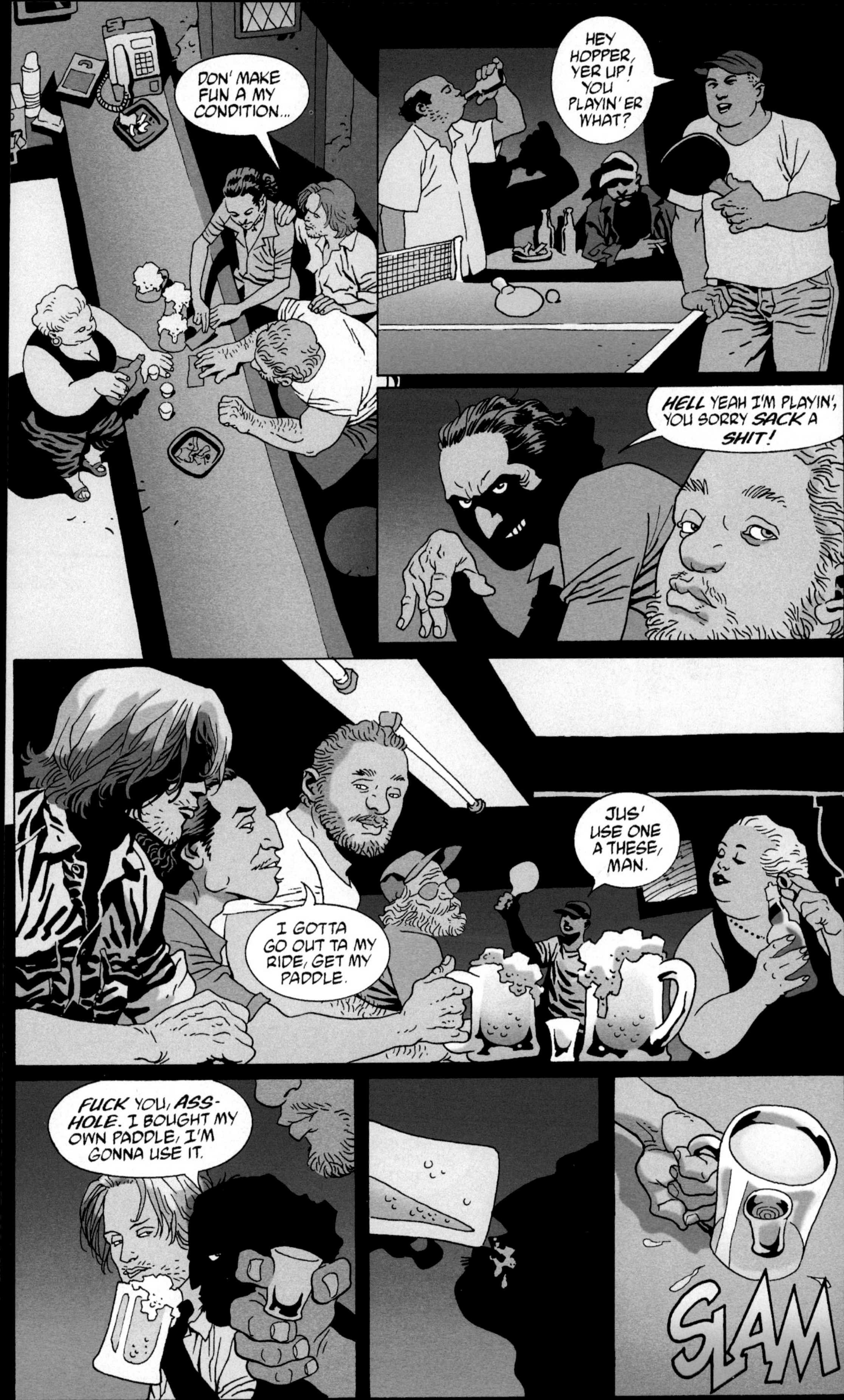
DON' MAKE FUN A MY CONDITION...
HEY HOPPER, YER UP! YOU PLAYIN' ER WHAT?
HELL YEAH I'M PLAYIN', YOU SORRY SACK A SHIT!
I GOTTA GO OUT TA MY RIDE, GET MY PADDLE.
JUS' USE ONE A THESE, MAN.
FUCK YOU, ASS-HOLE. I BOUGHT MY OWN PADDLE, I'M GONNA USE IT.
SLAM

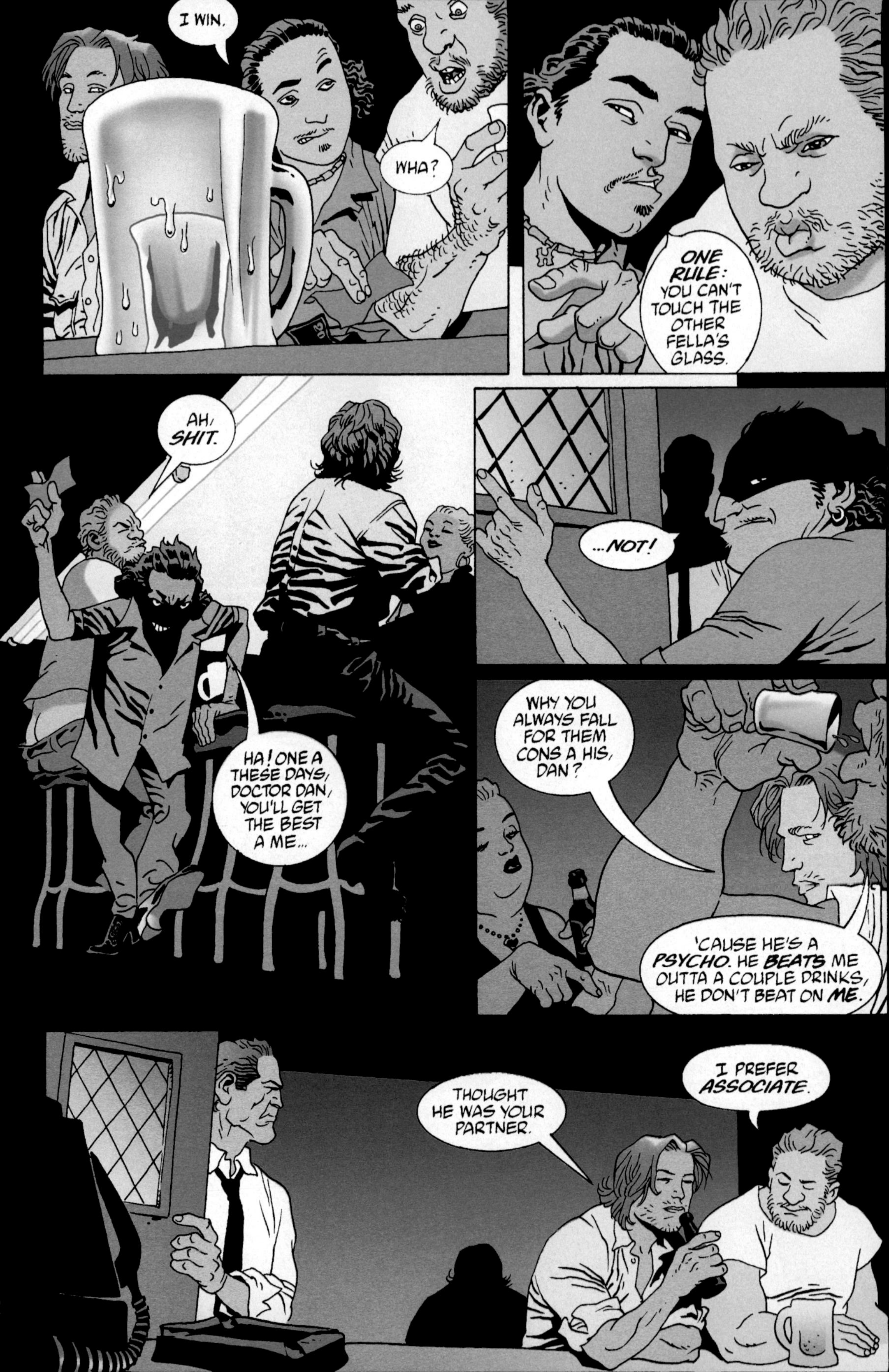

I WIN.
WHA?
ONE RULE: YOU CAN'T TOUCH THE OTHER FELLA'S GLASS.
AH, SHIT.
HA! ONE A THESE DAYS, DOCTOR DAN, YOU'LL GET THE BEST A ME...
...NOT!
WHY YOU ALWAYS FALL FOR THEM CONS A HIS, DAN?
'CAUSE HE'S A PSYCHO. HE BEATS ME OUTTA A COUPLE DRINKS, HE DON'T BEAT ON ME.
THOUGHT HE WAS YOUR PARTNER.
I PREFER ASSOCIATE.

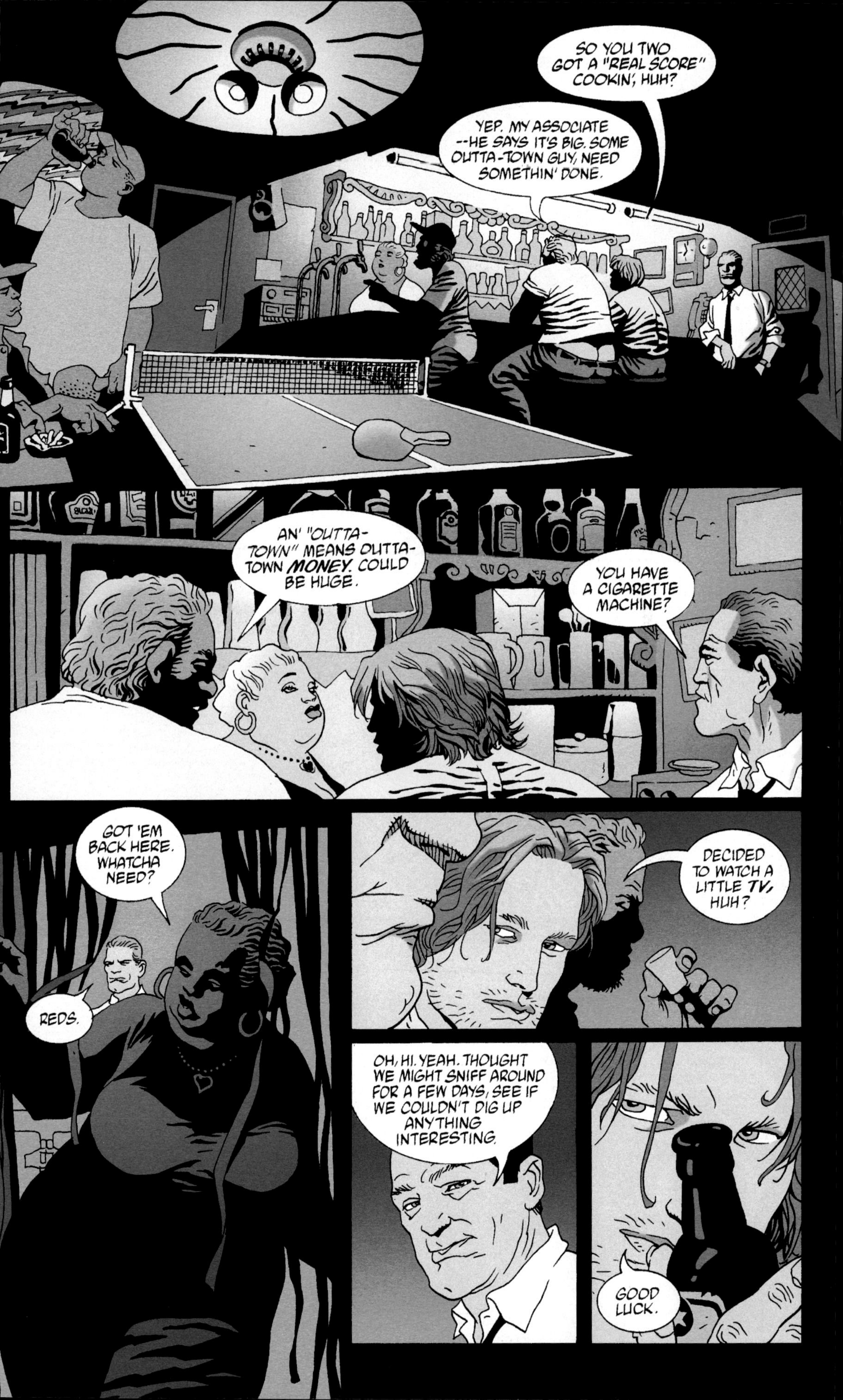
SO YOU TWO GOT A "REAL SCORE" COOKIN', HUH?
YEP. MY ASSOCIATE --HE SAYS IT'S BIG. SOME OUTTA-TOWN GUY, NEED SOMETHIN' DONE.
AN' "OUTTA-TOWN" MEANS OUTTA-TOWN MONEY. COULD BE HUGE.
YOU HAVE A CIGARETTE MACHINE?
GOT 'EM BACK HERE. WHATCHA NEED?
REDS.
DECIDED TO WATCH A LITTLE TV, HUH?
OH, HI. YEAH. THOUGHT WE MIGHT SNIFF AROUND FOR A FEW DAYS, SEE IF WE COULDN'T DIG UP ANYTHING INTERESTING.
GOOD LUCK.

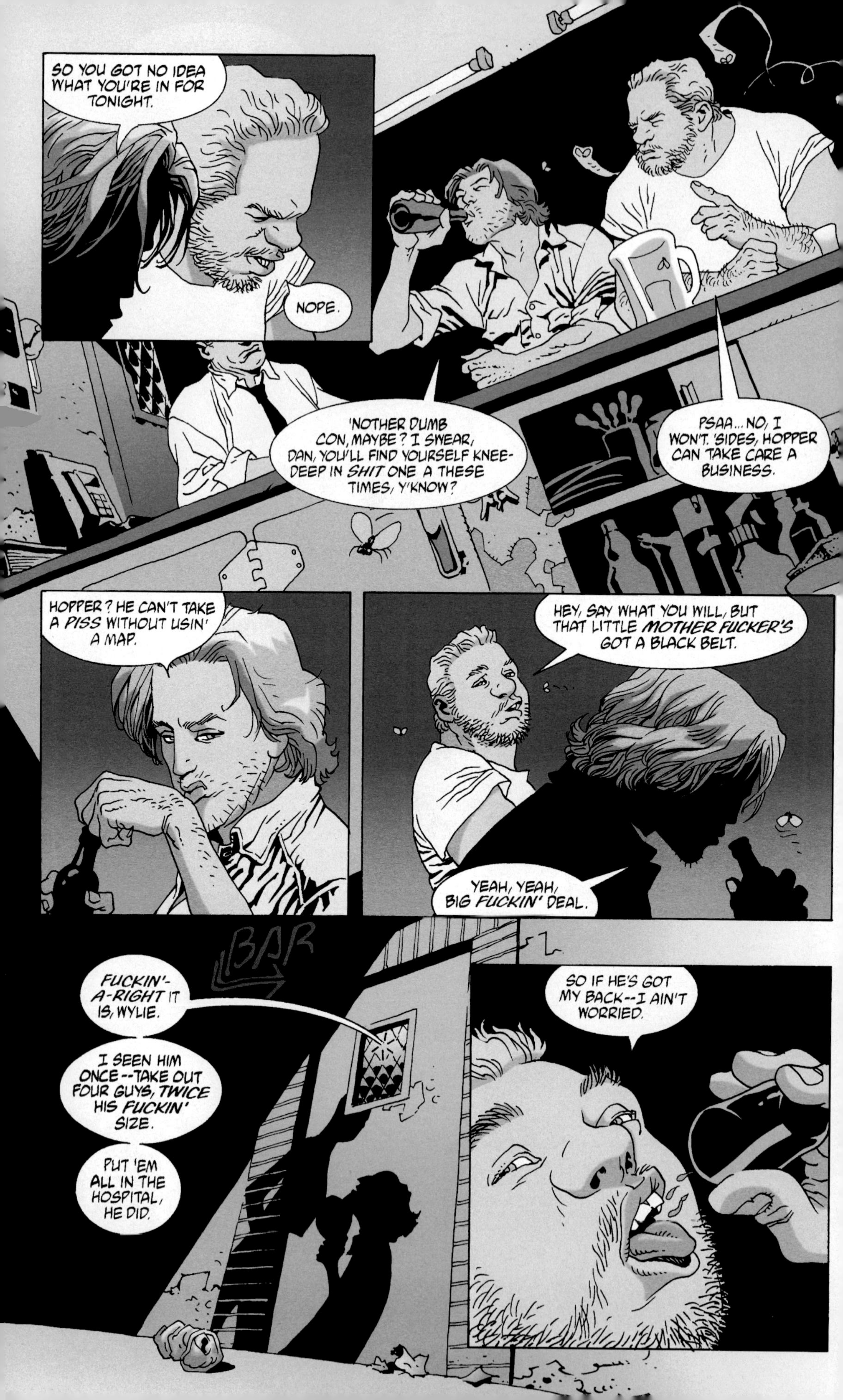
SO YOU GOT NO IDEA WHAT YOU'RE IN FOR TONIGHT.
NOPE.
'NOTHER DUMB CON, MAYBE? I SWEAR, DAN, YOU'LL FIND YOURSELF KNEE-DEEP IN *SHIT* ONE A THESE TIMES, Y'KNOW?
PSAA... NO, I WON'T. 'SIDES, HOPPER CAN TAKE CARE A BUSINESS.
HOPPER? HE CAN'T TAKE A *PISS* WITHOUT USIN' A MAP.
HEY, SAY WHAT YOU WILL, BUT THAT LITTLE *MOTHER FUCKER'S* GOT A BLACK BELT.
YEAH, YEAH, BIG *FUCKIN'* DEAL.
BAR
FUCKIN'-A-RIGHT IT IS, WYLIE.
I SEEN HIM ONCE--TAKE OUT FOUR GUYS, *TWICE* HIS *FUCKIN'* SIZE.
PUT 'EM ALL IN THE HOSPITAL, HE DID.
SO IF HE'S GOT MY BACK--I AIN'T WORRIED.

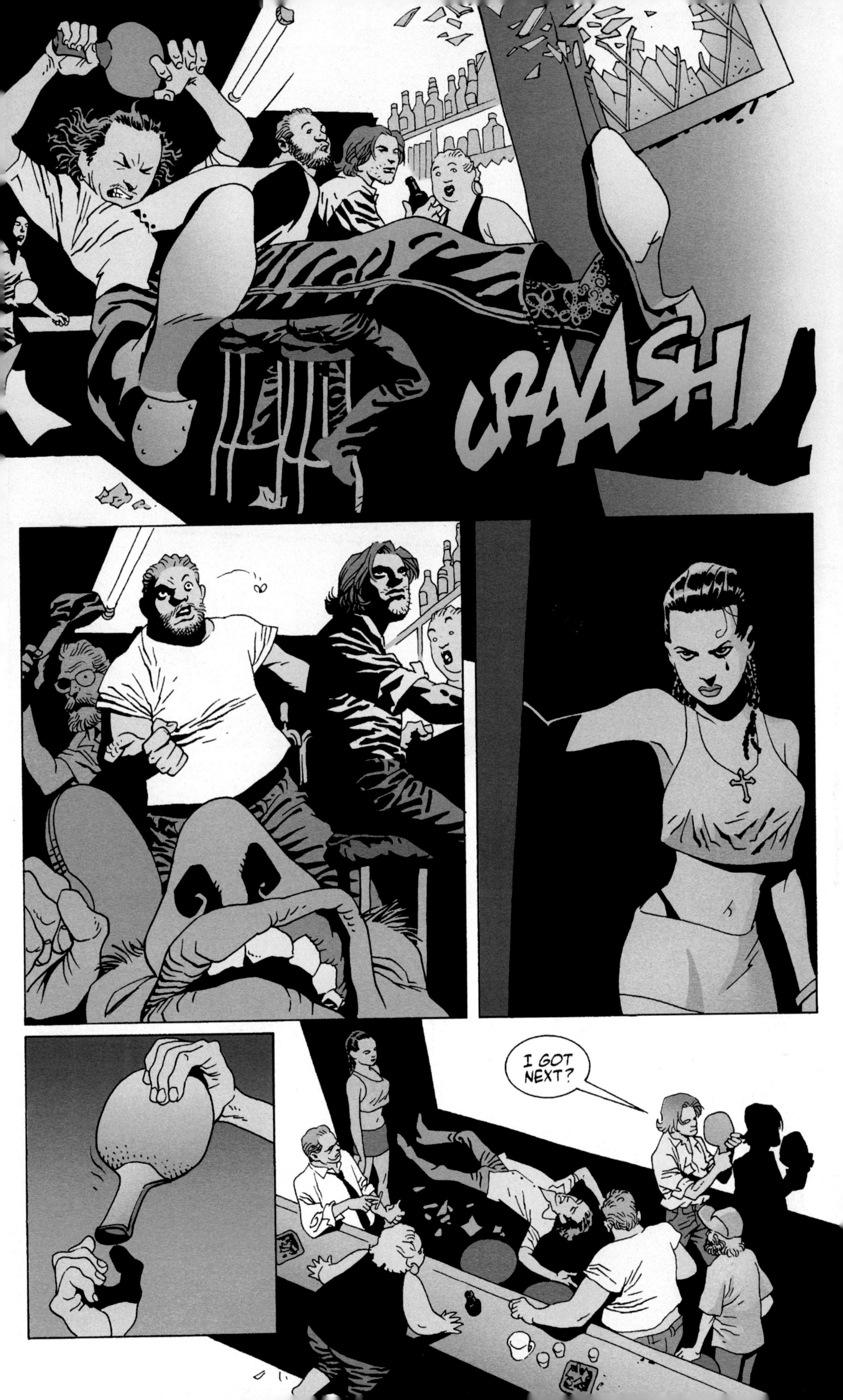
CRAASH
I GOT NEXT?

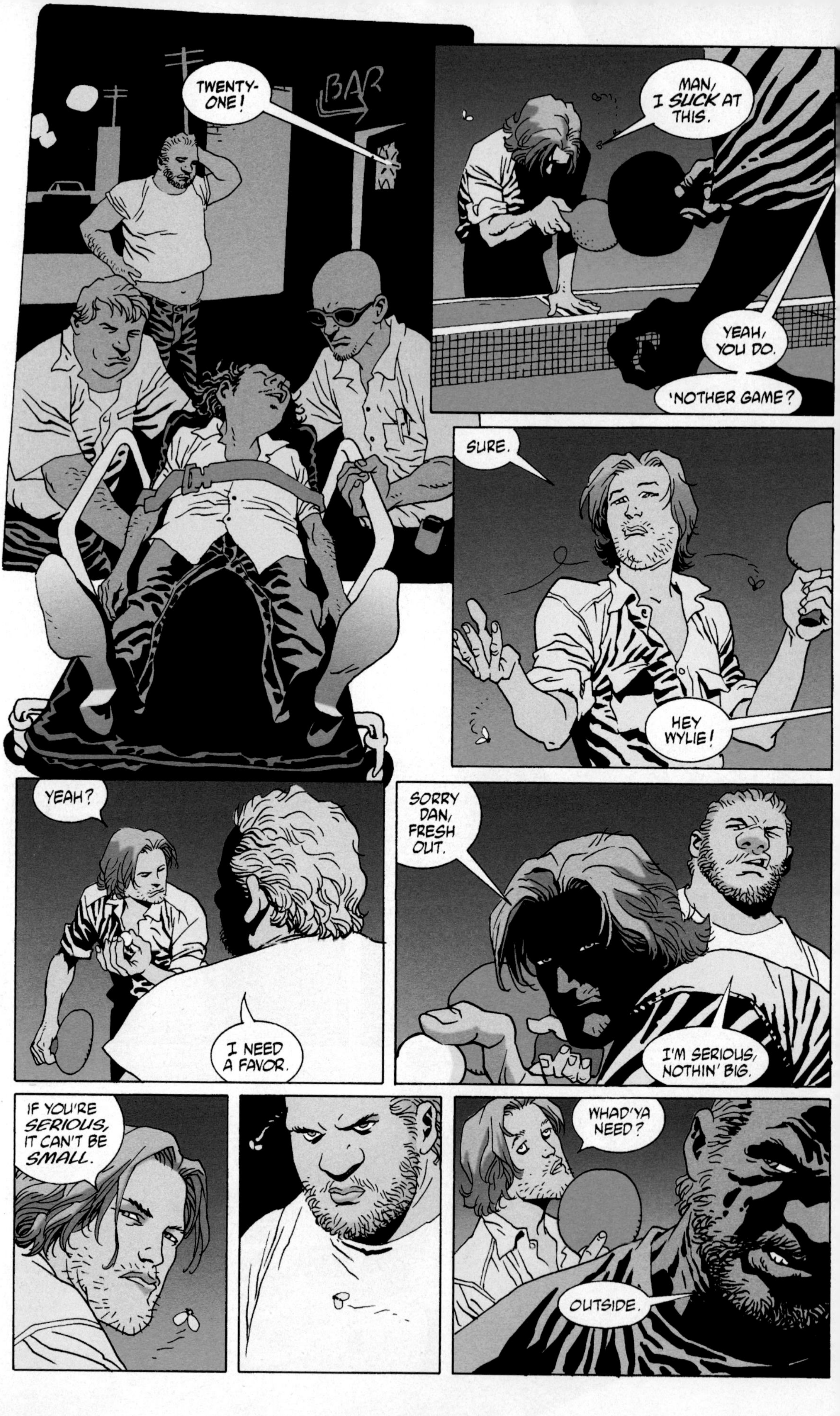
TWENTY-ONE!
BAR
MAN, I SUCK AT THIS.
YEAH, YOU DO.
'NOTHER GAME?
SURE.
HEY WYLIE!
YEAH?
I NEED A FAVOR.
SORRY DAN, FRESH OUT.
I'M SERIOUS, NOTHIN' BIG.
IF YOU'RE SERIOUS, IT CAN'T BE SMALL.
WHAD'YA NEED?
OUTSIDE.

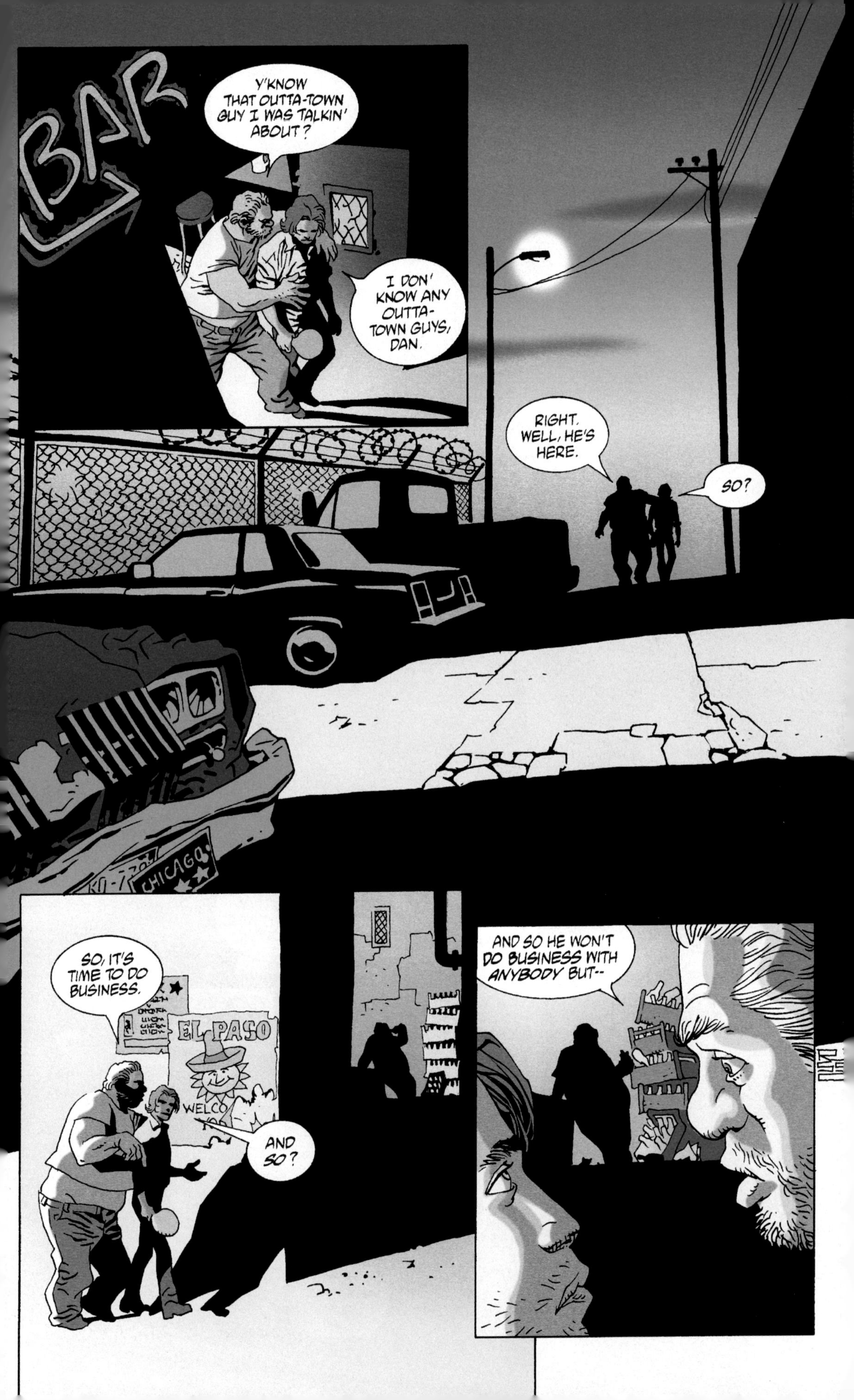
BAR
Y'KNOW THAT OUTTA-TOWN GUY I WAS TALKIN' ABOUT?
I DON' KNOW ANY OUTTA-TOWN GUYS, DAN.
RIGHT. WELL, HE'S HERE.
SO?
CHICAGO
SO, IT'S TIME TO DO BUSINESS.
EL PASO
WELCO
AND SO?
AND SO HE WON'T DO BUSINESS WITH ANYBODY BUT--

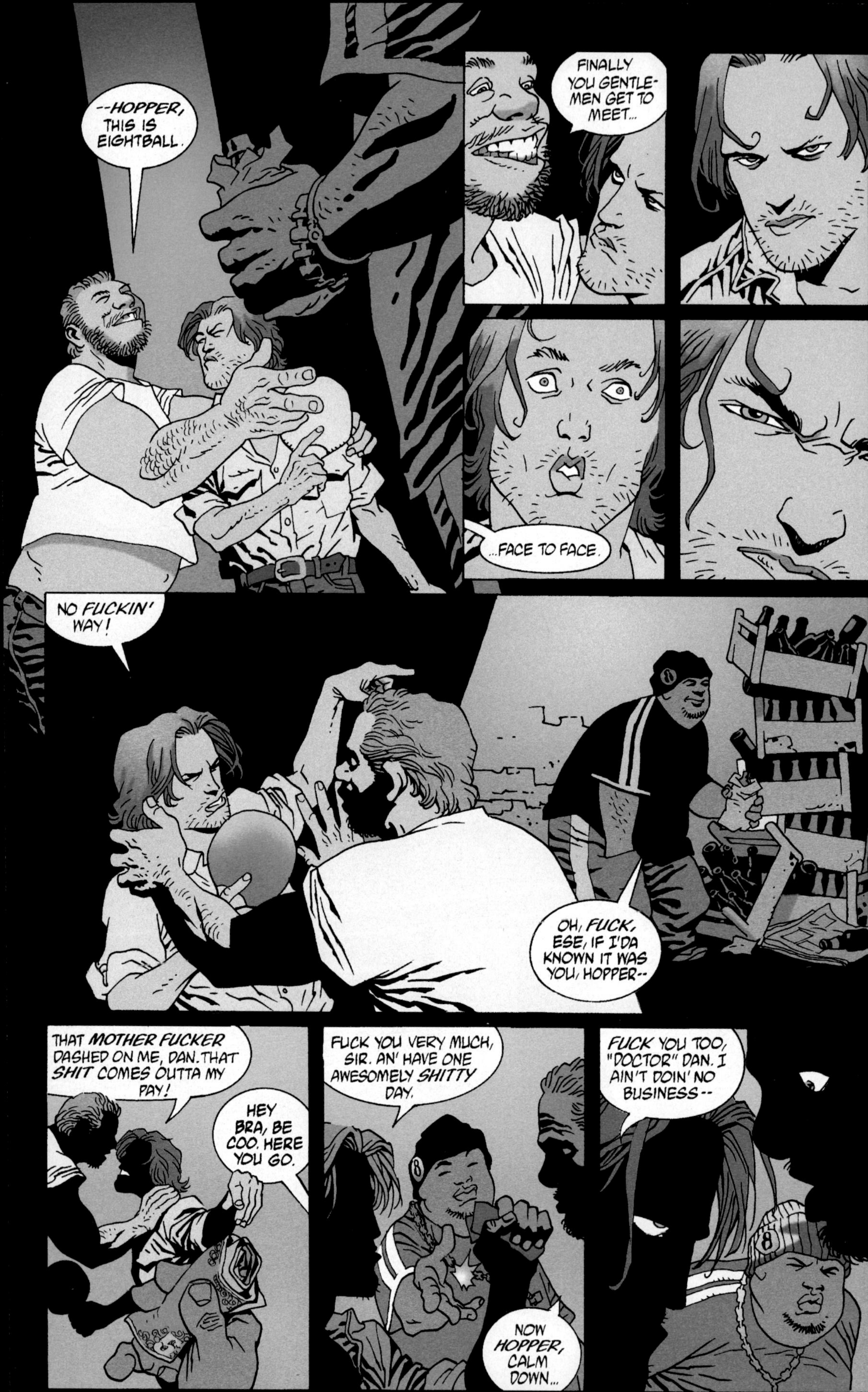
--HOPPER, THIS IS EIGHTBALL.
FINALLY YOU GENTLEMEN GET TO MEET...
...FACE TO FACE.
NO FUCKIN' WAY!
OH, FUCK, ESE, IF I'DA KNOWN IT WAS YOU, HOPPER--
THAT MOTHER FUCKER DASHED ON ME, DAN. THAT SHIT COMES OUTTA MY PAY!
HEY BRA, BE COO. HERE YOU GO.
FUCK YOU VERY MUCH, SIR. AN' HAVE ONE AWESOMELY SHITTY DAY.
NOW HOPPER, CALM DOWN...
FUCK YOU TOO, "DOCTOR" DAN. I AIN'T DOIN' NO BUSINESS--

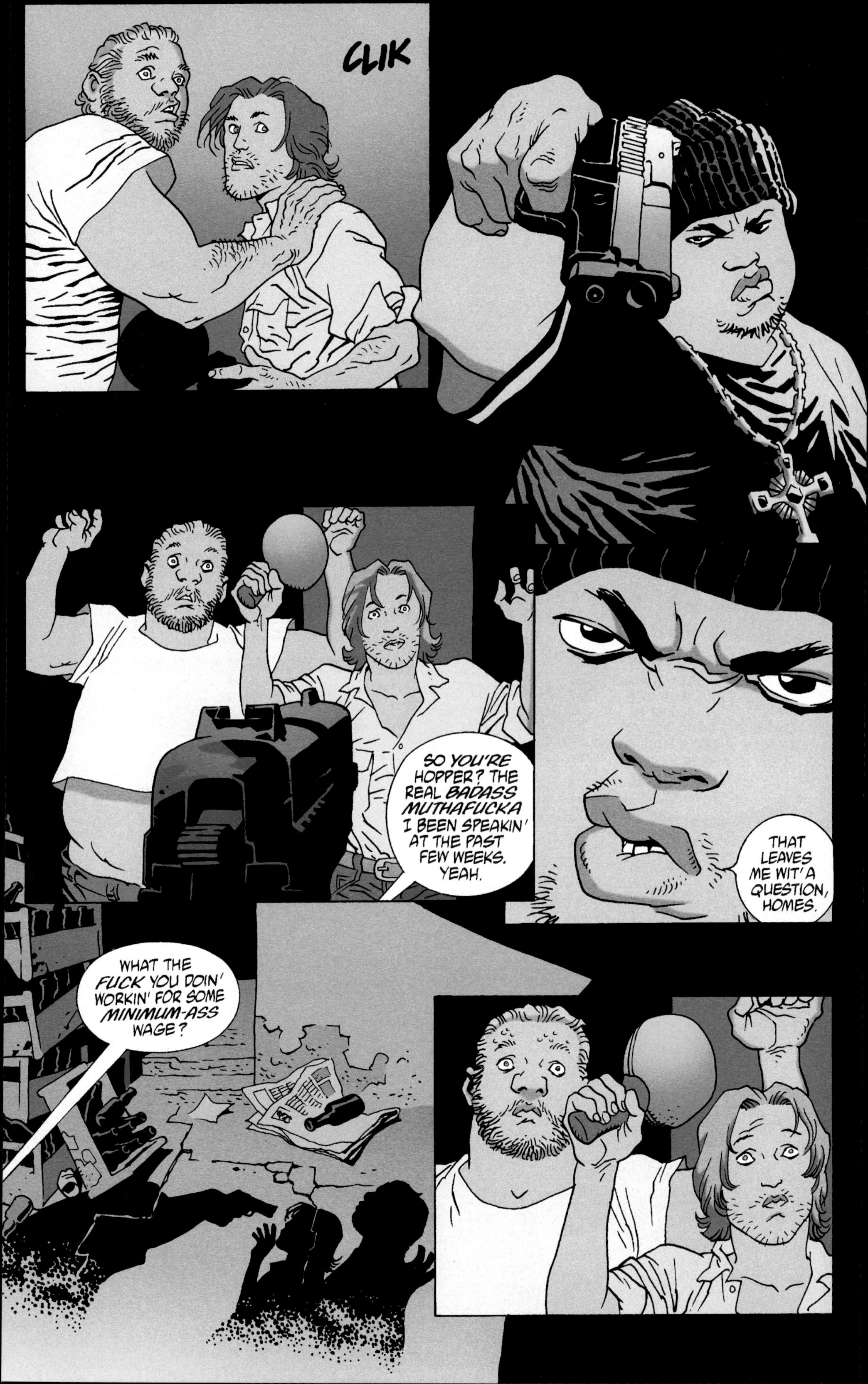
CLIK
SO YOU'RE HOPPER? THE REAL BADASS MUTHAFUCKA I BEEN SPEAKIN' AT THE PAST FEW WEEKS. YEAH.
THAT LEAVES ME WIT'A QUESTION, HOMES.
WHAT THE FUCK YOU DOIN' WORKIN' FOR SOME MINIMUM-ASS WAGE?

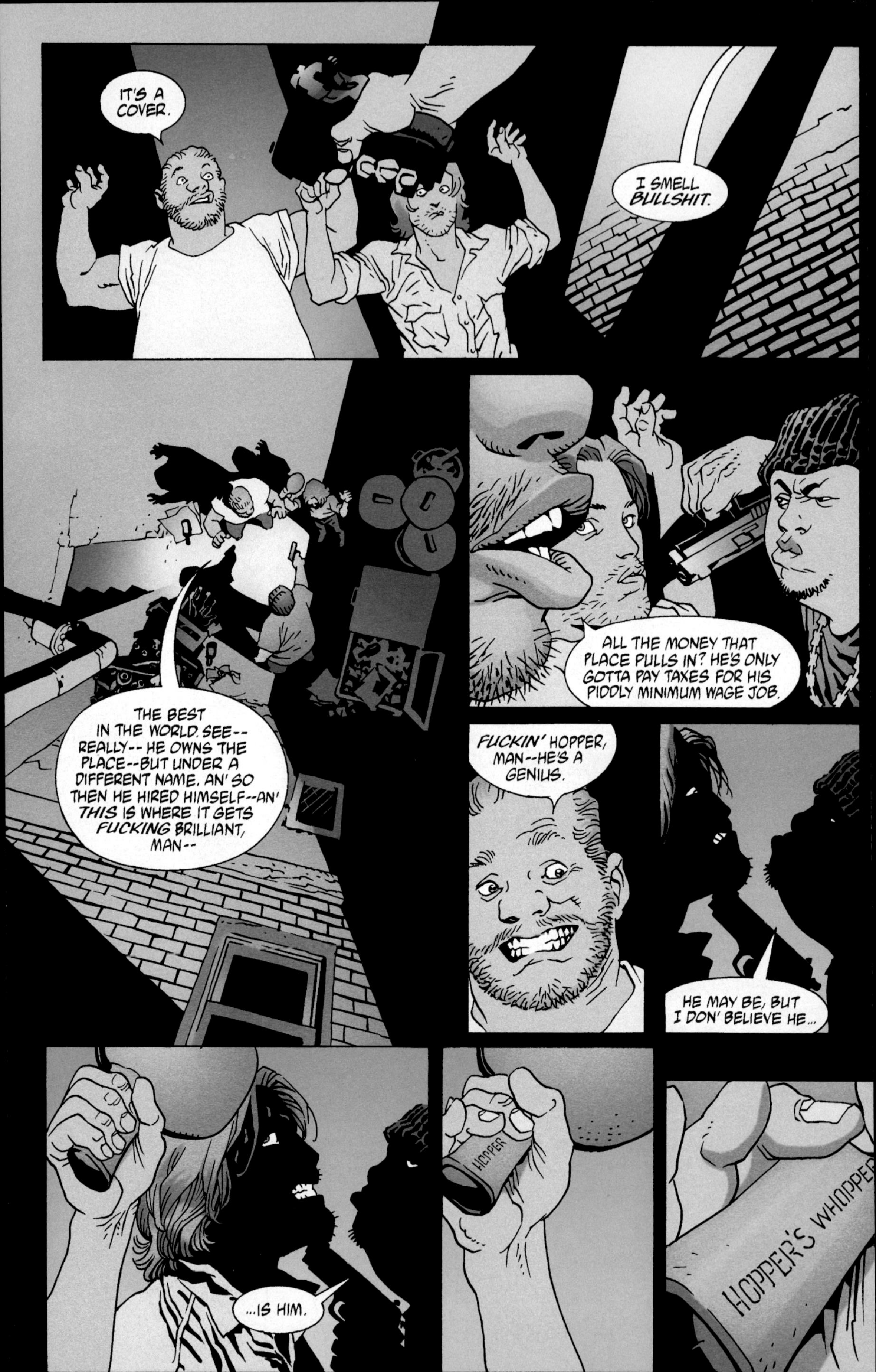
IT'S A COVER.
I SMELL BULLSHIT.
THE BEST IN THE WORLD. SEE-- REALLY-- HE OWNS THE PLACE--BUT UNDER A DIFFERENT NAME. AN' SO THEN HE HIRED HIMSELF--AN' THIS IS WHERE IT GETS FUCKING BRILLIANT, MAN--
ALL THE MONEY THAT PLACE PULLS IN? HE'S ONLY GOTTA PAY TAXES FOR HIS PIDDLY MINIMUM WAGE JOB.
FUCKIN' HOPPER, MAN--HE'S A GENIUS.
HE MAY BE, BUT I DON' BELIEVE HE...
...IS HIM.
HOPPER
HOPPER'S WHOPPER

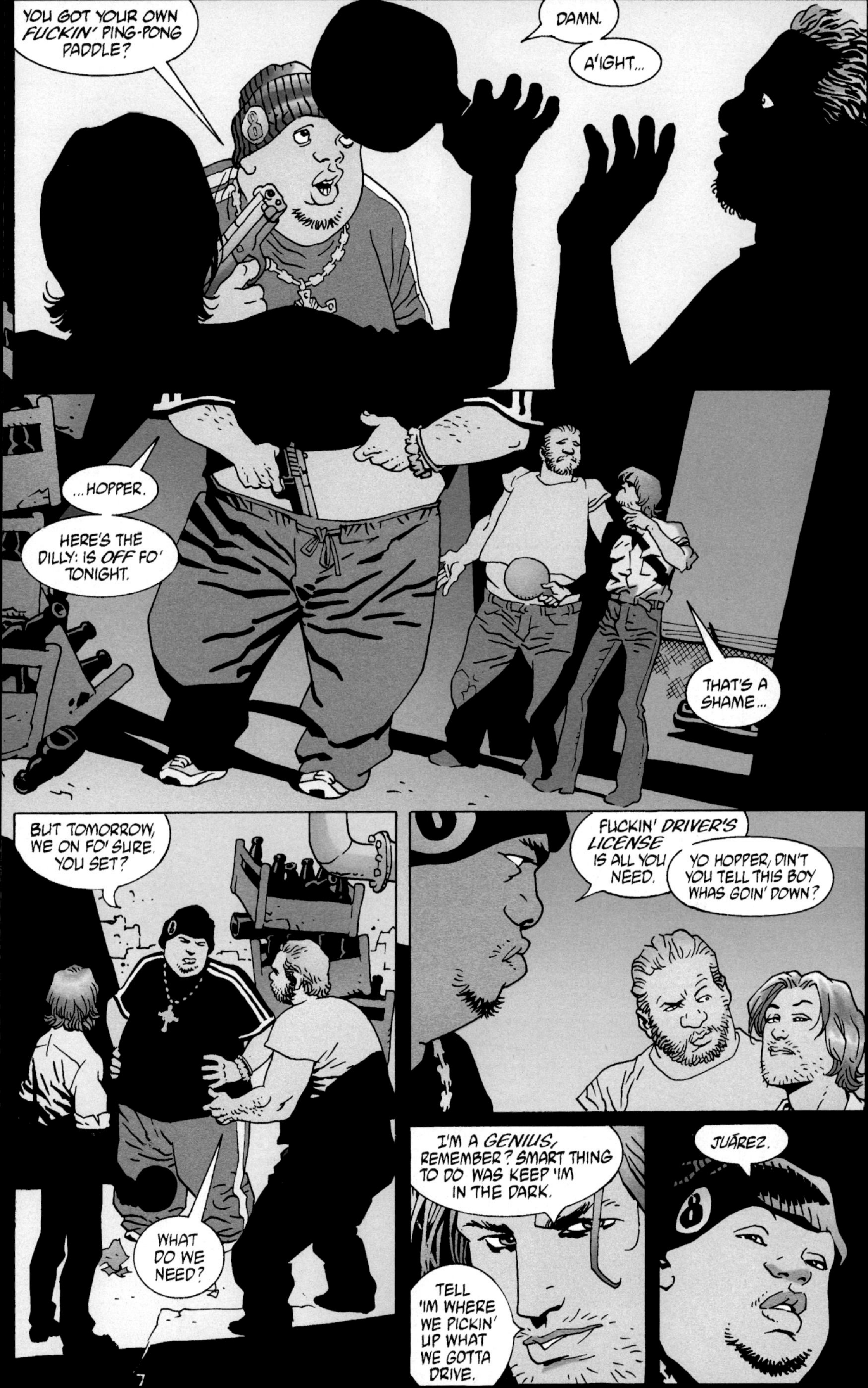
YOU GOT YOUR OWN FUCKIN' PING-PONG PADDLE?
DAMN.
A'IGHT...
...HOPPER.
HERE'S THE DILLY: IS OFF FO' TONIGHT.
THAT'S A SHAME...
BUT TOMORROW, WE ON FO' SURE. YOU SET?
WHAT DO WE NEED?
FUCKIN' DRIVER'S LICENSE IS ALL YOU NEED.
YO HOPPER, DIN'T YOU TELL THIS BOY WHAS GOIN' DOWN?
I'M A GENIUS, REMEMBER? SMART THING TO DO WAS KEEP 'IM IN THE DARK.
TELL 'IM WHERE WE PICKIN' UP WHAT WE GOTTA DRIVE.
JUÁREZ.

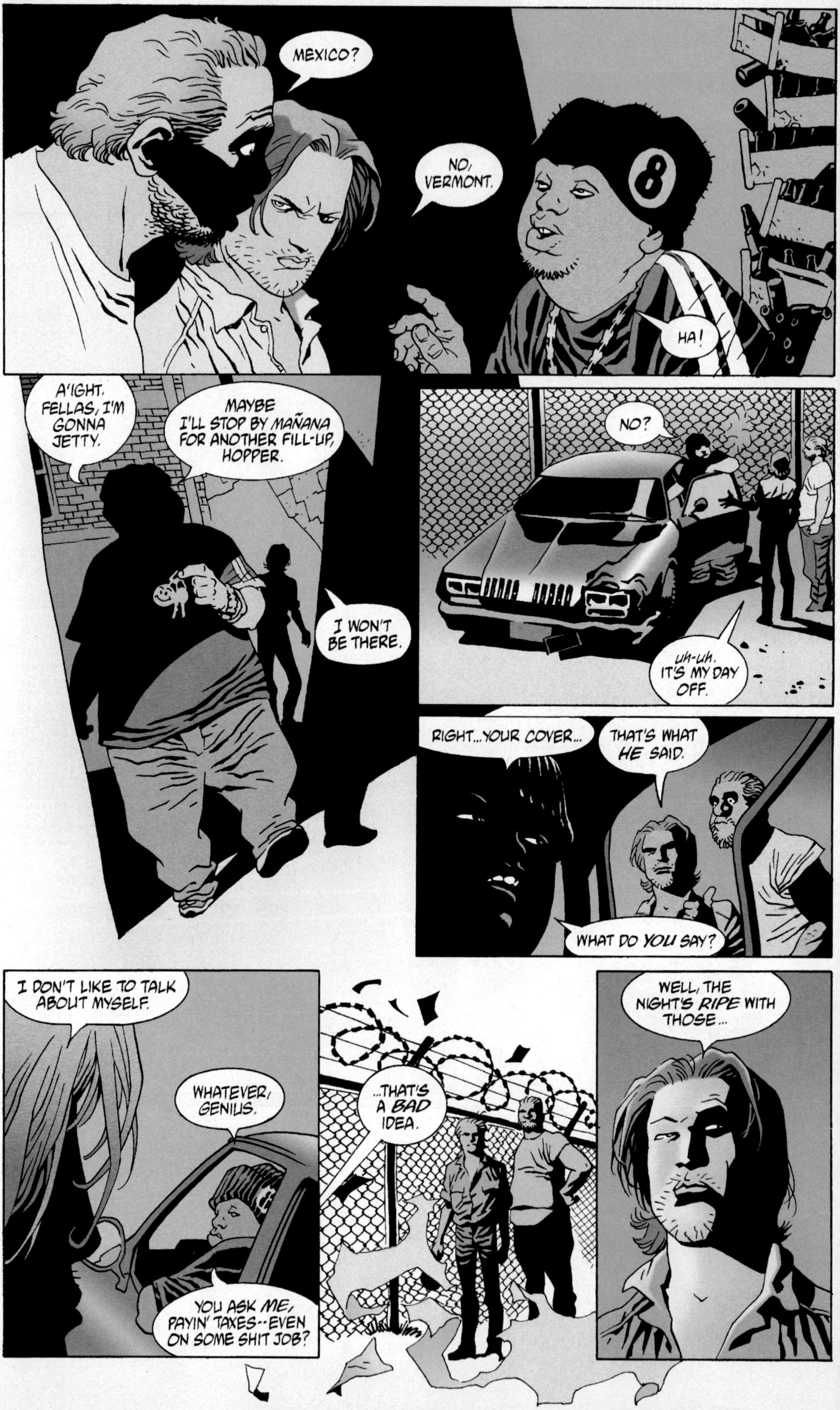
MEXICO?
NO, VERMONT.
HA!
A'IGHT. FELLAS, I'M GONNA JETTY.
MAYBE I'LL STOP BY MAÑANA FOR ANOTHER FILL-UP, HOPPER.
I WON'T BE THERE.
NO?
UH-UH. IT'S MY DAY OFF.
RIGHT... YOUR COVER...
THAT'S WHAT HE SAID.
WHAT DO YOU SAY?
I DON'T LIKE TO TALK ABOUT MYSELF.
WHATEVER, GENIUS.
YOU ASK ME, PAYIN' TAXES--EVEN ON SOME SHIT JOB?
...THAT'S A BAD IDEA.
WELL, THE NIGHT'S RIPE WITH THOSE...

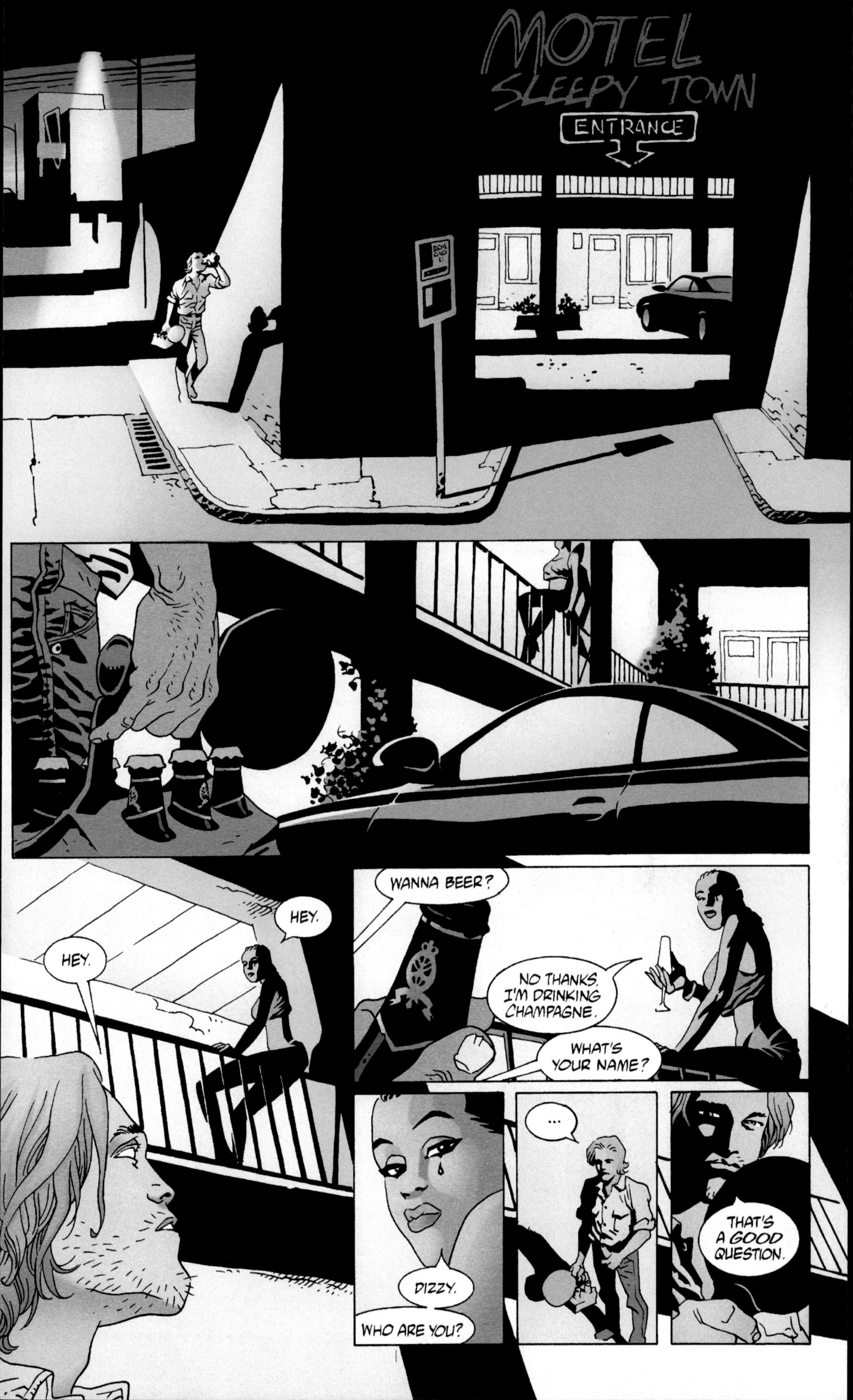
MOTEL
SLEEPY TOWN
ENTRANCE
HEY.
HEY.
WANNA BEER?
NO THANKS, I'M DRINKING CHAMPAGNE.
WHAT'S YOUR NAME?
DIZZY.
WHO ARE YOU?
...
THAT'S A GOOD QUESTION.

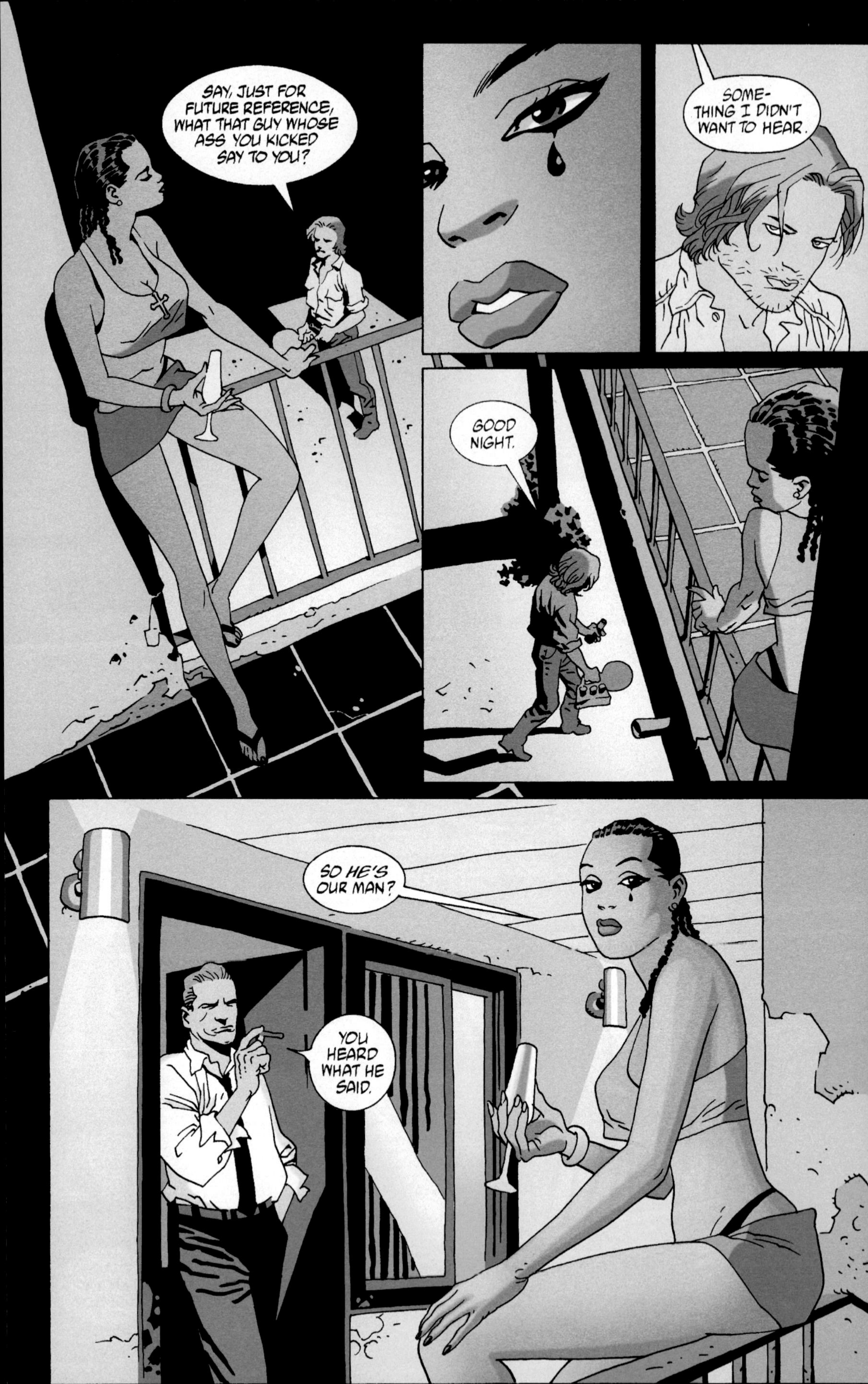
SAY, JUST FOR FUTURE REFERENCE, WHAT THAT GUY WHOSE ASS YOU KICKED SAY TO YOU?
SOME-THING I DIDN'T WANT TO HEAR.
GOOD NIGHT.
SO HE'S OUR MAN?
YOU HEARD WHAT HE SAID.

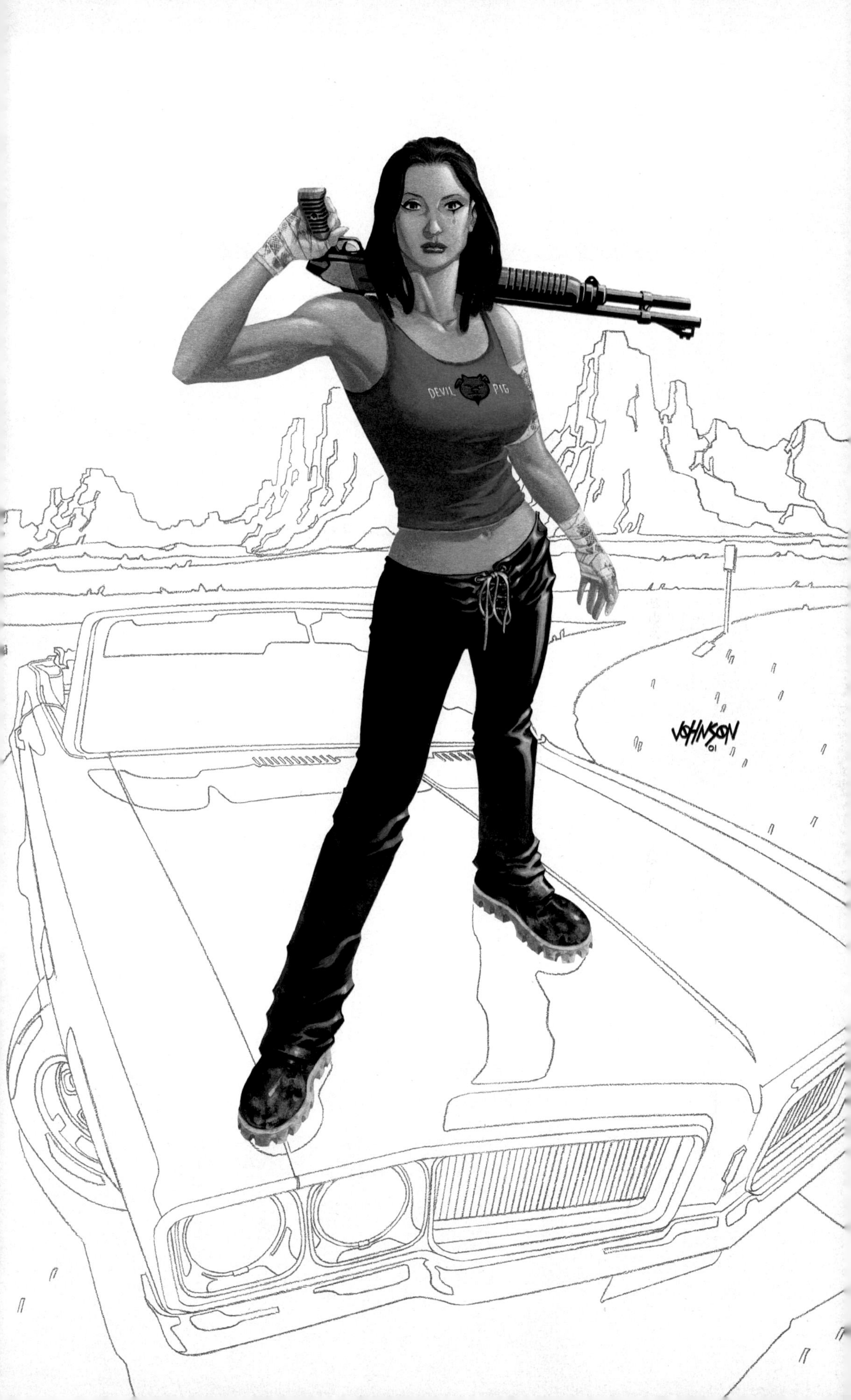
DEVIL PIG
JOHNSON '01

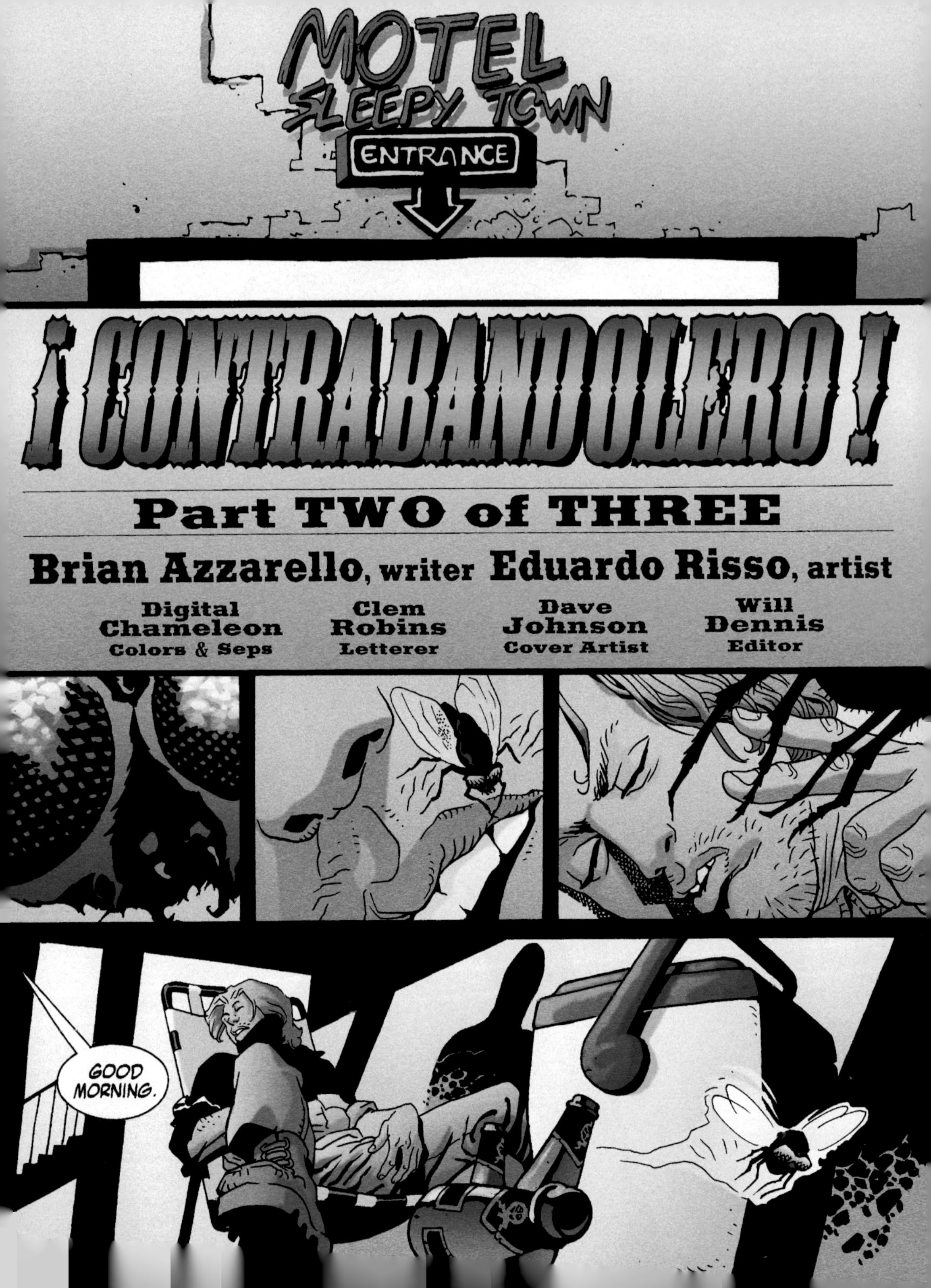
MOTEL
SLEEPY TOWN
ENTRANCE
¡CONTRABANDOLERO!
Part TWO of THREE
Brian Azzarello, writer Eduardo Risso, artist
Digital Chameleon Colors & Seps
Clem Robins Letterer
Dave Johnson Cover Artist
Will Dennis Editor
GOOD MORNING.

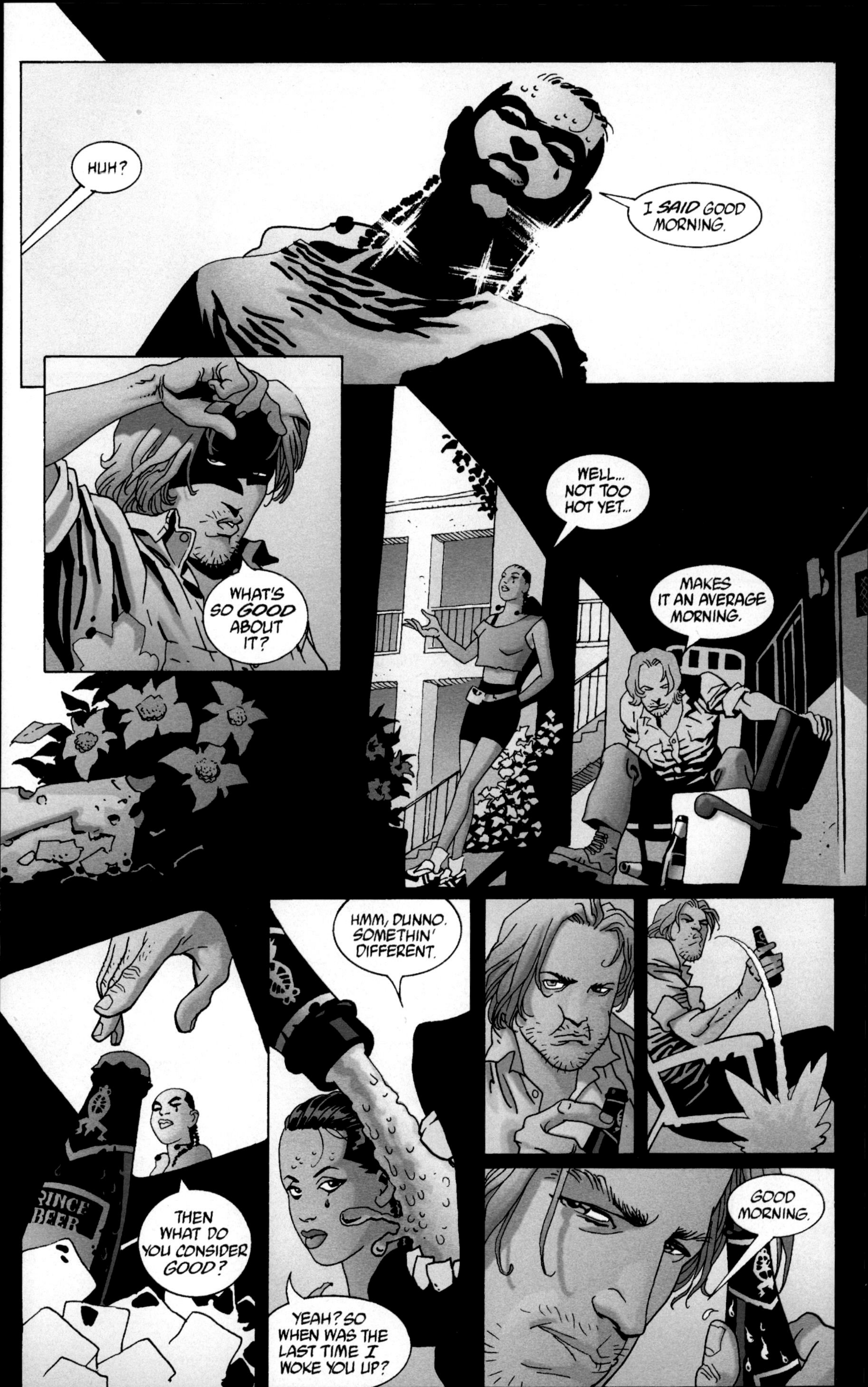

HUH?
I SAID GOOD MORNING.
WHAT'S SO GOOD ABOUT IT?
WELL... NOT TOO HOT YET...
MAKES IT AN AVERAGE MORNING.
THEN WHAT DO YOU CONSIDER GOOD?
HMM, DUNNO. SOMETHIN' DIFFERENT.
YEAH? SO WHEN WAS THE LAST TIME I WOKE YOU UP?
GOOD MORNING.
PRINCE BEER

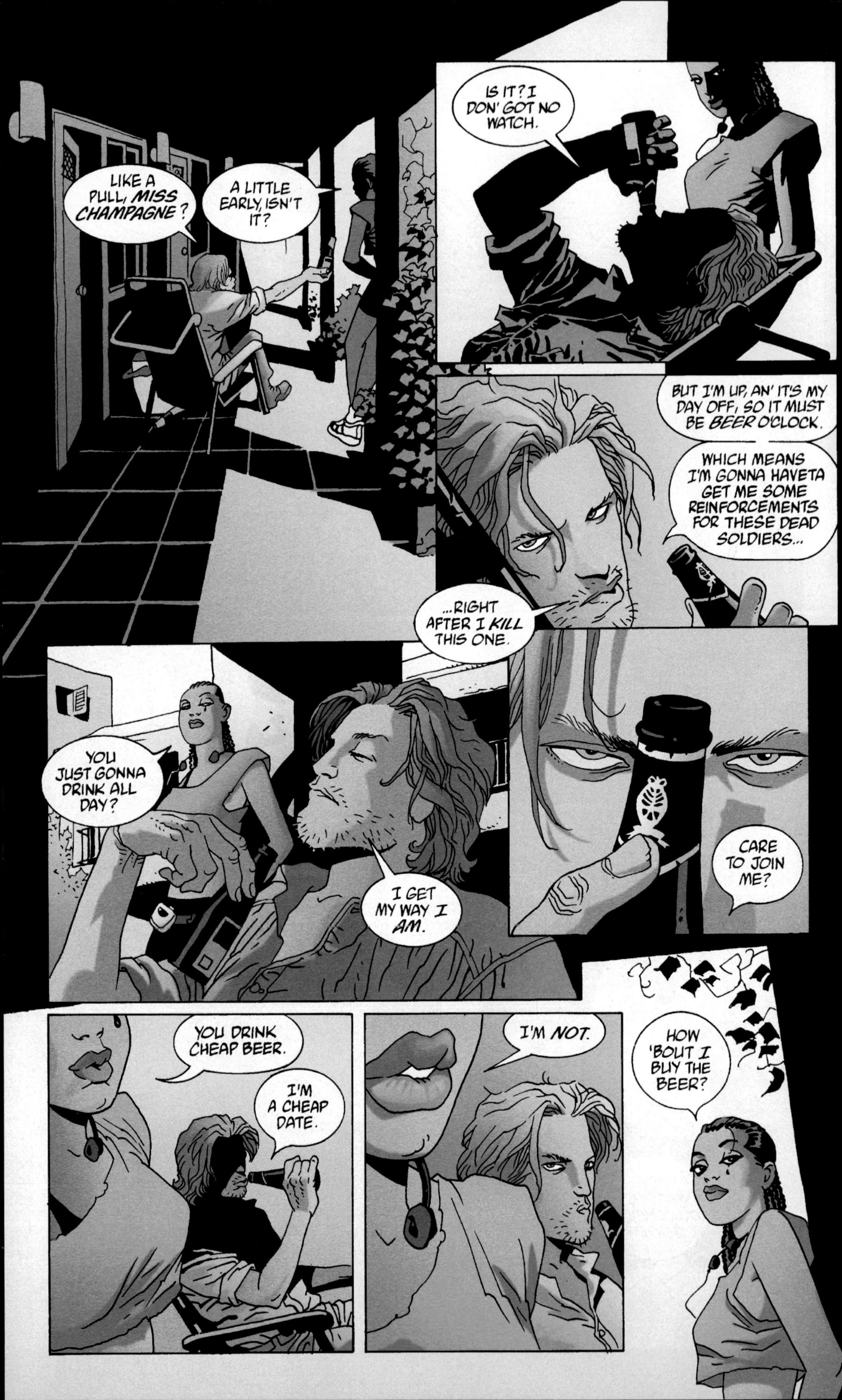
LIKE A PULL, MISS CHAMPAGNE?
A LITTLE EARLY, ISN'T IT?
IS IT? I DON' GOT NO WATCH.
BUT I'M UP, AN' IT'S MY DAY OFF, SO IT MUST BE BEER O'CLOCK.
WHICH MEANS I'M GONNA HAVETA GET ME SOME REINFORCEMENTS FOR THESE DEAD SOLDIERS...
...RIGHT AFTER I KILL THIS ONE.
YOU JUST GONNA DRINK ALL DAY?
I GET MY WAY I AM.
CARE TO JOIN ME?
YOU DRINK CHEAP BEER.
I'M A CHEAP DATE.
I'M NOT.
HOW 'BOUT I BUY THE BEER?

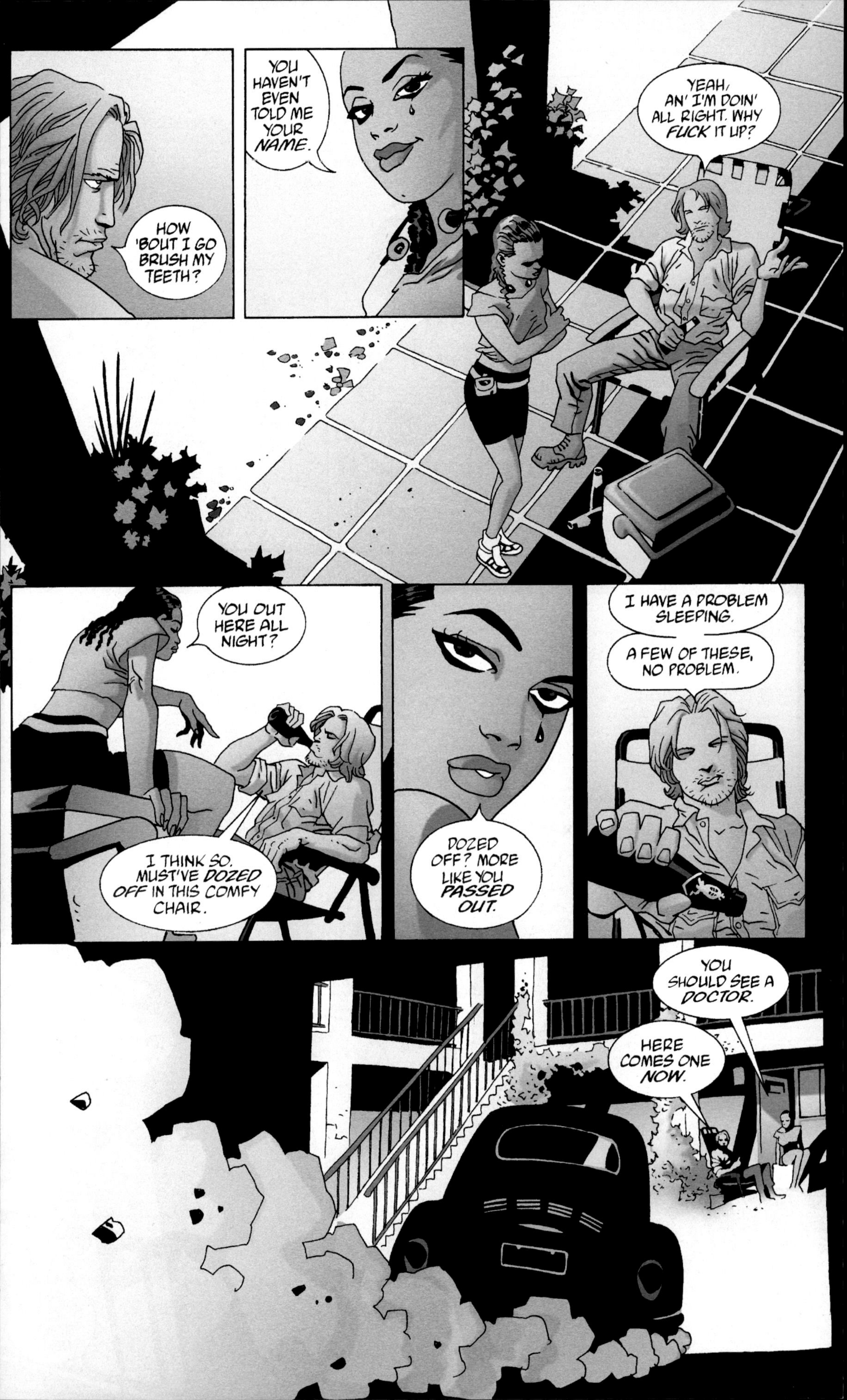
HOW 'BOUT I GO BRUSH MY TEETH?
YOU HAVEN'T EVEN TOLD ME YOUR NAME.
YEAH, AN' I'M DOIN' ALL RIGHT. WHY FUCK IT UP?
YOU OUT HERE ALL NIGHT?
I THINK SO. MUST'VE DOZED OFF IN THIS COMFY CHAIR.
DOZED OFF? MORE LIKE YOU PASSED OUT.
I HAVE A PROBLEM SLEEPING.
A FEW OF THESE, NO PROBLEM.
YOU SHOULD SEE A DOCTOR.
HERE COMES ONE NOW.

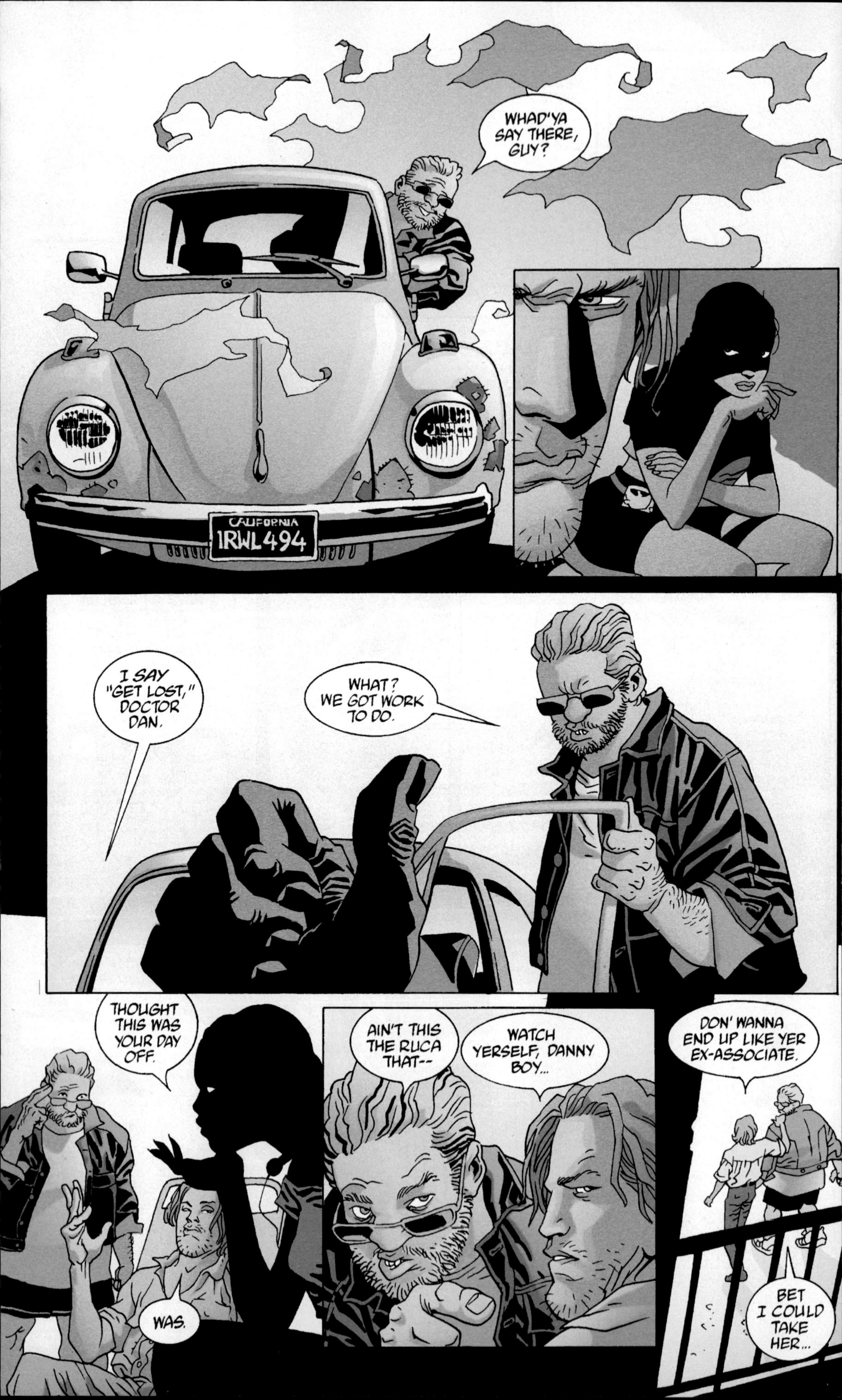
WHAD'YA SAY THERE, GUY?
CALIFORNIA 1RWL494
I SAY "GET LOST," DOCTOR DAN.
WHAT? WE GOT WORK TO DO.
THOUGHT THIS WAS YOUR DAY OFF.
WAS.
AIN'T THIS THE RUCA THAT--
WATCH YERSELF, DANNY BOY...
DON' WANNA END UP LIKE YER EX-ASSOCIATE.
BET I COULD TAKE HER...

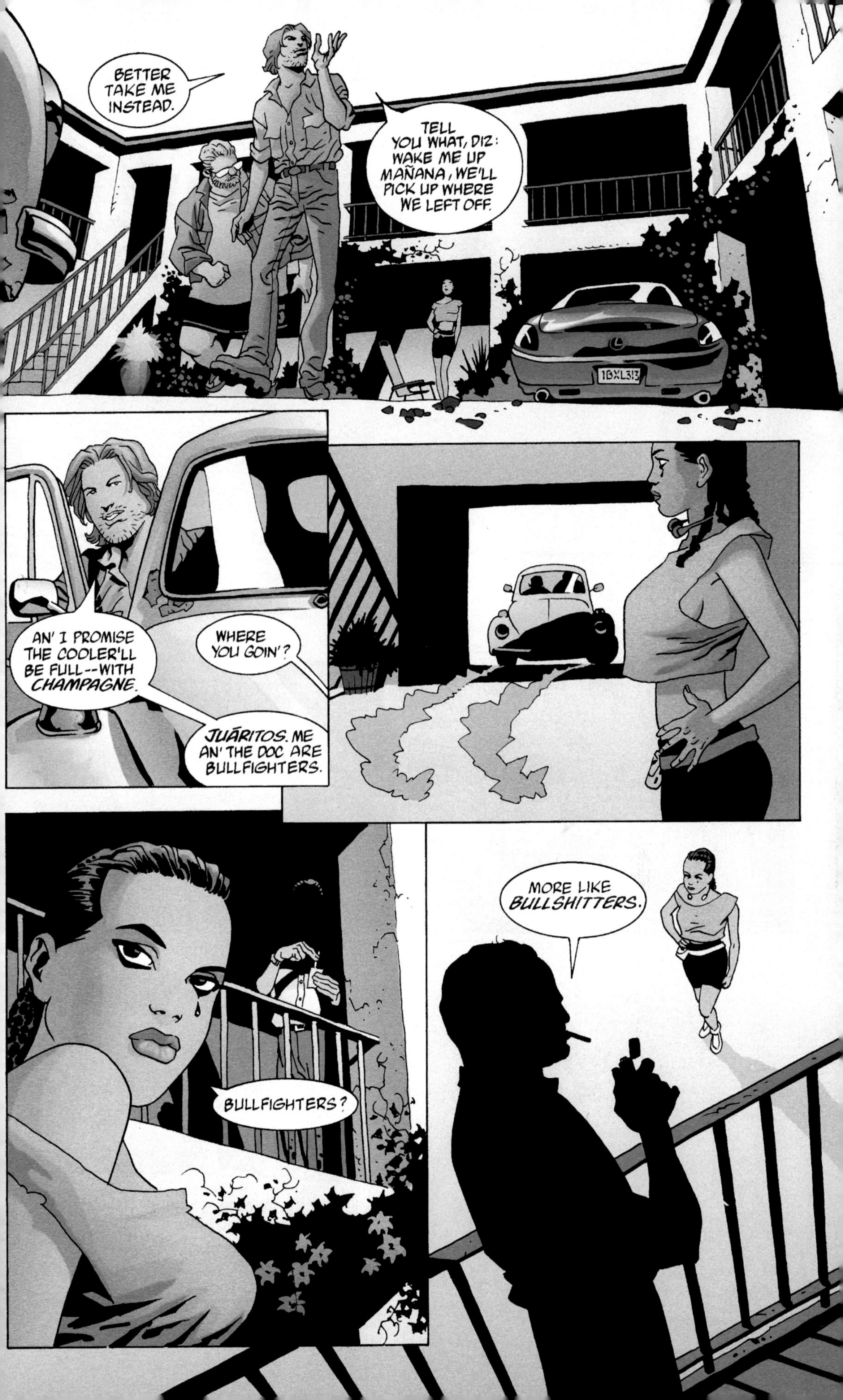
BETTER TAKE ME INSTEAD.
TELL YOU WHAT, DIZ: WAKE ME UP MAÑANA, WE'LL PICK UP WHERE WE LEFT OFF.
1BXL313
AN' I PROMISE THE COOLER'LL BE FULL--WITH CHAMPAGNE.
WHERE YOU GOIN'?
JUÁRITOS. ME AN' THE DOC ARE BULLFIGHTERS.
BULLFIGHTERS?
MORE LIKE BULLSHITTERS.

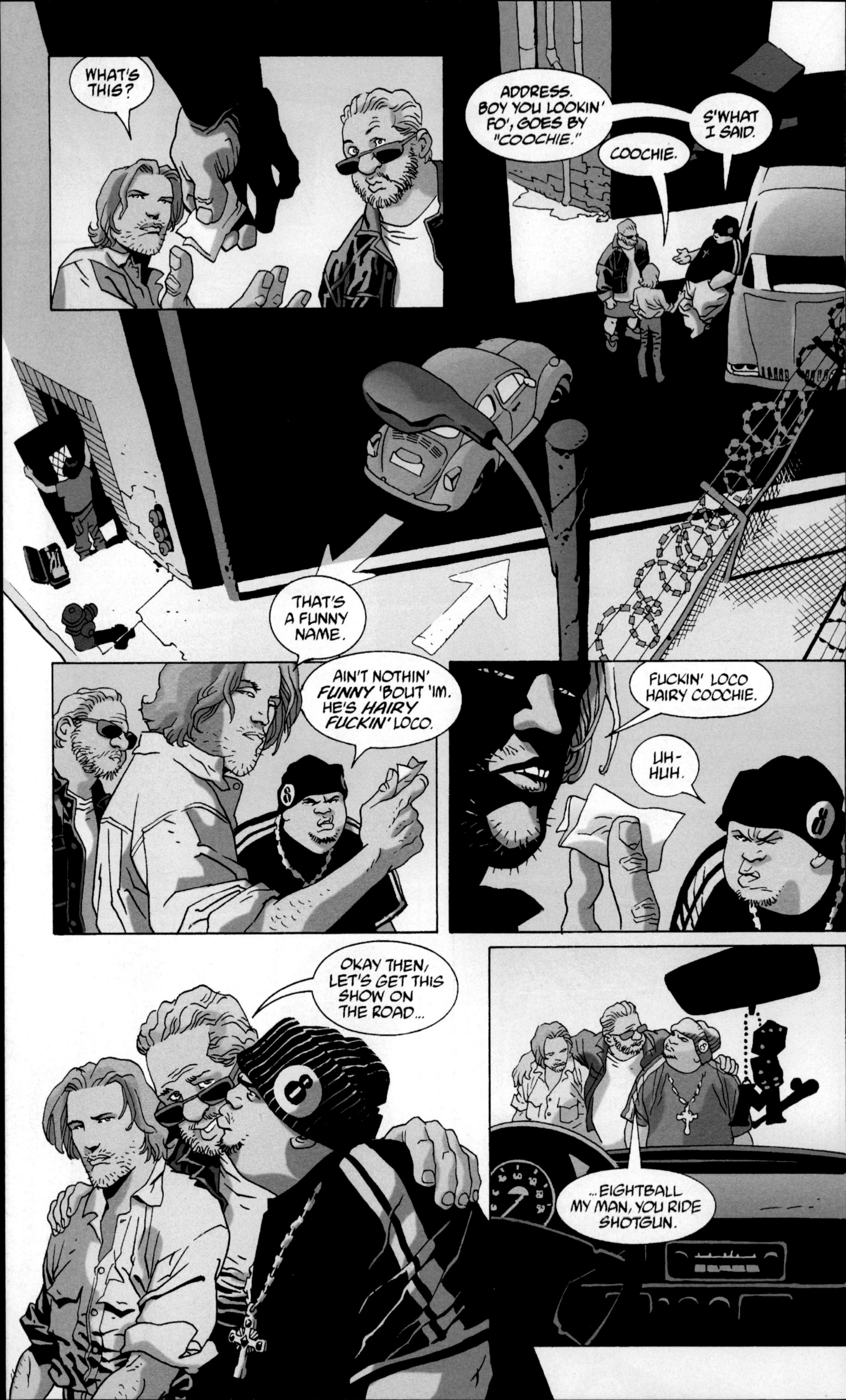
WHAT'S THIS?
ADDRESS. BOY YOU LOOKIN' FO', GOES BY "COOCHIE."
COOCHIE.
S'WHAT I SAID.
THAT'S A FUNNY NAME.
AIN'T NOTHIN' FUNNY 'BOUT 'IM. HE'S HAIRY FUCKIN' LOCO.
FUCKIN' LOCO HAIRY COOCHIE.
UH-HUH.
OKAY THEN, LET'S GET THIS SHOW ON THE ROAD...
...EIGHTBALL MY MAN, YOU RIDE SHOTGUN.

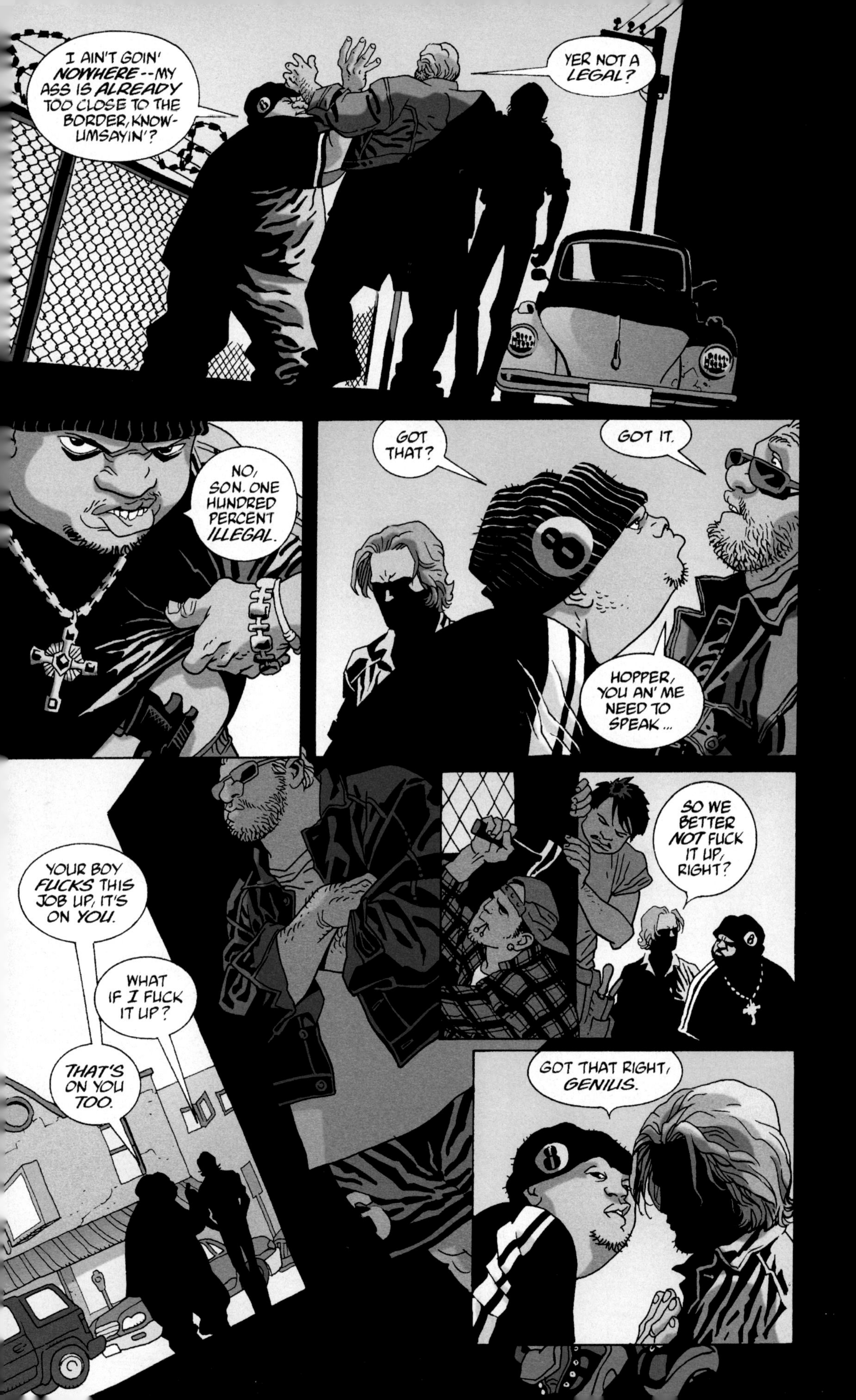
I AIN'T GOIN' NOWHERE--MY ASS IS ALREADY TOO CLOSE TO THE BORDER, KNOW-UMSAYIN'?
YER NOT A LEGAL?
NO, SON. ONE HUNDRED PERCENT ILLEGAL.
GOT THAT?
GOT IT.
HOPPER, YOU AN' ME NEED TO SPEAK...
YOUR BOY FUCKS THIS JOB UP, IT'S ON YOU.
WHAT IF I FUCK IT UP?
THAT'S ON YOU TOO.
SO WE BETTER NOT FUCK IT UP, RIGHT?
GOT THAT RIGHT, GENIUS.

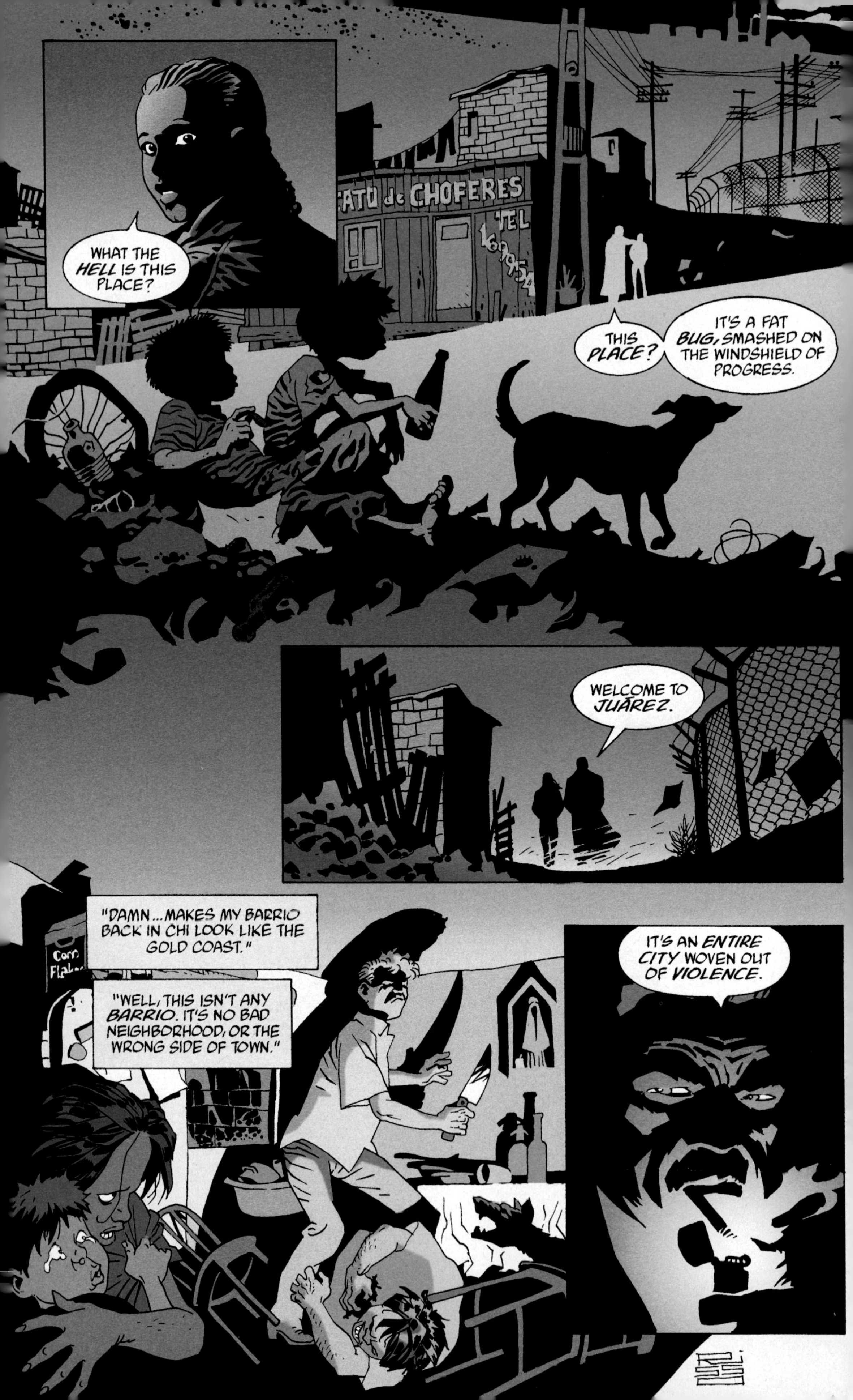
WHAT THE HELL IS THIS PLACE?
ATO de CHOFERES
TEL
THIS PLACE?
IT'S A FAT BUG, SMASHED ON THE WINDSHIELD OF PROGRESS.
WELCOME TO JUÁREZ.
"DAMN... MAKES MY BARRIO BACK IN CHI LOOK LIKE THE GOLD COAST."
"WELL, THIS ISN'T ANY BARRIO. IT'S NO BAD NEIGHBORHOOD, OR THE WRONG SIDE OF TOWN."
IT'S AN ENTIRE CITY WOVEN OUT OF VIOLENCE.

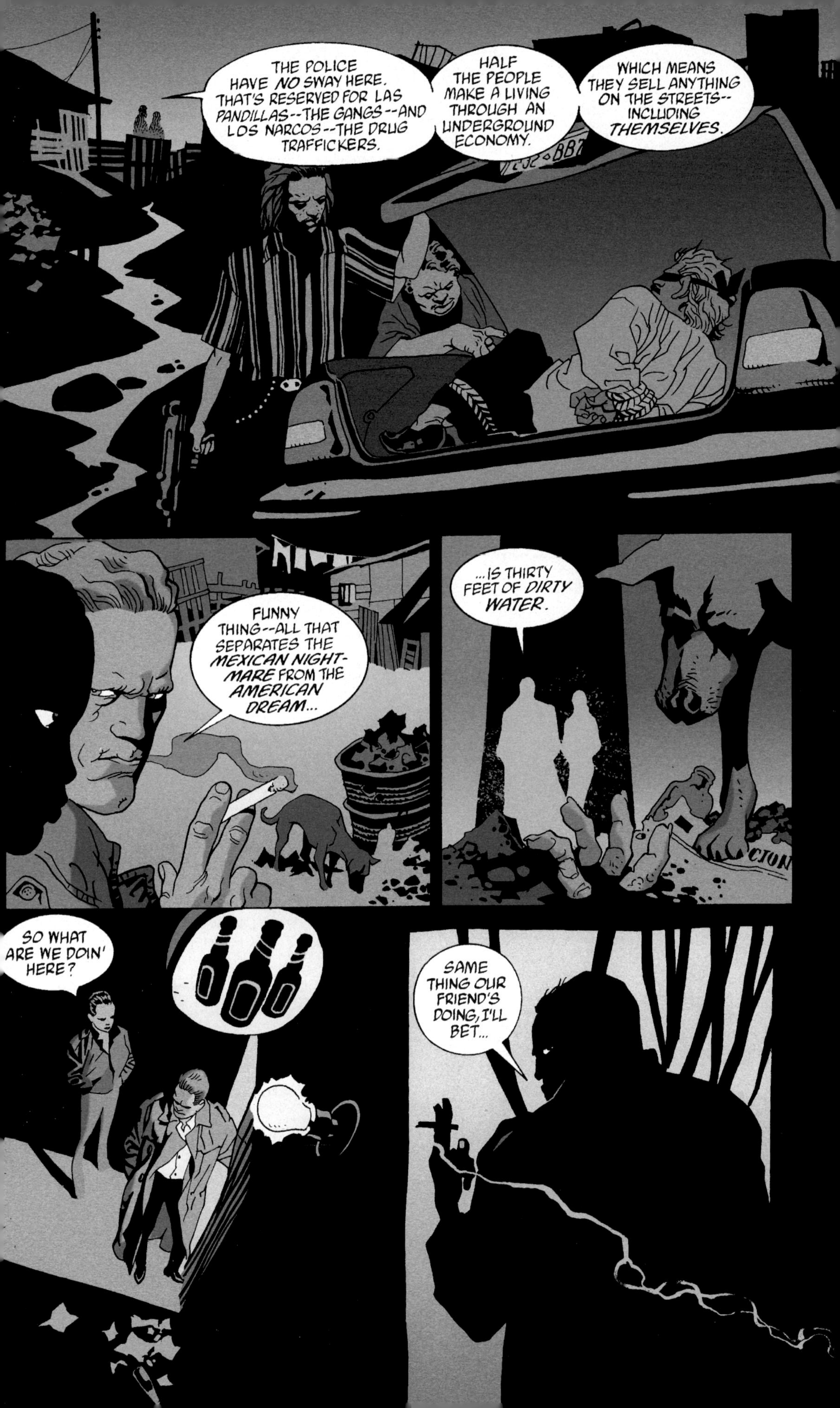
THE POLICE HAVE NO SWAY HERE. THAT'S RESERVED FOR LAS PANDILLAS--THE GANGS--AND LOS NARCOS--THE DRUG TRAFFICKERS.
HALF THE PEOPLE MAKE A LIVING THROUGH AN UNDERGROUND ECONOMY.
WHICH MEANS THEY SELL ANYTHING ON THE STREETS--INCLUDING THEMSELVES.
FUNNY THING--ALL THAT SEPARATES THE MEXICAN NIGHT-MARE FROM THE AMERICAN DREAM...
...IS THIRTY FEET OF DIRTY WATER.
SO WHAT ARE WE DOIN' HERE?
SAME THING OUR FRIEND'S DOING, I'LL BET...

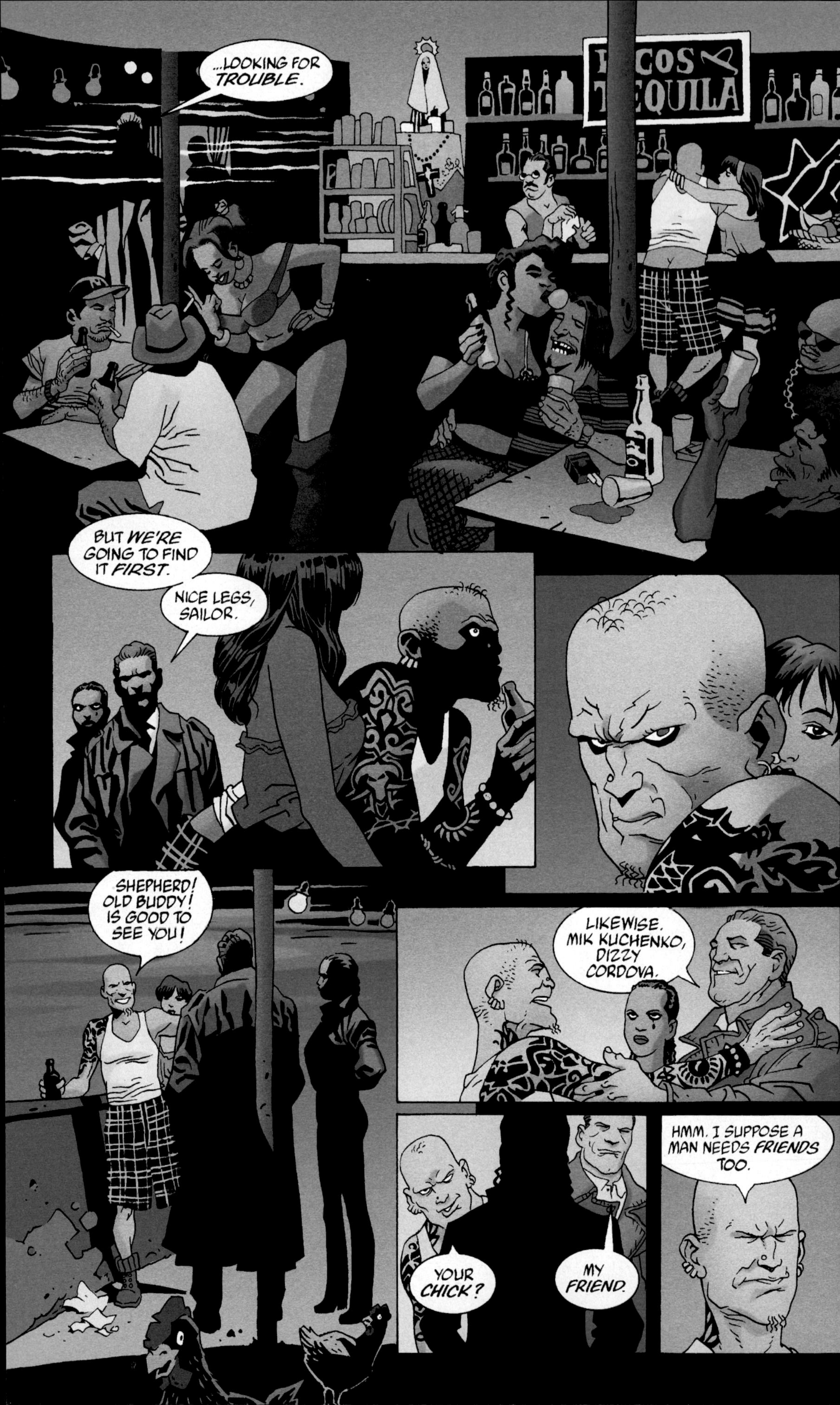
...LOOKING FOR TROUBLE.
BUT WE'RE GOING TO FIND IT FIRST.
NICE LEGS, SAILOR.
SHEPHERD! OLD BUDDY! IS GOOD TO SEE YOU!
LIKEWISE. MIK KUCHENKO, DIZZY CORDOVA.
YOUR CHICK?
MY FRIEND.
HMM. I SUPPOSE A MAN NEEDS FRIENDS TOO.

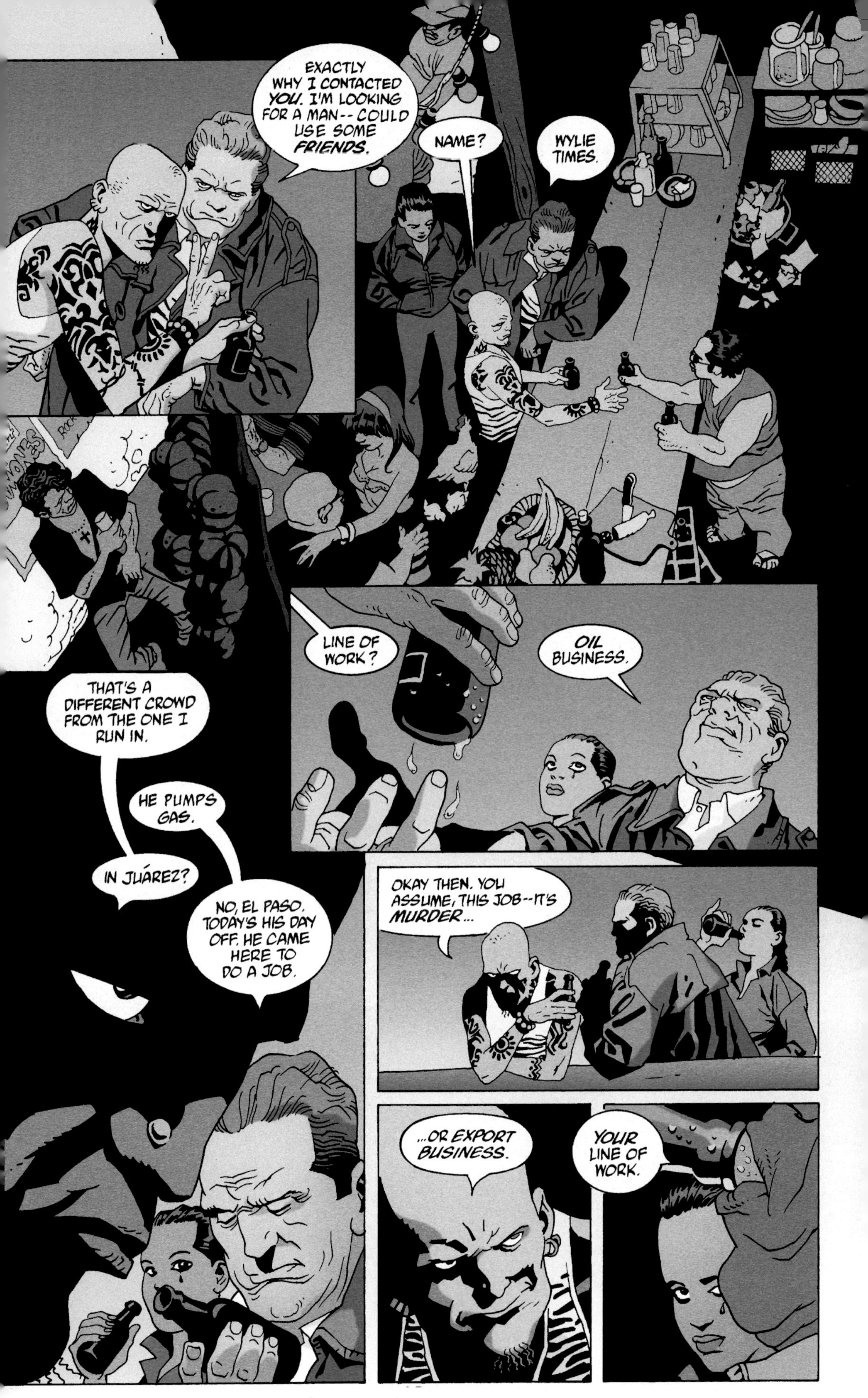
EXACTLY WHY I CONTACTED YOU. I'M LOOKING FOR A MAN-- COULD USE SOME FRIENDS.
NAME?
WYLIE TIMES.
LINE OF WORK?
OIL BUSINESS.
THAT'S A DIFFERENT CROWD FROM THE ONE I RUN IN.
HE PUMPS GAS.
IN JUÁREZ?
NO, EL PASO. TODAY'S HIS DAY OFF. HE CAME HERE TO DO A JOB.
OKAY THEN. YOU ASSUME, THIS JOB--IT'S MURDER...
...OR EXPORT BUSINESS.
YOUR LINE OF WORK.

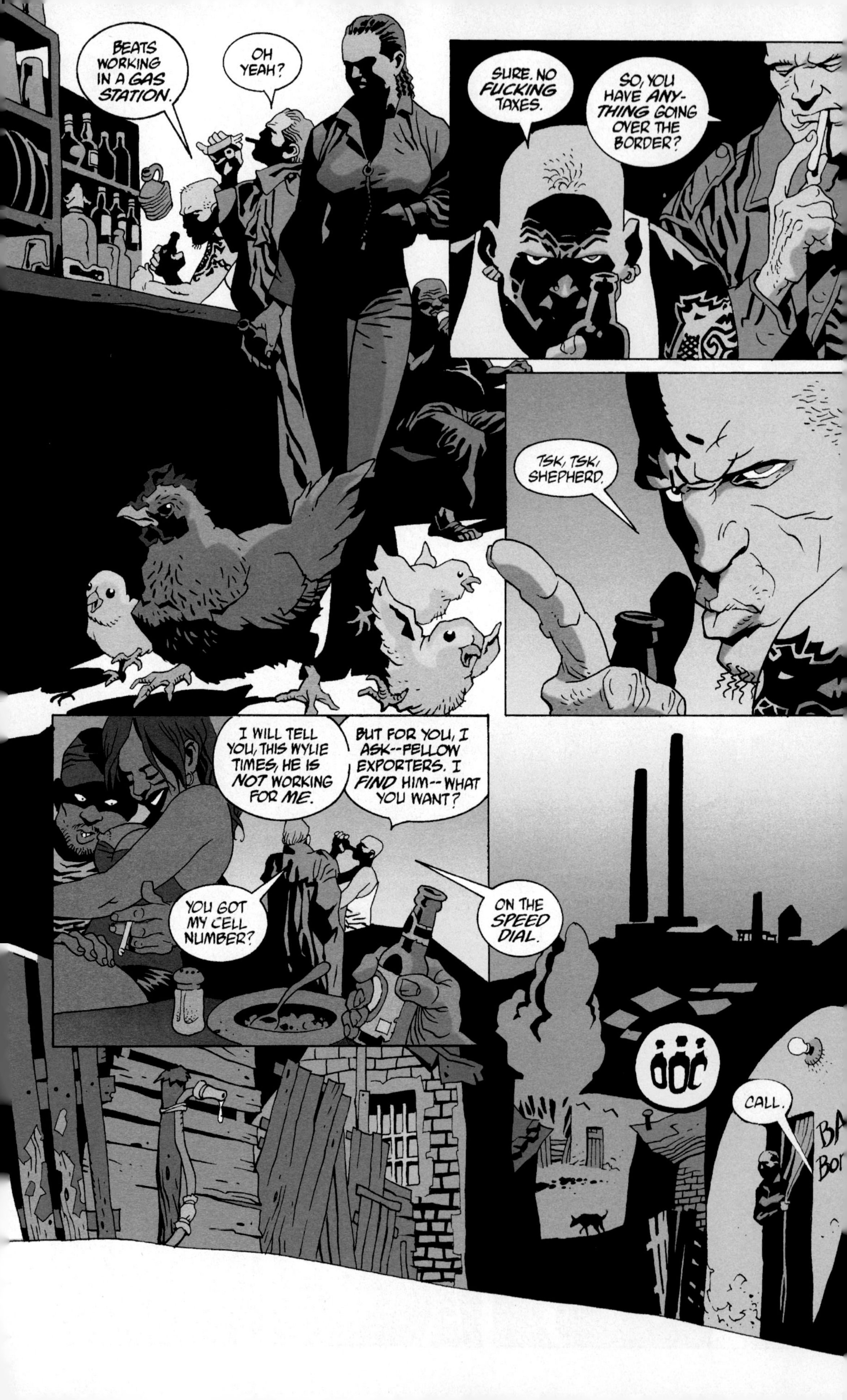
BEATS WORKING IN A GAS STATION.
OH YEAH?
SURE. NO FUCKING TAXES.
SO, YOU HAVE ANYTHING GOING OVER THE BORDER?
TSK, TSK, SHEPHERD.
I WILL TELL YOU, THIS WYLIE TIMES, HE IS NOT WORKING FOR ME.
BUT FOR YOU, I ASK--FELLOW EXPORTERS. I FIND HIM--WHAT YOU WANT?
YOU GOT MY CELL NUMBER?
ON THE SPEED DIAL.
CALL.

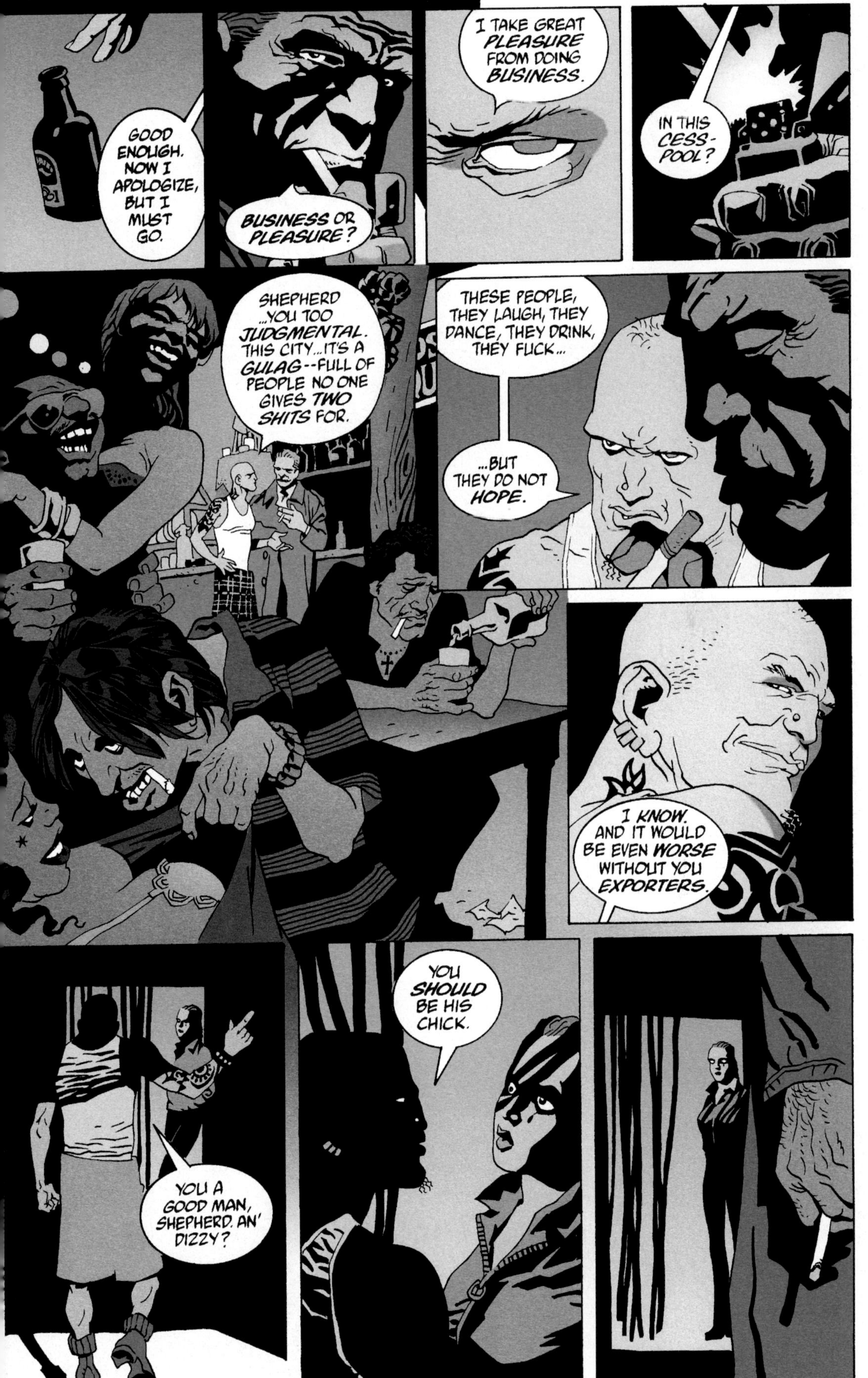
GOOD ENOUGH. NOW I APOLOGIZE, BUT I MUST GO.
BUSINESS OR PLEASURE?
I TAKE GREAT PLEASURE FROM DOING BUSINESS.
IN THIS CESS-POOL?
SHEPHERD ...YOU TOO JUDGMENTAL. THIS CITY... IT'S A GULAG--FULL OF PEOPLE NO ONE GIVES TWO SHITS FOR.
THESE PEOPLE, THEY LAUGH, THEY DANCE, THEY DRINK, THEY FUCK...
...BUT THEY DO NOT HOPE.
I KNOW. AND IT WOULD BE EVEN WORSE WITHOUT YOU EXPORTERS.
YOU A GOOD MAN, SHEPHERD. AN' DIZZY?
YOU SHOULD BE HIS CHICK.

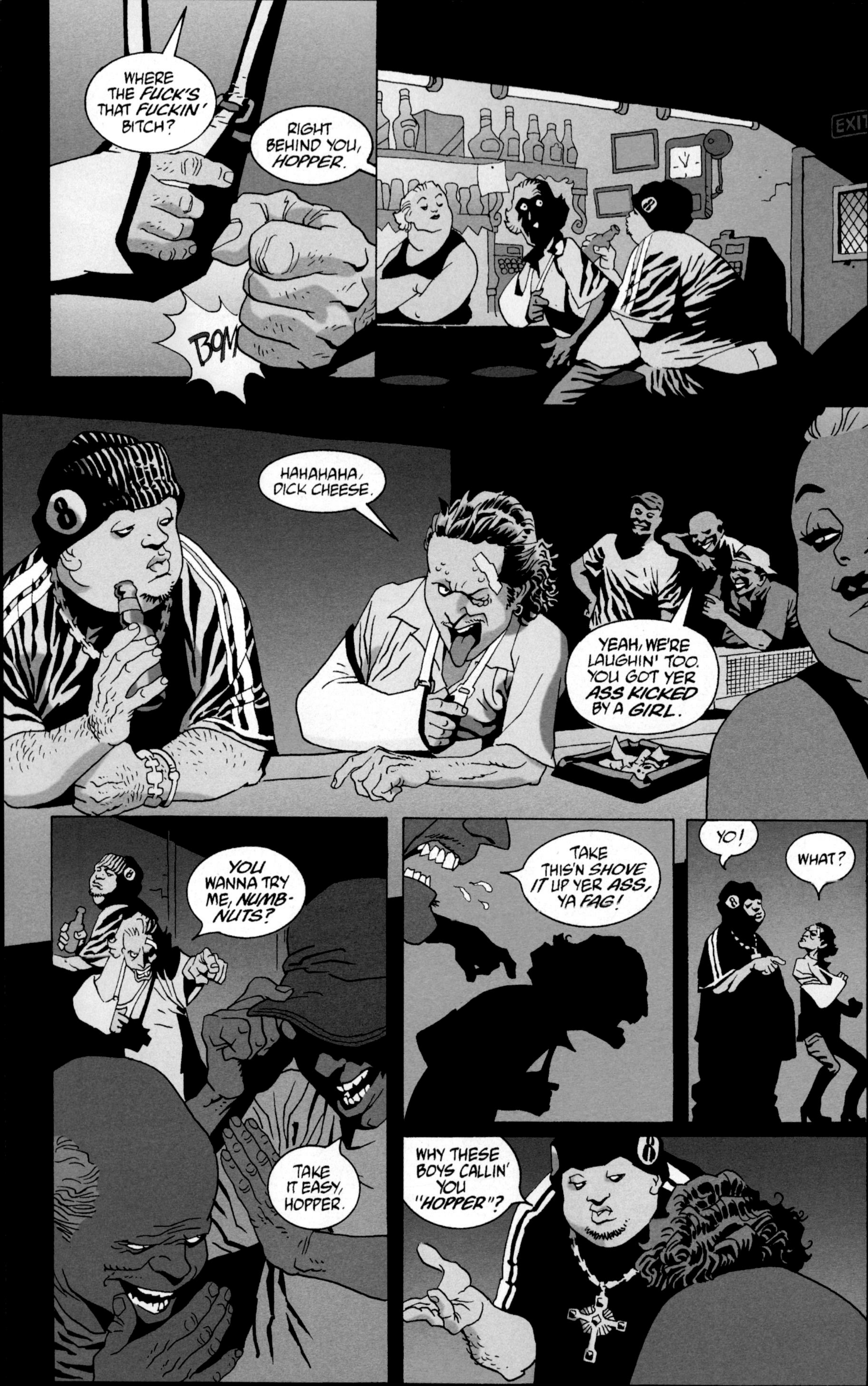
WHERE THE *FUCK'S* THAT *FUCKIN'* BITCH?
RIGHT BEHIND YOU, *HOPPER*.
BOM
HAHAHAHA, DICK CHEESE.
YEAH, WE'RE LAUGHIN' TOO. YOU GOT YER *ASS KICKED* BY A *GIRL*.
YOU WANNA TRY ME, *NUMB-NUTS?*
TAKE THIS'N *SHOVE IT* UP YER *ASS*, YA *FAG!*
YO!
WHAT?
TAKE IT EASY, HOPPER.
WHY THESE BOYS CALLIN' YOU "*HOPPER*"?

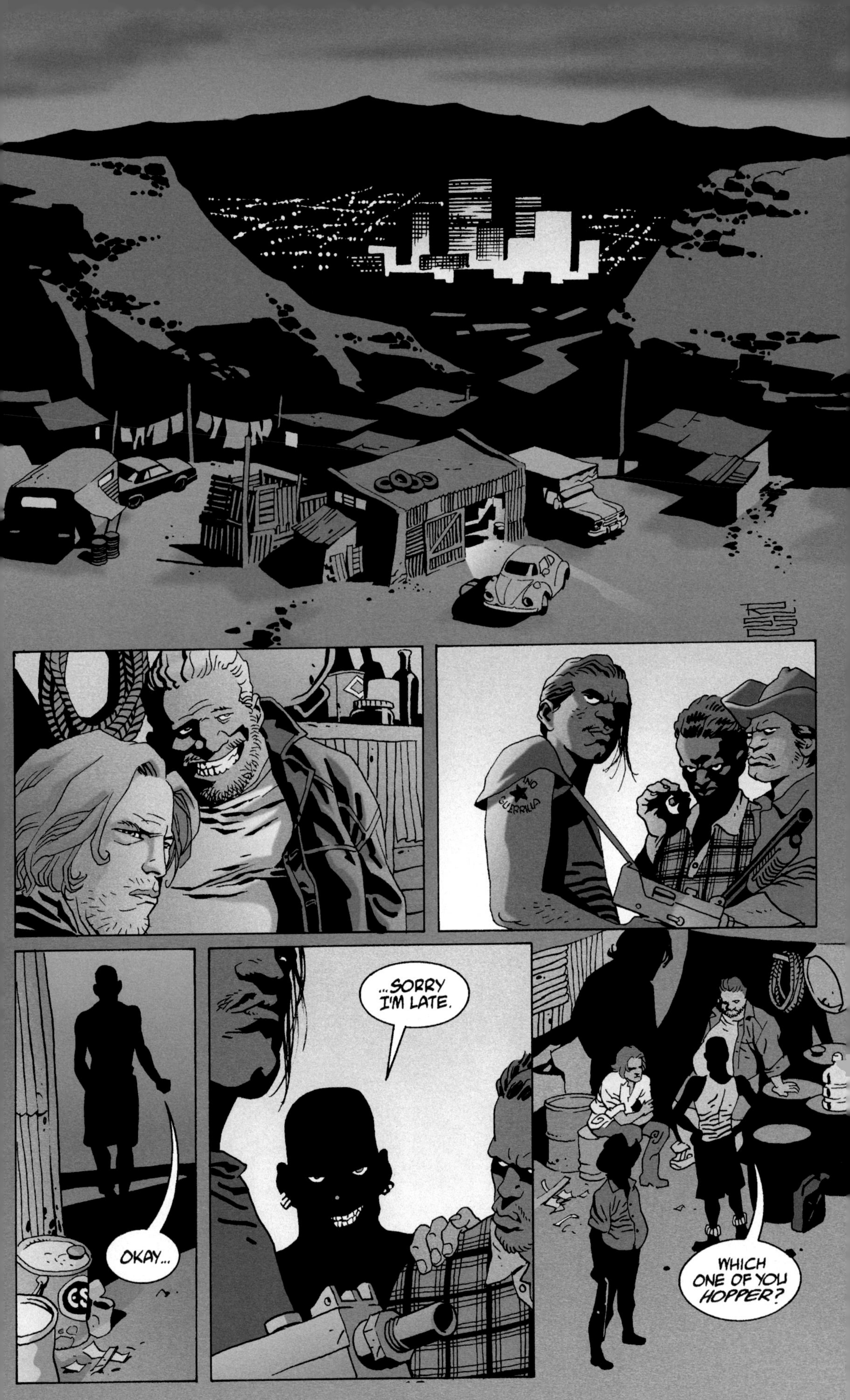
OKAY...
...SORRY I'M LATE.
WHICH ONE OF YOU HOPPER?

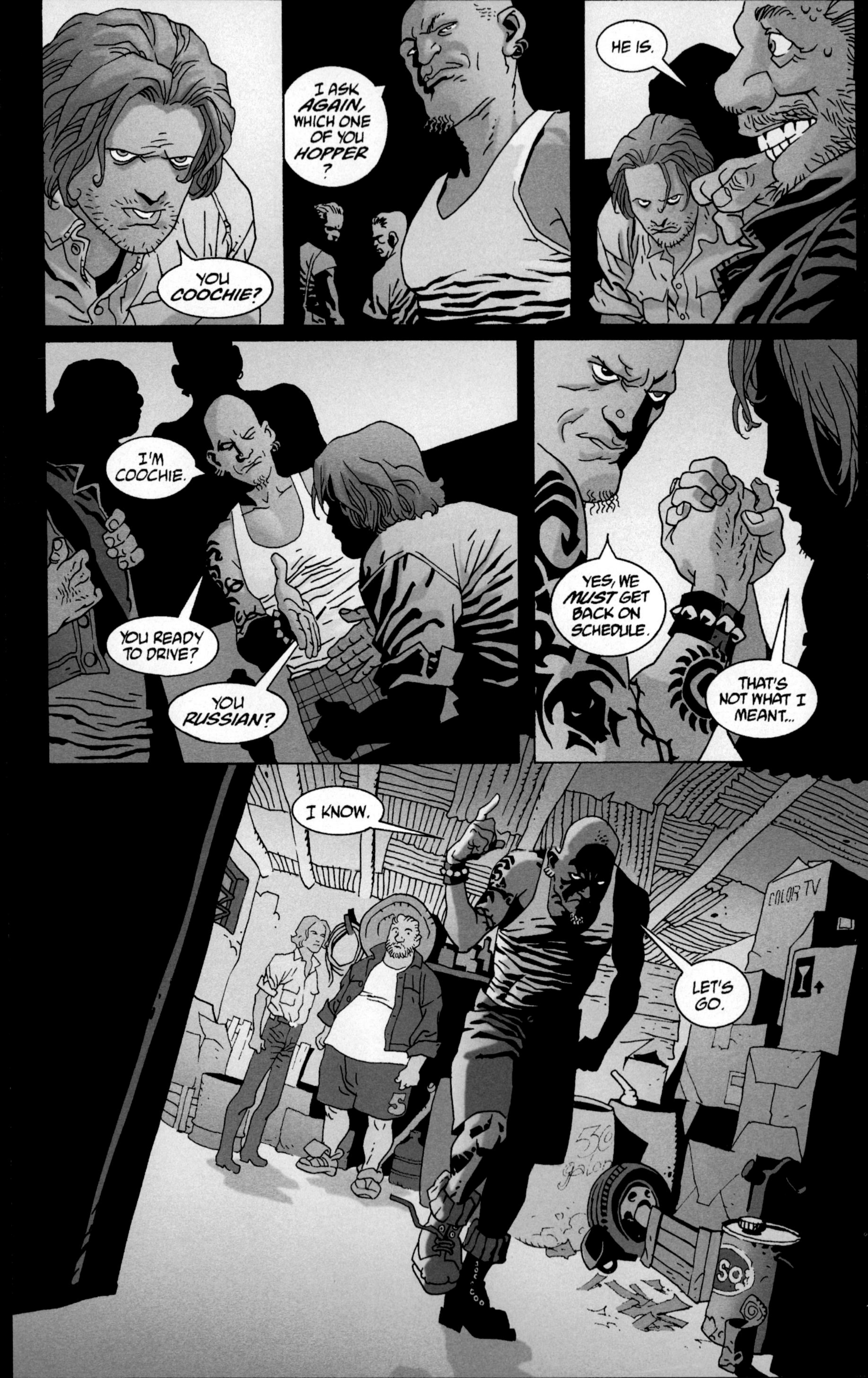
YOU COOCHIE?
I ASK AGAIN, WHICH ONE OF YOU HOPPER?
HE IS.
I'M COOCHIE.
YOU READY TO DRIVE?
YOU RUSSIAN?
YES, WE MUST GET BACK ON SCHEDULE.
THAT'S NOT WHAT I MEANT...
I KNOW.
LET'S GO.
COLOR TV

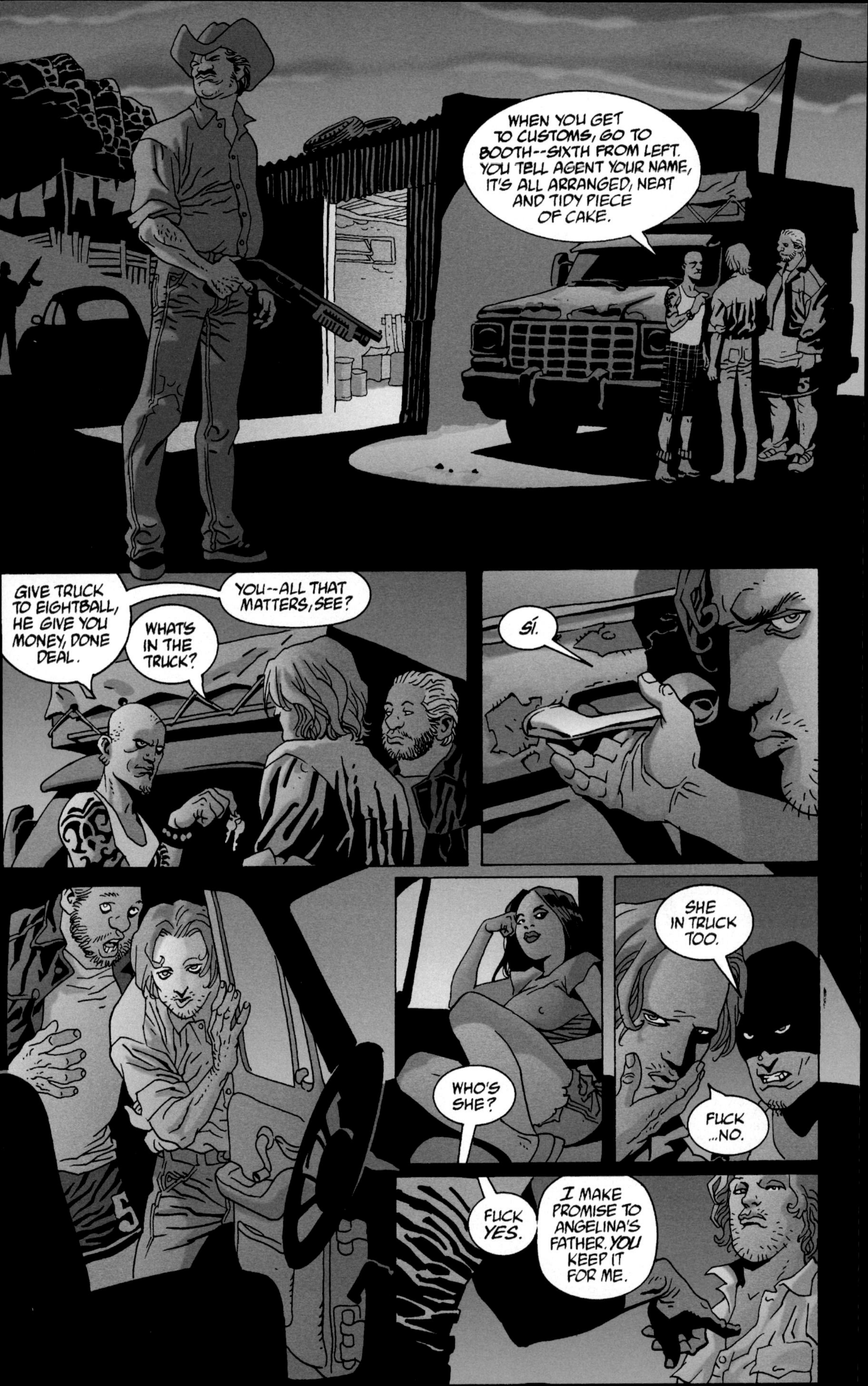

WHEN YOU GET TO CUSTOMS, GO TO BOOTH--SIXTH FROM LEFT. YOU TELL AGENT YOUR NAME, IT'S ALL ARRANGED, NEAT AND TIDY PIECE OF CAKE.
GIVE TRUCK TO EIGHTBALL, HE GIVE YOU MONEY, DONE DEAL.
WHAT'S IN THE TRUCK?
YOU--ALL THAT MATTERS, SEE?
SÍ.
WHO'S SHE?
SHE IN TRUCK TOO.
FUCK ...NO.
FUCK YES.
I MAKE PROMISE TO ANGELINA'S FATHER. YOU KEEP IT FOR ME.

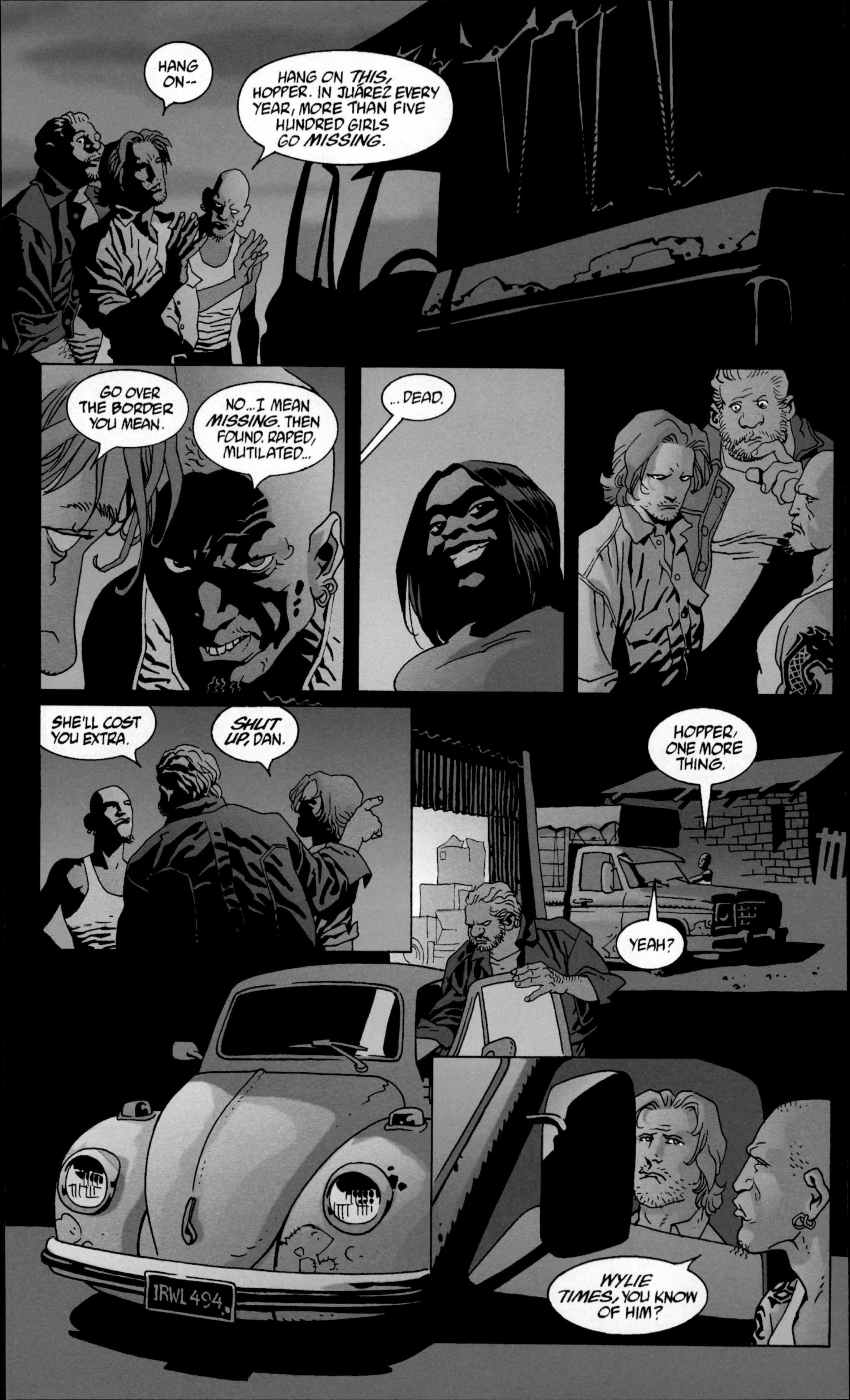
HANG ON--
HANG ON *THIS*, HOPPER. IN JUÁREZ EVERY YEAR, MORE THAN FIVE HUNDRED GIRLS GO *MISSING*.
GO OVER THE BORDER YOU MEAN.
NO...I MEAN *MISSING*. THEN FOUND. RAPED, MUTILATED...
...DEAD.
SHE'LL COST YOU EXTRA.
SHUT UP, DAN.
HOPPER, ONE MORE THING.
YEAH?
IRWL 494.
WYLIE TIMES, YOU KNOW OF HIM?

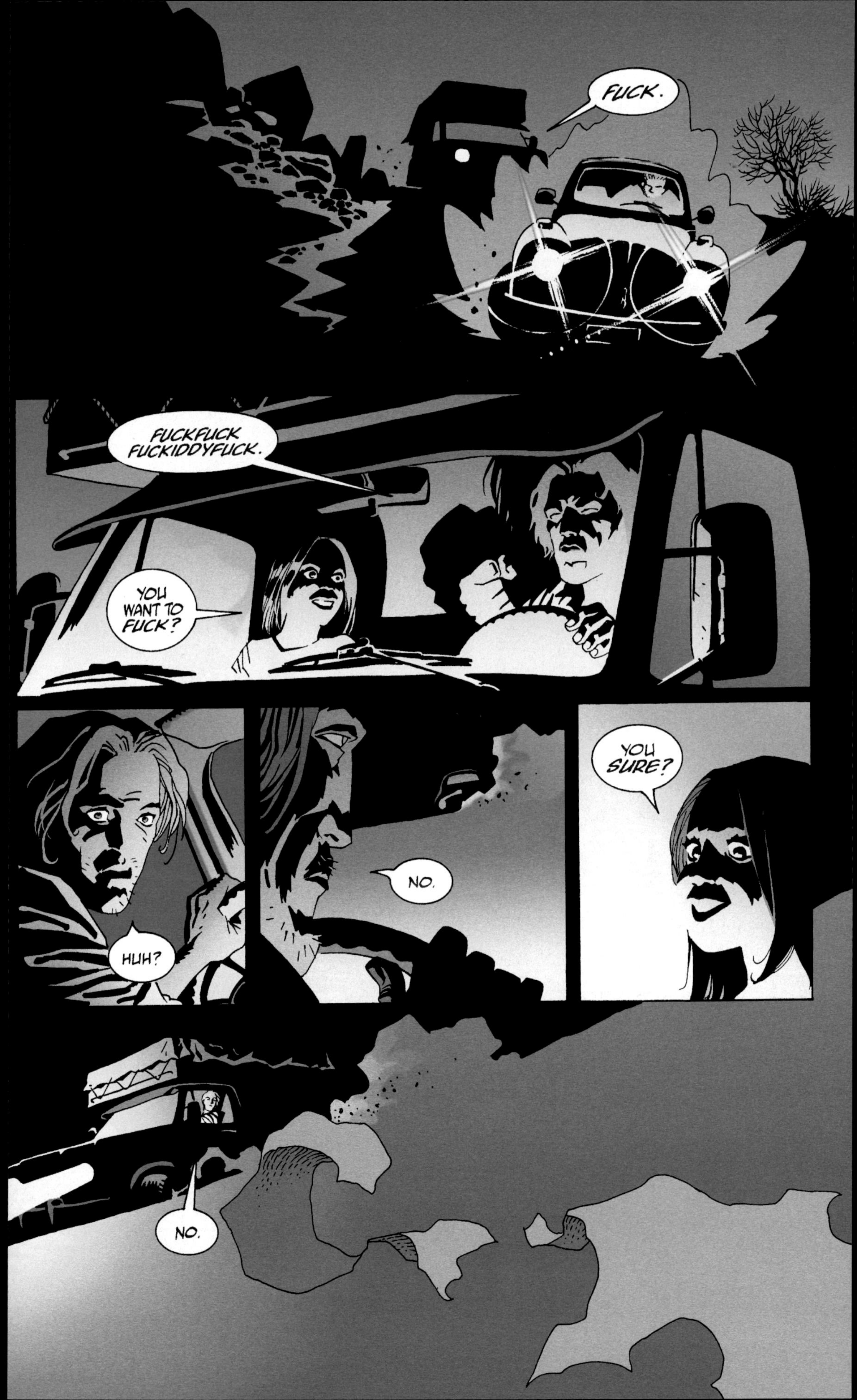
FUCK.
FUCKFUCK FUCKIDDYFUCK.
YOU WANT TO FUCK?
HUH?
NO.
YOU SURE?
NO.

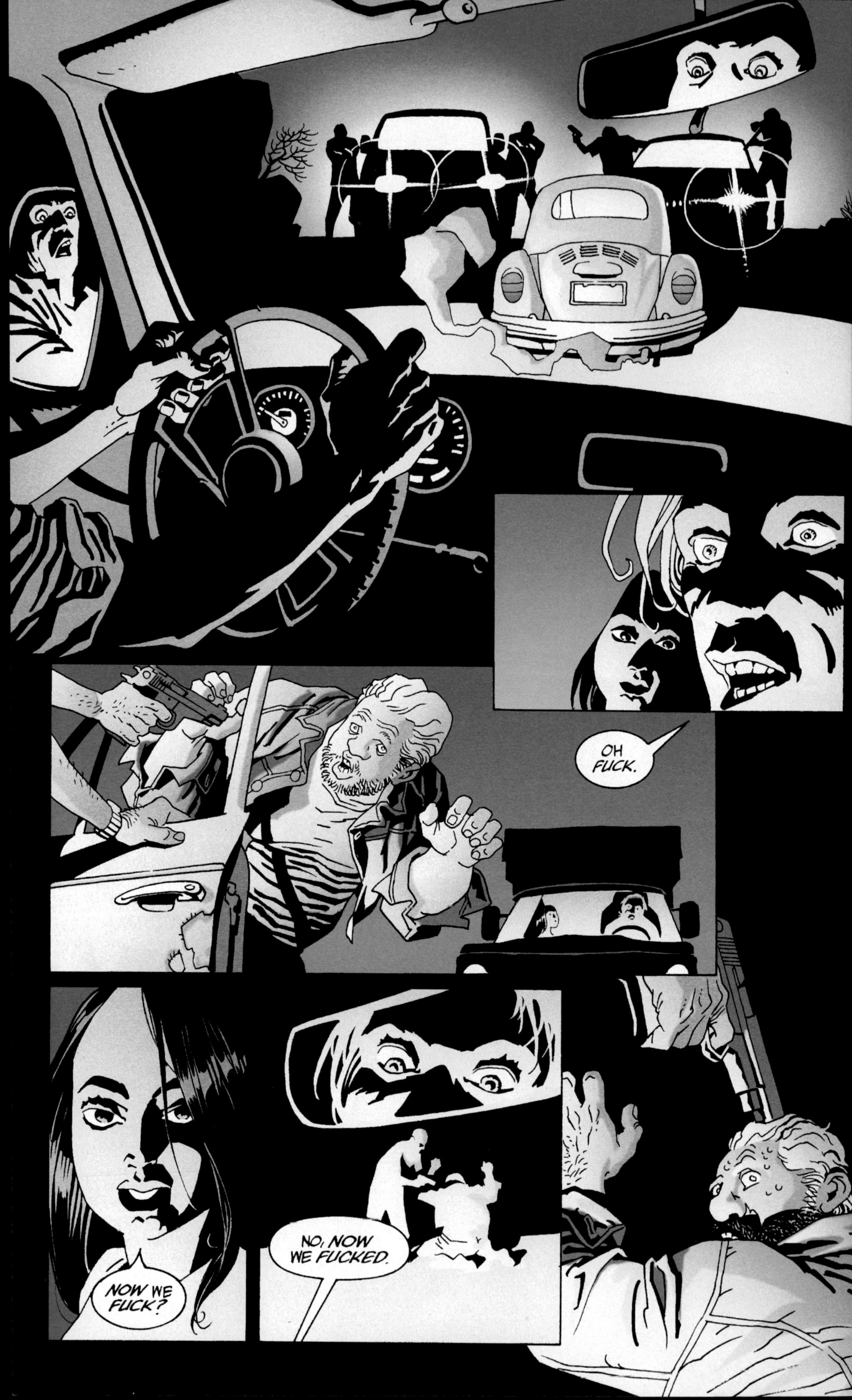
OH FUCK.
NOW WE FUCK?
NO, NOW WE FUCKED.

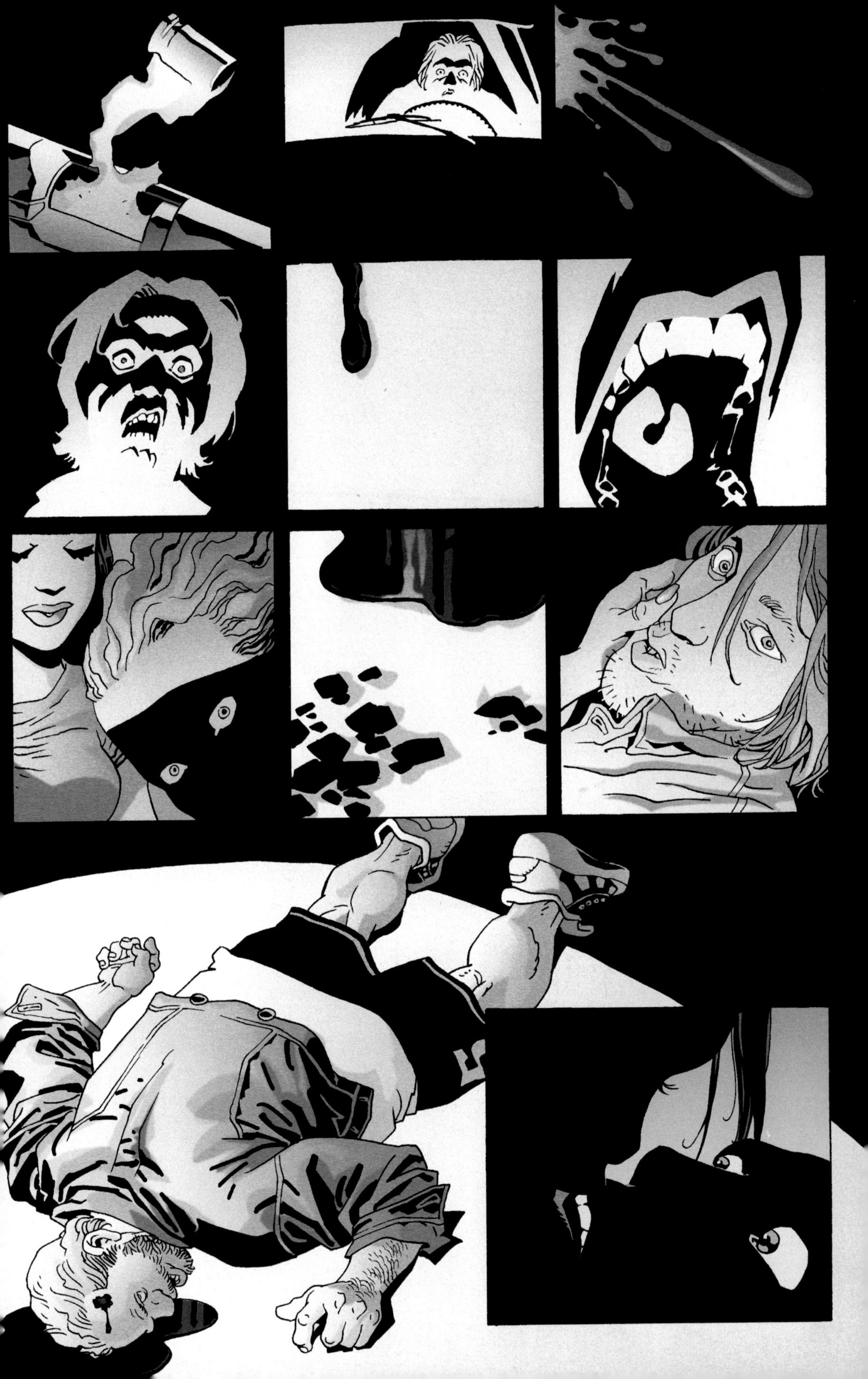

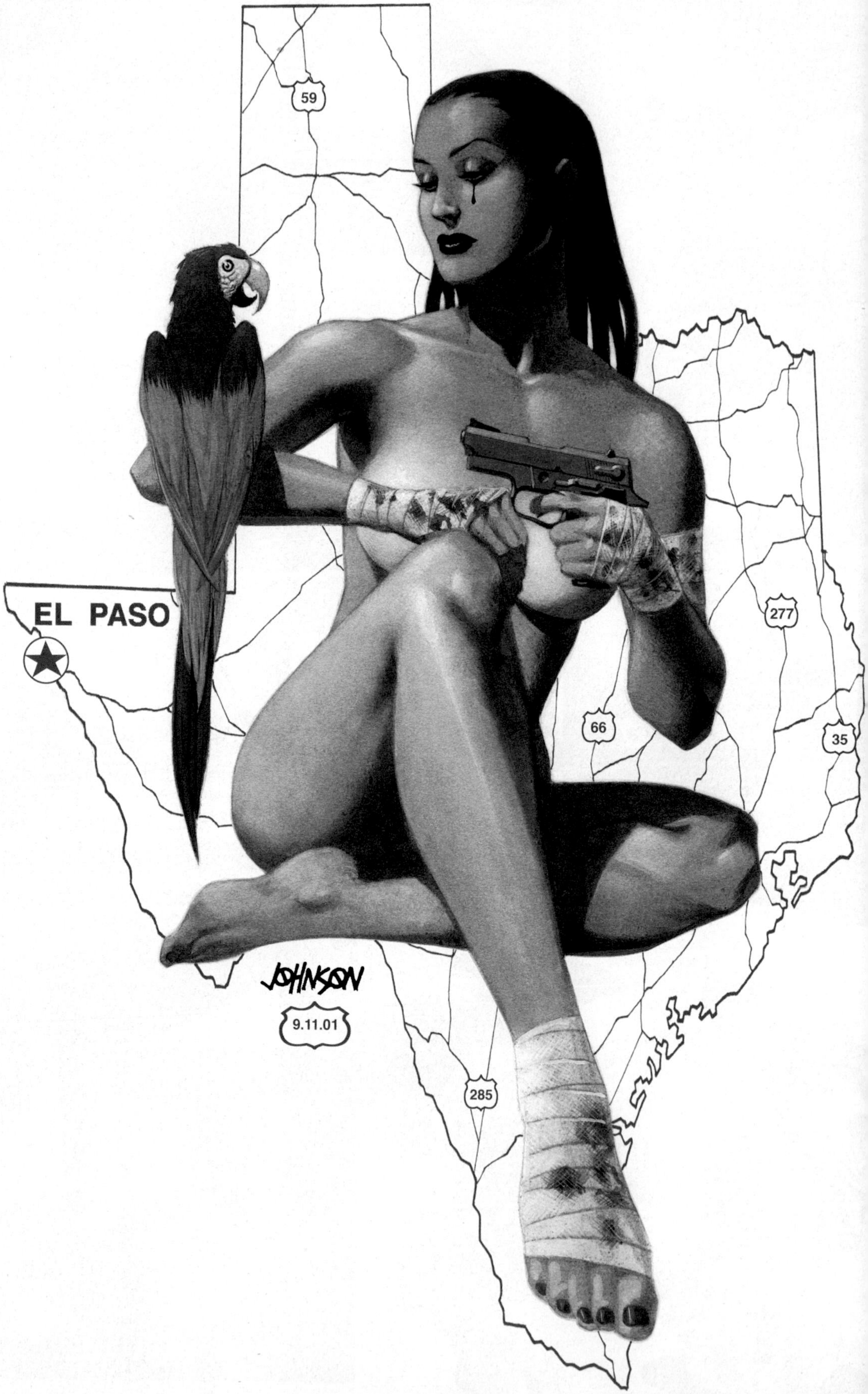
59
EL PASO
277
66
35
JOHNSON
9.11.01
285

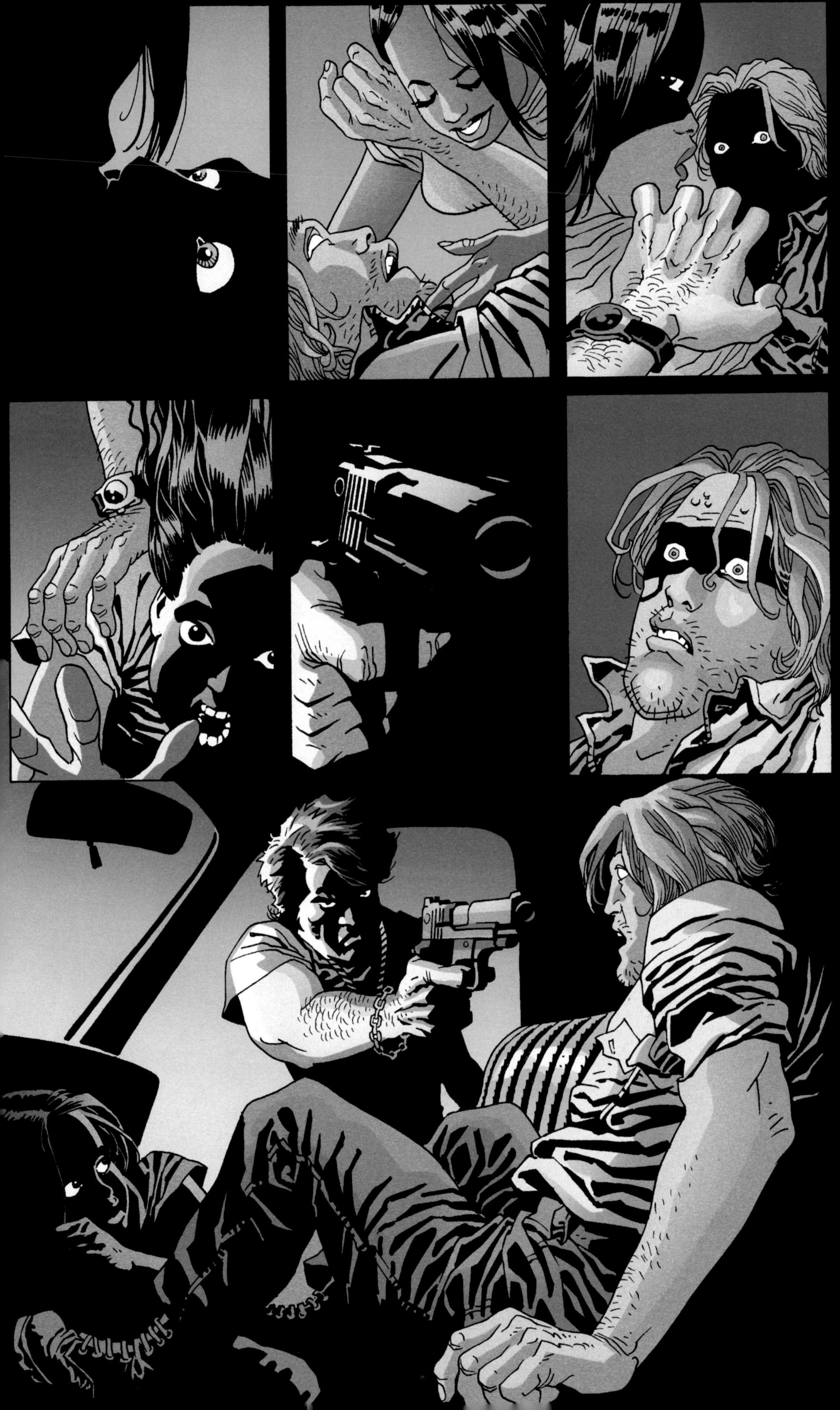

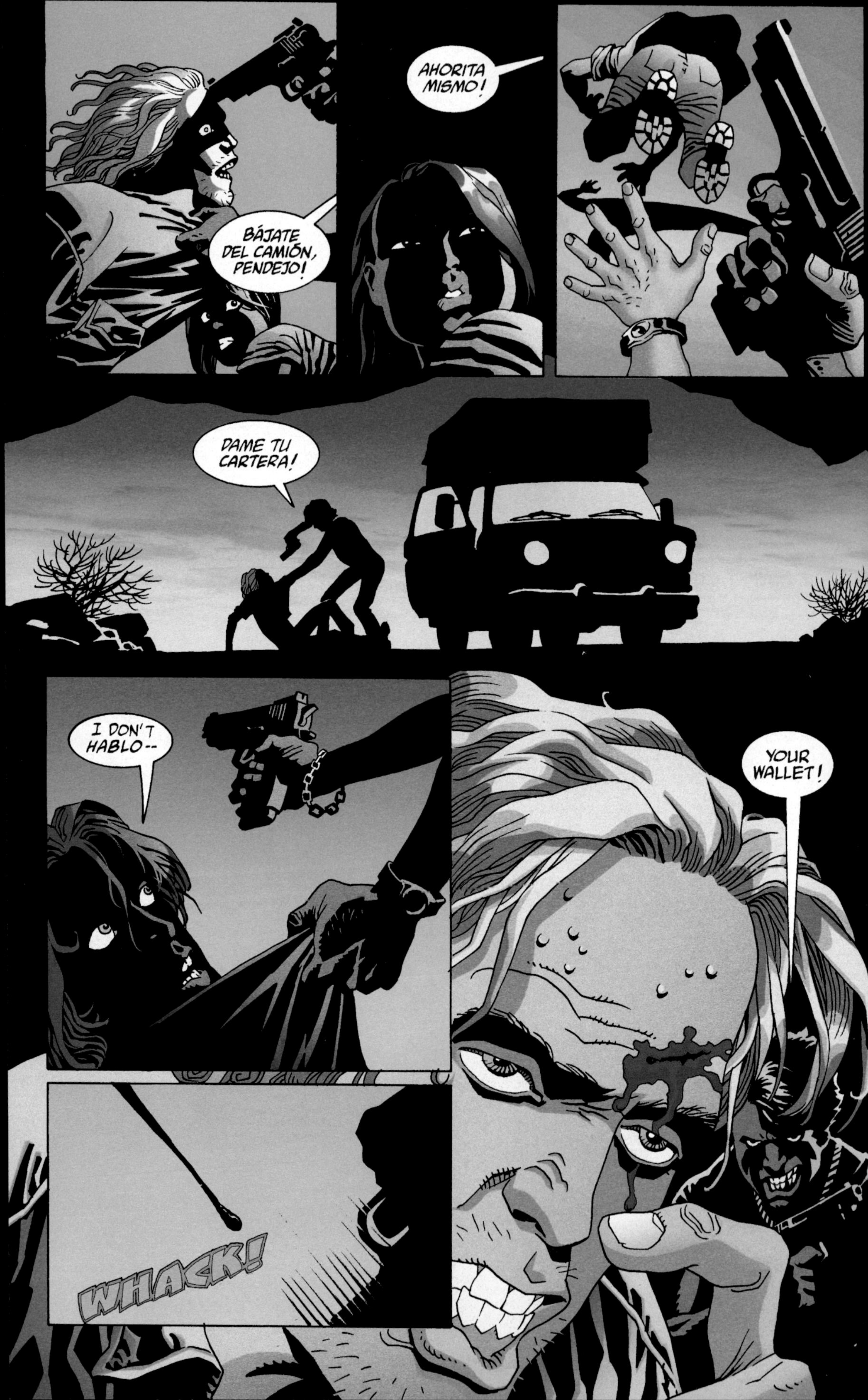
BÁJATE
DEL CAMIÓN,
PENDEJO!
AHORITA
MISMO!
DAME TU
CARTERA!
I DON'T
HABLO--
YOUR
WALLET!
WHACK!

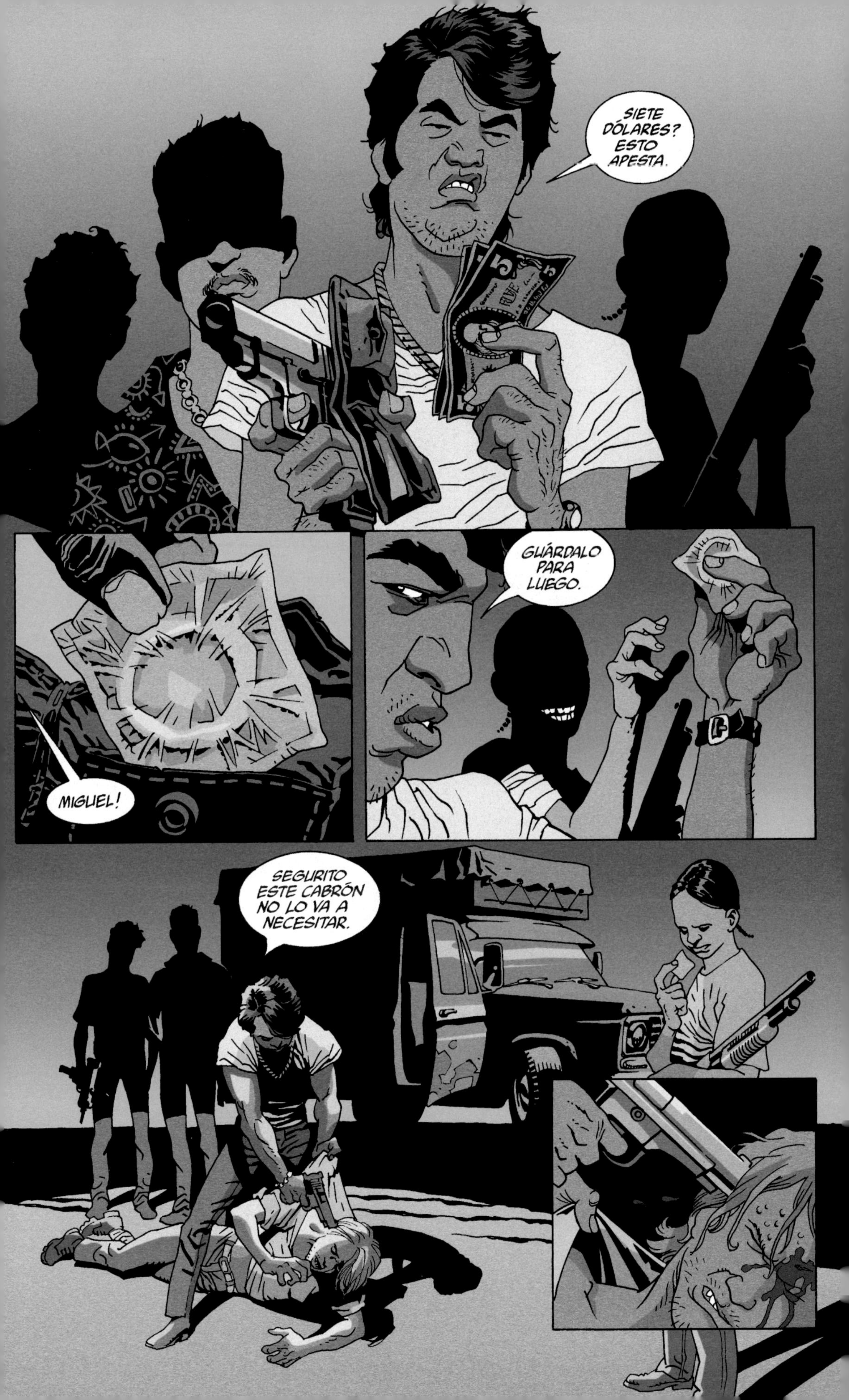

SIETE DÓLARES? ESTO APESTA.
MIGUEL!
GUÁRDALO PARA LUEGO.
SEGURITO ESTE CABRÓN NO LO VA A NECESITAR.

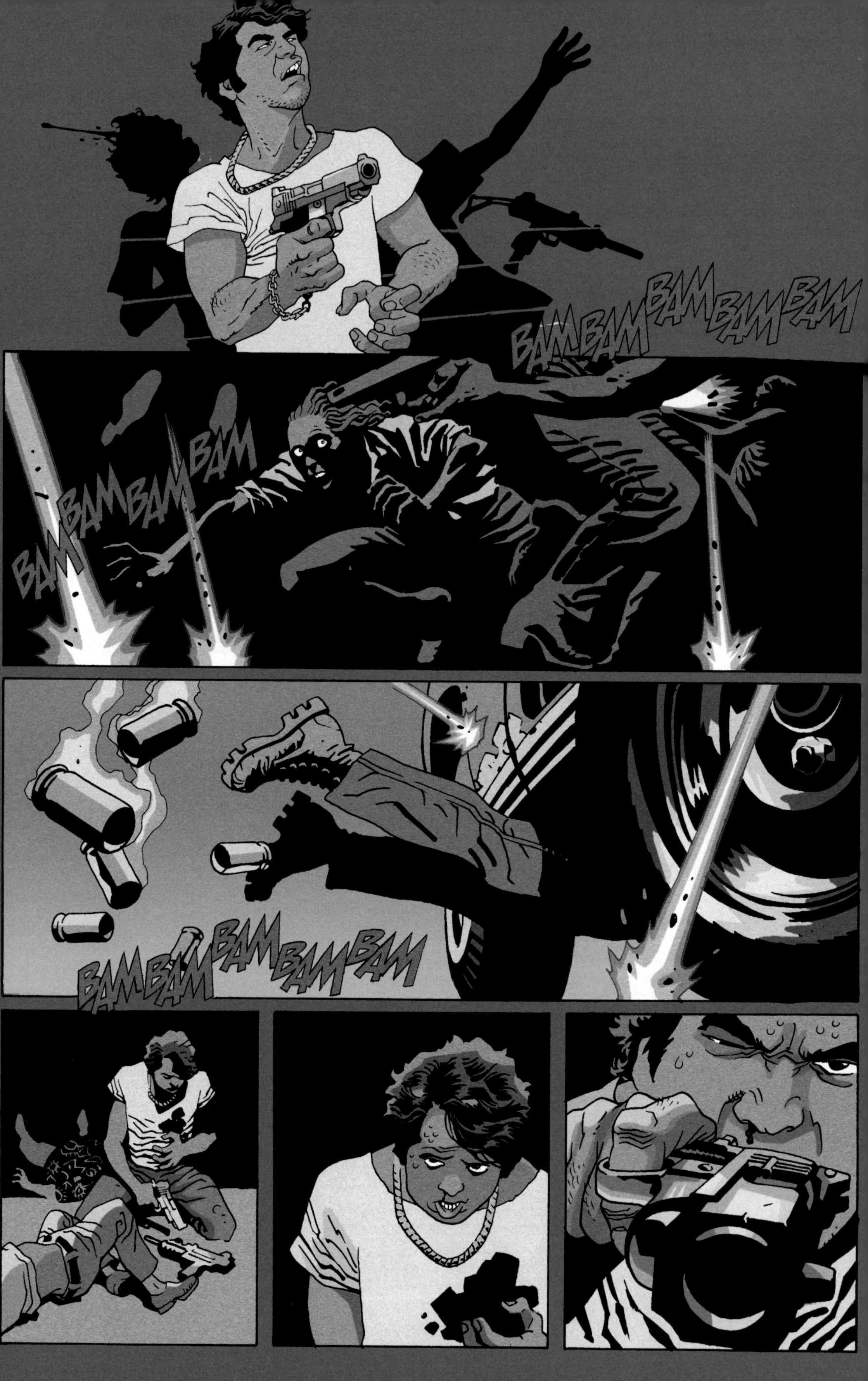
BAMBAMBAMBAMBAM
BAMBAMBAMBAM
BAMBAMBAMBAMBAM

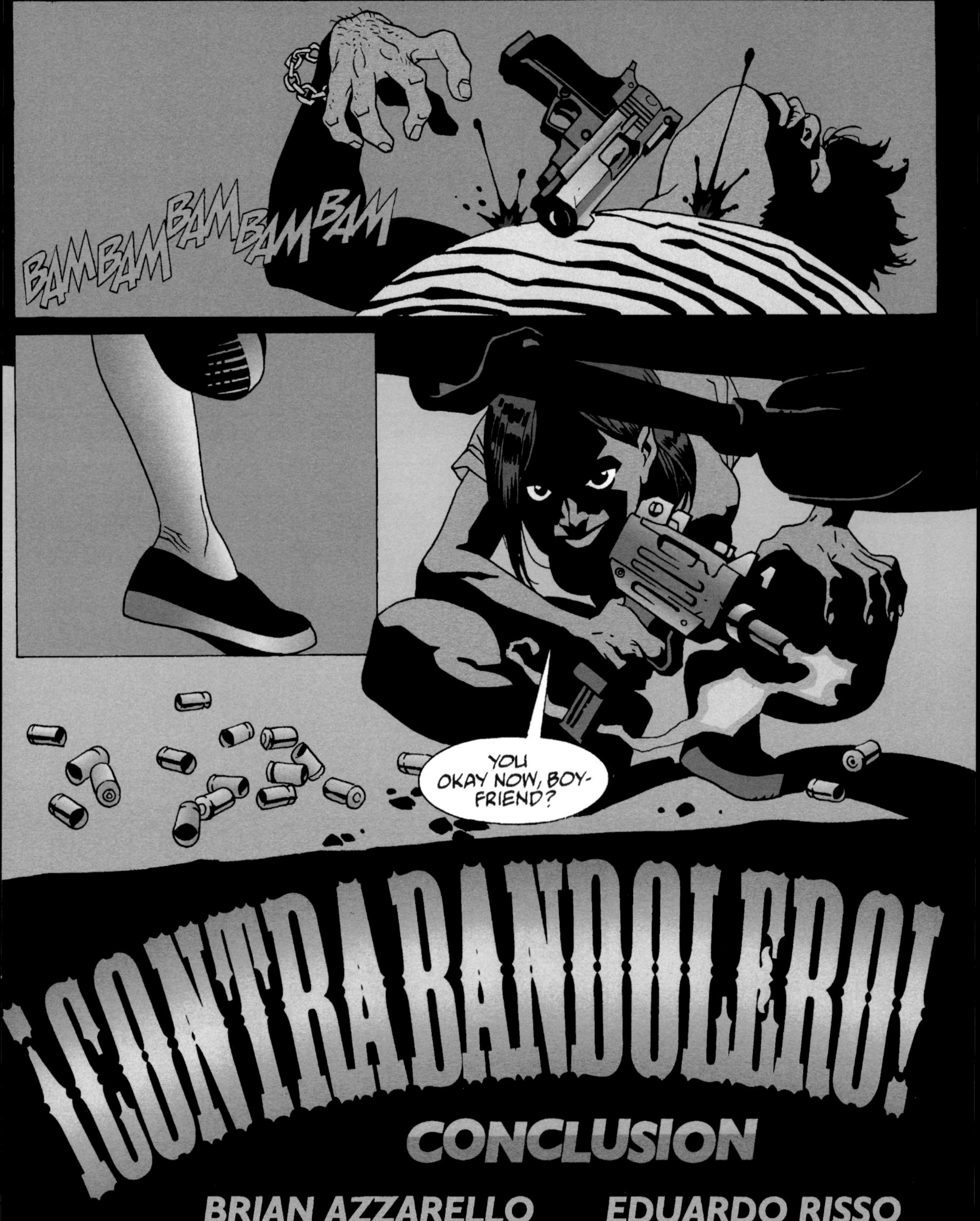
BAM BAM BAM BAM BAM
YOU OKAY NOW, BOY-FRIEND?
¡CONTRABANDOLERO!
CONCLUSION
BRIAN AZZARELLO
writer
EDUARDO RISSO
artist

PATRICIA MULVIHILL colorist | CLEM ROBINS letterer | DIGITAL CHAMELEON separator | DAVE JOHNSON cover artist | WILL DENNIS editor

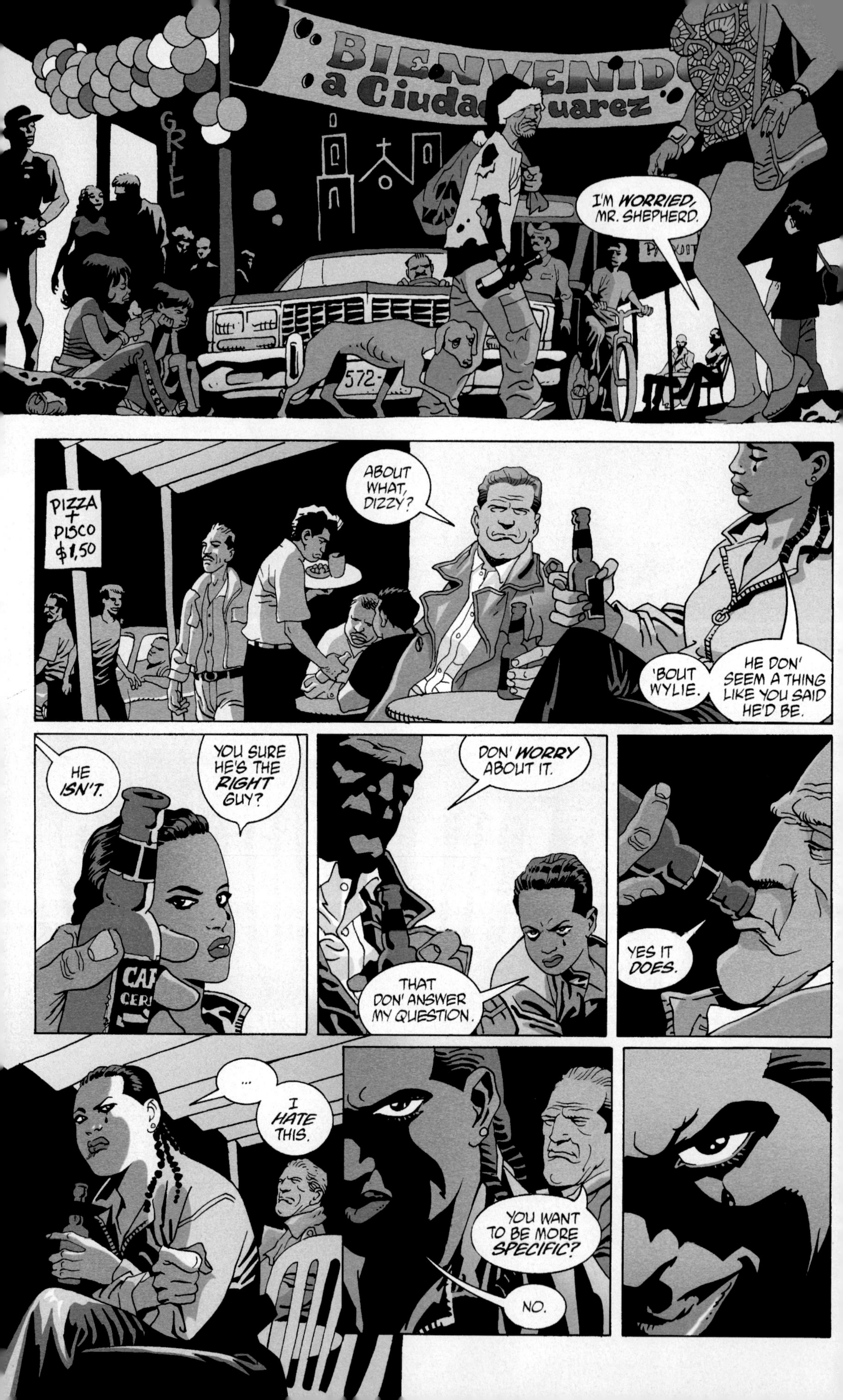
BIENVENIDO a Ciudad Juarez
GRILL
I'M WORRIED, MR. SHEPHERD.
572-
PIZZA + PISCO $1,50
ABOUT WHAT, DIZZY?
'BOUT WYLIE.
HE DON' SEEM A THING LIKE YOU SAID HE'D BE.
HE ISN'T.
YOU SURE HE'S THE RIGHT GUY?
DON' WORRY ABOUT IT.
THAT DON' ANSWER MY QUESTION.
YES IT DOES.
...
I HATE THIS.
YOU WANT TO BE MORE SPECIFIC?
NO.

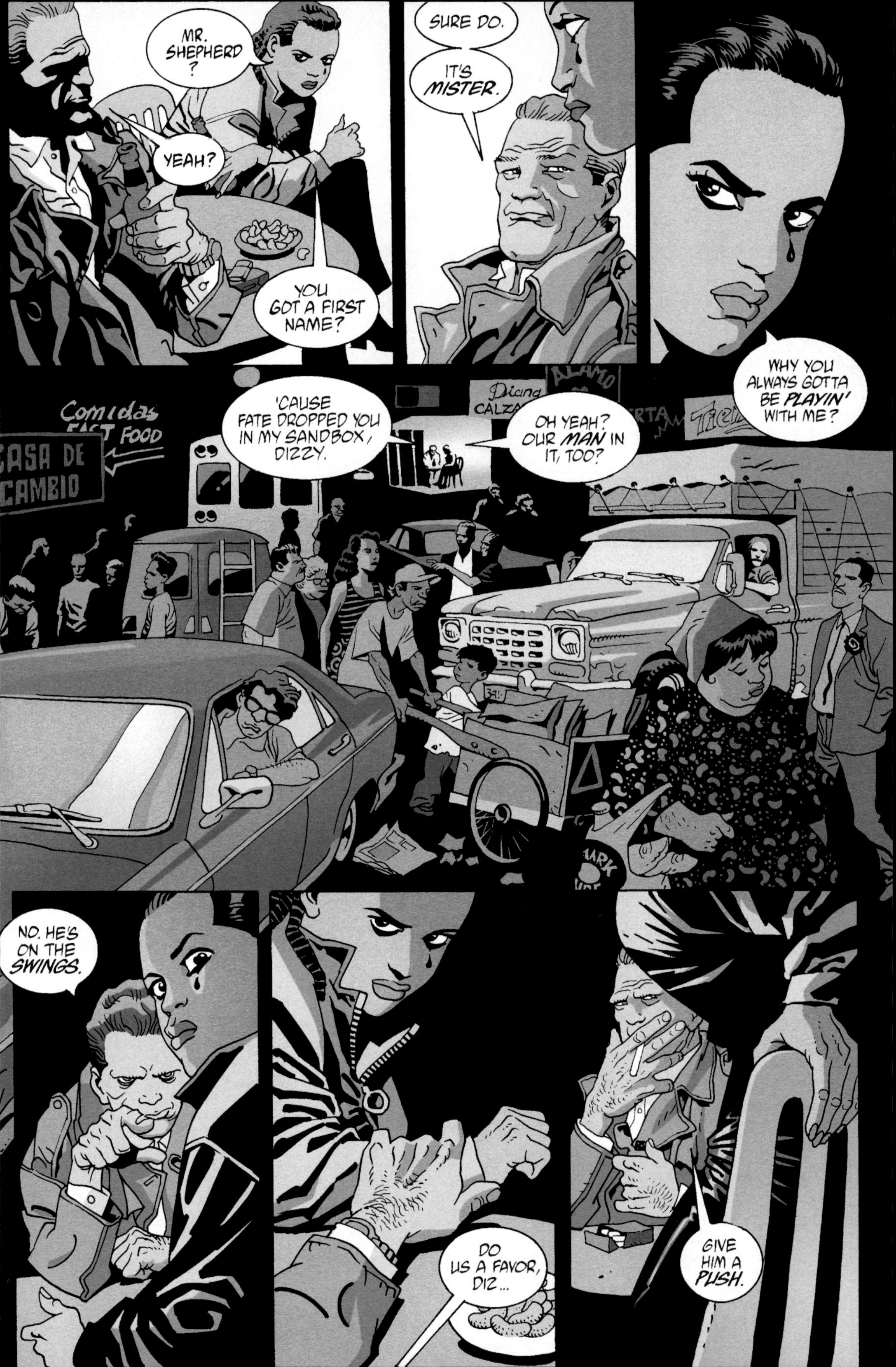
MR. SHEPHERD?
YEAH?
YOU GOT A FIRST NAME?
SURE DO.
IT'S MISTER.
Comidas FAST FOOD
CASA DE CAMBIO
'CAUSE FATE DROPPED YOU IN MY SANDBOX, DIZZY.
OH YEAH? OUR MAN IN IT, TOO?
WHY YOU ALWAYS GOTTA BE PLAYIN' WITH ME?
NO. HE'S ON THE SWINGS.
DO US A FAVOR, DIZ...
GIVE HIM A PUSH.

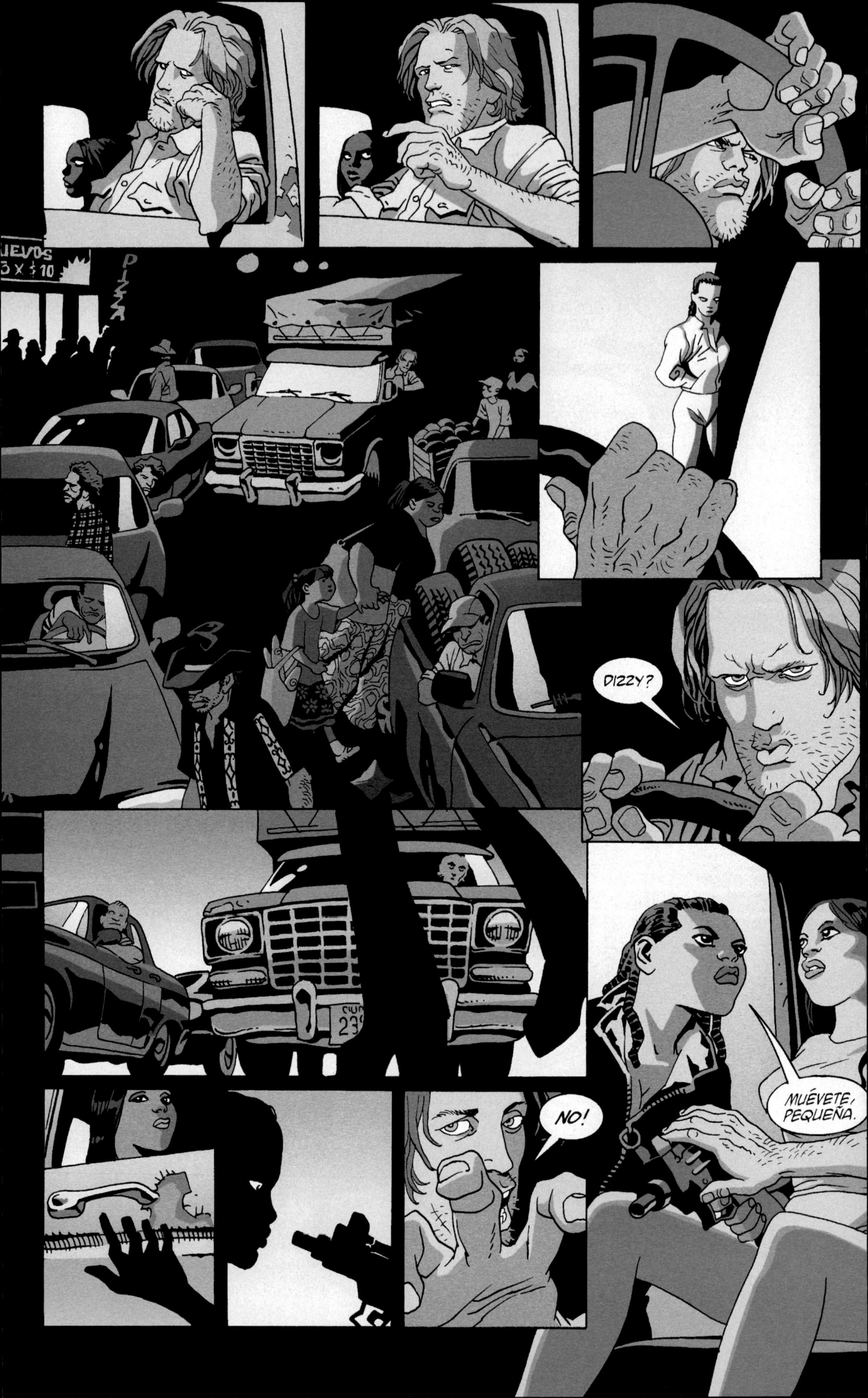

UEVOS
3 x $10
PIZZA
DIZZY?
MUÉVETE, PEQUEÑA.
NO!

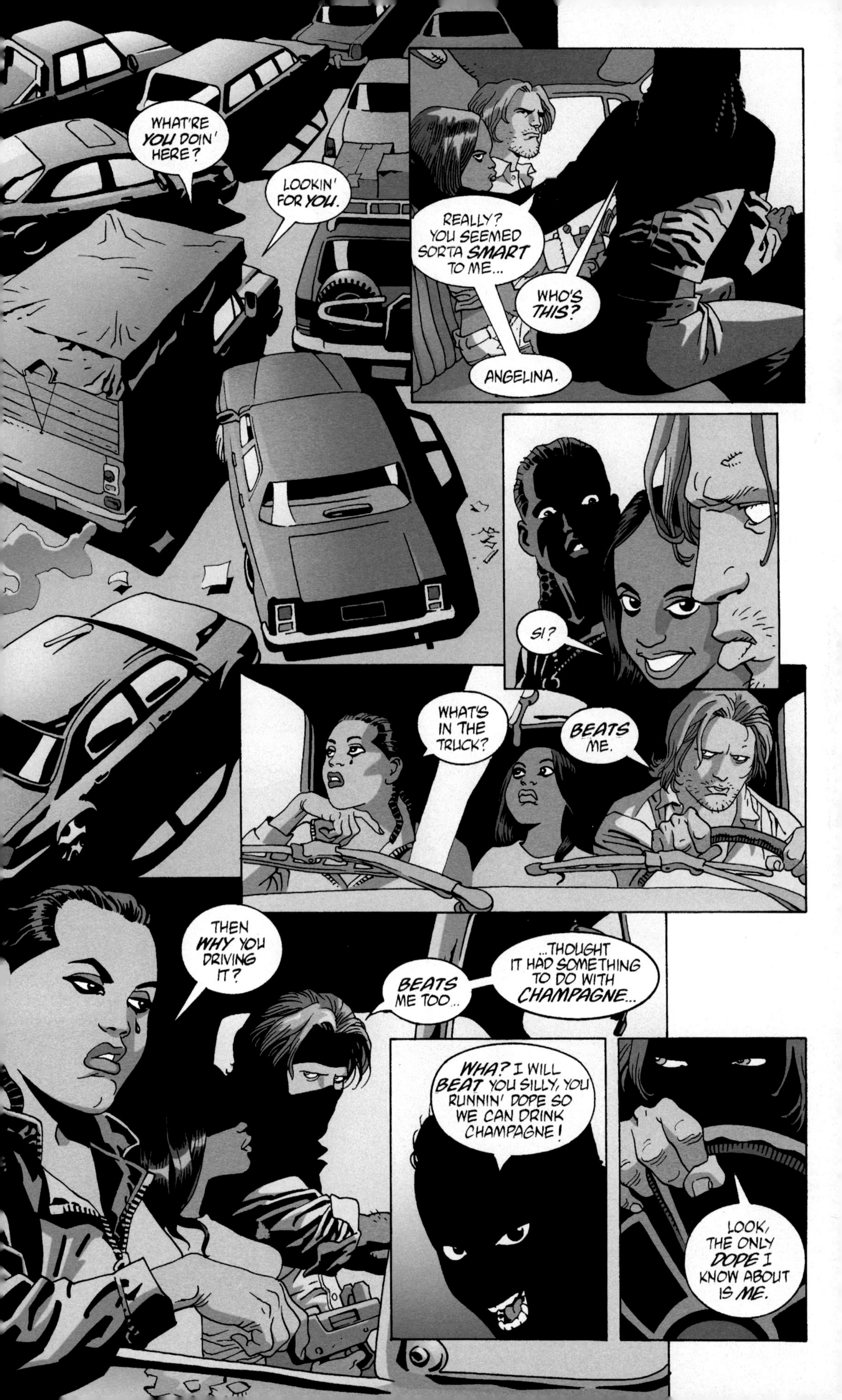
WHAT'RE YOU DOIN' HERE?
LOOKIN' FOR YOU.
REALLY? YOU SEEMED SORTA SMART TO ME...
WHO'S THIS?
ANGELINA.
SI?
WHAT'S IN THE TRUCK?
BEATS ME.
THEN WHY YOU DRIVING IT?
BEATS ME TOO...
...THOUGHT IT HAD SOMETHING TO DO WITH CHAMPAGNE...
WHA? I WILL BEAT YOU SILLY, YOU RUNNIN' DOPE SO WE CAN DRINK CHAMPAGNE!
LOOK, THE ONLY DOPE I KNOW ABOUT IS ME.

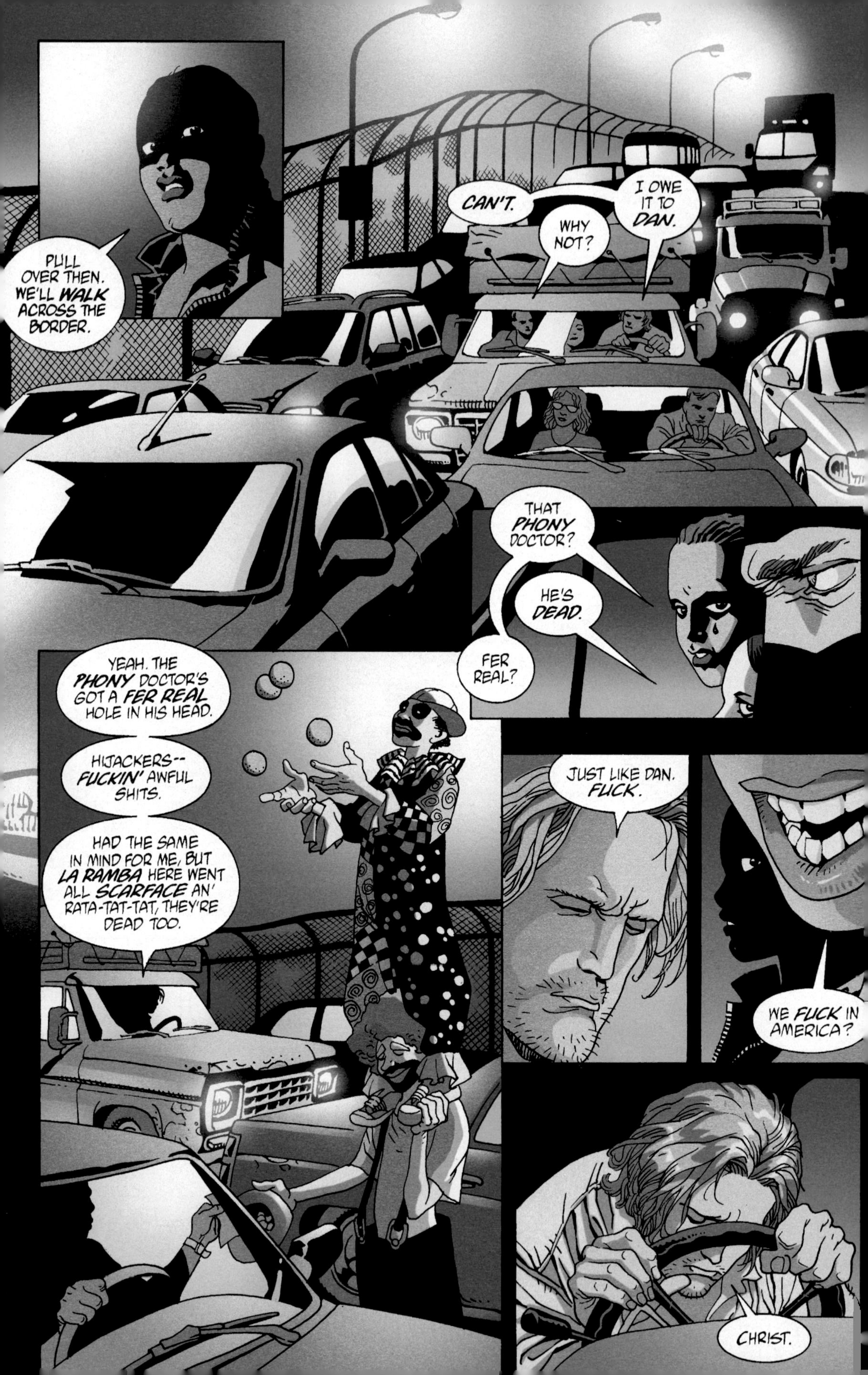
PULL OVER THEN. WE'LL WALK ACROSS THE BORDER.
CAN'T.
WHY NOT?
I OWE IT TO DAN.
THAT PHONY DOCTOR?
HE'S DEAD.
FER REAL?
YEAH. THE PHONY DOCTOR'S GOT A FER REAL HOLE IN HIS HEAD.
HIJACKERS-- FUCKIN' AWFUL SHITS.
HAD THE SAME IN MIND FOR ME, BUT LA RAMBA HERE WENT ALL SCARFACE AN' RATA-TAT-TAT, THEY'RE DEAD TOO.
JUST LIKE DAN. FUCK.
WE FUCK IN AMERICA?
CHRIST.

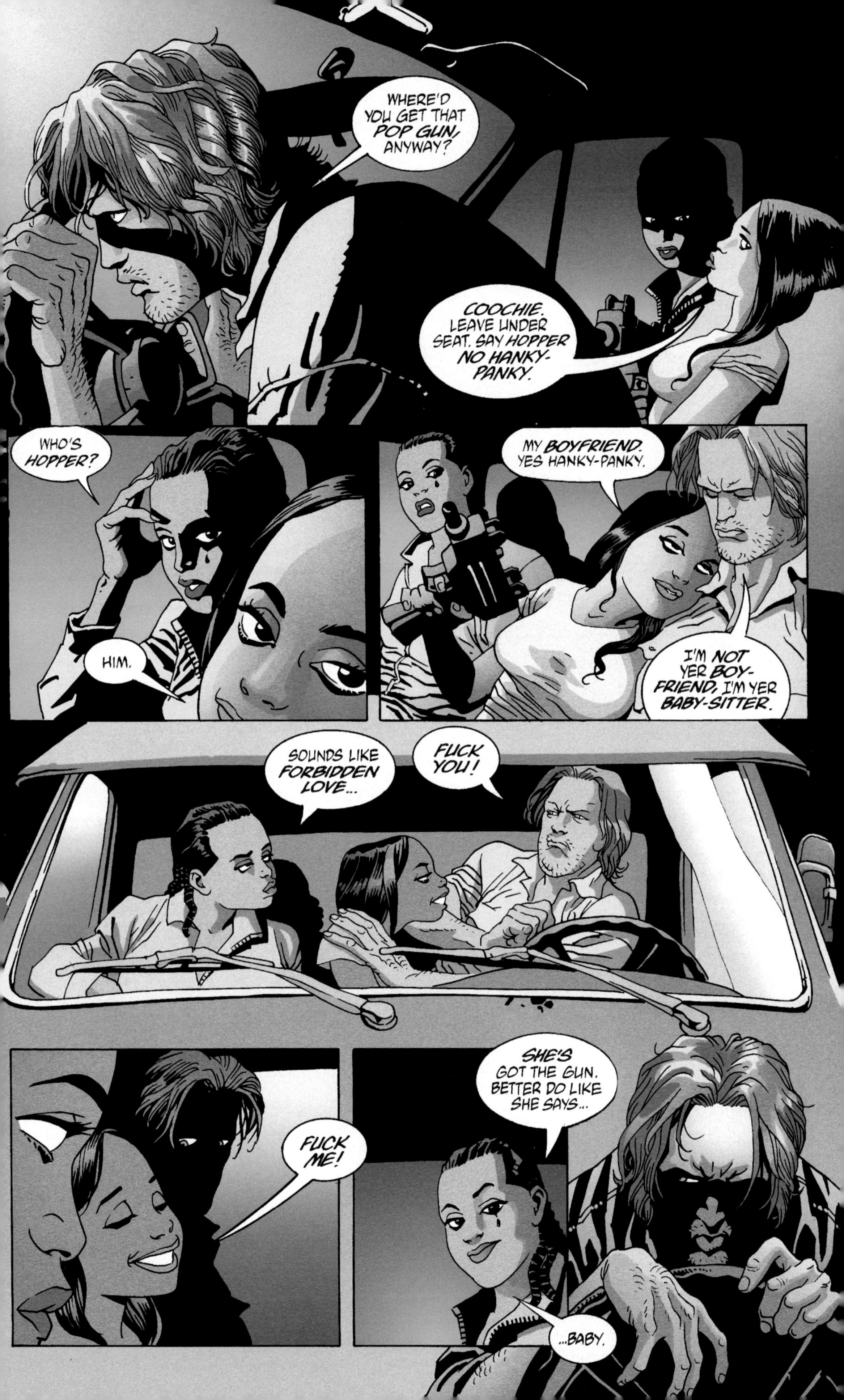

WHERE'D YOU GET THAT POP GUN, ANYWAY?
COOCHIE. LEAVE UNDER SEAT. SAY HOPPER NO HANKY-PANKY.
WHO'S HOPPER?
HIM.
MY BOYFRIEND. YES HANKY-PANKY.
I'M NOT YER BOY-FRIEND, I'M YER BABY-SITTER.
SOUNDS LIKE FORBIDDEN LOVE...
FUCK YOU!
FUCK ME!
SHE'S GOT THE GUN. BETTER DO LIKE SHE SAYS...
...BABY.

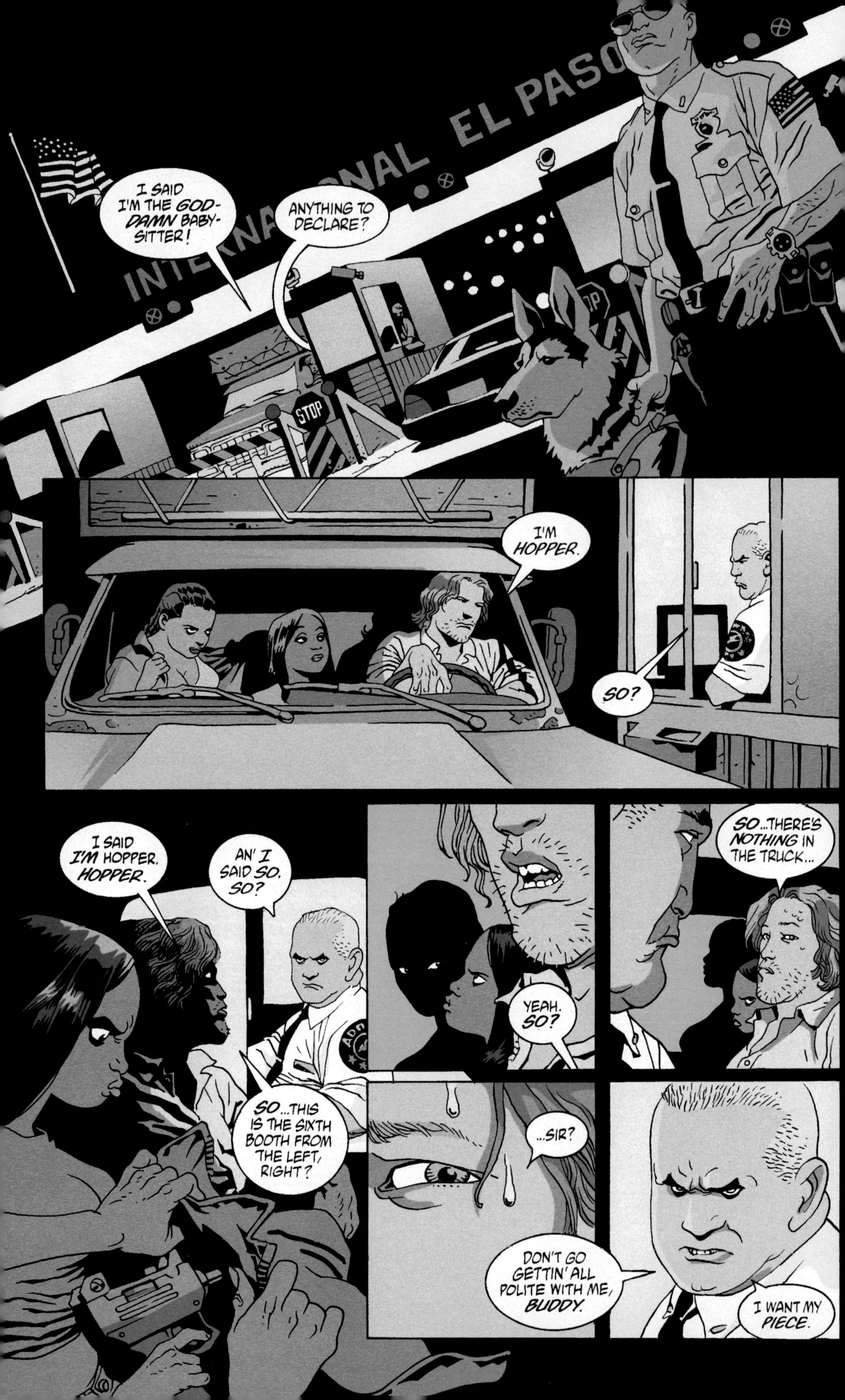
INTERNATIONAL EL PASO
STOP
I SAID I'M THE GOD-DAMN BABY-SITTER!
ANYTHING TO DECLARE?
I'M HOPPER.
SO?
I SAID I'M HOPPER. HOPPER.
AN' I SAID SO. SO?
YEAH. SO?
SO...THERE'S NOTHING IN THE TRUCK...
SO...THIS IS THE SIXTH BOOTH FROM THE LEFT, RIGHT?
...SIR?
DON'T GO GETTIN' ALL POLITE WITH ME, BUDDY.
I WANT MY PIECE.

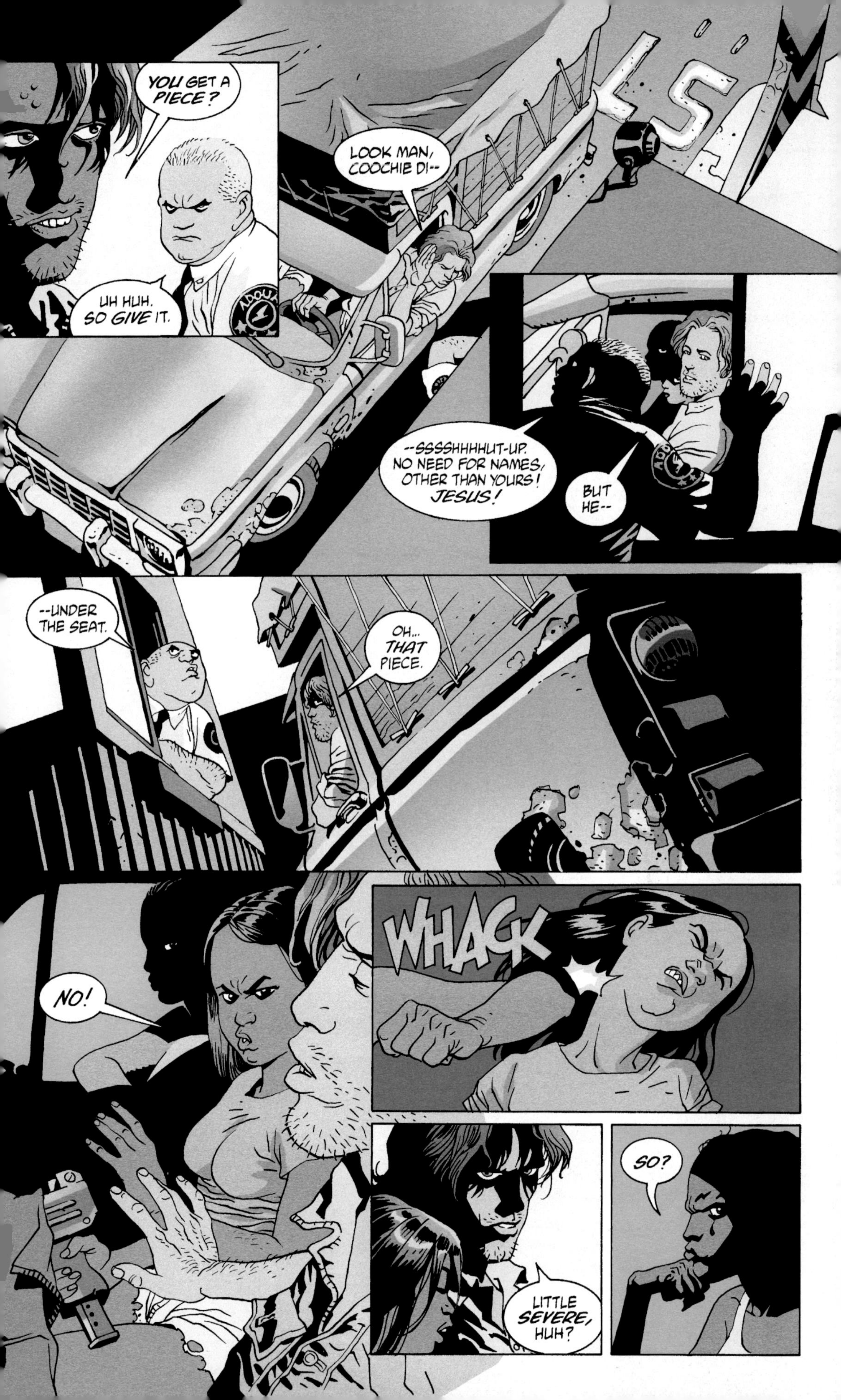
YOU GET A PIECE?
UH HUH. SO GIVE IT.
LOOK MAN, COOCHIE DI--
--SSSSHHHHUT-UP. NO NEED FOR NAMES, OTHER THAN YOURS! JESUS!
BUT HE--
--UNDER THE SEAT.
OH... THAT PIECE.
NO!
WHACK
LITTLE SEVERE, HUH?
SO?

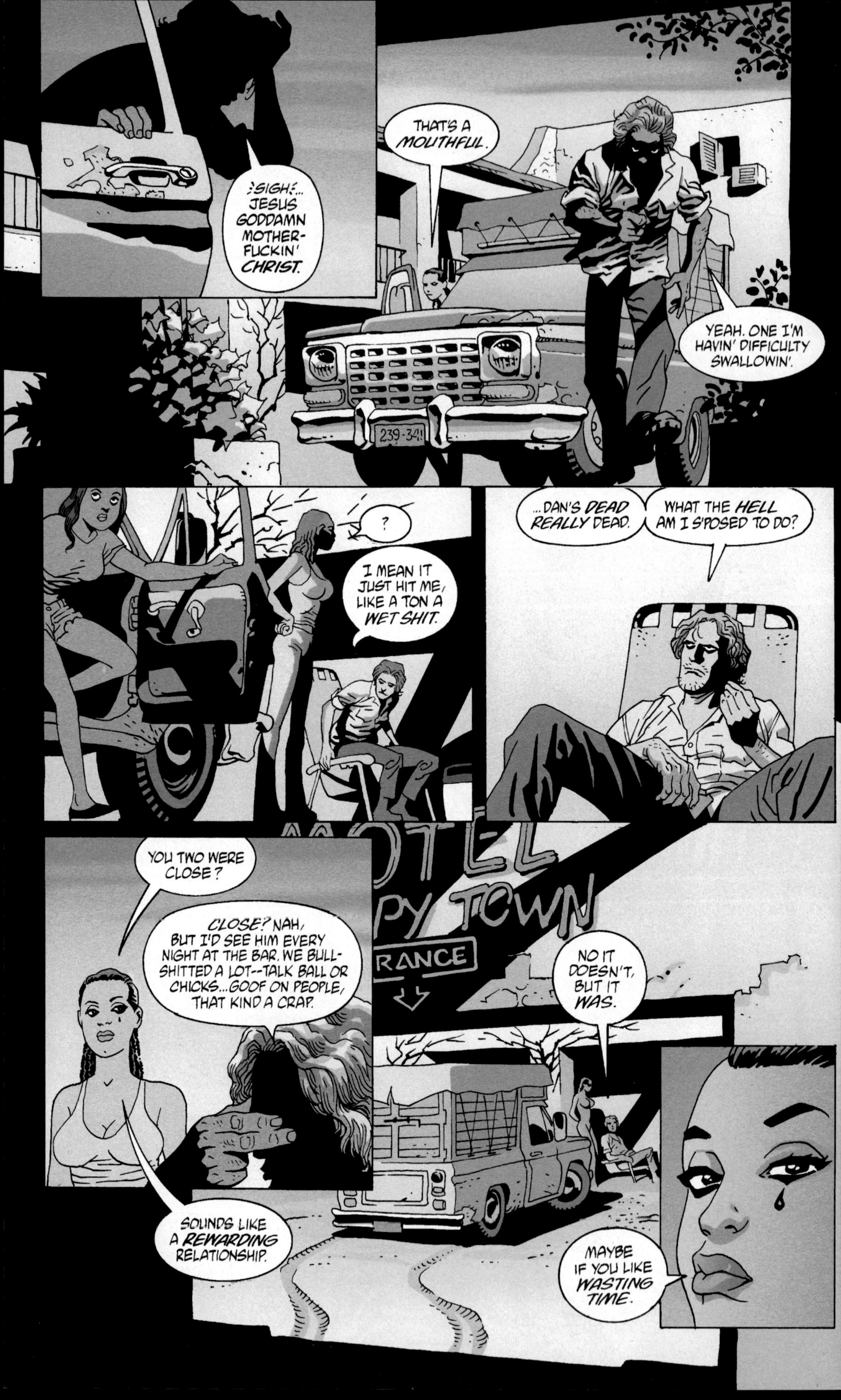

:SIGH:... JESUS GODDAMN MOTHER-FUCKIN' CHRIST.
THAT'S A MOUTHFUL.
YEAH. ONE I'M HAVIN' DIFFICULTY SWALLOWIN'.
239-341
?
I MEAN IT JUST HIT ME, LIKE A TON A WET SHIT.
...DAN'S DEAD REALLY DEAD.
WHAT THE HELL AM I S'POSED TO DO?
YOU TWO WERE CLOSE?
CLOSE? NAH, BUT I'D SEE HIM EVERY NIGHT AT THE BAR. WE BULL-SHITTED A LOT--TALK BALL OR CHICKS...GOOF ON PEOPLE, THAT KIND A CRAP.
SOUNDS LIKE A REWARDING RELATIONSHIP.
NO IT DOESN'T, BUT IT WAS.
MAYBE IF YOU LIKE WASTING TIME.

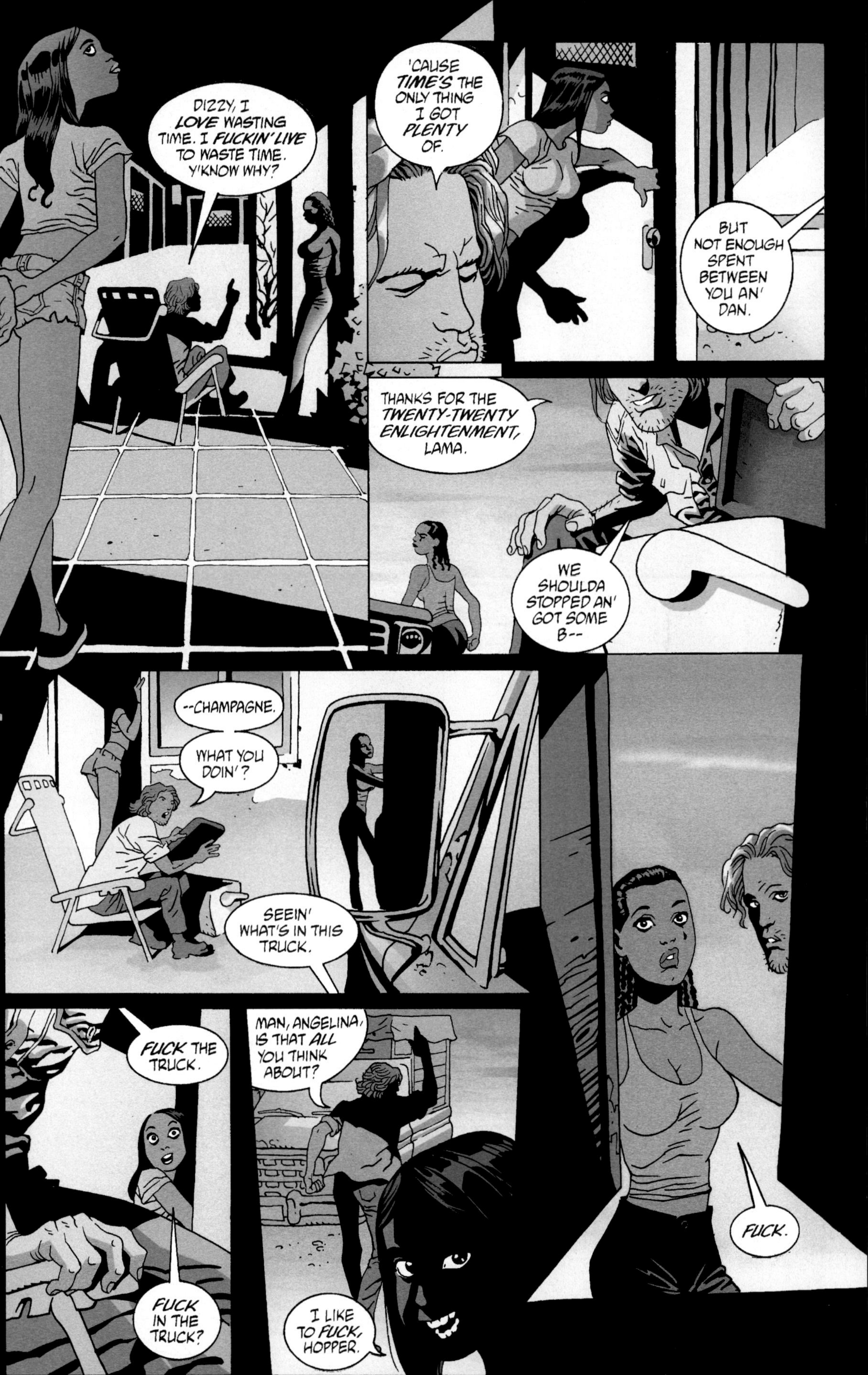
DIZZY, I *LOVE* WASTING TIME. I *FUCKIN' LIVE* TO WASTE TIME. Y'KNOW WHY?
'CAUSE *TIME'S* THE ONLY THING I GOT *PLENTY* OF.
BUT NOT ENOUGH SPENT BETWEEN YOU AN' DAN.
THANKS FOR THE *TWENTY-TWENTY ENLIGHTENMENT,* LAMA.
WE SHOULDA STOPPED AN' GOT SOME B--
--CHAMPAGNE.
WHAT YOU DOIN'?
SEEIN' WHAT'S IN THIS TRUCK.
FUCK.
FUCK THE TRUCK.
FUCK IN THE TRUCK?
MAN, ANGELINA, IS THAT *ALL* YOU THINK ABOUT?
I LIKE TO *FUCK,* HOPPER.

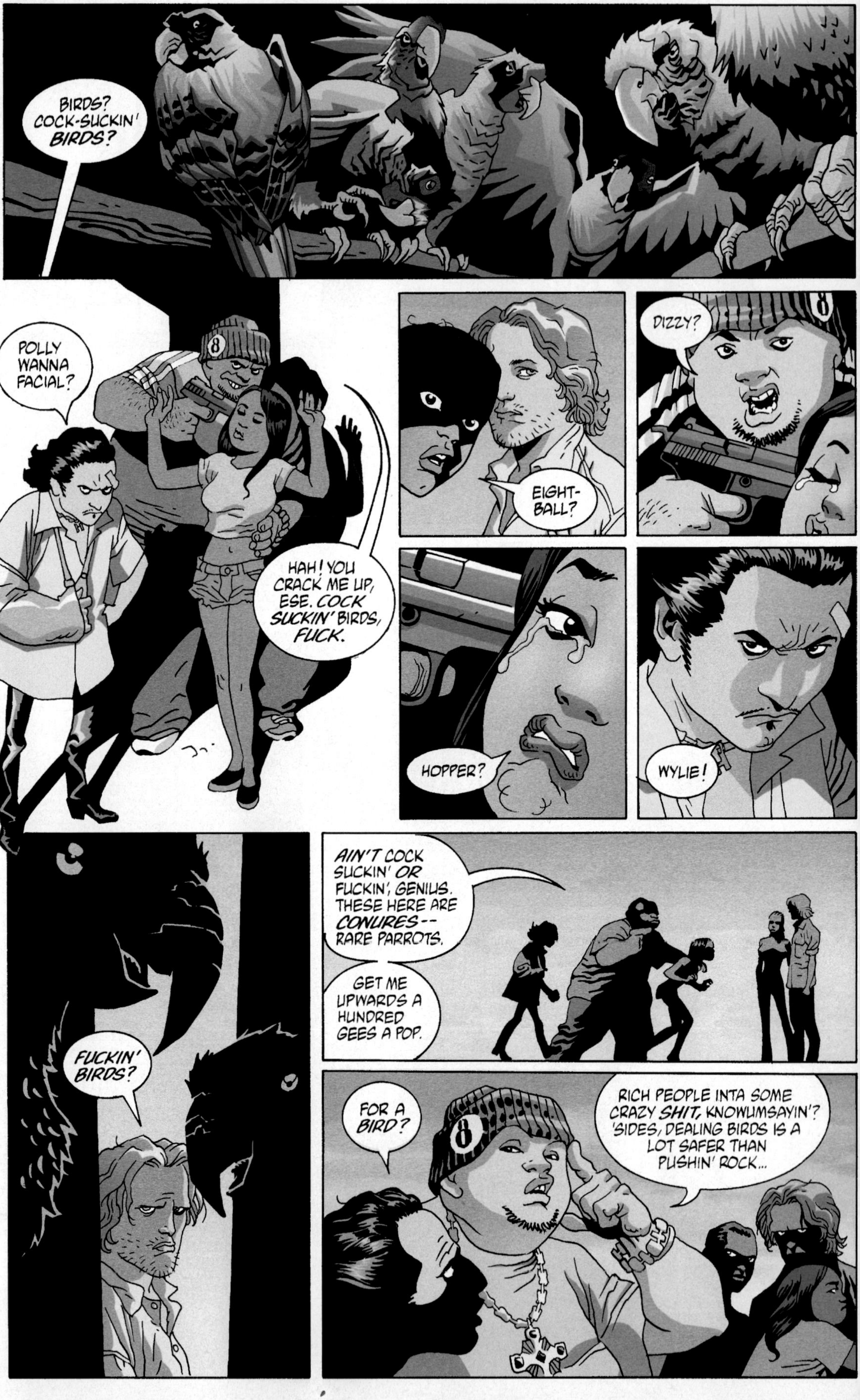
BIRDS? COCK-SUCKIN' BIRDS?
POLLY WANNA FACIAL?
HAH! YOU CRACK ME UP, ESE. COCK SUCKIN' BIRDS, FUCK.
EIGHT-BALL?
DIZZY?
HOPPER?
WYLIE!
FUCKIN' BIRDS?
AIN'T COCK SUCKIN' OR FUCKIN', GENIUS. THESE HERE ARE CONURES-- RARE PARROTS.
GET ME UPWARDS A HUNDRED GEES A POP.
FOR A BIRD?
RICH PEOPLE INTA SOME CRAZY SHIT, KNOWUMSAYIN'? 'SIDES, DEALING BIRDS IS A LOT SAFER THAN PUSHIN' ROCK...

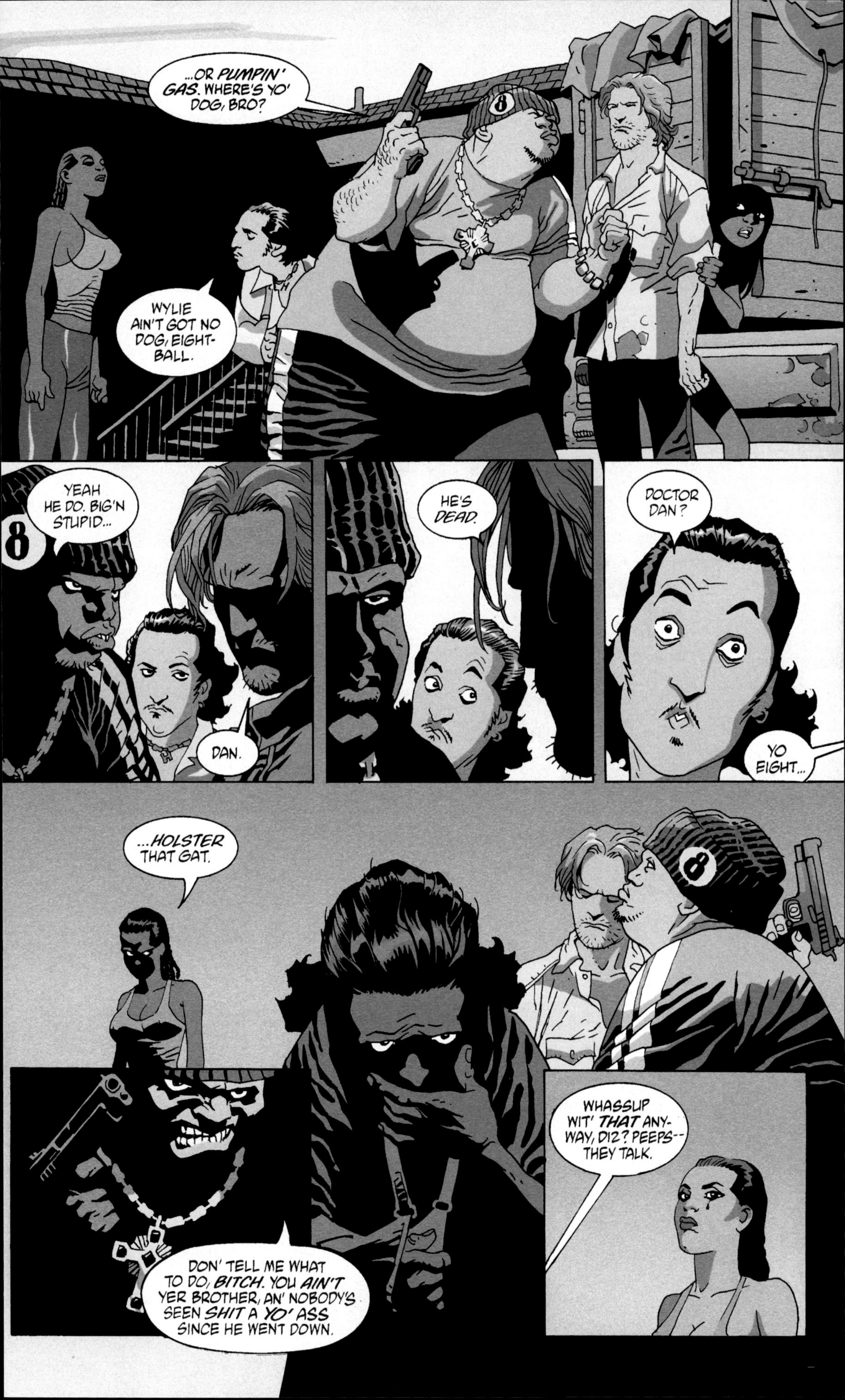
...OR PUMPIN' GAS. WHERE'S YO' DOG, BRO?
WYLIE AIN'T GOT NO DOG, EIGHT-BALL.
YEAH HE DO. BIG'N STUPID...
DAN.
HE'S DEAD.
DOCTOR DAN?
YO EIGHT...
...HOLSTER THAT GAT.
DON' TELL ME WHAT TO DO, BITCH. YOU AIN'T YER BROTHER, AN' NOBODY'S SEEN SHIT A YO' ASS SINCE HE WENT DOWN.
WHASSUP WIT' THAT ANY-WAY, DIZ? PEEPS--THEY TALK.

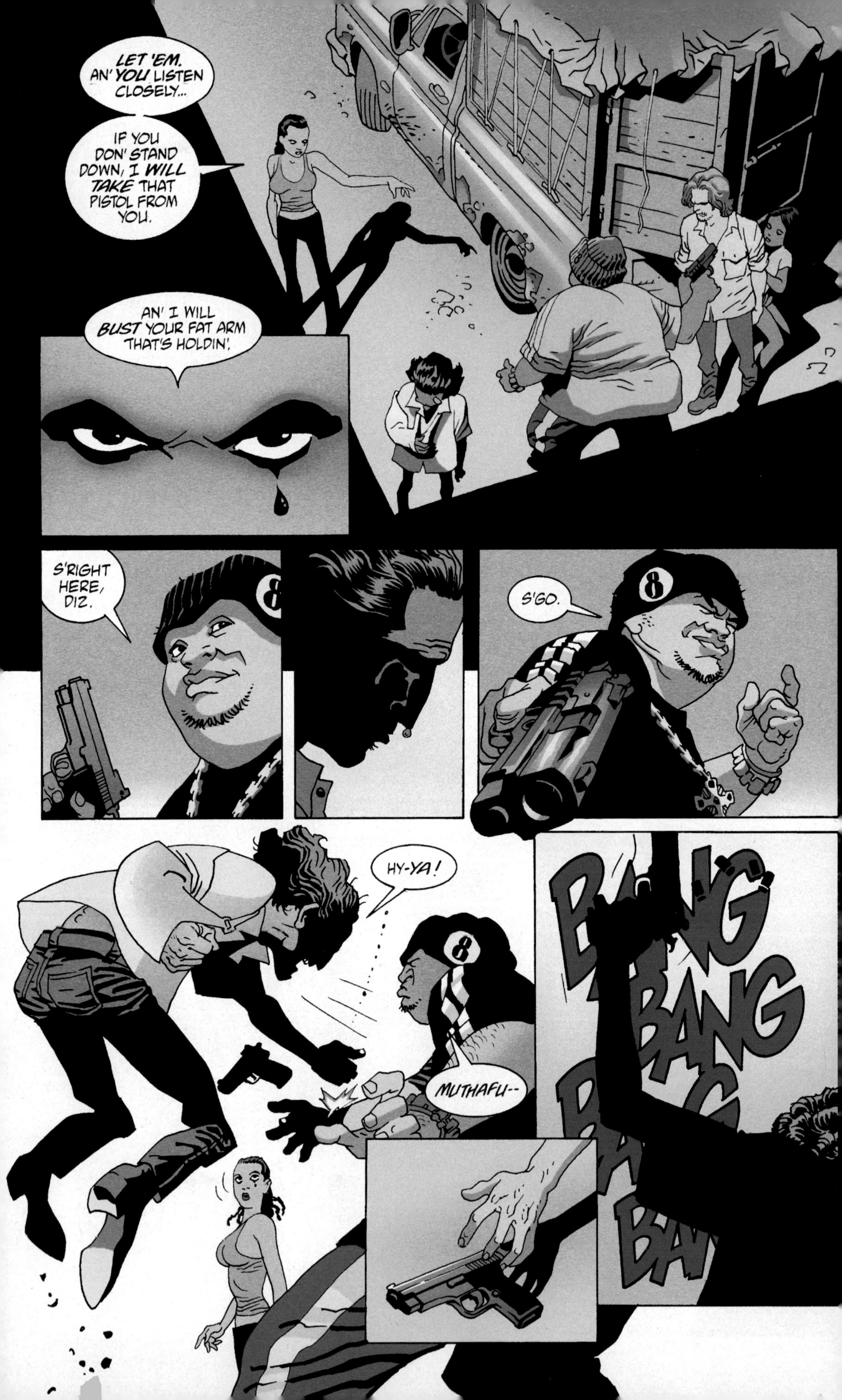
LET 'EM. AN' YOU LISTEN CLOSELY...
IF YOU DON' STAND DOWN, I WILL TAKE THAT PISTOL FROM YOU.
AN' I WILL BUST YOUR FAT ARM THAT'S HOLDIN'.
S'RIGHT HERE, DIZ.
S'GO.
HY-YA!
MUTHAFU--
BANG
BANG
BANG
BA

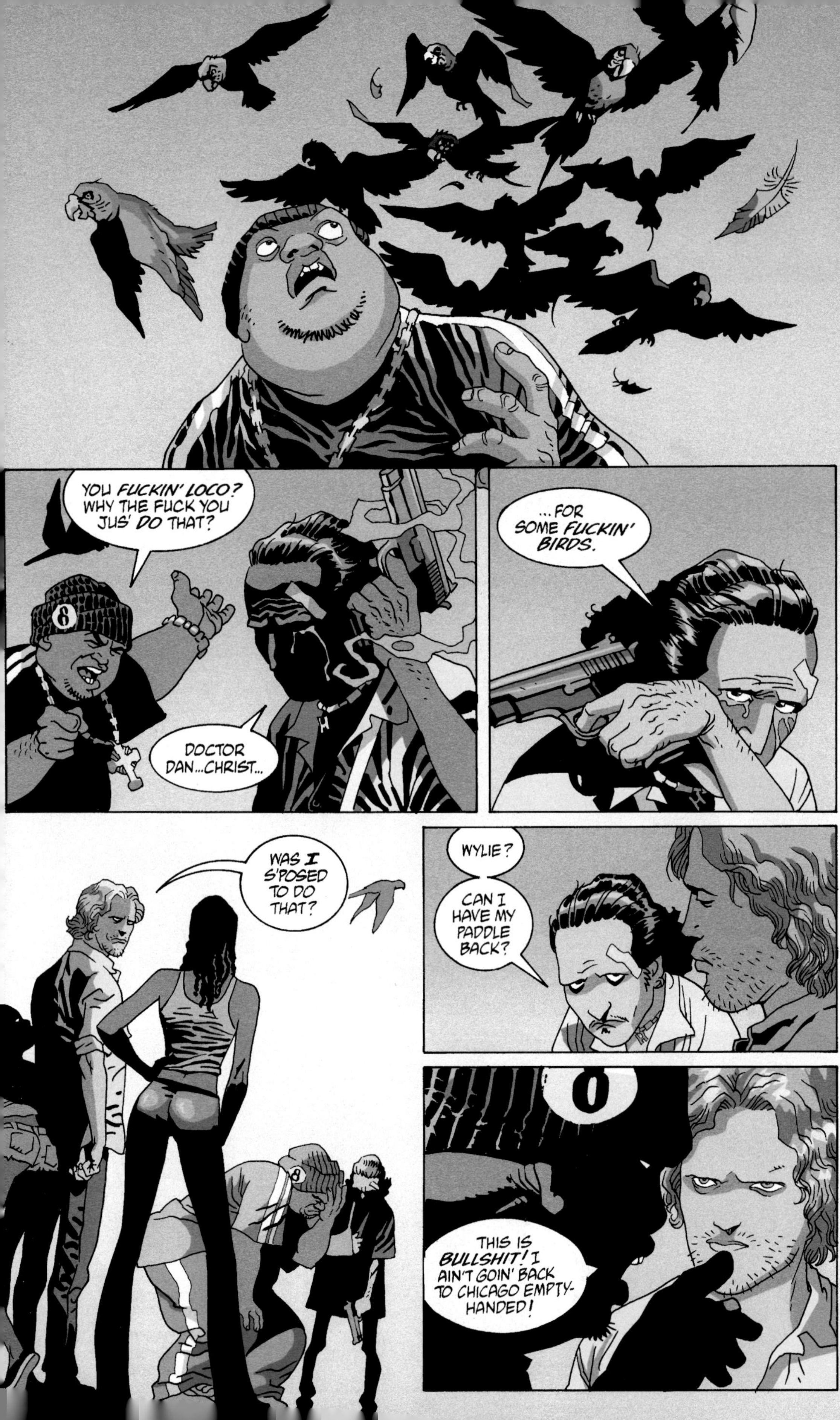

YOU FUCKIN' LOCO? WHY THE FUCK YOU JUS' DO THAT?
DOCTOR DAN...CHRIST...
...FOR SOME FUCKIN' BIRDS.
WAS I S'POSED TO DO THAT?
WYLIE?
CAN I HAVE MY PADDLE BACK?
THIS IS BULLSHIT! I AIN'T GOIN' BACK TO CHICAGO EMPTY-HANDED!

WHAT I MISS?

I'M NOT SURE...

GET YOUR THINGS, DIZZY. WE GOTTA GO.

HEY, THANKS, JUS' WHAT THE DOC--

Black BEER

--I COULD USE ONE.

DON'T MENTION IT, WYLIE.

I DON' REMEMBER TELLIN' YOU MY NAME...

WAS A LONG TIME AGO.

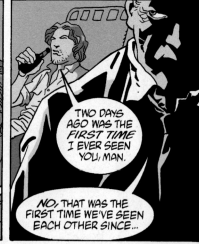

TWO DAYS AGO WAS THE FIRST TIME I EVER SEEN YOU, MAN.

NO, THAT WAS THE FIRST TIME WE'VE SEEN EACH OTHER SINCE...

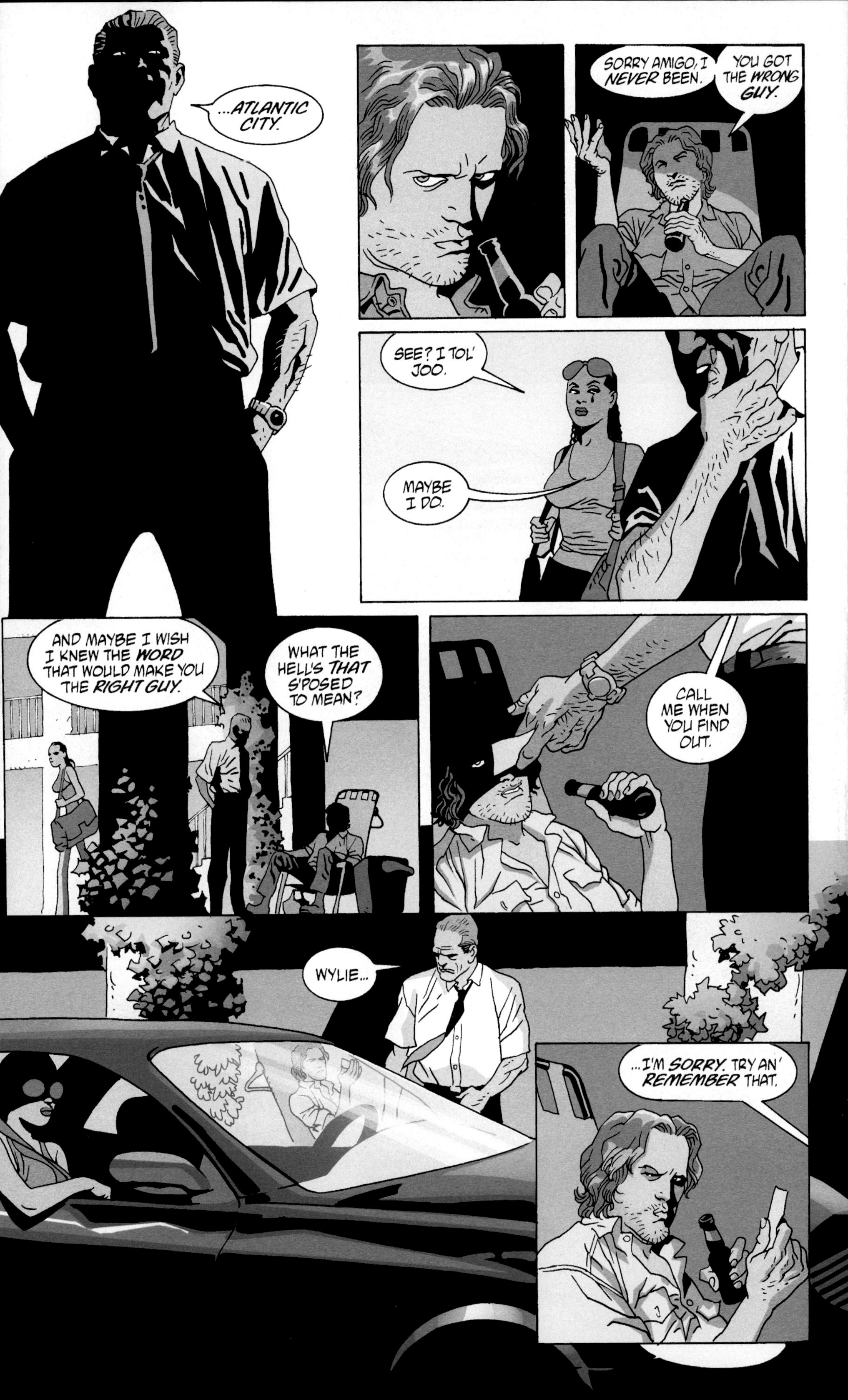
...ATLANTIC CITY.
SORRY AMIGO, I NEVER BEEN.
YOU GOT THE WRONG GUY.
SEE? I TOL' JOO.
MAYBE I DO.
AND MAYBE I WISH I KNEW THE WORD THAT WOULD MAKE YOU THE RIGHT GUY.
WHAT THE HELL'S THAT S'POSED TO MEAN?
CALL ME WHEN YOU FIND OUT.
WYLIE...
...I'M SORRY. TRY AN' REMEMBER THAT.

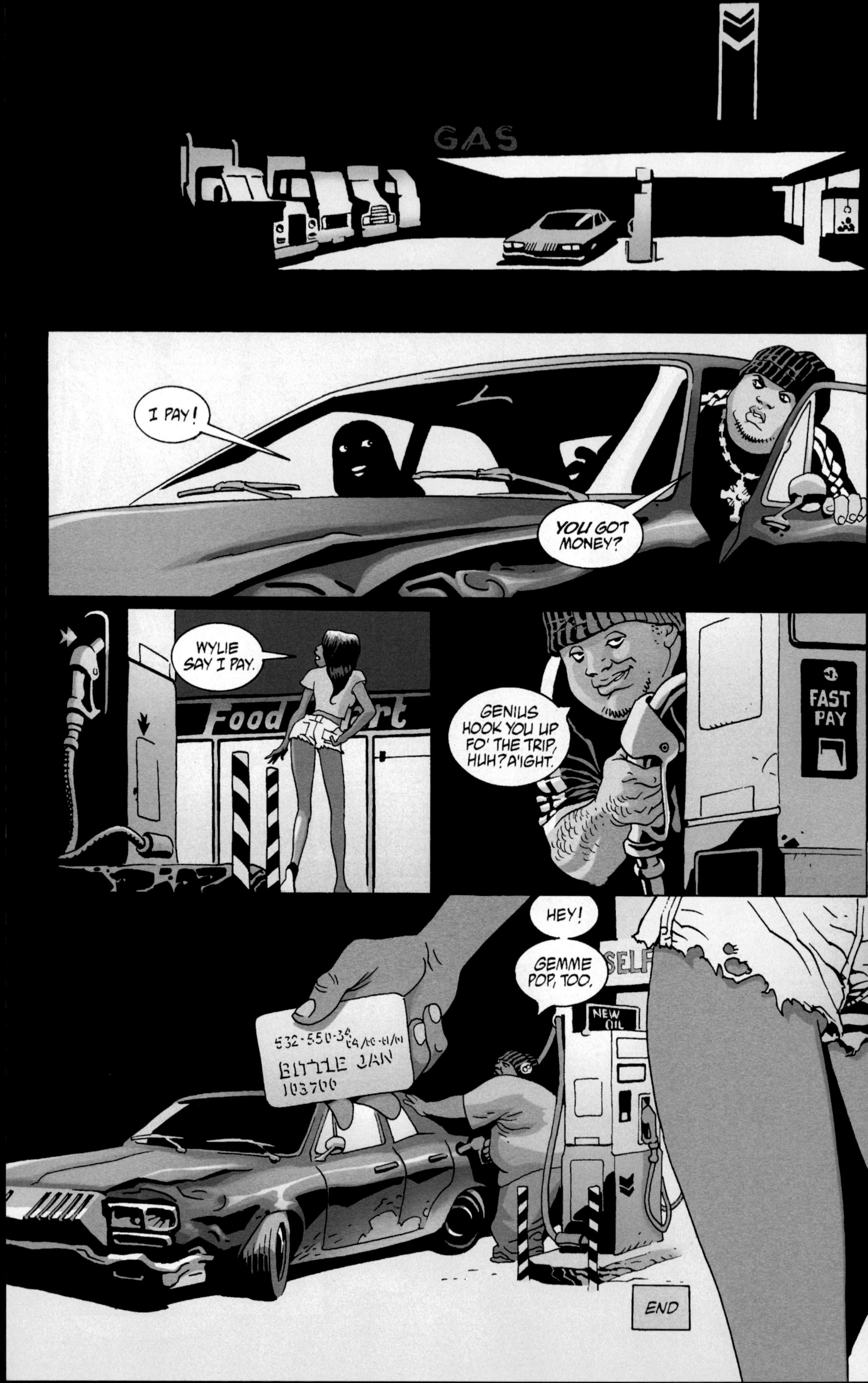
GAS
I PAY!
YOU GOT MONEY?
WYLIE SAY I PAY.
Food
GENIUS HOOK YOU UP FO' THE TRIP, HUH? A'IGHT.
FAST PAY
HEY!
GEMME POP, TOO.
NEW OIL
532-550-34
BITTLE JAN
103700
END

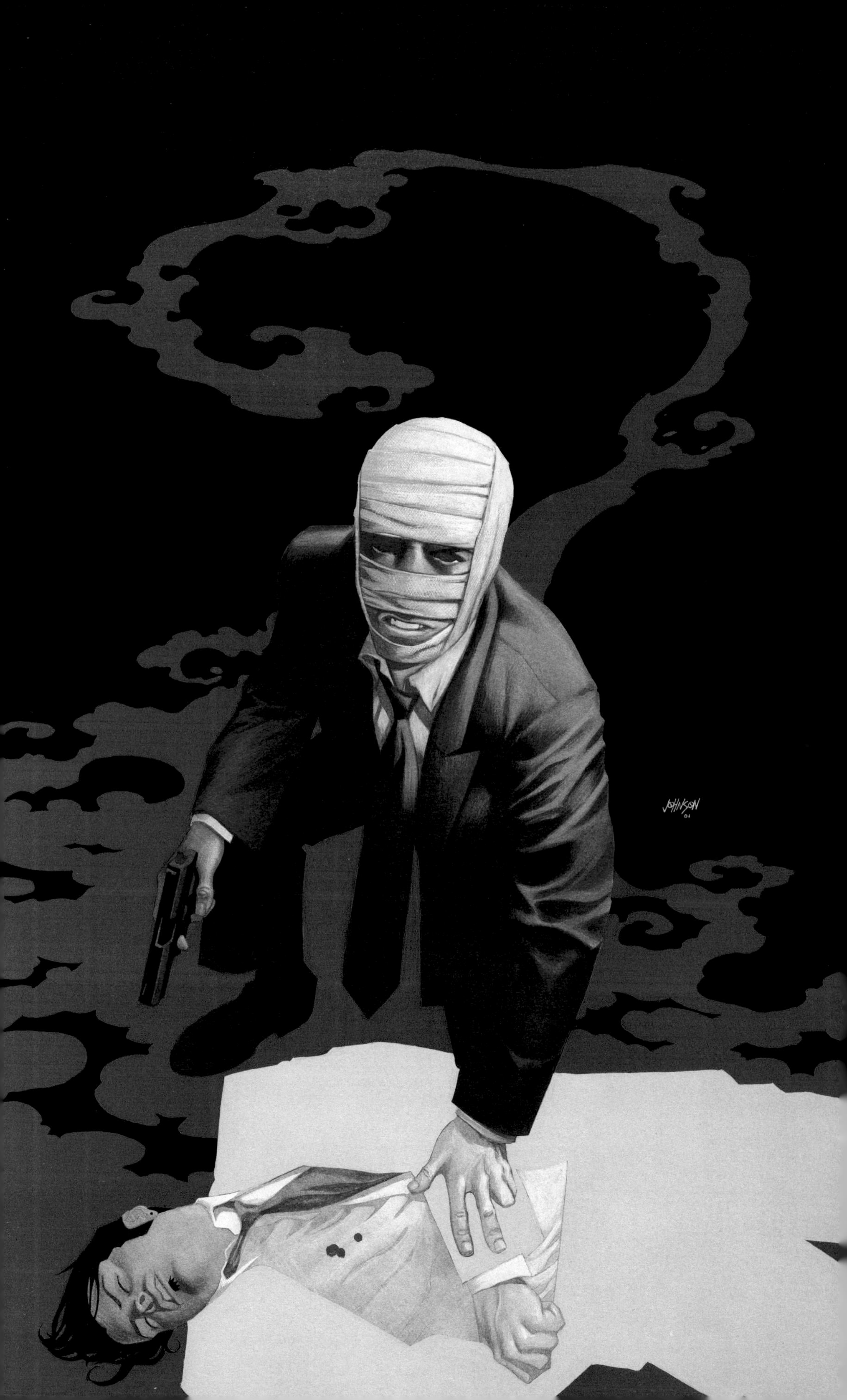
JOHNSON
'01

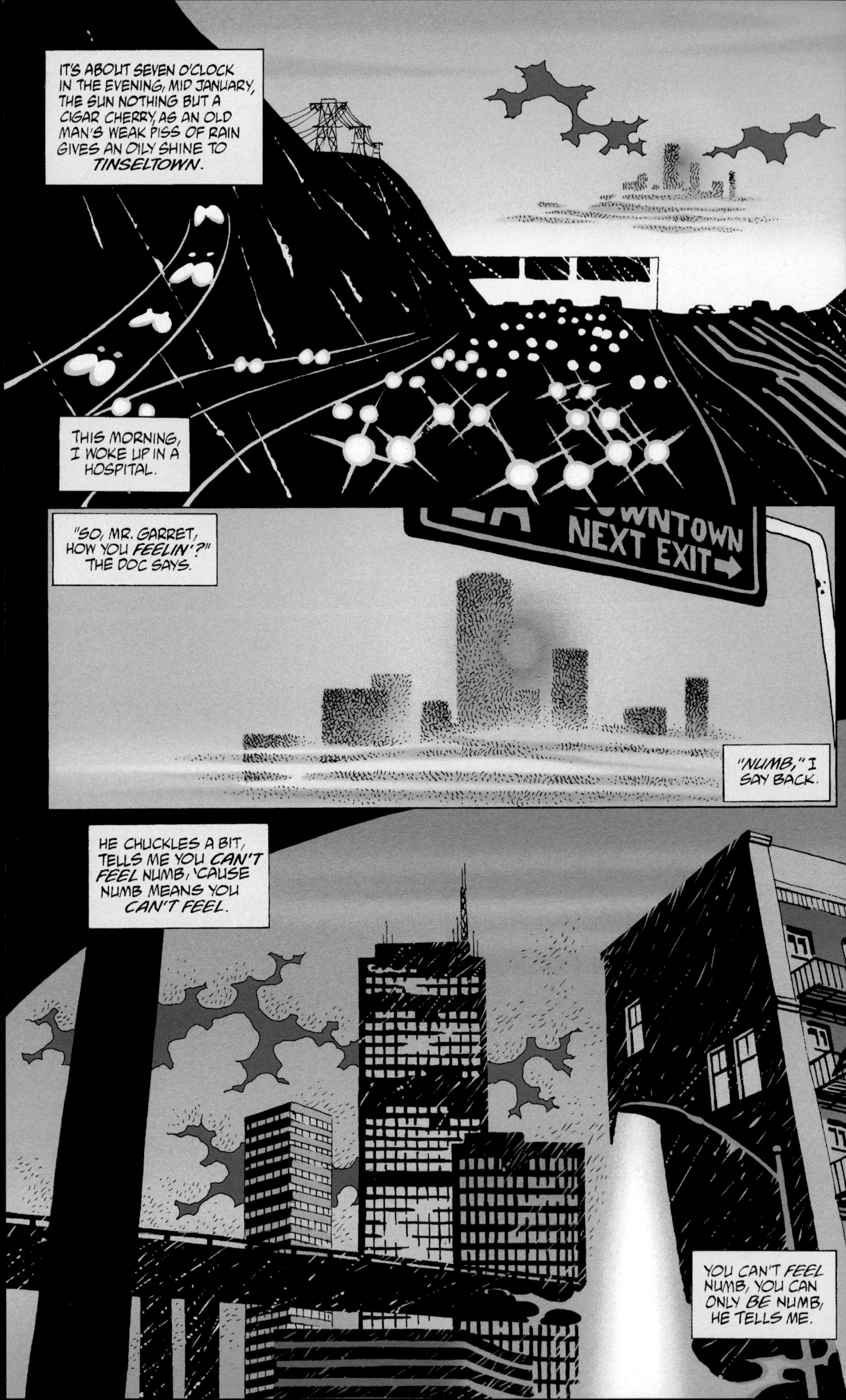
IT'S ABOUT SEVEN O'CLOCK IN THE EVENING, MID JANUARY, THE SUN NOTHING BUT A CIGAR CHERRY, AS AN OLD MAN'S WEAK PISS OF RAIN GIVES AN OILY SHINE TO TINSELTOWN.
THIS MORNING, I WOKE UP IN A HOSPITAL.
"SO, MR. GARRET, HOW YOU FEELIN'?" THE DOC SAYS.
NEXT EXIT
"NUMB," I SAY BACK.
HE CHUCKLES A BIT, TELLS ME YOU CAN'T FEEL NUMB, 'CAUSE NUMB MEANS YOU CAN'T FEEL.
YOU CAN'T FEEL NUMB, YOU CAN ONLY BE NUMB, HE TELLS ME.

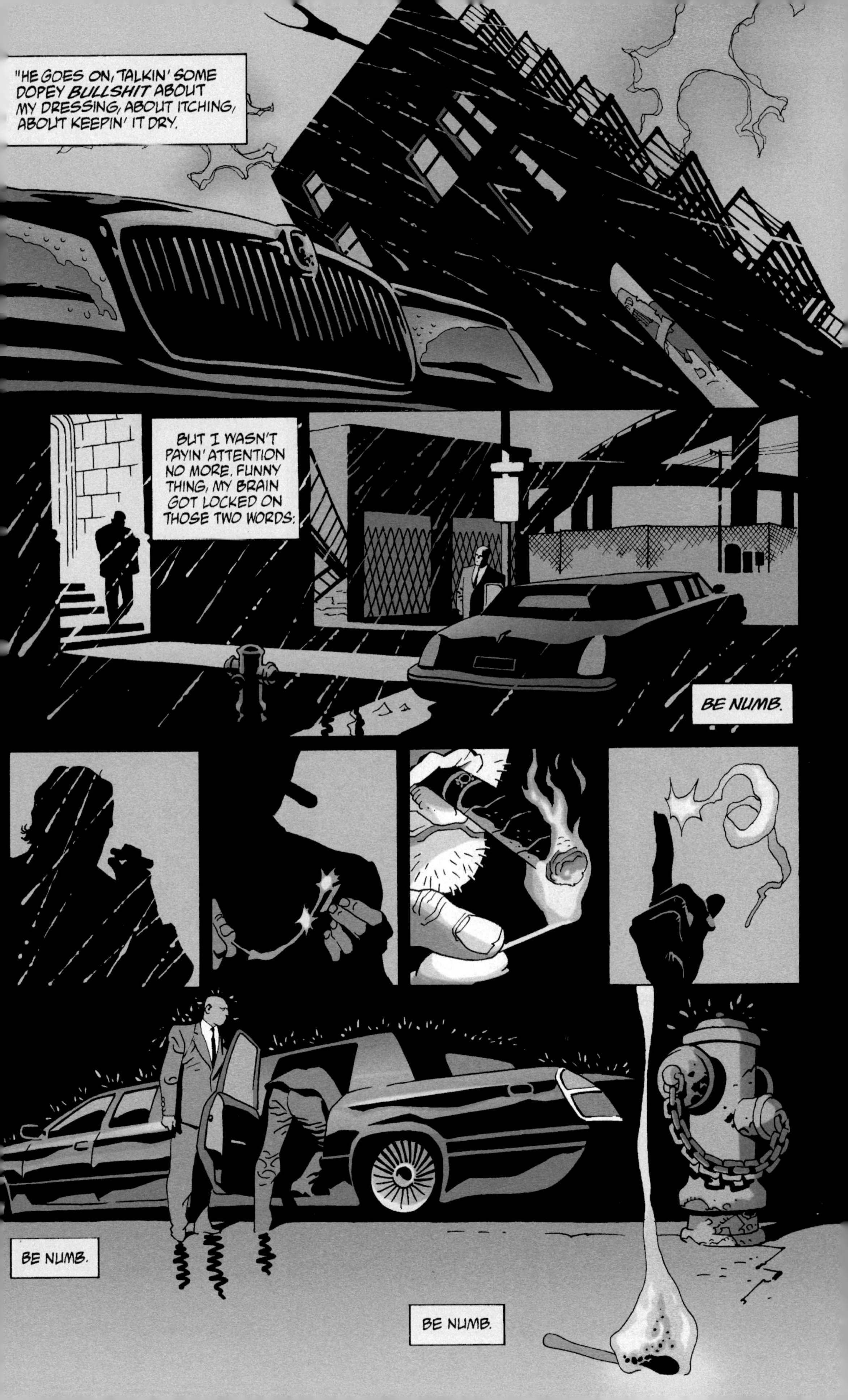
"HE GOES ON, TALKIN' SOME DOPEY BULLSHIT ABOUT MY DRESSING, ABOUT ITCHING, ABOUT KEEPIN' IT DRY.
BUT I WASN'T PAYIN' ATTENTION NO MORE. FUNNY THING, MY BRAIN GOT LOCKED ON THOSE TWO WORDS:
BE NUMB.
BE NUMB.
BE NUMB.

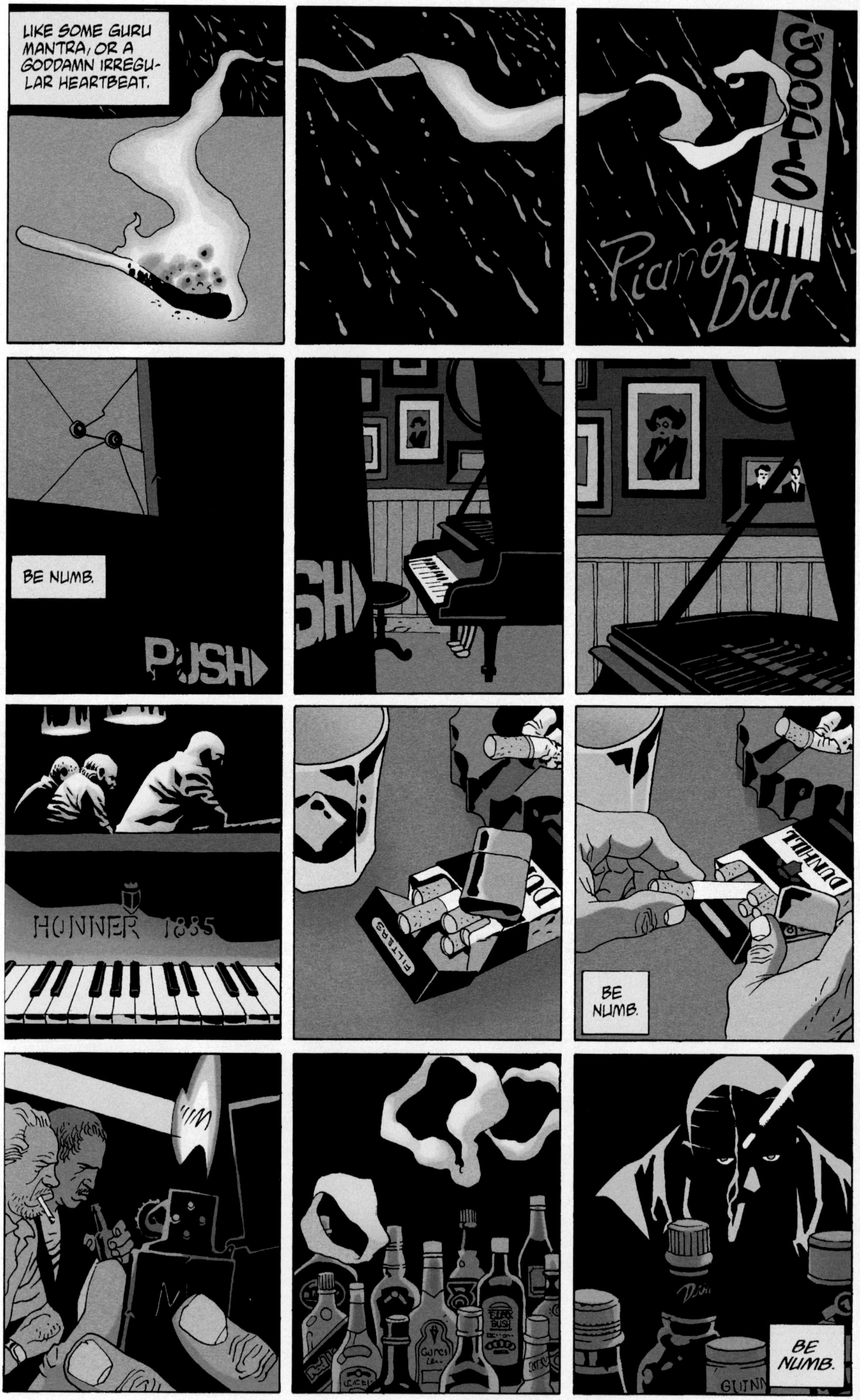
LIKE SOME GURU MANTRA, OR A GODDAMN IRREGULAR HEARTBEAT.
GOODIS
Piano bar
BE NUMB.
PUSH
HONNER 1885
DUNHILL
FILTERS
BE NUMB.
BE NUMB.

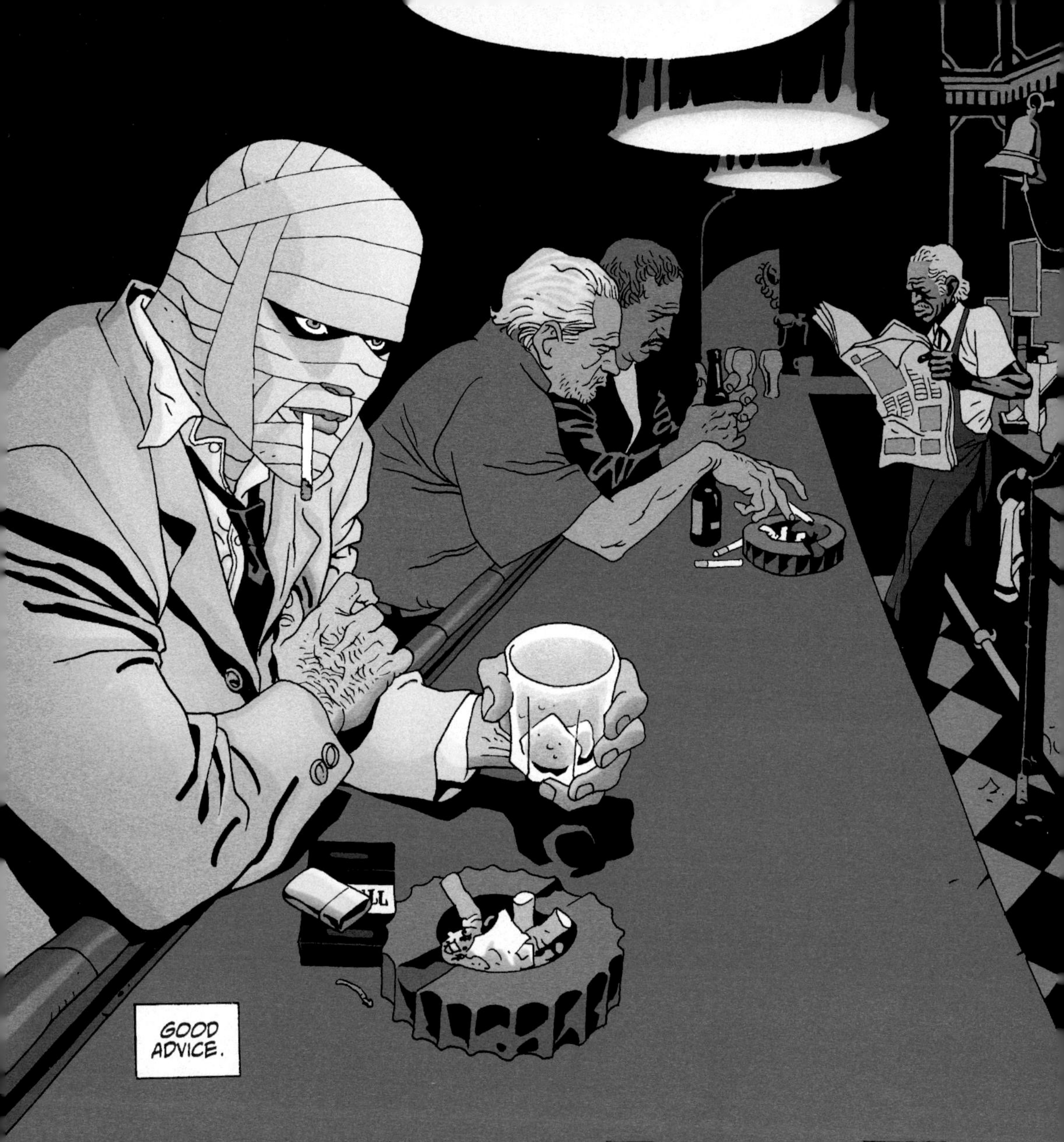
GOOD ADVICE.

THE COUNTERFIFTH DETECTIVE PART ONE

BRIAN AZZARELLO writer
EDUARDO RISSO artist
PATRICIA MULVIHILL colorist
CLEM ROBINS letterer
DIGITAL CHAMELEON separations
DAVE JOHNSON cover artist
ZACHARY RAU ass't ed.
WILL DENNIS editor

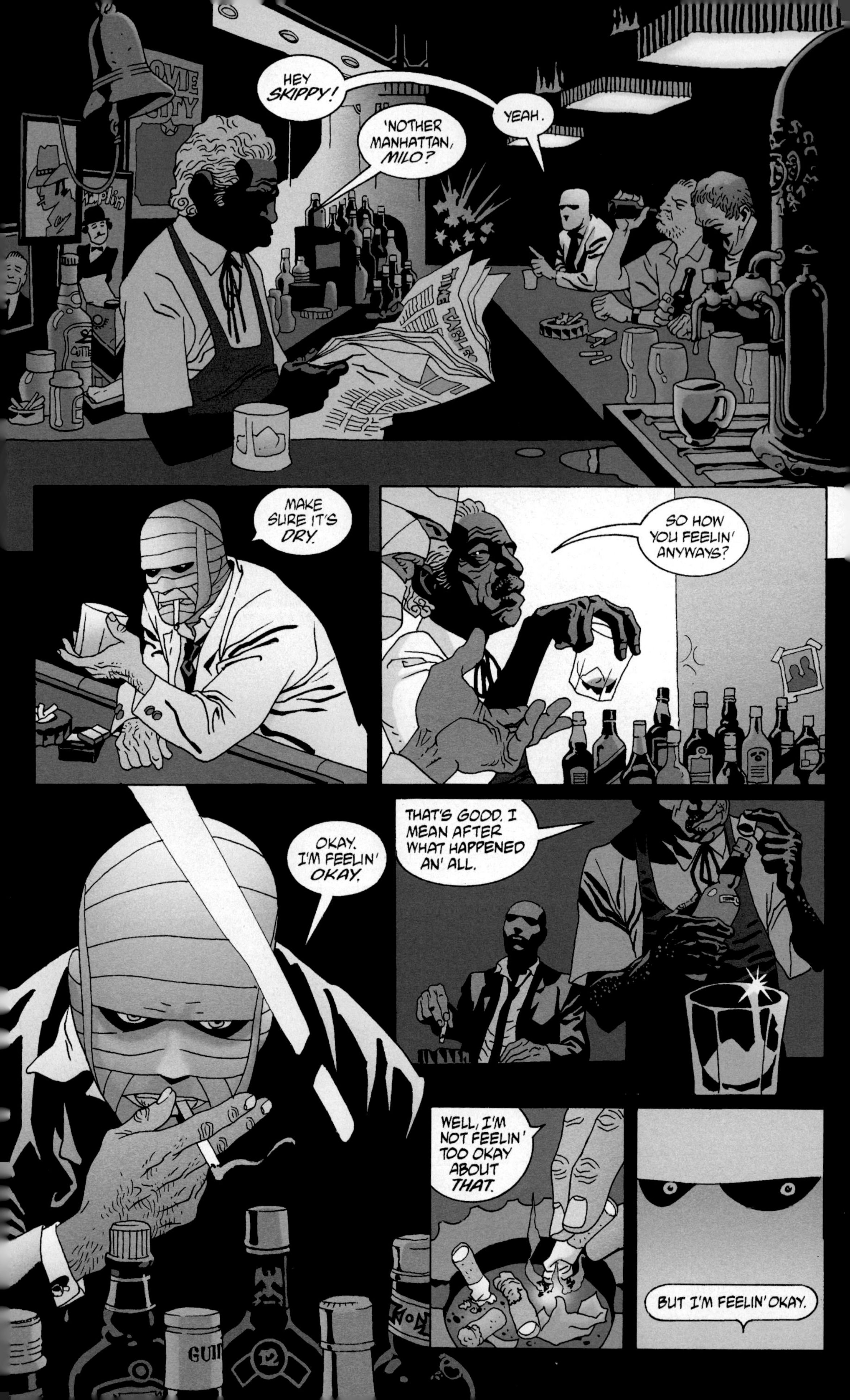
HEY SKIPPY!
'NOTHER MANHATTAN, MILO?
YEAH.
MAKE SURE IT'S DRY.
SO HOW YOU FEELIN' ANYWAYS?
OKAY. I'M FEELIN' OKAY.
THAT'S GOOD. I MEAN AFTER WHAT HAPPENED AN' ALL.
WELL, I'M NOT FEELIN' TOO OKAY ABOUT THAT.
BUT I'M FEELIN' OKAY.

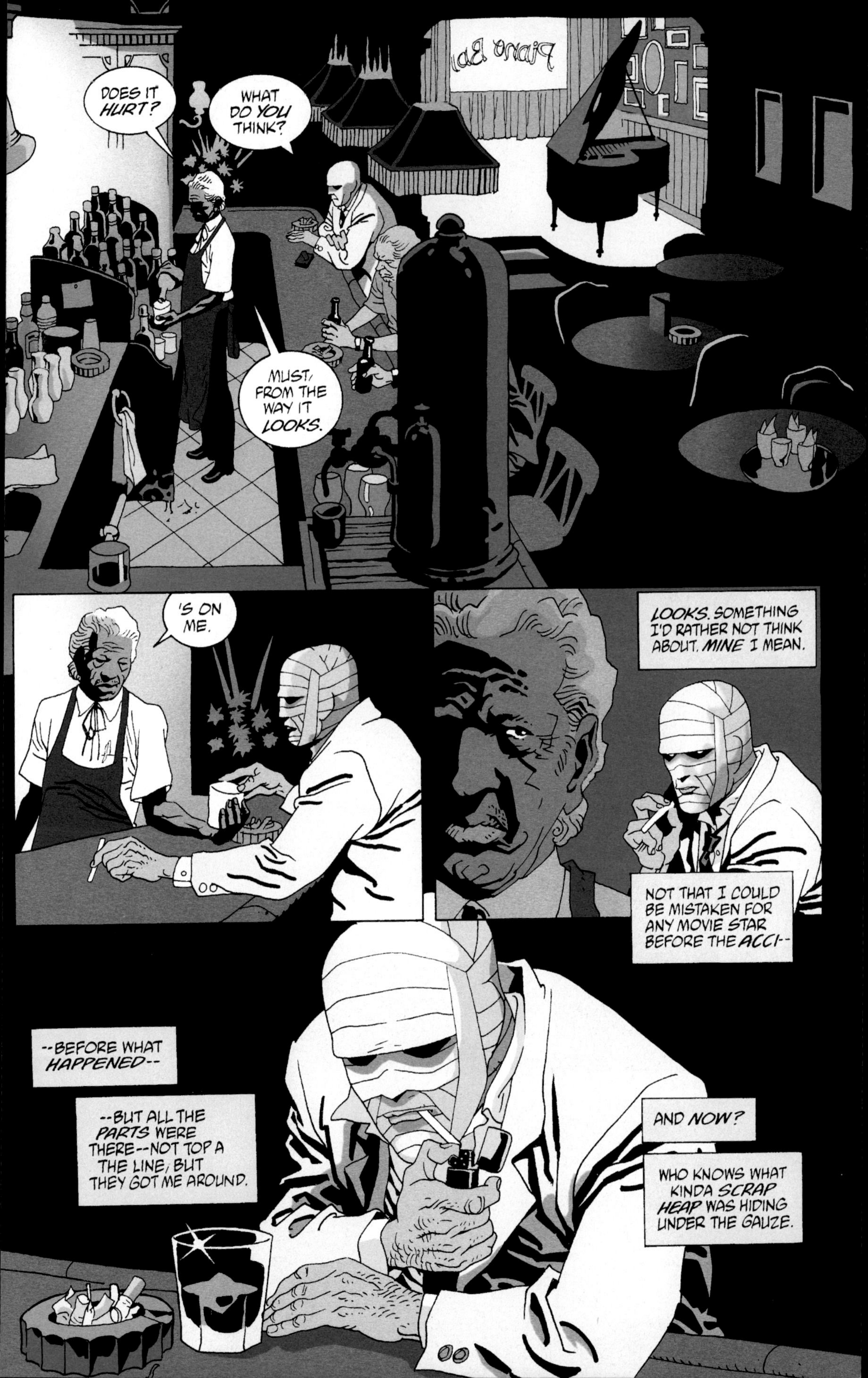
Piano Bar
DOES IT HURT?
WHAT DO YOU THINK?
MUST, FROM THE WAY IT LOOKS.
'S ON ME.
LOOKS. SOMETHING I'D RATHER NOT THINK ABOUT. MINE I MEAN.
NOT THAT I COULD BE MISTAKEN FOR ANY MOVIE STAR BEFORE THE ACCI-
--BEFORE WHAT HAPPENED--
--BUT ALL THE PARTS WERE THERE--NOT TOP A THE LINE, BUT THEY GOT ME AROUND.
AND NOW?
WHO KNOWS WHAT KINDA SCRAP HEAP WAS HIDING UNDER THE GAUZE.

AFTER BEING DRY FOR A COUPLE A WEEKS, THREE COCKTAILS WENT DOWN QUICKER THAN A *BONER* IN A *BUSTED RUBBER.*

AN' LIKE *ALWAYS,* THE BOOZE HAD DONE ITS *THANKLESS JOB.*

ONE MORE MIGHT PUSH ME *OVER* THE EDGE...

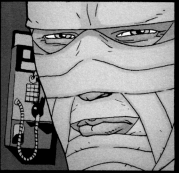

...WHEN WHERE I *WANTED* TO BE WAS *ON* IT.

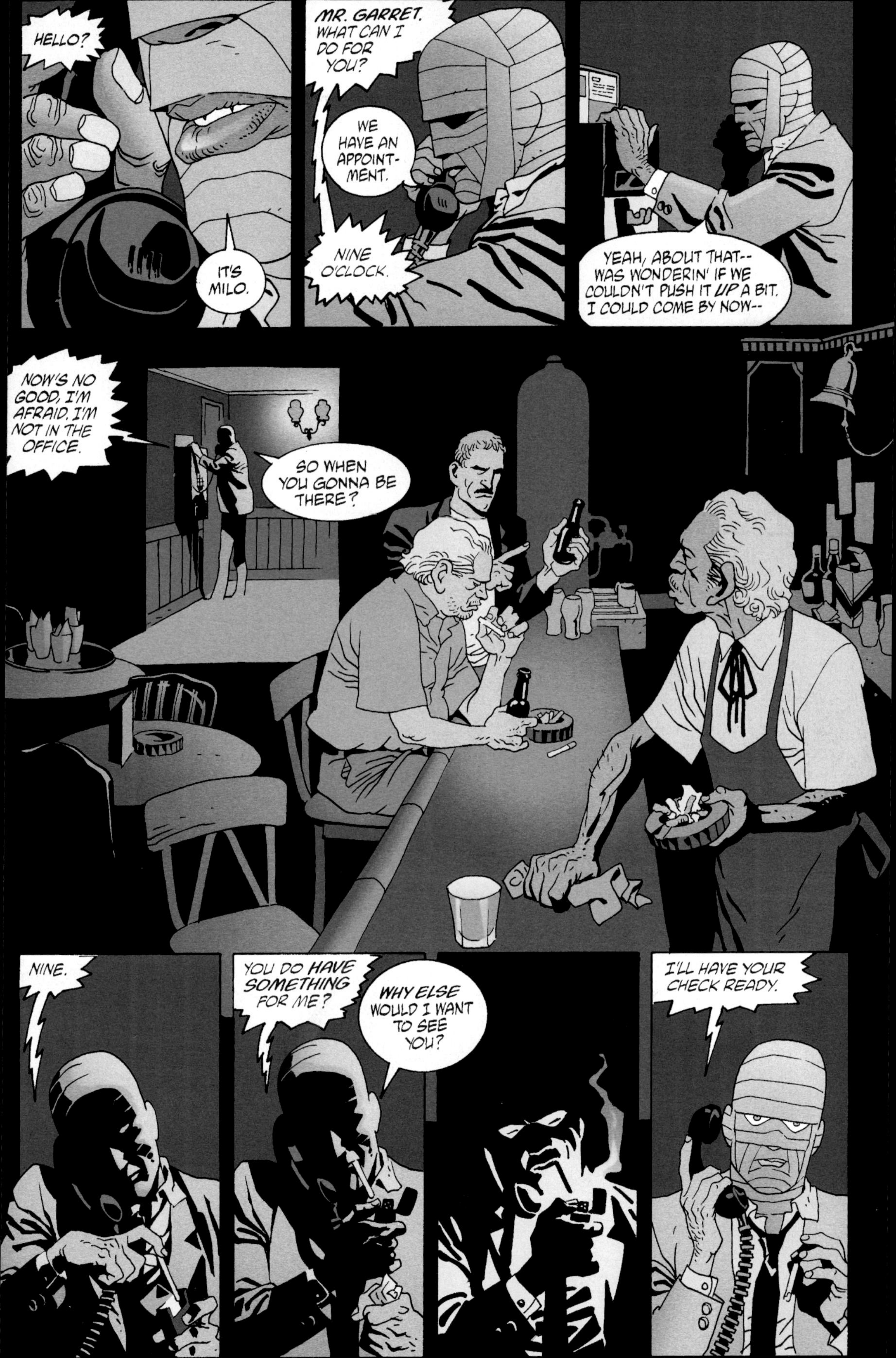
HELLO?
IT'S MILO.
MR. GARRET. WHAT CAN I DO FOR YOU?
WE HAVE AN APPOINT-MENT.
NINE O'CLOCK.
YEAH, ABOUT THAT-- WAS WONDERIN' IF WE COULDN'T PUSH IT UP A BIT. I COULD COME BY NOW--
NOW'S NO GOOD, I'M AFRAID. I'M NOT IN THE OFFICE.
SO WHEN YOU GONNA BE THERE?
NINE.
YOU DO HAVE SOMETHING FOR ME?
WHY ELSE WOULD I WANT TO SEE YOU?
I'LL HAVE YOUR CHECK READY.

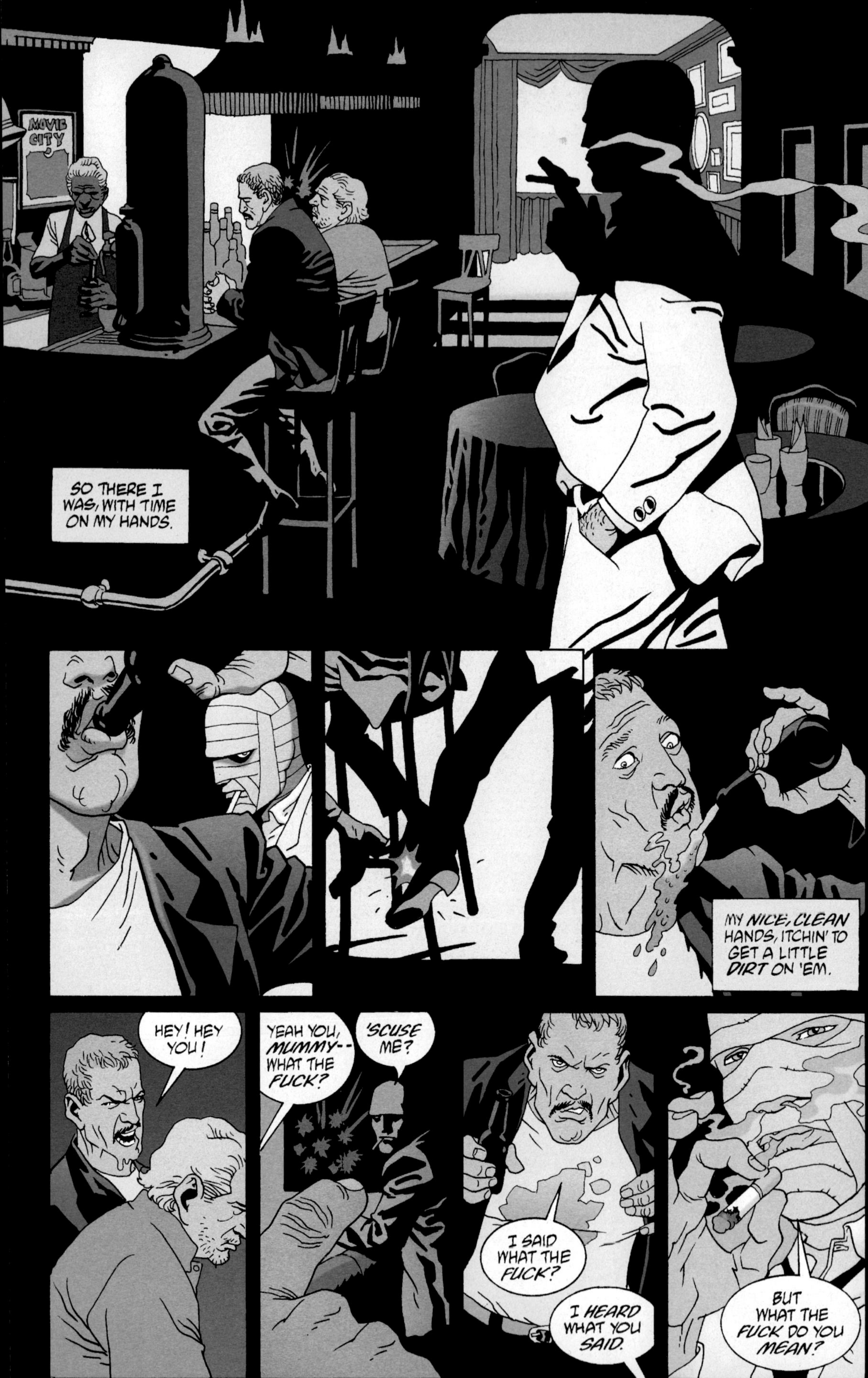
MOVIE CITY
SO THERE I WAS, WITH TIME ON MY HANDS.
MY NICE, CLEAN HANDS, ITCHIN' TO GET A LITTLE DIRT ON 'EM.
HEY! HEY YOU!
YEAH YOU, MUMMY-- WHAT THE FUCK?
'SCUSE ME?
I SAID WHAT THE FUCK?
I HEARD WHAT YOU SAID.
BUT WHAT THE FUCK DO YOU MEAN?

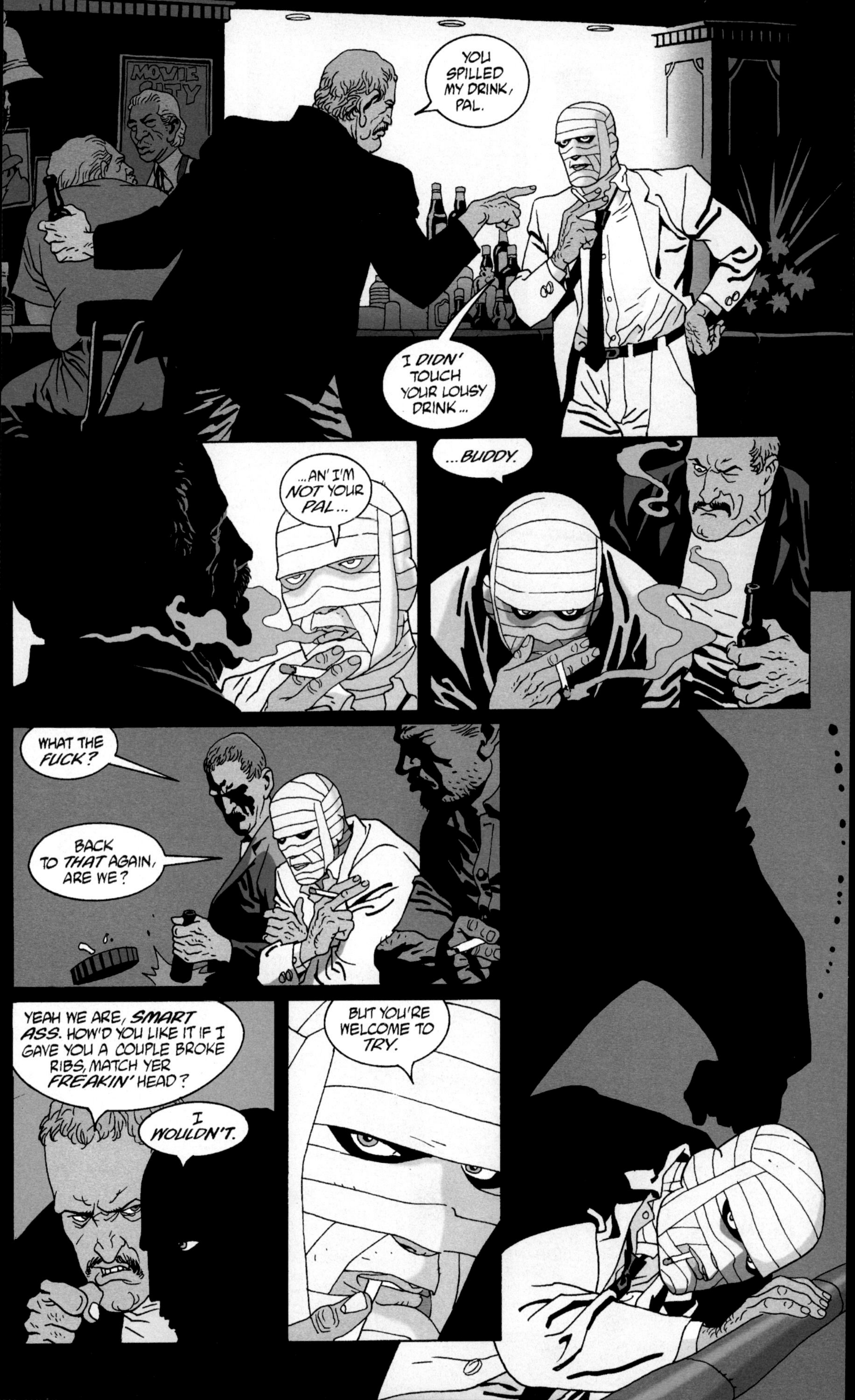

YOU SPILLED MY DRINK, PAL.
I DIDN' TOUCH YOUR LOUSY DRINK...
...AN' I'M NOT YOUR PAL...
...BUDDY.
WHAT THE FUCK?
BACK TO THAT AGAIN, ARE WE?
YEAH WE ARE, SMART ASS. HOW'D YOU LIKE IT IF I GAVE YOU A COUPLE BROKE RIBS, MATCH YER FREAKIN' HEAD?
I WOULDN'T.
BUT YOU'RE WELCOME TO TRY.
MOVIE CITY

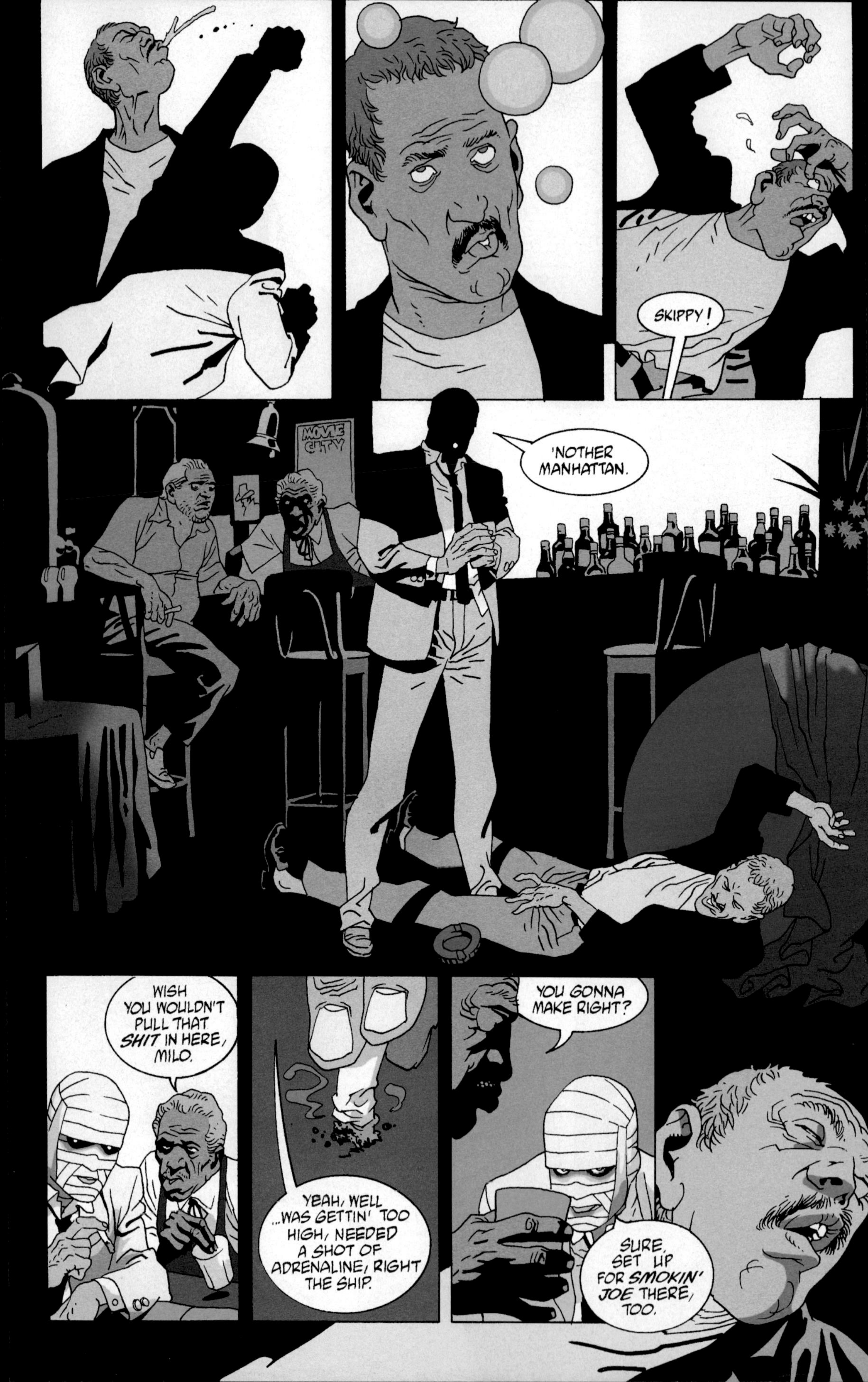
SKIPPY!
'NOTHER MANHATTAN.
MOVIE CITY
WISH YOU WOULDN'T PULL THAT *SHIT* IN HERE, MILO.
YEAH, WELL ...WAS GETTIN' TOO HIGH, NEEDED A SHOT OF ADRENALINE, RIGHT THE SHIP.
YOU GONNA MAKE RIGHT?
SURE, SET UP FOR *SMOKIN' JOE* THERE, TOO.

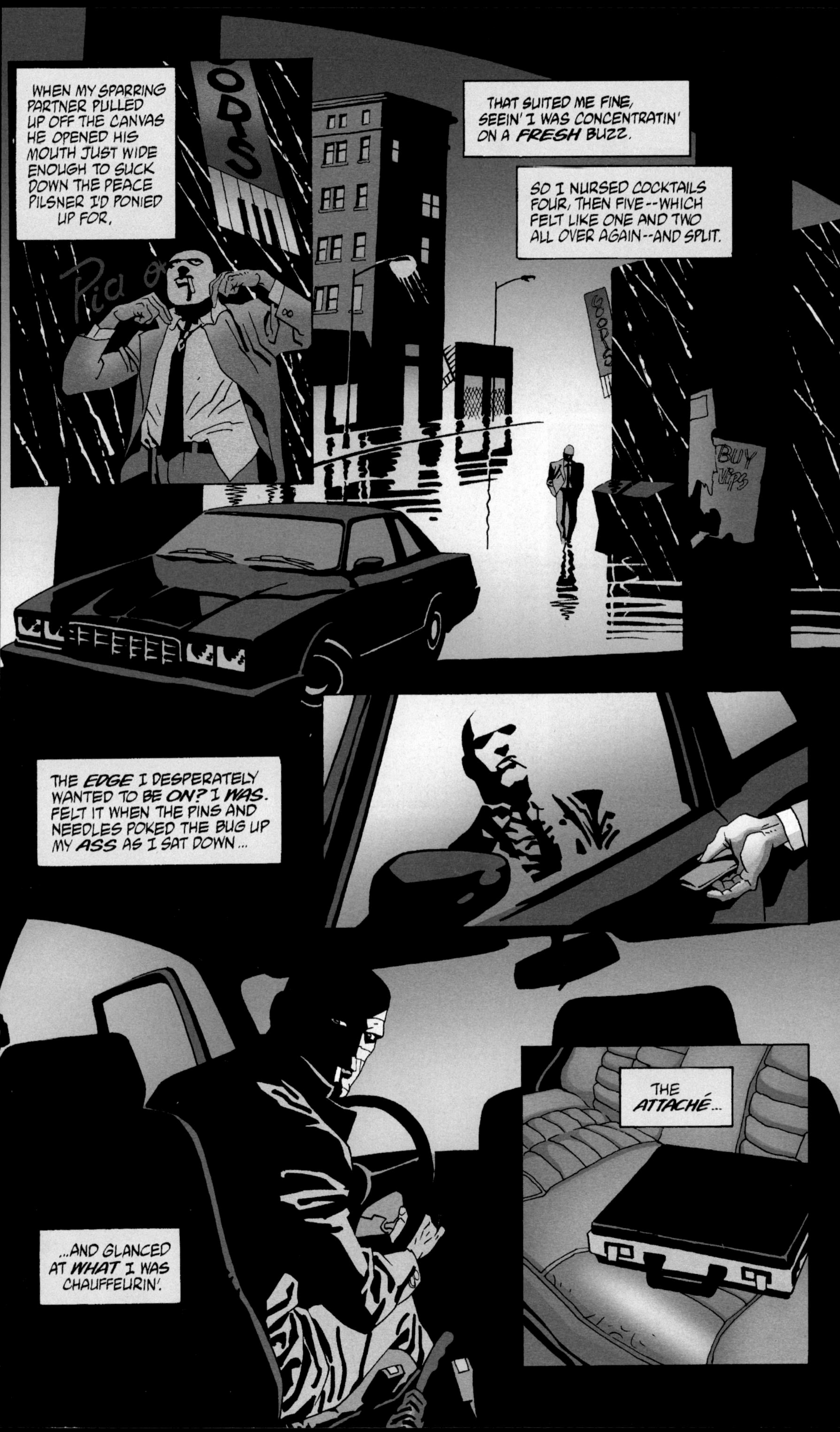
WHEN MY SPARRING PARTNER PULLED UP OFF THE CANVAS HE OPENED HIS MOUTH JUST WIDE ENOUGH TO SUCK DOWN THE PEACE PILSNER I'D PONIED UP FOR.
THAT SUITED ME FINE, SEEIN' I WAS CONCENTRATIN' ON A FRESH BUZZ.
SO I NURSED COCKTAILS FOUR, THEN FIVE--WHICH FELT LIKE ONE AND TWO ALL OVER AGAIN--AND SPLIT.
BUY
THE EDGE I DESPERATELY WANTED TO BE ON? I WAS. FELT IT WHEN THE PINS AND NEEDLES POKED THE BUG UP MY ASS AS I SAT DOWN...
THE ATTACHÉ...
...AND GLANCED AT WHAT I WAS CHAUFFEURIN'.

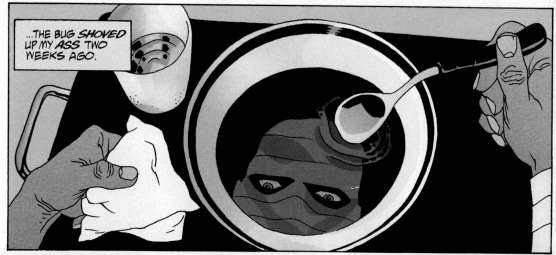

...THE BUG *SHOVED* UP MY *ASS* TWO WEEKS AGO.

MILO GARRET?

I'M *AGENT* GRAVES.

PEACHY. I'VE BEEN *WAITIN'* FOR FOR YOU TO SHOW UP.

HAVE YOU?

GODDAMN RIGHT.

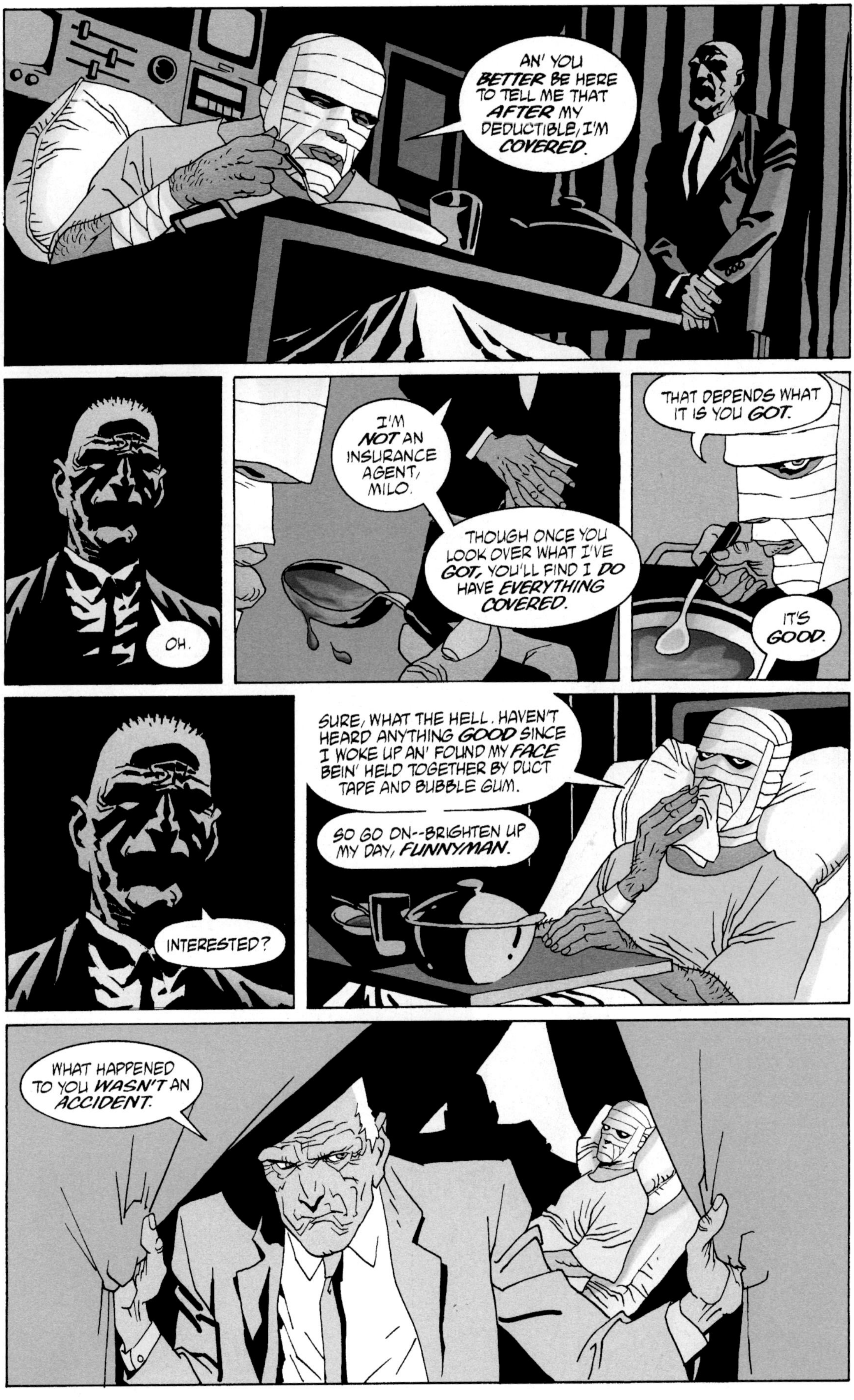
AN' YOU BETTER BE HERE TO TELL ME THAT AFTER MY DEDUCTIBLE, I'M COVERED.
OH.
I'M NOT AN INSURANCE AGENT, MILO.
THOUGH ONCE YOU LOOK OVER WHAT I'VE GOT, YOU'LL FIND I DO HAVE EVERYTHING COVERED.
THAT DEPENDS WHAT IT IS YOU GOT.
IT'S GOOD.
INTERESTED?
SURE, WHAT THE HELL. HAVEN'T HEARD ANYTHING GOOD SINCE I WOKE UP AN' FOUND MY FACE BEIN' HELD TOGETHER BY DUCT TAPE AND BUBBLE GUM.
SO GO ON--BRIGHTEN UP MY DAY, FUNNYMAN.
WHAT HAPPENED TO YOU WASN'T AN ACCIDENT.

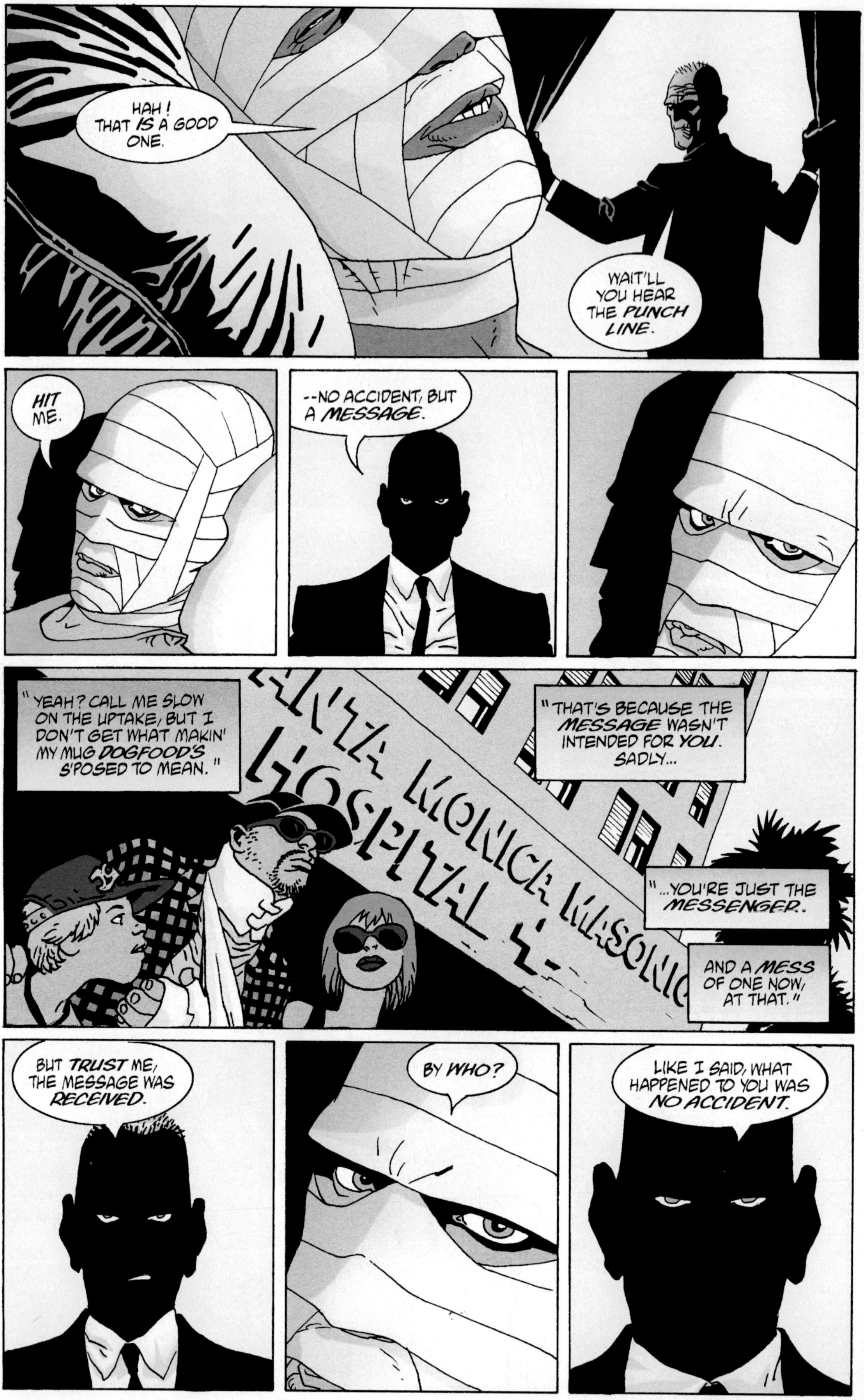
HAH! THAT IS A GOOD ONE.
WAIT'LL YOU HEAR THE PUNCH LINE.
HIT ME.
--NO ACCIDENT, BUT A MESSAGE.
"YEAH? CALL ME SLOW ON THE UPTAKE, BUT I DON'T GET WHAT MAKIN' MY MUG DOGFOOD'S S'POSED TO MEAN."
"THAT'S BECAUSE THE MESSAGE WASN'T INTENDED FOR YOU. SADLY...
"...YOU'RE JUST THE MESSENGER.
AND A MESS OF ONE NOW, AT THAT."
ANTA MONICA MASONIC GOSPITAL
BUT TRUST ME, THE MESSAGE WAS RECEIVED.
BY WHO?
LIKE I SAID, WHAT HAPPENED TO YOU WAS NO ACCIDENT.

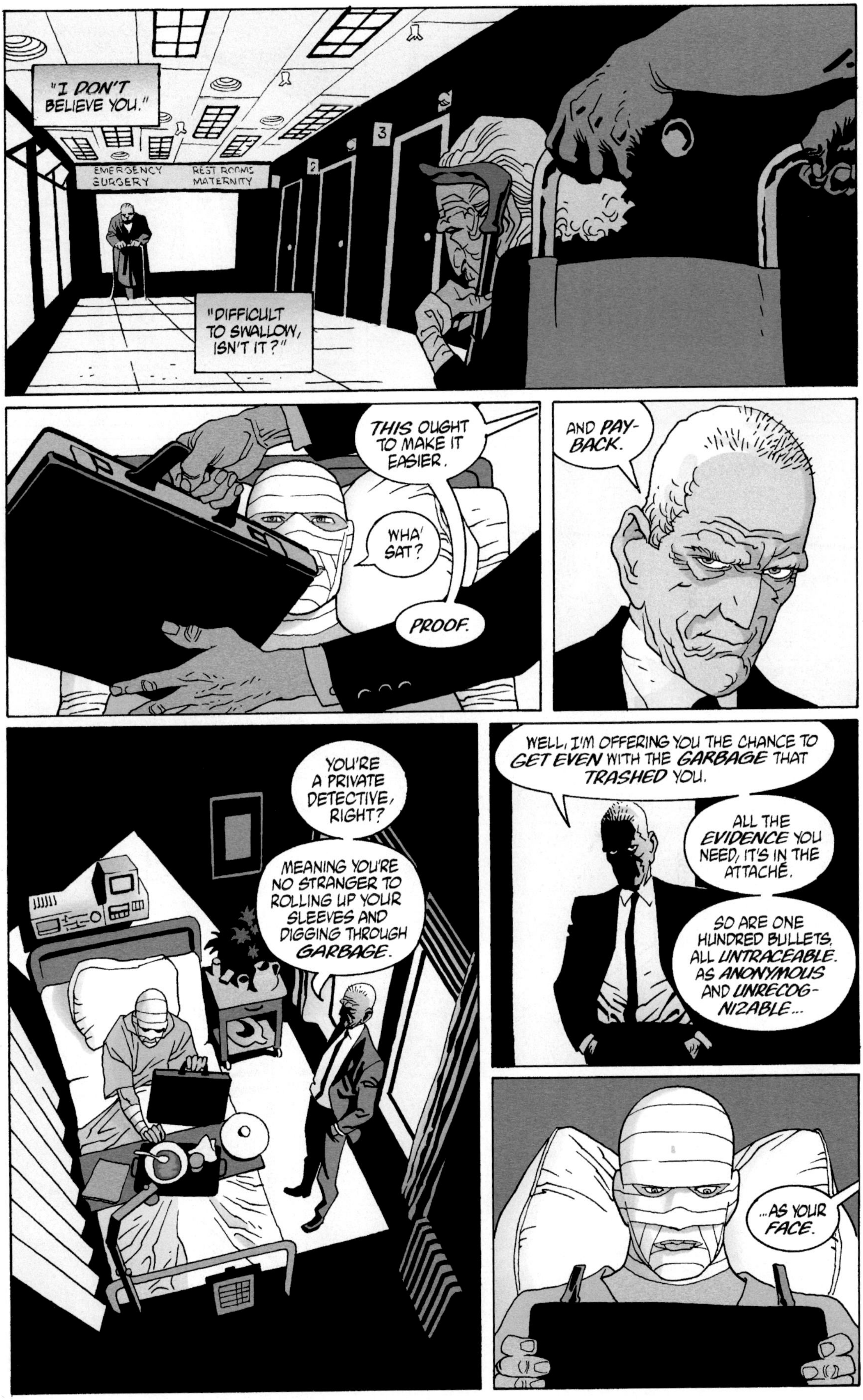
"I DON'T BELIEVE YOU."
EMERGENCY SURGERY
REST ROOMS MATERNITY
3
"DIFFICULT TO SWALLOW, ISN'T IT?"
THIS OUGHT TO MAKE IT EASIER.
WHA' SAT?
PROOF.
AND PAY-BACK.
YOU'RE A PRIVATE DETECTIVE, RIGHT?
MEANING YOU'RE NO STRANGER TO ROLLING UP YOUR SLEEVES AND DIGGING THROUGH GARBAGE.
WELL, I'M OFFERING YOU THE CHANCE TO GET EVEN WITH THE GARBAGE THAT TRASHED YOU.
ALL THE EVIDENCE YOU NEED, IT'S IN THE ATTACHÉ.
SO ARE ONE HUNDRED BULLETS, ALL UNTRACEABLE. AS ANONYMOUS AND UNRECOG-NIZABLE...
...AS YOUR FACE.

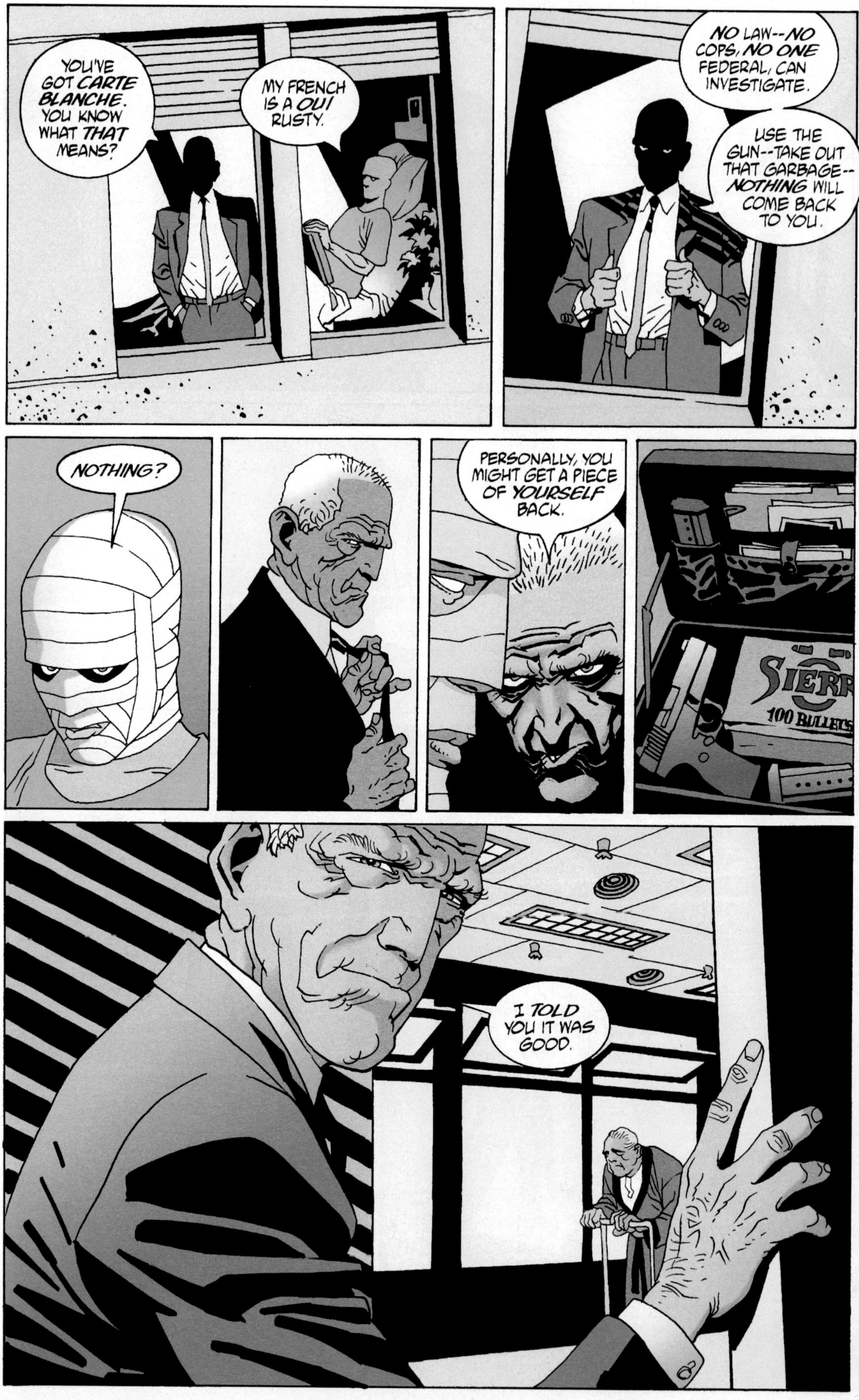
YOU'VE GOT CARTE BLANCHE. YOU KNOW WHAT THAT MEANS?
MY FRENCH IS A OUI RUSTY.
NO LAW--NO COPS, NO ONE FEDERAL, CAN INVESTIGATE.
USE THE GUN--TAKE OUT THAT GARBAGE--NOTHING WILL COME BACK TO YOU.
NOTHING?
PERSONALLY, YOU MIGHT GET A PIECE OF YOURSELF BACK.
SIERR
100 BULLETS
I TOLD YOU IT WAS GOOD.

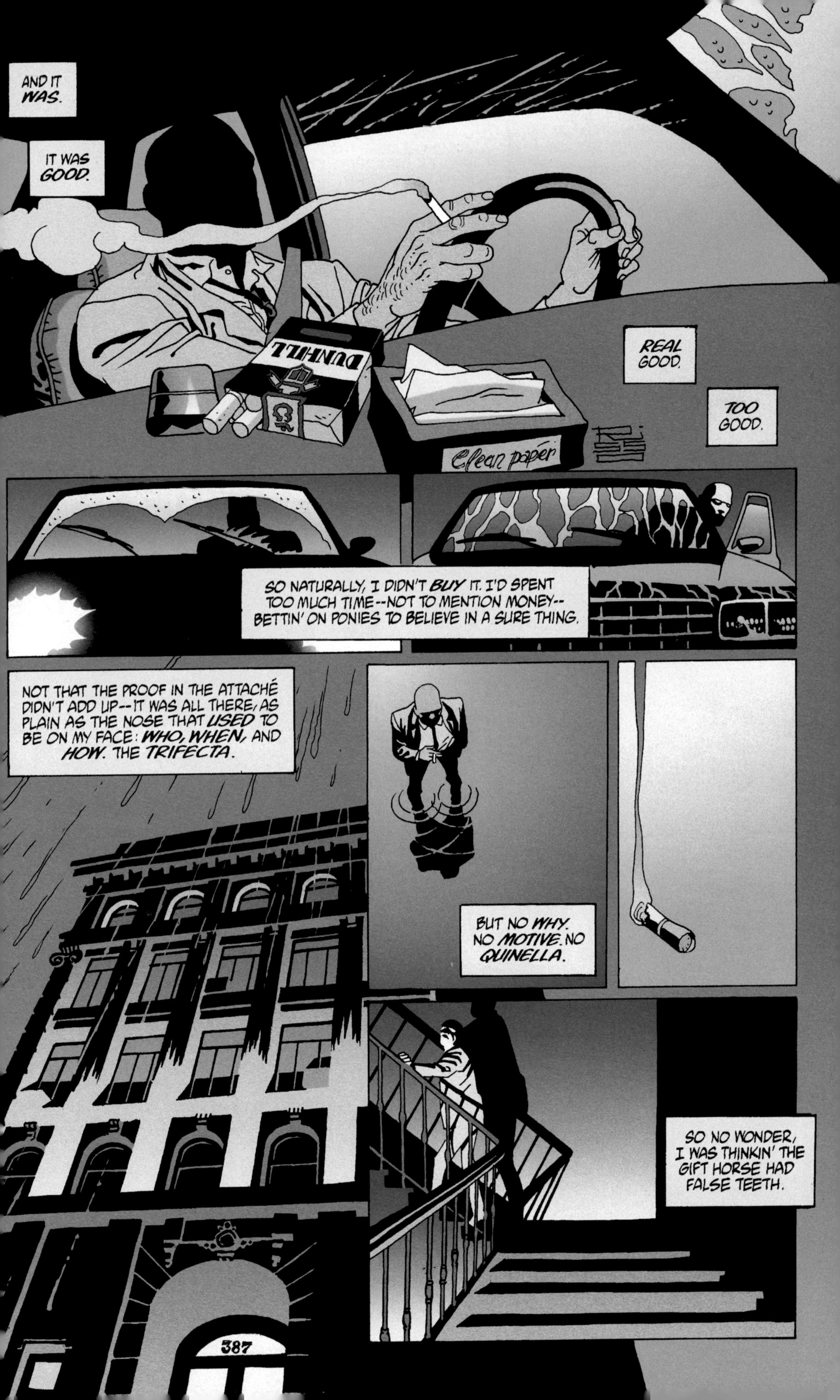
AND IT WAS.
IT WAS GOOD.
DUNHILL
Clean paper
REAL GOOD.
TOO GOOD.
SO NATURALLY, I DIDN'T BUY IT. I'D SPENT TOO MUCH TIME--NOT TO MENTION MONEY--BETTIN' ON PONIES TO BELIEVE IN A SURE THING.
NOT THAT THE PROOF IN THE ATTACHÉ DIDN'T ADD UP--IT WAS ALL THERE, AS PLAIN AS THE NOSE THAT USED TO BE ON MY FACE: WHO, WHEN, AND HOW. THE TRIFECTA.
BUT NO WHY. NO MOTIVE. NO QUINELLA.
SO NO WONDER, I WAS THINKIN' THE GIFT HORSE HAD FALSE TEETH.
387

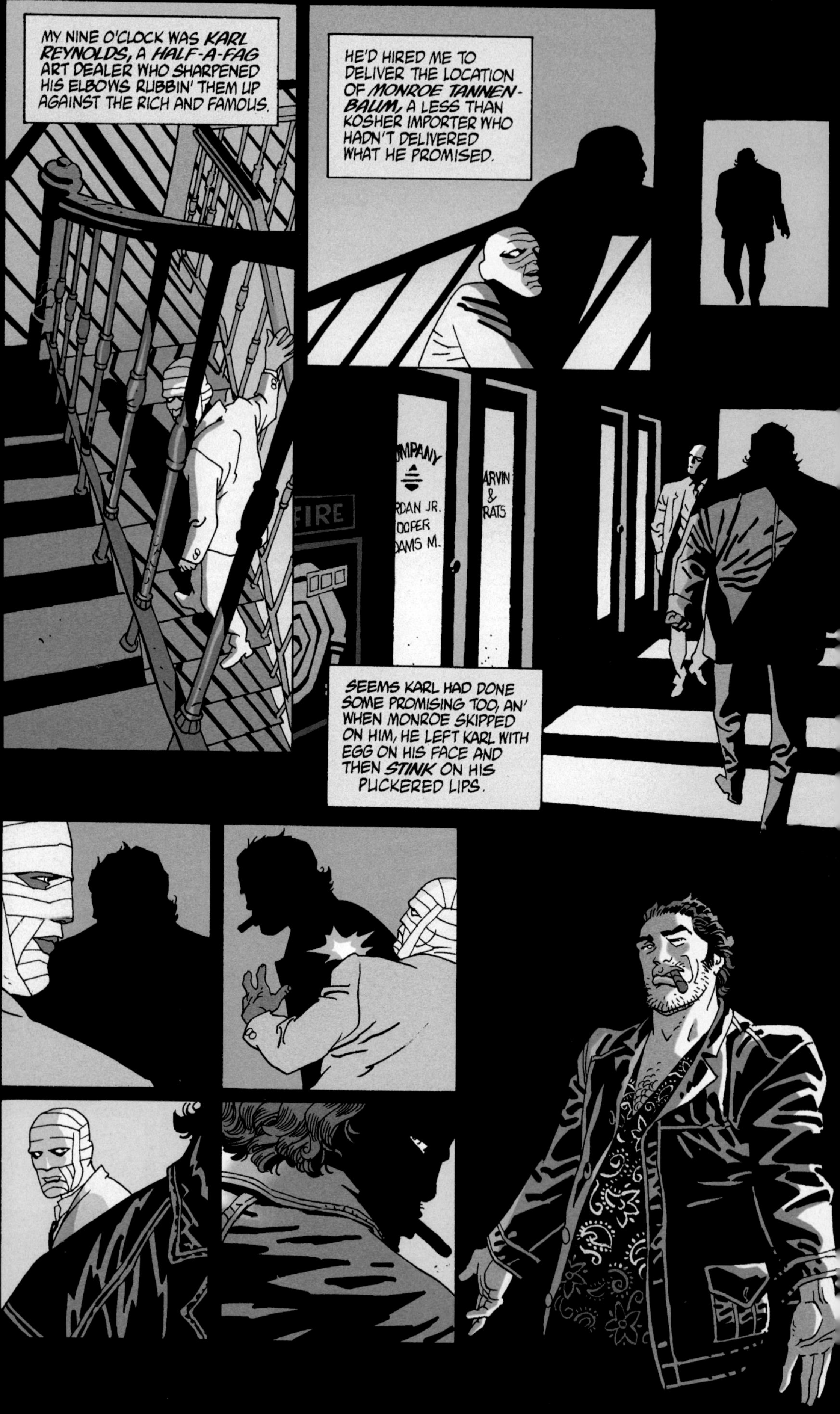
MY NINE O'CLOCK WAS KARL REYNOLDS, A HALF-A-FAG ART DEALER WHO SHARPENED HIS ELBOWS RUBBIN' THEM UP AGAINST THE RICH AND FAMOUS.
HE'D HIRED ME TO DELIVER THE LOCATION OF MONROE TANNEN-BAUM, A LESS THAN KOSHER IMPORTER WHO HADN'T DELIVERED WHAT HE PROMISED.
FIRE
SEEMS KARL HAD DONE SOME PROMISING TOO, AN' WHEN MONROE SKIPPED ON HIM, HE LEFT KARL WITH EGG ON HIS FACE AND THEN STINK ON HIS PUCKERED LIPS.

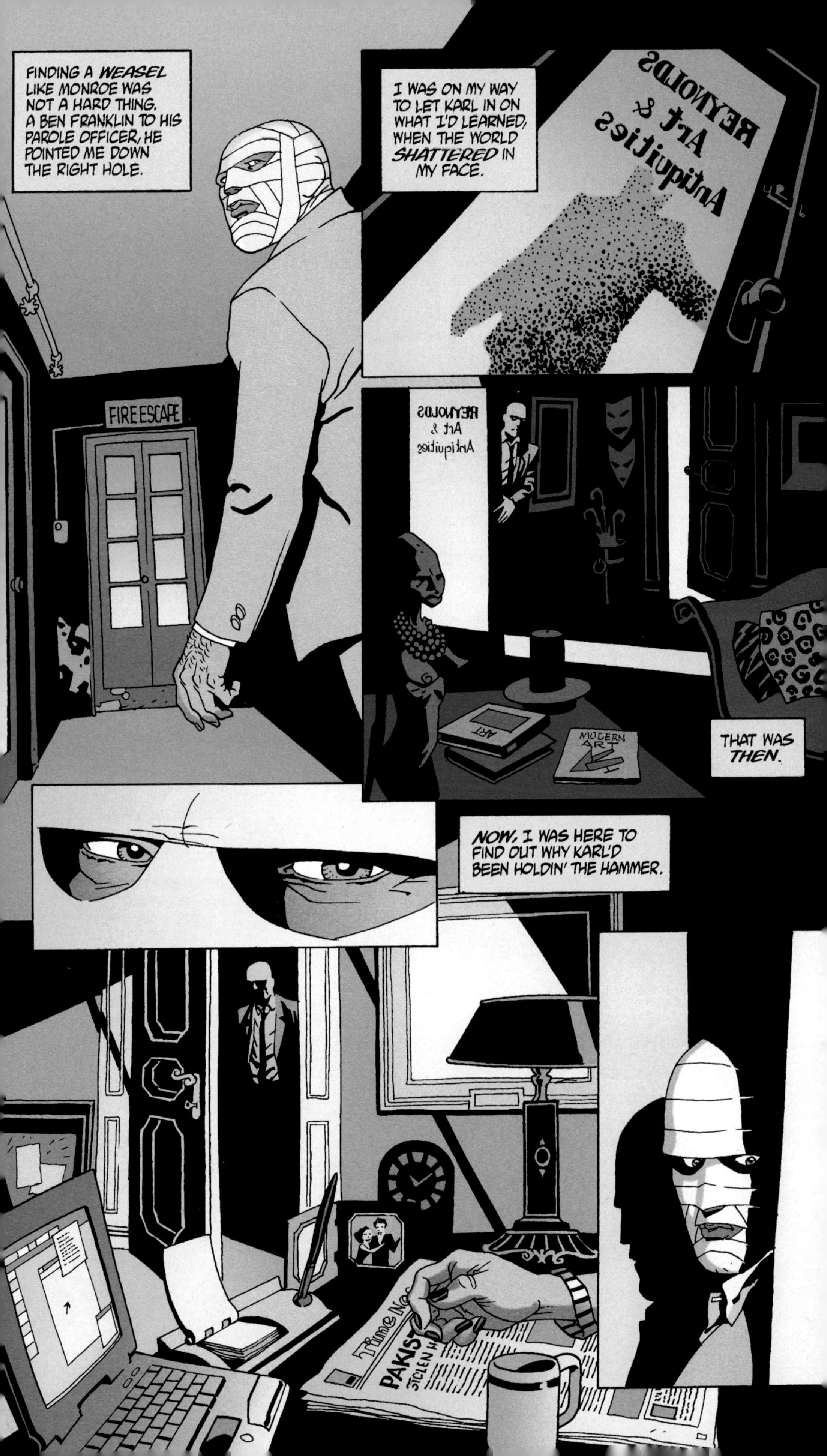

FINDING A WEASEL LIKE MONROE WAS NOT A HARD THING. A BEN FRANKLIN TO HIS PAROLE OFFICER, HE POINTED ME DOWN THE RIGHT HOLE.
FIRE ESCAPE
I WAS ON MY WAY TO LET KARL IN ON WHAT I'D LEARNED, WHEN THE WORLD SHATTERED IN MY FACE.
REYNOLDS & Art Antiquities
ART
MODERN ART
THAT WAS THEN.
NOW, I WAS HERE TO FIND OUT WHY KARL'D BEEN HOLDIN' THE HAMMER.
PAKIST

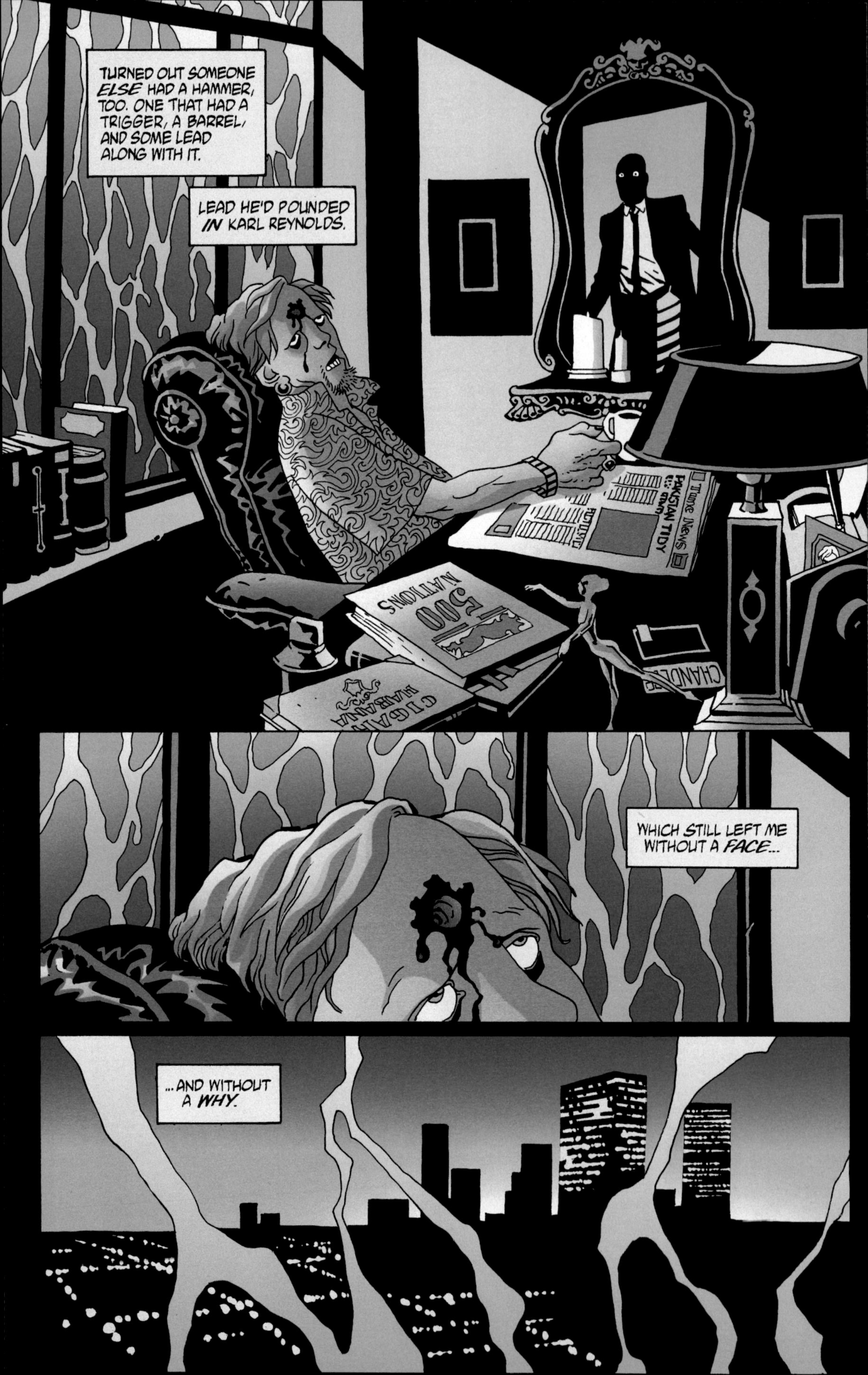
TURNED OUT SOMEONE ELSE HAD A HAMMER, TOO. ONE THAT HAD A TRIGGER, A BARREL, AND SOME LEAD ALONG WITH IT.
LEAD HE'D POUNDED IN KARL REYNOLDS.
WHICH STILL LEFT ME WITHOUT A FACE...
...AND WITHOUT A WHY.

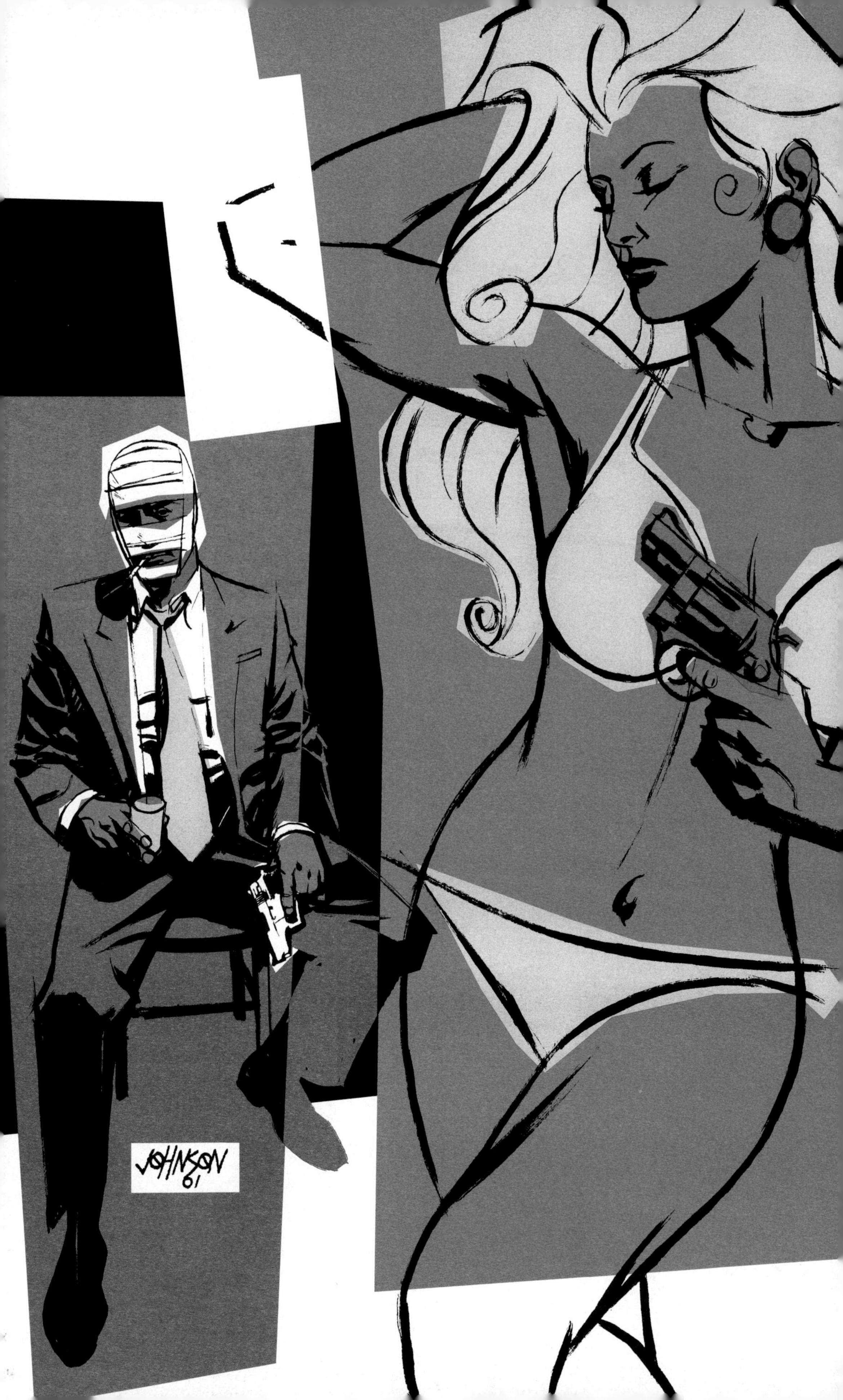
JOHNSON
61

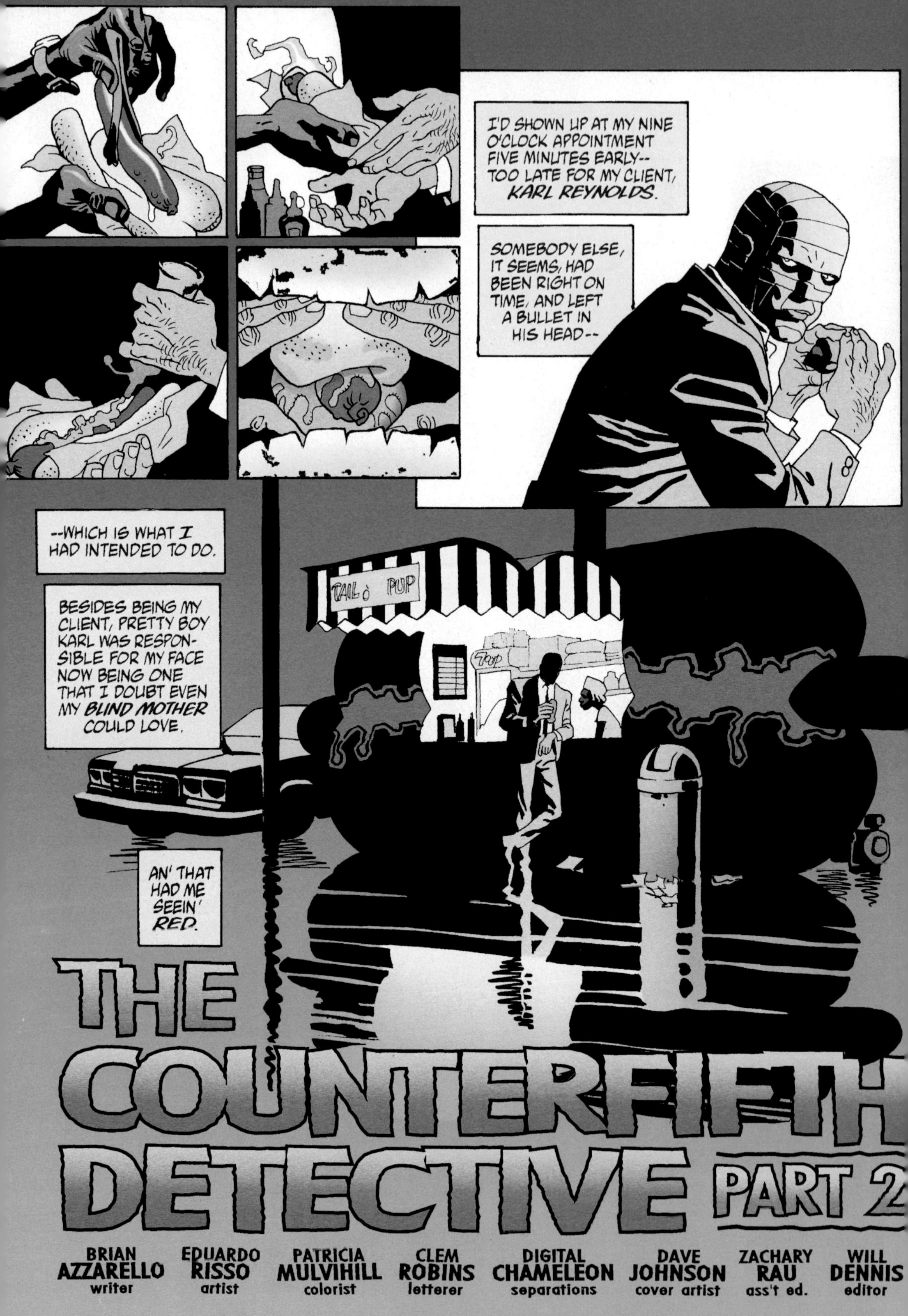

I'D SHOWN UP AT MY NINE O'CLOCK APPOINTMENT FIVE MINUTES EARLY-- TOO LATE FOR MY CLIENT, KARL REYNOLDS.
SOMEBODY ELSE, IT SEEMS, HAD BEEN RIGHT ON TIME, AND LEFT A BULLET IN HIS HEAD--
--WHICH IS WHAT I HAD INTENDED TO DO.
BESIDES BEING MY CLIENT, PRETTY BOY KARL WAS RESPON-SIBLE FOR MY FACE NOW BEING ONE THAT I DOUBT EVEN MY BLIND MOTHER COULD LOVE.
TAIL o' PUP
AN' THAT HAD ME SEEIN' RED.
THE COUNTERFIFTH DETECTIVE PART 2
BRIAN AZZARELLO writer
EDUARDO RISSO artist
PATRICIA MULVIHILL colorist
CLEM ROBINS letterer
DIGITAL CHAMELEON separations
DAVE JOHNSON cover artist
ZACHARY RAU ass't ed.
WILL DENNIS editor

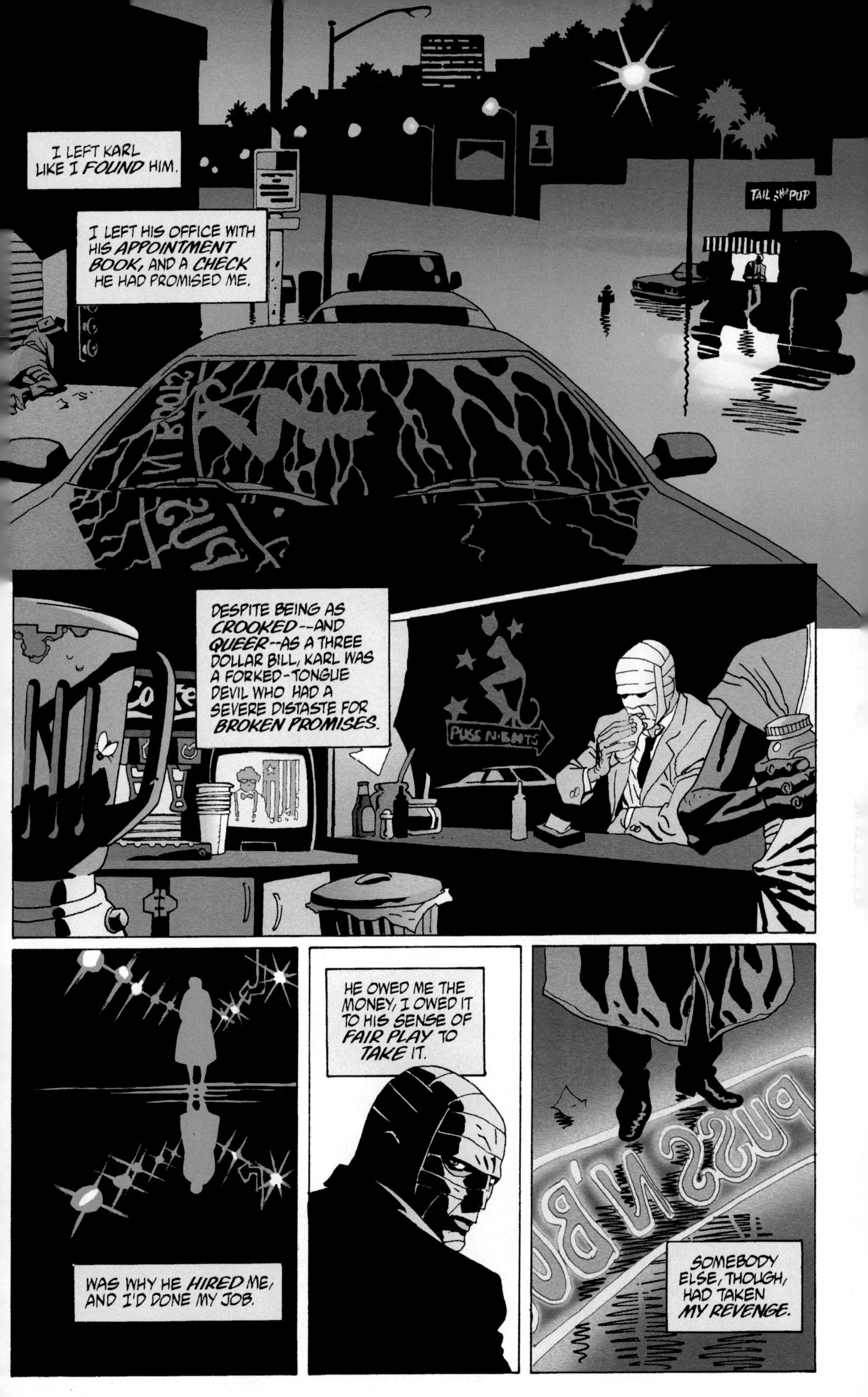
I LEFT KARL LIKE I *FOUND* HIM.
I LEFT HIS OFFICE WITH HIS *APPOINTMENT BOOK*, AND A *CHECK* HE HAD PROMISED ME.
TAIL O' THE PUP
DESPITE BEING AS *CROOKED*--AND *QUEER*--AS A THREE DOLLAR BILL, KARL WAS A FORKED-TONGUE DEVIL WHO HAD A SEVERE DISTASTE FOR *BROKEN PROMISES*.
PUSS N BOOTS
WAS WHY HE *HIRED* ME, AND I'D DONE MY JOB.
HE OWED ME THE MONEY, I OWED IT TO HIS SENSE OF *FAIR PLAY* TO *TAKE* IT.
SOMEBODY ELSE, THOUGH, HAD TAKEN *MY REVENGE*.

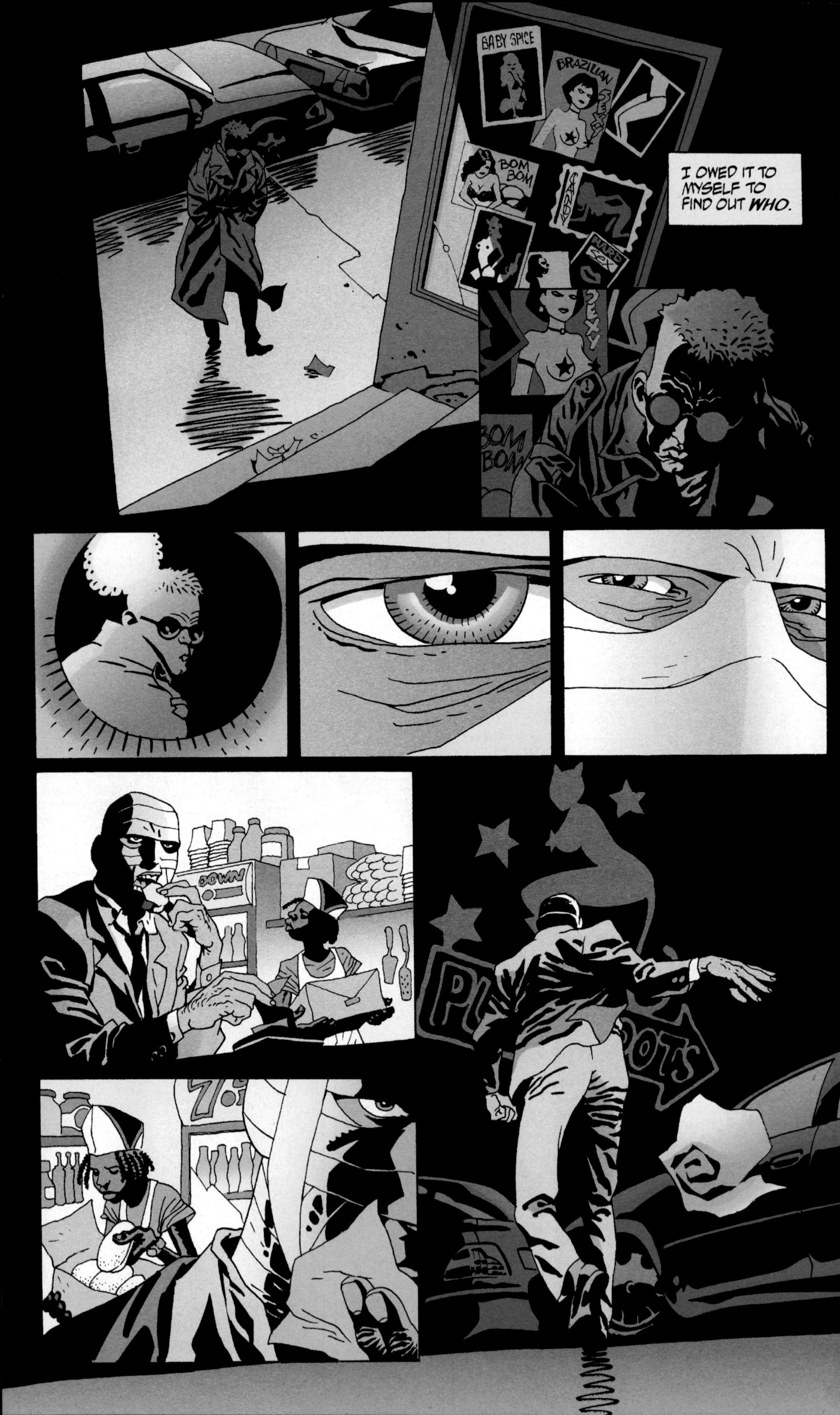
BABY SPICE
BRAZILIAN
BOM BOM
CANDY
HARD SEX
I OWED IT TO MYSELF TO FIND OUT ***WHO***.
SEXY
BOM BOM
DOWN

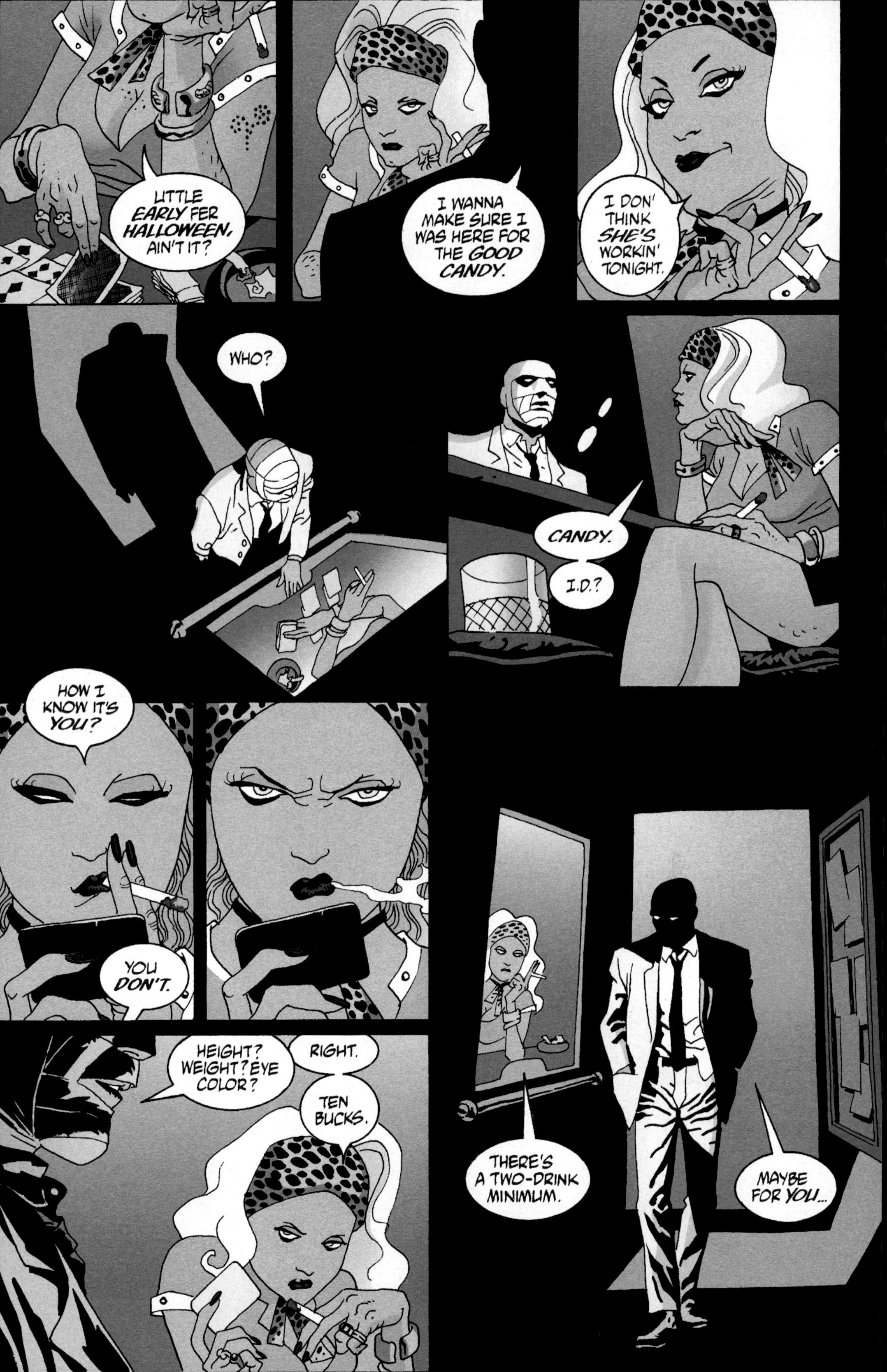
LITTLE EARLY FER HALLOWEEN, AIN'T IT?
I WANNA MAKE SURE I WAS HERE FOR THE GOOD CANDY.
I DON' THINK SHE'S WORKIN' TONIGHT.
WHO?
CANDY.
I.D.?
HOW I KNOW IT'S YOU?
YOU DON'T.
HEIGHT? WEIGHT? EYE COLOR?
RIGHT.
TEN BUCKS.
THERE'S A TWO-DRINK MINIMUM.
MAYBE FOR YOU...

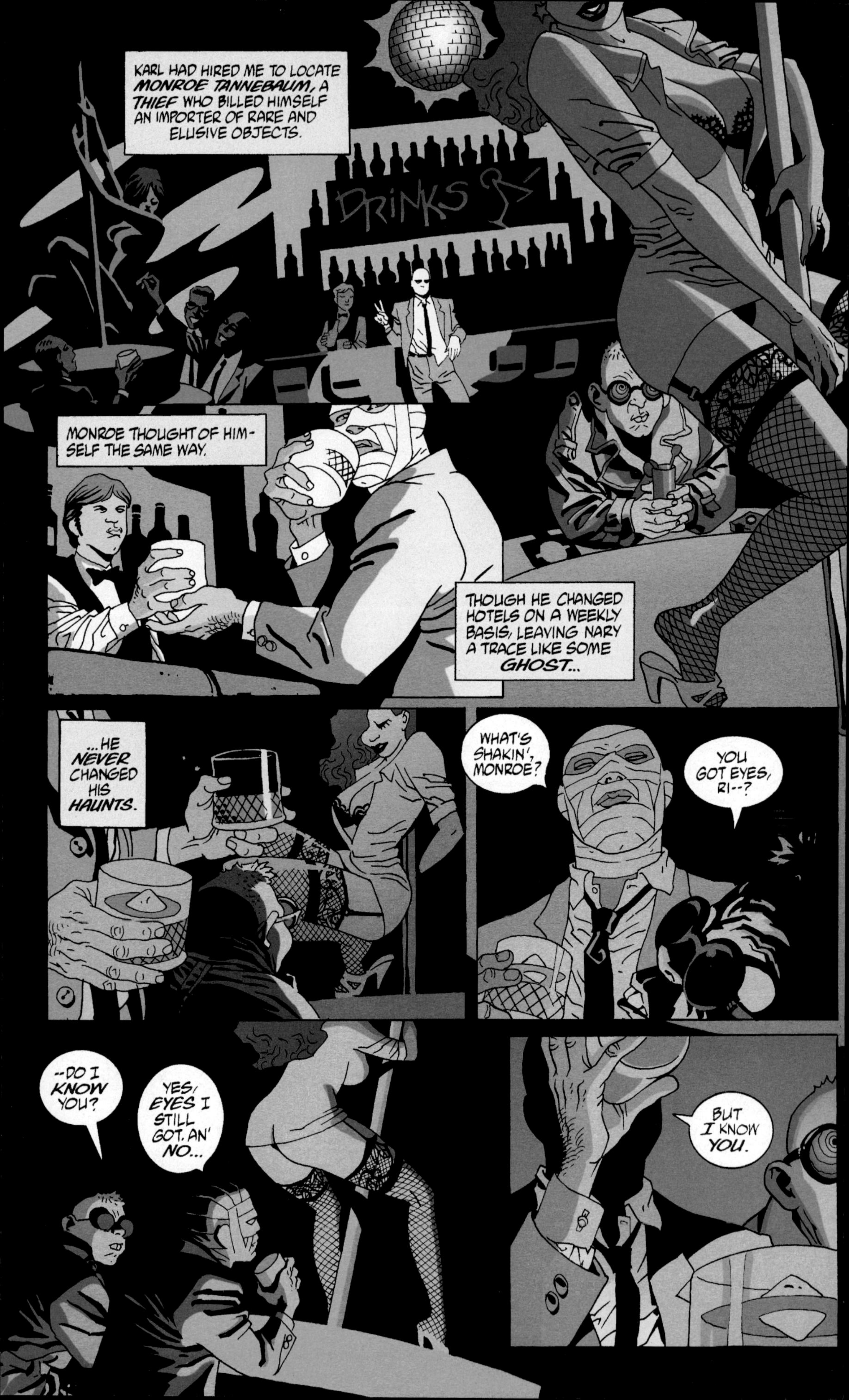
KARL HAD HIRED ME TO LOCATE MONROE TANNEBAUM, A THIEF WHO BILLED HIMSELF AN IMPORTER OF RARE AND ELUSIVE OBJECTS.
DRINKS
MONROE THOUGHT OF HIMSELF THE SAME WAY.
THOUGH HE CHANGED HOTELS ON A WEEKLY BASIS, LEAVING NARY A TRACE LIKE SOME GHOST...
...HE NEVER CHANGED HIS HAUNTS.
WHAT'S SHAKIN', MONROE?
YOU GOT EYES, RI--?
--DO I KNOW YOU?
YES, EYES I STILL GOT. AN' NO...
BUT I KNOW YOU.

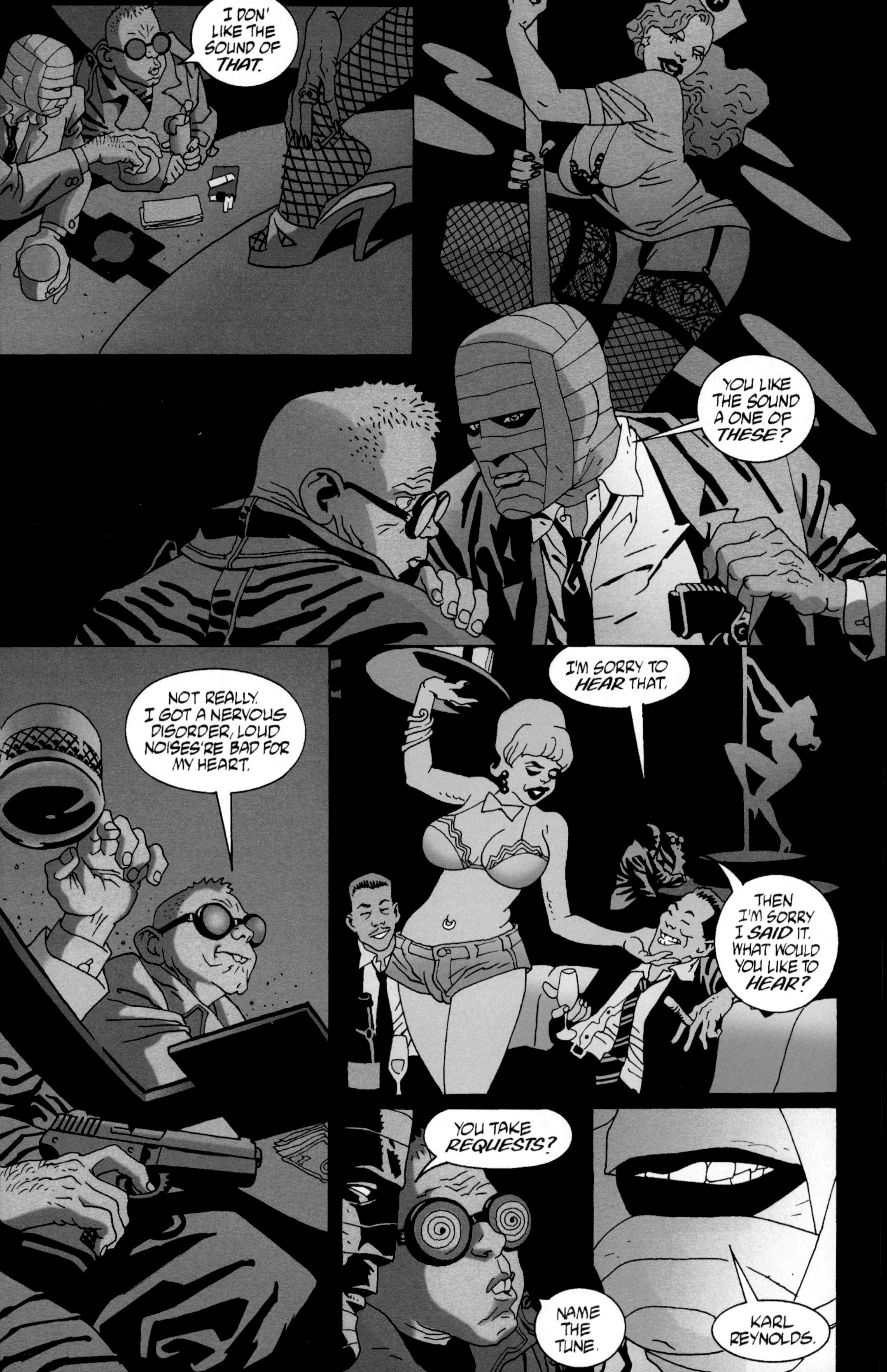
I DON' LIKE THE SOUND OF THAT.
YOU LIKE THE SOUND A ONE OF THESE?
NOT REALLY. I GOT A NERVOUS DISORDER, LOUD NOISES'RE BAD FOR MY HEART.
I'M SORRY TO HEAR THAT.
THEN I'M SORRY I SAID IT. WHAT WOULD YOU LIKE TO HEAR?
YOU TAKE REQUESTS?
NAME THE TUNE.
KARL REYNOLDS.

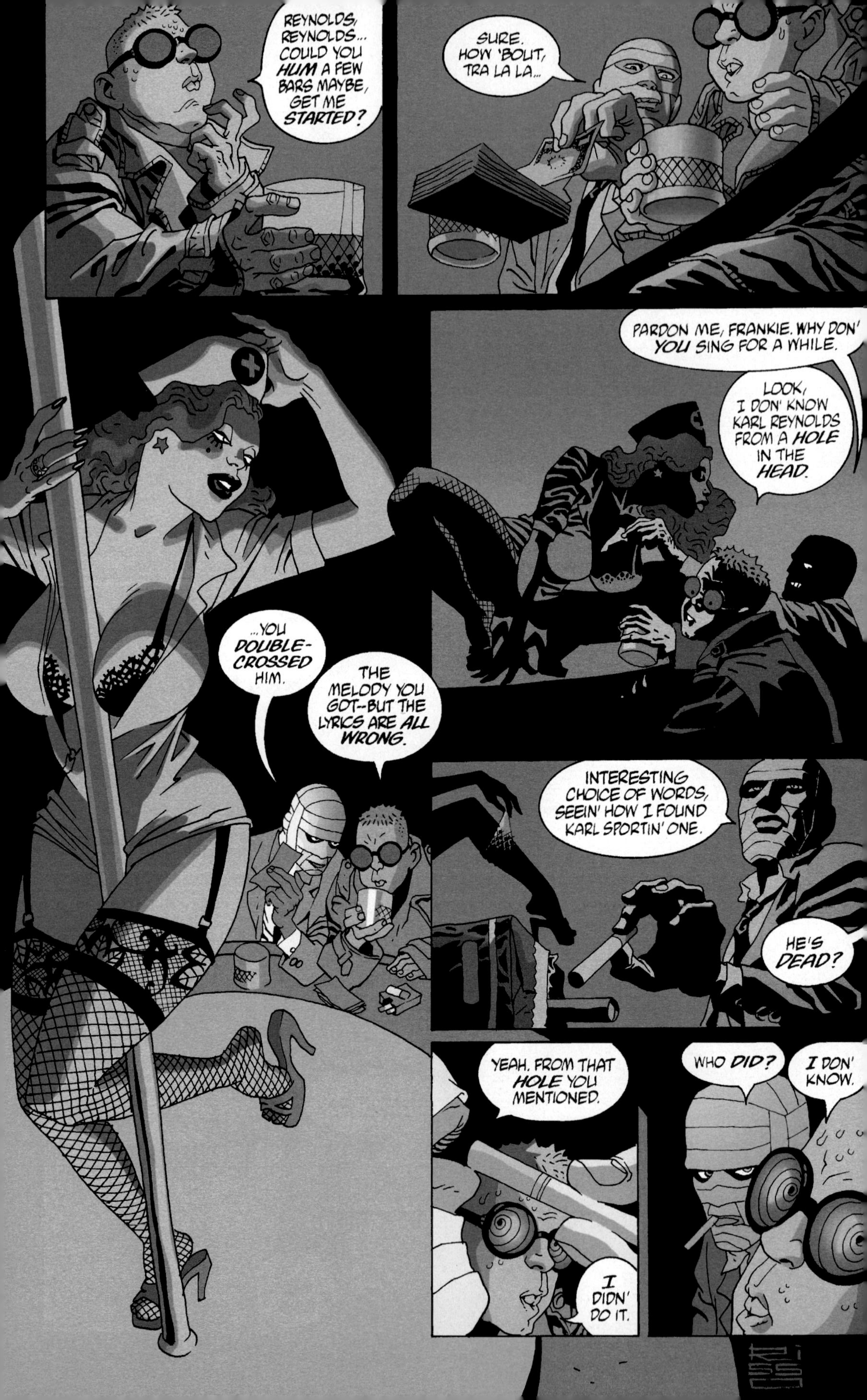
REYNOLDS, REYNOLDS... COULD YOU HUM A FEW BARS MAYBE, GET ME STARTED?
SURE. HOW 'BOUT, TRA LA LA...
PARDON ME, FRANKIE. WHY DON' YOU SING FOR A WHILE.
LOOK, I DON' KNOW KARL REYNOLDS FROM A HOLE IN THE HEAD.
...YOU DOUBLE-CROSSED HIM.
THE MELODY YOU GOT--BUT THE LYRICS ARE ALL WRONG.
INTERESTING CHOICE OF WORDS, SEEIN' HOW I FOUND KARL SPORTIN' ONE.
HE'S DEAD?
YEAH. FROM THAT HOLE YOU MENTIONED.
I DIDN' DO IT.
WHO DID?
I DON' KNOW.

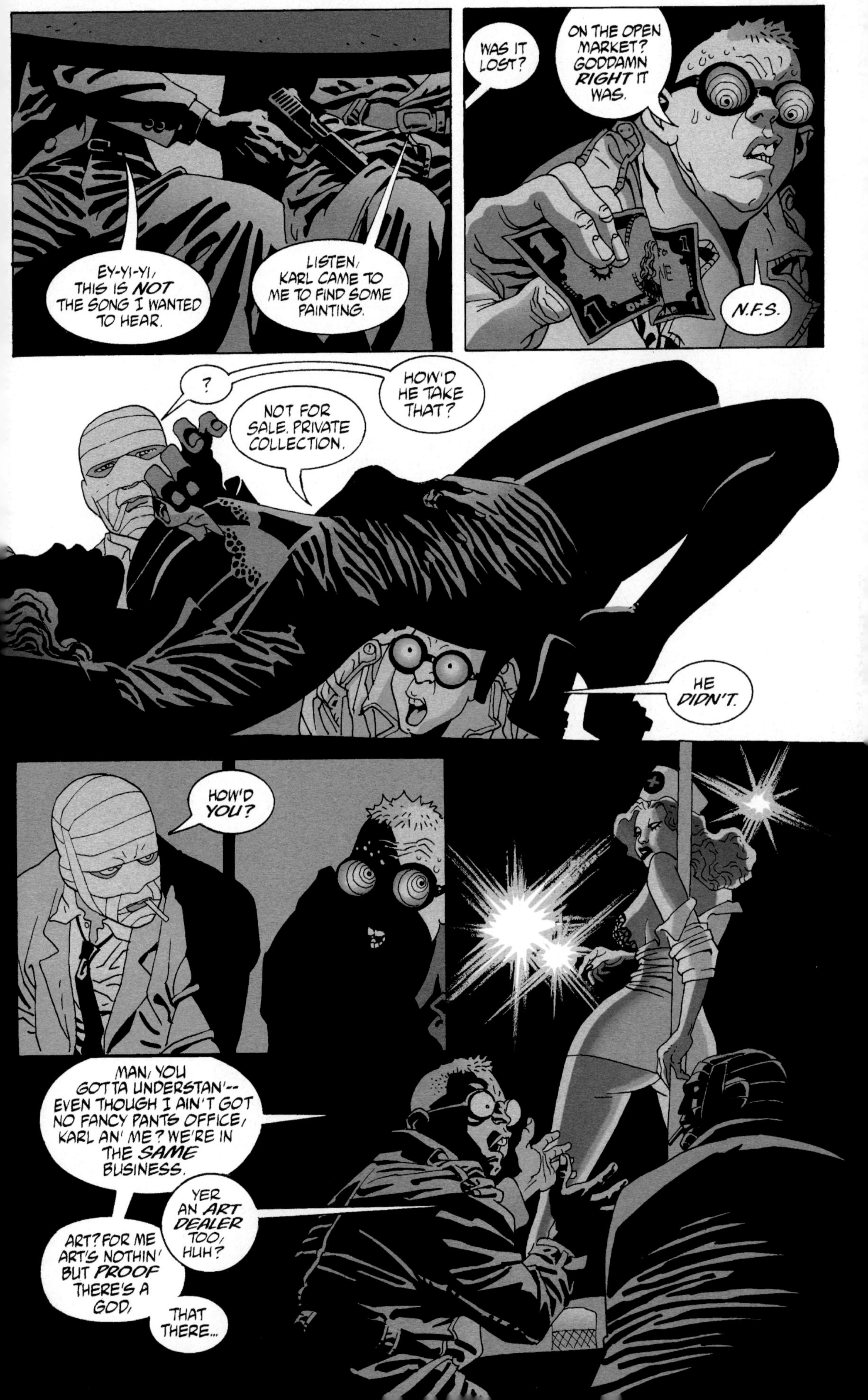
EY-YI-YI, THIS IS NOT THE SONG I WANTED TO HEAR.
LISTEN, KARL CAME TO ME TO FIND SOME PAINTING.
WAS IT LOST?
ON THE OPEN MARKET? GODDAMN RIGHT IT WAS.
N.F.S.
?
NOT FOR SALE. PRIVATE COLLECTION.
HOW'D HE TAKE THAT?
HE DIDN'T.
HOW'D YOU?
MAN, YOU GOTTA UNDERSTAN'-- EVEN THOUGH I AIN'T GOT NO FANCY PANTS OFFICE, KARL AN' ME? WE'RE IN THE SAME BUSINESS.
YER AN ART DEALER TOO, HUH?
ART? FOR ME ART'S NOTHIN' BUT PROOF THERE'S A GOD,
THAT THERE...

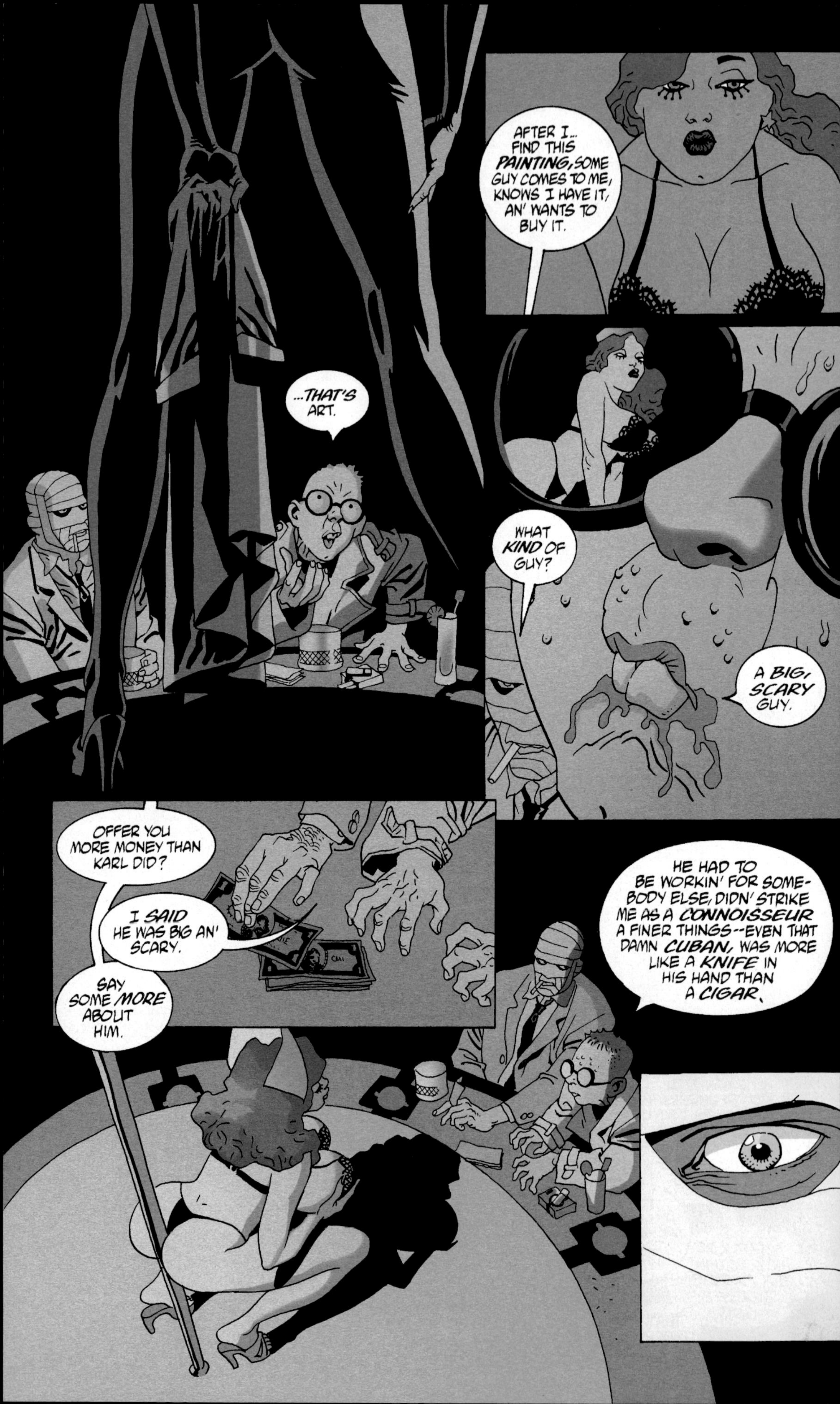
AFTER I... FIND THIS PAINTING, SOME GUY COMES TO ME, KNOWS I HAVE IT, AN' WANTS TO BUY IT.
...THAT'S ART.
WHAT KIND OF GUY?
A BIG, SCARY GUY.
OFFER YOU MORE MONEY THAN KARL DID?
I SAID HE WAS BIG AN' SCARY.
SAY SOME MORE ABOUT HIM.
HE HAD TO BE WORKIN' FOR SOMEBODY ELSE, DIDN' STRIKE ME AS A CONNOISSEUR A FINER THINGS--EVEN THAT DAMN CUBAN, WAS MORE LIKE A KNIFE IN HIS HAND THAN A CIGAR.

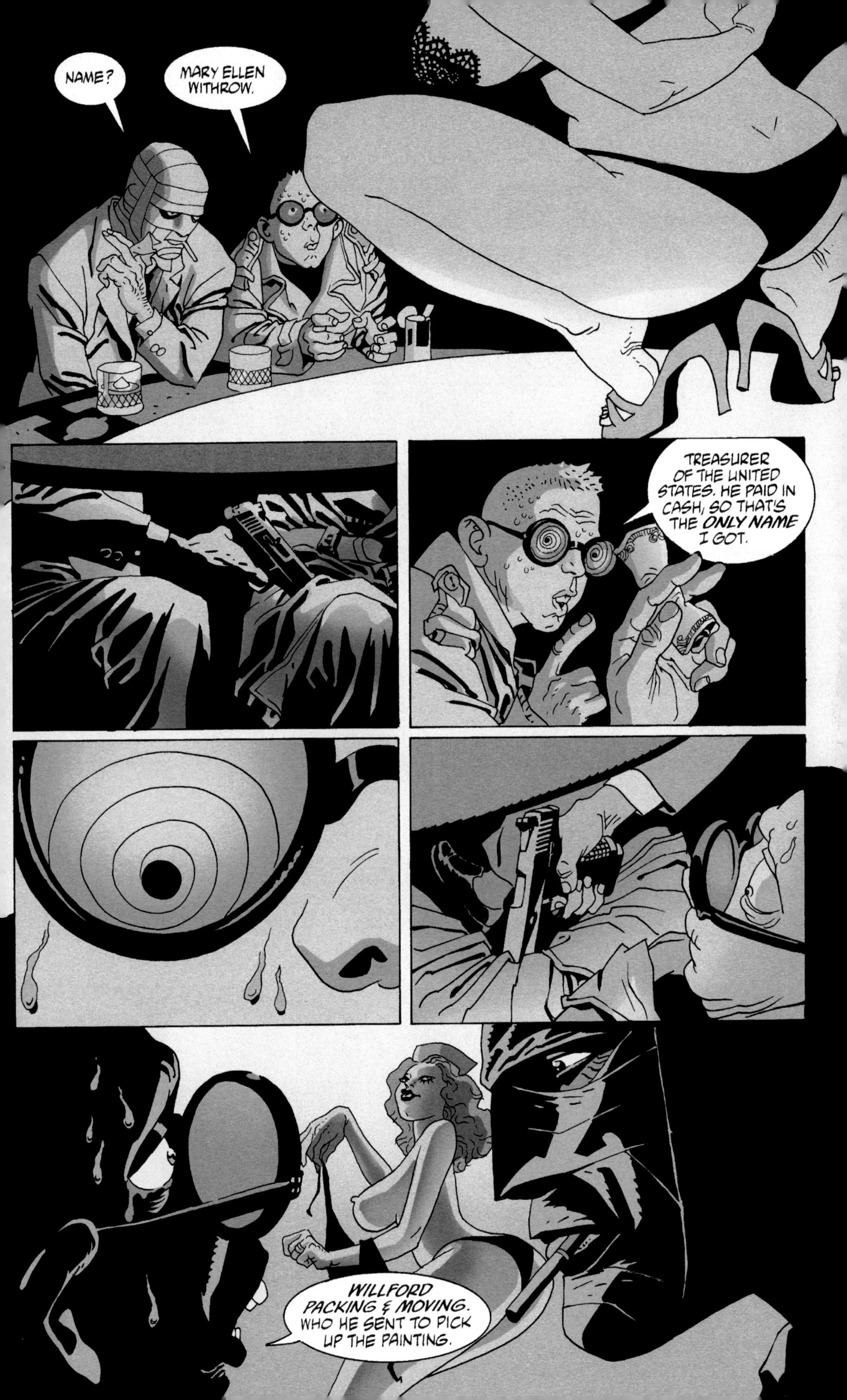
NAME?
MARY ELLEN WITHROW.
TREASURER OF THE UNITED STATES. HE PAID IN CASH, SO THAT'S THE ONLY NAME I GOT.
WILLFORD PACKING & MOVING. WHO HE SENT TO PICK UP THE PAINTING.

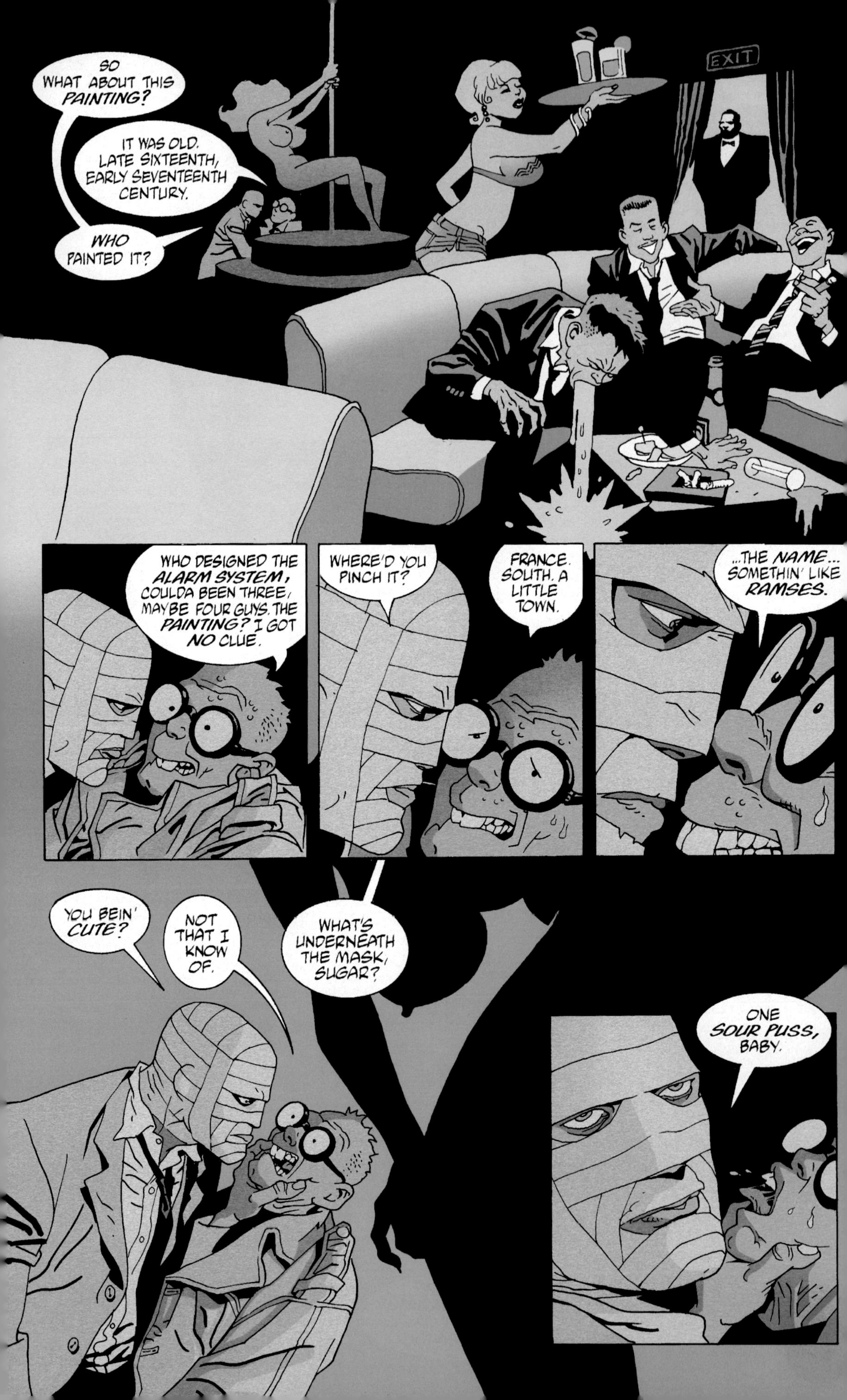

EXIT
SO WHAT ABOUT THIS PAINTING?
IT WAS OLD. LATE SIXTEENTH, EARLY SEVENTEENTH CENTURY.
WHO PAINTED IT?
WHO DESIGNED THE ALARM SYSTEM, COULDA BEEN THREE, MAYBE FOUR GUYS. THE PAINTING? I GOT NO CLUE.
WHERE'D YOU PINCH IT?
FRANCE. SOUTH. A LITTLE TOWN.
...THE NAME... SOMETHIN' LIKE RAMSES.
YOU BEIN' CUTE?
NOT THAT I KNOW OF.
WHAT'S UNDERNEATH THE MASK, SUGAR?
ONE SOUR PUSS, BABY.

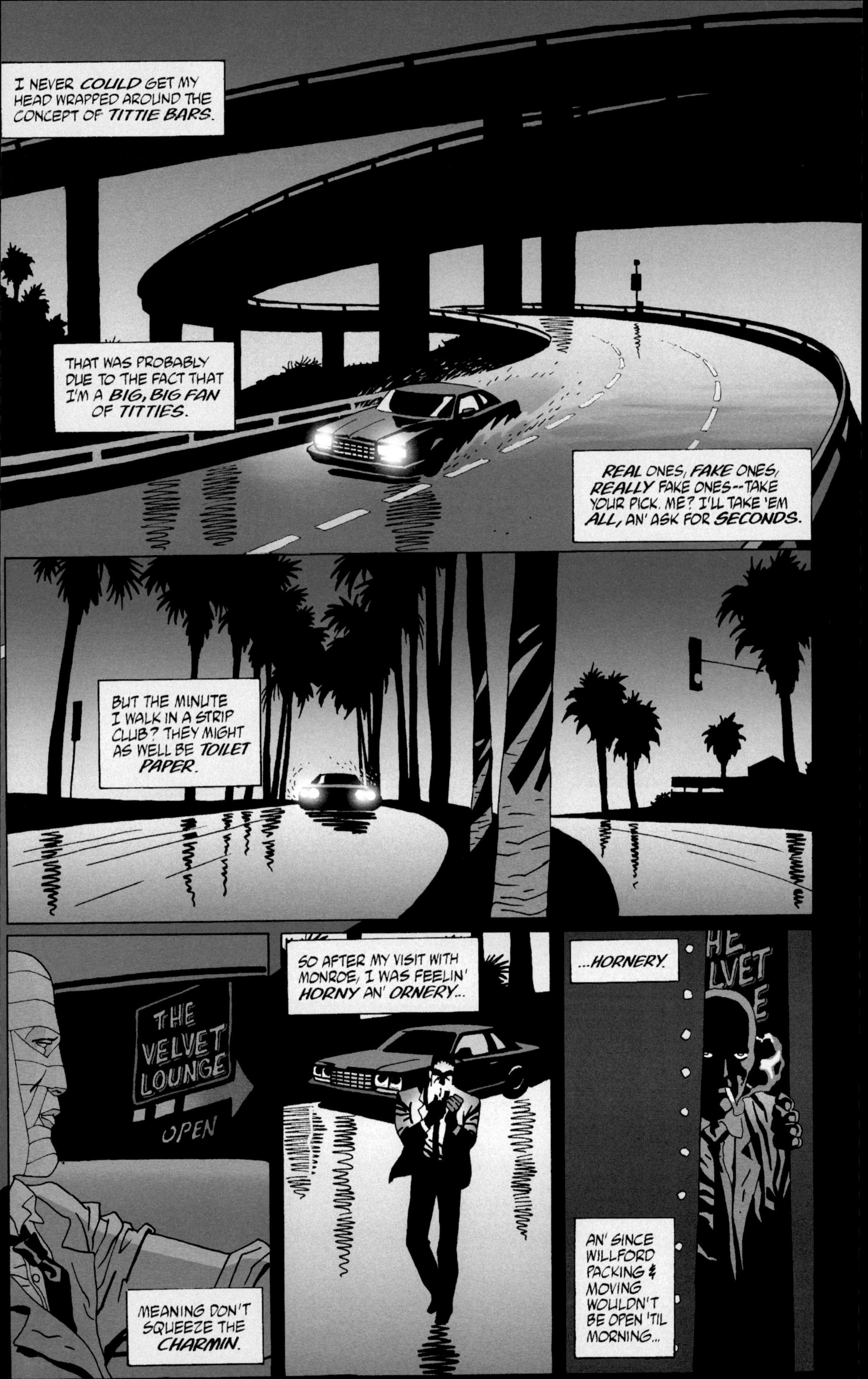

I NEVER COULD GET MY HEAD WRAPPED AROUND THE CONCEPT OF TITTIE BARS.
THAT WAS PROBABLY DUE TO THE FACT THAT I'M A BIG, BIG FAN OF TITTIES.
REAL ONES, FAKE ONES, REALLY FAKE ONES--TAKE YOUR PICK. ME? I'LL TAKE 'EM ALL, AN' ASK FOR SECONDS.
BUT THE MINUTE I WALK IN A STRIP CLUB? THEY MIGHT AS WELL BE TOILET PAPER.
THE VELVET LOUNGE
OPEN
MEANING DON'T SQUEEZE THE CHARMIN.
SO AFTER MY VISIT WITH MONROE, I WAS FEELIN' HORNY AN' ORNERY...
...HORNERY.
AN' SINCE WILLFORD PACKING & MOVING WOULDN'T BE OPEN 'TIL MORNING...

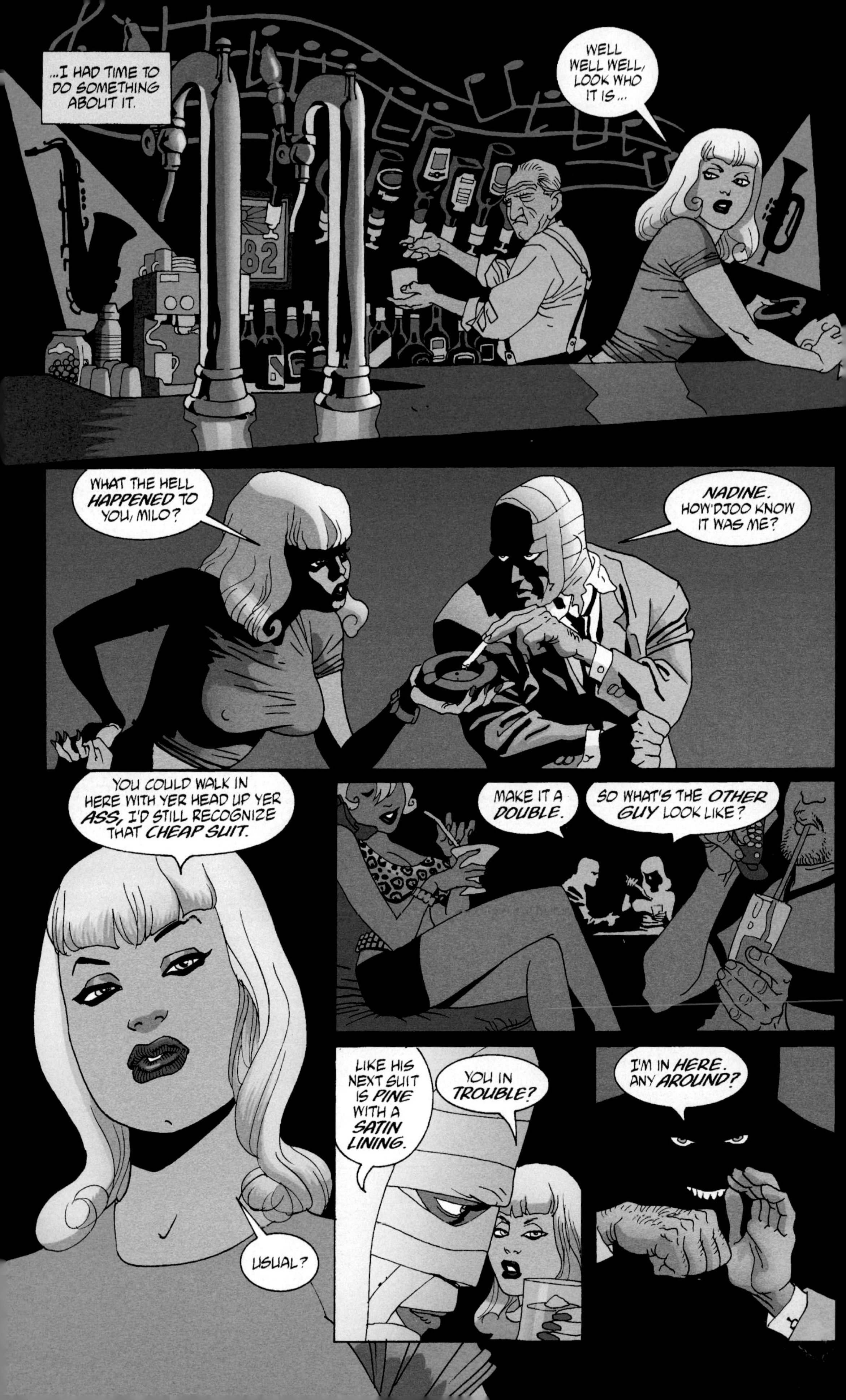

...I HAD TIME TO DO SOMETHING ABOUT IT.
WELL WELL WELL, LOOK WHO IT IS...
WHAT THE HELL HAPPENED TO YOU, MILO?
NADINE. HOW'DJOO KNOW IT WAS ME?
YOU COULD WALK IN HERE WITH YER HEAD UP YER ASS, I'D STILL RECOGNIZE THAT CHEAP SUIT.
USUAL?
MAKE IT A DOUBLE.
SO WHAT'S THE OTHER GUY LOOK LIKE?
LIKE HIS NEXT SUIT IS PINE WITH A SATIN LINING.
YOU IN TROUBLE?
I'M IN HERE. ANY AROUND?

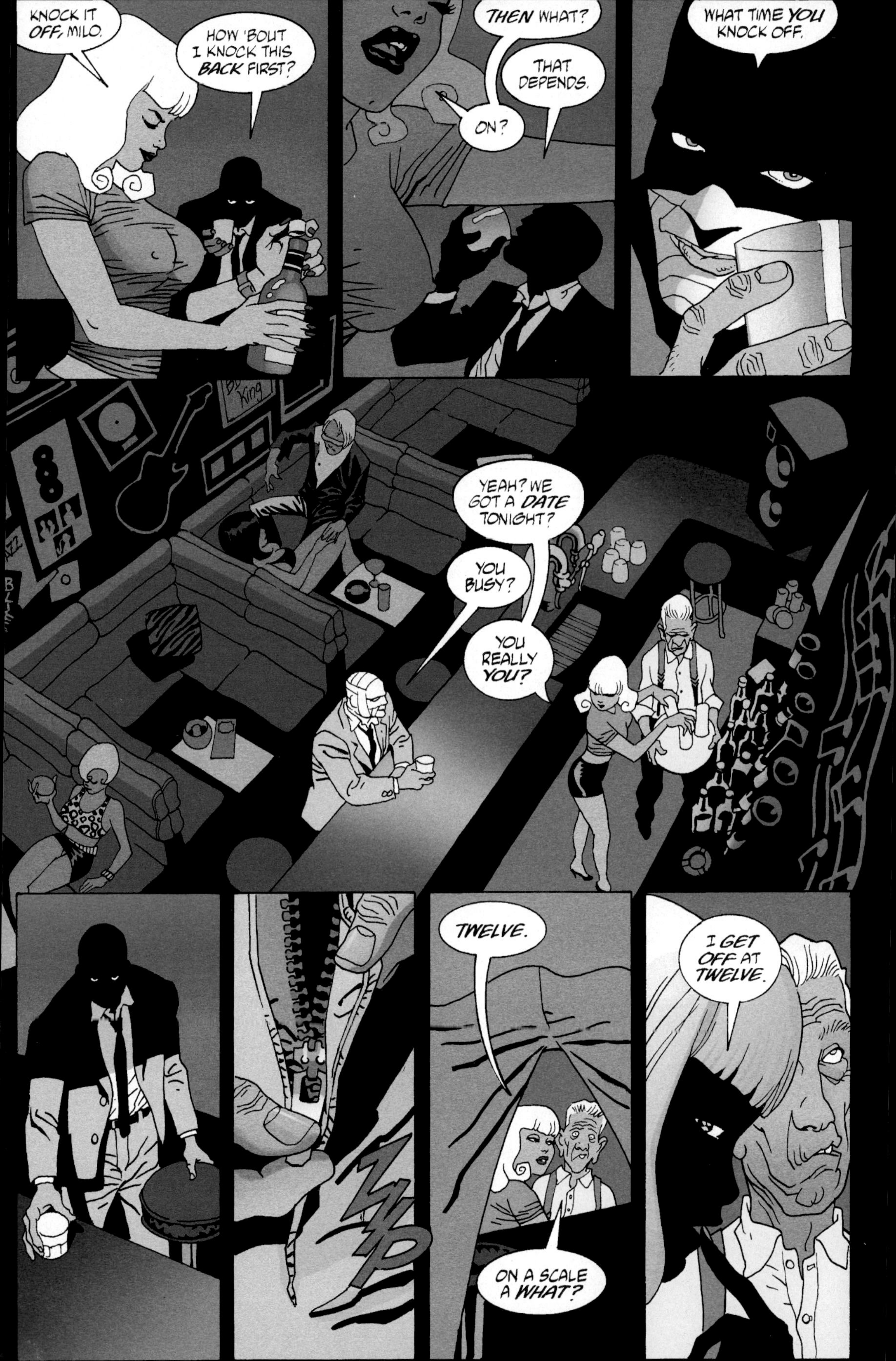
KNOCK IT OFF, MILO.
HOW 'BOUT I KNOCK THIS BACK FIRST?
THEN WHAT?
THAT DEPENDS.
ON?
WHAT TIME YOU KNOCK OFF.
YEAH? WE GOT A DATE TONIGHT?
YOU BUSY?
YOU REALLY YOU?
TWELVE.
ON A SCALE A WHAT?
I GET OFF AT TWELVE.

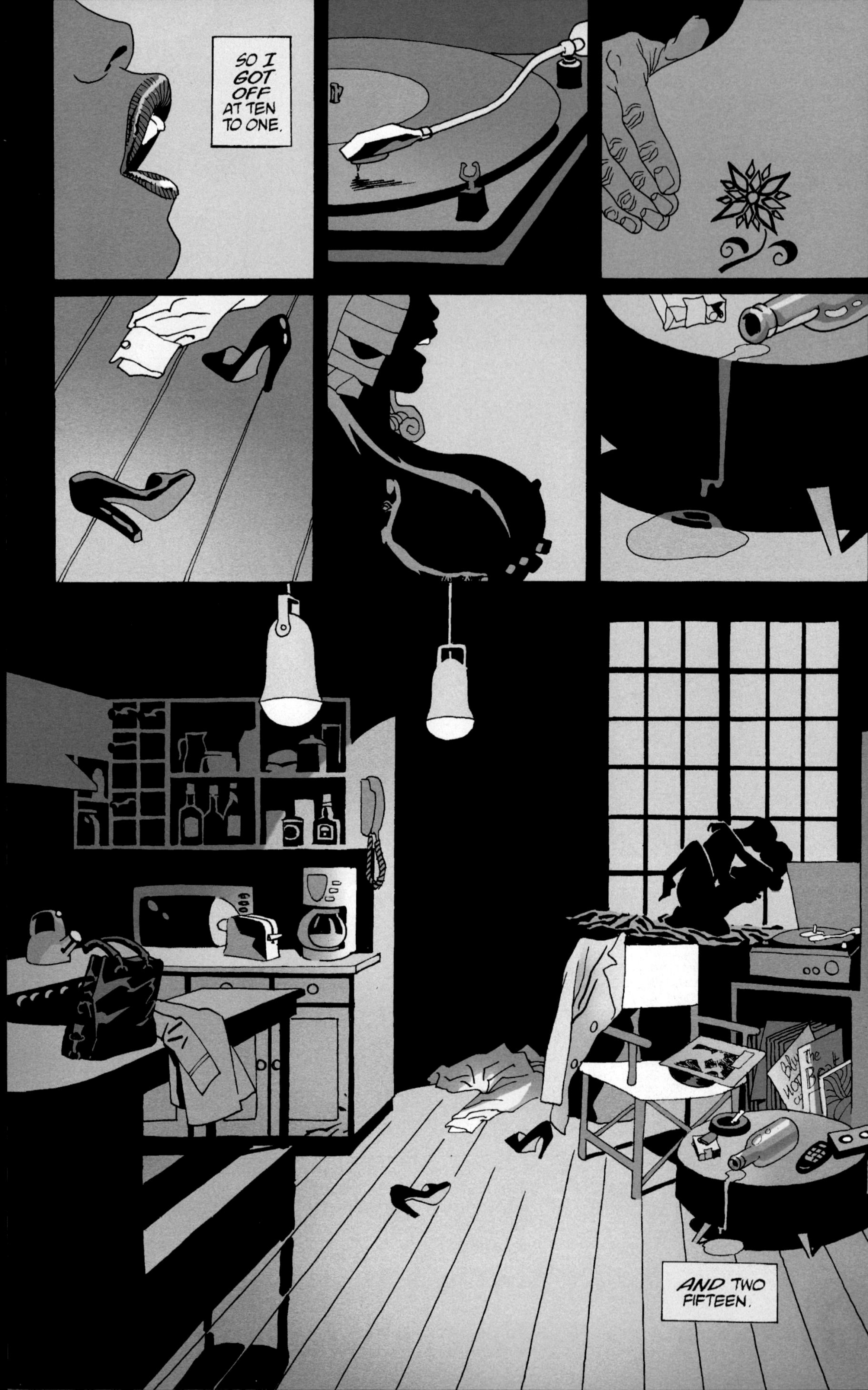
SO I GOT OFF AT TEN TO ONE.
AND TWO FIFTEEN.

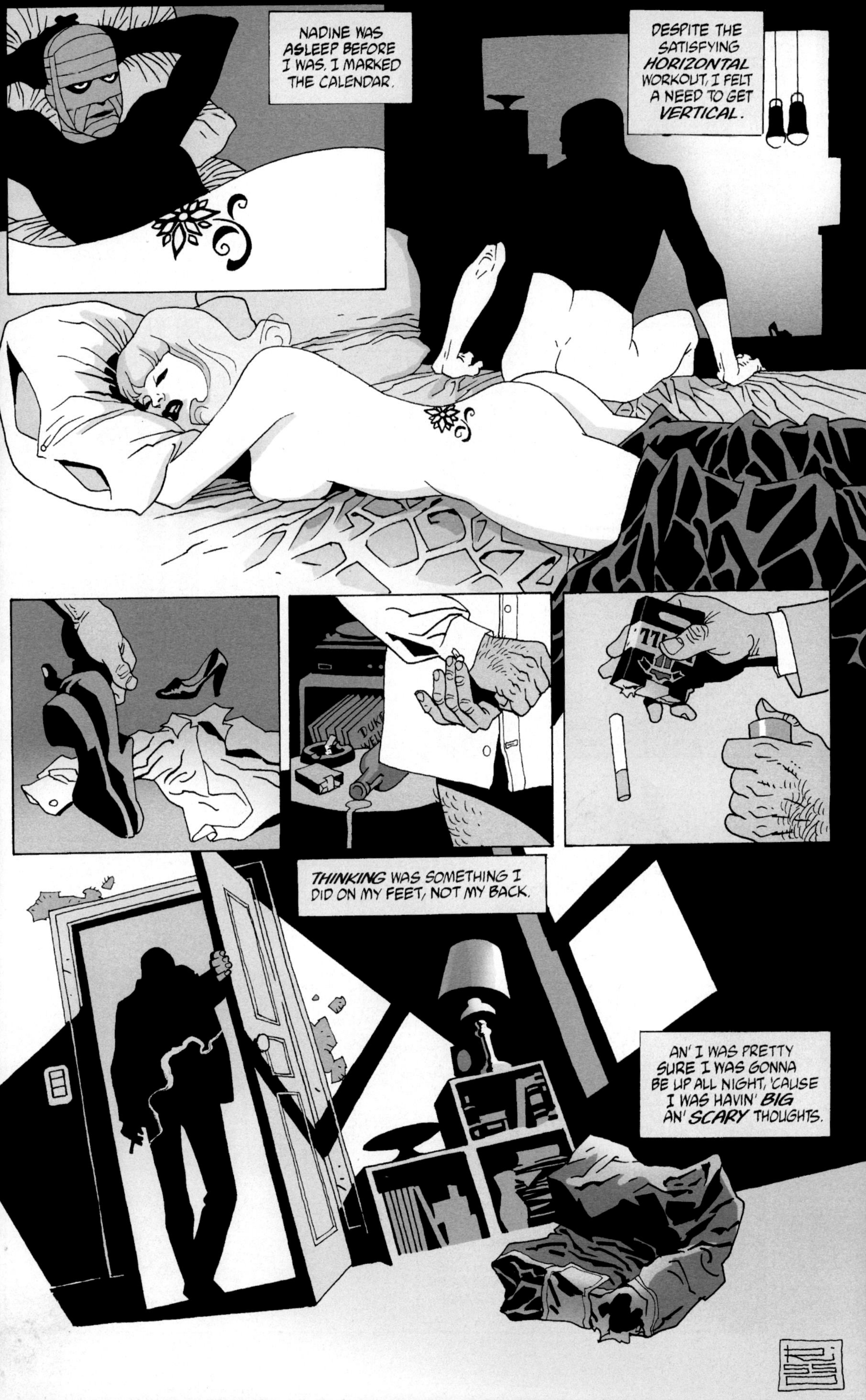
NADINE WAS ASLEEP BEFORE I WAS. I MARKED THE CALENDAR.
DESPITE THE SATISFYING HORIZONTAL WORKOUT, I FELT A NEED TO GET VERTICAL.
THINKING WAS SOMETHING I DID ON MY FEET, NOT MY BACK.
AN' I WAS PRETTY SURE I WAS GONNA BE UP ALL NIGHT, 'CAUSE I WAS HAVIN' BIG AN' SCARY THOUGHTS.

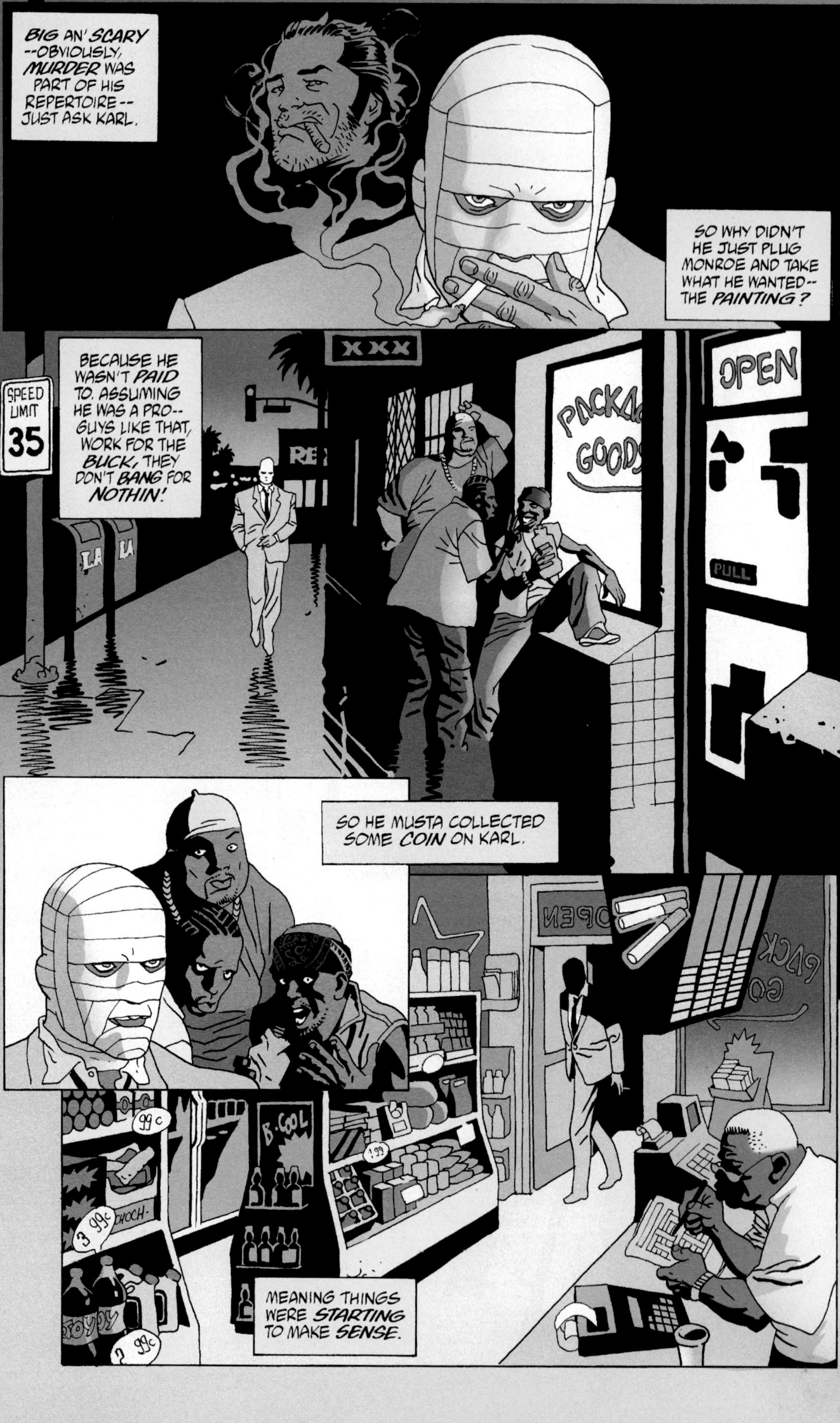
BIG AN' SCARY --OBVIOUSLY, MURDER WAS PART OF HIS REPERTOIRE -- JUST ASK KARL.
SO WHY DIDN'T HE JUST PLUG MONROE AND TAKE WHAT HE WANTED-- THE PAINTING?
XXX
SPEED LIMIT 35
BECAUSE HE WASN'T PAID TO. ASSUMING HE WAS A PRO-- GUYS LIKE THAT, WORK FOR THE BUCK, THEY DON'T BANG FOR NOTHIN'.
OPEN
PACKAG GOODS
PULL
SO HE MUSTA COLLECTED SOME COIN ON KARL.
99¢
B-COOL
1.99
MEANING THINGS WERE STARTING TO MAKE SENSE.

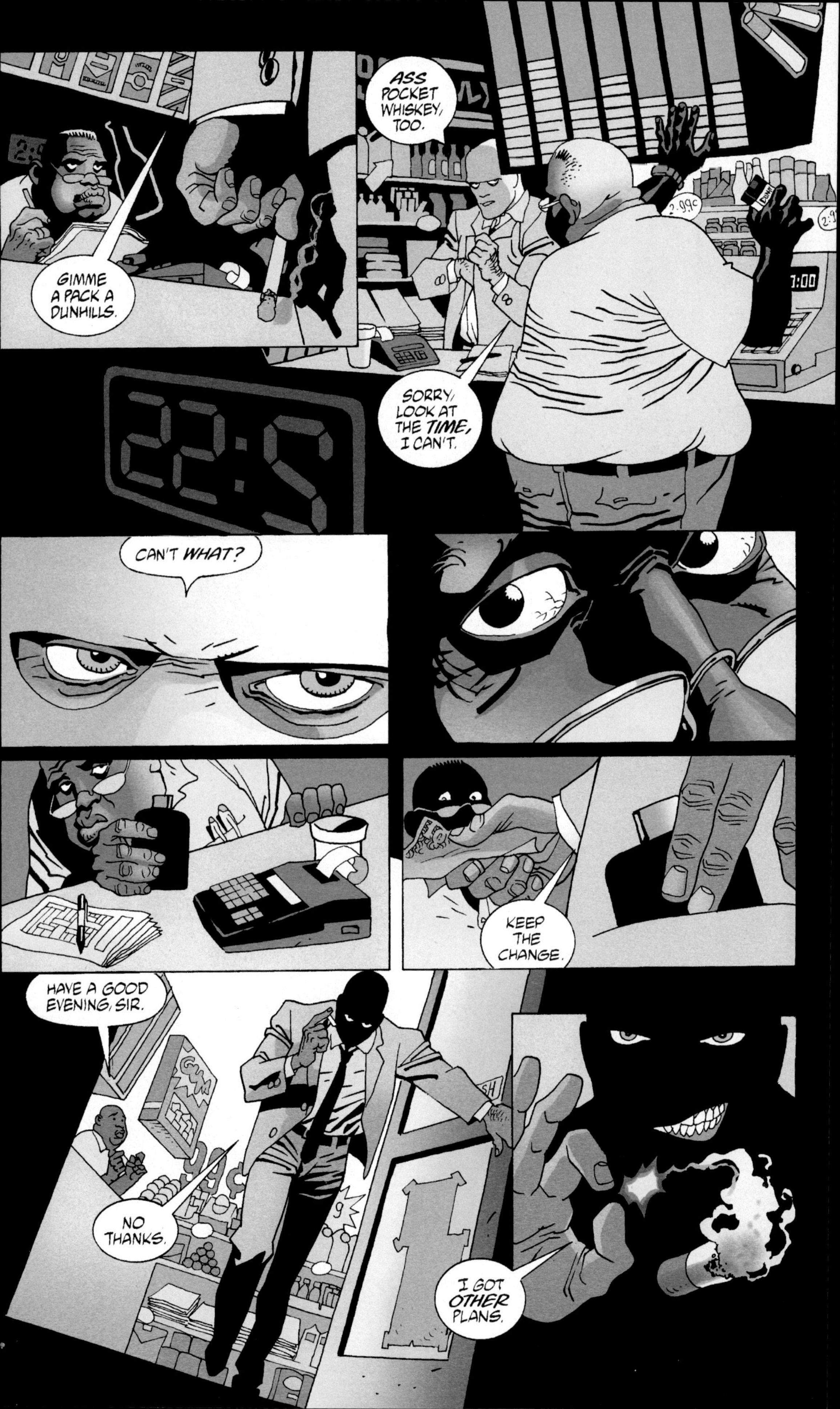
GIMME A PACK A DUNHILLS.
ASS POCKET WHISKEY, TOO.
SORRY, LOOK AT THE TIME, I CAN'T.
CAN'T WHAT?
KEEP THE CHANGE.
HAVE A GOOD EVENING, SIR.
NO THANKS.
I GOT OTHER PLANS.

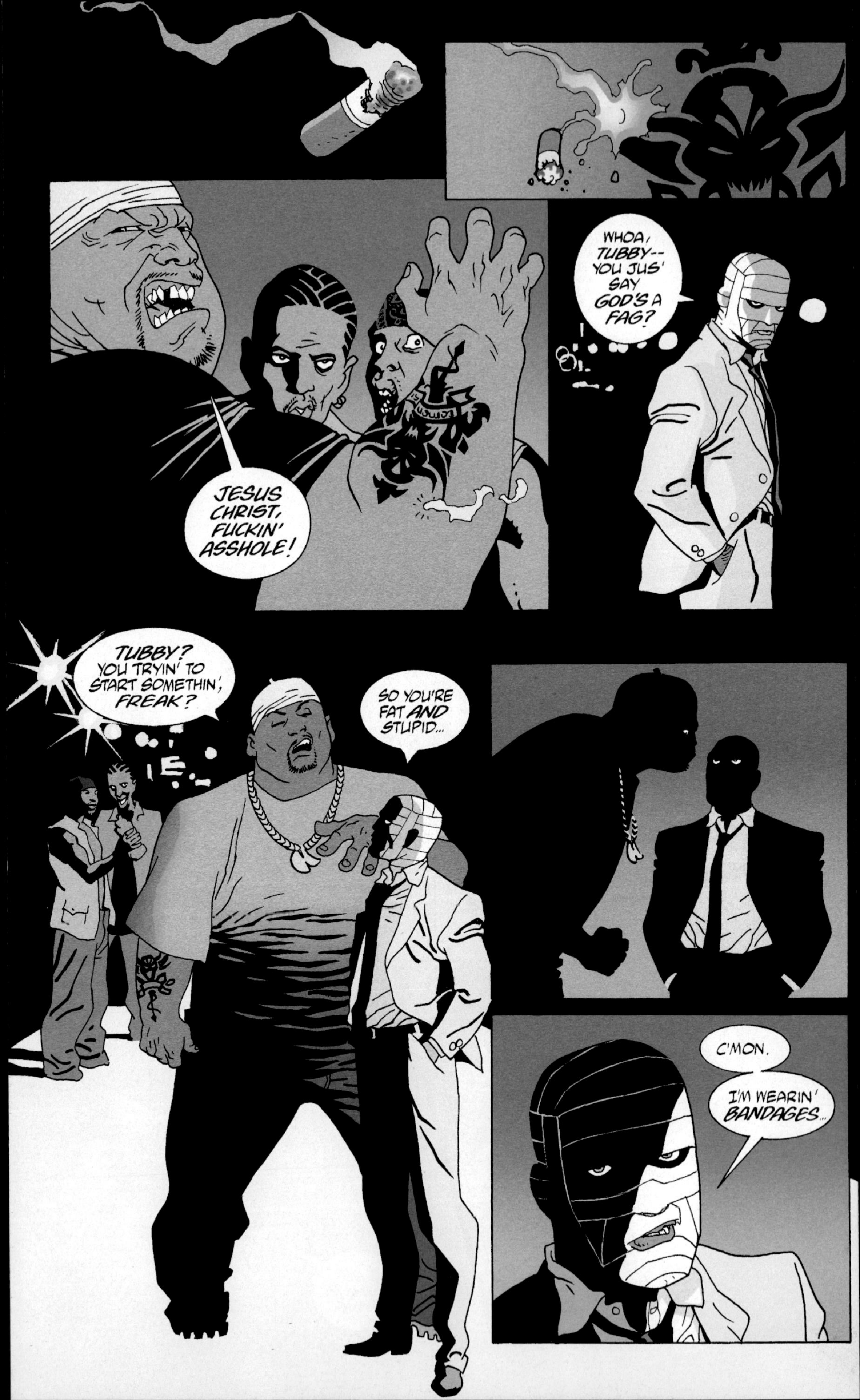

WHOA, TUBBY-- YOU JUS' SAY GOD'S A FAG?
JESUS CHRIST, FUCKIN' ASSHOLE!
TUBBY? YOU TRYIN' TO START SOMETHIN', FREAK?
SO YOU'RE FAT AND STUPID...
C'MON.
I'M WEARIN' BANDAGES...

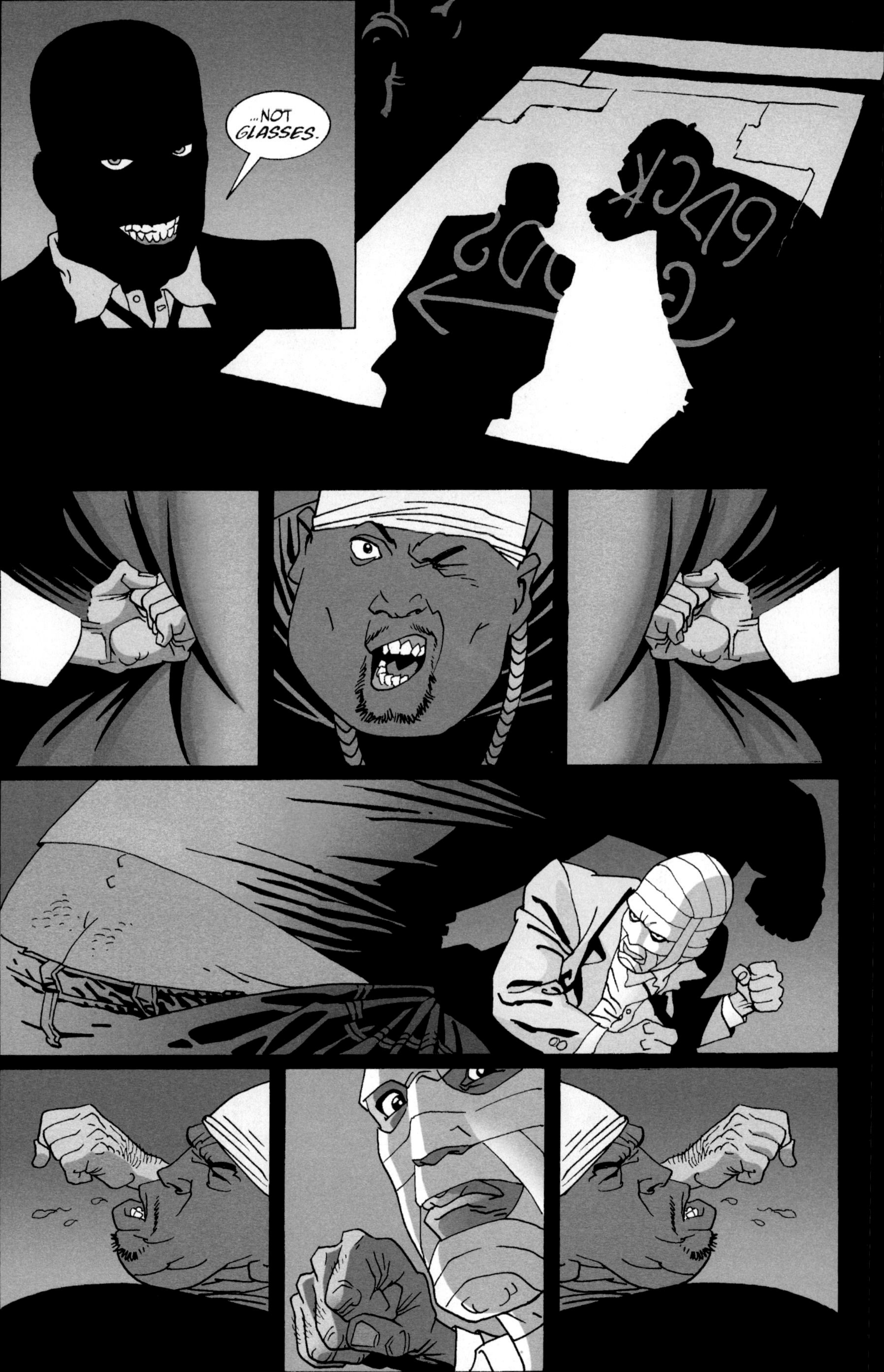
...NOT GLASSES.

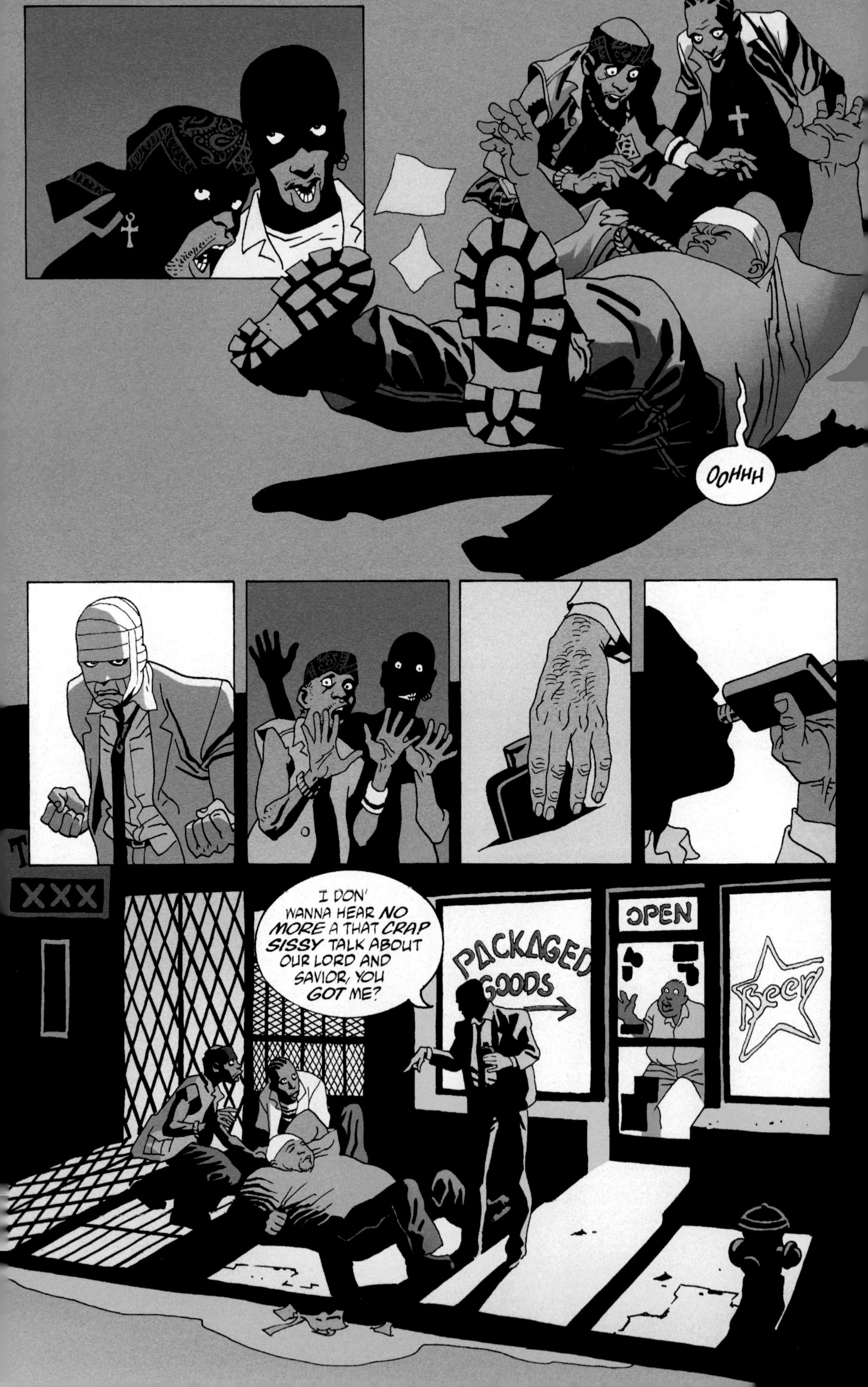
OOHHH
XXX
I DON' WANNA HEAR NO MORE A THAT CRAP SISSY TALK ABOUT OUR LORD AND SAVIOR, YOU GOT ME?
OPEN
PACKAGED GOODS
Beer

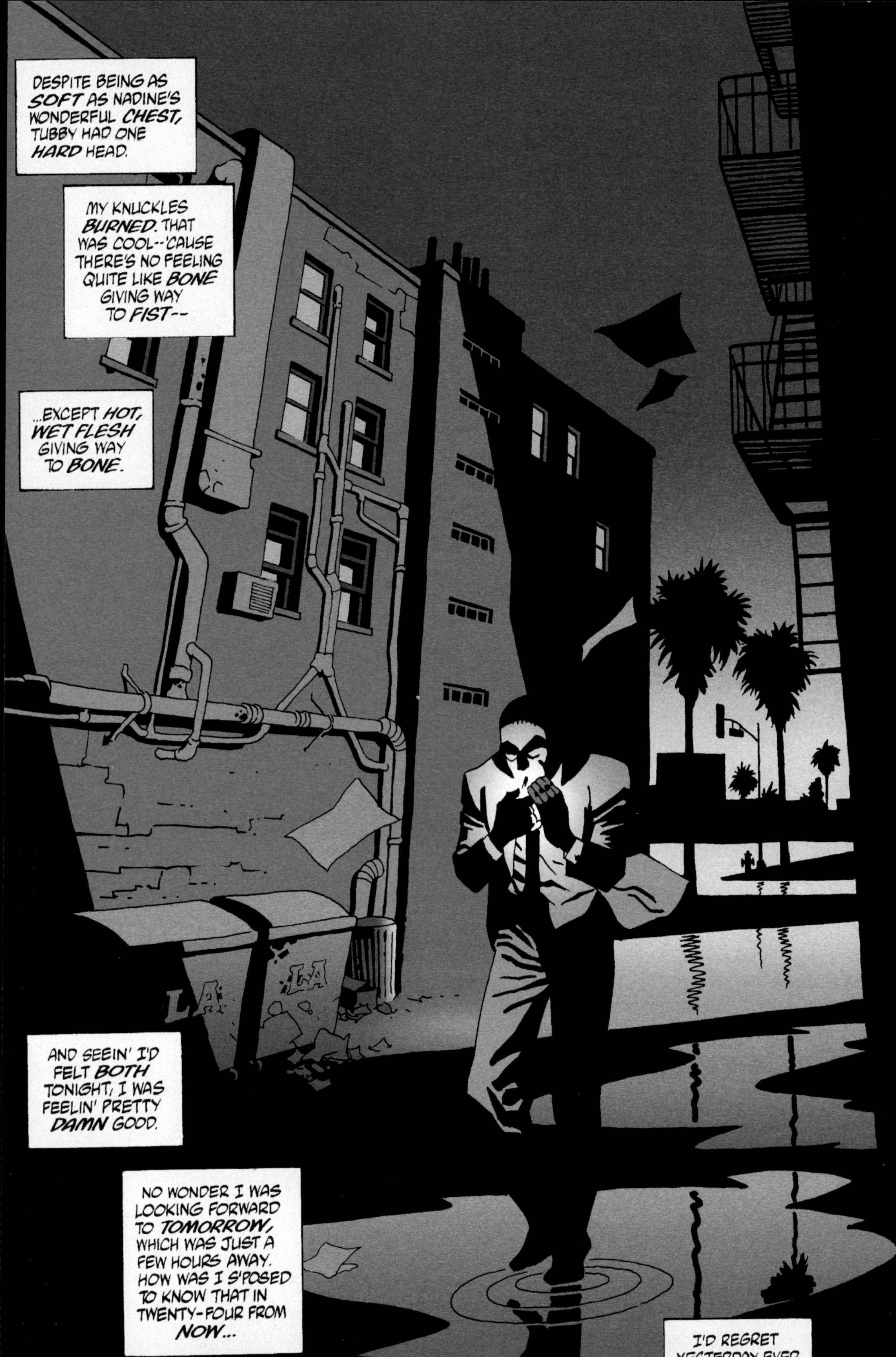
DESPITE BEING AS SOFT AS NADINE'S WONDERFUL CHEST, TUBBY HAD ONE HARD HEAD.
MY KNUCKLES BURNED. THAT WAS COOL--'CAUSE THERE'S NO FEELING QUITE LIKE BONE GIVING WAY TO FIST--
...EXCEPT HOT, WET FLESH GIVING WAY TO BONE.
LA
LA
AND SEEIN' I'D FELT BOTH TONIGHT, I WAS FEELIN' PRETTY DAMN GOOD.
NO WONDER I WAS LOOKING FORWARD TO TOMORROW, WHICH WAS JUST A FEW HOURS AWAY. HOW WAS I S'POSED TO KNOW THAT IN TWENTY-FOUR FROM NOW...
I'D REGRET

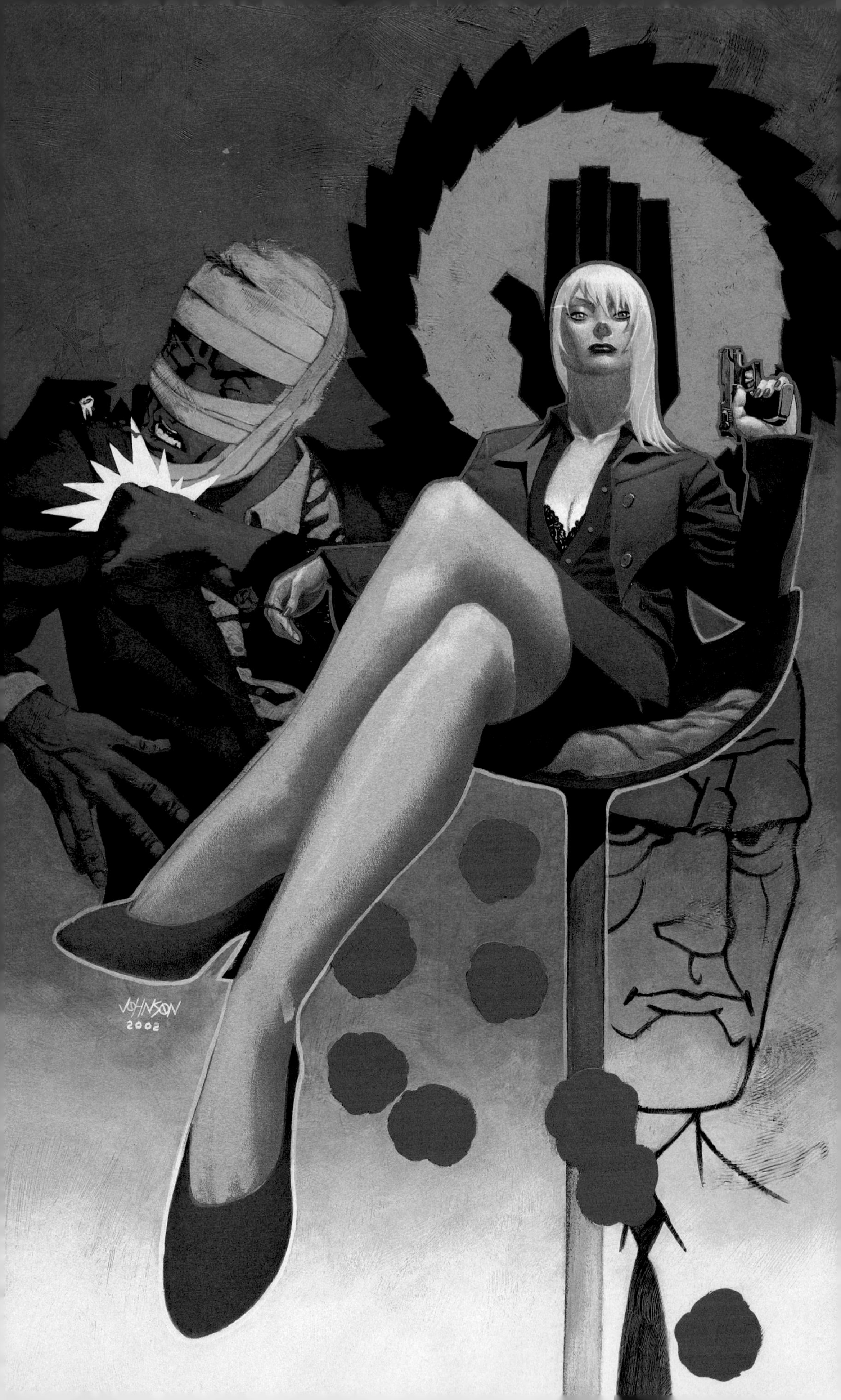
JOHNSON
2002

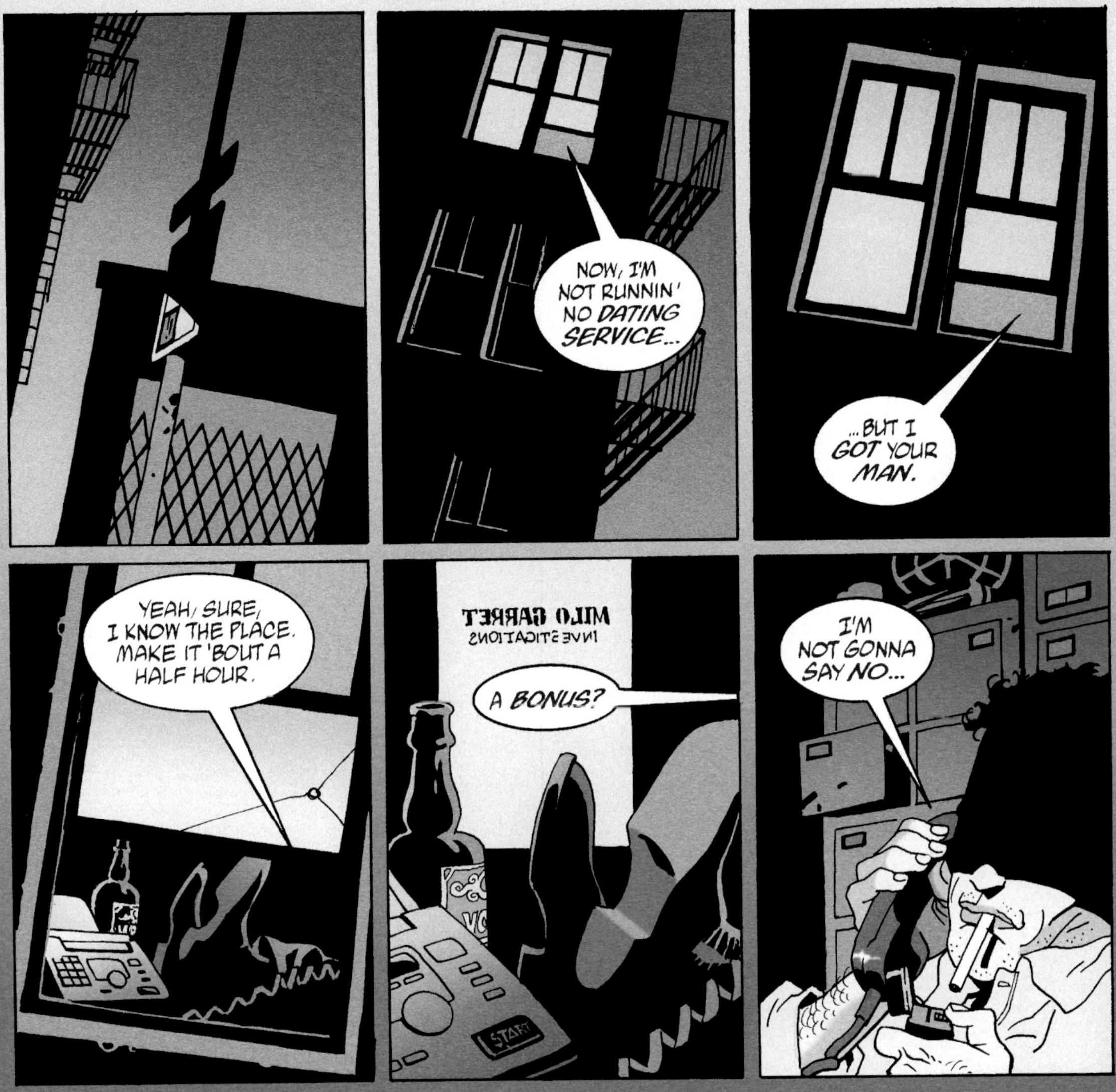
NOW, I'M NOT RUNNIN' NO DATING SERVICE...
...BUT I GOT YOUR MAN.
YEAH, SURE, I KNOW THE PLACE. MAKE IT 'BOUT A HALF HOUR.
MILO GARRET INVESTIGATIONS
A BONUS?
START
I'M NOT GONNA SAY NO...

THE COUNTERFIFTH DETECTIVE PART 3

BRIAN AZZARELLO writer
EDUARDO RISSO artist
PATRICIA MULVIHILL colorist
CLEM ROBINS letterer
DIGITAL CHAMELEON separations
DAVE JOHNSON cover artist
ZACHARY RAU ass't ed.
WILL DENNIS editor

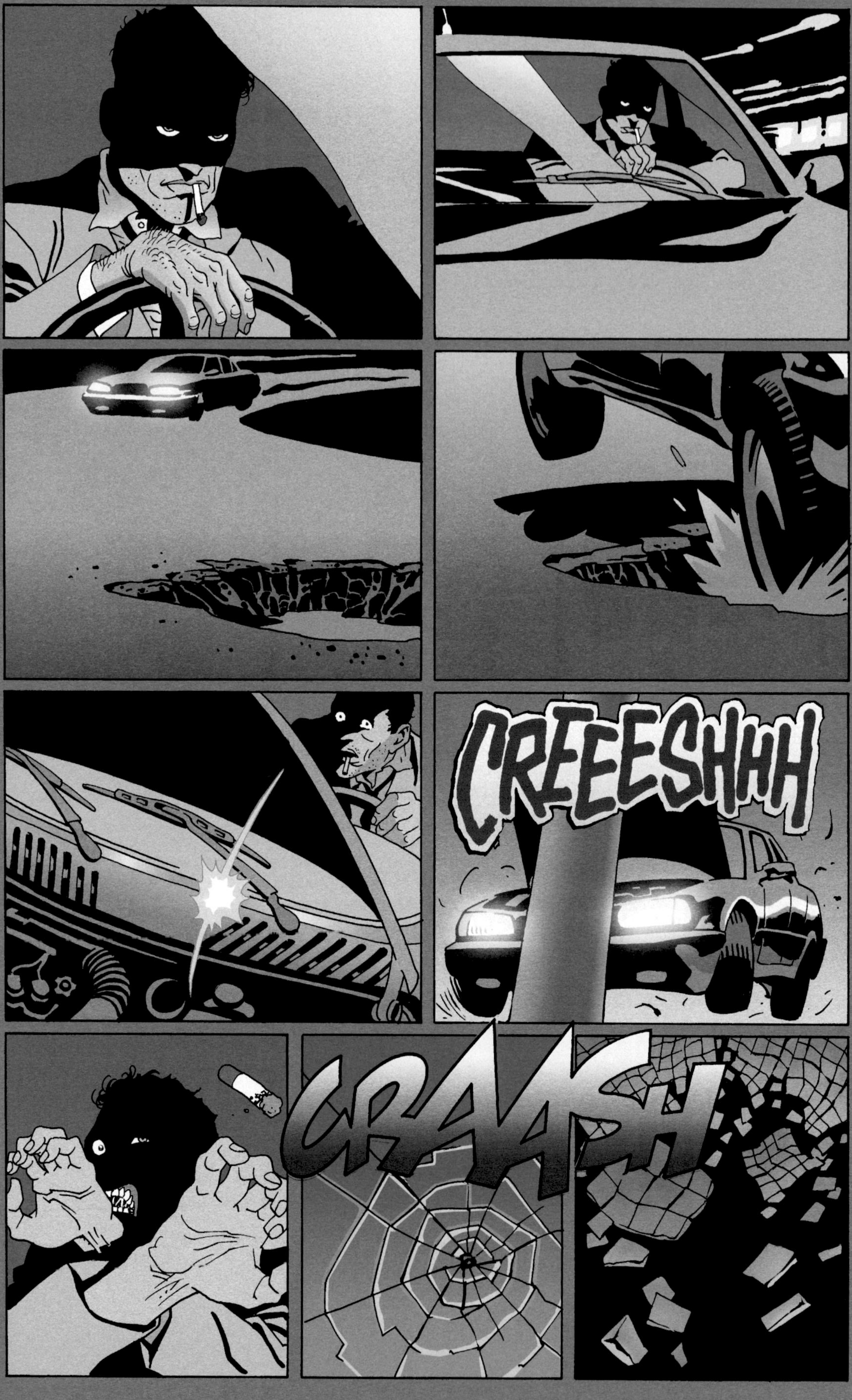
CREEESHHH
CRAASH

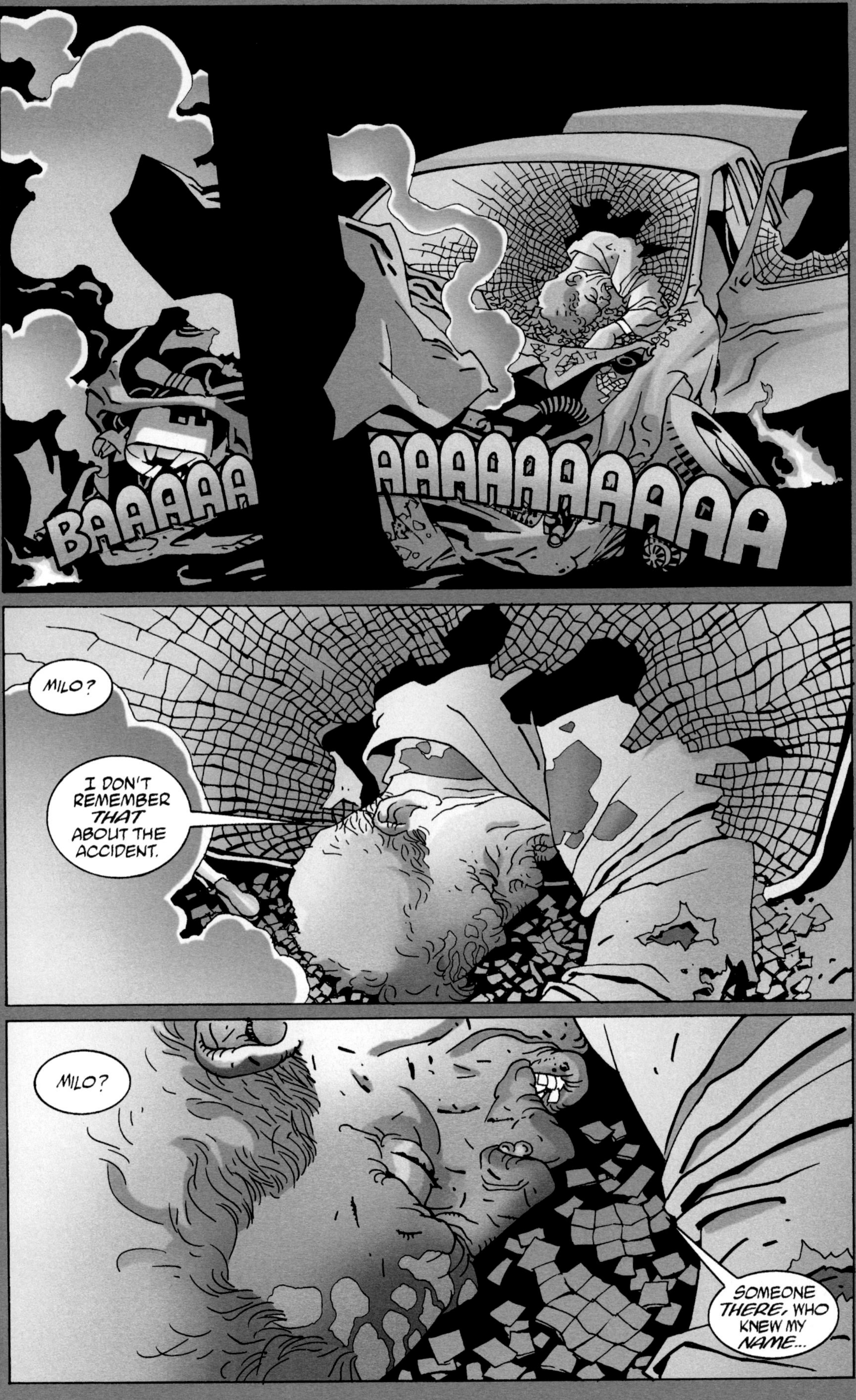
BAAAAAAAAAAAAAAAAAA
MILO?
I DON'T REMEMBER THAT ABOUT THE ACCIDENT.
MILO?
SOMEONE THERE, WHO KNEW MY NAME...

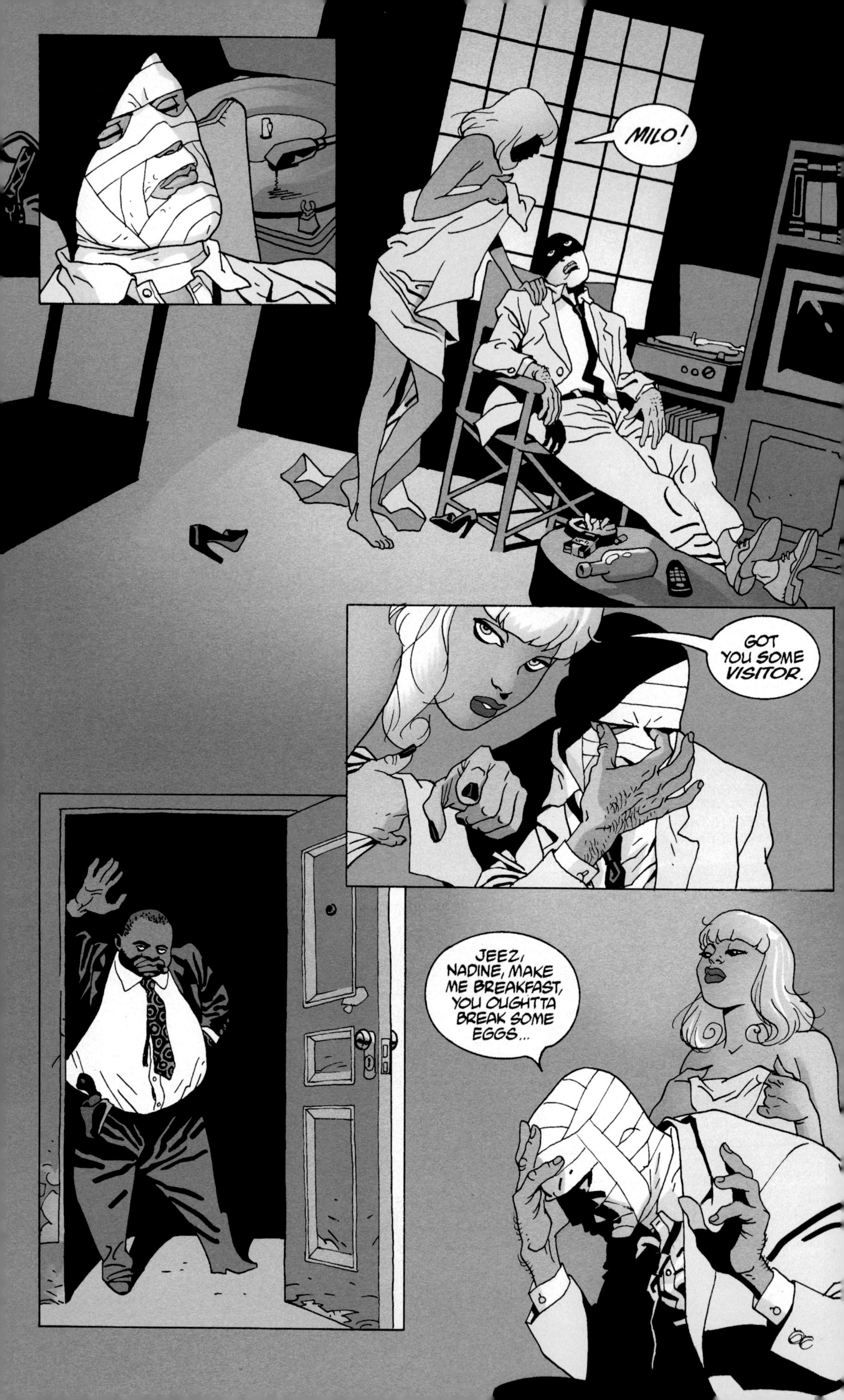
MILO!
GOT YOU SOME VISITOR.
JEEZ, NADINE, MAKE ME BREAKFAST, YOU OUGHTTA BREAK SOME EGGS...

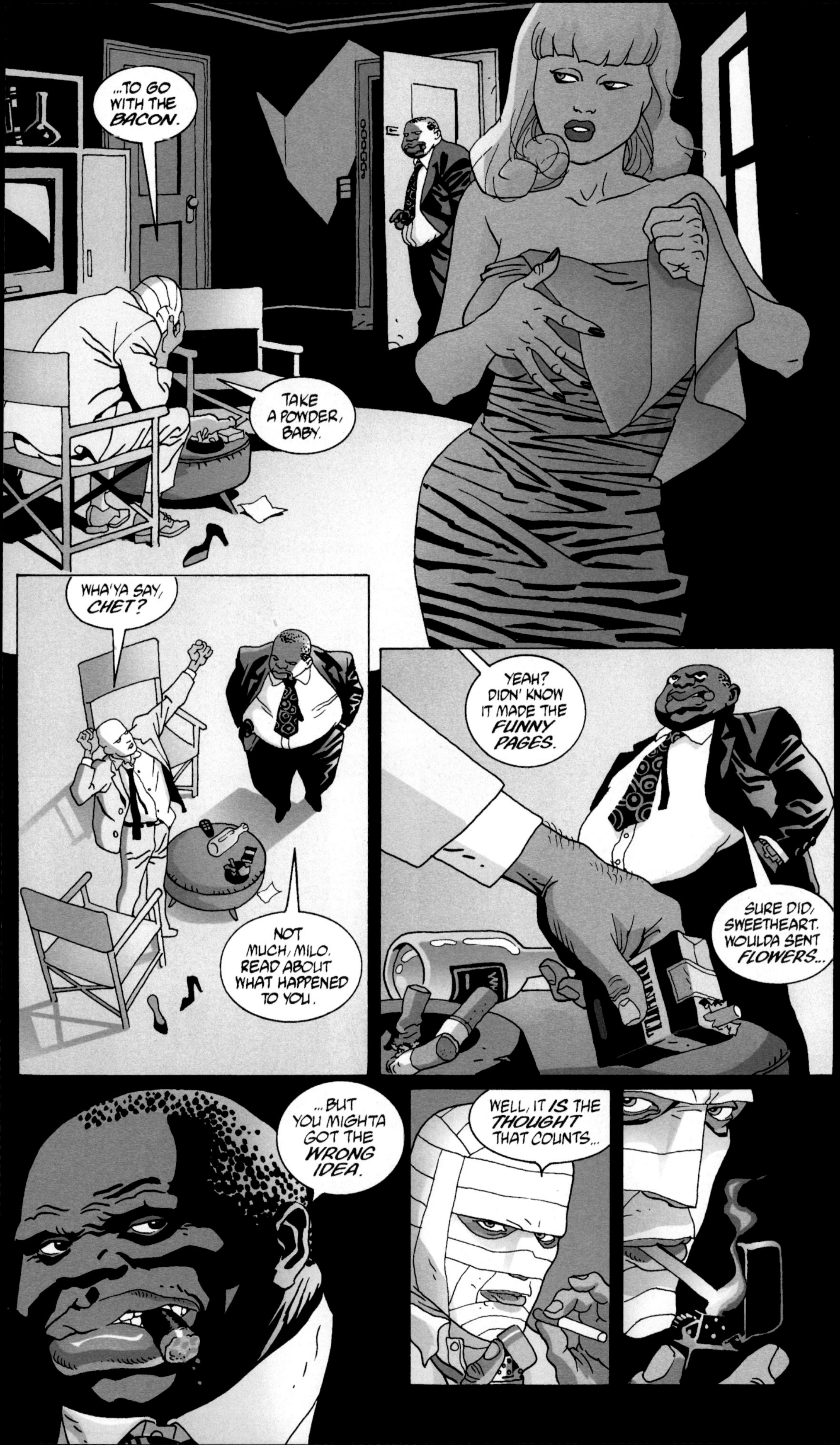
...TO GO WITH THE BACON.
TAKE A POWDER, BABY.
WHA'YA SAY, CHET?
NOT MUCH, MILO. READ ABOUT WHAT HAPPENED TO YOU.
YEAH? DIDN' KNOW IT MADE THE FUNNY PAGES.
SURE DID, SWEETHEART. WOULDA SENT FLOWERS...
...BUT YOU MIGHTA GOT THE WRONG IDEA.
WELL, IT IS THE THOUGHT THAT COUNTS...

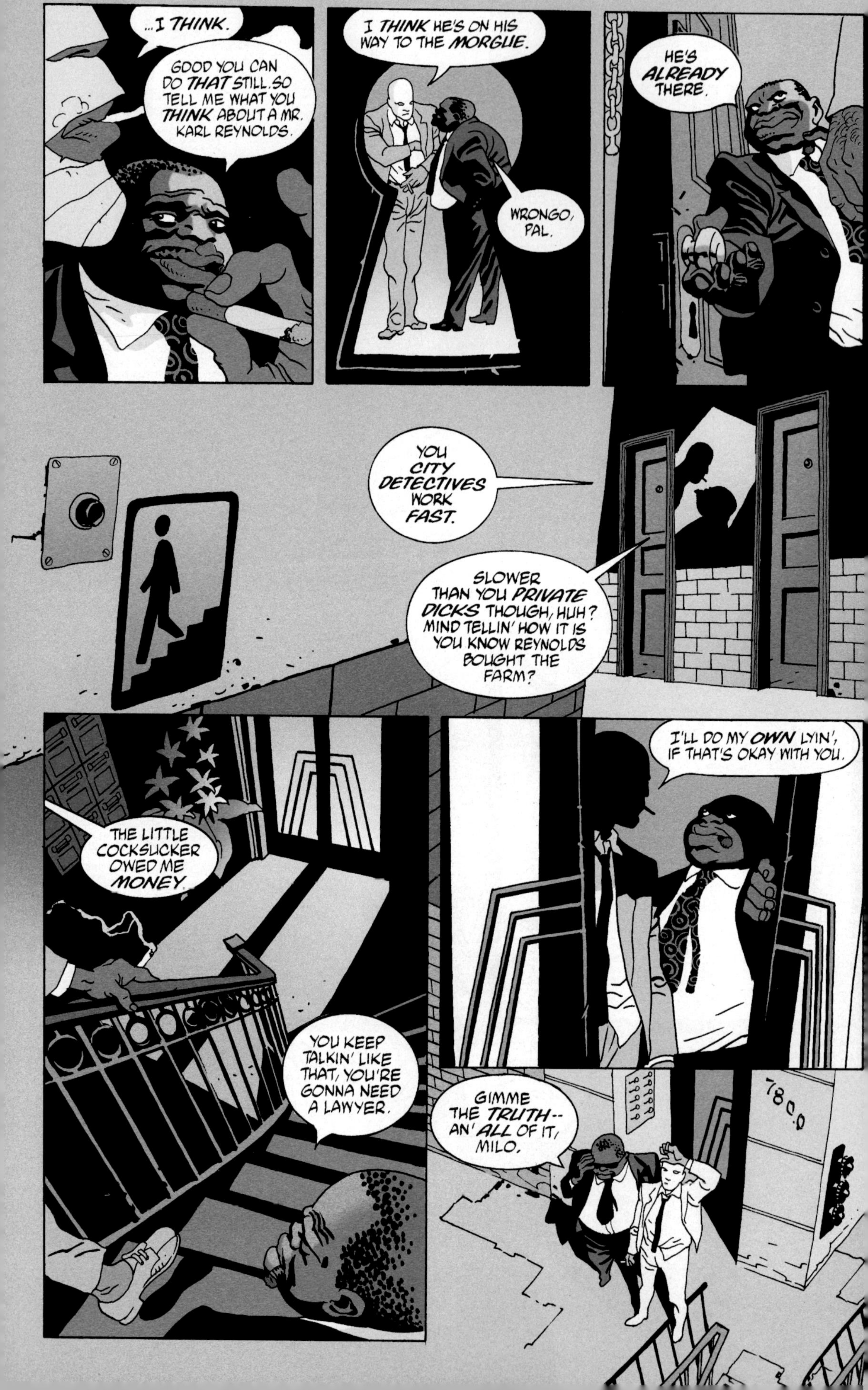
...I THINK.
GOOD YOU CAN DO THAT STILL. SO TELL ME WHAT YOU THINK ABOUT A MR. KARL REYNOLDS.
I THINK HE'S ON HIS WAY TO THE MORGUE.
WRONGO, PAL.
HE'S ALREADY THERE.
YOU CITY DETECTIVES WORK FAST.
SLOWER THAN YOU PRIVATE DICKS THOUGH, HUH? MIND TELLIN' HOW IT IS YOU KNOW REYNOLDS BOUGHT THE FARM?
THE LITTLE COCKSUCKER OWED ME MONEY.
YOU KEEP TALKIN' LIKE THAT, YOU'RE GONNA NEED A LAWYER.
I'LL DO MY OWN LYIN', IF THAT'S OKAY WITH YOU.
GIMME THE TRUTH-- AN' ALL OF IT, MILO.
7800

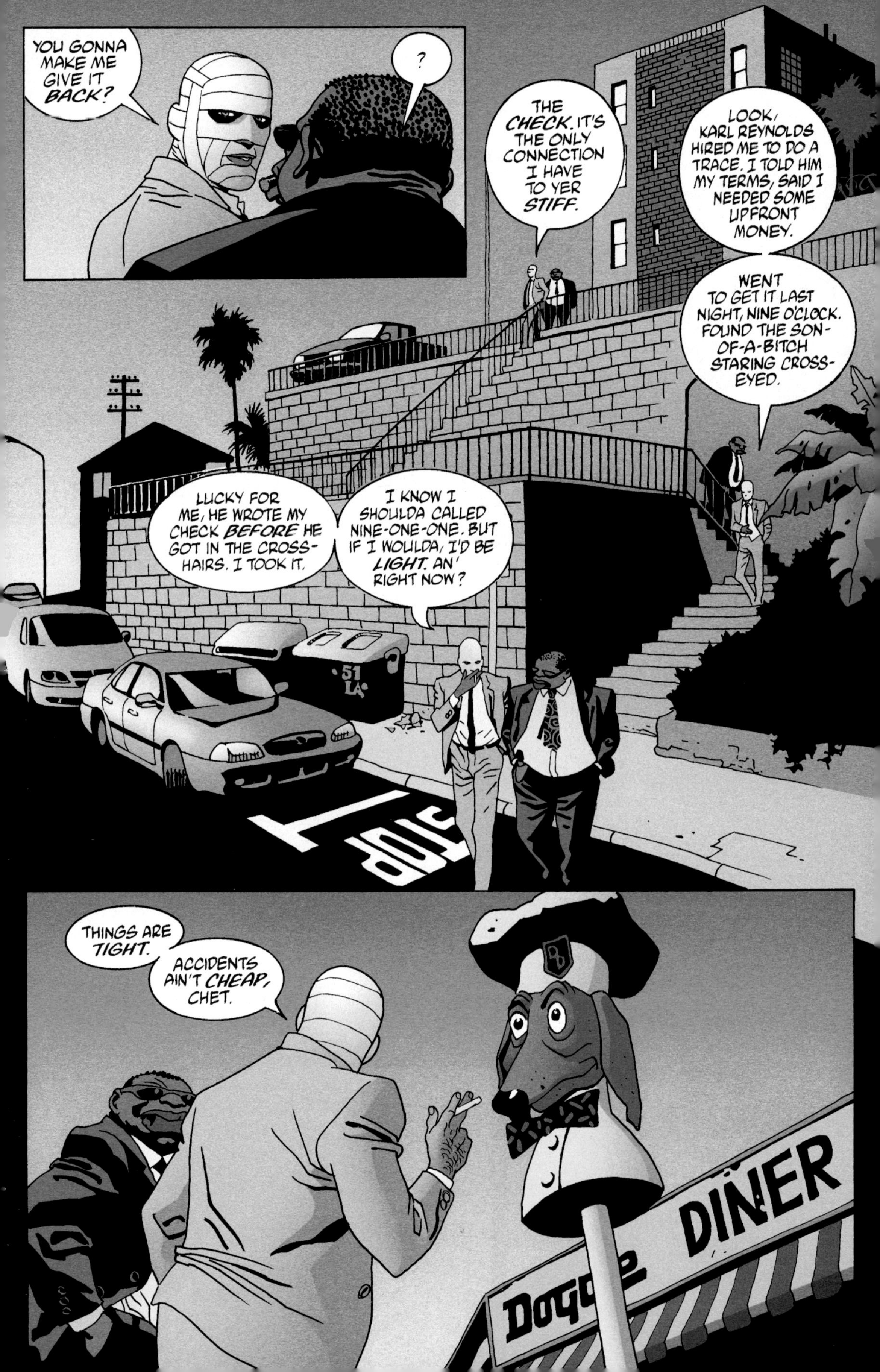

YOU GONNA MAKE ME GIVE IT *BACK?*
?
THE *CHECK*. IT'S THE ONLY CONNECTION I HAVE TO YER *STIFF*.
LOOK, KARL REYNOLDS HIRED ME TO DO A TRACE. I TOLD HIM MY TERMS, SAID I NEEDED SOME UPFRONT MONEY.
WENT TO GET IT LAST NIGHT, NINE O'CLOCK. FOUND THE SON-OF-A-BITCH STARING CROSS-EYED.
LUCKY FOR ME, HE WROTE MY CHECK *BEFORE* HE GOT IN THE CROSS-HAIRS. I TOOK IT.
I KNOW I SHOULDA CALLED NINE-ONE-ONE. BUT IF I WOULDA, I'D BE *LIGHT*. AN' RIGHT NOW?
51 LA
STOP
THINGS ARE *TIGHT*.
ACCIDENTS AIN'T *CHEAP*, CHET.
DB
DINER

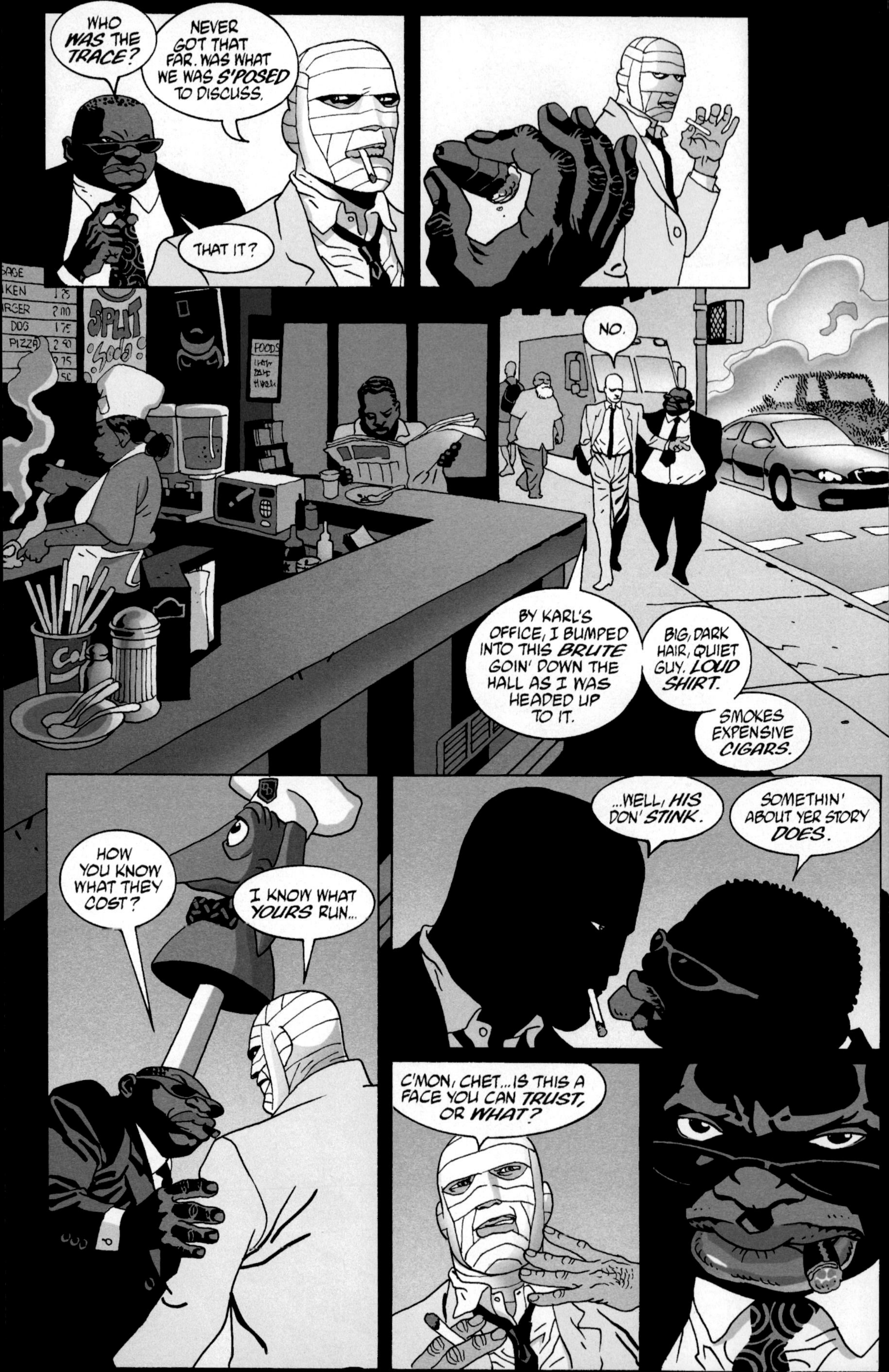
WHO WAS THE TRACE?
NEVER GOT THAT FAR. WAS WHAT WE WAS S'POSED TO DISCUSS.
THAT IT?
NO.
BY KARL'S OFFICE, I BUMPED INTO THIS BRUTE GOIN' DOWN THE HALL AS I WAS HEADED UP TO IT.
BIG, DARK HAIR, QUIET GUY. LOUD SHIRT.
SMOKES EXPENSIVE CIGARS.
HOW YOU KNOW WHAT THEY COST?
I KNOW WHAT YOURS RUN...
...WELL, HIS DON' STINK.
SOMETHIN' ABOUT YER STORY DOES.
C'MON, CHET... IS THIS A FACE YOU CAN TRUST, OR WHAT?

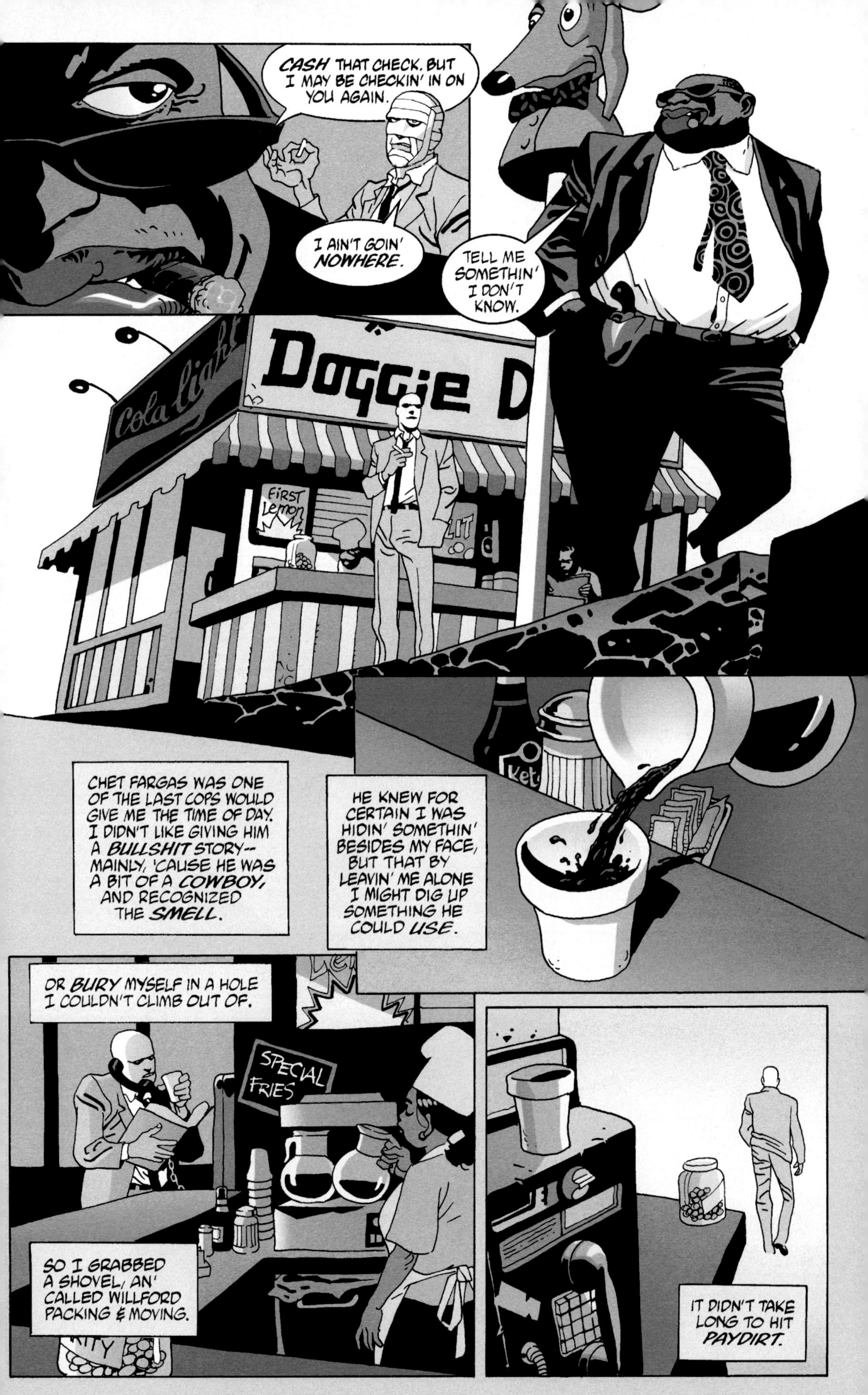
CASH THAT CHECK. BUT I MAY BE CHECKIN' IN ON YOU AGAIN.
I AIN'T GOIN' NOWHERE.
TELL ME SOMETHIN' I DON'T KNOW.
Doggie D
Cola light
First Lemon
CHET FARGAS WAS ONE OF THE LAST COPS WOULD GIVE ME THE TIME OF DAY. I DIDN'T LIKE GIVING HIM A BULLSHIT STORY-- MAINLY, 'CAUSE HE WAS A BIT OF A COWBOY, AND RECOGNIZED THE SMELL.
HE KNEW FOR CERTAIN I WAS HIDIN' SOMETHIN' BESIDES MY FACE, BUT THAT BY LEAVIN' ME ALONE I MIGHT DIG UP SOMETHING HE COULD USE.
OR BURY MYSELF IN A HOLE I COULDN'T CLIMB OUT OF.
SPECIAL FRIES
SO I GRABBED A SHOVEL, AN' CALLED WILLFORD PACKING & MOVING.
IT DIDN'T TAKE LONG TO HIT PAYDIRT.

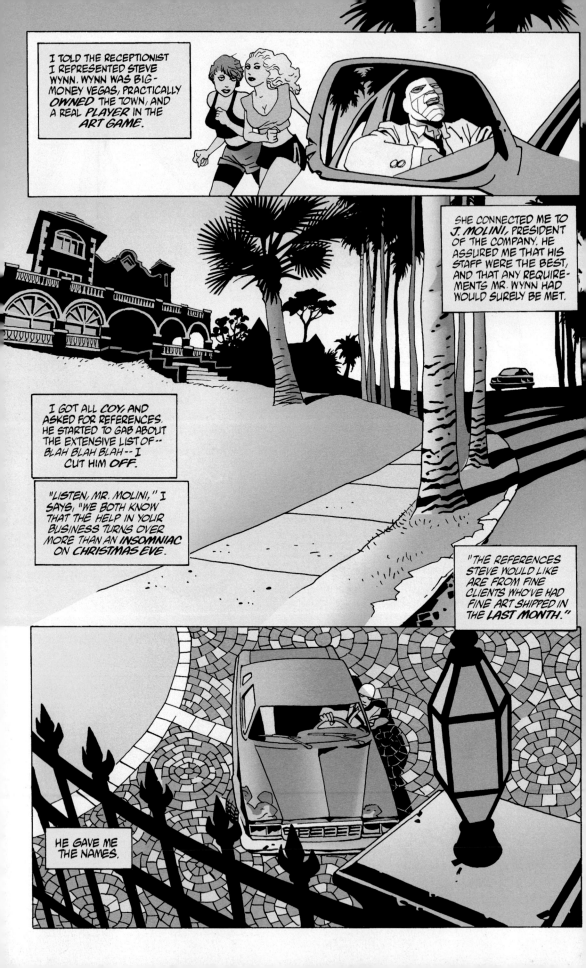

I TOLD THE RECEPTIONIST I REPRESENTED STEVE WYNN. WYNN WAS BIG-MONEY VEGAS, PRACTICALLY *OWNED* THE TOWN, AND A REAL *PLAYER* IN THE *ART GAME.*

SHE CONNECTED ME TO *J. MOLINI,* PRESIDENT OF THE COMPANY. HE ASSURED ME THAT HIS STAFF WERE THE BEST, AND THAT ANY REQUIRE-MENTS MR. WYNN HAD WOULD SURELY BE MET.

I GOT ALL *COY,* AND ASKED FOR REFERENCES. HE STARTED TO GAB ABOUT THE EXTENSIVE LIST OF-- BLAH BLAH BLAH-- I CUT HIM *OFF.*

"LISTEN, MR. MOLINI," I SAYS, *"WE BOTH KNOW THAT THE HELP IN YOUR BUSINESS TURNS OVER MORE THAN AN INSOMNIAC ON CHRISTMAS EVE.*

"THE REFERENCES STEVE WOULD LIKE ARE FROM FINE CLIENTS WHO'VE HAD FINE ART SHIPPED IN THE LAST MONTH."

HE GAVE ME THE NAMES.

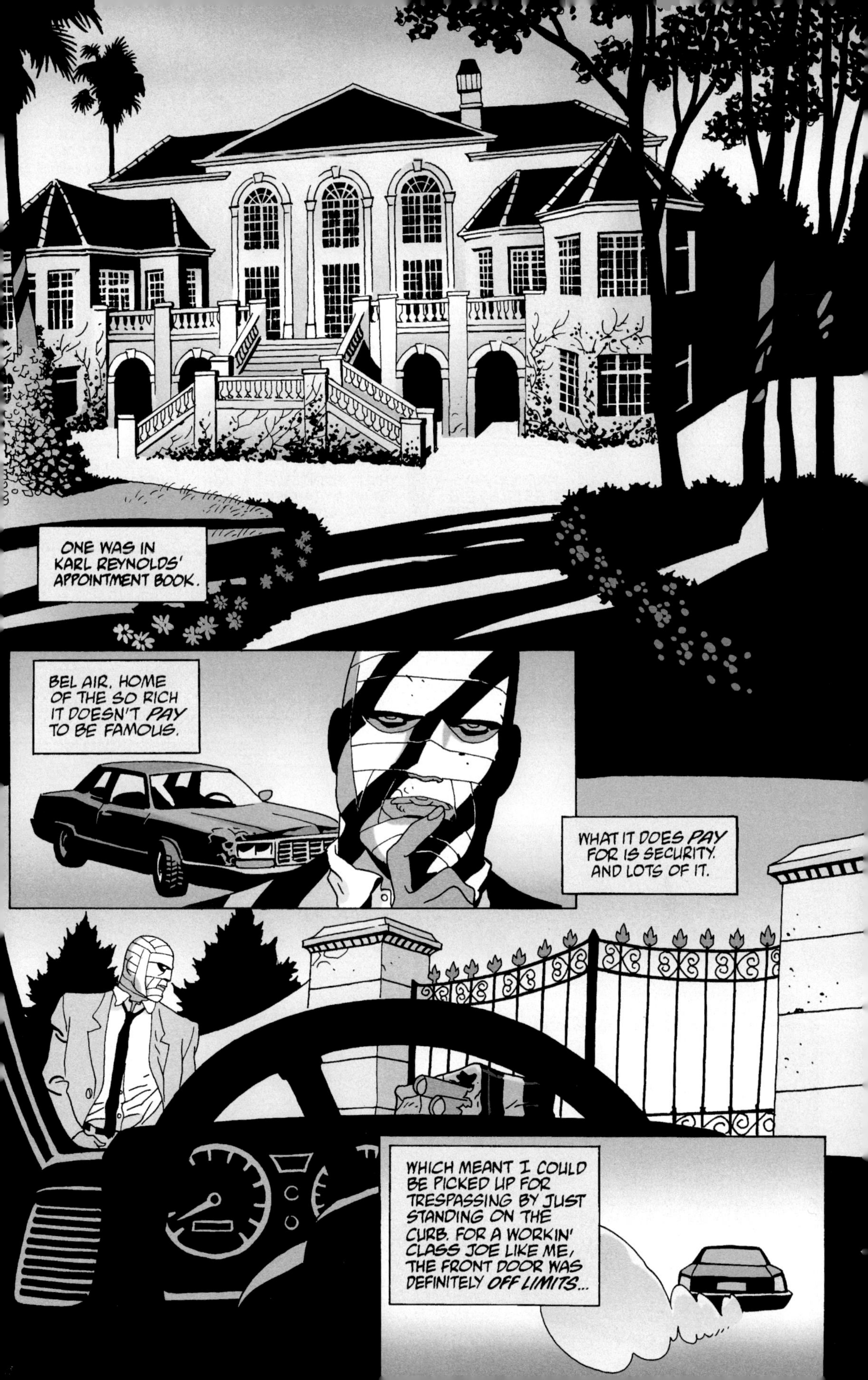
ONE WAS IN KARL REYNOLDS' APPOINTMENT BOOK.
BEL AIR. HOME OF THE SO RICH IT DOESN'T PAY TO BE FAMOUS.
WHAT IT DOES PAY FOR IS SECURITY. AND LOTS OF IT.
WHICH MEANT I COULD BE PICKED UP FOR TRESPASSING BY JUST STANDING ON THE CURB. FOR A WORKIN' CLASS JOE LIKE ME, THE FRONT DOOR WAS DEFINITELY OFF LIMITS...

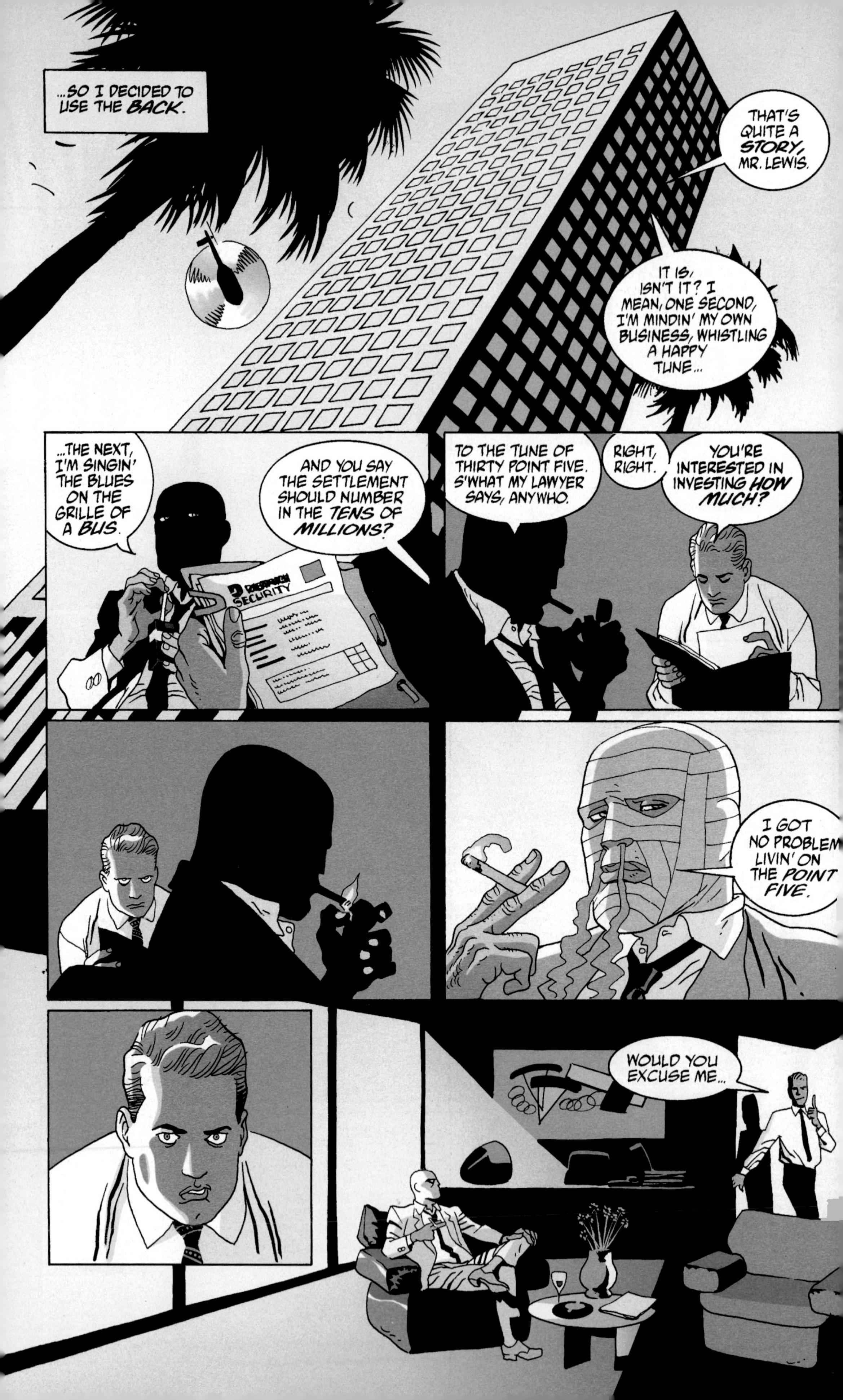
...SO I DECIDED TO USE THE BACK.
THAT'S QUITE A STORY, MR. LEWIS.
IT IS, ISN'T IT? I MEAN, ONE SECOND, I'M MINDIN' MY OWN BUSINESS, WHISTLING A HAPPY TUNE...
...THE NEXT, I'M SINGIN' THE BLUES ON THE GRILLE OF A BUS.
AND YOU SAY THE SETTLEMENT SHOULD NUMBER IN THE TENS OF MILLIONS?
SECURITY
TO THE TUNE OF THIRTY POINT FIVE. S'WHAT MY LAWYER SAYS, ANYWHO.
RIGHT, RIGHT.
YOU'RE INTERESTED IN INVESTING HOW MUCH?
I GOT NO PROBLEM LIVIN' ON THE POINT FIVE.
WOULD YOU EXCUSE ME...

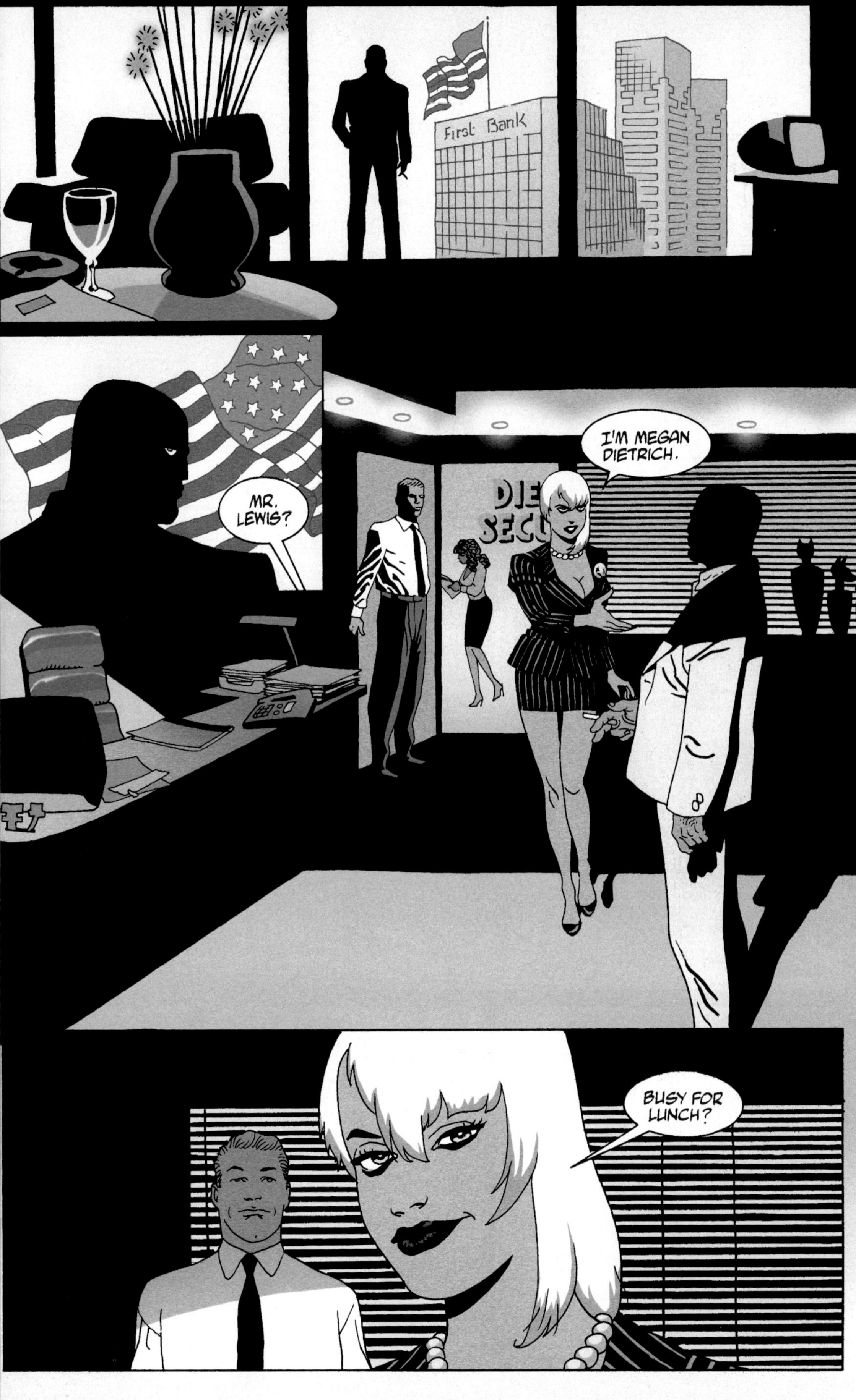
First Bank
MR. LEWIS?
I'M MEGAN DIETRICH.
BUSY FOR LUNCH?

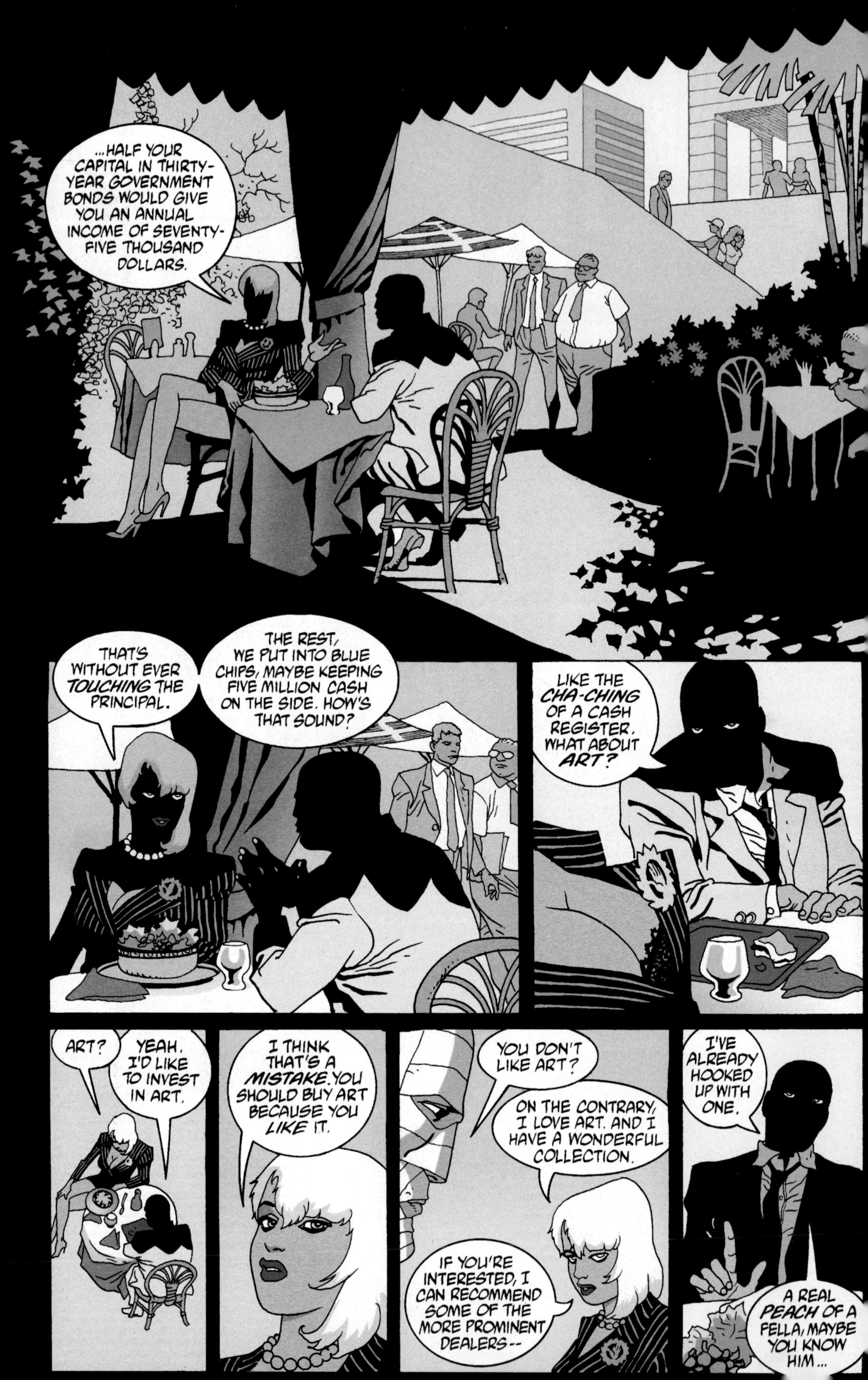
...HALF YOUR CAPITAL IN THIRTY-YEAR GOVERNMENT BONDS WOULD GIVE YOU AN ANNUAL INCOME OF SEVENTY-FIVE THOUSAND DOLLARS.
THAT'S WITHOUT EVER TOUCHING THE PRINCIPAL.
THE REST, WE PUT INTO BLUE CHIPS, MAYBE KEEPING FIVE MILLION CASH ON THE SIDE. HOW'S THAT SOUND?
LIKE THE CHA-CHING OF A CASH REGISTER. WHAT ABOUT ART?
ART?
YEAH. I'D LIKE TO INVEST IN ART.
I THINK THAT'S A MISTAKE. YOU SHOULD BUY ART BECAUSE YOU LIKE IT.
YOU DON'T LIKE ART?
ON THE CONTRARY, I LOVE ART. AND I HAVE A WONDERFUL COLLECTION.
IF YOU'RE INTERESTED, I CAN RECOMMEND SOME OF THE MORE PROMINENT DEALERS--
I'VE ALREADY HOOKED UP WITH ONE.
A REAL PEACH OF A FELLA, MAYBE YOU KNOW HIM...

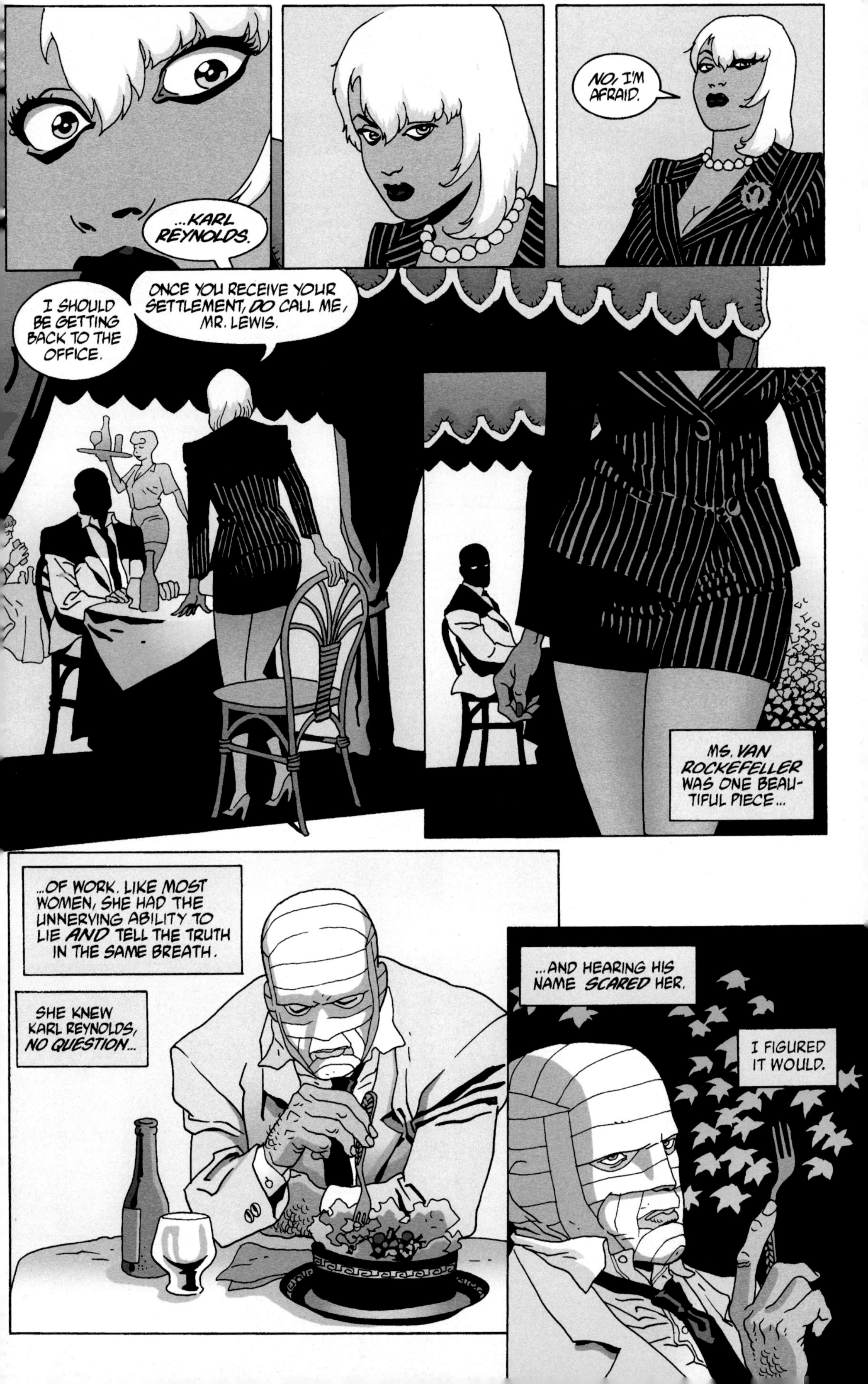
...KARL REYNOLDS.
NO, I'M AFRAID.
I SHOULD BE GETTING BACK TO THE OFFICE.
ONCE YOU RECEIVE YOUR SETTLEMENT, DO CALL ME, MR. LEWIS.
MS. VAN ROCKEFELLER WAS ONE BEAUTIFUL PIECE...
...OF WORK. LIKE MOST WOMEN, SHE HAD THE UNNERVING ABILITY TO LIE AND TELL THE TRUTH IN THE SAME BREATH.
SHE KNEW KARL REYNOLDS, NO QUESTION...
...AND HEARING HIS NAME SCARED HER.
I FIGURED IT WOULD.

WAY I SAW IT? LITTLE MISS RICHIE RICH DIETRICH--THOUGH SHE HAD A *BRICK SHIT HOUSE* OF A *FRONT*-- WAS *BEHIND* EVERYTHING.

SHE'D CONTACTED KARL REYNOLDS ABOUT A PAINTING SHE WANTED TO GET HER HANDS ON.

WHEN NANCY-BOY KARL FOUND OUT IT WASN'T UP FOR *GRABS*, HE THUMBED A RIDE OVER BY MONROE TANNENBAUM, WHO *FIVE-FINGERED* IT FOR HIM.

FELLAS LIKE KARL-- WANNABE *HIGH STEPPERS*-- LOVE NOTHING MORE THAN GABBIN' ABOUT THEIR *LOW LIFE* CONNECTIONS.

SO MEGAN GETS WIND OF KARL'S HOT AIR, AND SENDS *BIG AND SCARY* TO MAKE THE DEAL WITH MONROE. HE PUTS THE SQUEEZE ON, AND MONROE CHOKES UP THE PAINTING, WHICH LEAVES KARL OUT FLAPPIN' IN THE BREEZE.

MAKES DOLLARS AND SENSE.

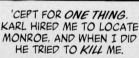

'CEPT FOR *ONE THING*. KARL HIRED ME TO LOCATE MONROE, AND WHEN I DID HE TRIED TO *KILL* ME.

A THROUGH *X* I GOT.

THAT LEFT ME STUCK AT *WHY*...

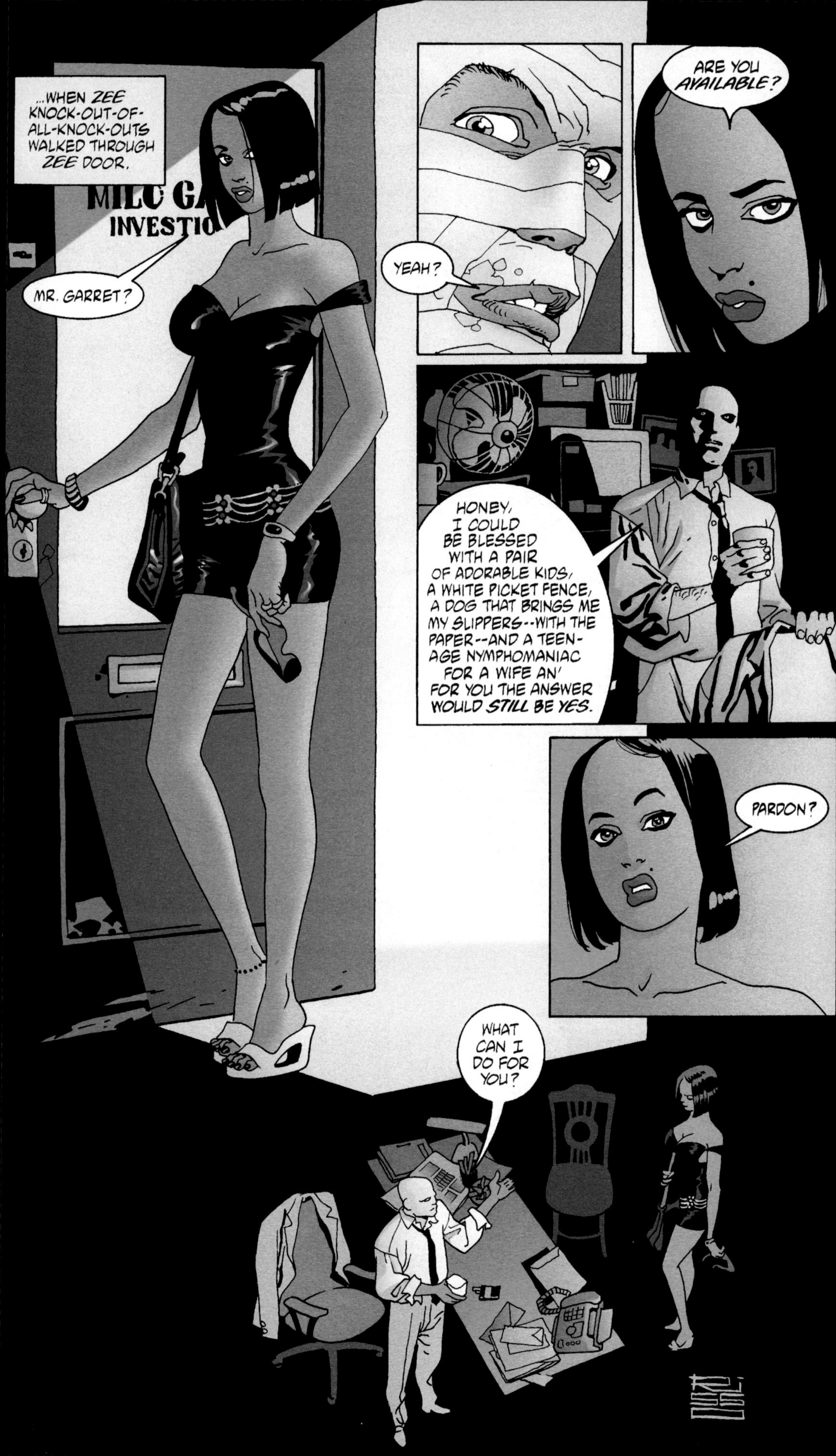
...WHEN ZEE KNOCK-OUT-OF-ALL-KNOCK-OUTS WALKED THROUGH ZEE DOOR.
MILO GA
INVESTIG
MR. GARRET?
YEAH?
ARE YOU AVAILABLE?
HONEY, I COULD BE BLESSED WITH A PAIR OF ADORABLE KIDS, A WHITE PICKET FENCE, A DOG THAT BRINGS ME MY SLIPPERS--WITH THE PAPER--AND A TEEN-AGE NYMPHOMANIAC FOR A WIFE AN' FOR YOU THE ANSWER WOULD STILL BE YES.
PARDON?
WHAT CAN I DO FOR YOU?

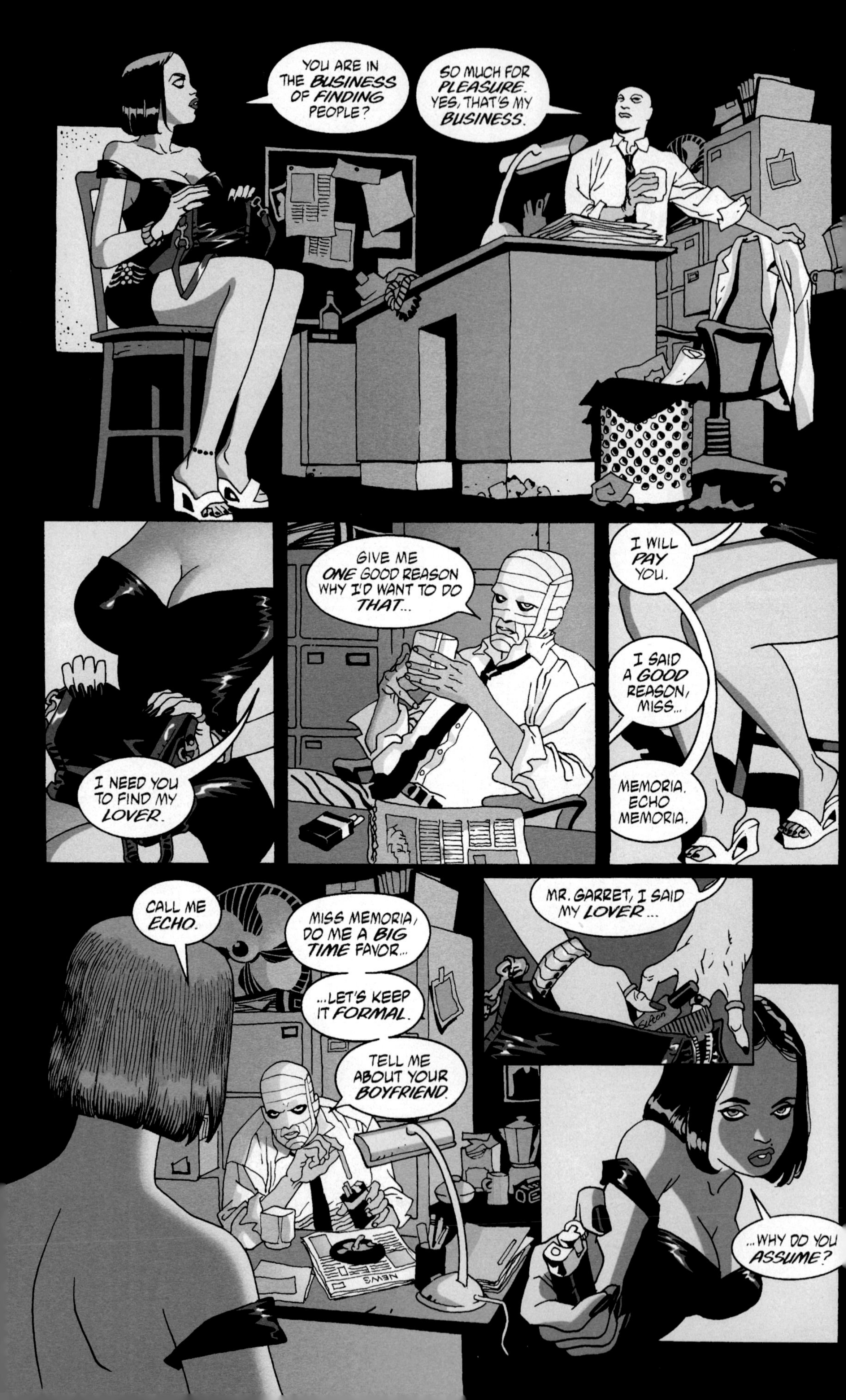
YOU ARE IN THE BUSINESS OF FINDING PEOPLE?
SO MUCH FOR PLEASURE. YES, THAT'S MY BUSINESS.
I NEED YOU TO FIND MY LOVER.
GIVE ME ONE GOOD REASON WHY I'D WANT TO DO THAT...
I WILL PAY YOU.
I SAID A GOOD REASON, MISS...
MEMORIA. ECHO MEMORIA.
CALL ME ECHO.
MISS MEMORIA, DO ME A BIG TIME FAVOR...
...LET'S KEEP IT FORMAL.
TELL ME ABOUT YOUR BOYFRIEND.
MR. GARRET, I SAID MY LOVER...
...WHY DO YOU ASSUME?
NEWS

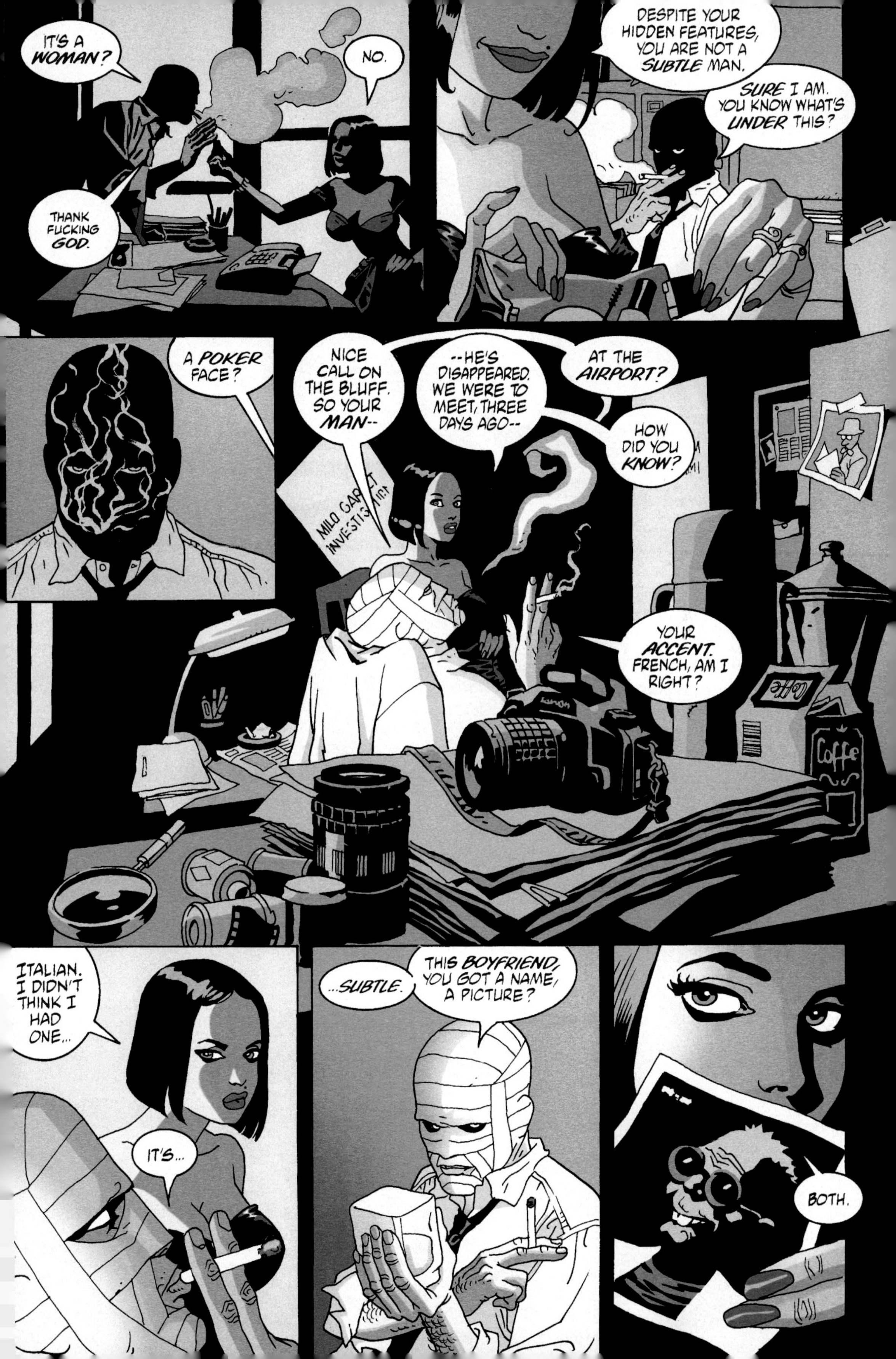
IT'S A WOMAN?
NO.
THANK FUCKING GOD.
DESPITE YOUR HIDDEN FEATURES, YOU ARE NOT A SUBTLE MAN.
SURE I AM. YOU KNOW WHAT'S UNDER THIS?
A POKER FACE?
NICE CALL ON THE BLUFF. SO YOUR MAN--
--HE'S DISAPPEARED. WE WERE TO MEET, THREE DAYS AGO--
AT THE AIRPORT?
HOW DID YOU KNOW?
YOUR ACCENT. FRENCH, AM I RIGHT?
ITALIAN. I DIDN'T THINK I HAD ONE...
IT'S...
...SUBTLE.
THIS BOYFRIEND, YOU GOT A NAME, A PICTURE?
BOTH.

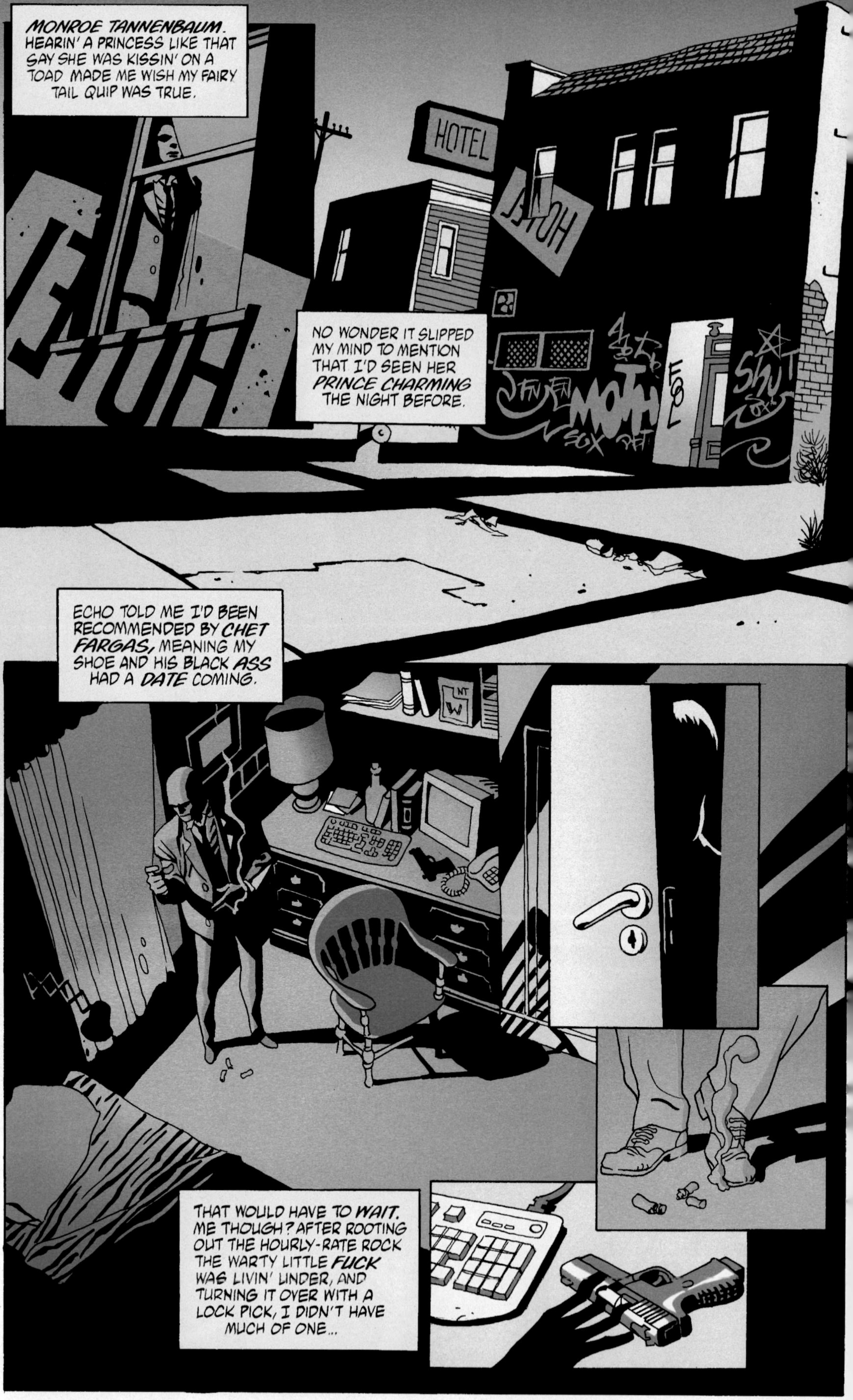
MONROE TANNENBAUM. HEARIN' A PRINCESS LIKE THAT SAY SHE WAS KISSIN' ON A TOAD MADE ME WISH MY FAIRY TAIL QUIP WAS TRUE.
HOTEL
NO WONDER IT SLIPPED MY MIND TO MENTION THAT I'D SEEN HER PRINCE CHARMING THE NIGHT BEFORE.
ECHO TOLD ME I'D BEEN RECOMMENDED BY CHET FARGAS, MEANING MY SHOE AND HIS BLACK ASS HAD A DATE COMING.
THAT WOULD HAVE TO WAIT. ME THOUGH? AFTER ROOTING OUT THE HOURLY-RATE ROCK THE WARTY LITTLE FUCK WAS LIVIN' UNDER, AND TURNING IT OVER WITH A LOCK PICK, I DIDN'T HAVE MUCH OF ONE...

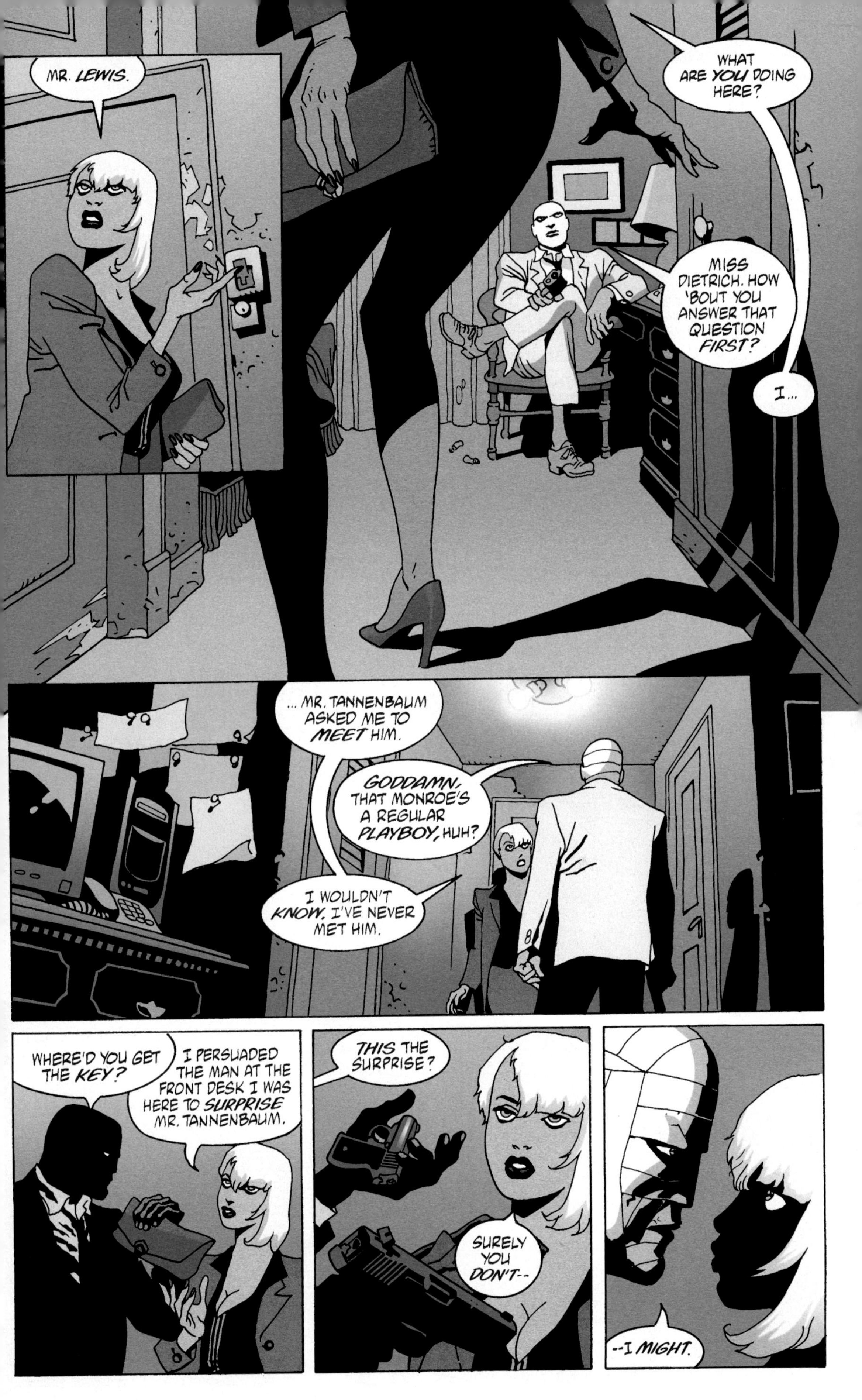

MR. LEWIS.
WHAT ARE YOU DOING HERE?
MISS DIETRICH. HOW 'BOUT YOU ANSWER THAT QUESTION FIRST?
I...
... MR. TANNENBAUM ASKED ME TO MEET HIM.
GODDAMN, THAT MONROE'S A REGULAR PLAYBOY, HUH?
I WOULDN'T KNOW. I'VE NEVER MET HIM.
WHERE'D YOU GET THE KEY?
I PERSUADED THE MAN AT THE FRONT DESK I WAS HERE TO SURPRISE MR. TANNENBAUM.
THIS THE SURPRISE?
SURELY YOU DON'T--
--I MIGHT.

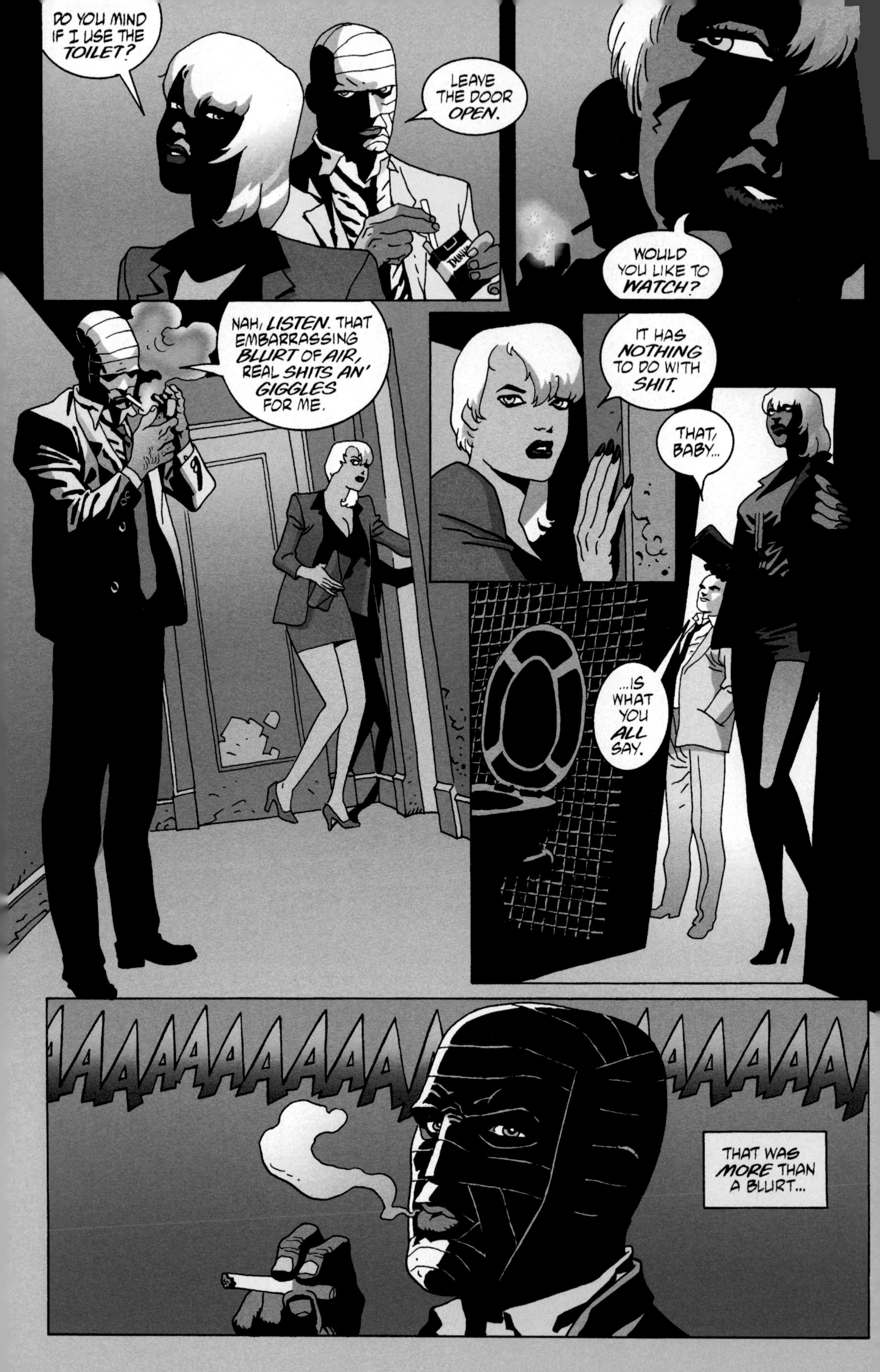
DO YOU MIND IF I USE THE TOILET?
LEAVE THE DOOR OPEN.
WOULD YOU LIKE TO WATCH?
NAH, LISTEN. THAT EMBARRASSING BLURT OF AIR, REAL SHITS AN' GIGGLES FOR ME.
IT HAS NOTHING TO DO WITH SHIT.
THAT, BABY...
...IS WHAT YOU ALL SAY.
AAAAAAAAAAAAAAAAAAAAA
THAT WAS MORE THAN A BLURT...

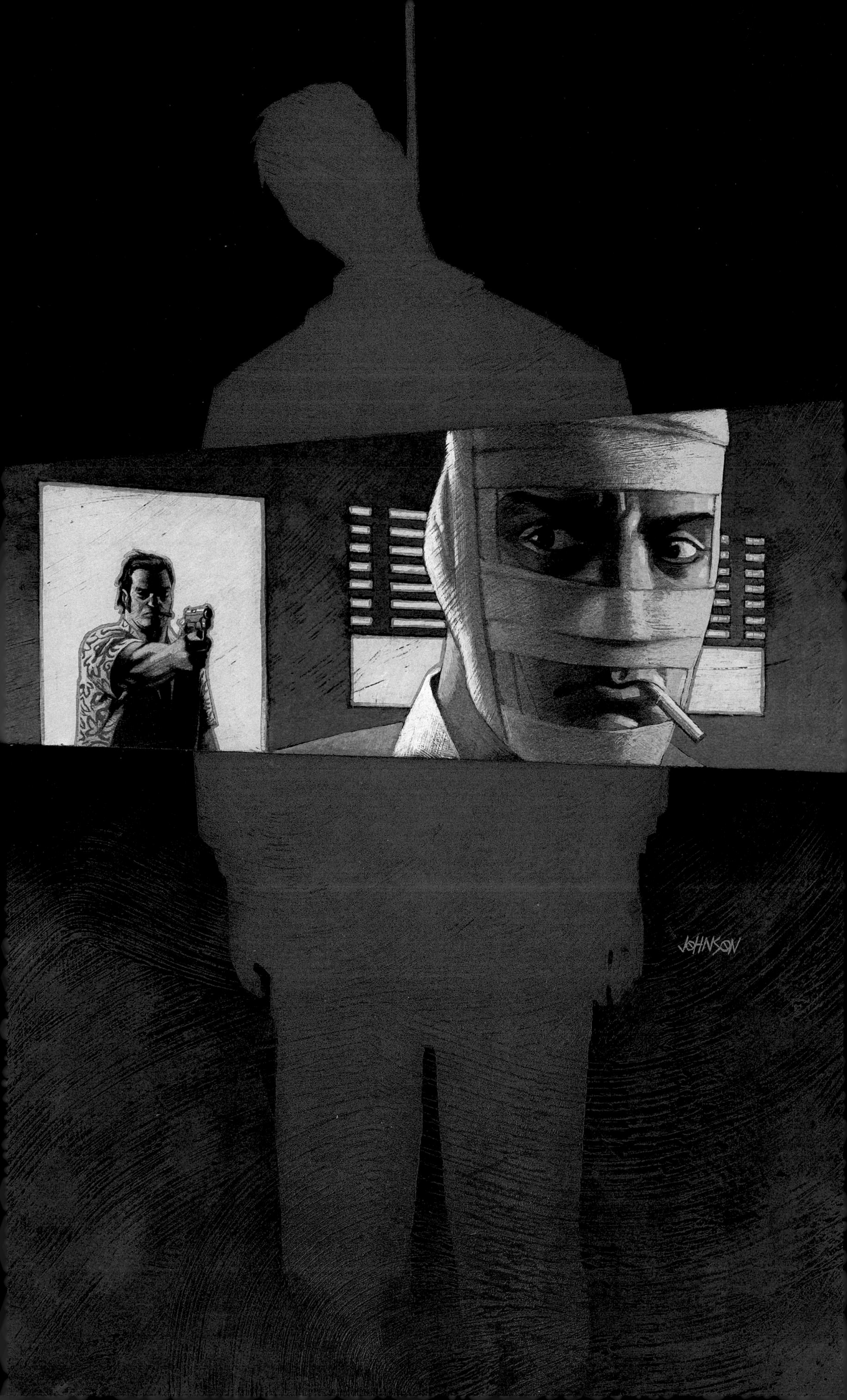
JOHNSON

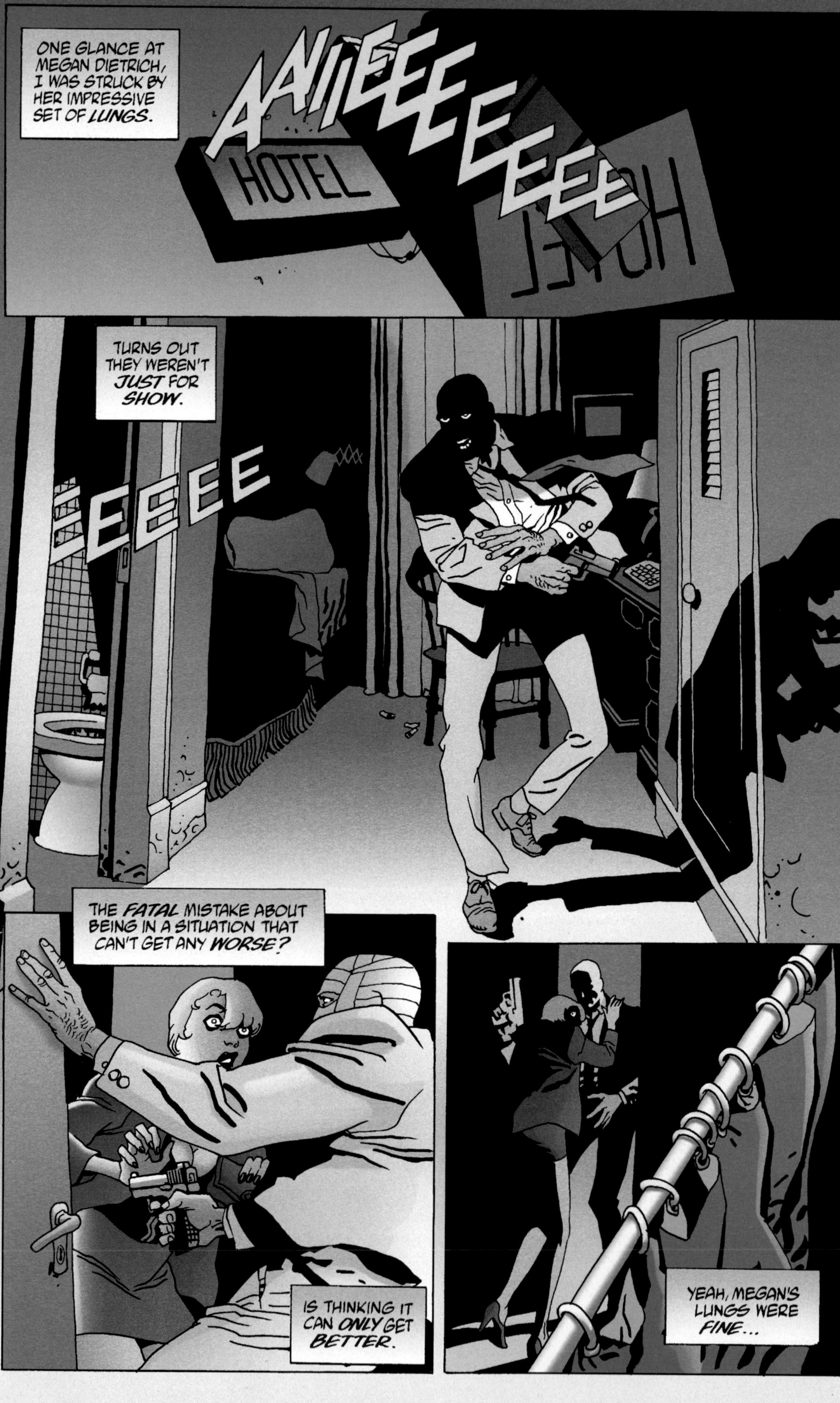

ONE GLANCE AT MEGAN DIETRICH, I WAS STRUCK BY HER IMPRESSIVE SET OF *LUNGS*.
AAIIEEEEEEEE
HOTEL
TURNS OUT THEY WEREN'T *JUST* FOR *SHOW*.
EEEEE
THE *FATAL* MISTAKE ABOUT BEING IN A SITUATION THAT CAN'T GET ANY *WORSE*?
IS THINKING IT CAN *ONLY* GET *BETTER*.
YEAH, MEGAN'S LUNGS WERE *FINE*...

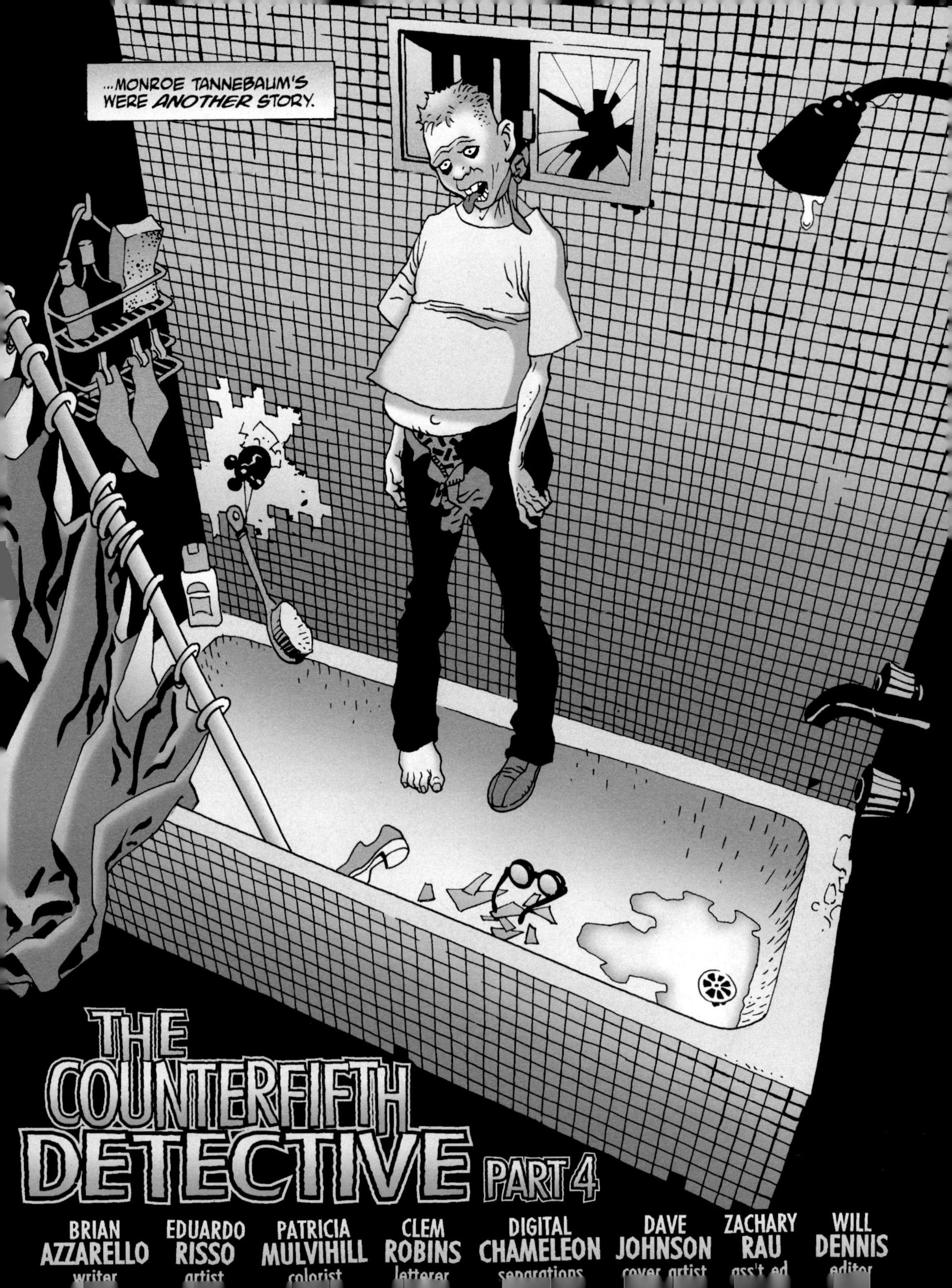

...MONROE TANNEBAUM'S WERE ANOTHER STORY.
THE COUNTERFIFTH DETECTIVE PART 4
BRIAN AZZARELLO writer
EDUARDO RISSO artist
PATRICIA MULVIHILL colorist
CLEM ROBINS letterer
DIGITAL CHAMELEON separations
DAVE JOHNSON cover artist
ZACHARY RAU ass't ed
WILL DENNIS editor

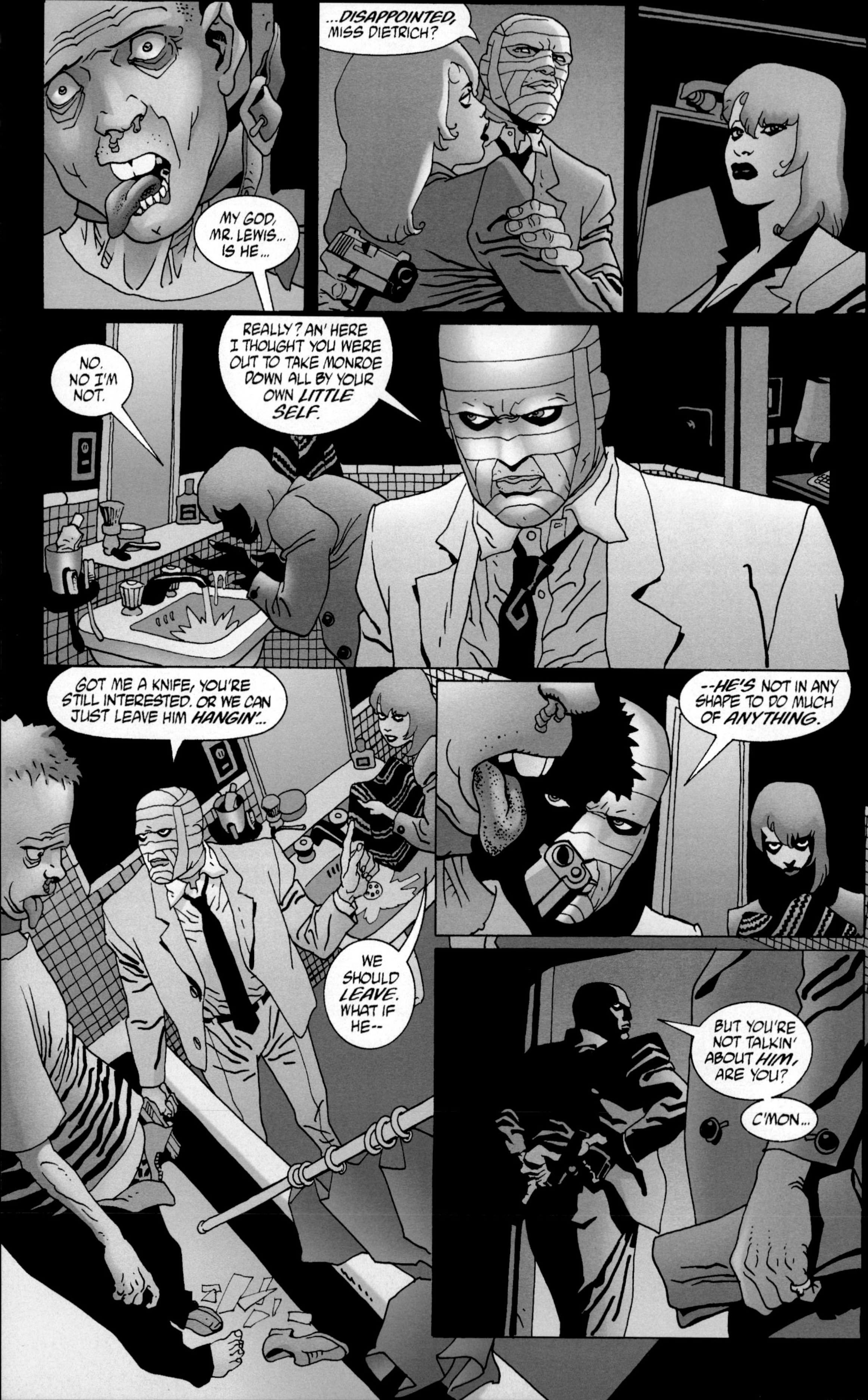
MY GOD, MR. LEWIS... IS HE...
...DISAPPOINTED, MISS DIETRICH?
NO. NO I'M NOT.
REALLY? AN' HERE I THOUGHT YOU WERE OUT TO TAKE MONROE DOWN ALL BY YOUR OWN LITTLE SELF.
GOT ME A KNIFE, YOU'RE STILL INTERESTED. OR WE CAN JUST LEAVE HIM HANGIN'...
WE SHOULD LEAVE. WHAT IF HE--
--HE'S NOT IN ANY SHAPE TO DO MUCH OF ANYTHING.
BUT YOU'RE NOT TALKIN' ABOUT HIM, ARE YOU?
C'MON...

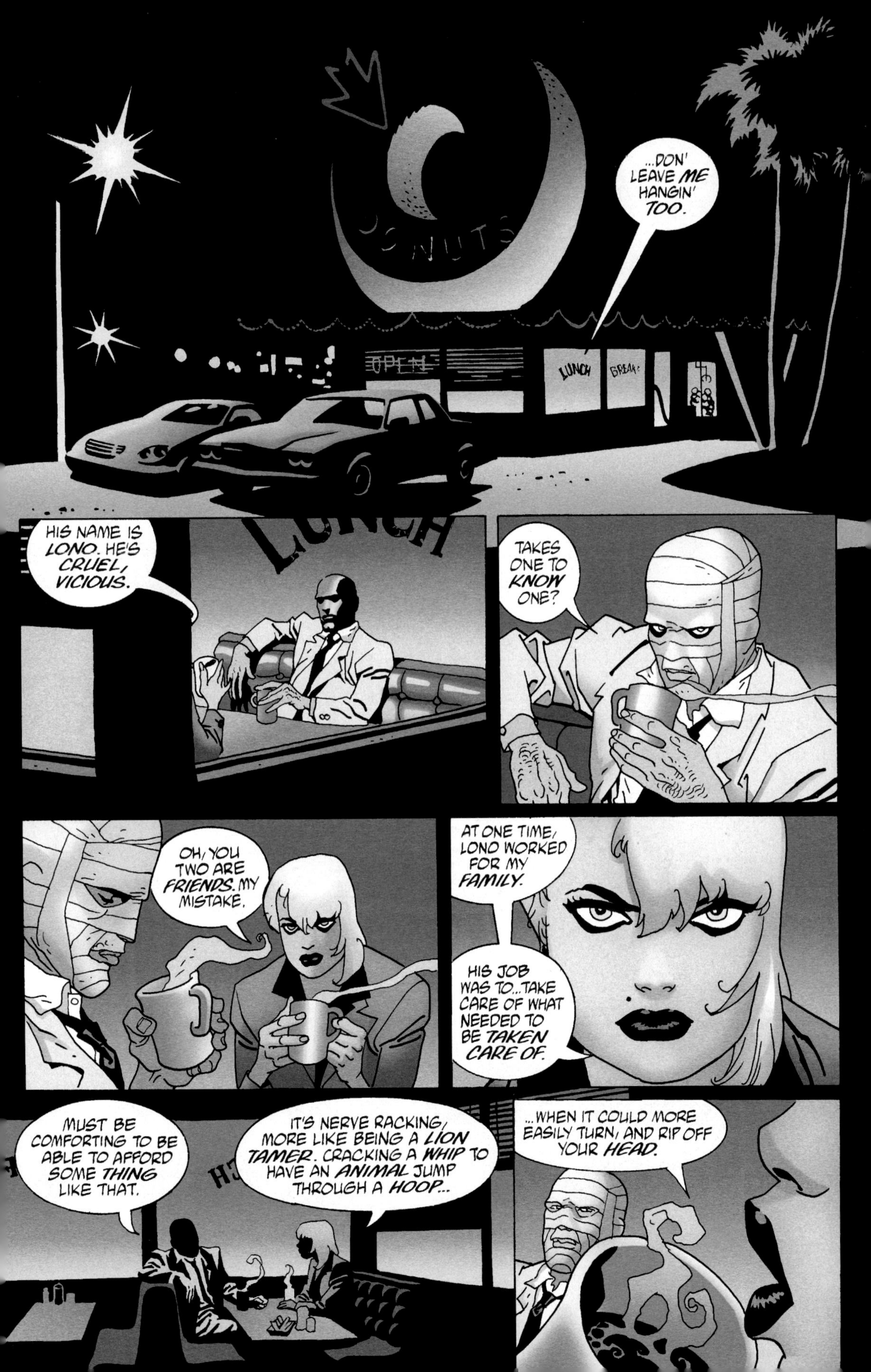
DONUTS
OPEN
LUNCH
BREAK
...DON' LEAVE ME HANGIN' TOO.
HIS NAME IS LONO. HE'S CRUEL, VICIOUS.
LUNCH
TAKES ONE TO KNOW ONE?
OH, YOU TWO ARE FRIENDS. MY MISTAKE.
AT ONE TIME, LONO WORKED FOR MY FAMILY.
HIS JOB WAS TO...TAKE CARE OF WHAT NEEDED TO BE TAKEN CARE OF.
MUST BE COMFORTING TO BE ABLE TO AFFORD SOME THING LIKE THAT.
IT'S NERVE RACKING, MORE LIKE BEING A LION TAMER. CRACKING A WHIP TO HAVE AN ANIMAL JUMP THROUGH A HOOP...
...WHEN IT COULD MORE EASILY TURN, AND RIP OFF YOUR HEAD.

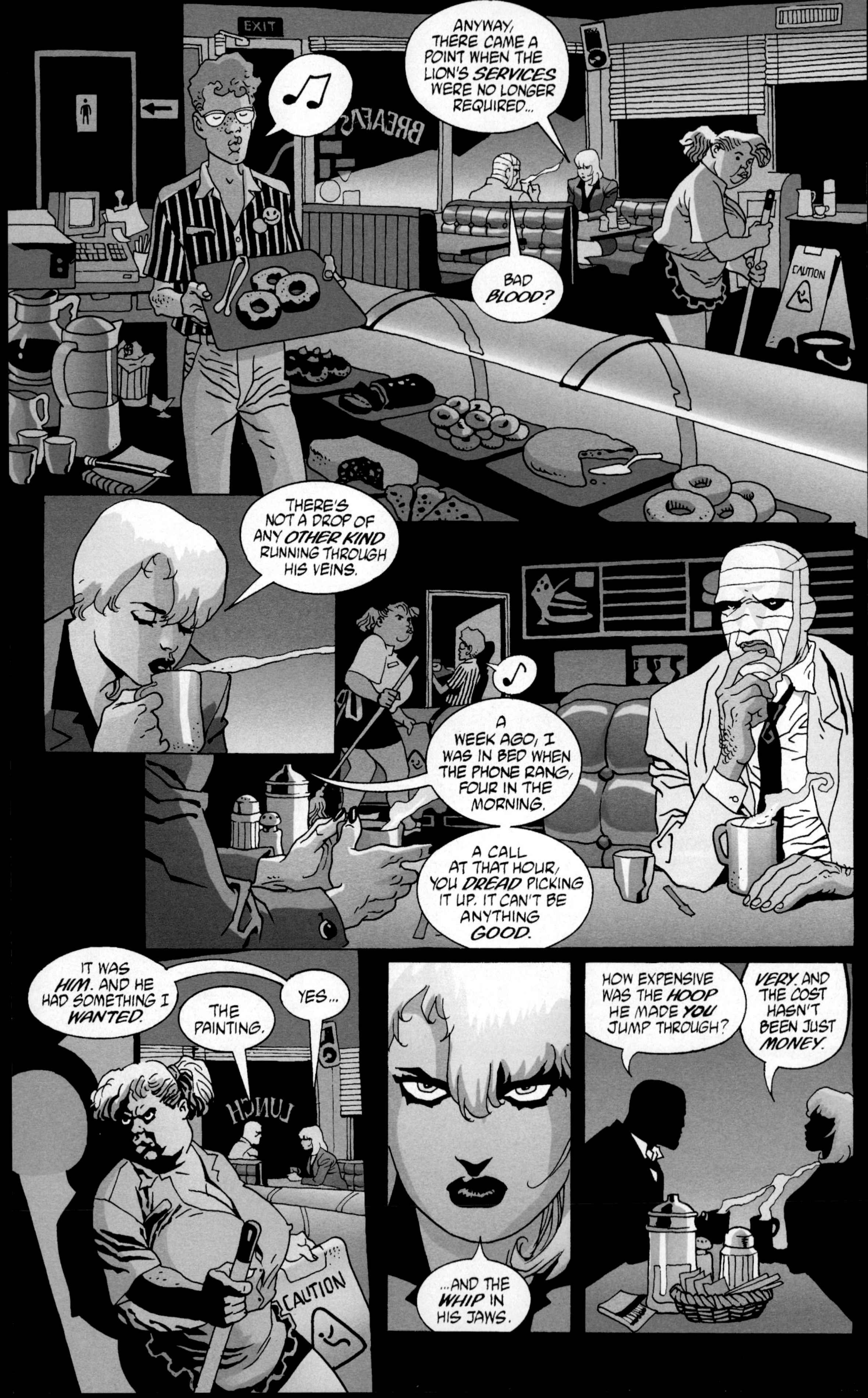
EXIT
BREAKFAST
♫
ANYWAY, THERE CAME A POINT WHEN THE LION'S SERVICES WERE NO LONGER REQUIRED...
BAD BLOOD?
CAUTION
THERE'S NOT A DROP OF ANY OTHER KIND RUNNING THROUGH HIS VEINS.
♪
A WEEK AGO, I WAS IN BED WHEN THE PHONE RANG, FOUR IN THE MORNING.
A CALL AT THAT HOUR, YOU DREAD PICKING IT UP. IT CAN'T BE ANYTHING GOOD.
IT WAS HIM. AND HE HAD SOMETHING I WANTED.
THE PAINTING.
YES...
LUNCH
CAUTION
...AND THE WHIP IN HIS JAWS.
HOW EXPENSIVE WAS THE HOOP HE MADE YOU JUMP THROUGH?
VERY. AND THE COST HASN'T BEEN JUST MONEY.

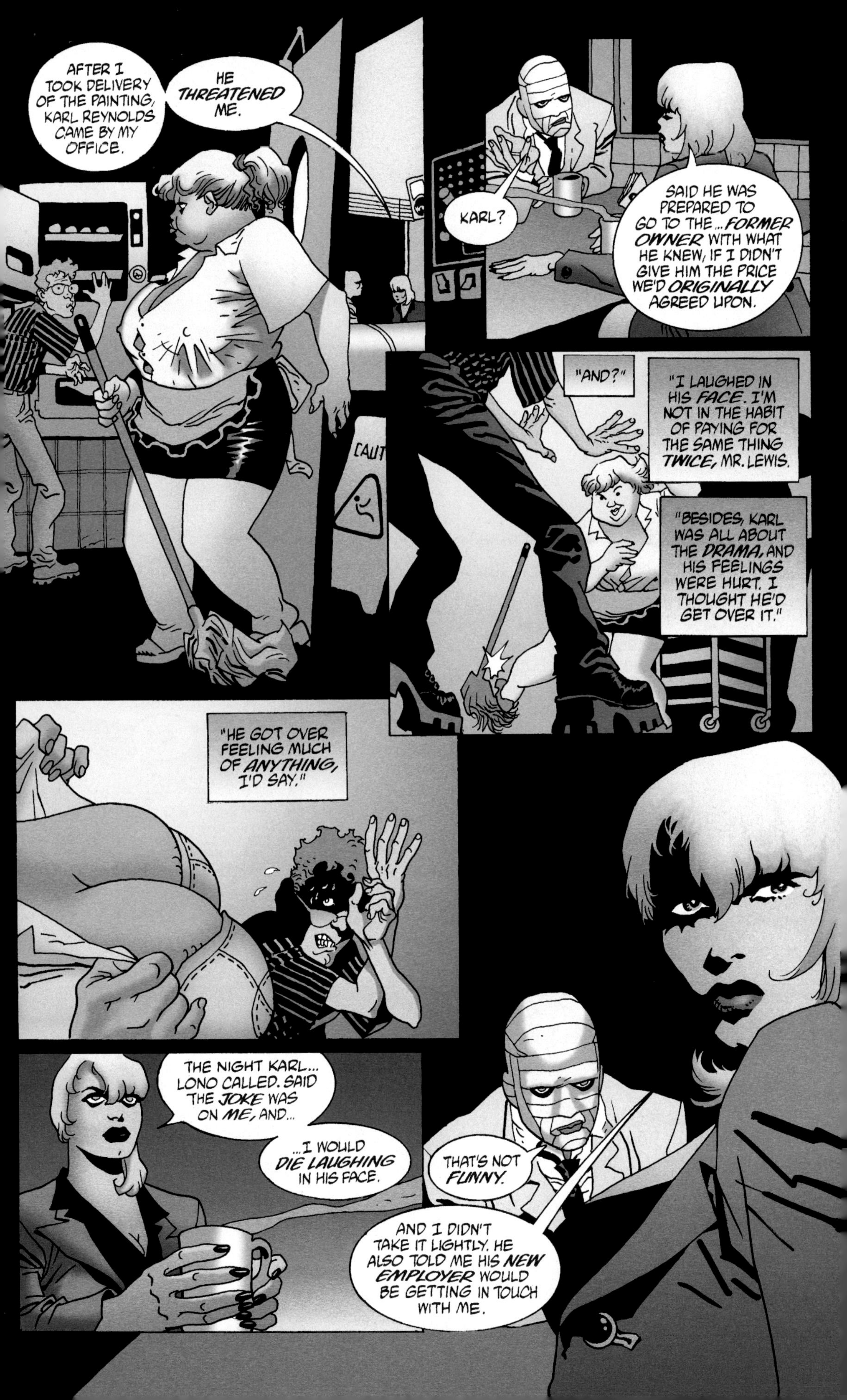
AFTER I TOOK DELIVERY OF THE PAINTING, KARL REYNOLDS CAME BY MY OFFICE.
HE THREATENED ME.
KARL?
SAID HE WAS PREPARED TO GO TO THE... FORMER OWNER WITH WHAT HE KNEW, IF I DIDN'T GIVE HIM THE PRICE WE'D ORIGINALLY AGREED UPON.
"AND?"
"I LAUGHED IN HIS FACE. I'M NOT IN THE HABIT OF PAYING FOR THE SAME THING TWICE, MR. LEWIS.
"BESIDES, KARL WAS ALL ABOUT THE DRAMA, AND HIS FEELINGS WERE HURT. I THOUGHT HE'D GET OVER IT."
"HE GOT OVER FEELING MUCH OF ANYTHING, I'D SAY."
THE NIGHT KARL... LONO CALLED. SAID THE JOKE WAS ON ME, AND...
...I WOULD DIE LAUGHING IN HIS FACE.
THAT'S NOT FUNNY.
AND I DIDN'T TAKE IT LIGHTLY. HE ALSO TOLD ME HIS NEW EMPLOYER WOULD BE GETTING IN TOUCH WITH ME.

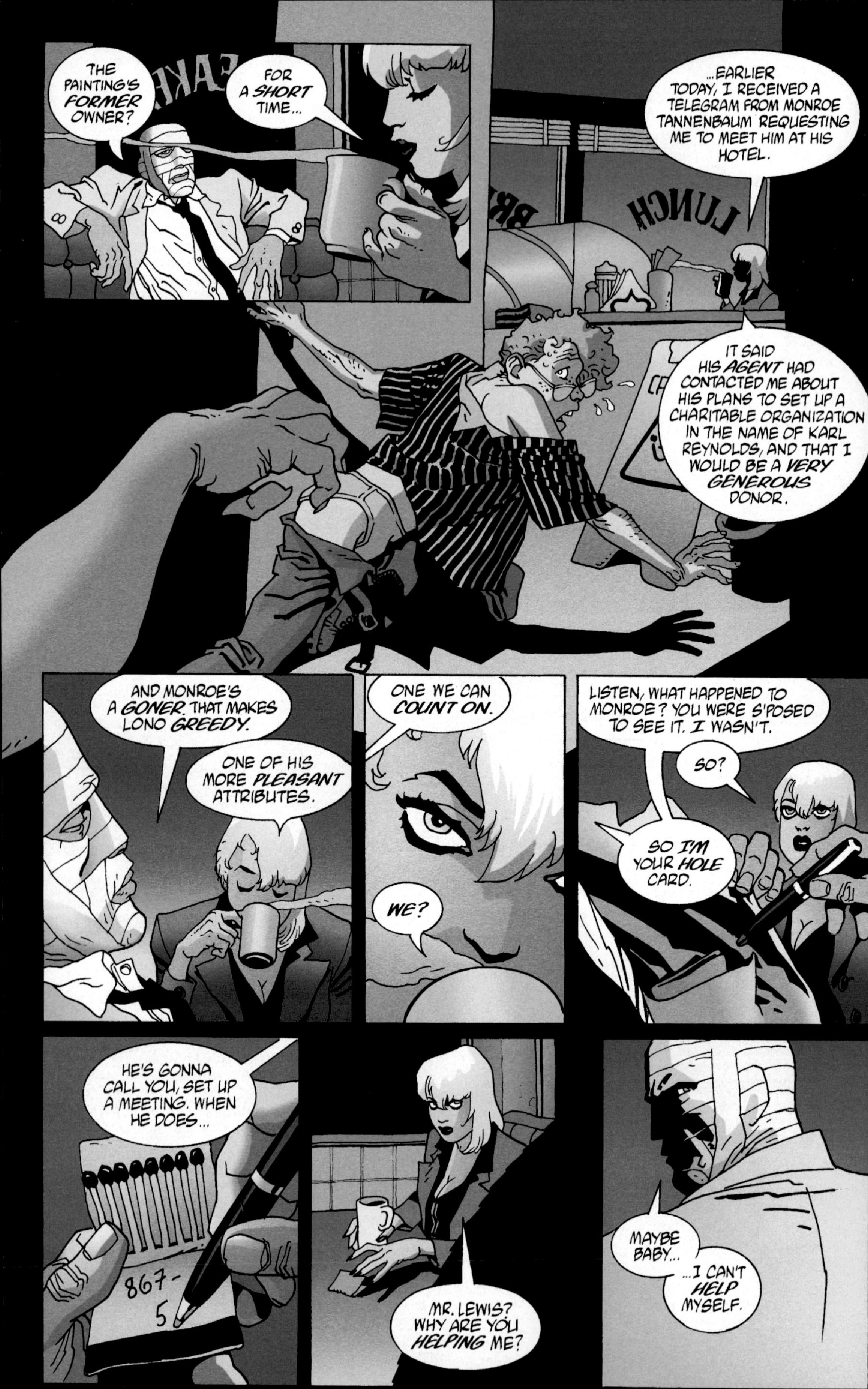
THE PAINTING'S FORMER OWNER?
FOR A SHORT TIME...
...EARLIER TODAY, I RECEIVED A TELEGRAM FROM MONROE TANNENBAUM REQUESTING ME TO MEET HIM AT HIS HOTEL.
LUNCH
IT SAID HIS AGENT HAD CONTACTED ME ABOUT HIS PLANS TO SET UP A CHARITABLE ORGANIZATION IN THE NAME OF KARL REYNOLDS, AND THAT I WOULD BE A VERY GENEROUS DONOR.
AND MONROE'S A GONER. THAT MAKES LONO GREEDY.
ONE OF HIS MORE PLEASANT ATTRIBUTES.
ONE WE CAN COUNT ON.
WE?
LISTEN, WHAT HAPPENED TO MONROE? YOU WERE S'POSED TO SEE IT. I WASN'T.
SO?
SO I'M YOUR HOLE CARD.
HE'S GONNA CALL YOU, SET UP A MEETING. WHEN HE DOES...
867-
5
MR. LEWIS? WHY ARE YOU HELPING ME?
MAYBE BABY...
...I CAN'T HELP MYSELF.

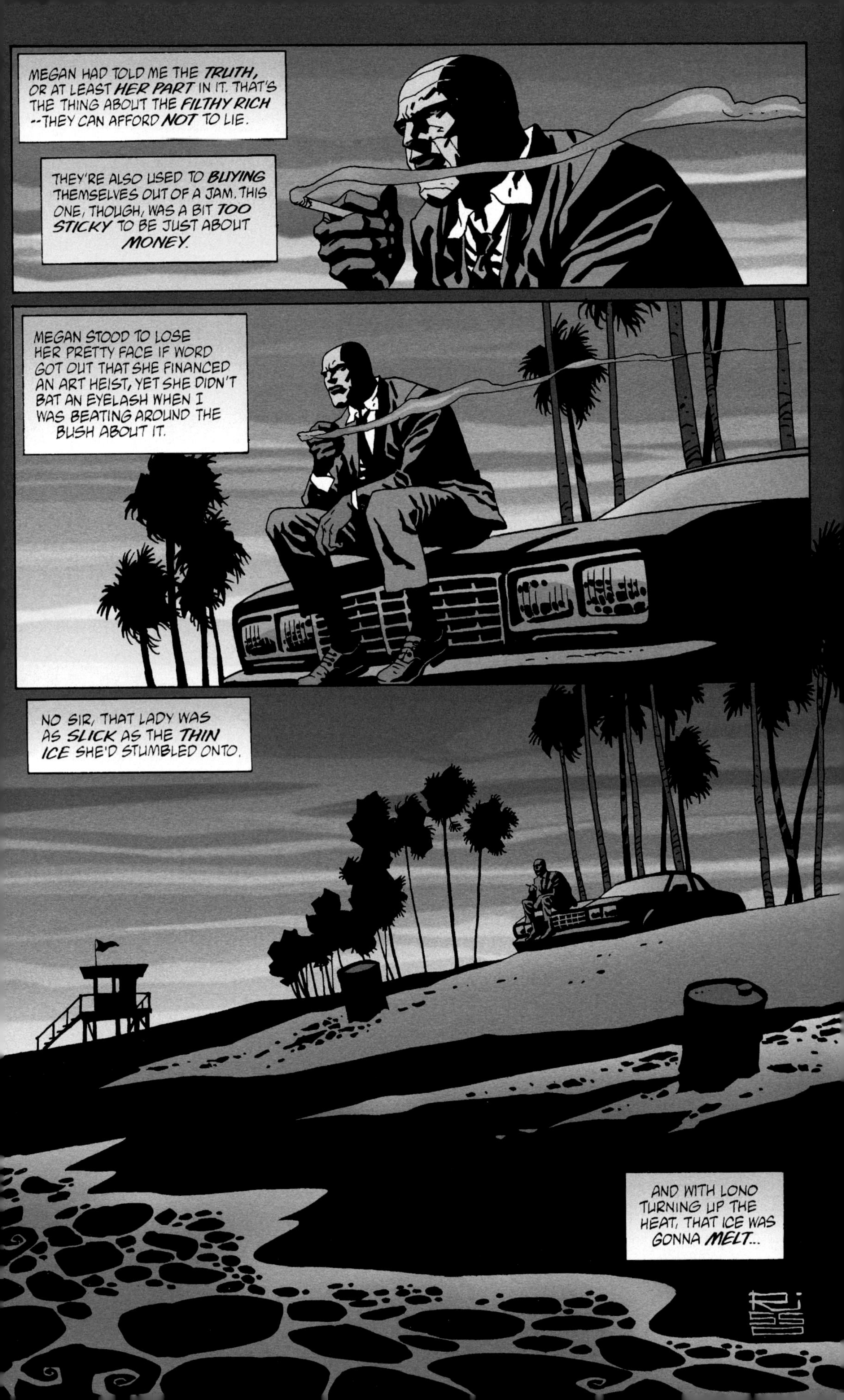
MEGAN HAD TOLD ME THE TRUTH, OR AT LEAST HER PART IN IT. THAT'S THE THING ABOUT THE FILTHY RICH --THEY CAN AFFORD NOT TO LIE.
THEY'RE ALSO USED TO BUYING THEMSELVES OUT OF A JAM. THIS ONE, THOUGH, WAS A BIT TOO STICKY TO BE JUST ABOUT MONEY.
MEGAN STOOD TO LOSE HER PRETTY FACE IF WORD GOT OUT THAT SHE FINANCED AN ART HEIST, YET SHE DIDN'T BAT AN EYELASH WHEN I WAS BEATING AROUND THE BUSH ABOUT IT.
NO SIR, THAT LADY WAS AS SLICK AS THE THIN ICE SHE'D STUMBLED ONTO.
AND WITH LONO TURNING UP THE HEAT, THAT ICE WAS GONNA MELT...

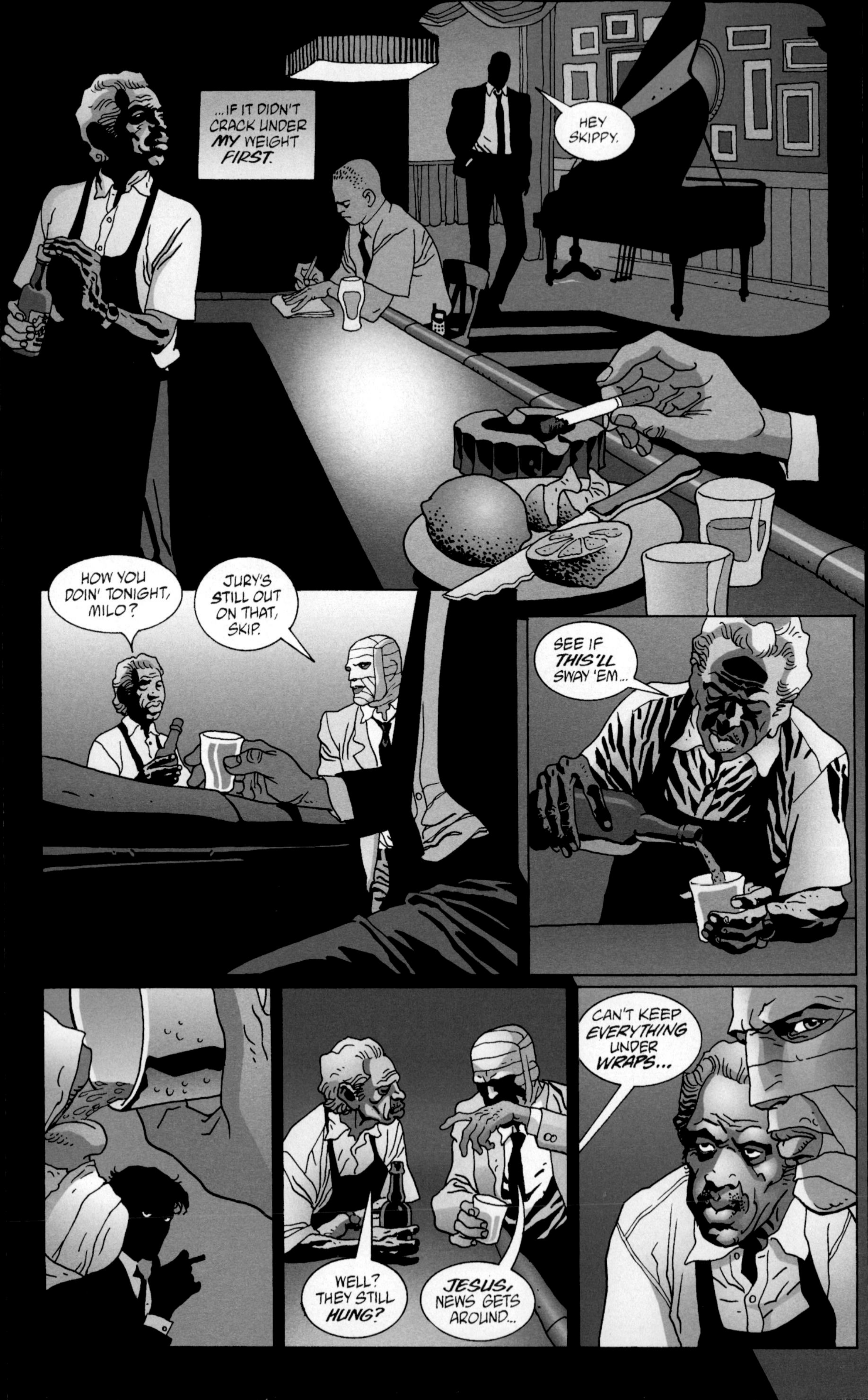
...IF IT DIDN'T CRACK UNDER MY WEIGHT FIRST.
HEY SKIPPY.
HOW YOU DOIN' TONIGHT, MILO?
JURY'S STILL OUT ON THAT, SKIP.
SEE IF THIS'LL SWAY 'EM...
WELL? THEY STILL HUNG?
JESUS, NEWS GETS AROUND...
CAN'T KEEP EVERYTHING UNDER WRAPS...

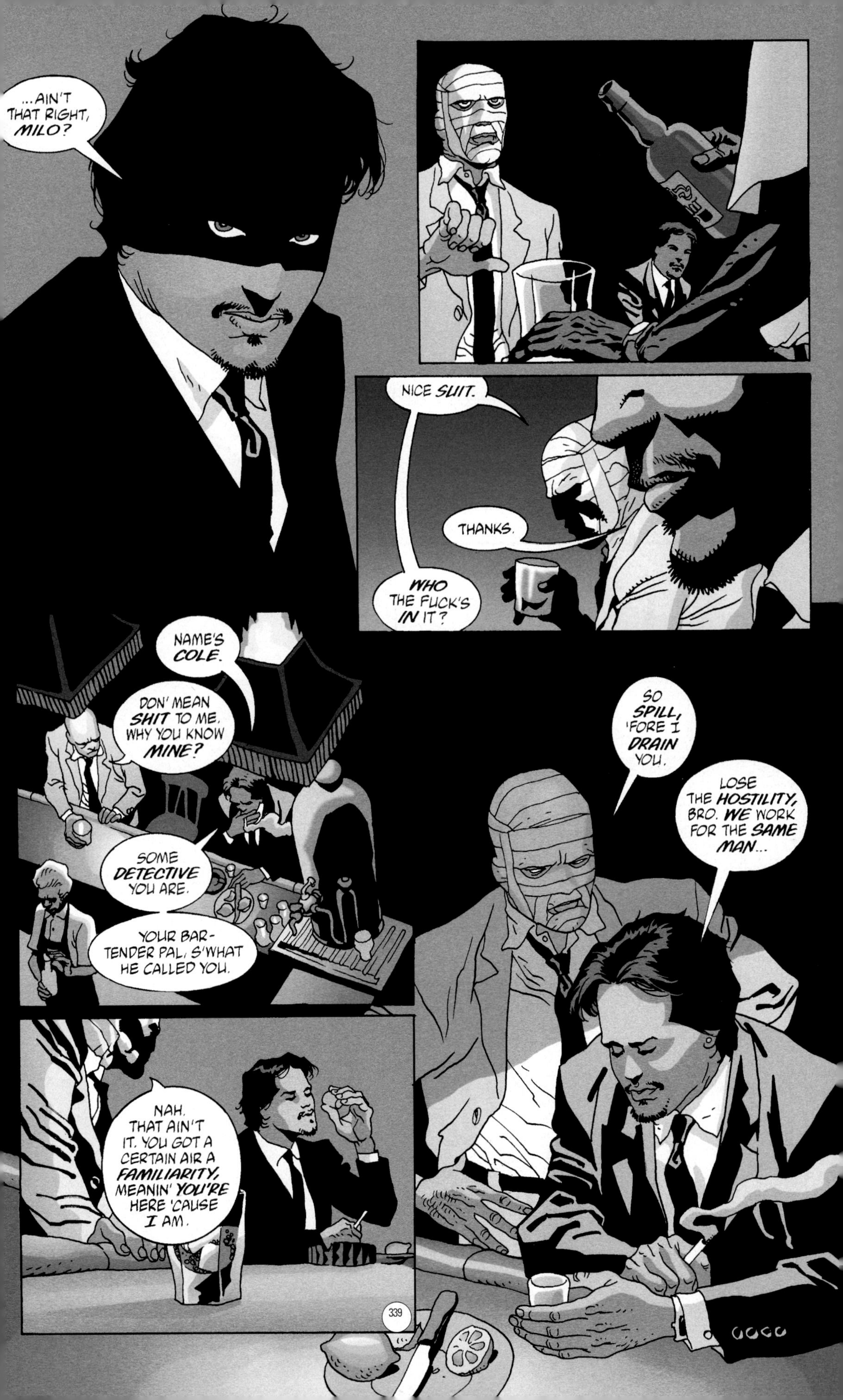
...AIN'T THAT RIGHT, MILO?
NICE SUIT.
THANKS.
WHO THE FUCK'S IN IT?
NAME'S COLE.
DON' MEAN SHIT TO ME. WHY YOU KNOW MINE?
SOME DETECTIVE YOU ARE.
YOUR BAR-TENDER PAL, S'WHAT HE CALLED YOU.
SO SPILL, 'FORE I DRAIN YOU.
LOSE THE HOSTILITY, BRO. WE WORK FOR THE SAME MAN...
NAH. THAT AIN'T IT. YOU GOT A CERTAIN AIR A FAMILIARITY, MEANIN' YOU'RE HERE 'CAUSE I AM.

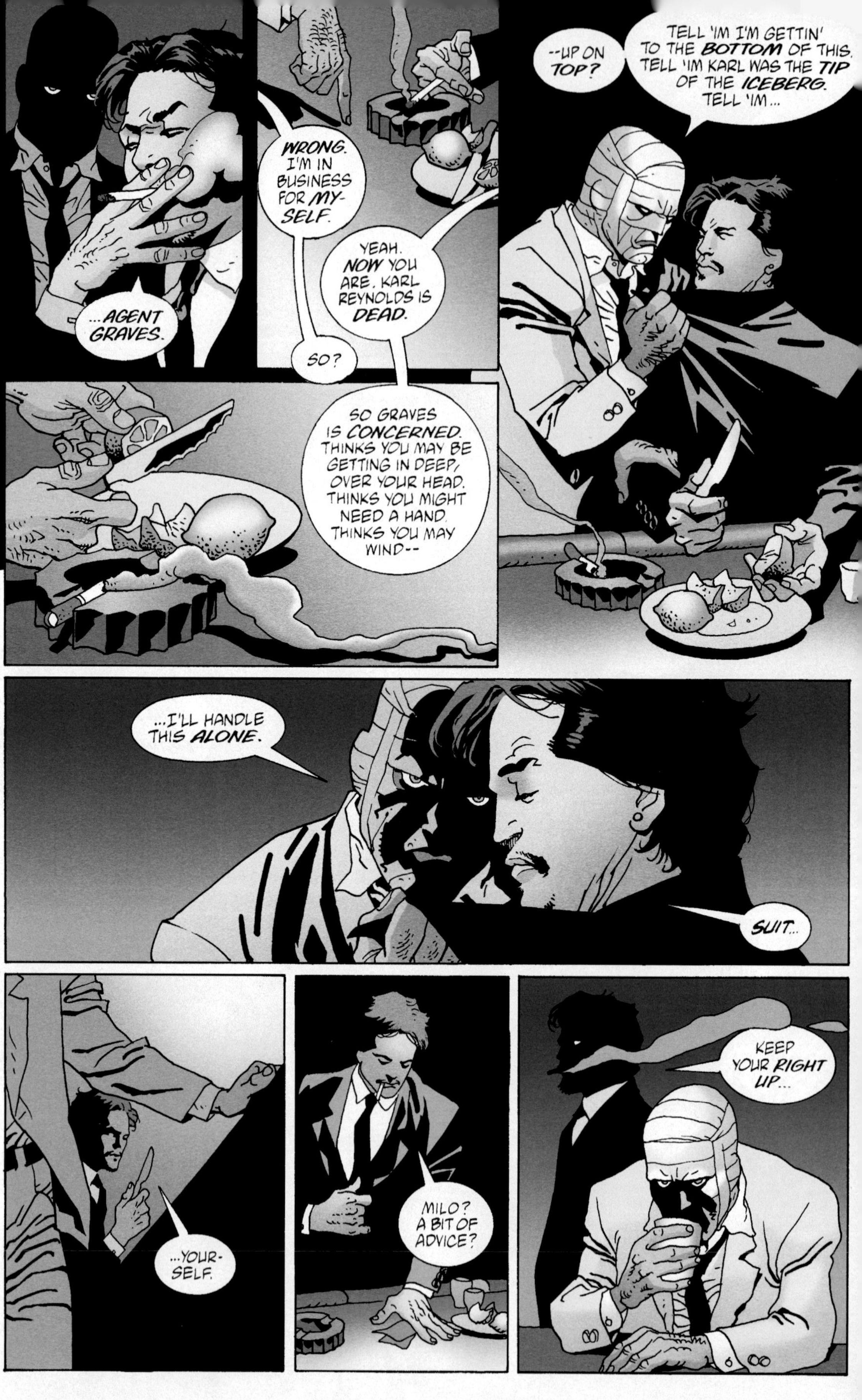
...AGENT GRAVES.
WRONG. I'M IN BUSINESS FOR MYSELF.
SO?
YEAH. NOW YOU ARE. KARL REYNOLDS IS DEAD.
SO GRAVES IS CONCERNED. THINKS YOU MAY BE GETTING IN DEEP, OVER YOUR HEAD. THINKS YOU MIGHT NEED A HAND. THINKS YOU MAY WIND--
--UP ON TOP?
TELL 'IM I'M GETTIN' TO THE BOTTOM OF THIS. TELL 'IM KARL WAS THE TIP OF THE ICEBERG. TELL 'IM ...
...I'LL HANDLE THIS ALONE.
SUIT...
...YOURSELF.
MILO? A BIT OF ADVICE?
KEEP YOUR RIGHT UP...

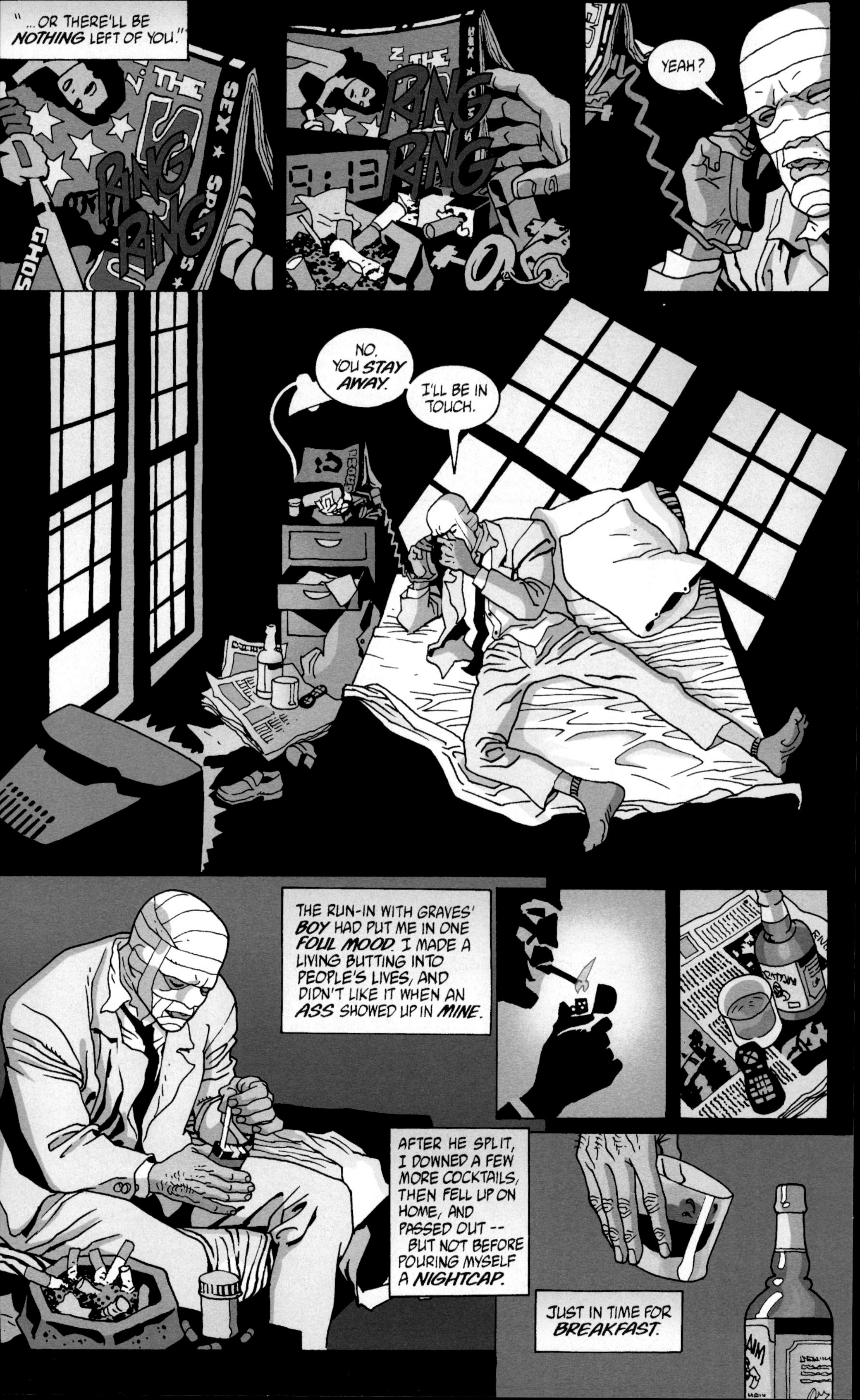
"...OR THERE'LL BE NOTHING LEFT OF YOU."
RANG RANG
9:13
RANG RANG
YEAH?
NO. YOU STAY AWAY.
I'LL BE IN TOUCH.
THE RUN-IN WITH GRAVES' BOY HAD PUT ME IN ONE FOUL MOOD. I MADE A LIVING BUTTING INTO PEOPLE'S LIVES, AND DIDN'T LIKE IT WHEN AN ASS SHOWED UP IN MINE.
AFTER HE SPLIT, I DOWNED A FEW MORE COCKTAILS, THEN FELL UP ON HOME, AND PASSED OUT -- BUT NOT BEFORE POURING MYSELF A NIGHTCAP.
JUST IN TIME FOR BREAKFAST.

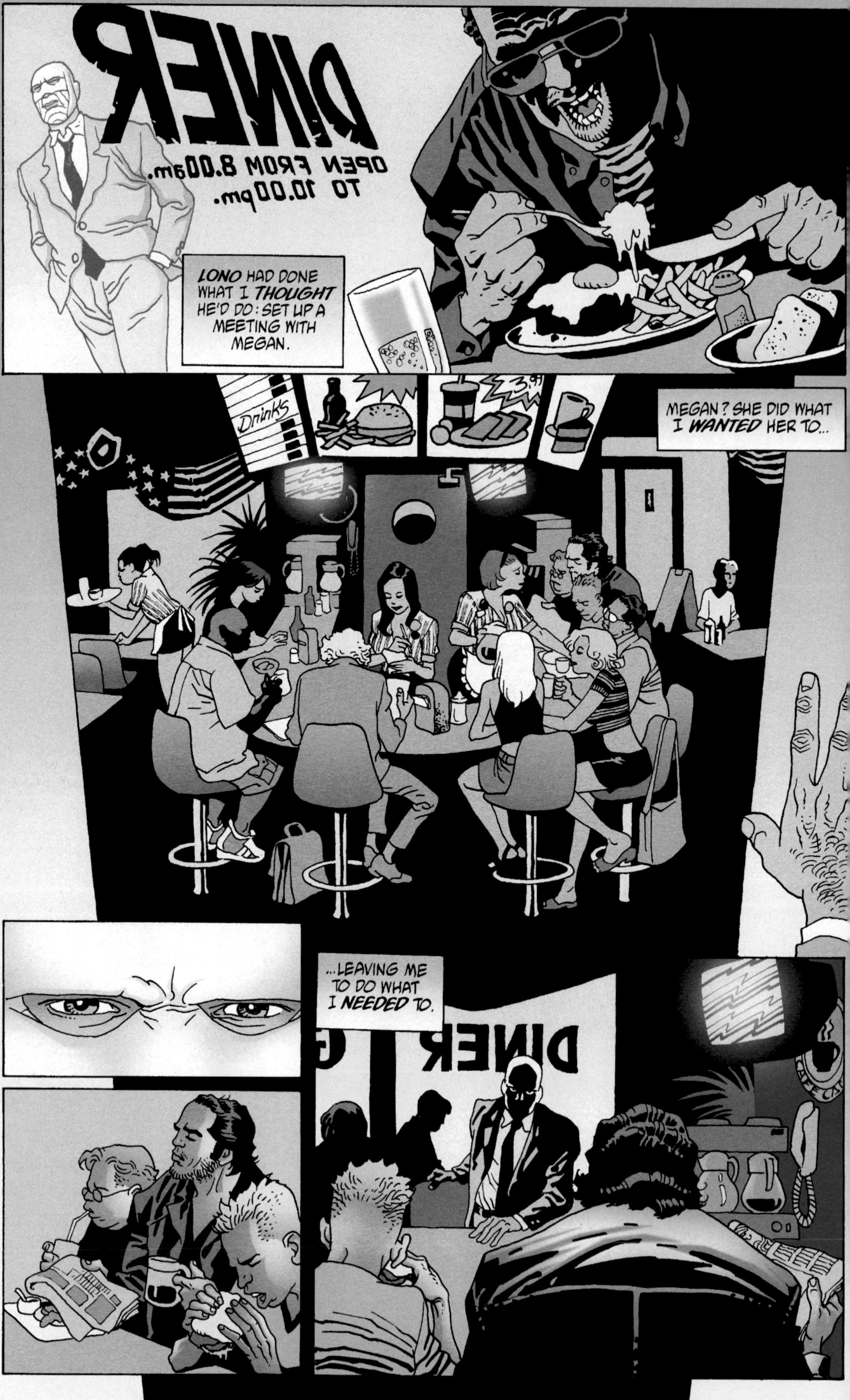
DINER
OPEN FROM 8.00am. TO 10.00pm.
LONO HAD DONE WHAT I THOUGHT HE'D DO: SET UP A MEETING WITH MEGAN.
Drinks
MEGAN? SHE DID WHAT I WANTED HER TO...
...LEAVING ME TO DO WHAT I NEEDED TO.
DINER

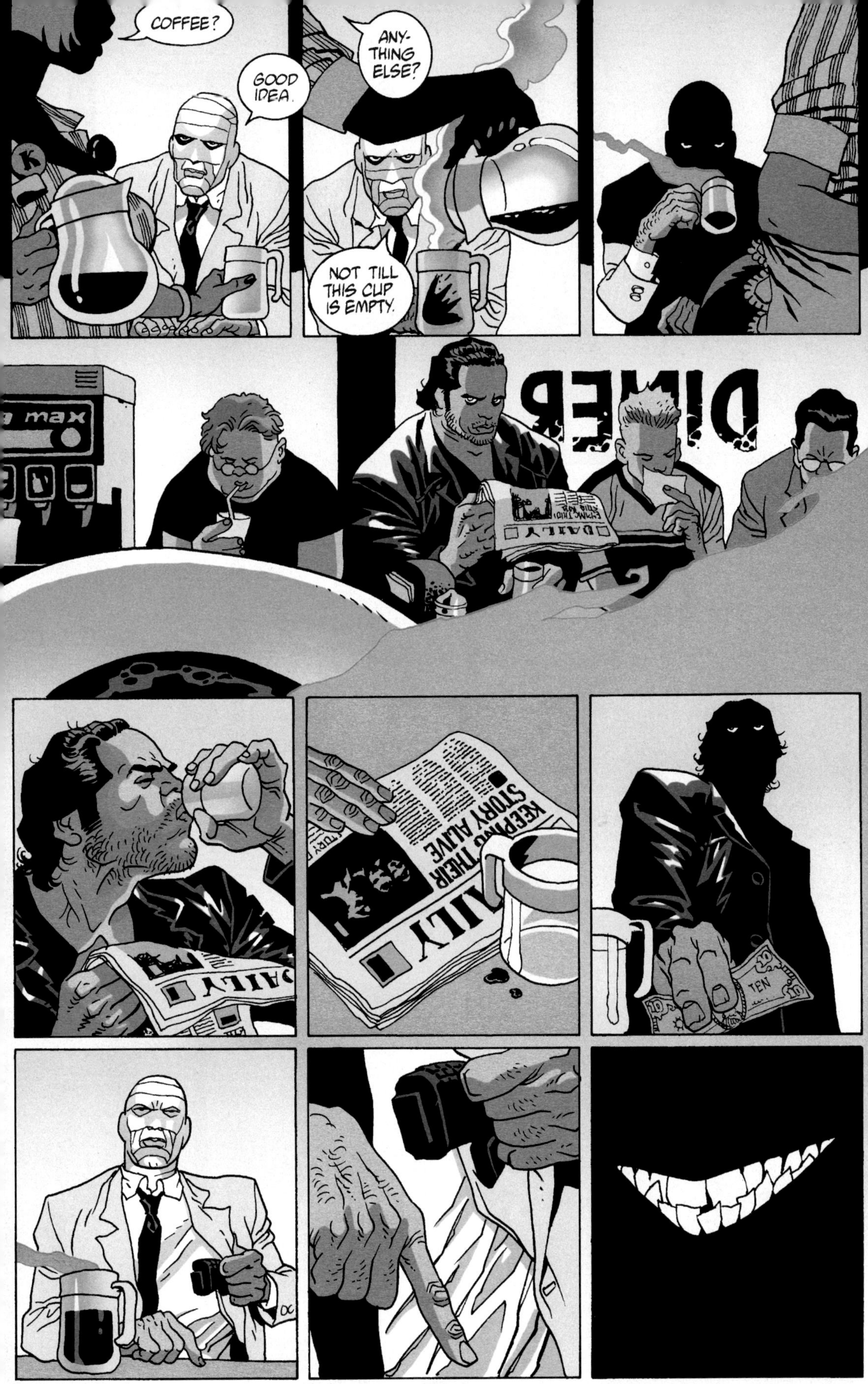
COFFEE?
GOOD IDEA.
ANY-THING ELSE?
NOT TILL THIS CUP IS EMPTY.
TEN

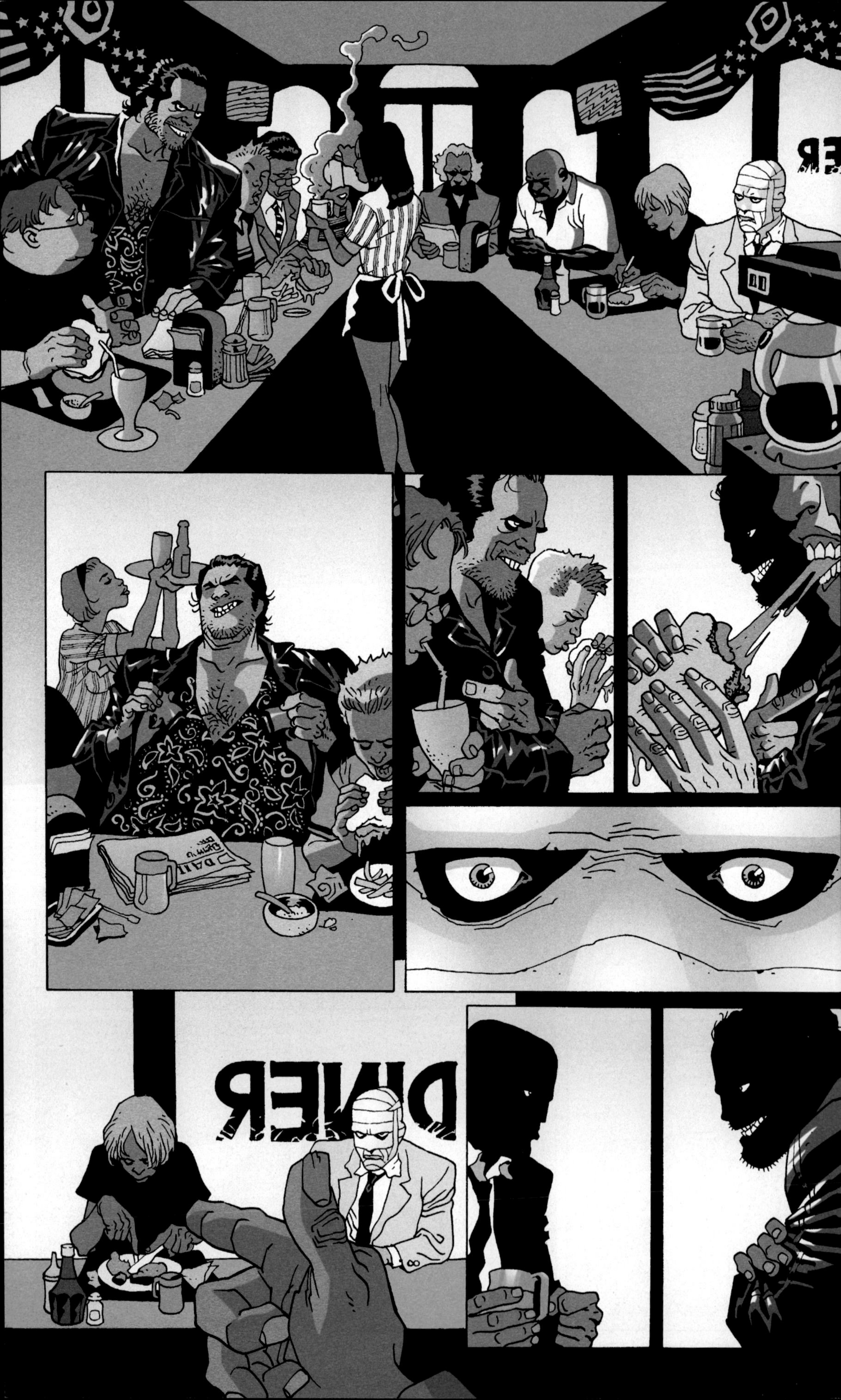

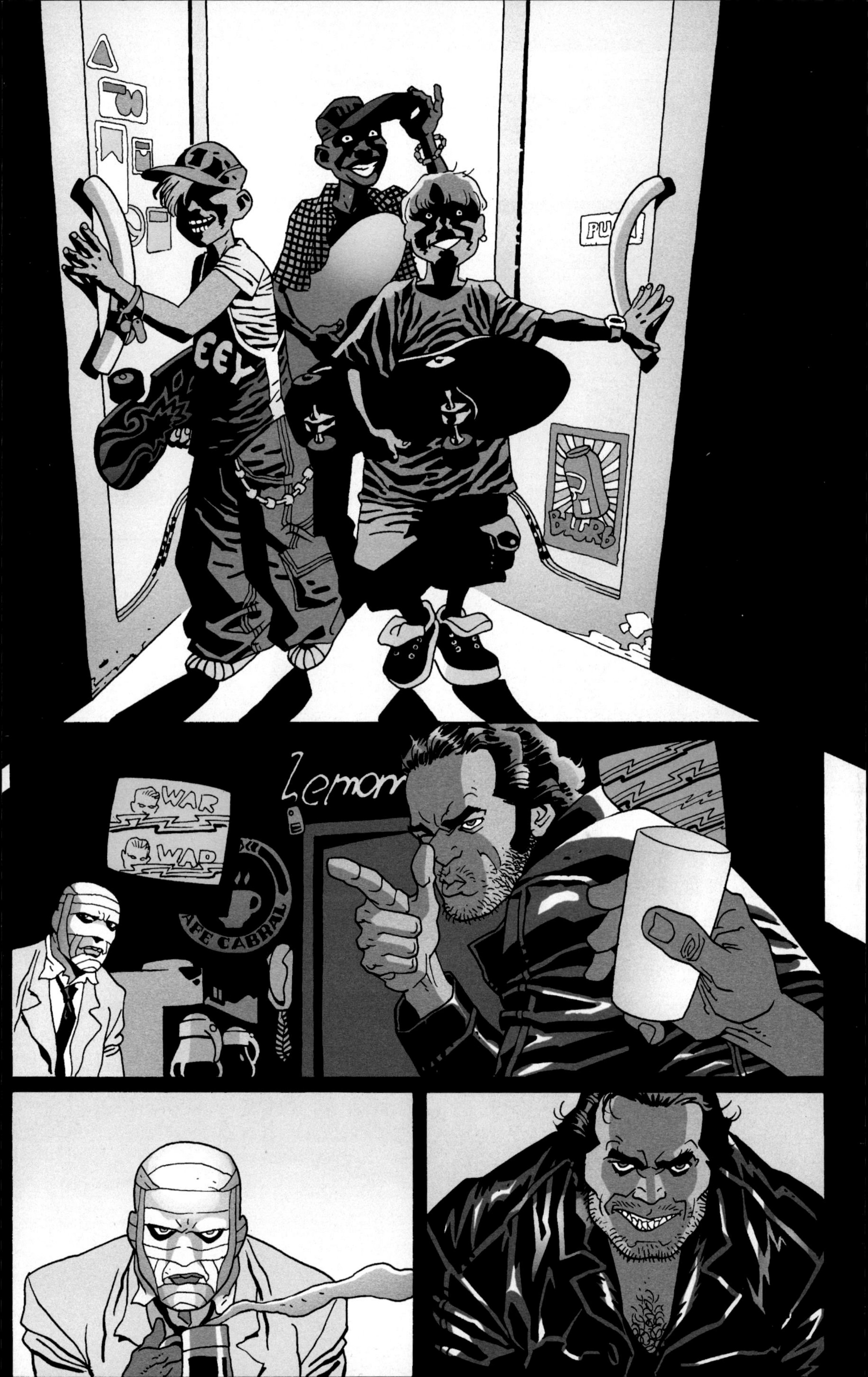
EEY
BLURB
Lemon
WAR
WAP
AFE CABRAL

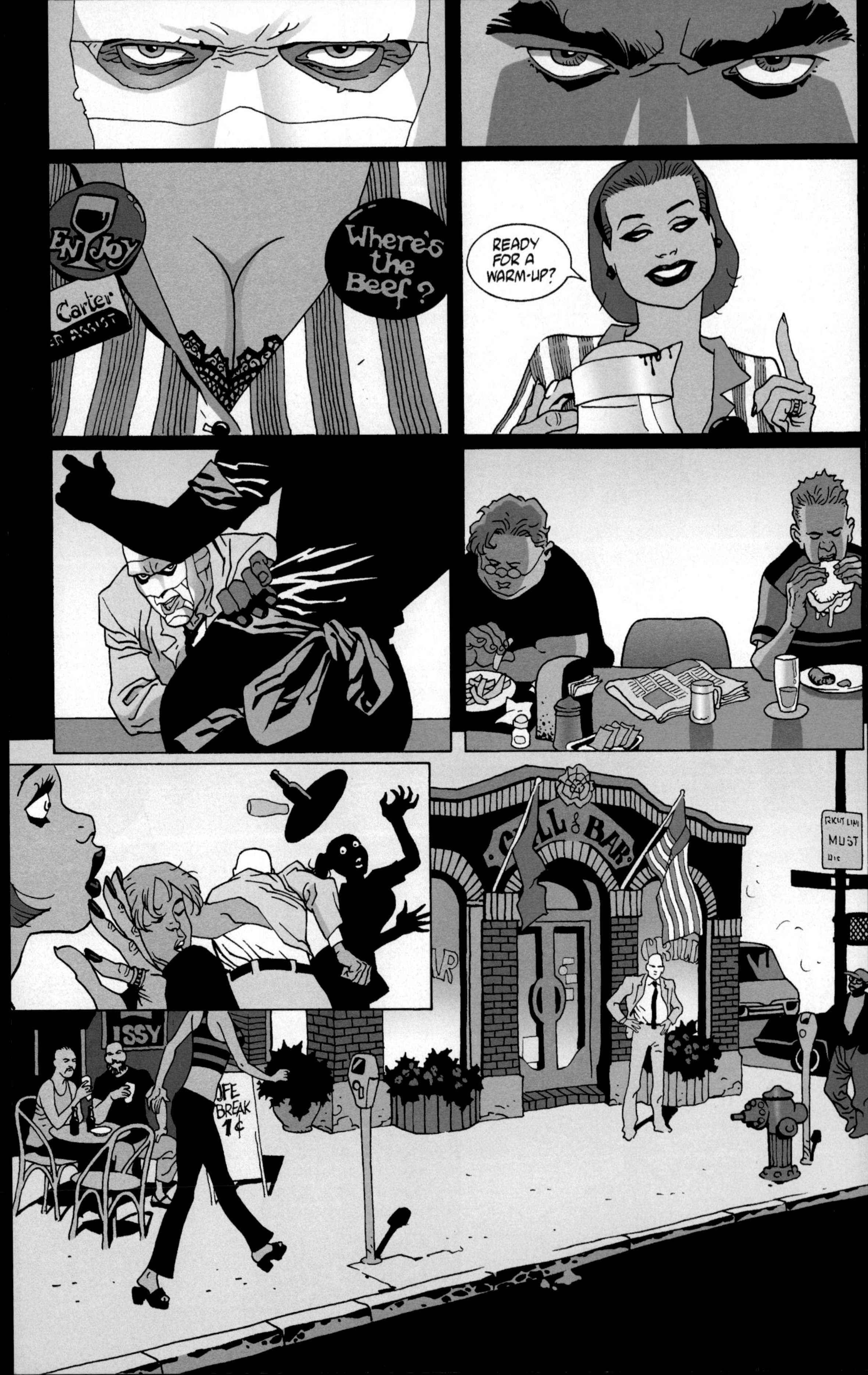
EN JOY
Carter
Where's the Beef?
READY FOR A WARM-UP?
BAR
MUST
ISSY
BREAK
1¢

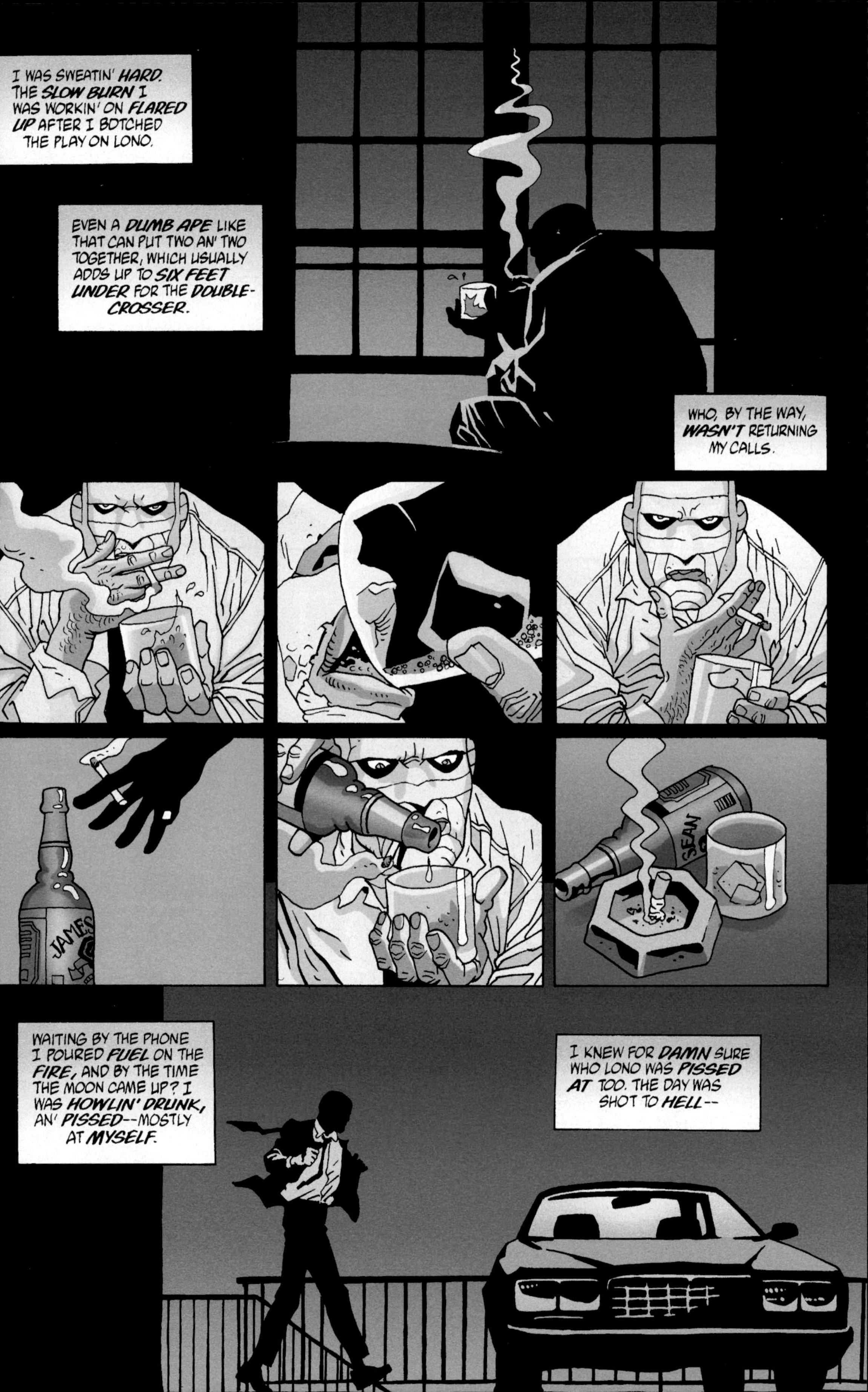
I WAS SWEATIN' HARD. THE SLOW BURN I WAS WORKIN' ON FLARED UP AFTER I BOTCHED THE PLAY ON LONO.
EVEN A DUMB APE LIKE THAT CAN PUT TWO AN' TWO TOGETHER, WHICH USUALLY ADDS UP TO SIX FEET UNDER FOR THE DOUBLE-CROSSER.
WHO, BY THE WAY, WASN'T RETURNING MY CALLS.
JAMES
SEAN
WAITING BY THE PHONE I POURED FUEL ON THE FIRE, AND BY THE TIME THE MOON CAME UP? I WAS HOWLIN' DRUNK, AN' PISSED--MOSTLY AT MYSELF.
I KNEW FOR DAMN SURE WHO LONO WAS PISSED AT TOO. THE DAY WAS SHOT TO HELL--

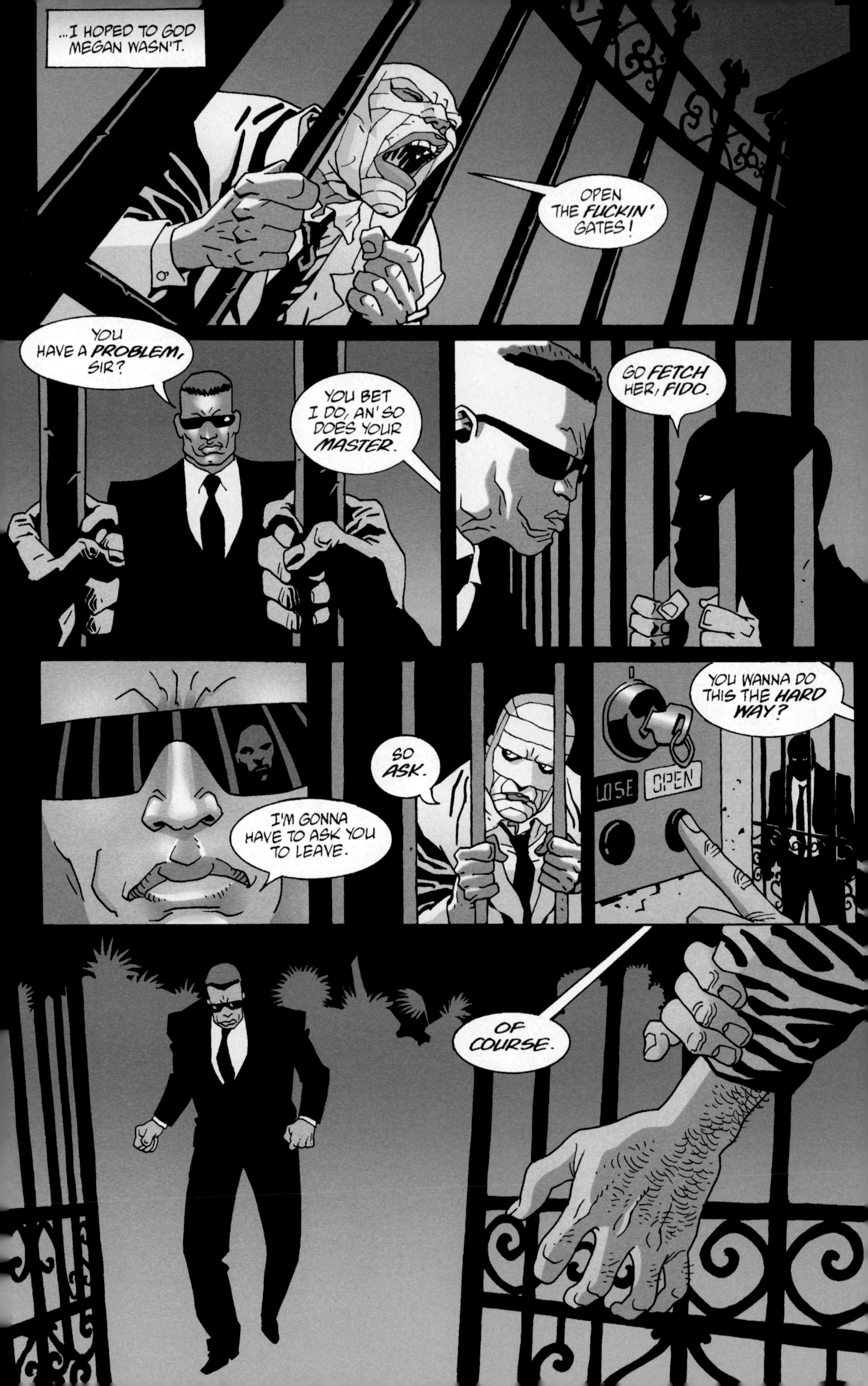
...I HOPED TO GOD MEGAN WASN'T.
OPEN THE FUCKIN' GATES!
YOU HAVE A PROBLEM, SIR?
YOU BET I DO, AN' SO DOES YOUR MASTER.
GO FETCH HER, FIDO.
I'M GONNA HAVE TO ASK YOU TO LEAVE.
SO ASK.
YOU WANNA DO THIS THE HARD WAY?
LOSE
OPEN
OF COURSE.

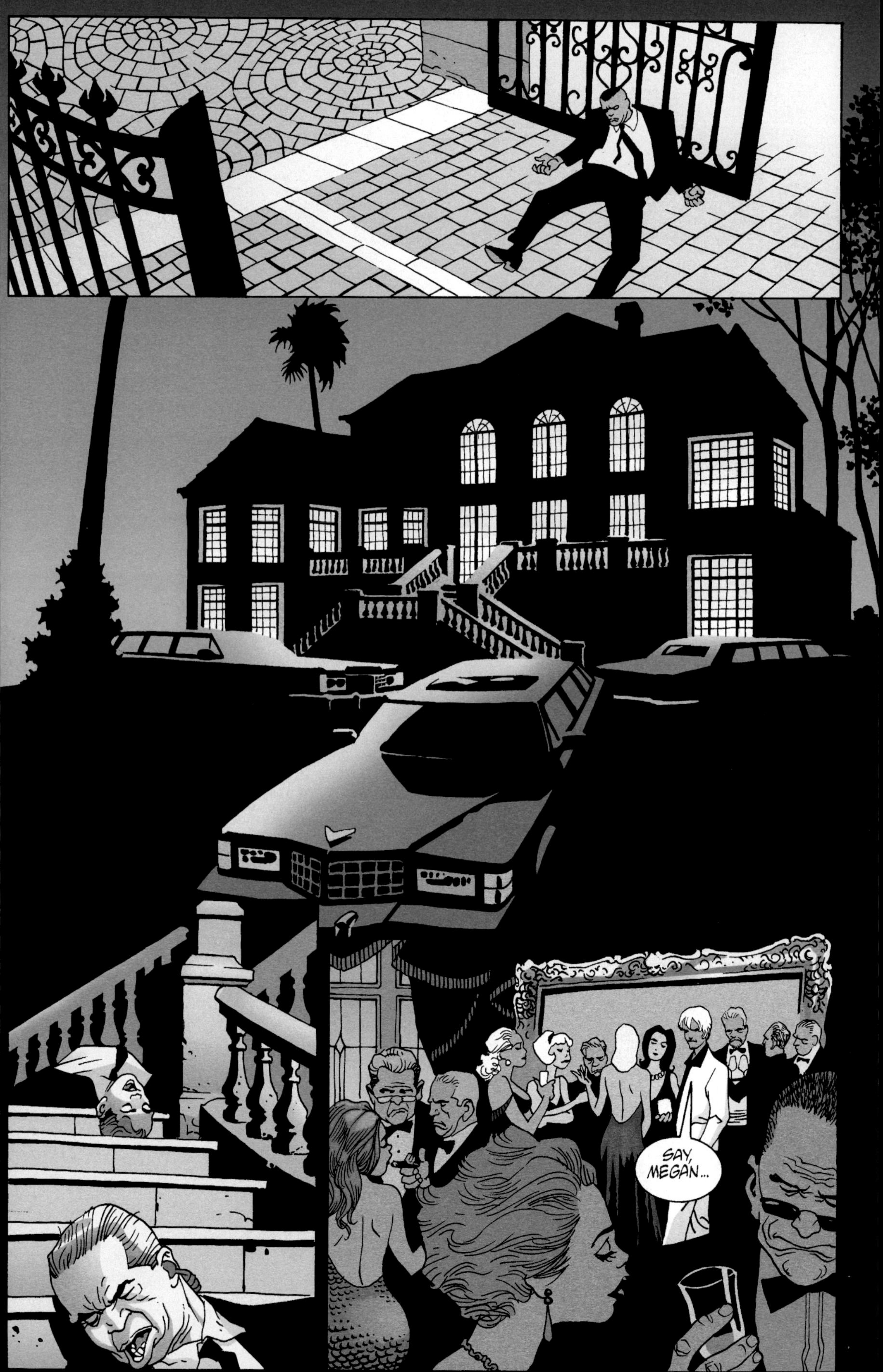
SAY, MEGAN...

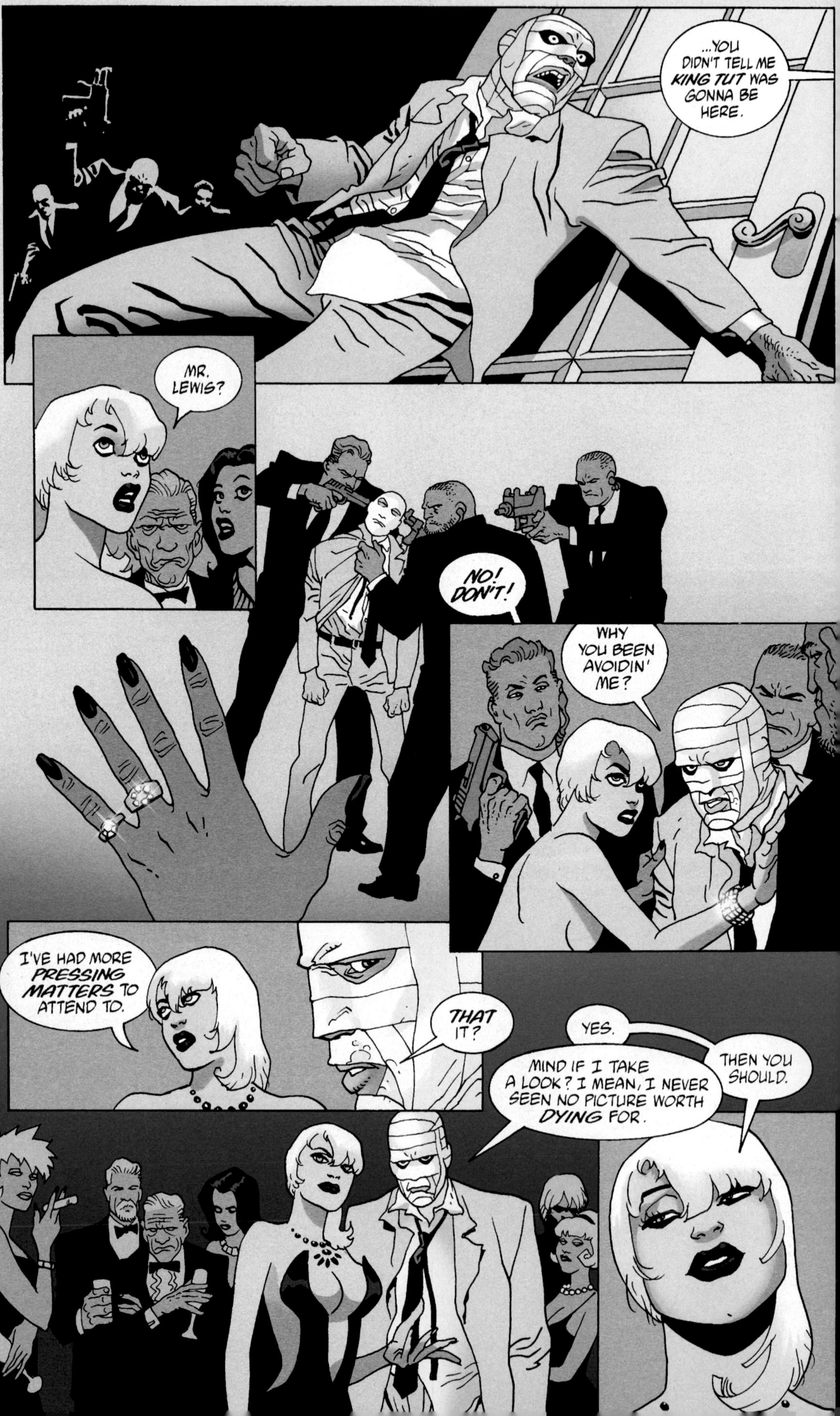
...YOU DIDN'T TELL ME KING TUT WAS GONNA BE HERE.
MR. LEWIS?
NO! DON'T!
WHY YOU BEEN AVOIDIN' ME?
I'VE HAD MORE PRESSING MATTERS TO ATTEND TO.
THAT IT?
YES.
THEN YOU SHOULD.
MIND IF I TAKE A LOOK? I MEAN, I NEVER SEEN NO PICTURE WORTH DYING FOR.

LA MORTE DIL CESARE

MR. LEWIS...

ARE YOU *ALL RIGHT?*

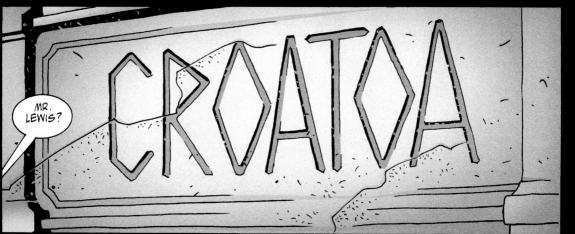

MR. LEWIS?

CROATOA

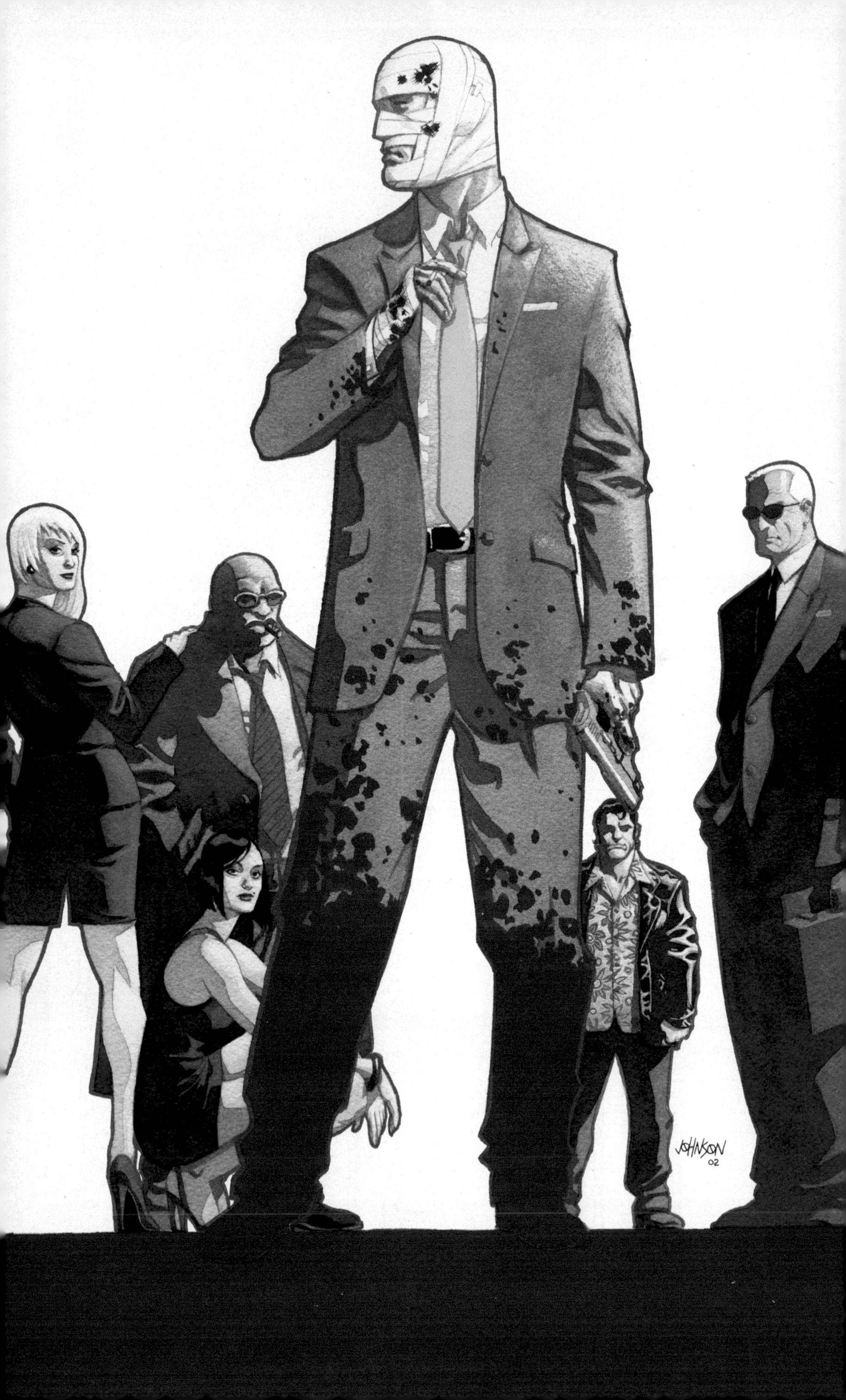
JOHNSON
02

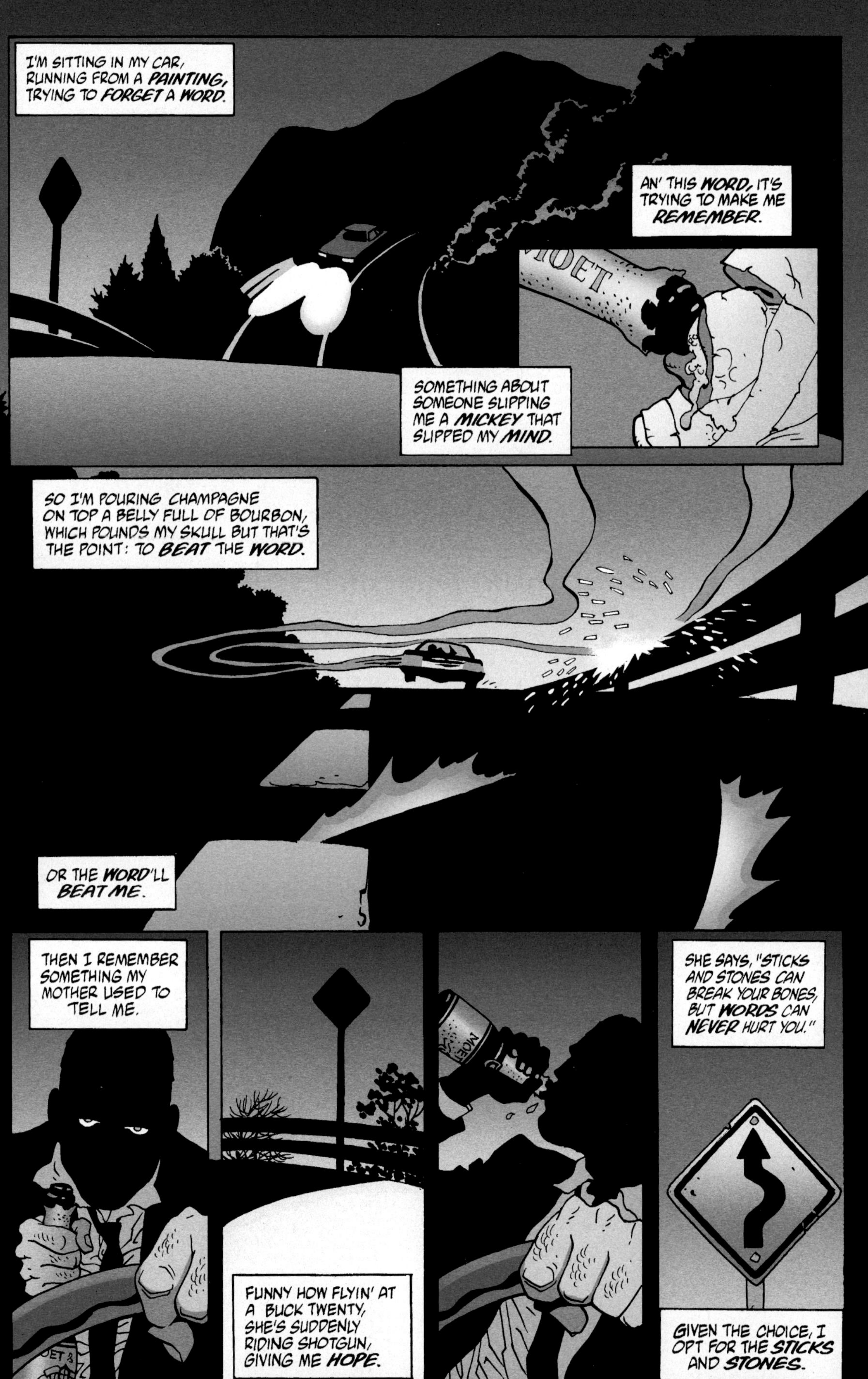
I'M SITTING IN MY CAR, RUNNING FROM A PAINTING, TRYING TO FORGET A WORD.
AN' THIS WORD, IT'S TRYING TO MAKE ME REMEMBER.
MOET
SOMETHING ABOUT SOMEONE SLIPPING ME A MICKEY THAT SLIPPED MY MIND.
SO I'M POURING CHAMPAGNE ON TOP A BELLY FULL OF BOURBON, WHICH POUNDS MY SKULL BUT THAT'S THE POINT: TO BEAT THE WORD.
OR THE WORD'LL BEAT ME.
THEN I REMEMBER SOMETHING MY MOTHER USED TO TELL ME.
FUNNY HOW FLYIN' AT A BUCK TWENTY, SHE'S SUDDENLY RIDING SHOTGUN, GIVING ME HOPE.
SHE SAYS, "STICKS AND STONES CAN BREAK YOUR BONES, BUT WORDS CAN NEVER HURT YOU."
GIVEN THE CHOICE, I OPT FOR THE STICKS AND STONES.

THANKS, MOM.

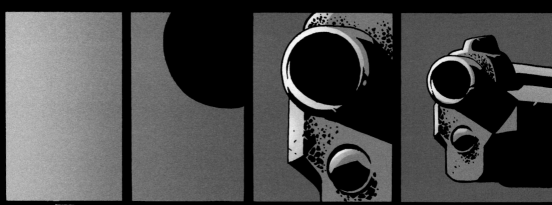

THE COUNTERFIFTH DETECTIVE PART 5

BRIAN AZZARELLO
writer

EDUARDO RISSO
artist

PATRICIA MULVIHILL
colorist

CLEM ROBINS
letterer

DIGITAL CHAMELEON
separations

DAVE JOHNSON
cover artist

ZACHARY RAU
ass't ed.

WILL DENNIS
editor

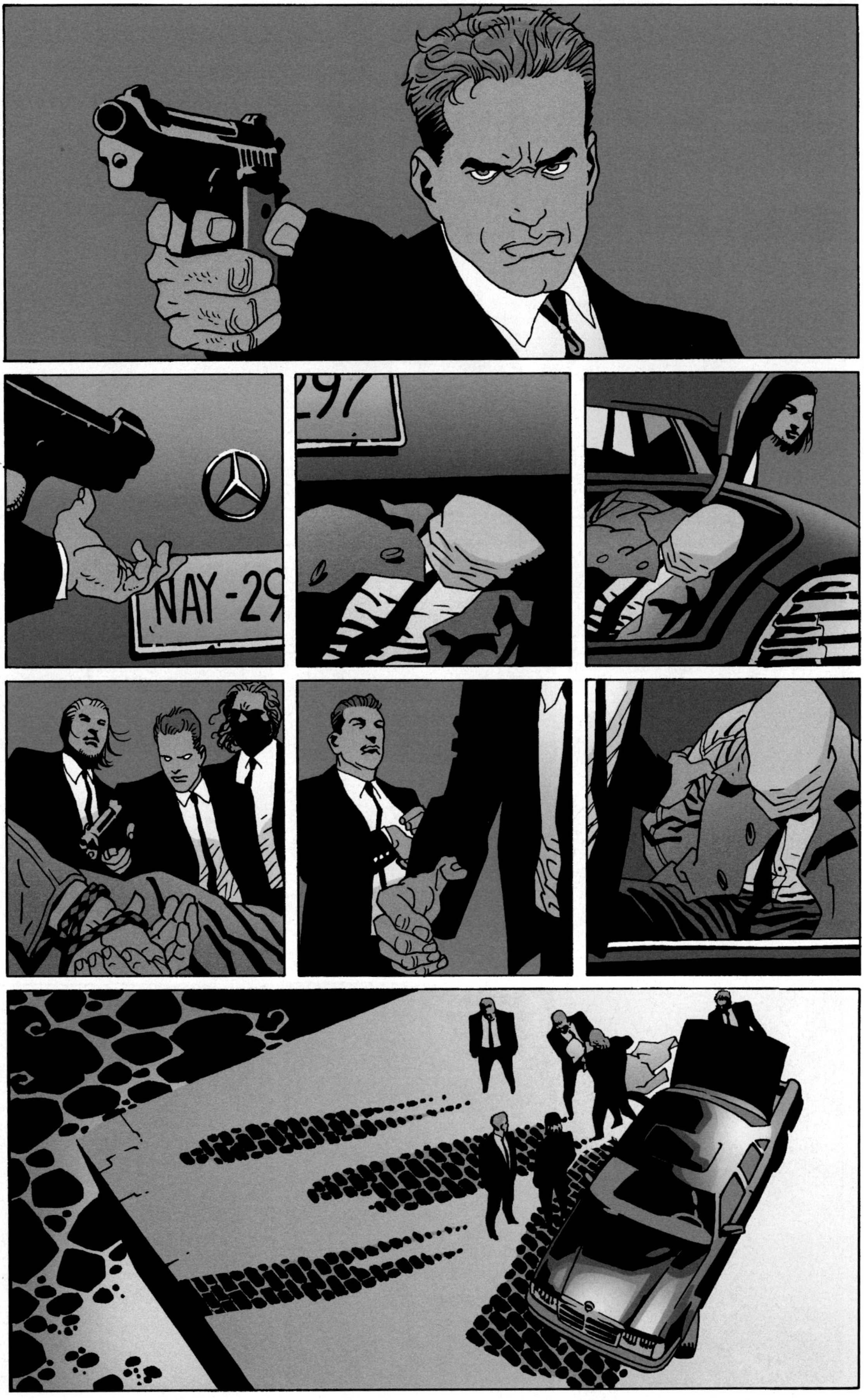
NAY-29
297

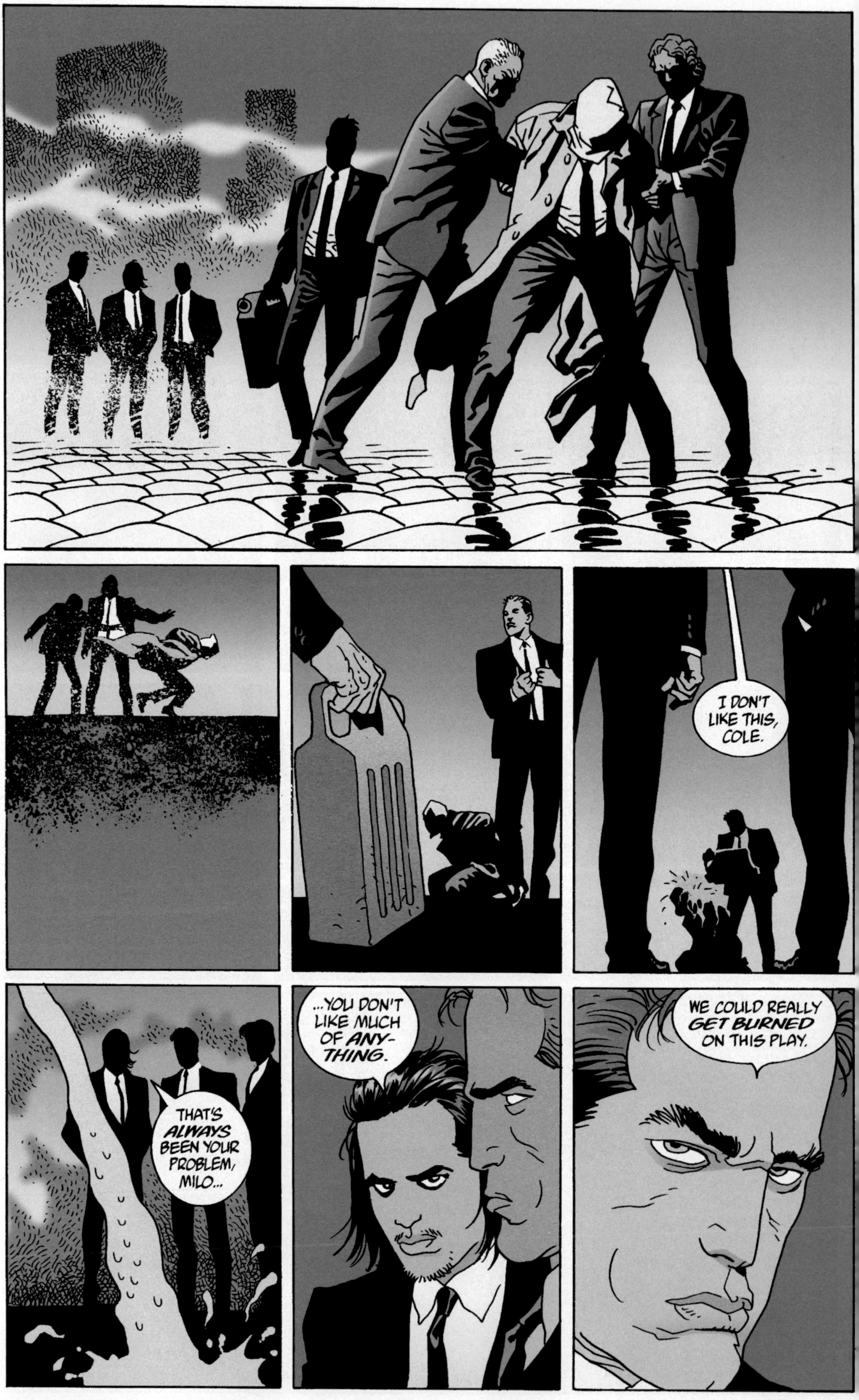
I DON'T LIKE THIS, COLE.
THAT'S *ALWAYS* BEEN YOUR PROBLEM, MILO...
...YOU DON'T LIKE MUCH OF *ANY-THING*.
WE COULD REALLY *GET BURNED* ON THIS PLAY.

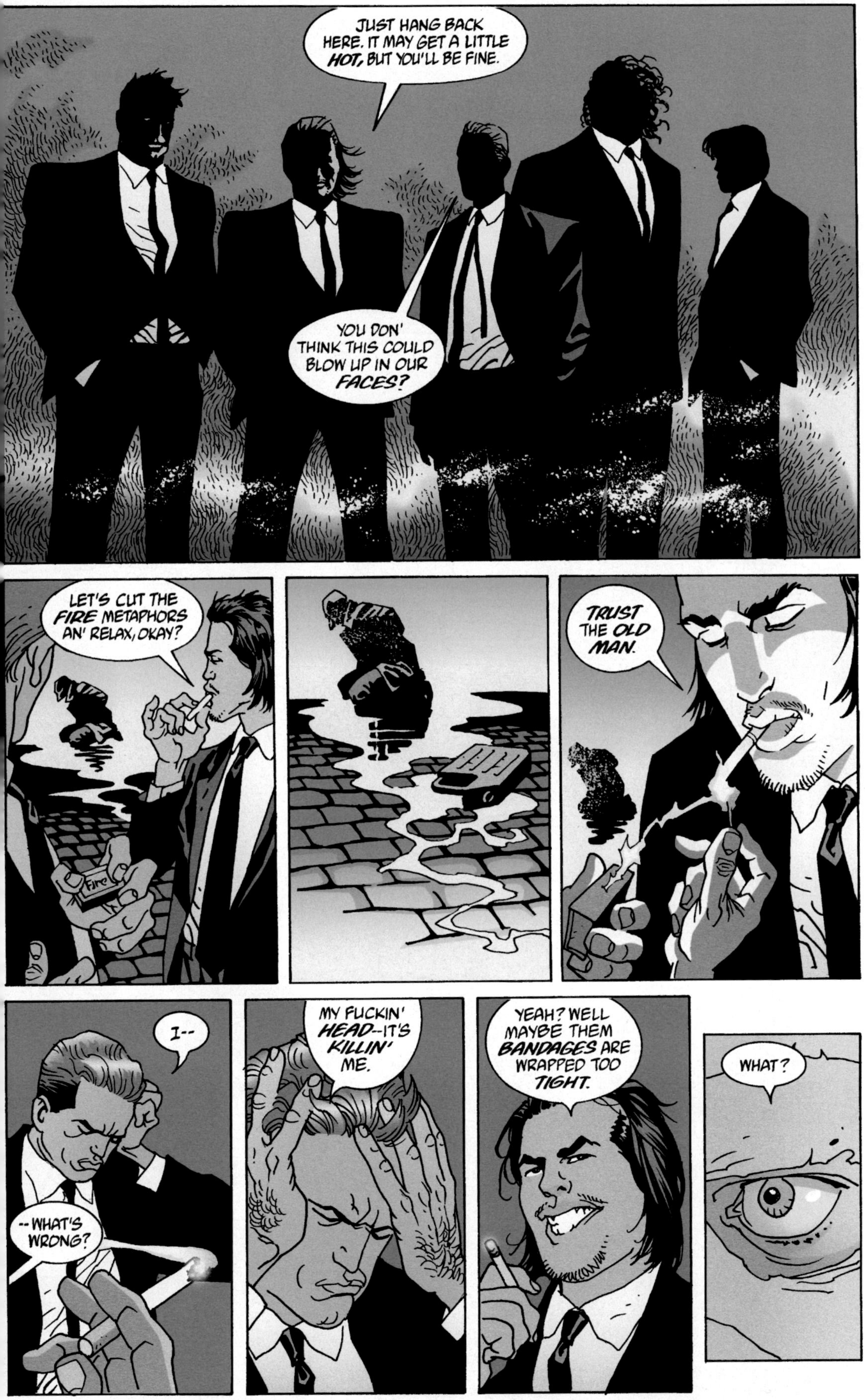
JUST HANG BACK HERE. IT MAY GET A LITTLE HOT, BUT YOU'LL BE FINE.
YOU DON' THINK THIS COULD BLOW UP IN OUR FACES?
LET'S CUT THE FIRE METAPHORS AN' RELAX, OKAY?
Fire
TRUST THE OLD MAN.
I--
--WHAT'S WRONG?
MY FUCKIN' HEAD--IT'S KILLIN' ME.
YEAH? WELL MAYBE THEM BANDAGES ARE WRAPPED TOO TIGHT.
WHAT?

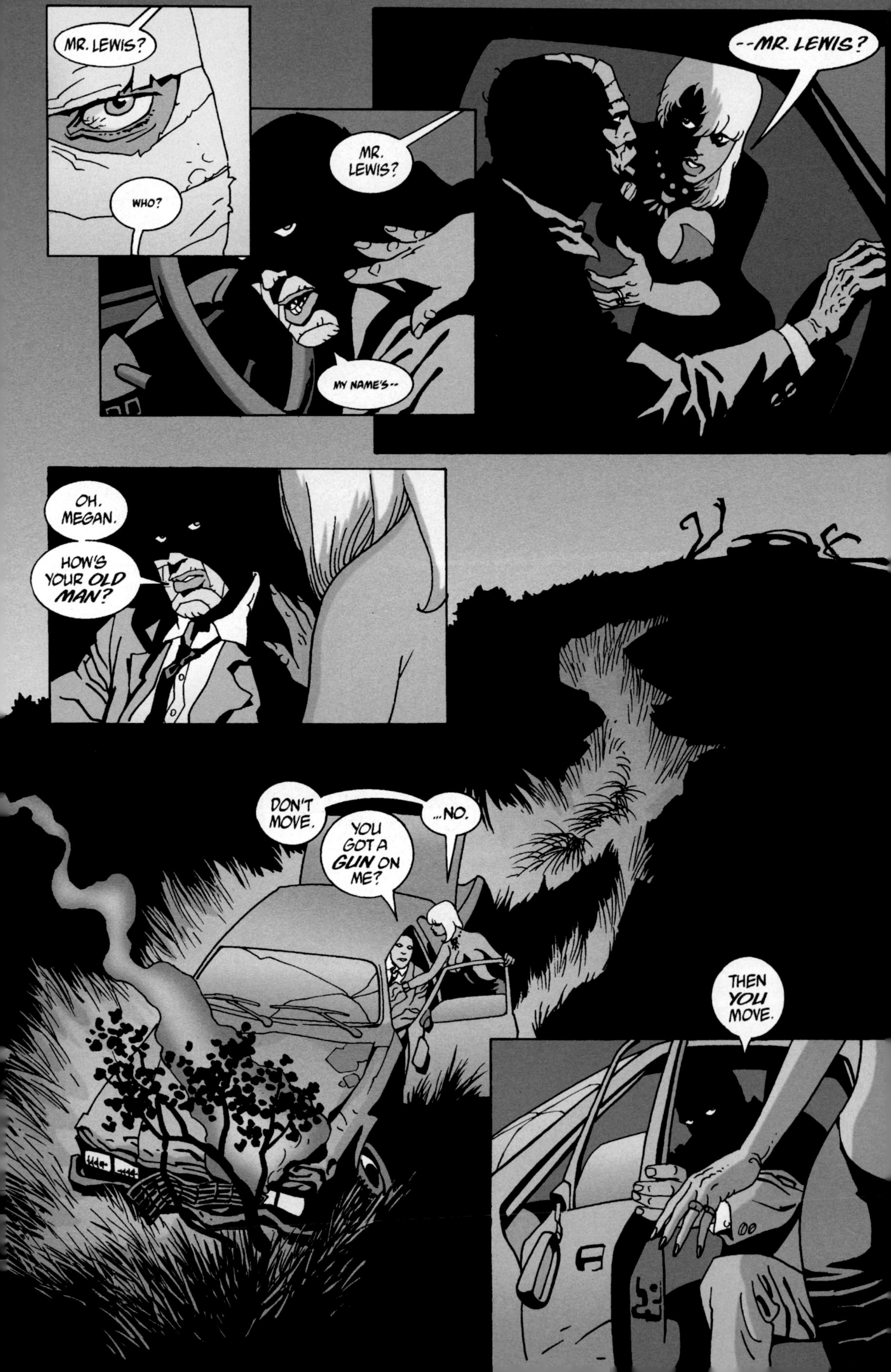
MR. LEWIS?
WHO?
MR. LEWIS?
MY NAME'S--
--MR. LEWIS?
OH. MEGAN.
HOW'S YOUR OLD MAN?
DON'T MOVE.
...NO.
YOU GOT A GUN ON ME?
THEN YOU MOVE.

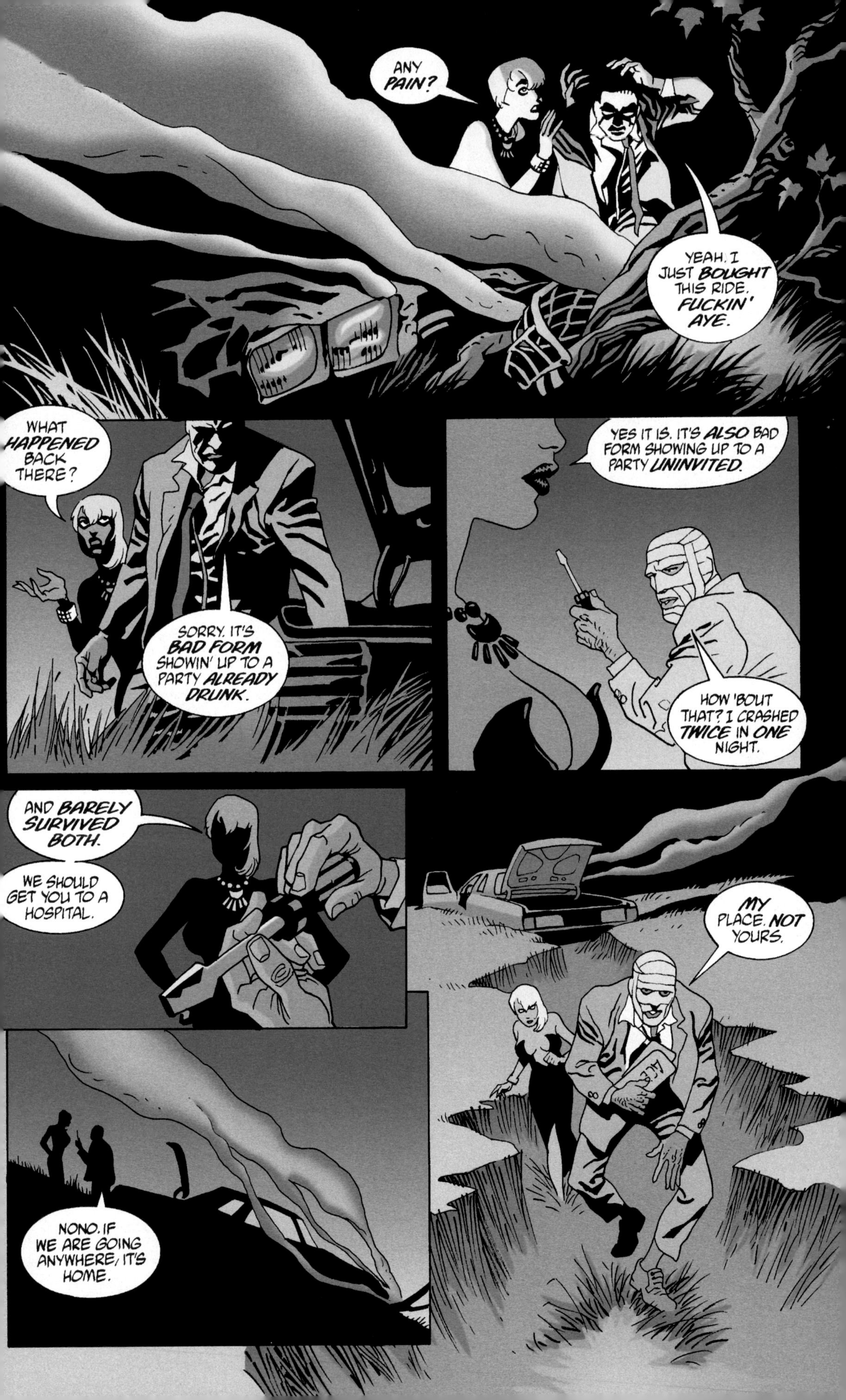
ANY PAIN?
YEAH. I JUST BOUGHT THIS RIDE. FUCKIN' AYE.
WHAT HAPPENED BACK THERE?
SORRY. IT'S BAD FORM SHOWIN' UP TO A PARTY ALREADY DRUNK.
YES IT IS. IT'S ALSO BAD FORM SHOWING UP TO A PARTY UNINVITED.
HOW 'BOUT THAT? I CRASHED TWICE IN ONE NIGHT.
AND BARELY SURVIVED BOTH.
WE SHOULD GET YOU TO A HOSPITAL.
NONO. IF WE ARE GOING ANYWHERE, IT'S HOME.
MY PLACE. NOT YOURS.

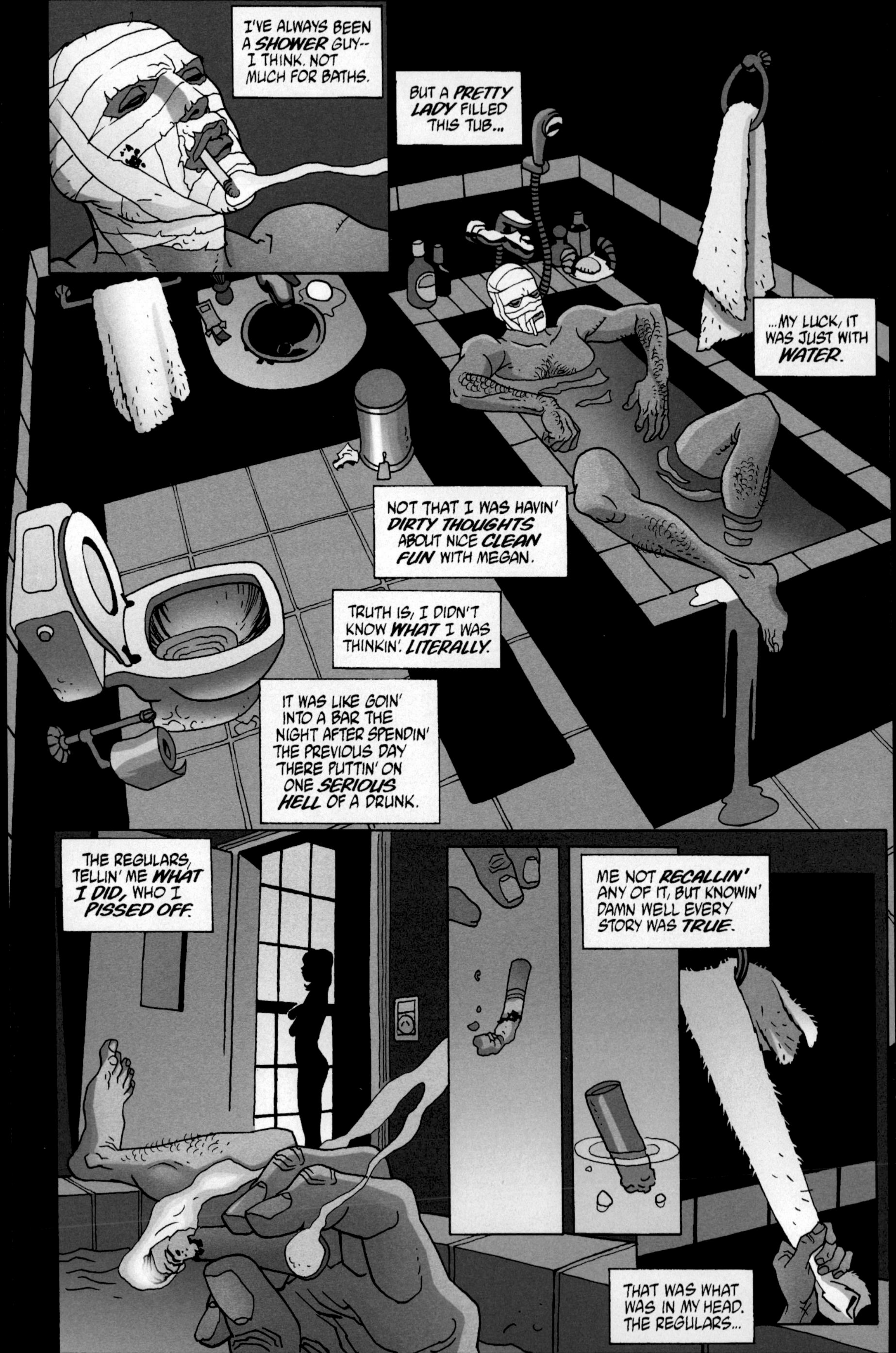
I'VE ALWAYS BEEN A SHOWER GUY-- I THINK. NOT MUCH FOR BATHS.
BUT A PRETTY LADY FILLED THIS TUB...
...MY LUCK, IT WAS JUST WITH WATER.
NOT THAT I WAS HAVIN' DIRTY THOUGHTS ABOUT NICE CLEAN FUN WITH MEGAN.
TRUTH IS, I DIDN'T KNOW WHAT I WAS THINKIN'. LITERALLY.
IT WAS LIKE GOIN' INTO A BAR THE NIGHT AFTER SPENDIN' THE PREVIOUS DAY THERE PUTTIN' ON ONE SERIOUS HELL OF A DRUNK.
THE REGULARS, TELLIN' ME WHAT I DID, WHO I PISSED OFF.
ME NOT RECALLIN' ANY OF IT, BUT KNOWIN' DAMN WELL EVERY STORY WAS TRUE.
THAT WAS WHAT WAS IN MY HEAD. THE REGULARS...

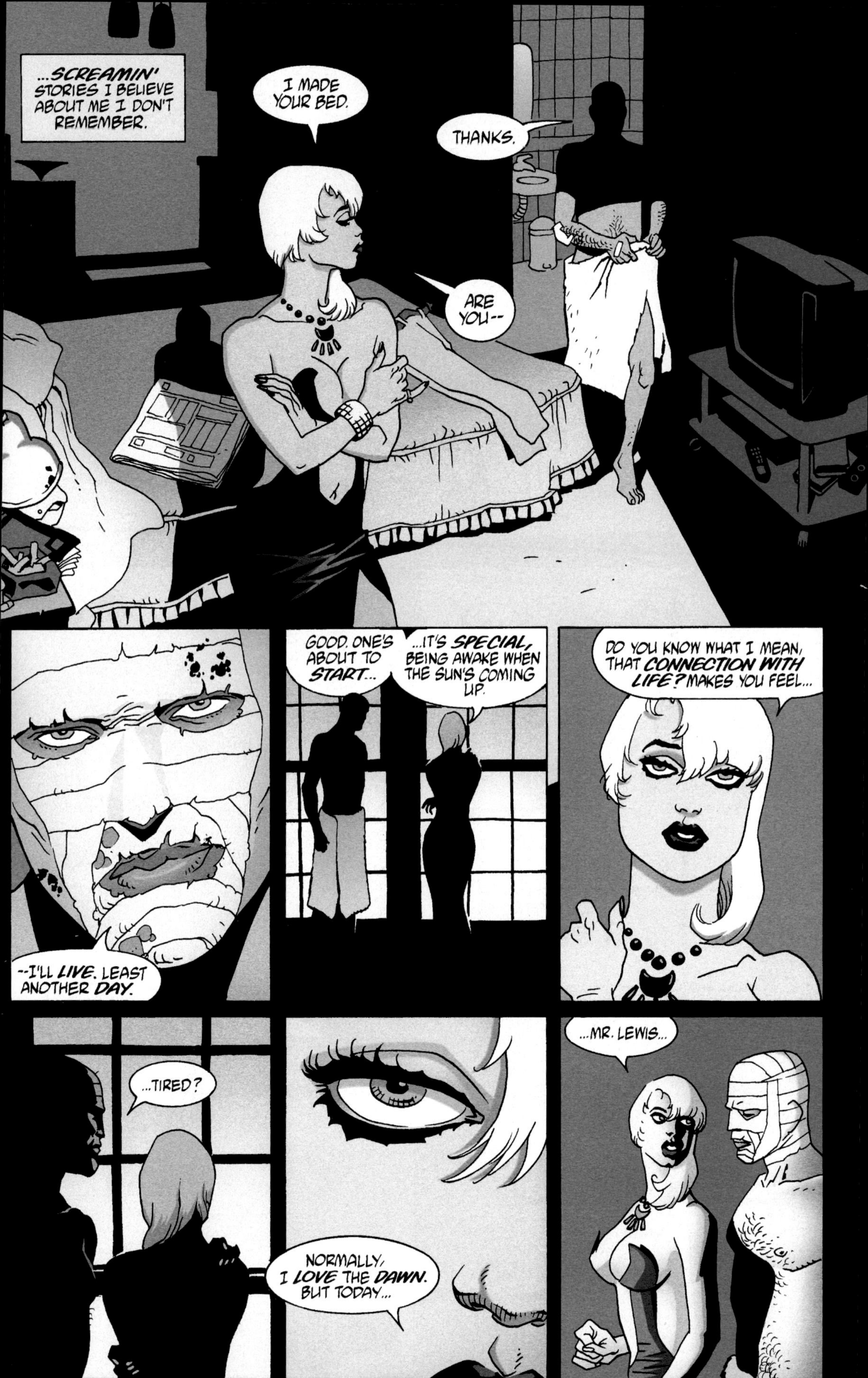
...SCREAMIN' STORIES I BELIEVE ABOUT ME I DON'T REMEMBER.
I MADE YOUR BED.
THANKS.
ARE YOU--
--I'LL LIVE. LEAST ANOTHER DAY.
GOOD. ONE'S ABOUT TO START...
...IT'S SPECIAL, BEING AWAKE WHEN THE SUN'S COMING UP.
DO YOU KNOW WHAT I MEAN, THAT CONNECTION WITH LIFE? MAKES YOU FEEL...
...TIRED?
NORMALLY, I LOVE THE DAWN. BUT TODAY...
...MR. LEWIS...

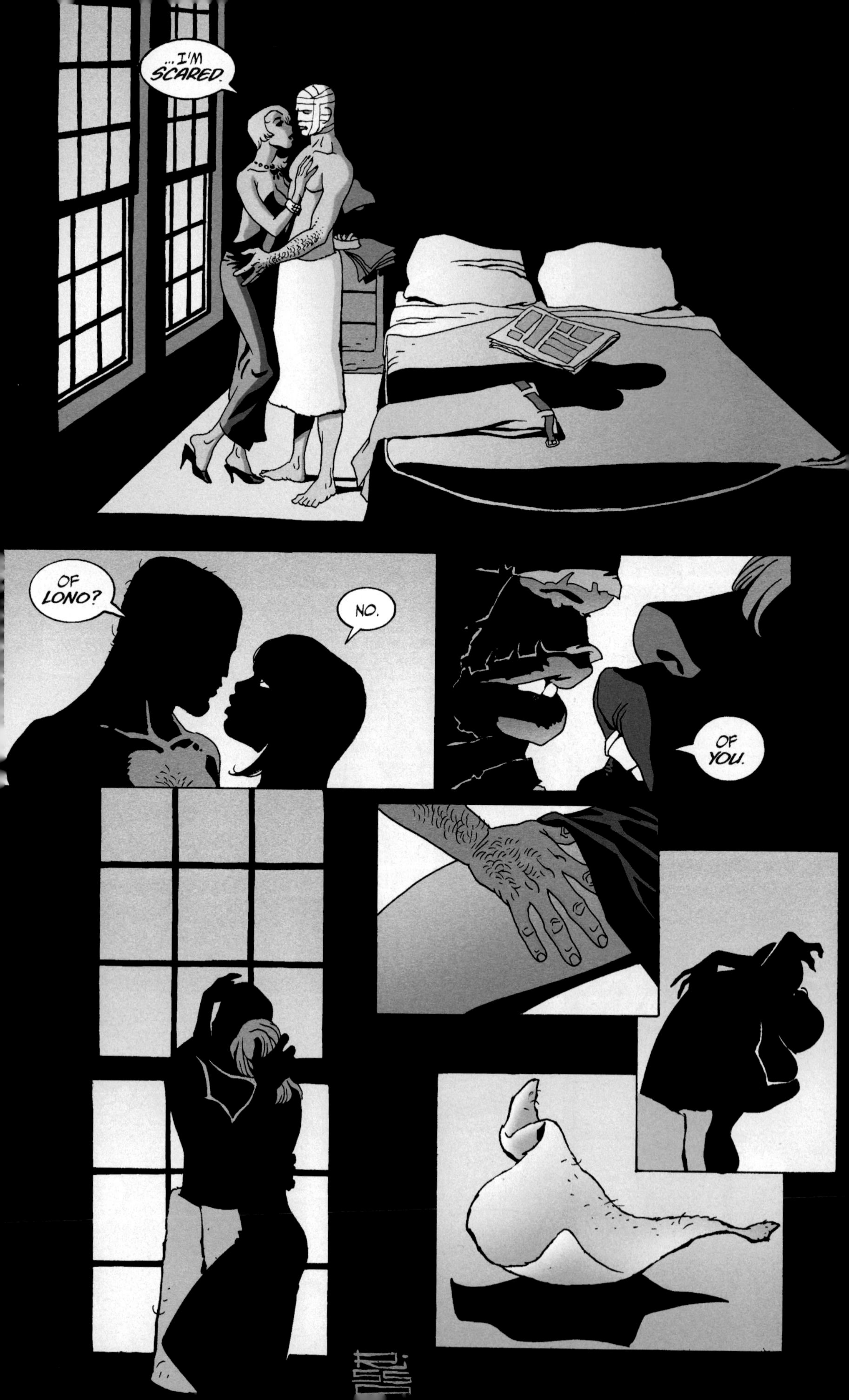
...I'M SCARED.
OF LONO?
NO.
OF YOU.

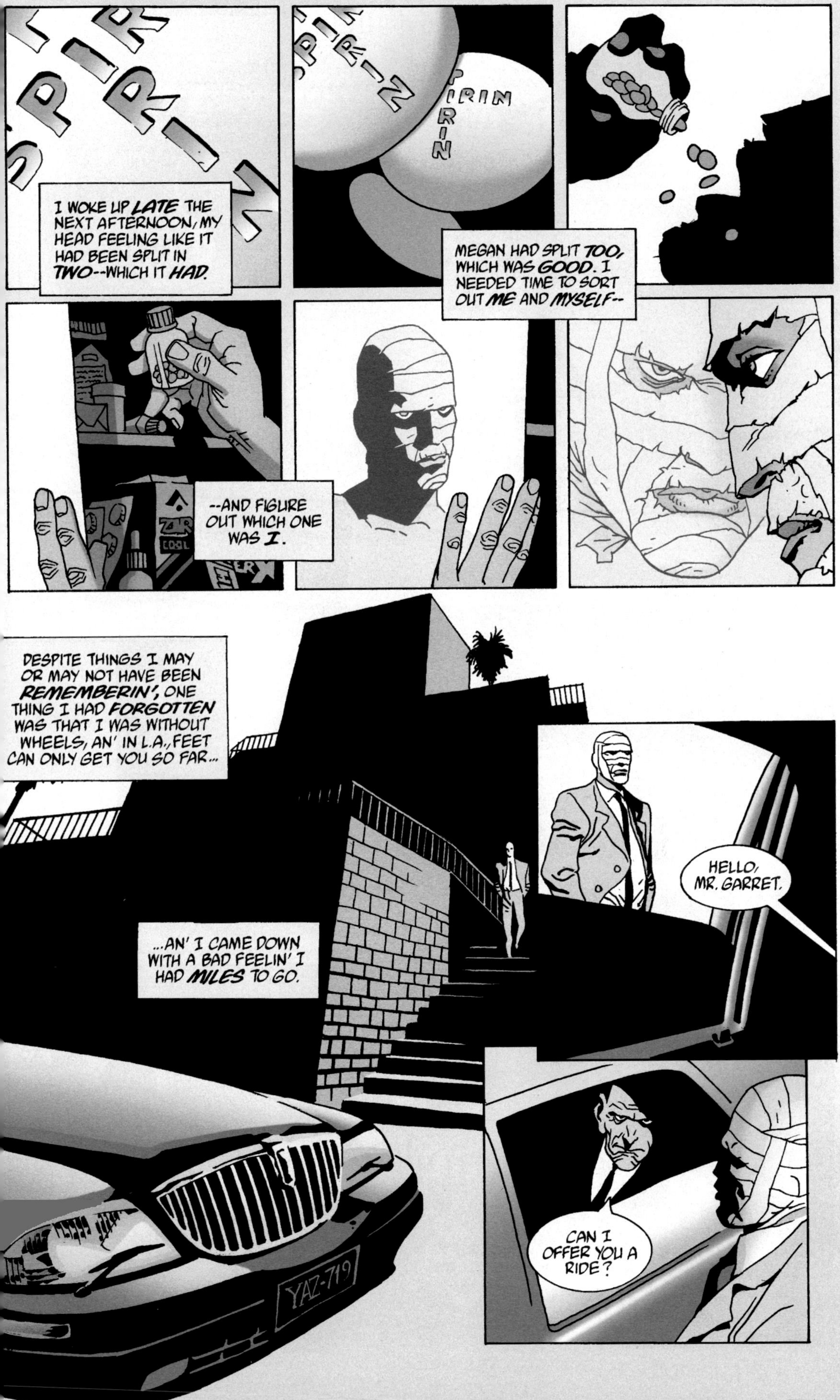
SPIRIN
I WOKE UP LATE THE NEXT AFTERNOON, MY HEAD FEELING LIKE IT HAD BEEN SPLIT IN TWO--WHICH IT HAD.
PIR R-I-N
IRIN
RIN
MEGAN HAD SPLIT TOO, WHICH WAS GOOD. I NEEDED TIME TO SORT OUT ME AND MYSELF--
--AND FIGURE OUT WHICH ONE WAS I.
DESPITE THINGS I MAY OR MAY NOT HAVE BEEN REMEMBERIN', ONE THING I HAD FORGOTTEN WAS THAT I WAS WITHOUT WHEELS, AN' IN L.A., FEET CAN ONLY GET YOU SO FAR...
...AN' I CAME DOWN WITH A BAD FEELIN' I HAD MILES TO GO.
HELLO, MR. GARRET.
CAN I OFFER YOU A RIDE?
YAZ-719

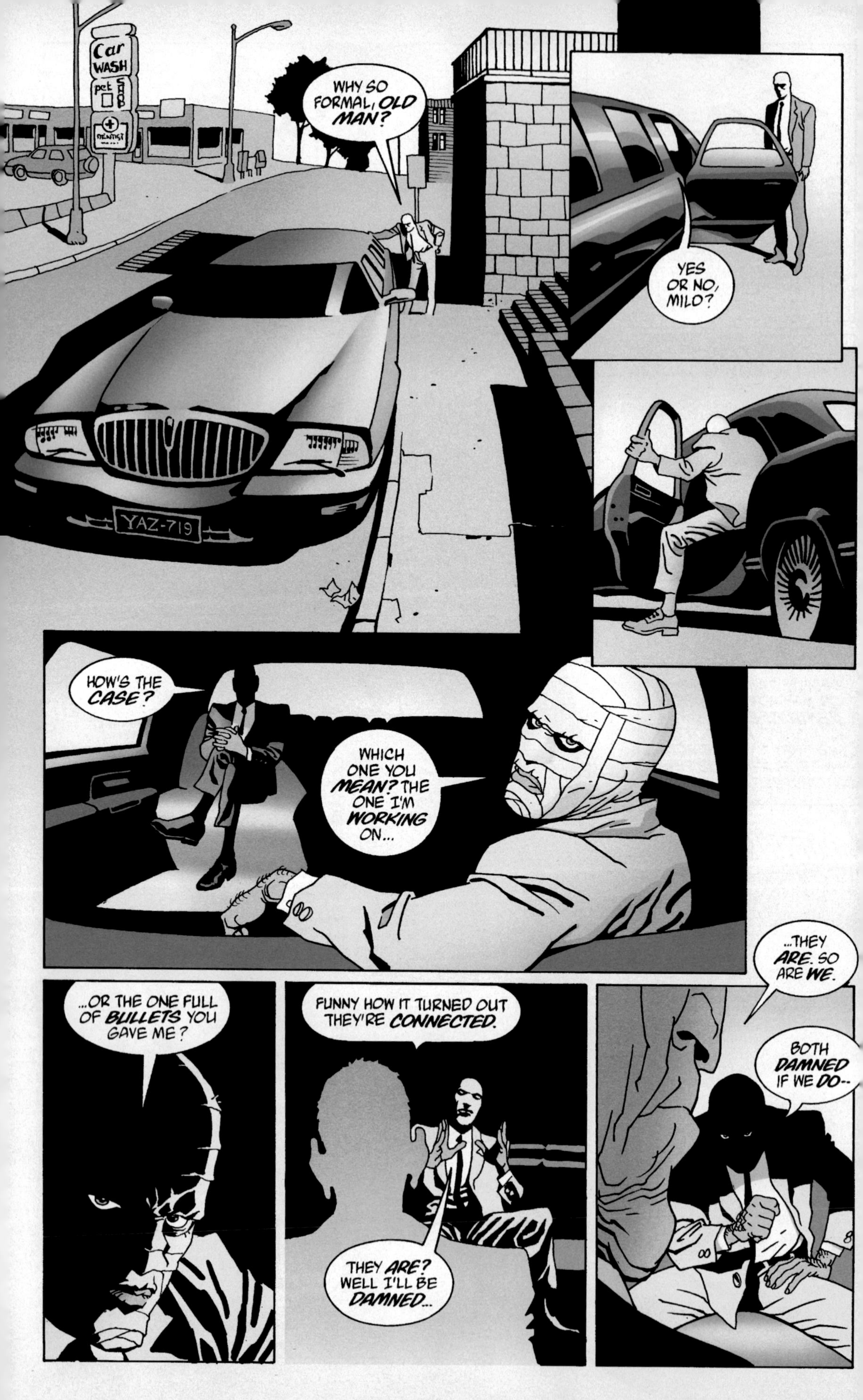
Car WASH
pet SHOP
DENTIST
WHY SO FORMAL, OLD MAN?
YAZ-719
YES OR NO, MILO?
HOW'S THE CASE?
WHICH ONE YOU MEAN? THE ONE I'M WORKING ON...
...OR THE ONE FULL OF BULLETS YOU GAVE ME?
FUNNY HOW IT TURNED OUT THEY'RE CONNECTED.
THEY ARE? WELL I'LL BE DAMNED...
...THEY ARE. SO ARE WE.
BOTH DAMNED IF WE DO--

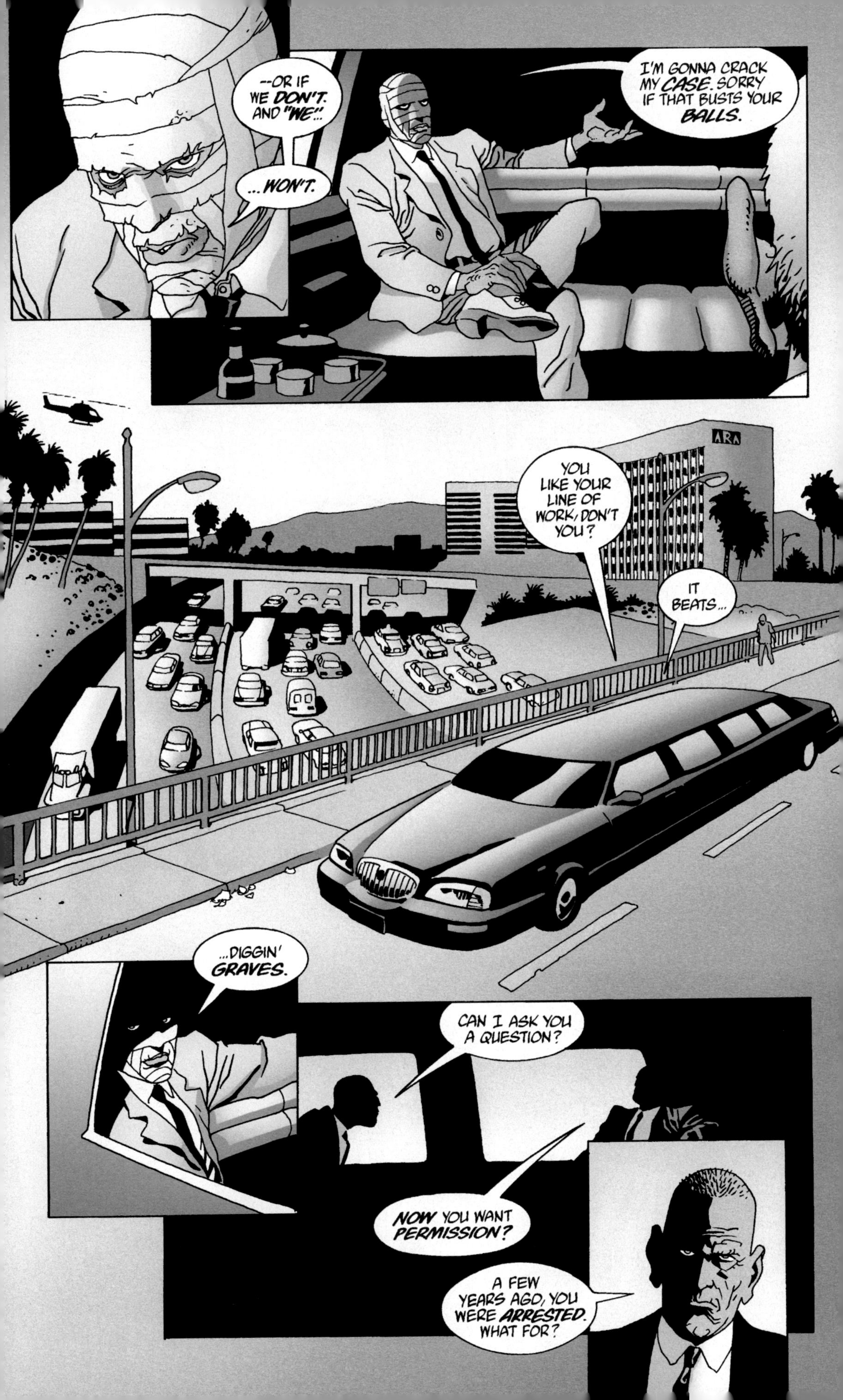

--OR IF WE DON'T. AND "WE"...
...WON'T.
I'M GONNA CRACK MY CASE. SORRY IF THAT BUSTS YOUR BALLS.
ARA
YOU LIKE YOUR LINE OF WORK, DON'T YOU?
IT BEATS...
...DIGGIN' GRAVES.
CAN I ASK YOU A QUESTION?
NOW YOU WANT PERMISSION?
A FEW YEARS AGO, YOU WERE ARRESTED. WHAT FOR?

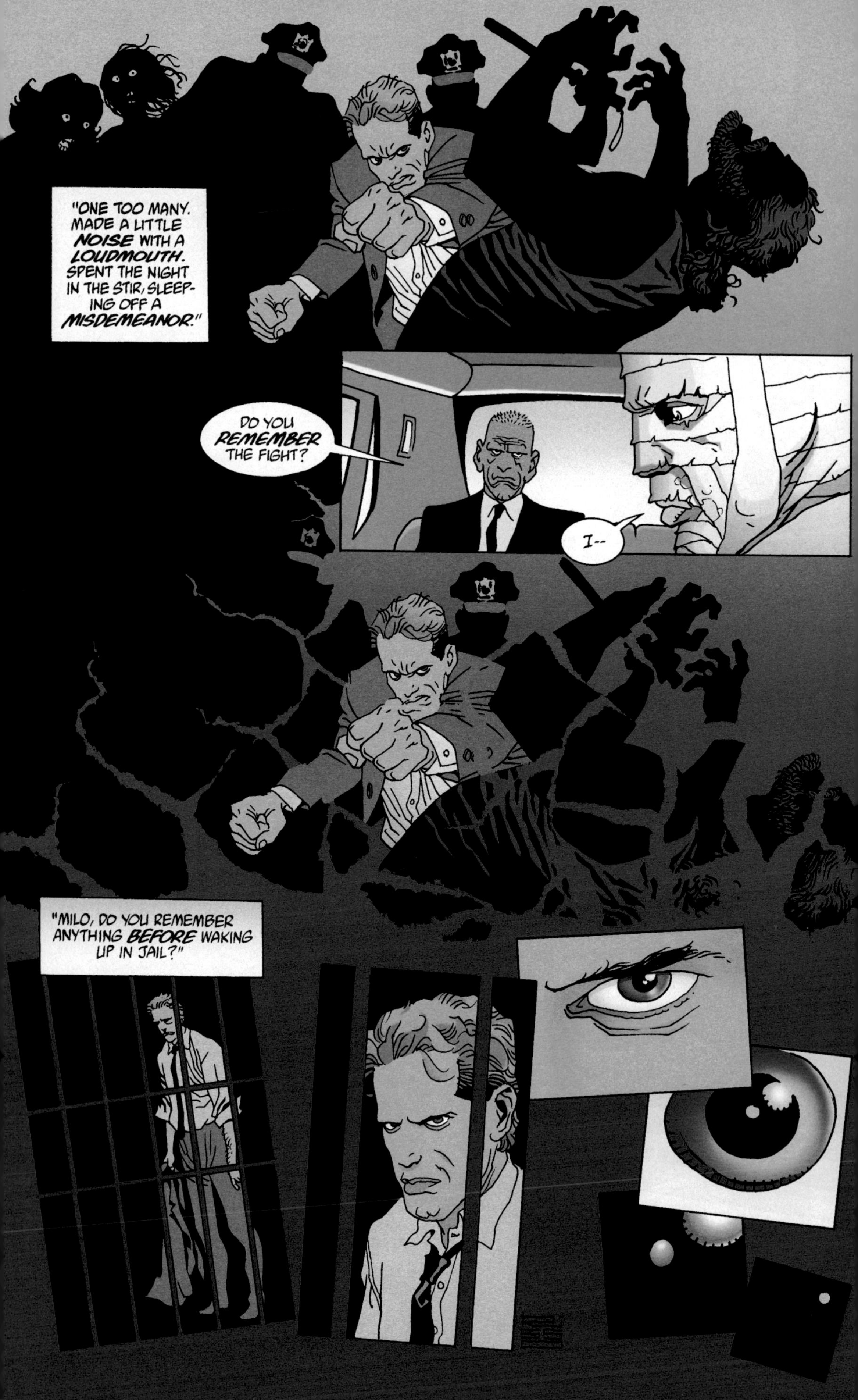
"ONE TOO MANY. MADE A LITTLE NOISE WITH A LOUDMOUTH. SPENT THE NIGHT IN THE STIR, SLEEPING OFF A MISDEMEANOR."
DO YOU REMEMBER THE FIGHT?
I--
"MILO, DO YOU REMEMBER ANYTHING BEFORE WAKING UP IN JAIL?"

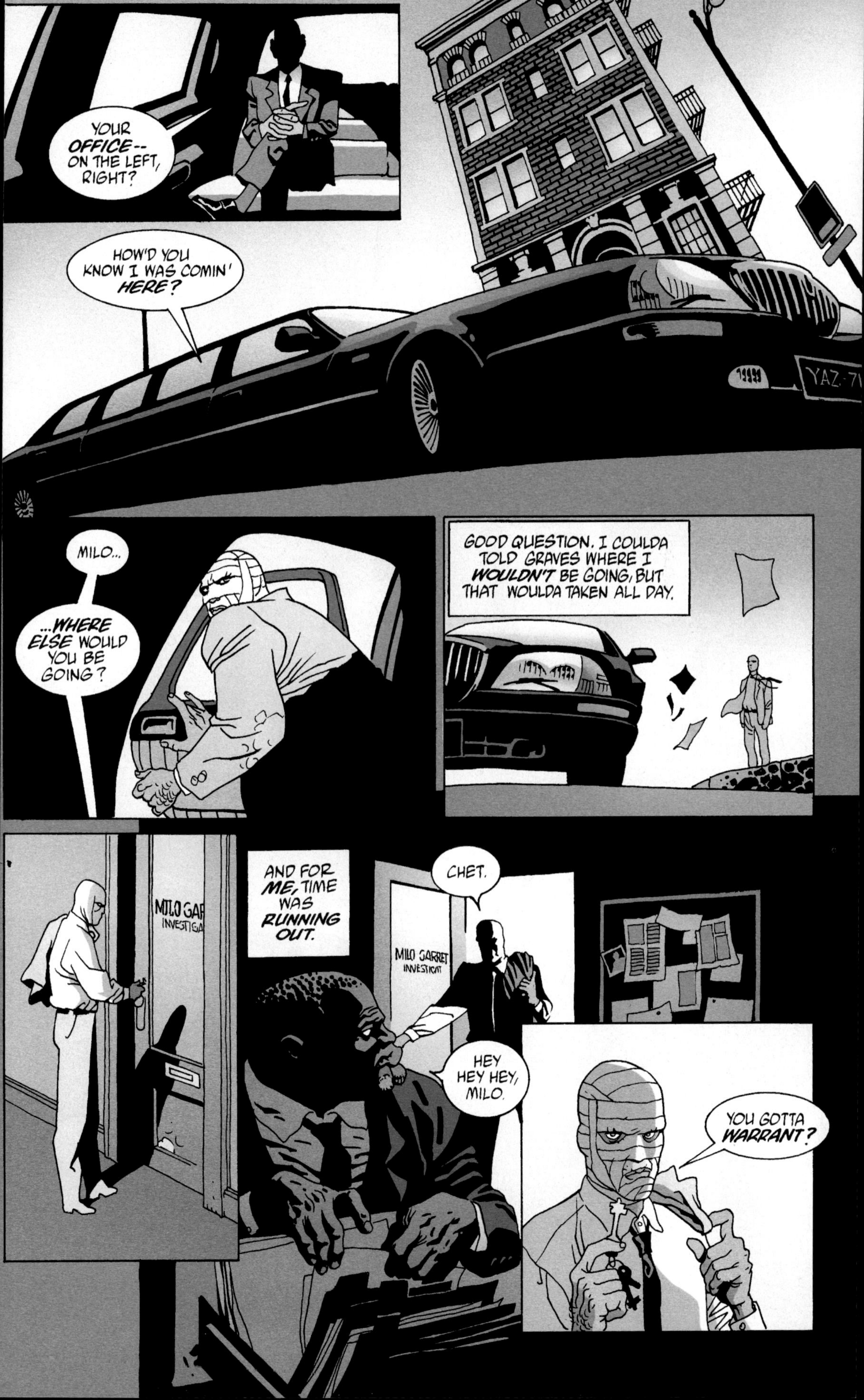
YOUR OFFICE -- ON THE LEFT, RIGHT?
HOW'D YOU KNOW I WAS COMIN' HERE?
YAZ-7
MILO...
...WHERE ELSE WOULD YOU BE GOING?
GOOD QUESTION. I COULDA TOLD GRAVES WHERE I WOULDN'T BE GOING, BUT THAT WOULDA TAKEN ALL DAY.
MILO GARR INVESTIGA
AND FOR ME, TIME WAS RUNNING OUT.
CHET.
MILO GARRET INVESTIGAT
HEY HEY HEY, MILO.
YOU GOTTA WARRANT?

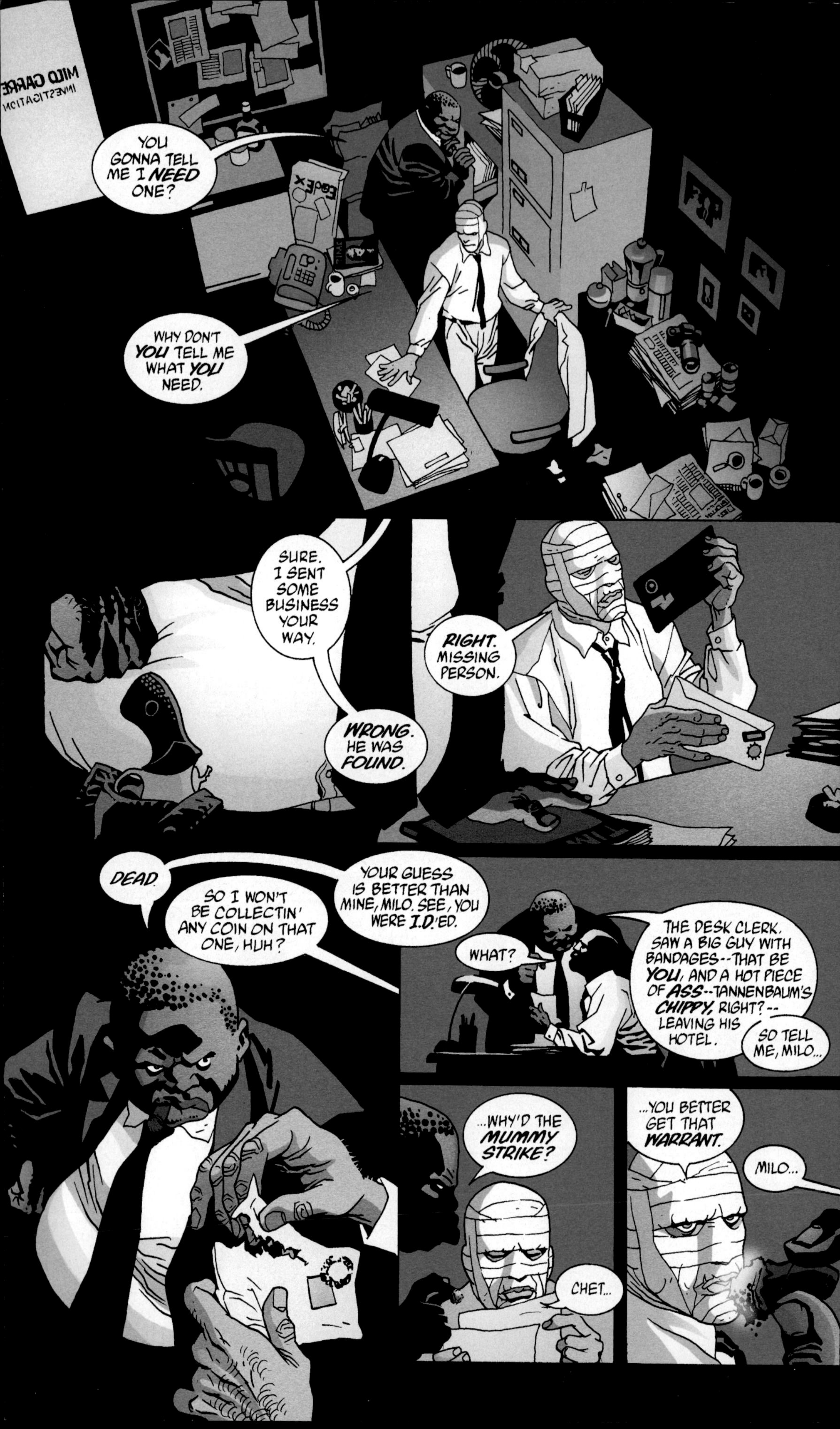
MILO GARRE
INVESTIGATION
YOU GONNA TELL ME I NEED ONE?
WHY DON'T YOU TELL ME WHAT YOU NEED.
SURE. I SENT SOME BUSINESS YOUR WAY.
RIGHT. MISSING PERSON.
WRONG. HE WAS FOUND.
DEAD.
SO I WON'T BE COLLECTIN' ANY COIN ON THAT ONE, HUH?
YOUR GUESS IS BETTER THAN MINE, MILO. SEE, YOU WERE I.D.'ED.
WHAT?
THE DESK CLERK, SAW A BIG GUY WITH BANDAGES--THAT BE YOU, AND A HOT PIECE OF ASS--TANNENBAUM'S CHIPPY, RIGHT?--LEAVING HIS HOTEL.
SO TELL ME, MILO...
...WHY'D THE MUMMY STRIKE?
CHET...
...YOU BETTER GET THAT WARRANT.
MILO...

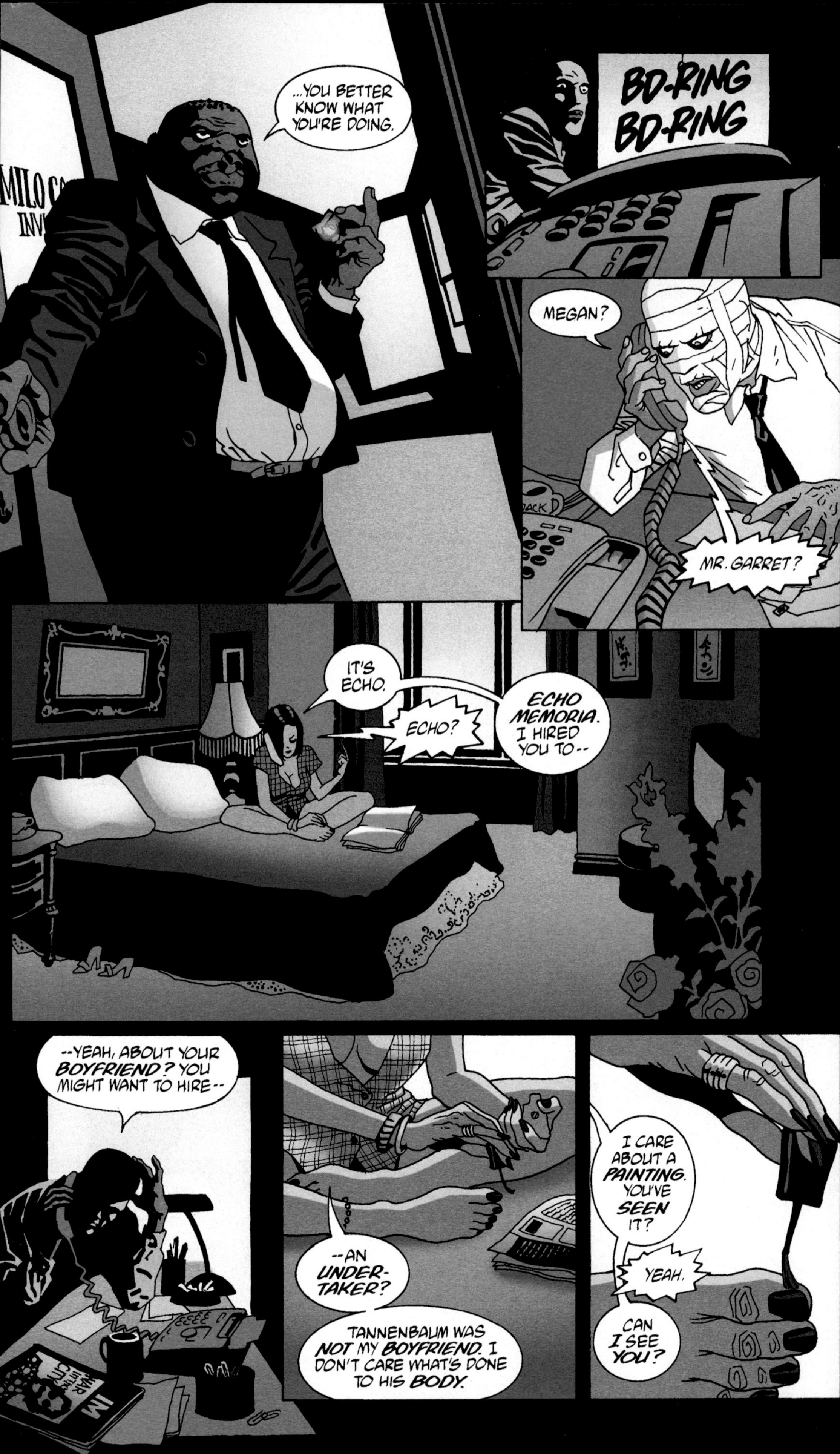
...YOU BETTER KNOW WHAT YOU'RE DOING.
MILO C
INV
BD-RING BD-RING
MEGAN?
MR. GARRET?
IT'S ECHO.
ECHO?
ECHO MEMORIA. I HIRED YOU TO--
--YEAH, ABOUT YOUR BOYFRIEND? YOU MIGHT WANT TO HIRE--
--AN UNDER-TAKER?
TANNENBAUM WAS NOT MY BOYFRIEND. I DON'T CARE WHAT'S DONE TO HIS BODY.
I CARE ABOUT A PAINTING. YOU'VE SEEN IT?
YEAH.
CAN I SEE YOU?

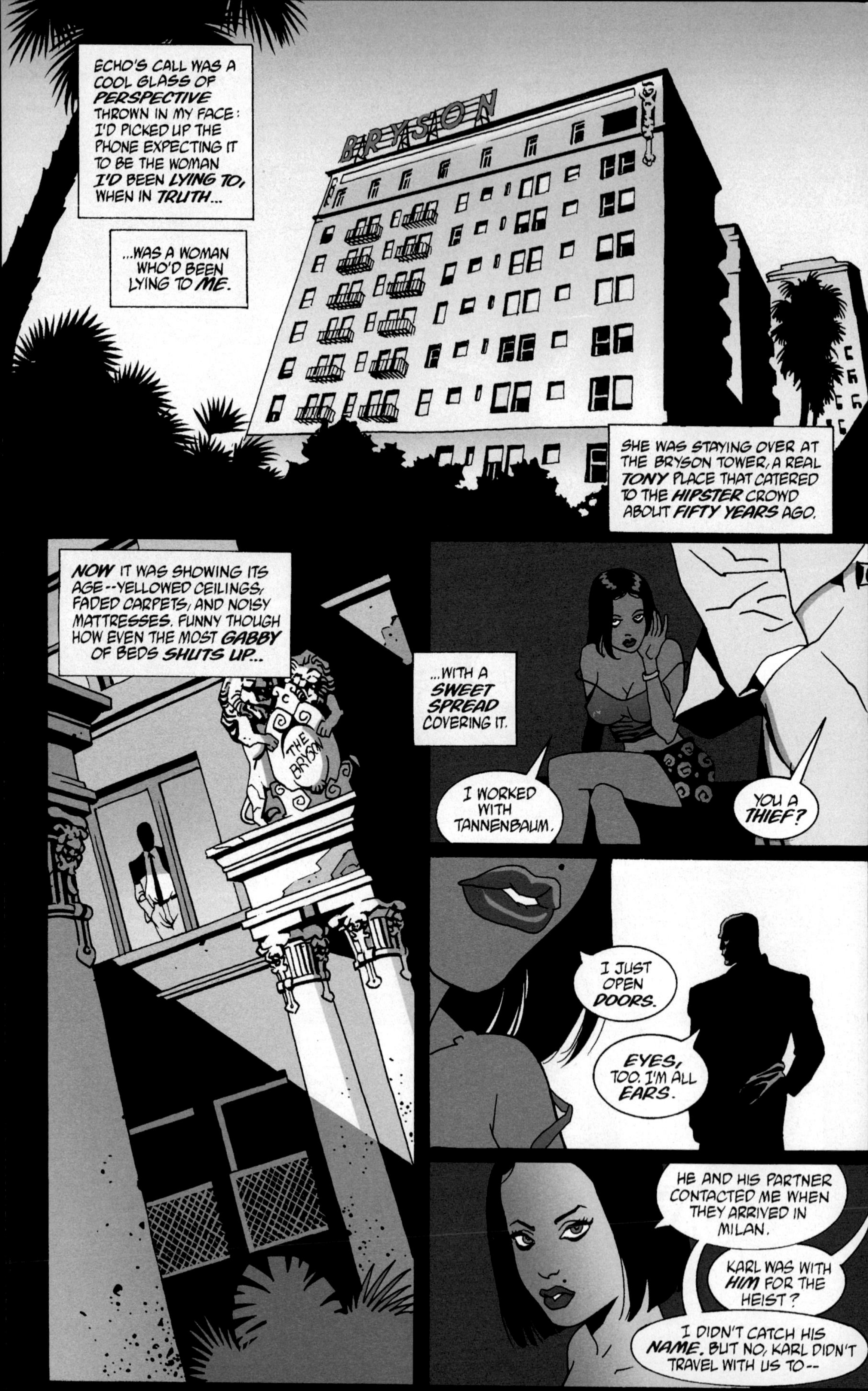

ECHO'S CALL WAS A COOL GLASS OF PERSPECTIVE THROWN IN MY FACE: I'D PICKED UP THE PHONE EXPECTING IT TO BE THE WOMAN I'D BEEN LYING TO, WHEN IN TRUTH...
...WAS A WOMAN WHO'D BEEN LYING TO ME.
BRYSON
SHE WAS STAYING OVER AT THE BRYSON TOWER, A REAL TONY PLACE THAT CATERED TO THE HIPSTER CROWD ABOUT FIFTY YEARS AGO.
NOW IT WAS SHOWING ITS AGE--YELLOWED CEILINGS, FADED CARPETS, AND NOISY MATTRESSES. FUNNY THOUGH HOW EVEN THE MOST GABBY OF BEDS SHUTS UP...
THE BRYSON
...WITH A SWEET SPREAD COVERING IT.
I WORKED WITH TANNENBAUM.
YOU A THIEF?
I JUST OPEN DOORS.
EYES, TOO. I'M ALL EARS.
HE AND HIS PARTNER CONTACTED ME WHEN THEY ARRIVED IN MILAN.
KARL WAS WITH HIM FOR THE HEIST?
I DIDN'T CATCH HIS NAME. BUT NO, KARL DIDN'T TRAVEL WITH US TO--

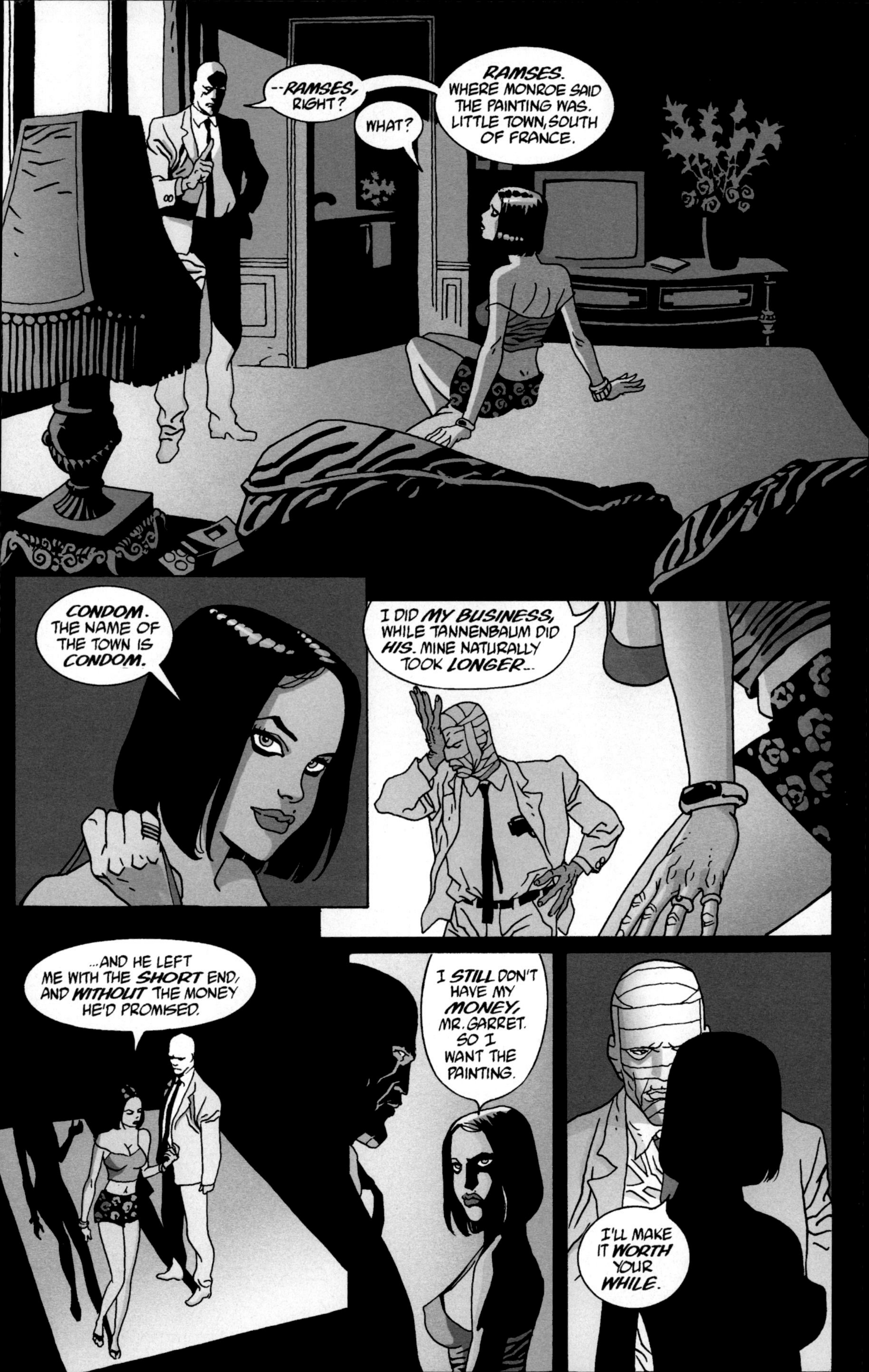
--RAMSES, RIGHT?
WHAT?
RAMSES. WHERE MONROE SAID THE PAINTING WAS. LITTLE TOWN, SOUTH OF FRANCE.
CONDOM. THE NAME OF THE TOWN IS CONDOM...
I DID MY BUSINESS, WHILE TANNENBAUM DID HIS. MINE NATURALLY TOOK LONGER...
...AND HE LEFT ME WITH THE SHORT END, AND WITHOUT THE MONEY HE'D PROMISED.
I STILL DON'T HAVE MY MONEY, MR. GARRET. SO I WANT THE PAINTING.
I'LL MAKE IT WORTH YOUR WHILE.

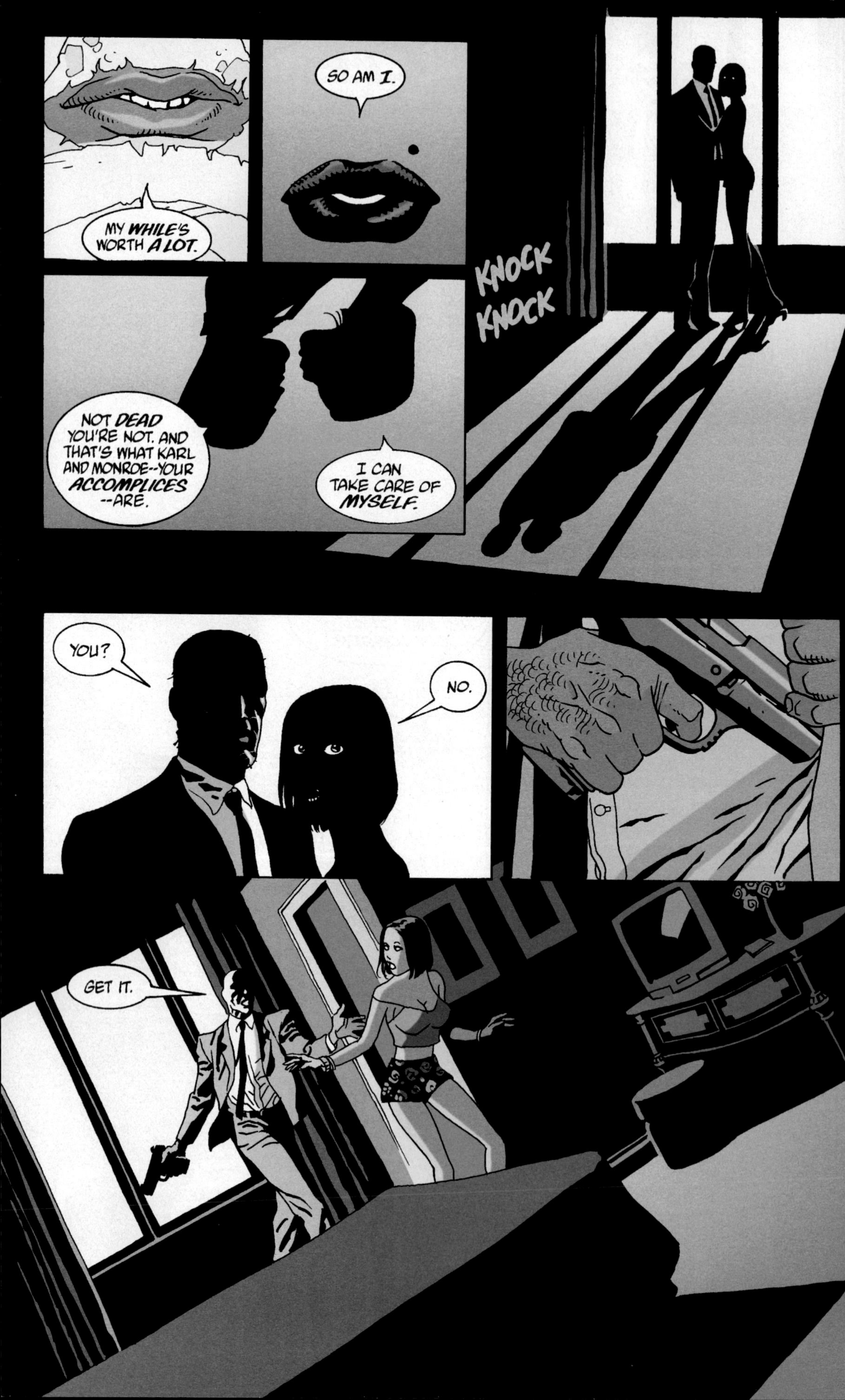
MY WHILE'S WORTH A LOT.
SO AM I.
KNOCK KNOCK
NOT DEAD YOU'RE NOT. AND THAT'S WHAT KARL AND MONROE--YOUR ACCOMPLICES --ARE.
I CAN TAKE CARE OF MYSELF.
YOU?
NO.
GET IT.

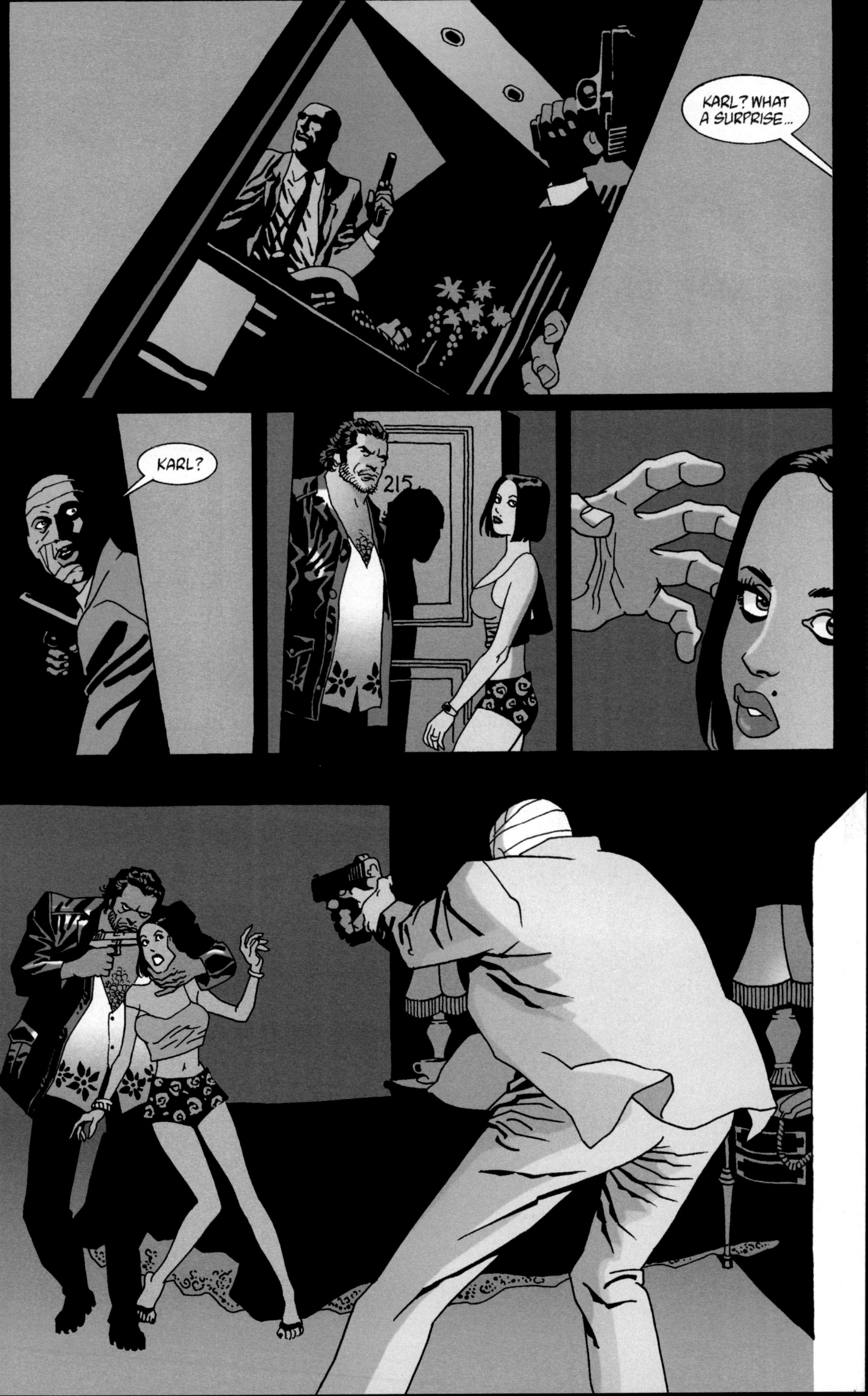
KARL? WHAT
A SURPRISE...
KARL?

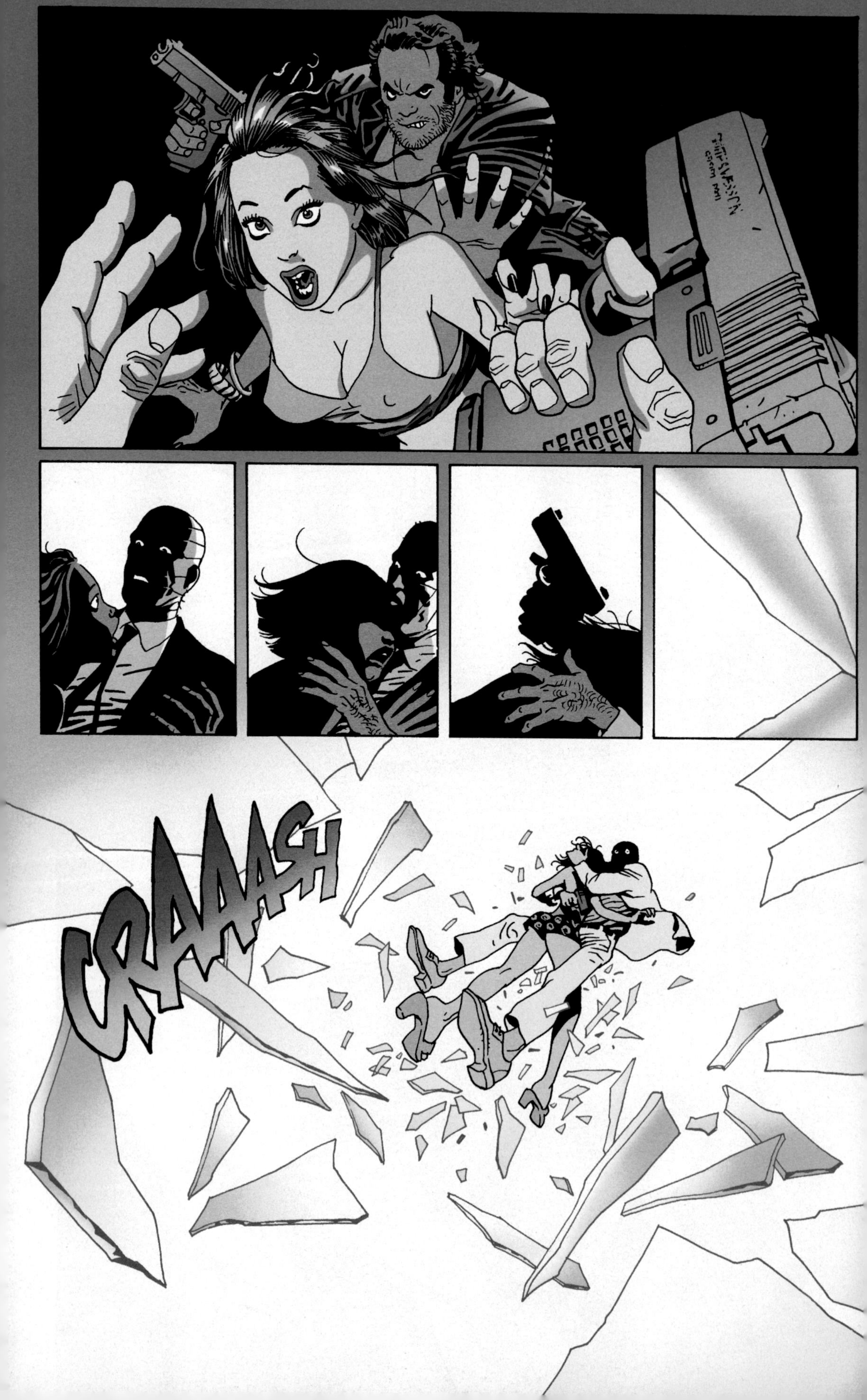
CRAAASH

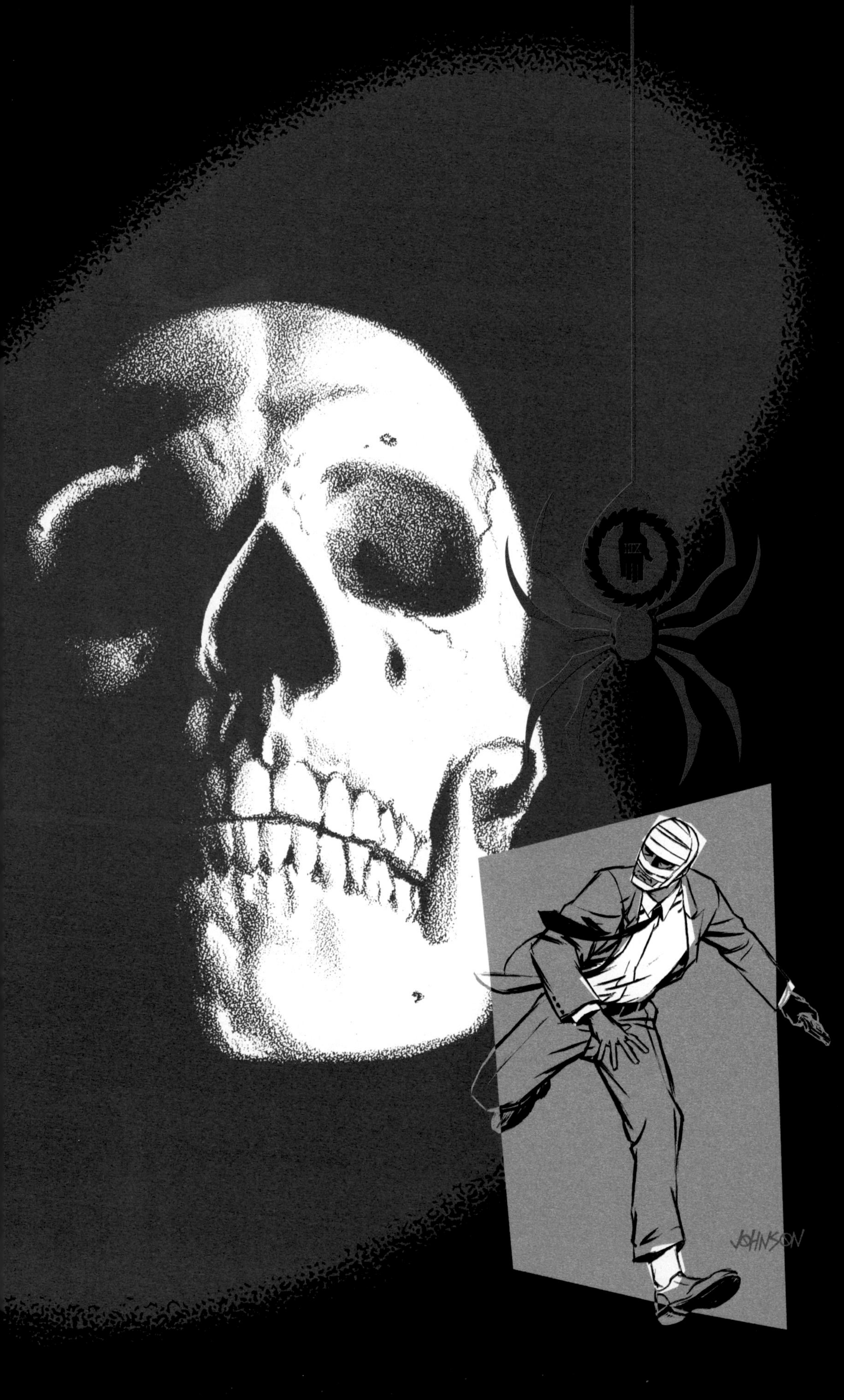
JOHNSON

FRESH, CLEAN SHEETS.

ALONG WITH THE ACHES AN' BRUISES *IN* ME AN' *ON* ME, CLEAN SHEETS WAS WHAT I WAS FEELIN' NEXT TO ME.

MEANING I WASN'T *ANYWHERE NEAR* MY OWN CRIB.

NO, I HAD TAKEN A TWO-STORY TUMBLE OUT A WINDOW AND RIGHT INTO A HOSPITAL BED.

SANTA MONICA MASO HOSPITAL

TWO *STORIES.* ONE *FALL.*

MY LIFE.

THE COUNTERFIFTH DETECTIVE
CONCLUSION

BRIAN **AZZARELLO** writer

EDUARDO **RISSO** artist

PATRICIA **MULVIHILL** colorist

CLEM **ROBINS** letterer

DIGITAL **CHAMELEON** separations

DAVE **JOHNSON** cover artist

ZACHARY **RAU** ass't ed

WILL **DENNIS** editor

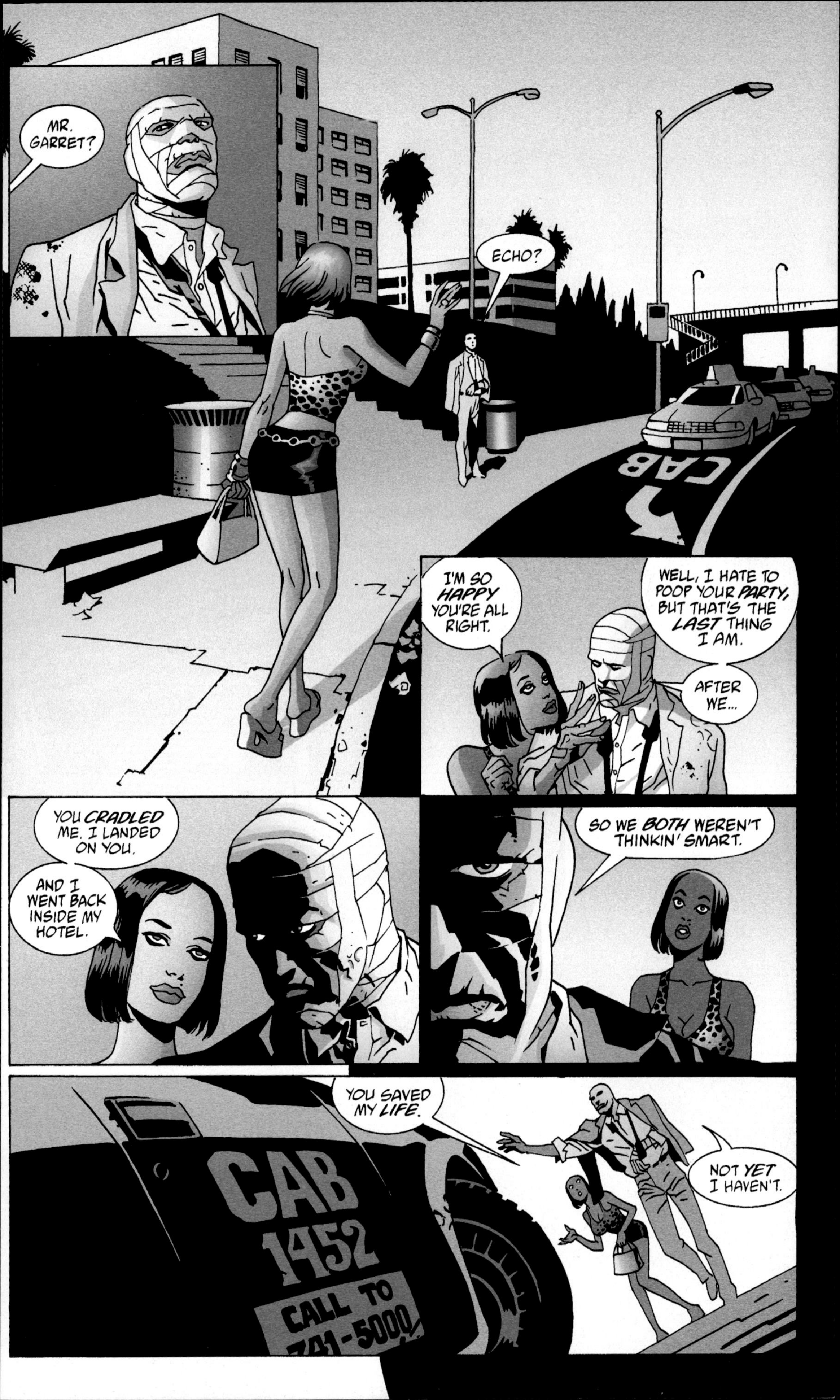
MR. GARRET?
ECHO?
CAB
I'M SO HAPPY YOU'RE ALL RIGHT.
WELL, I HATE TO POOP YOUR PARTY, BUT THAT'S THE LAST THING I AM.
AFTER WE...
YOU CRADLED ME. I LANDED ON YOU.
AND I WENT BACK INSIDE MY HOTEL.
SO WE BOTH WEREN'T THINKIN' SMART.
CAB
1452
CALL TO
741-5000
YOU SAVED MY LIFE.
NOT YET I HAVEN'T.

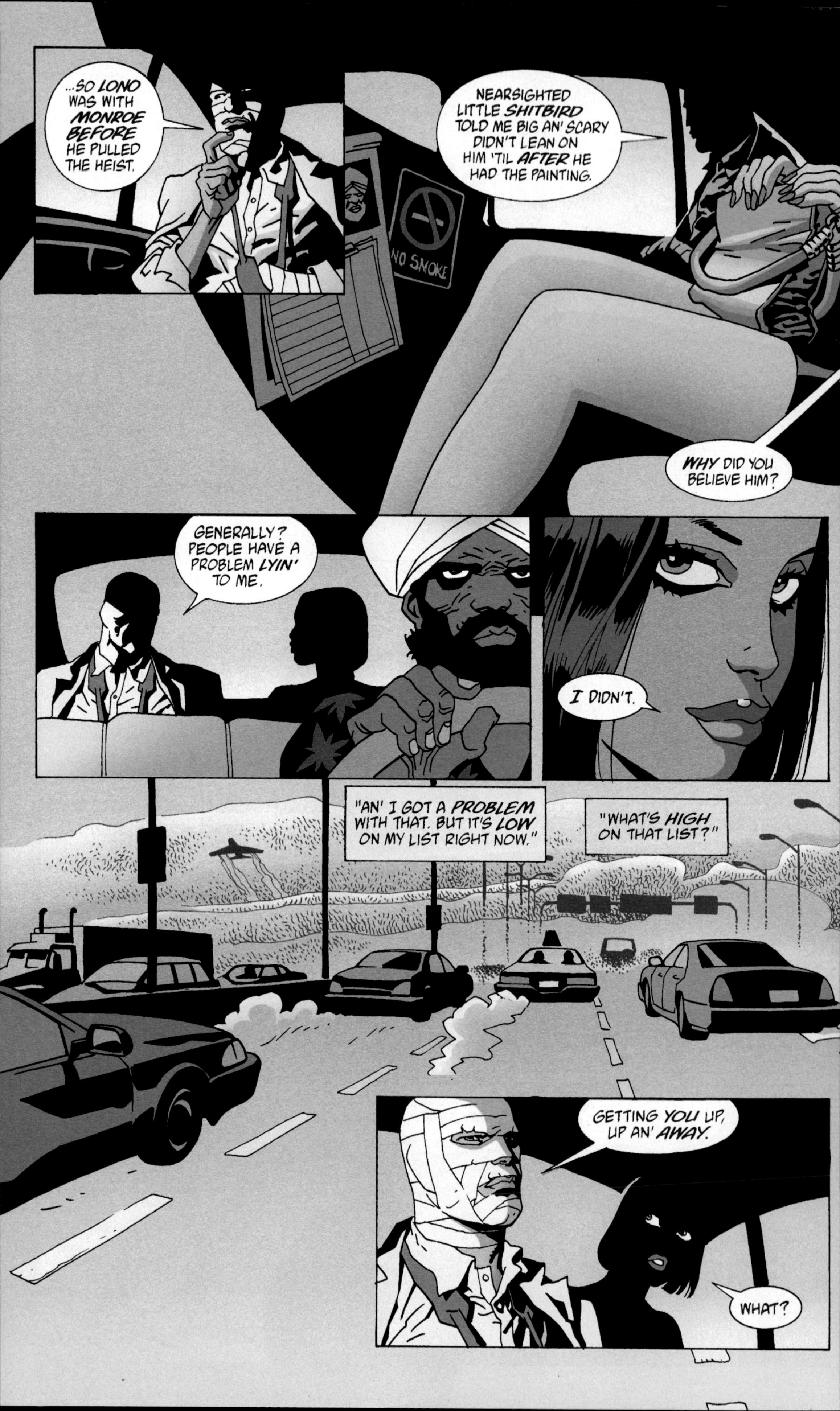
...SO LONO WAS WITH MONROE BEFORE HE PULLED THE HEIST.
NEARSIGHTED LITTLE SHITBIRD TOLD ME BIG AN' SCARY DIDN'T LEAN ON HIM 'TIL AFTER HE HAD THE PAINTING.
NO SMOKE
WHY DID YOU BELIEVE HIM?
GENERALLY? PEOPLE HAVE A PROBLEM LYIN' TO ME.
I DIDN'T.
"AN' I GOT A PROBLEM WITH THAT. BUT IT'S LOW ON MY LIST RIGHT NOW."
"WHAT'S HIGH ON THAT LIST?"
GETTING YOU UP, UP AN' AWAY.
WHAT?

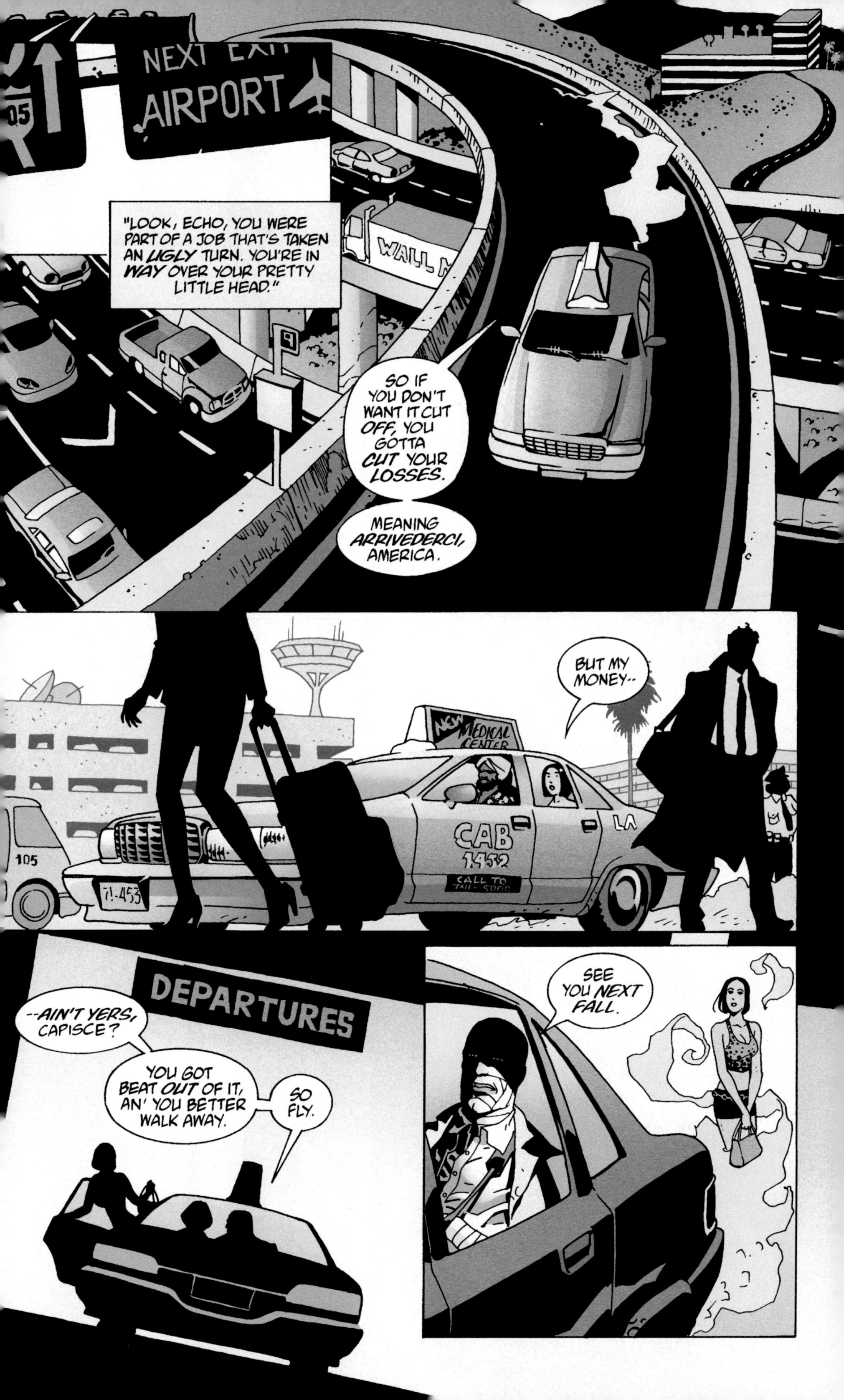

NEXT EXIT
AIRPORT
105
"LOOK, ECHO, YOU WERE PART OF A JOB THAT'S TAKEN AN UGLY TURN. YOU'RE IN WAY OVER YOUR PRETTY LITTLE HEAD."
SO IF YOU DON'T WANT IT CUT OFF, YOU GOTTA CUT YOUR LOSSES.
MEANING ARRIVEDERCI, AMERICA.
BUT MY MONEY--
CAB
LA
DEPARTURES
--AIN'T YERS, CAPISCE?
YOU GOT BEAT OUT OF IT, AN' YOU BETTER WALK AWAY.
SO FLY.
SEE YOU NEXT FALL.

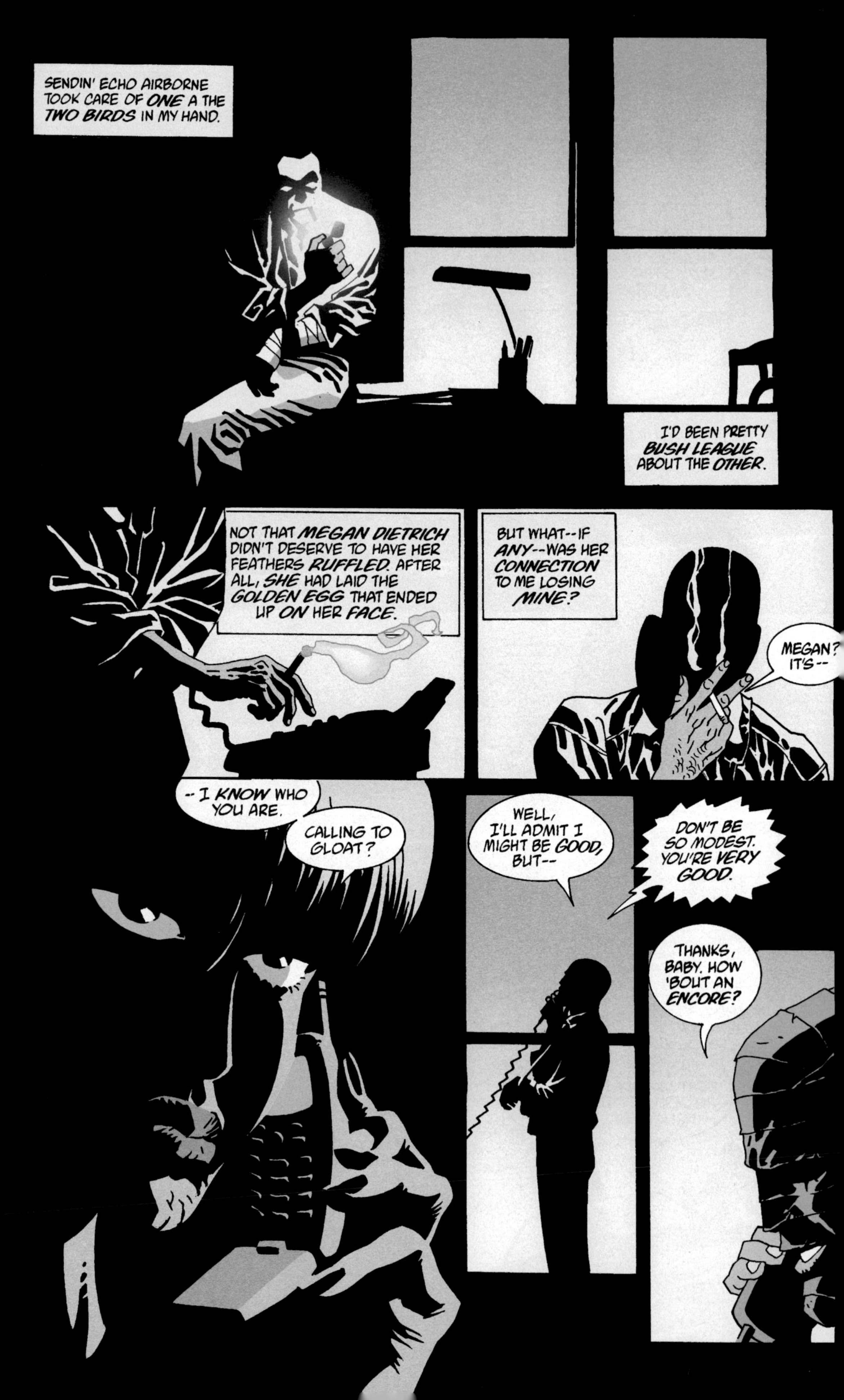
SENDIN' ECHO AIRBORNE TOOK CARE OF ONE A THE TWO BIRDS IN MY HAND.
I'D BEEN PRETTY BUSH LEAGUE ABOUT THE OTHER.
NOT THAT MEGAN DIETRICH DIDN'T DESERVE TO HAVE HER FEATHERS RUFFLED. AFTER ALL, SHE HAD LAID THE GOLDEN EGG THAT ENDED UP ON HER FACE.
BUT WHAT--IF ANY--WAS HER CONNECTION TO ME LOSING MINE?
MEGAN? IT'S--
--I KNOW WHO YOU ARE.
CALLING TO GLOAT?
WELL, I'LL ADMIT I MIGHT BE GOOD, BUT--
DON'T BE SO MODEST. YOU'RE VERY GOOD.
THANKS, BABY. HOW 'BOUT AN ENCORE?

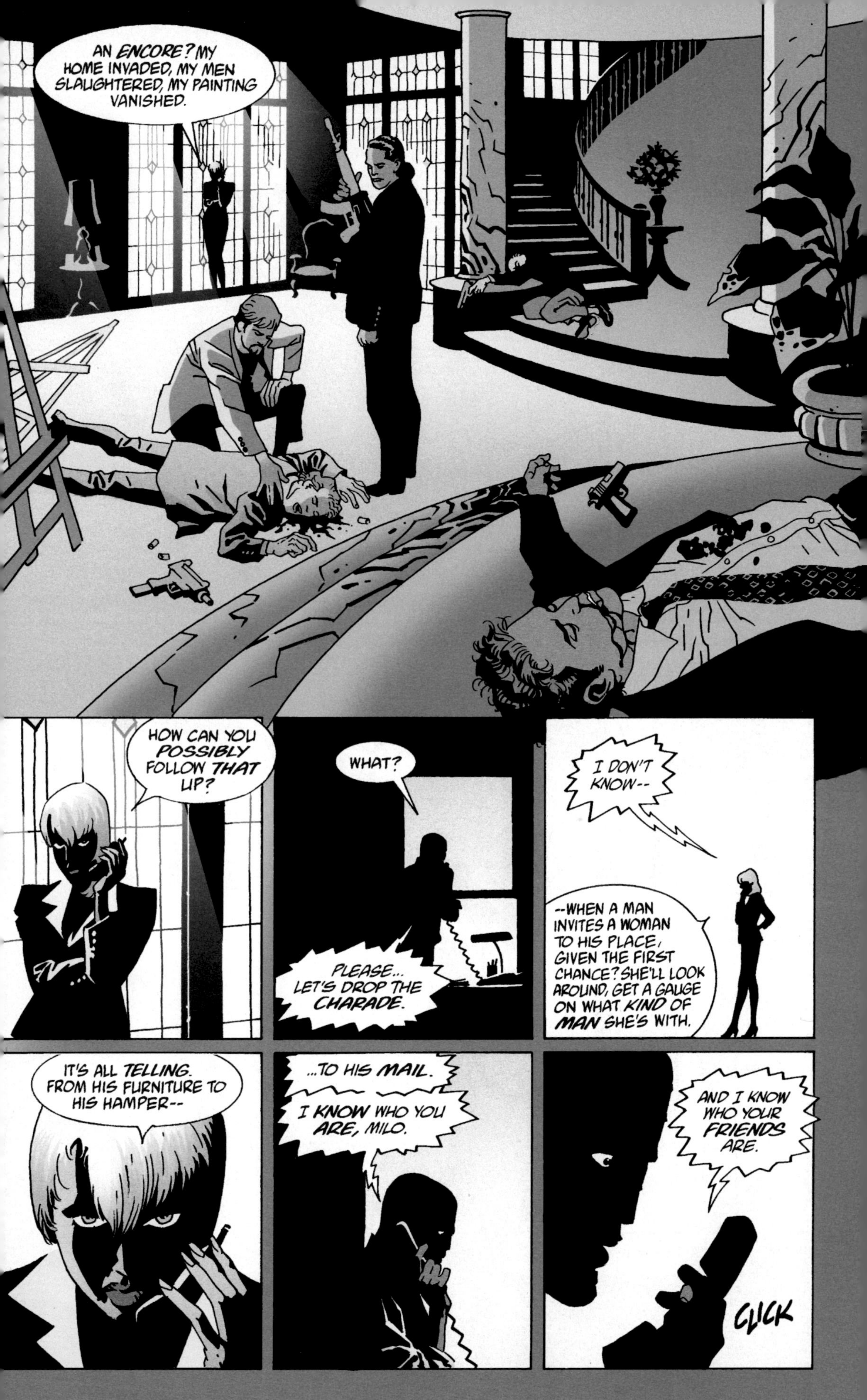
AN ENCORE? MY HOME INVADED, MY MEN SLAUGHTERED, MY PAINTING VANISHED.
HOW CAN YOU POSSIBLY FOLLOW THAT UP?
WHAT?
PLEASE... LET'S DROP THE CHARADE.
I DON'T KNOW--
--WHEN A MAN INVITES A WOMAN TO HIS PLACE, GIVEN THE FIRST CHANCE? SHE'LL LOOK AROUND, GET A GAUGE ON WHAT KIND OF MAN SHE'S WITH.
IT'S ALL TELLING. FROM HIS FURNITURE TO HIS HAMPER--
...TO HIS MAIL.
I KNOW WHO YOU ARE, MILO.
AND I KNOW WHO YOUR FRIENDS ARE.
CLICK

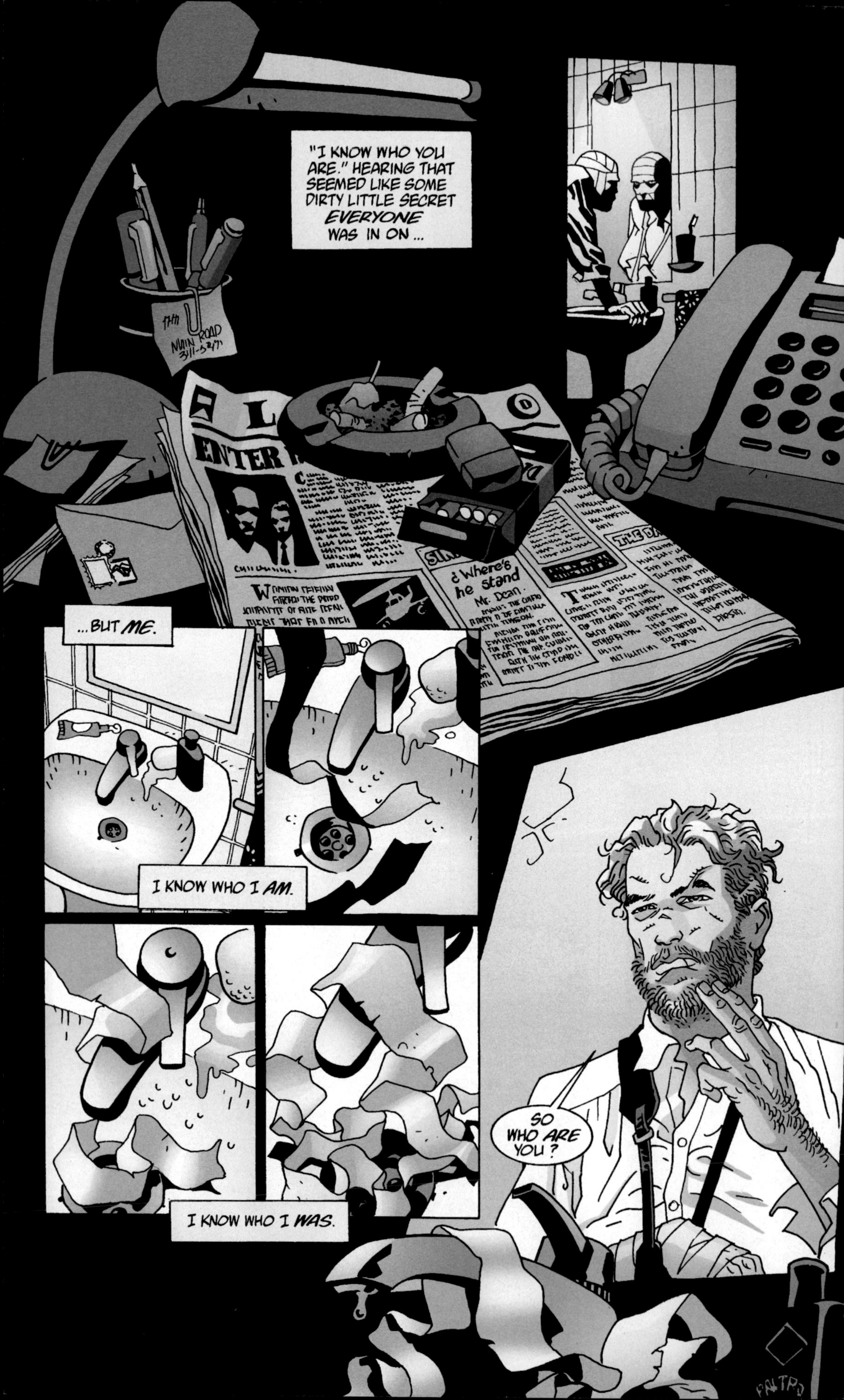
"I KNOW WHO YOU ARE." HEARING THAT SEEMED LIKE SOME DIRTY LITTLE SECRET EVERYONE WAS IN ON ...
...BUT ME.
I KNOW WHO I AM.
I KNOW WHO I WAS.
SO WHO ARE YOU?

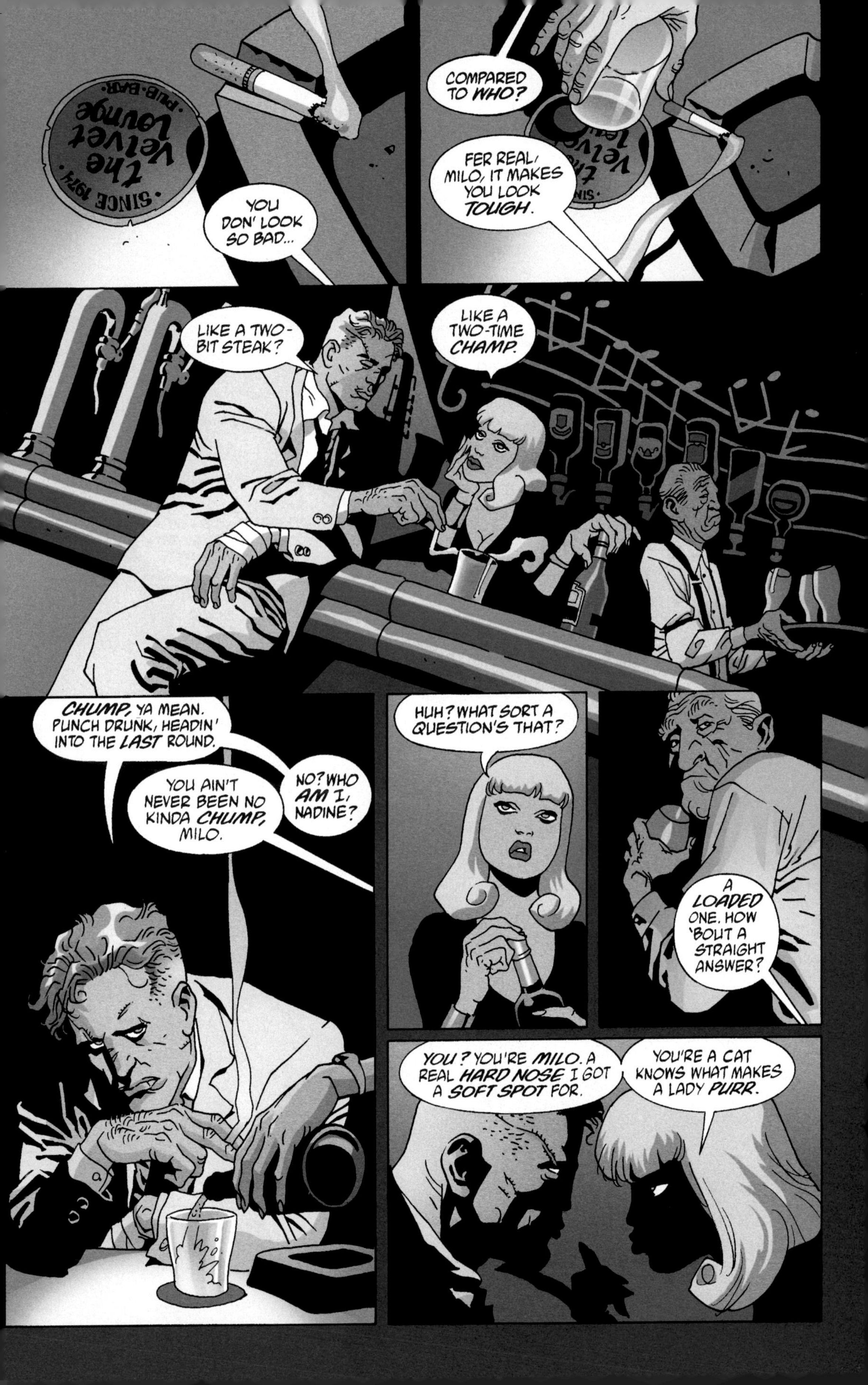

The Velvet Lounge
·PUB·BAR·
·SINCE 1974·
YOU DON' LOOK SO BAD...
COMPARED TO WHO?
FER REAL, MILO, IT MAKES YOU LOOK TOUGH.
LIKE A TWO-BIT STEAK?
LIKE A TWO-TIME CHAMP.
CHUMP, YA MEAN. PUNCH DRUNK, HEADIN' INTO THE LAST ROUND.
YOU AIN'T NEVER BEEN NO KINDA CHUMP, MILO.
NO? WHO AM I, NADINE?
HUH? WHAT SORT A QUESTION'S THAT?
A LOADED ONE. HOW 'BOUT A STRAIGHT ANSWER?
YOU? YOU'RE MILO. A REAL HARD NOSE I GOT A SOFT SPOT FOR.
YOU'RE A CAT KNOWS WHAT MAKES A LADY PURR.

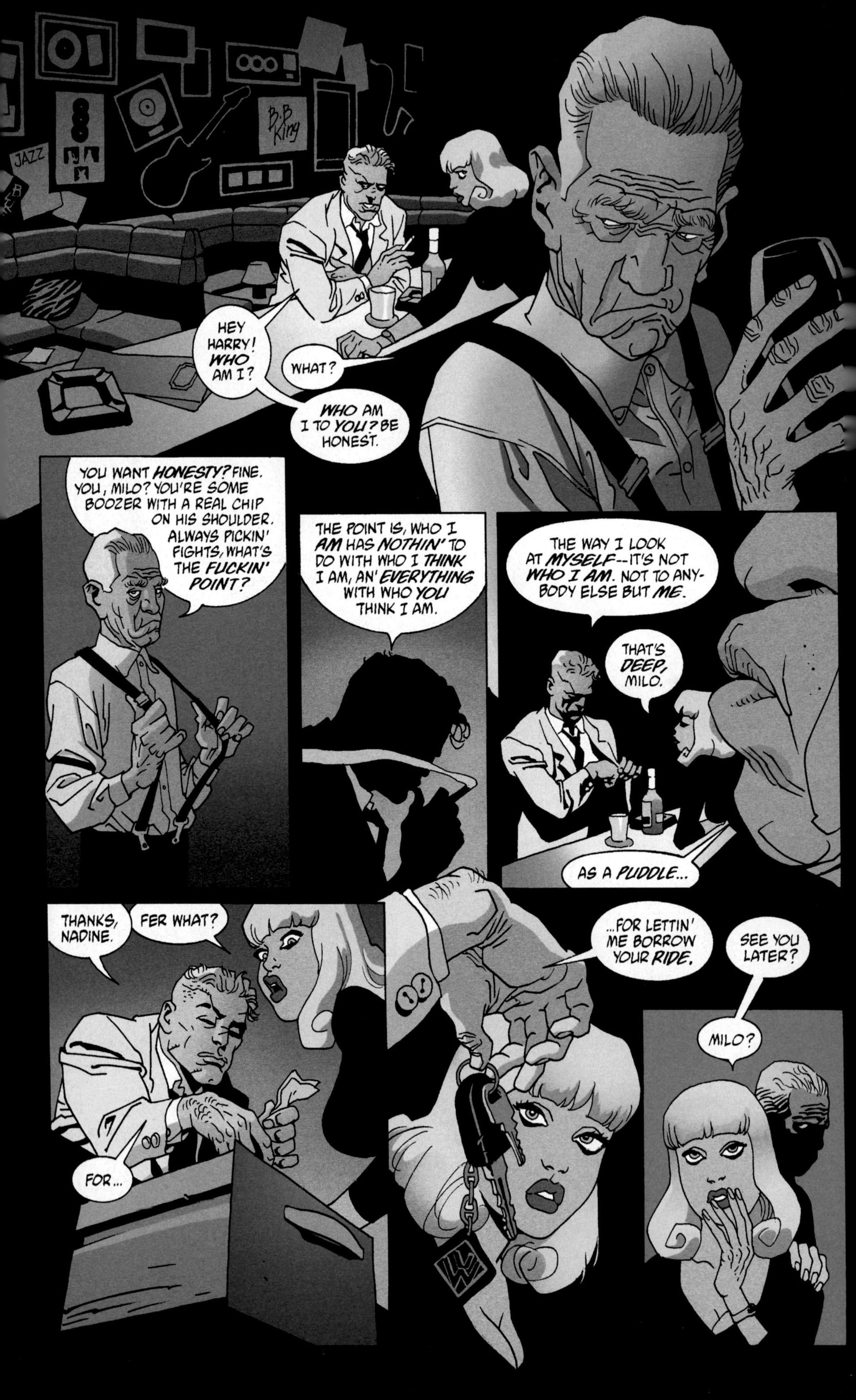
HEY HARRY! WHO AM I?
WHAT?
WHO AM I TO YOU? BE HONEST.
YOU WANT HONESTY? FINE. YOU, MILO? YOU'RE SOME BOOZER WITH A REAL CHIP ON HIS SHOULDER. ALWAYS PICKIN' FIGHTS, WHAT'S THE FUCKIN' POINT?
THE POINT IS, WHO I AM HAS NOTHIN' TO DO WITH WHO I THINK I AM, AN' EVERYTHING WITH WHO YOU THINK I AM.
THE WAY I LOOK AT MYSELF--IT'S NOT WHO I AM. NOT TO ANYBODY ELSE BUT ME.
THAT'S DEEP, MILO.
AS A PUDDLE...
THANKS, NADINE.
FER WHAT?
FOR...
...FOR LETTIN' ME BORROW YOUR RIDE.
SEE YOU LATER?
MILO?

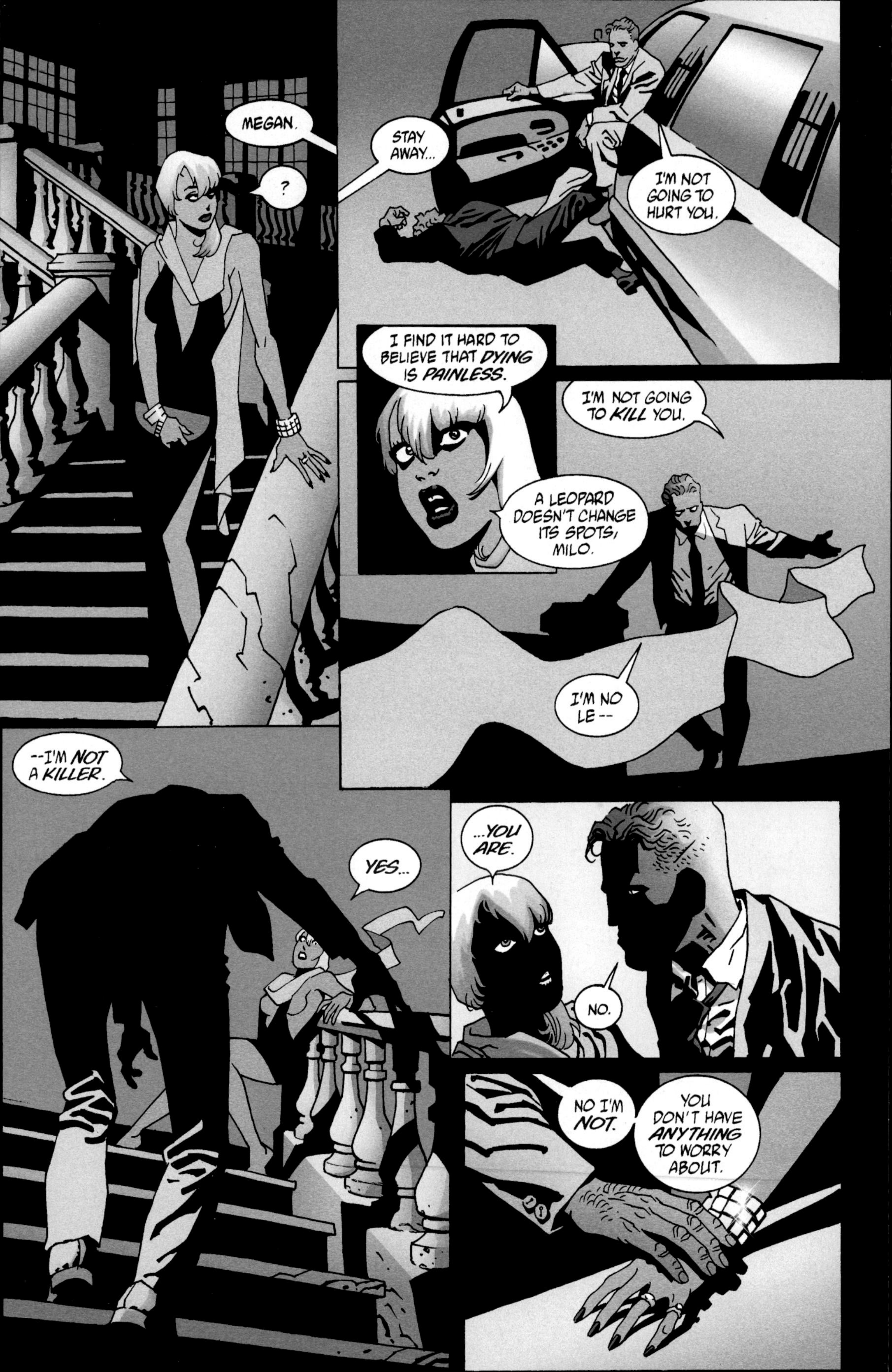
MEGAN.
?
STAY AWAY...
I'M NOT GOING TO HURT YOU.
I FIND IT HARD TO BELIEVE THAT DYING IS PAINLESS.
I'M NOT GOING TO KILL YOU.
A LEOPARD DOESN'T CHANGE ITS SPOTS, MILO.
I'M NO LE--
--I'M NOT A KILLER.
YES...
...YOU ARE.
NO.
NO I'M NOT.
YOU DON'T HAVE ANYTHING TO WORRY ABOUT.

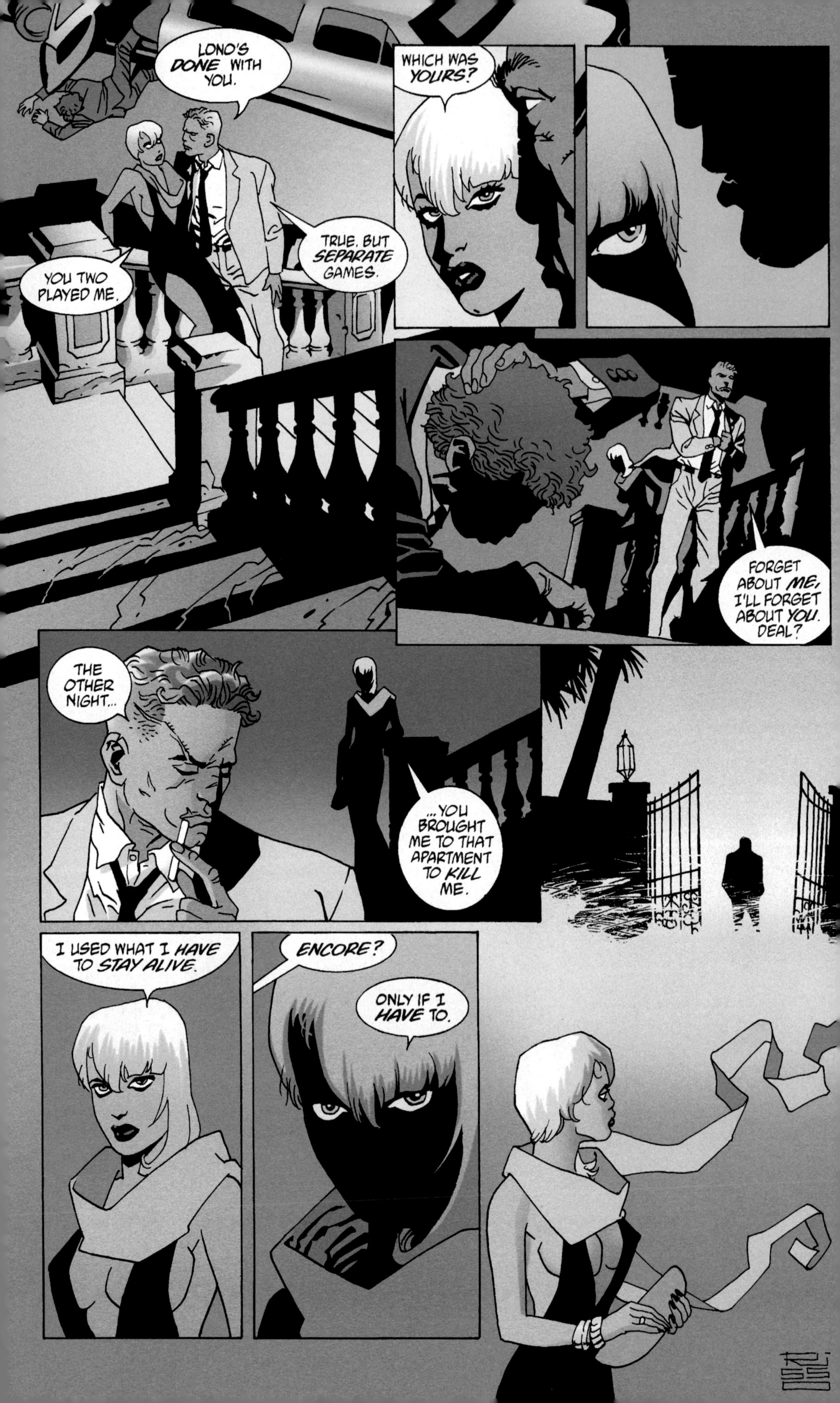
LONO'S DONE WITH YOU.
YOU TWO PLAYED ME.
TRUE, BUT SEPARATE GAMES.
WHICH WAS YOURS?
FORGET ABOUT ME, I'LL FORGET ABOUT YOU. DEAL?
THE OTHER NIGHT...
...YOU BROUGHT ME TO THAT APARTMENT TO KILL ME.
I USED WHAT I HAVE TO STAY ALIVE.
ENCORE?
ONLY IF I HAVE TO.

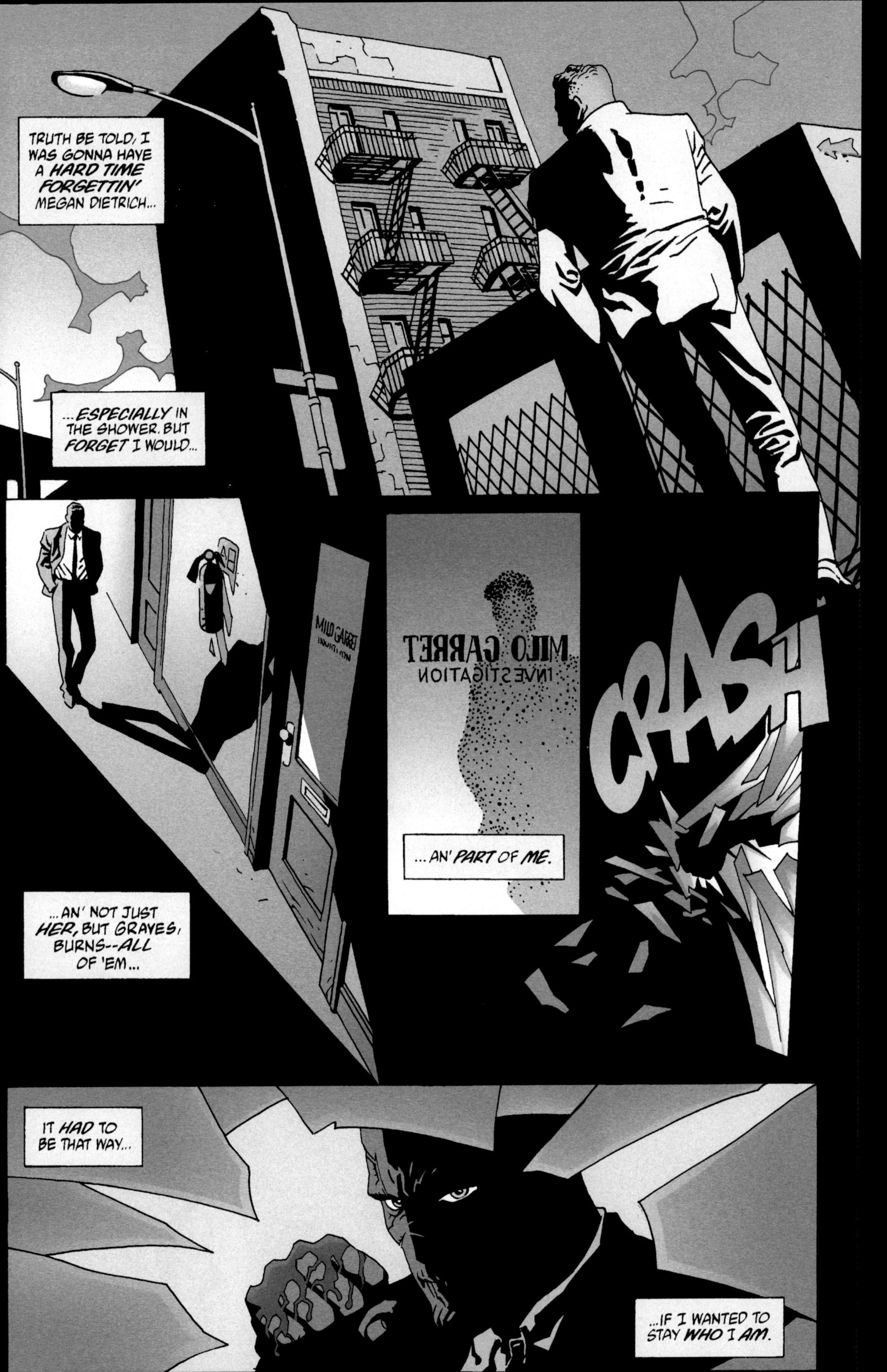
TRUTH BE TOLD, I WAS GONNA HAVE A HARD TIME FORGETTIN' MEGAN DIETRICH...
...ESPECIALLY IN THE SHOWER. BUT FORGET I WOULD...
...AN' NOT JUST HER, BUT GRAVES, BURNS--ALL OF 'EM...
MILO GARRET
INVESTIGATION
...AN' PART OF ME.
CRASH
IT HAD TO BE THAT WAY...
...IF I WANTED TO STAY WHO I AM.

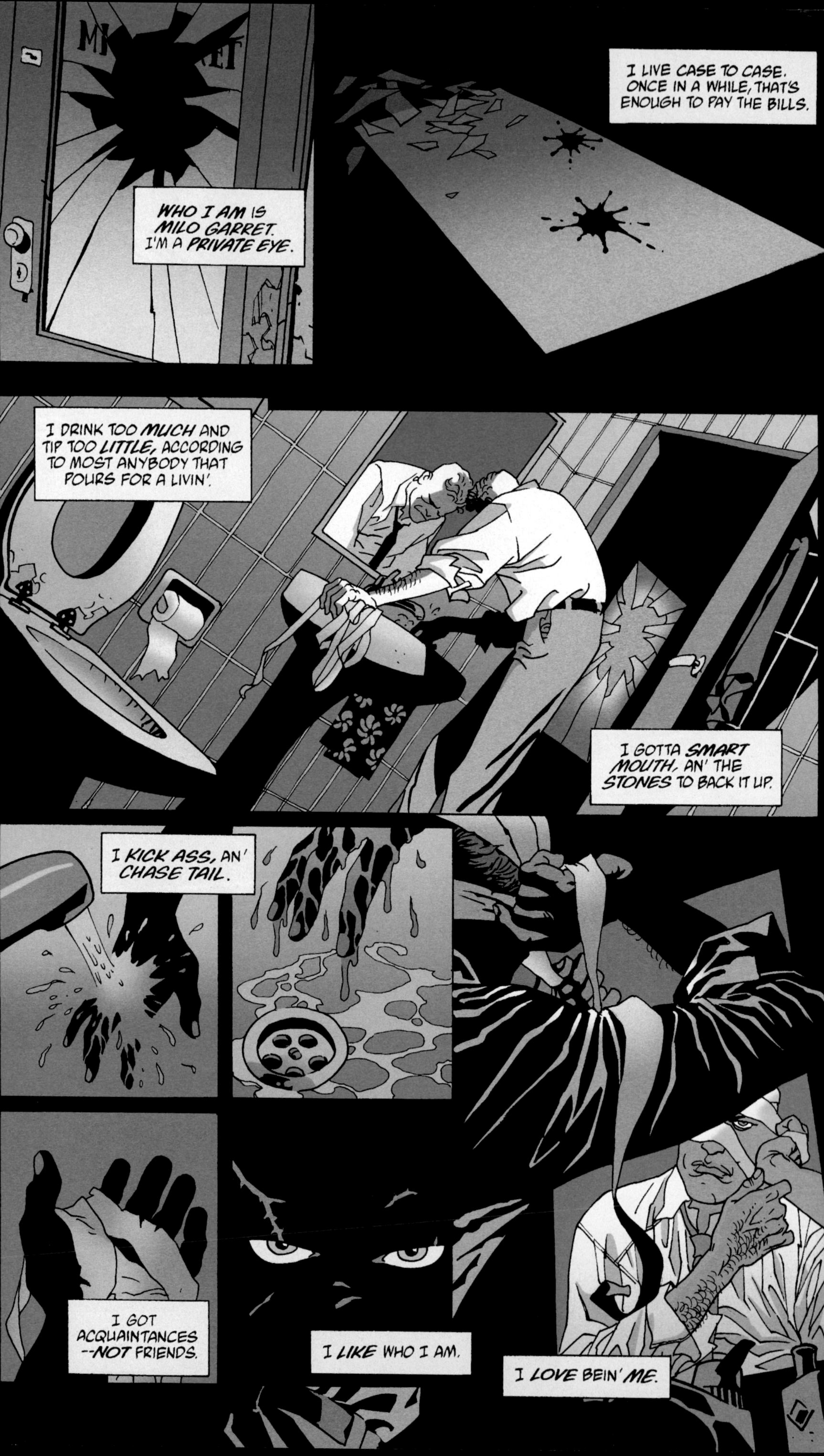

I LIVE CASE TO CASE. ONCE IN A WHILE, THAT'S ENOUGH TO PAY THE BILLS.
WHO I AM IS MILO GARRET. I'M A PRIVATE EYE.
I DRINK TOO MUCH AND TIP TOO LITTLE, ACCORDING TO MOST ANYBODY THAT POURS FOR A LIVIN'.
I GOTTA SMART MOUTH, AN' THE STONES TO BACK IT UP.
I KICK ASS, AN' CHASE TAIL.
I GOT ACQUAINTANCES --NOT FRIENDS.
I LIKE WHO I AM.
I LOVE BEIN' ME.

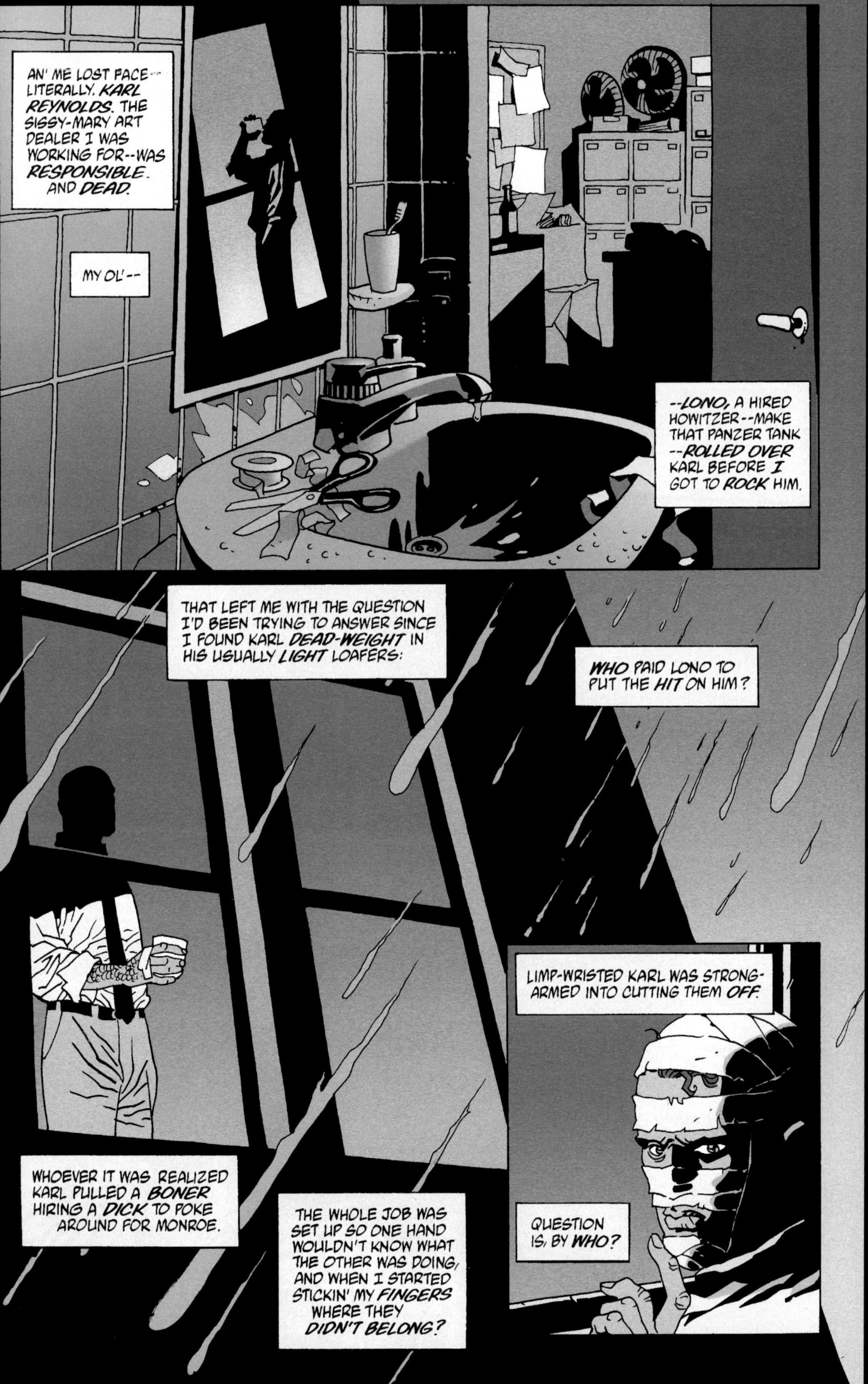
AN' ME LOST FACE-- LITERALLY. KARL REYNOLDS. THE SISSY-MARY ART DEALER I WAS WORKING FOR--WAS RESPONSIBLE. AND DEAD.
MY OL'--
--LONO, A HIRED HOWITZER--MAKE THAT PANZER TANK --ROLLED OVER KARL BEFORE I GOT TO ROCK HIM.
THAT LEFT ME WITH THE QUESTION I'D BEEN TRYING TO ANSWER SINCE I FOUND KARL DEAD-WEIGHT IN HIS USUALLY LIGHT LOAFERS:
WHO PAID LONO TO PUT THE HIT ON HIM?
LIMP-WRISTED KARL WAS STRONG-ARMED INTO CUTTING THEM OFF.
WHOEVER IT WAS REALIZED KARL PULLED A BONER HIRING A DICK TO POKE AROUND FOR MONROE.
THE WHOLE JOB WAS SET UP SO ONE HAND WOULDN'T KNOW WHAT THE OTHER WAS DOING, AND WHEN I STARTED STICKIN' MY FINGERS WHERE THEY DIDN'T BELONG?
QUESTION IS, BY WHO?

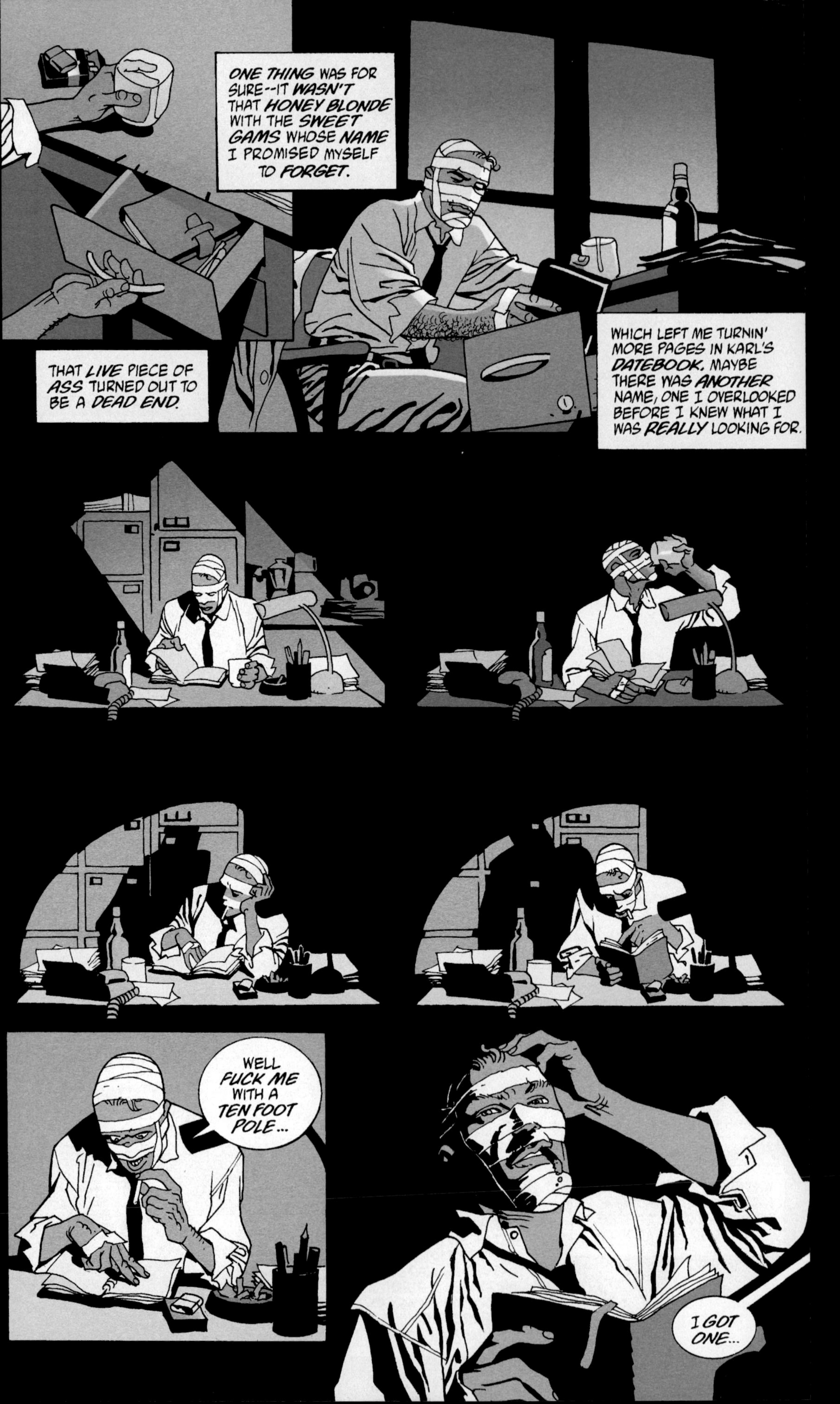

ONE THING WAS FOR SURE--IT WASN'T THAT HONEY BLONDE WITH THE SWEET GAMS WHOSE NAME I PROMISED MYSELF TO FORGET.
THAT LIVE PIECE OF ASS TURNED OUT TO BE A DEAD END.
WHICH LEFT ME TURNIN' MORE PAGES IN KARL'S DATEBOOK. MAYBE THERE WAS ANOTHER NAME, ONE I OVERLOOKED BEFORE I KNEW WHAT I WAS REALLY LOOKING FOR.
WELL FUCK ME WITH A TEN FOOT POLE...
I GOT ONE...

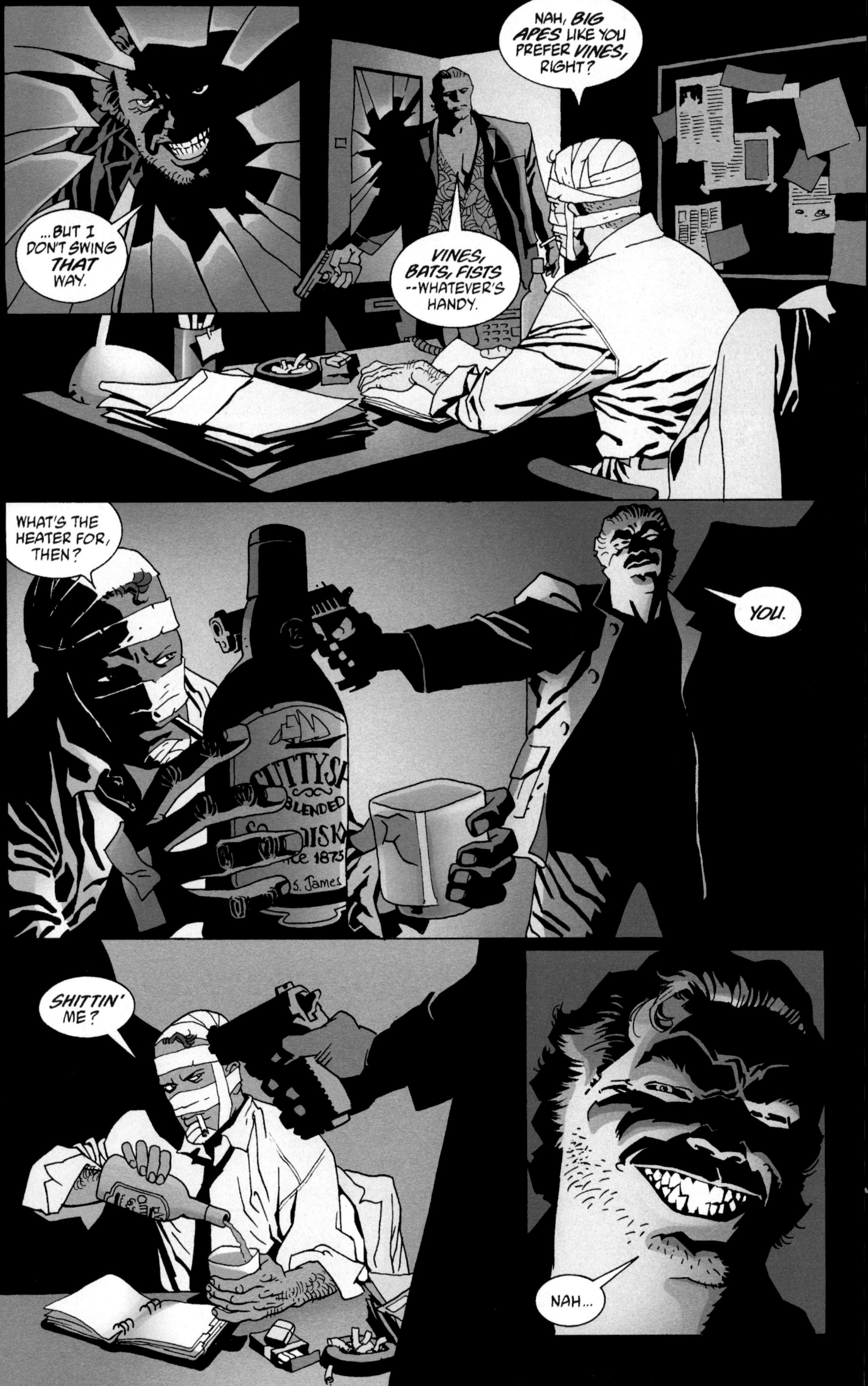
...BUT I DON'T SWING THAT WAY.
NAH, BIG APES LIKE YOU PREFER VINES, RIGHT?
VINES, BATS, FISTS --WHATEVER'S HANDY.
WHAT'S THE HEATER FOR, THEN?
YOU.
SHITTIN' ME?
NAH...

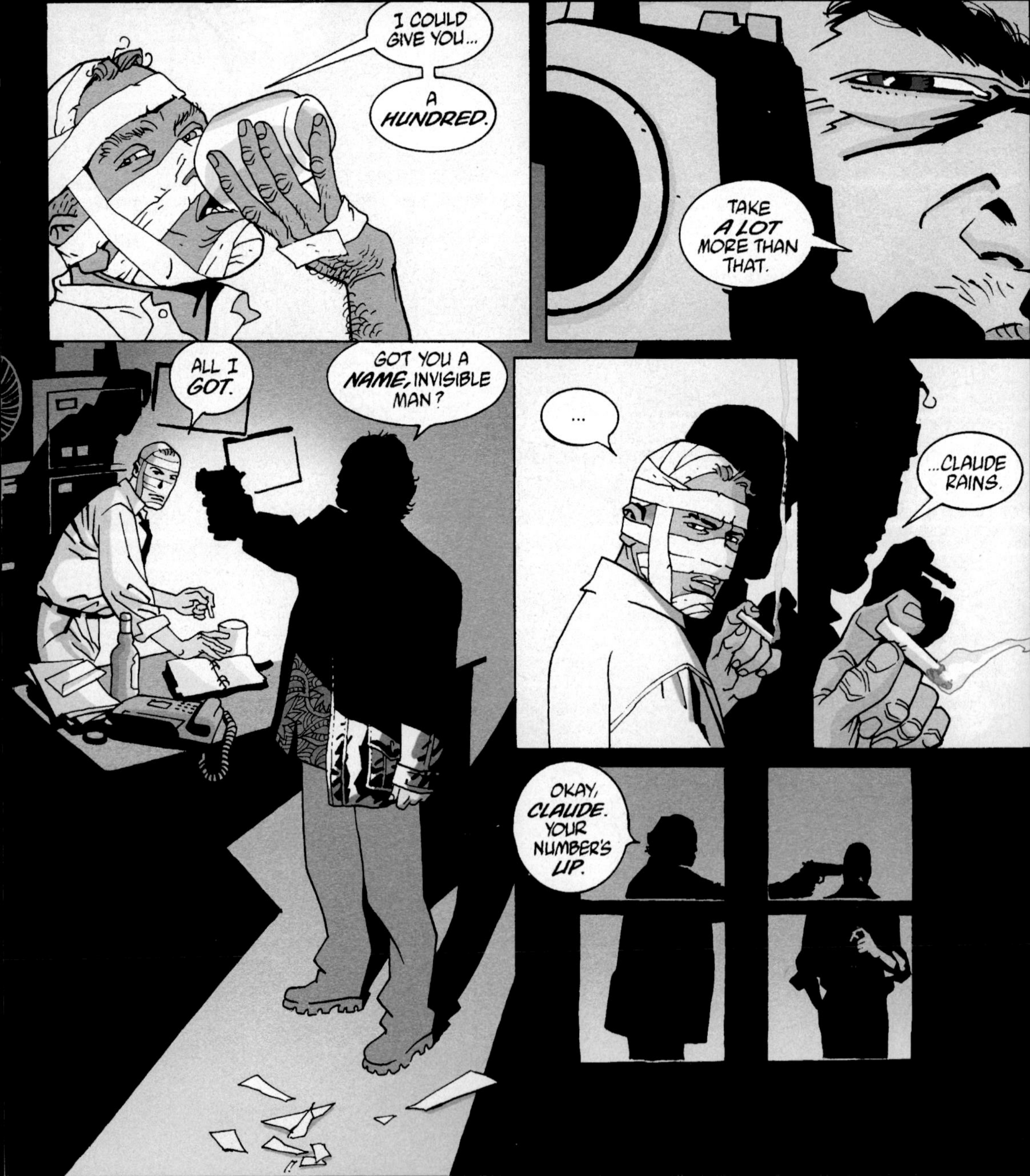
I COULD GIVE YOU...
A HUNDRED.
TAKE A LOT MORE THAN THAT.
ALL I GOT.
GOT YOU A NAME, INVISIBLE MAN?
...
...CLAUDE RAINS.
OKAY, CLAUDE. YOUR NUMBER'S UP.

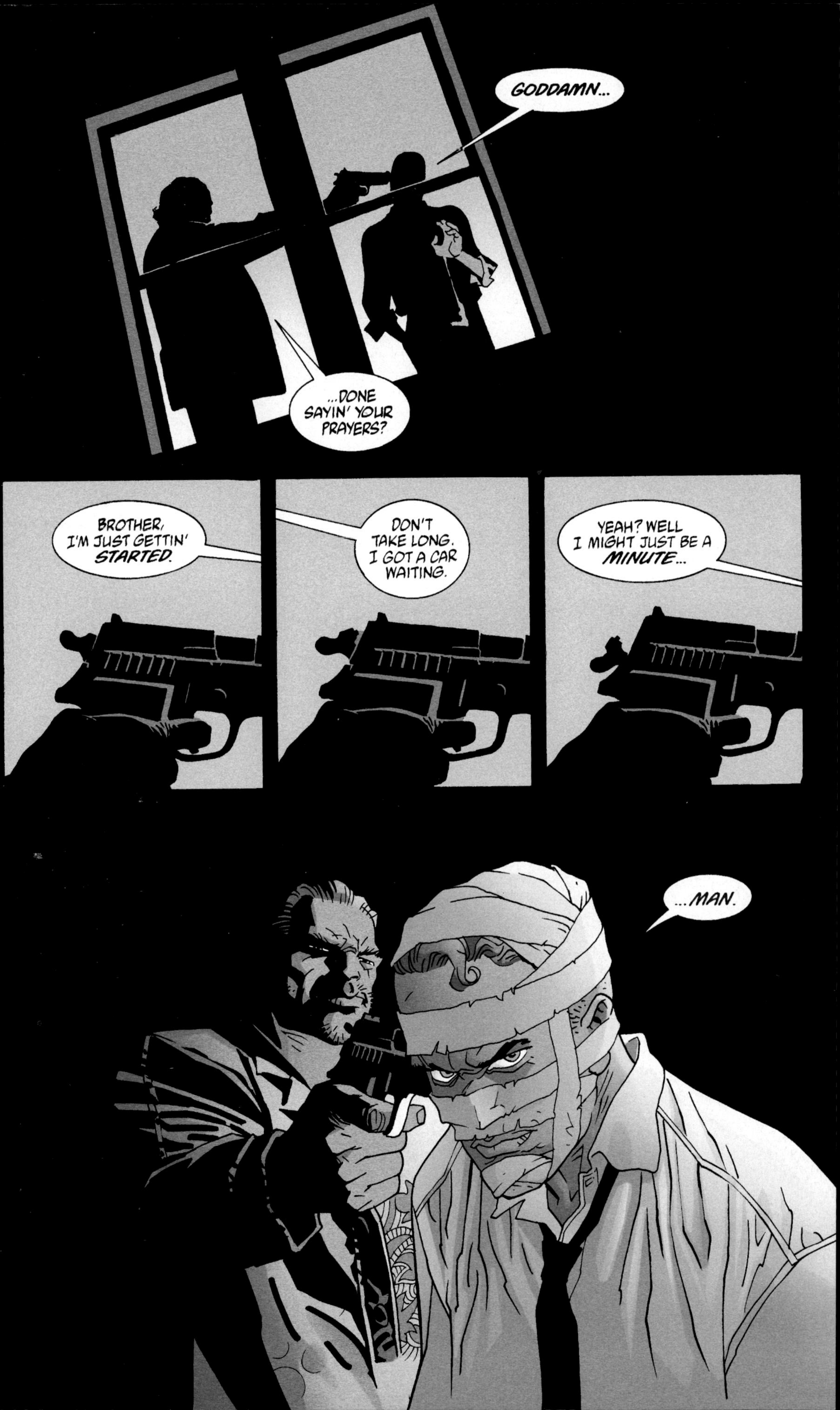
GODDAMN...
...DONE SAYIN' YOUR PRAYERS?
BROTHER, I'M JUST GETTIN' STARTED.
DON'T TAKE LONG. I GOT A CAR WAITING.
YEAH? WELL I MIGHT JUST BE A MINUTE...
...MAN.

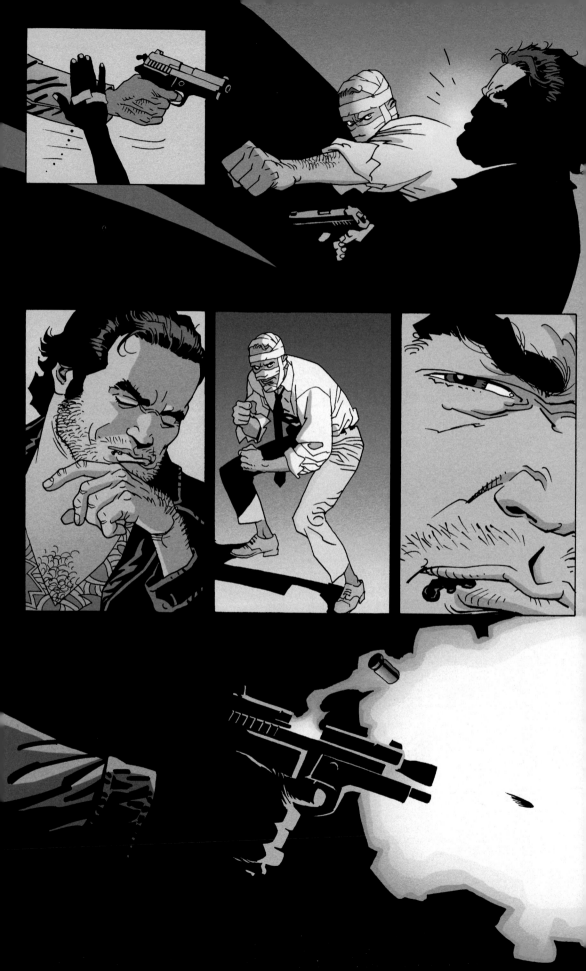

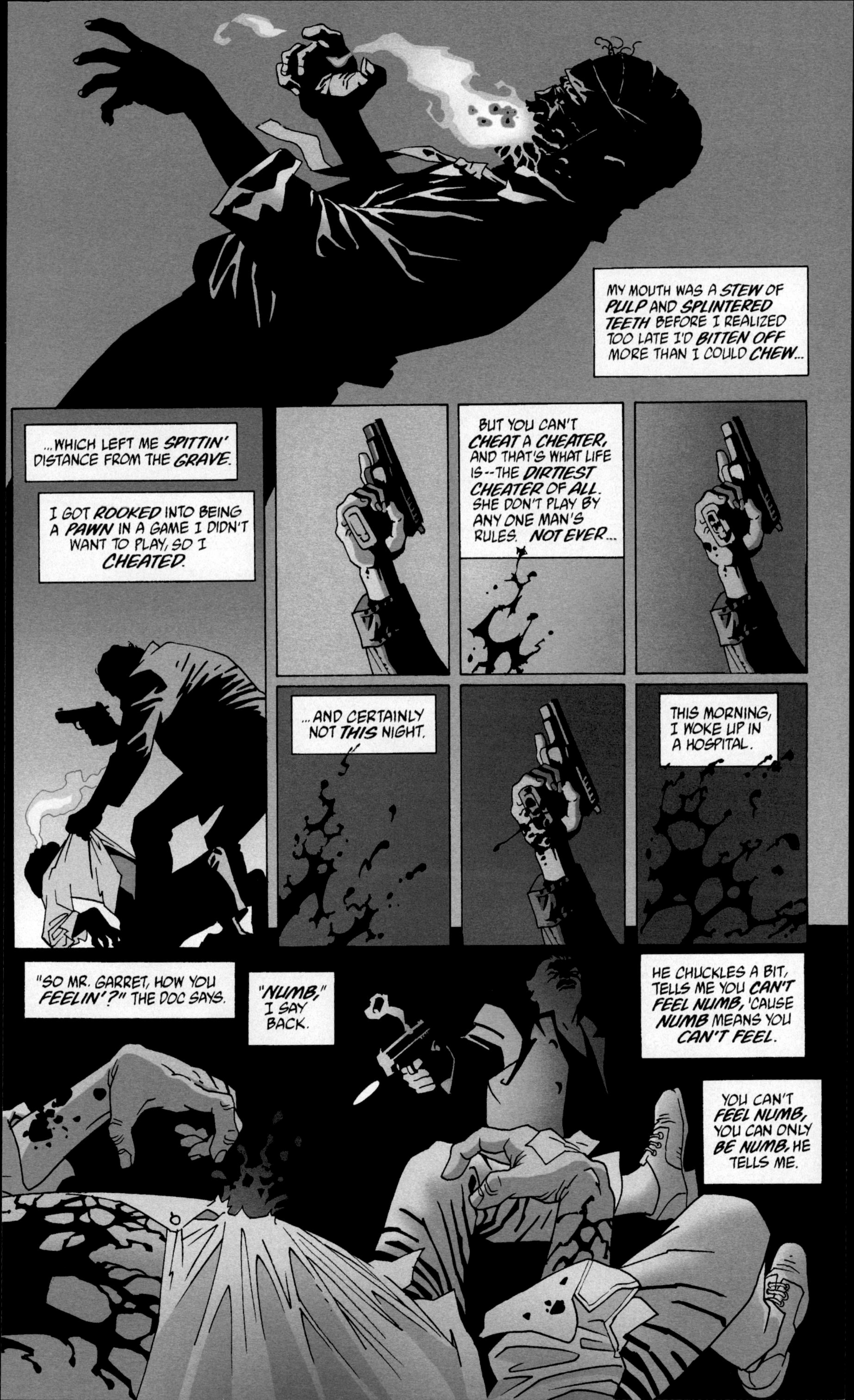

MY MOUTH WAS A STEW OF PULP AND SPLINTERED TEETH BEFORE I REALIZED TOO LATE I'D BITTEN OFF MORE THAN I COULD CHEW...
...WHICH LEFT ME SPITTIN' DISTANCE FROM THE GRAVE.
I GOT ROOKED INTO BEING A PAWN IN A GAME I DIDN'T WANT TO PLAY, SO I CHEATED.
BUT YOU CAN'T CHEAT A CHEATER, AND THAT'S WHAT LIFE IS--THE DIRTIEST CHEATER OF ALL. SHE DON'T PLAY BY ANY ONE MAN'S RULES. NOT EVER...
...AND CERTAINLY NOT THIS NIGHT.
THIS MORNING, I WOKE UP IN A HOSPITAL.
"SO MR. GARRET, HOW YOU FEELIN'?" THE DOC SAYS.
"NUMB," I SAY BACK.
HE CHUCKLES A BIT, TELLS ME YOU CAN'T FEEL NUMB, 'CAUSE NUMB MEANS YOU CAN'T FEEL.
YOU CAN'T FEEL NUMB, YOU CAN ONLY BE NUMB, HE TELLS ME.

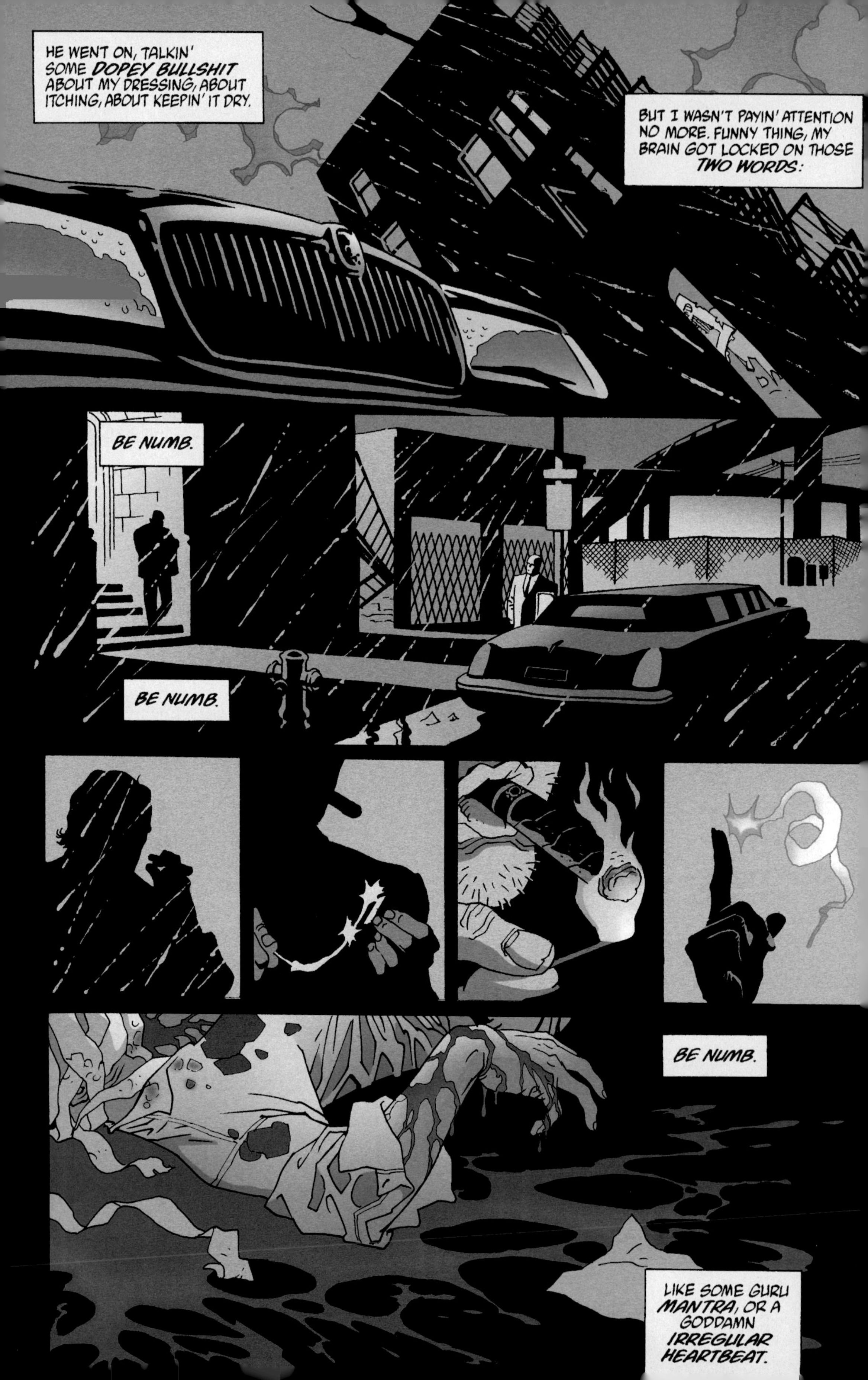
HE WENT ON, TALKIN' SOME DOPEY BULLSHIT ABOUT MY DRESSING, ABOUT ITCHING, ABOUT KEEPIN' IT DRY.
BUT I WASN'T PAYIN' ATTENTION NO MORE. FUNNY THING, MY BRAIN GOT LOCKED ON THOSE TWO WORDS:
BE NUMB.
BE NUMB.
BE NUMB.
LIKE SOME GURU MANTRA, OR A GODDAMN IRREGULAR HEARTBEAT.

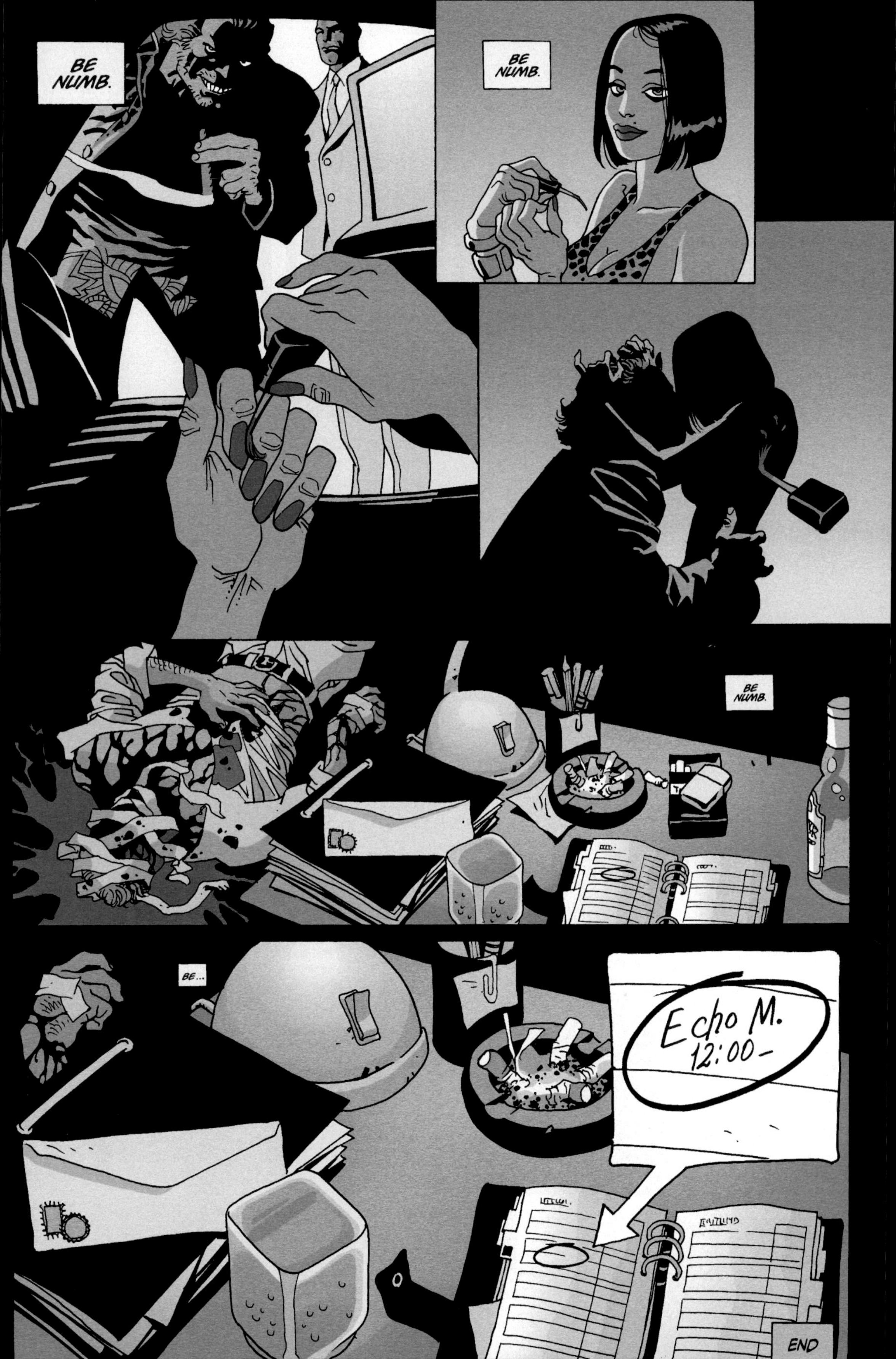
BE NUMB.
BE NUMB.
BE NUMB.
BE...
Echo M.
12:00 -
END

"THE MIMIC"

The complete script to
100 BULLETS #20
by Brian Azzarello.

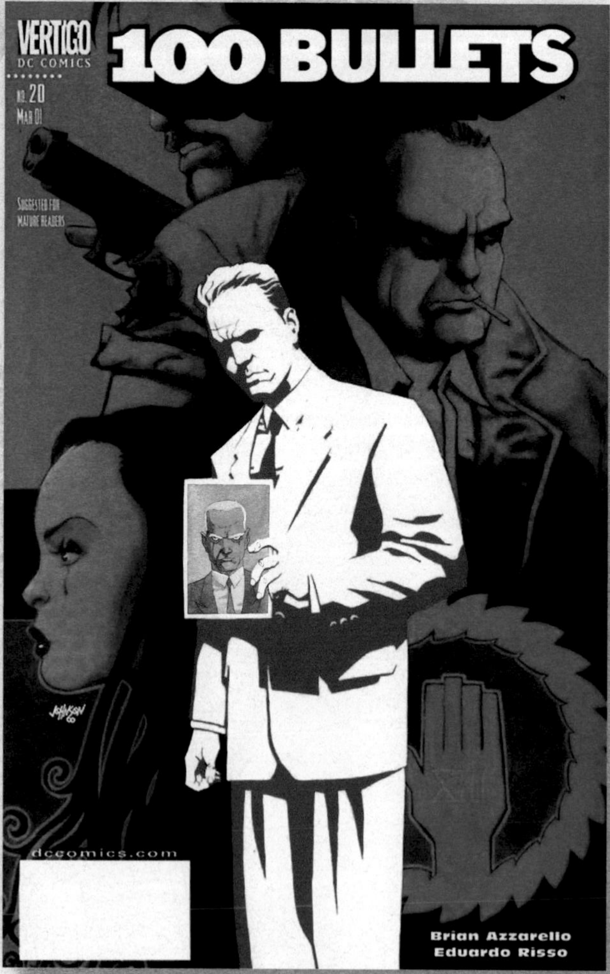
VERTIGO
DC COMICS
100 BULLETS
NO. 20
MAR 01
SUGGESTED FOR MATURE READERS
dccomics.com
Brian Azzarello
Eduardo Risso

100 BULLETS #20 — "HOT HOUSE (THE MIMIC)" 1st Draft

PAGE 1 — Eight Panels

1.1
This issue takes place entirely in NYC's Washington Square Park. Let's set this issue in winter, so everybody's got coats on, and there's a smattering of snow on the ground. BOPPA, a black drug dealer in his early twenties, is sitting up on a park bench, ass on the backrest, feet on the seat. He's dressed in baggy clothes, a parka, and give him a knit cap, pulled down right to his eyes. As people walk by, he mentions what he's selling to them.

BOPPA: S'UP SMOKE.

1.2
Two college girls walk by.

BOPPA: S'UP WEED.

1.3
Couple of punk rockers walk by.

BOPPA: S'UP EX.

1.4
A Wall Street broker dude walks by.

BOPPA: S'UP SMOKE.

1.5
KENNY, another black guy and friend of Boppa's, comes and sits all splay-legged on the bench.

KENNY: YO BOPPA.

BOPPA: YO BACK, SON. HOW YOU DOIN'?

1.6
Same. More people walk by.

KENNY: S'AIGHT, S'AIGHT. YOU KNOW.

BOPPA: TRUE.

1.7
Kenny leans forward, looking left.

KENNY: SAY, YOU SCOPE WHO'S HANGIN'?

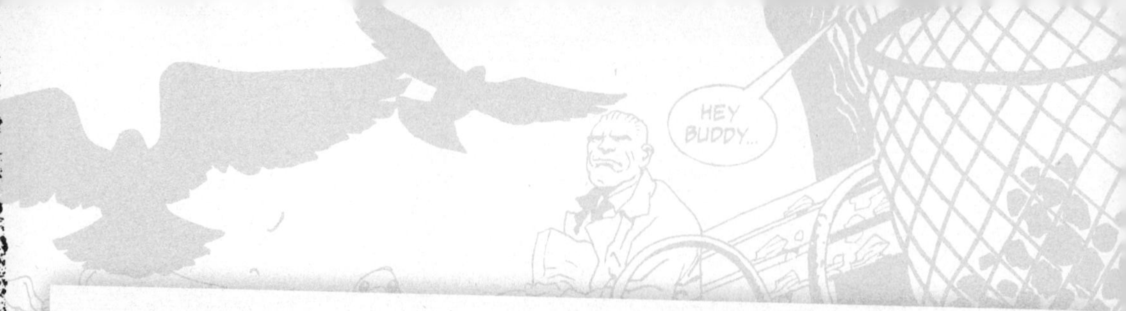
HEY BUDDY...

1.8
Boppa looks left too.

BOPPA: MUTHAFUCK...

PAGE 2 — SPLASH

Wide shot. Lots of people, so we don't know who Boppa is referring to. Most importantly, Mr. Shepherd sits on another bench, feeding pigeons. As for the people, make them diverse-- mothers with strollers, punk rockers, b-boys, skate rats, old-timers, you know, the type of people who hang out in a large urban park. In the background is ISCO, another dealer, wearing a parka with the hood up over his head. He's the man Boppa is referring to.

CAPTION: ...THAT BITCH GOT HIM SOME BALLS.

PAGE 3 — Six Panels

3.1
Pull in on Shepherd.

BENITO (OFF PANEL): HEY BUDDY...

3.2
Pull back a bit, so we see BENITO. He's in his late twenties, extremely good looking, and extremely wealthy. Dress him accordingly, with an expensive leather jacket. He's connected to The Trust-- his father is our man on the beach from issue 5.

BENITO: ...CAN I BUM A SMOKE?

SHEPHERD: BENITO. THANKS FOR MEETING ME. HOW'S YOUR FATHER?

3.3
Benito sits down next to Shepherd, who offers him a cigarette.

BENITO: EXTREMELY ANGRY WITH YOU, MR. SHEPHERD.

SHEPHERD: YES, WELL, HE HAS EVERY RIGHT TO BE, DOESN'T HE?

BENITO: AND THEN SOME. SO WHAT HAPPENED?

3.4
Shepherd leans forward.

SHEPHERD: I WISH I COULD TELL YOU.

3.5
Benito leans down next to him.

BENITO: "I WISH I COULD TELL YOU." NOW, DOES THAT MEAN YOU DON'T KNOW, OR THAT THERE ARE EXTENUATING CIRCUMSTANCES WHICH PREVENT YOU?

3.6
Shepherd looks at Benito, understanding he's just been accused of a cover-up.

PAGE 4 — Five Panels

4.1
They sit back.

SHEPHERD: SO THAT'S THE VERDICT, COUNSELOR?

BENITO: UP IN THE IVORY TOWER, IT MIGHT BE. ME THOUGH, I THINK BETTER OF YOU.

SHEPHERD: THANK YOU.

4.2
Two shot.

BENITO: DON'T THANK ME, THANK YOURSELF. YOU'VE ALWAYS BEEN STRAIGHT, AND YOU TAUGHT ME A LOT. WHEN YOU REPORTED THE JOB WAS DONE, I BELIEVE YOU BELIEVED IT WAS.

SHEPHERD: I SAW THE BODIES.

4.3
Same.

BENITO: NOT <u>THE</u> BODIES, OBVIOUSLY.

4.4
Close-up on Shepherd.

4.5
Two shot.

BENITO: SO WHY IS GRAVES STILL ALIVE?

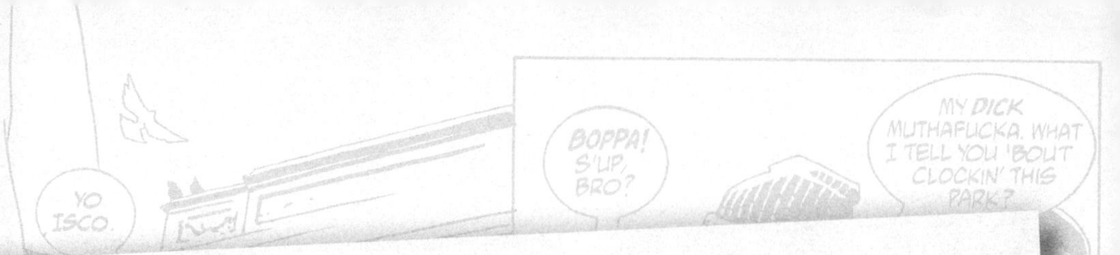
YO ISCO.
BOPPA! S'UP, BRO?
MY DICK MUTHAFUCKA. WHAT I TELL YOU 'BOUT CLOCKIN' THIS PARK?

PAGE 5 — Five Panels

5.1
Two shot. Boppa and Kenny walk by, on their way to confront Isco.

SHEPHERD: THAT'S A GOOD QUESTION, BUT NOT THE IMPORTANT ONE.

5.2
Close-up on Benito.

BENITO: OH NO? AND THAT WOULD BE...

5.3
Close-up on Shepherd.

SHEPHERD: WHAT'S HE UP TO?

5.4
Two shot.

BENITO: THAT IS AN IMPORTANT QUESTION. I'M SURE IT'S NO SURPRISE THAT MY FATHER WOULD LIKE SOME ANSWERS.

BENITO: GOT ANY?

SHEPHERD: THEORIES, NOTHING CONCRETE.

5.5
Wide shot.

BENITO: LET'S HEAR 'EM.

PAGE 6 — Six Panels

6.1
Boppa and Kenny approach Isco. Boppa is angry.

BOPPA: YO ISCO.

6.2
Isco is all smiles. Like I said, Boppa is angry. Kenny's got his back.

ISCO: BOPPA! S'UP, BRO?

BOPPA: MY DICK MUTHAFUCKA. WHAT I TELL YOU 'BOUT CLOCKIN' THIS PARK?

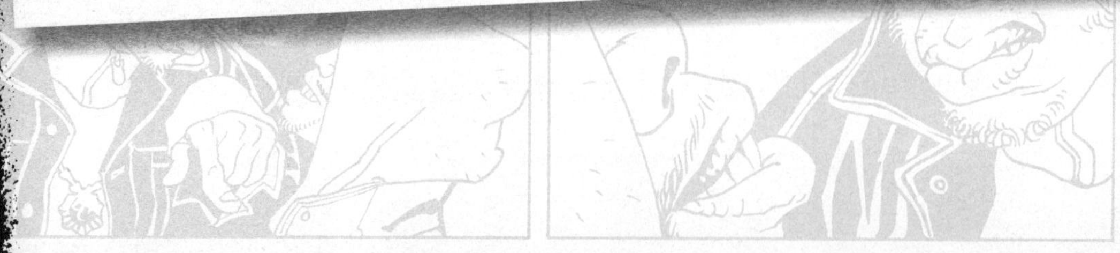

6.3
Same.

ISCO: YOU TOL' ME THERE AIN'T NO ROOM FO' NO CLOWN NIGGAS IN THE DOPE
GAME.

6.4
Same.

BOPPA: S'RIGHT I DID, CLOWN NIGGA.

ISCO: YEAH, WELL CHECK MY RÉSUMÉ, SON. THIS "CLOWN NIGGA'S" WORKIN' FO'
SPAIN NOW.

6.5
Close-up on Boppa.

BOPPA: WHA? DON' EVEN TRY TO FRONT, ISCO. NUMBA ONE, SPAIN AIN'T GOT NO
TIME FO' YO' NAPPY ASS.

BOPPA: AN' NUMBA TWO, SPAIN DON' WORK THIS CORNER.

6.6
Two shot. Boppa's getting really angry.

ISCO: HE DO NOW. AN' IF YOU WANNA KEEP WORKIN', YOU GONNA DO IT FO' HIM.

PAGE 7 — Six Panels

7.1
Boppa pulls a gun, and puts it in Isco's defiant face.

7.2
Kenny gets right up to Boppa's ear.

KENNY: DON' BE TRIPPIN' BOPPA. FO' ALL WE KNOW, THIS BOY MIGHT BE JUS'
TALKIN' SOME CRAZY SHIT.

7.3
Close-up on Boppa.

7.4
Same.

BOPPA: YEAH.

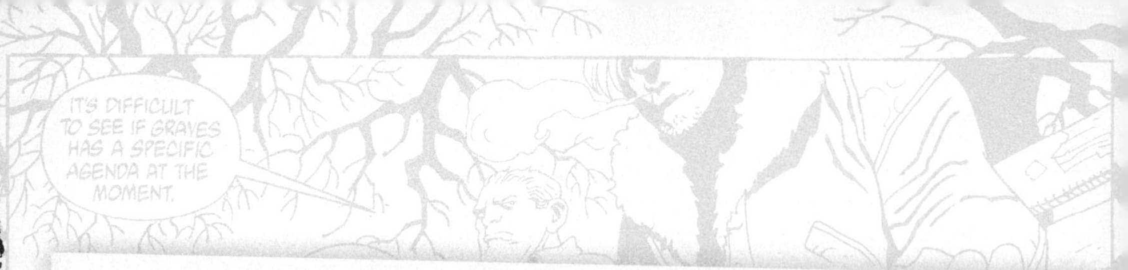
IT'S DIFFICULT TO SEE IF GRAVES HAS A SPECIFIC AGENDA AT THE MOMENT.

7.5
Boppa puts his gun away.

BOPPA: JUS' SOME CRAZY SHIT.

7.6
Boppa and Kenny leave, heading back towards the bench they came from.

ISCO: LATER, BRO.

BOPPA: FUCK YO' ASS.

PAGE 8 — Seven Panels

8.1
Back to Shepherd and Benito. (EDUARDO — I saw pages 1-6 and loved them. Keep up with that kid on the skateboard in the backgrounds — he'll play a major part in the outcome of this story)

SHEPHERD: IT'S DIFFICULT TO SEE IF GRAVES HAS A SPECIFIC AGENDA AT THE MOMENT.

BENITO: WELL, YOU MIGHT NOT BE ABLE TO SEE IT--

8.2
The two men verbally joust.

SHEPHERD: --BUT IT'S THERE, I KNOW. IT SEEMS HE'S INCORPORATED IT INTO--

BENITO: --HIS GAME?

8.3
Close-up on Shepherd.

SHEPHERD: IT'S NOT A GAME, BENITO. NOT TO HIM. IT'S HIS MISSION.

8.4
Two shot. They both looks straight ahead.

8.5
Same. Benito's had an idea.

BENITO: WHY DON'T WE ABORT IT THEN?

SHEPHERD: I THOUGHT THAT'S WHAT WE TRIED...

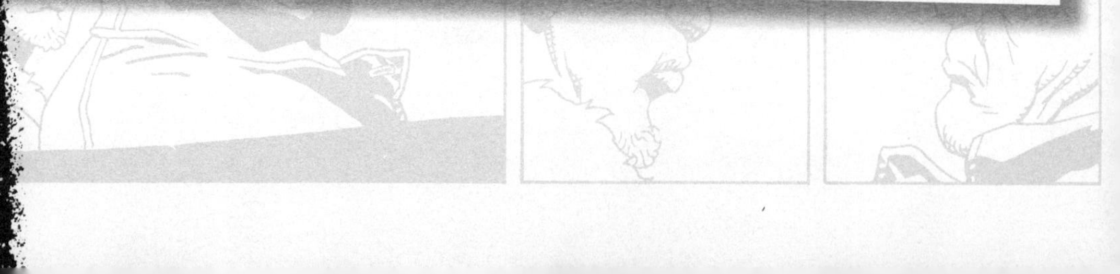

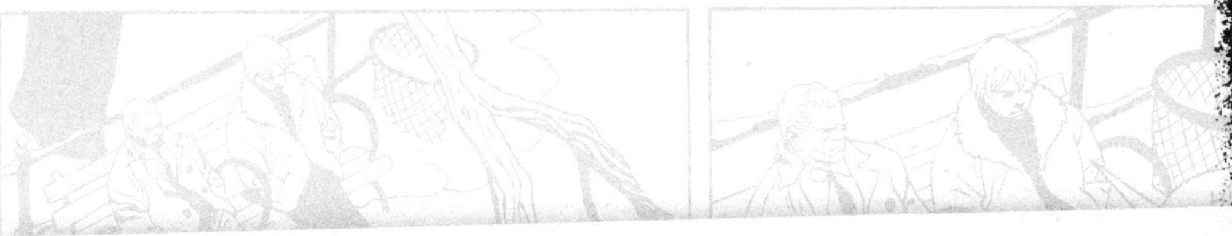

8.6
Close-up on Benito.

BENITO: NO, YOU TRIED TO KILL HIM. THAT DIDN'T WORK. OKAY.

8.7
Close-up on Shepherd.

BENITO: SO WHAT IF YOU HIT HIM HARD, RIGHT WHERE IT HURTS?

PAGE 9 — Five Panels

9.1
Two shot.

SHEPHERD: AND WHERE MIGHT THAT BE?

9.2
Pull into Benito.

BENITO: HIS MISSIONS. THE GAME. TAKE AWAY HIS ABILITY TO PLAY IT.

BENITO: THE ATTACHÉS, THE GUNS, ALL OF IT. JUST CUT HIM OFF.

9.3
Close-up on Shepherd as he considers what Benito has said.

9.4
Same.

SHEPHERD: BENITO...HYPOTHETICALLY, THAT MAKES SENSE. IN REALITY...

9.5
Wide shot. (Back to Boppa next page.)

SHEPHERD: ...WE'D HAVE WAR.

PAGE 10 — Five Panels

10.1
Back to Boppa. Close-up. He's super-pissed.

BOPPA: I'M GONNA KILL THAT BITCH!

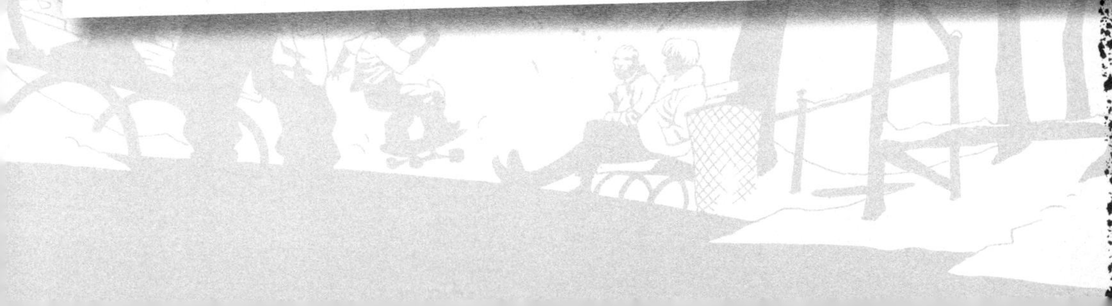

10.2
Pull back. We see Kenny is still with him. SCOONIE (the skateboard kid from PAGE 4, PANEL 1) cuts in front of Boppa, startling him.

BOPPA: DAMN, SCOONIE!

10.2
Boppa yells at Scoonie, who's skating away. If we see Scoonie's face, he should remain expressionless.

BOPPA: STAY THE FUCK OUT MY WAY!

KENNY: COO YO' JETS, BOPPA!

BOPPA: THAT MUTHAFUCKA COMES INTA MY HOUSE, TALKIN' THAT TRASH 'BOUT SPAIN N'SHIT?

10.3
Boppa and Kenny.

BOPPA: FUCK THAT PUNK!

KENNY: SON, WHY YOU GETTIN' ALL AMPED WHEN YOU DON' EVEN KNOW IF'N WHAT HE SAYS IS FER REAL?

KENNY: YOU OUGHT TO SPEAK WIT' SPAIN.

10.4
Boppa "throws down."

BOPPA: I KNOW WHAT I OUGHTTA DO N'SHIT, KENNY. SHIT.

CLUB KID (OFF PANEL, BEHIND BOPPA): HEY.

PAGE 11 — Seven Panels

11.1
Boppa turns, still angry until he sees who it is-- the punk rock girl from PAGE 6, PANEL 4.

BOPPA: WHA? OH.

11.2
Boppa gets all business, not looking at her, but scanning his surroundings for cops.

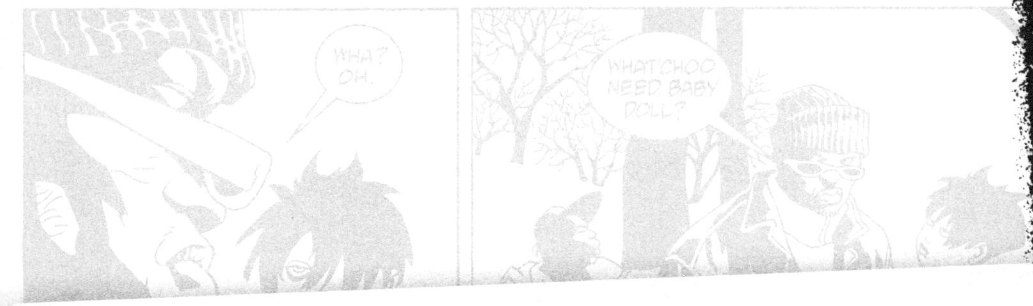
WHAT? OH.
WHAT'CHOO NEED BABY DOLL?

BOPPA: HOW Y'ALL DOIN'?

GIRL: ALL RIGHT.

BOPPA: WHAT'CHOO NEED, BABY DOLL?

GIRL: EIGHT HITS.

11.3
Boppa flashes two fingers at the girl.

11.4
Off a bit, a kid wearing a red sweatshirt, hood up, watches the girl hand Boppa some money.

11.5
Back to Boppa and the girl. Boppa is holding up both his hands, flashing eight fingers. The both are looking off panel, at the kid with the red sweatshirt.

BOPPA: SEE MY PARTNA OVAH THERE WIT' THE RED HOODIE?

BOPPA: FIVE MINUTES.

11.6
Boppa looks over towards Isco. He sees Isco and some college guy, who's handing Isco money.

11.7
Boppa walks off, as if to leave the park.

KENNY: WHERE YOU GOIN'?

PAGE 12 — Eight Panels

12.1
Back to Shepherd and Benito.

BENITO: SO WHAT DO YOU SUGGEST WE DO?

SHEPHERD: FOR THE MOMENT? WAIT.

12.2
Benito smiles slightly.

BENITO: WAIT? I'M NOT SO SURE DAD'S IN A PATIENT MOOD...

SHEPHERD: WELL, THEN WE'LL HAVE TO CONVINCE HIM.

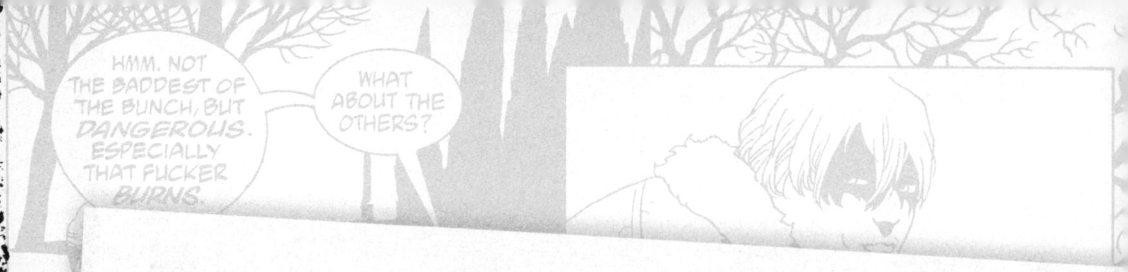
HMM. NOT THE BADDEST OF THE BUNCH, BUT DANGEROUS. ESPECIALLY THAT FUCKER BURNS.
WHAT ABOUT THE OTHERS?

12.3
Same.

BENITO: WE?

12.4
Close-up on Shepherd.

SHEPHERD: BENITO, FOR THE TIME BEING IT WOULD BE PRUDENT TO LET GRAVES MAKE ALL THE MOVES. LET A PATTERN EMERGE.

12.5
Two shot of the men, considering what Shepherd proposes.

12.6
Same.

BENITO: WHAT ABOUT THE MINUTEMEN?

12.7
Close-up on Shepherd.

SHEPHERD: AS FAR AS I KNOW?

12.8
Close-up on Shepherd.

SHEPHERD: TWO ARE ALIVE. LONO AND COLE BURNS.

PAGE 13 — Seven Panels

13.1
Two shot.

BENITO: HMM. NOT THE BADDEST OF THE BUNCH, BUT DANGEROUS. ESPECIALLY THAT FUCKER BURNS.

BENITO: WHAT ABOUT THE OTHERS?

SHEPHERD: I DON'T KNOW. LONO WASN'T IN ATLANTIC CITY WHEN WE STRUCK, BUT BURNS WAS. SO WE HAVE TO ASSUME--

13.2
Close-up on Benito.

BENITO: --THEY'RE ALL STILL KICKING.

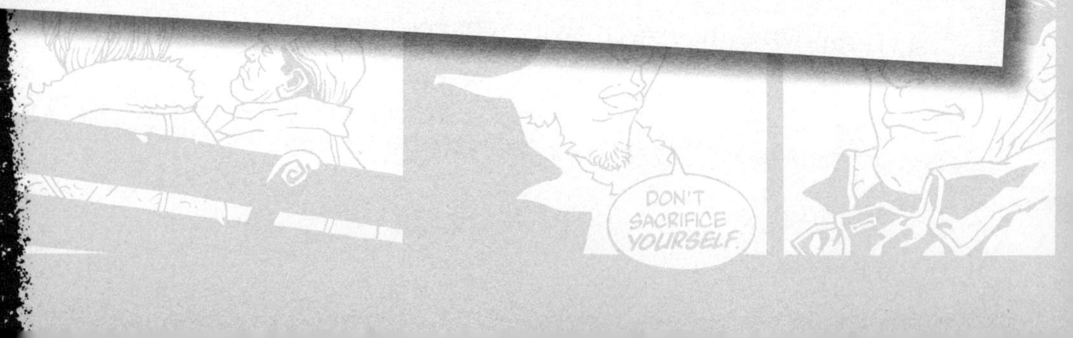
DON'T SACRIFICE YOURSELF.

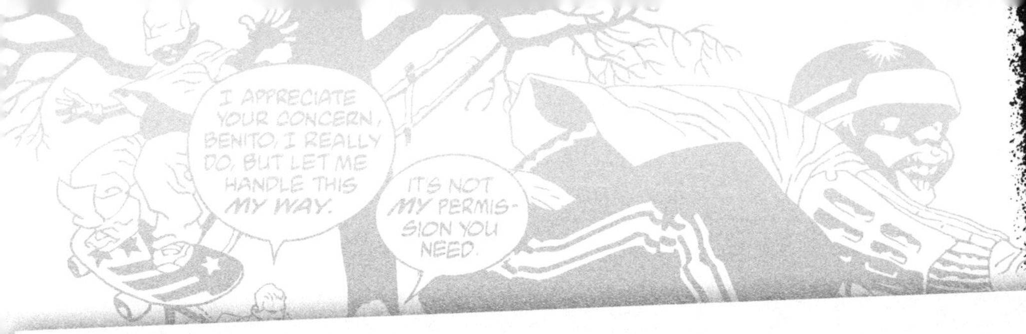
I APPRECIATE YOUR CONCERN, BENITO, I REALLY DO, BUT LET ME HANDLE THIS MY WAY.
IT'S NOT MY PERMISSION YOU NEED.

13.3
Same.

SHEPHERD: YES, BUT, NOT EVERY MINUTEMAN SAW THINGS GRAVES' WAY. GIVEN THE SITUATION, I WOULDN'T PUT IT PAST HIM TO SACRIFICE SOME OF THEM.

13.4
Two shot, as the men consider what Shepherd has said.

13.5
Same.

BENITO: MR. SHEPHERD?

SHEPHERD: HMM?

13.6
Close-up on Benito. He looks a bit sheepish.

BENITO: DON'T SACRIFICE YOURSELF.

13.7
Close-up on Shepherd, a slight smile on his face.

PAGE 14 — Six Panels

14.1
Two shot.

SHEPHERD: I APPRECIATE YOUR CONCERN, BENITO, I REALLY DO, BUT LET ME HANDLE THIS MY WAY.

14.2
Same.

BENITO: IT'S NOT MY PERMISSION YOU NEED.

SHEPHERD: NOT YET, ANYWAY.

14.3
Same.

BENITO: HEY, THAT'S A LONG WAY OFF, I FIGURE. THE LONGER THE BETTER.

SHEPHERD: WELL, FOR BETTER OR FOR WORSE, YOU'RE IN LINE--

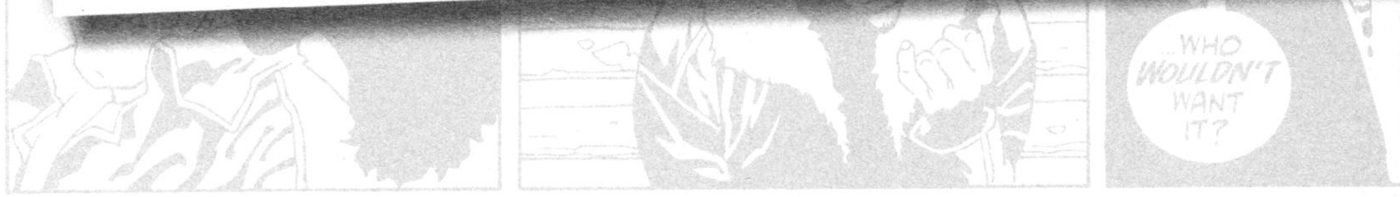
...WHO WOULDN'T WANT IT?

TWO SIXTY-EIGHT.
WHA? SAYS ONE NINETY-NINE ON THE COOLER.
TAXES, MY FRIEND. UNCLE SAM.

14.4
Benito raises his arm a bit, gesturing at his surroundings.

BENITO: --YEAH YEAH, I KNOW-- THE KEYS TO THE FUCKING KINGDOM. "SOMEDAY, THIS WILL ALL BE YOURS..."

14.5
Two shot. Benito appears uninterested now.

SHEPHERD: IT'S A RESPONSIBILITY. ONE, BY THE WAY, I THINK YOU'RE UP FOR--

BENITO: --NO, IT'S ONE I HAVE NO GODDAMN CHOICE IN ACCEPTING. WHO SAYS I WANT IT?

14.6
Close-up on Shepherd.

SHEPHERD: BENITO...

SHEPHERD: ...WHO WOULDN'T WANT IT?

PAGE 15 — Five Panels

15.1
Cut to a close-up on a 40 oz. bottle of malt liquor.

GROCER: TWO SIXTY-EIGHT.

15.2
Pull back. Boppa is standing at a counter in a small grocery store across the street from the park. A Middle Eastern clerk is at the counter.

BOPPA: WHA? SAYS ONE NINEY-NINE ON THE COOLER.

GROCER: TAXES, MY FRIEND. UNCLE SAM.

15.3
Boppa throws another dollar on the counter.

BOPPA: MUTHAFUCK...

15.4
Boppa exits the grocery, carrying the bottle in a tight fitting brown paper bag.

BOPPA (MUTTERING): EVERY NIGGA'S GETTIN' PAID BUT ME...

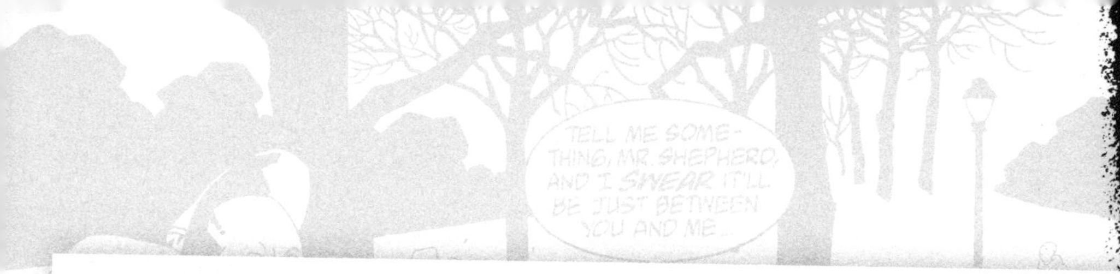
TELL ME SOMETHING, MR. SHEPHERD, AND I SWEAR IT'LL BE JUST BETWEEN YOU AND ME...

15.5
Looking across the street, Boppa sees a tricked-out BMW, with black tinted windows.

BOPPA: SHIT.

PAGE 16 — Four Panels

16.1
Cut back to the park. Kenny is looking at the same BMW. The kid with the red hoodie is there too, handing off the drugs to the punk rock girl.

KENNY: SHIT.

16.2
Hoodie joins Kenny, who looks worried.

HOODIE: WHAT?

16.3
Boppa saunters over to the BMW.

16.4
Back to Kenny and hoodie.

KENNY: MUTHAFUCKIN' SPAIN.

PAGE 17 — Seven Panels

17.1
Back to Shepherd and Benito.

BENITO: TELL ME SOMETHING, MR. SHEPHERD, AND I SWEAR IT'LL BE JUST BETWEEN YOU AND ME...

17.2
Two shot.

BENITO:...DID YOU KNOW GRAVES WAS ALIVE BEFORE HE MADE HIS MOVE AGAINST MEGAN DIETRICH?

SHEPHERD: YES. HE SURFACED A FEW MONTHS PRIOR, IN CHICAGO.

17.3
Same.

HE MADE HIS MOVE; HE WANTED THE TRUST TO KNOW HE WAS STILL ALIVE-- THAT HE COULD TOUCH THEM.

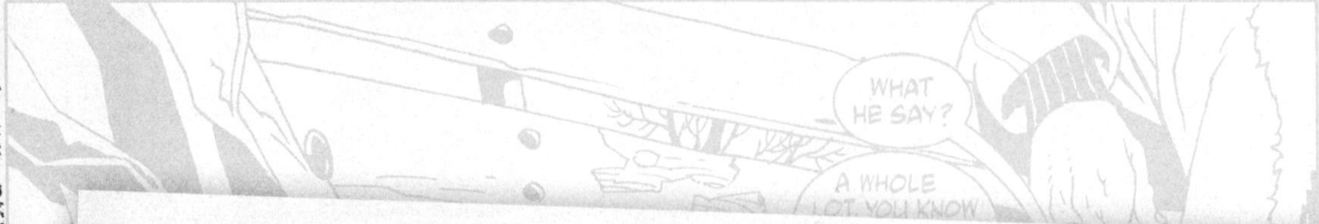
WHAT HE SAY?
A WHOLE

BENITO: OKAY...WHY DIDN'T YOU INFORM THE TRUST?

SHEPHERD: WHY WOULD I DO THAT?

17.4
Close-up on Benito.

BENITO: WHY? HOW 'BOUT 'CAUSE YOU WORK FOR THEM.

17.5
Close-up on Shepherd.

SHEPHERD: SERVICE, NOT SERVITUDE, BENITO. IT WAS MORE IMPORTANT TO LEARN WHAT GRAVES WAS PLANNING.

SHEPHERD: REMEMBER: BEFORE I WAS "RETIRED," I WAS A MINUTEMAN. I WORKED FOR HIM.

17.6
Two shot.

BENITO: YOU WEREN'T RETIRED, YOU WERE PROMOTED.

SHEPHERD: AND AS FOR MY DECISION, I STAND BY IT. HELL, GRAVES HIMSELF PROVED ME RIGHT. HE MADE HIS MOVE; HE WANTED THE TRUST TO KNOW HE WAS STILL ALIVE--THAT HE COULD TOUCH THEM.

17.7
Close-up on Shepherd.

SHEPHERD: BESIDES, CHICAGO WAS INCONSEQUENTIAL. JUST GRAVES PLAYING HIS "GAME," AS YOU CALL IT.

PAGE 18 — Six Panels

18.1
Cut back to Kenny and hoodie. Boppa joins them, drinking from his 40.

KENNY: WHAT HE SAY?

BOPPA: A WHOLE LOT. YOU KNOW SPAIN, NIGGA RUNS HIS MOUTH.

KENNY: HE GOT ISCO'S BACK?

18.2
Boppa looks down. Kenny and hoodie look shaken.

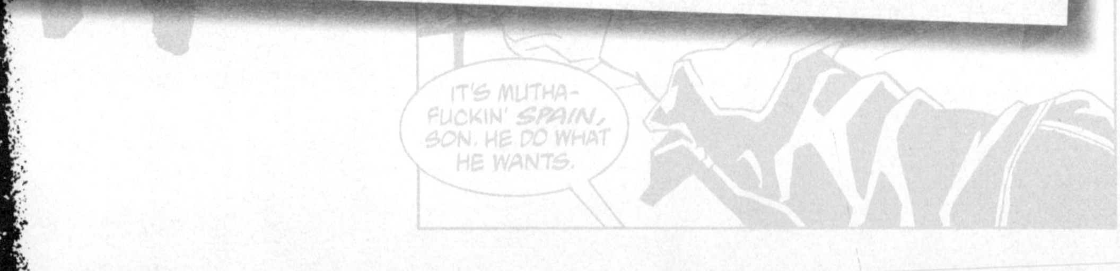
IT'S MUTHA-FUCKIN' SPAIN, SON. HE DO WHAT HE WANTS.

BOPPA: YEAH.

HOODIE: DAMN.

18.3
Close-up on Boppa. He's not angry, but resigned.

BOPPA: MUTHAFUCKIN' GODDAMN'S WHAT IT IS. LOOK HERE, SEE; SPAIN'S MAKIN'
A PLAY FO' THE PARK, AN' HE'S READY TO GO BAD ON ANY MUTHAFUCKA AIN'T
DOWN WITH THAT.

18.4
Three shot.

KENNY: WE IN THE SHIT.

HOODIE: HOW DEEP?

18.5
Same.

BOPPA: MUTHAFUCKIN' REAL DEEP. NIGGA SAYS WE RE-UP ALL WE ROLL FROM HIM
NOW, OR WE OUT THE GAME.

HOODIE: THAT AIN'T RIGHT. CIN HE DO THAT?

18.6
Wide shot of the park. We see Shepherd looking their way.

KENNY: IT'S MUTHAFUCKIN' SPAIN, SON. HE DO WHAT HE WANTS.

PAGE 19 — Six Panels

19.1
All right, let's bring our two stories together. Kenny seems resigned.

KENNY: GUESS ISCO WAS RIGHT...

19.2
Boppa starts to exhibit a quiet rage. Don't make him look angry, make him looked determined.

KENNY: WE WORKIN' FO THAT NIGGA NOW.

BOPPA: BULLSHIT. MUTHAFUCKA'S A PIMP S'ALL, AN I AIN'T GONNA BE HIS BITCH.

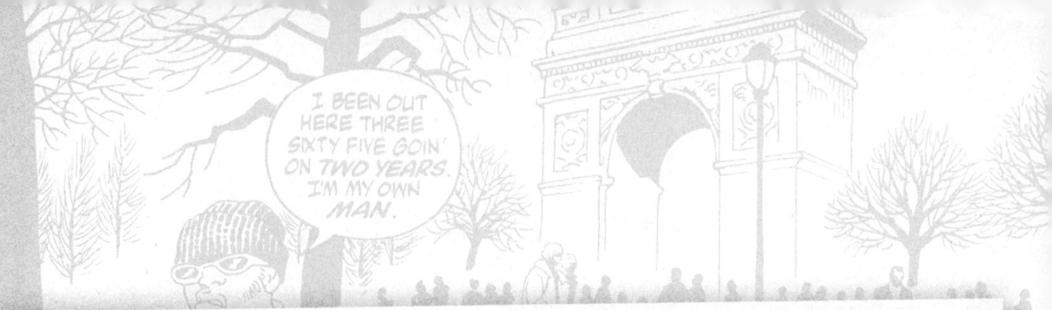
I BEEN OUT HERE THREE SIXTY FIVE GOIN' ON TWO YEARS. I'M MY OWN MAN.

19.3
Back to Shepherd. He's getting up, because he knows there's going to be trouble.

SHEPHERD: WE SHOULD GO.

19.4
Shepherd and Benito start to walk in the direction of Boppa and his crew.

SHEPHERD: ONE THING YOU SHOULD UNDERSTAND ABOUT GRAVES, BENITO: HE HAS A VERY RIGID CODE OF CONDUCT. IT'S WHAT DRIVES HIM.

19.5
Back to Boppa.

HOODIE: YOU TELLIN' ME YOU LEAVIN' THE LIFE? SHIT.

BOPPA: THAT AIN'T WHAT I'M SAYIN', MELLOW.

19.6
Back to Shepherd.

SHEPHERD: EVERY DECISION HE MAKES IS IN KEEPING WITH HIS CODE, AND WHILE HIS STRICT ADHERENCE TO IT IS HIS ALONE, HE BELIEVES SHARING IT A NECESSARY GESTURE.

PAGE 20 — Six Panels

20.1
Pull in on Boppa.

BOPPA: I BEEN OUT HERE THREE SIXTY FIVE GOIN' ON TWO YEARS. I'M MY OWN MAN, AIN'T BOUT TO CHANGE CUZ SOME SKUNK NIGGA SAYS I GOTTA BE INTA HIM.

20.2
Back to Shepherd and Benito.

SHEPHERD: IT GIVES HIM PURPOSE.

SHEPHERD: IT'S WHAT MADE HIM SO VALUABLE TO THE TRUST; IT WAS PART OF THE JOB. NOW, IT'S PERSONAL.

20.3
Back to Boppa.

KENNY: BOPPA...

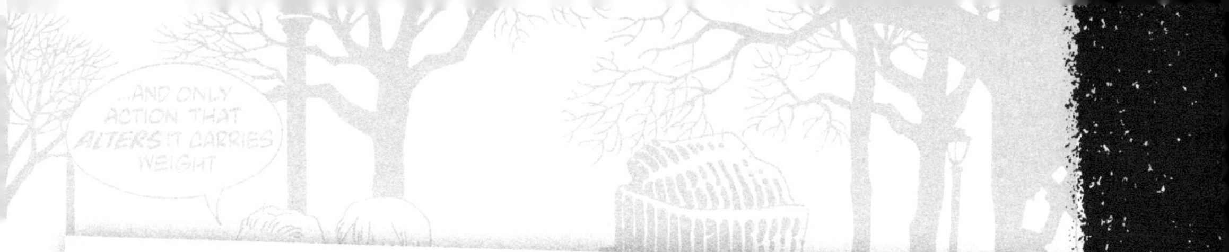
...AND ONLY ACTION THAT ALTERS IT CARRIES WEIGHT

BOPPA: IT'S GOTTA BE THIS WAY, KENNY.

KENNY: WHY?

20.4
Close-up on Boppa.

BOPPA: CUZ IT'S THE ONLY WAY I KNOW.

20.5
Back to Shepherd and Benito.

BENITO: HIS PERSONAL CODE.

SHEPHERD: WHICH, IF WE PLAY OUR CARDS RIGHT...

20.6
Boppa has now headed in the direction of Shepherd and Benito. He's alone.

SHEPHERD: ...WILL BE HIS UNDOING. SO WE'LL HANDLE THIS LIKE HE WOULD...

SHEPHERD: ...KNOWING FULL WELL THAT FUTILE ACTION IS NO VIABLE WAY OF CONFRONTING THE WORLD...

PAGE 21 — Five Panels

21.1
Shepherd passes Boppa, and wishes him good luck.

SHEPHERD: ...AND ONLY ACTION WHICH ALTERS IT CARRIES WEIGHT.

SHEPHERD: GOOD LUCK.

21.2
Boppa stops for a second.

BOPPA: ?

21.3
At the street, Benito and Shepherd get into a cab, as Benito looks back towards the park.

BENITO: I ALWAYS LIKED THIS PARK.

SHEPHERD: WELL, IT'S CHANGED A LOT.

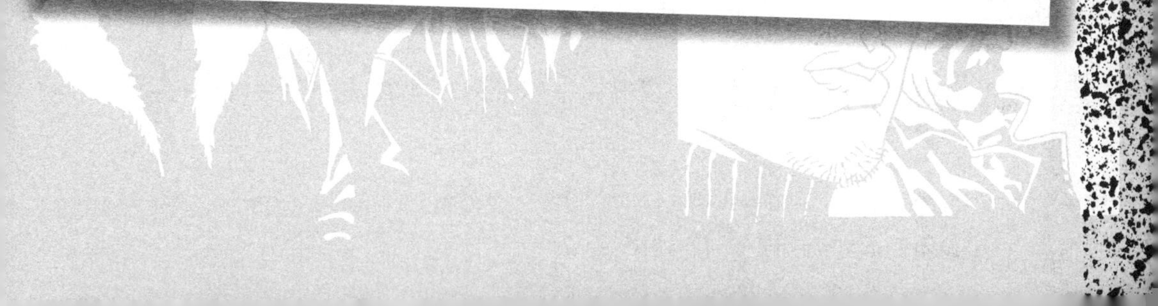

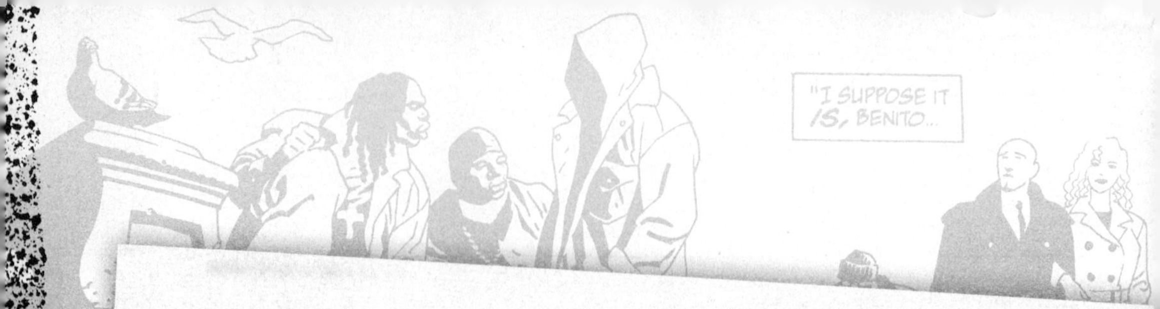
"I SUPPOSE IT IS, BENITO...

21.4
Inside the cab.

BENITO: YEAH, FOR THE BETTER. THIS WHOLE CITY HAS.

SHEPHERD: YOU THINK SO?

21.5
Same.

BENITO: I KNOW SO. IT'S A HELL OF A LOT SAFER THESE DAYS.

PAGE 22 — Eight Panels

22.1
Boppa approaches Isco and a few of his homies. Other people are around too.

CAPTION: "I SUPPOSE IT IS, BENITO...

22.2
Boppa pulls his gun and fires.

22.3
Isco and his crew open fire back. They looked panicked.

22.4
Bullets fly, people run. Some are falling, caught in the hail of bullets.

22.5
Skateboard kid gets shot off his board.

22.6
The board rolls into Boppa's feet. Boppa's been shot.

22.7
Boppa falls, dead.

CAPTION: "...FOR SOME."

CAPTION: END

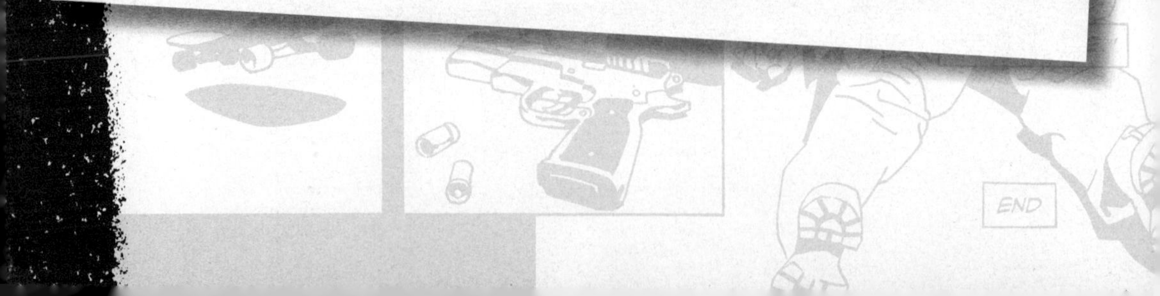
END